C0-AUF-077

370.193 CI VI

THE STRUGGLE FOR EQUAL EDUCATION$ NEW

3 2711 00002 6565

APR '98

ENTERED JUL 0 1 1993

COLUMBIA COLLEGE
LIBRARY

RACE, LAW, and American History 1700-1990

The African-American EXPERIENCE

An eleven-volume anthology of scholarly articles

edited by
Paul Finkelman
BROOKLYN LAW SCHOOL

a garland series

Contents
of the Series

Volume 7

Part I

The Struggle for EQUAL EDUCATION

edited by
Paul Finkelman

Garland Publishing, Inc.
New York & London

370.19342 S927f v.1

The Struggle for equal
education

Introductions © 1992 Paul Finkelman
All rights reserved

Library of Congress Cataloging-in-Publication Data

The Struggle for equal education / edited with introductions by
    Paul Finkelman.
        p.   cm.—(Race, law and American history, 1700–1990. The
    African-American experience ; v. 7, pt. 1)
    Includes bibliographical references.
    ISBN 0-8153-0540-0
    1. Afro-Americans—Education—History. 2. Educational
equalization—United States—History. 3. Educational
equalization—Law and legislation—United States—History. 4.
School integration—United States—History.   I. Finkelman, Paul,
1949–   . II. Series.
LC2741.S77   1992
370.19'342'0973—dc20
                                                            91-42939
                                                                CIP

Printed on acid-free, 250-year-life paper
MANUFACTURED IN THE UNITED STATES OF AMERICA

Series Introduction

Race relations have dominated much of American history. The place that became the United States began as a multicultural, multiracial society. By 1619 Native Americans, Africans, and Europeans lived side by side in Virginia. Initially relations between blacks and whites were unregulated by either law or custom. The first blacks brought to Virginia were treated as indentured servants. Some soon gained their freedom; a few subsequently became landowners and even owned other servants.

However, as early as the 1630s Virginia's courts and law-making bodies began to make distinctions between Africans and their American-born children and Europeans and their white children. By the 1640s Euro-Virginians were beginning to treat some Afro-Virginians as slaves. By 1660 statutes in Virginia recognized, and to some extent regulated, slavery.

Since the colonial period black–white relations in this country have been increasingly legalistic. The first records we have of enslavement are from court orders in the first half of the seventeenth century. At the Philadelphia Convention of 1787 delegates debated, often acrimoniously, the place of slavery in the new constitutional order. One of the most important and famous Supreme Court decisions of the antebellum era—*Dred Scott* v. *Sandford* (1857)—involved slavery. While the Civil War ostensibly settled the constitutional and legal question of secession, the three constitutional amendments following the war—the Thirteenth, Fourteenth, and Fifteenth—involved race relations. Since the adoption of those amendments many of our most important Supreme Court cases, such as *Plessy* v. *Ferguson* (1896) and *Brown* v. *Board of Education of Topeka* (1954), have involved race relations. The Twenty-Fourth Amendment, although not on its face about race, was adopted mostly to prevent voting discrimination against African Americans through taxes. Each term of the United States Supreme Court leads to new and important cases involving race and the law. Politics and the media are permeated by issues such as affirmative action, multicultural education, and racial bias in the legal system.

As this series went to press the nation watched the Senate debate the confirmation of a black judge to the United States Supreme Court. The outcome of the Senate's deliberations and the debates themselves underscore the importance of race to our nation's legal system and constitutional structure. This series is designed to provide a better understanding of that order by bringing together the most significant scholarly articles on African-American legal history. To avoid overlap with other Garland publications, most of the articles in this set are on race relations since Emancipation. Only one volume deals directly with the history of race and law before Emancipation. A few of the articles in other volumes also cover pre-Civil War topics. Most of the articles in this series come from a large variety of history journals and law reviews. However, articles are also drawn from journals specializing in political science, economics, geography, race relations, social policy, education, and social work.

Organized by topics, these volumes are designed to give scholars and students quick access to the major scholarly articles in various subfields— such as education, voting, and criminal justice—as well as in the overall legal history of black–white relations in America. For this reason, I have not covered the important disciplinary and scholarly issues raised by the work of critical race theorists, the law and economics schools, or the critical legal studies movement. These, and other new modes of inquiry, are important for our understanding of how law impacts on society and thus some of the scholarship coming out of these new schools of thought has been included in these volumes.

Because of the mix of articles, this series allows for a multidisciplinary approach to the issues of African Americans, law, and United States history. Future Garland volumes will bring together a similar literature on Asian Americans, Hispanic Americans, and Native Americans. When completed, these volumes will give all scholars better access to the literature that helps us understand how race has been a factor in the development of law and how our legal system in turn has defined concepts of race.

It would not have been possible to put this series together without the help of librarians, fellow scholars, and students. The library staff at Brooklyn Law School, especially Sara Robbins, Linda Holmes, Howard Brenner, James Gordon, and Jean M. Jablonski, went out of their way to quickly get me materials and articles on interlibrary loan. Michael Kent Curtis, Robert Cottrol, M. J. Dupont, John Hope Franklin, J. Morgan Kousser, Kermit Hall, and Earl Maltz were generous with their time in discussing the literature of race and law. My research assistants, Degna Levister, Elayna Nacci, Philip Presby, Marni Schlissel, Marci Silverman, and Jordan Tamagni, were creative and diligent in helping with this project.

Introduction

S chooling and education, more than anything else, have defined the problem of segregation and integration in the twentieth century. What is arguably the single most important Supreme Court case of this century— *Brown* v. *Board of Education of Topeka* (1954)—was a school desegregation case. Civil rights lawyers and legal historians think of case law and historical developments in terms of "pre-*Brown*" and "post-*Brown*." Beyond destroying the constitutional basis for separate schools, *Brown* undermined the entire basis of segregation and racial classification in American law. Thus, it is *the* case of the century. The fact that it stemmed from cases involving schools underscores the importance of education to the struggle for equality in America.

Many of the articles in this volume focus on *Brown* and the response to it. The first eight articles deal generally with the legitimacy of the *Brown* decision itself. Some of these are "classics" in the literature of law and jurisprudence. Other articles, found elsewhere in this volume, illuminate the history and background to *Brown*. While the most important case in twentieth-century race relations, *Brown* must be seen in the context of a larger history of the African-American struggle for education.

Discrimination against blacks in schools is almost as old as public education itself. As early as 1798 there was a private school for blacks in Boston. In 1800 the city refused to appropriate public funds to support this school. However, in 1820 the city established a segregated school as part of the public school system. In 1846 members of Boston's black community, led by William C. Nell, petitioned the Boston school board to integrate its schools. This petition eventually led to the nation's first school desegregation case, argued by the future U.S. Senator Charles Sumner. In *Roberts* v. *City of Boston* (1849) the Massachusetts Supreme Judicial Court rejected Sumner's arguments. Chief Justice Lemuel Shaw determined that the Massachusetts constitution did not prohibit segregation in the public schools. In 1855, however, the Massachusetts legislature effectively reversed Shaw's opinion by adopting legislation that prohibited segregation in the public schools.

The story of the Boston public schools shows how long blacks have struggled for equal educational opportunity. The history of schooling in other northern states has a similar pattern. In some states abolitionists tried to create integrated private schools with mixed success. In others, abolitionists created private schools for blacks where public education was not available to them. In still other communities, abolitionists, blacks, and eventually Republicans in the 1850s fought for integrated public schools.

Boston's experience was repeated in other places, with mixed results. Schooling for blacks in the antebellum North was not great, although an increasing number of blacks did find their way into the schools in this period.

After the Civil War access to schooling in the North remained mixed. Some states prohibited all segregation; others allowed it at the local level. In large northern cities segregation arose in the twentieth century as a result of housing patterns, economics, and transportation networks. Blacks living in predominantly black neighborhoods found themselves going to virtually or completely all-black schools. This type of segregation was eventually labeled *de facto*. However, after the *Brown* decision revolutionized discrimination law in America, scholars, lawyers, and activists began to demonstrate that segregation in some northern public schools was not solely a result of housing patterns. Decisions by school boards, planning commissions, and other government agencies also led to segregation that was much closer to the *de jure* segregation created by statutes in the South and a few places in the North.

In the antebellum South segregated education was the rule, where there was education at all for blacks. All of the southern states prohibited teaching slaves to read and write. At various times some of the slave South also prohibited the education of free blacks. In 1860 the U.S. census reported that fewer than 3,000 of the more than 90,000 free black children living in the fifteen slave states attended school. In the eleven states that would make up the Confederacy barely a thousand free black children out of a population of over 50,000 attended school. In Virginia only 41 blacks of school age attended school out of a population of over 22,000. For virtually all antebellum southern free blacks education was neither segregated nor integrated: it was nonexistent.

The end of slavery brought some education to southern blacks. This education was almost always segregated and almost always unequal to that afforded whites. The struggle of the next century was to integrate and equalize education. That struggle intensified after *Brown*. In some places federal troops were required to end racial segregation. In other places segregation ended more peacefully. However, an end to segregation did not always mean either integration or educational equality. In much of the South, and many cities in the North, "white flight" to suburbs or to private schools created *de facto* segregation. Urban schools were left to decay as tax revenues declined and the state and federal governments failed to provide adequate resources to create urban public schools that were equal to suburban public schools or to private schools.

To a great extent *Brown* has left us with an ambiguous legacy. *Brown* led to the end to all forms of statutory segregation. Nowhere are public institutions and facilities legally segregated. To a great extent the positive legacy of *Brown* has been the end to segregated seating on public transportation and segregation in restaurants, waiting rooms, and other public facilities. Ironically, however, the one area where segregation— albeit *de facto* segregation—is most obvious, and where the lack of equal opportunity is most painful, is in the public schools of America. The articles in this volume help us better understand the history behind this situation.

Further Reading

The literature on black education and law is enormous. The citations only touch the surface of this large literature. Many of the articles listed here could not be included in this series due to size, budgetary, and copyright restraints. Some of these articles are also reprinted in other volumes of this series.

Baltimore, Roderick T., and Robert F. Williams. "The State Constitutional Roots of the 'Separate But Equal' Doctrine: *Roberts v. City of Boston*," *Rutgers Law Journal* 17 (1986).

Baratz, Joan C. "Court Decisions and Educational Change: A Case History of the D.C. Public Schools, 1954–1974," *Journal of Law Education* 4 (1975).

Bass, Jack. *Unlikely Heroes* (1981).

Bell, Derrick A., Jr. "Serving Two Masters: Integration Ideals and Client Interests in School Desegregation Litigation," *Yale Law Journal* 85 (1976).

Bond, Horace Mann. *The Education of the Negro in the American Social Order* (1965).

Bullock, Henry Allen. *A History of Negro Education in the South from 1619 to the Present* (1967).

Freyer, Tony. *The Little Rock Crisis: A Constitutional Interpretation* (1984).

Graglia, Lino. *Disaster by Decree: The Supreme Court Decisions on Race and the Schools* (1976).

Hubbell, John T. "Some Reactions to the Desegregation of the University of Oklahoma," *Phylon* 34 (1973).

"In Honor of *Brown* v. *Board of Education:* A Symposium," *Yale Law Journal* 93 (1984).

Kluger, Richard. *Simple Justice* (1975).

Kousser, J. Morgan. *Dead End: The Development of Nineteenth-Century Litigation on Racial Discriminiation in Schools* (1986).

Kousser, J. Morgan. "Making Separate Equal: Integration of Black and White School Funds in Kentucky," *Journal of Interdisciplinary History* 10 (1980).

Kousser, J. Morgan. "'The Supremacy of Equal Rights: The Struggle Against Racial Discrimination in Antebellum Massachusetts and the Foundations of the Fourteenth Amendment." *Northwestern University Law Review* 82 (1988).

Meier, August, and Elliott Rudwick. "Early Boycott of Segregated Schools: The Alton, Illinois Case, 1897–1908," *Journal of Negro Education* 36 (1967).

McPherson, James M. "White Liberals and Black Power in Negro Education, 1865–1915," *American Historical Review* 75 (1970).

Orfield, Gary. *Must We Bus? Segregated Schools and National Policy* (1979).

Orfield, Gary. *The Reconstruction of Southern Education* (1969).

Savage, W. Sherman. "Legal Provisions for Negro Schools in Missouri From 1865–1890," *Journal of Negro History* 16 (1931).

Savage, W. Sherman. "Legal Provisions for Negro Schools in Missouri From 1890–1934," *Journal of Negro History* 22 (1937).

Schwartz, Bernard. *Swann's Way: The School Busing Case and the Supreme Court* (1986).

Rabinowitz, Howard N. "Half a Loaf: The Shift from Black Teachers in the Negro Schools of the Urban South, 1865–1890." *Journal of Southern History* 60 (1974).

Tushnet, Mark. *The NAACP's Campaign Against Segregated Education* (1987).

Wilkinson, J. Harvie, III. *From Brown to Bakke: The Supreme Court and School Integration, 1954–1978* (1979).

Wolf, Ealeanor P. *Trial and Error: The Detroit School Desegregation Case* (1981).

Contents

THE FOURTEENTH AMENDMENT AND SCHOOL SEGREGATION

HOWARD JAY GRAHAM*

Once again intense interest and scrutiny are focused on the Fourteenth Amendment. The immediate occasion is the decision now pending in the *School Segregation Cases*.[1] Held over from 1952 term at the Supreme Court's request, these five cases were rebriefed and on December 7-9, 1953, elaborately reargued upon a series of five questions framed by the justices. The five queries[2] dealt with the purpose of the Amendment, the intent of framers and ratifiers, and the respective powers, under Sections One and Five, of Congress and the Judiciary. The first two questions sought "evidence" of the intention with regard to the school segregation issue. Question three related to the Court's existent powers under the text of the Amendment, regardless of framer-intent, in case historic evidence proved unclear or indecisive. Questions four and five concerned the judicial mechanics for ending segregation "assuming it is decided that segregation in public schools violates the Fourteenth Amendment."

A Rip Van Winkle, awakening from an eighty-year nap, would pinch himself in disbelief at these developments. The Fourteenth Amendment,[3] he would exclaim, had been drafted in 1866 to make the former slaves citizens—to remove doubt about constitutionality of the Civil Rights Act of that year. That Act in turn, drawn

---

* Bibliographer, Los Angeles County Law Library (on leave of absence) and Guggenheim Fellow, 1953-54.

1. Supreme Court of the United States, October, 1953 Term, docket numbers 1, 2, 4, 8, 10: *Brown v. Board of Education of Topeka; Briggs v. Elliott; Davis v. County School Board of Prince Edward County; Bolling v. Sharpe; Gebhart v. Belton*. The corresponding docket numbers of the cases, 1952 Term, were 8, 101, 191, 413, 448.

2. 345 U. S. 972 (1953) (memorandum decision).

3. Basic monographs and articles on the history of the Fourteenth Amendment and its major clauses are: FLACK, THE ADOPTION OF THE FOURTEENTH AMENDMENT (1908); KENDRICK, JOURNAL OF THE JOINT COMMITTEE OF FIFTEEN ON RECONSTRUCTION (1914); Fairman, *Does the Fourteenth Amendment Incorporate the Bill of Rights? The Original Understanding*, 2 STAN. L. REV. 5 (1949); Frank and Munro, *The Original Understanding of the "Equal Protection of the Laws"*, 50 COL. L. REV. 131 (1950); Graham, *The "Conspiracy Theory" of the Fourteenth Amendment*, 47 YALE L. J. 371 (1938), 48 YALE L. J. 171 (1938); 1 SELECTED ESSAYS CONSTITUTIONAL LAW 236 (1938); McLaughlin, *The Court, the Constitution and Conkling*, 46 AM. HIST. REV. 45 (1940); Boudin, *Truth and Fiction About the Fourteenth Amendment*, 16 N. Y. U. L. Q. REV. 19 (1938); WARSOFF, EQUALITY AND THE LAW (1938); Graham, *Early Antislavery Backgrounds of the Fourteenth Amendment*, [1950] WIS. L. REV. 479 and 610; Graham, *Procedure to Substance—Extra-Judicial Rise of Due Process, 1830-1860*, 40 CALIF. L. REV. 483 (1953); TENBROEK, THE ANTISLAVERY ORIGINS OF THE FOURTEENTH AMENDMENT (1951); CROSSKEY, POLITICS AND THE CONSTITUTION IN THE HISTORY OF THE UNITED STATES vol. 2, c. 31-32 (1953).

1

by Senator Trumbull,[3a] had been designed to secure to the freedmen actual as well as nominal freedom, to root out slavery's "badges and incidents," to outlaw public race discrimination.[4] The Fourteenth Amendment—universally understood as "embodying" or "incorporating" this bill—and hence as reconstituting the powers of the Federal government to the extent needed to erase the color line from American life—was ratified in 1868. Five years later, in the *Slaughter-House Cases*, the Supreme Court declared that the "one pervading purpose" of the Amendment, and indeed of all three War Amendments, had been "the freedom of the slave race [and] the security and firm establishment of that freedom."[5] One can imagine Rip's puzzlement therefore on learning that since 1896,[6] this Amendment, securing to all "persons" the "equal protection of the laws," had nonetheless sanctioned racial segregation in public schools, transportation, amusement, etc. Chide us, this awakened sleeper well might, for proof *he alone* had been napping!

Assuredly a sensitive American with an eye to the headlines as well as histories[7] would have a very bad time bringing the old gentleman down to date. These are the darkest chapters in our past: Gradual, systematic breakdown of Reconstruction; betrayal of the South and Negroes alike; vindictive partisanship, reckless Executive-Legislative warfare; shameless exploitation of sectional hatreds and Negro suffrage; at length, military rule at dead end, sectional stalemate, the freedmen and Negro race jettisoned through this "separate but equal" cynicism, with its evasions and insulting defenses.

To convey this—the combined substance of Reconstruction history and of Myrdal's *An American Dilemma*[8]—to one who had experienced the thrill of Emancipation and shared the hopes and idealism of the Trumbulls, would be a harrowing task. To under-

---

3a. WHITE, LIFE OF TRUMBULL (1913).

4. See TENBROEK, *op. cit. supra* note 3, c. 9-12; FLACK, *op. cit. supra* note 3, c. 1; Graham, *Our "Declaratory" Fourteenth Amendment*, to be published.

5. 16 Wall. 36, 71 (U. S. 1873).

6. *Plessy v. Ferguson*, 163 U. S. 537 (1896); two excellent recent critiques are Hyman, *Segregation and the Fourteenth Amendment*, 4 VAND. L. REV. 555 (1951); Ramsmeir, *The Fourteenth Amendment and the "Separate But Equal" Doctrine*, 50 MICH. L. REV. 203 (1951).

7. For "revisionist" views and bibliographies, see also Beale, *On Rewriting Reconstruction History*, 45 AM. HIST. REV. 807 (1940); Williams, *An Analysis of Some Reconstruction Attitudes*, 12 JL. OF SOUTHERN HIST. 469 (1946); BUCK, THE ROAD TO REUNION, 1865-1900 (1937); RANDALL, THE CIVIL WAR AND RECONSTRUCTION (1937); COULTER, THE SOUTH DURING RECONSTRUCTION (1947); DUBOIS, BLACK RECONSTRUCTION (1935); BEALE, THE CRITICAL YEAR (1930). An indispensible bibliographic aid on the legal side of civil rights history is POLITICAL AND CIVIL RIGHTS IN THE UNITED STATES (Emerson and Haber, eds. 1952).

8. (1944).

2

take it now, when every headline is a reminder of farflung American interests, and of the necessity for moral leadership in a world only one-third of whose population is white, would be a sobering, depressing experience for any citizen.

The initial reaction, after incredulity, at national frustration and failures of this magnitude, is anger, and search for historic villains or scapegoats. Thaddeus Stevens and Charles Sumner, the leading Ultra-Radicals and Vindictives; Andrew Johnson, the vain, pugnacious little President, as courageous (and occasionally as right) as he was inept, have served in countless histories and speeches in this regard. So have innumerable lesser, general fry—"Abolitionist fanatics," "Black Republicans," "Grant Stalwarts," "Carpetbaggers," "Scalawags" and the rest. And on the other side, their opposites, the "unrepentent Rebels, Traitors and Secesh" that figured in stump speeches for fifty years.

Our generation fortunately has outgrown such history. The Civil War and Reconstruction now are uniformly viewed as failures of statesmanship and of resource on both sides. Fanaticism was no monoply of abolitionists. Slavery was not a "positive good;" nor its abolition "evil," nor protection of freedmen's rights "unconstitutional and unnecessary." On the other hand, neither were immediate Negro suffrage and military government the panaceas naive and designing men pretended. Negation and polarized programs at length brought both sides to near disaster. Reunion was largely at the expense of the Negro Race.[9]

Constitutional history barely has begun to benefit from this revisionism. Indeed, the whole subject has fallen on evil days. Once a favored form of American history, today it is the most neglected. McLaughlin's volume,[10] published in 1935, is still the latest general coverage as such. Constitutional *Law,* of course has split off as a discipline in its own right—abstruse, technical, increasingly viewed and taught merely as a system of rules with little regard for political and social context.[11] The residue ob-

---

9. This view is taken now in nearly all modern discussions, but corrective judicial interpretation still lags. For brilliant revisionary studies of the so-called "redemptionist" movement, see WOODWARD, THE ORIGINS OF THE NEW SOUTH (1951); and for the politics of the Reconstruction settlement of 1877, the same author's, REUNION AND REACTION (1951).

10. McLAUGHLIN, A CONSTITUTIONAL HISTORY OF THE UNITED STATES (1935); KELLY AND HARBISON, THE AMERICAN CONSTITUTION; ITS ORIGINS AND DEVELOPMENT (1948) and SWISHER, AMERICAN CONSTITUTIONAL DEVELOPMENT (1943) are admirable academic works; the writer is here speaking of the decline of the subject in the popular sense. Professor Crosskey's *tour de force,* cited *supra* note 3, promises to quicken popular interest in the subject.

11. For exploration of some of the consequences, see Graham, *Procedure to Substance—Extra-Judicial Rise of Due Process, 1830-1860,* 40 CALIF. L. REV. 483 (1953).

3

viously is difficult to manage. Even monographic treatments and judicial biographies have grown fewer. A widening gap is thus created, not only by differential rates of institutional growth, but by shifts of research interest as well.

An undesired consequence is that Americans generally are losing touch with a vital part of their past—and are doing so despite tremendous emphasis, in colleges and secondary schools, on American history and government. Constitutional democracy rests, in the long run, on popular understanding of its bases and operations. It is evident, therefore, that this growing neglect of constitutional history, and our tendency to build up arrearages of research and understanding, are by no means healthy signs.

In so far as popular—and even professional—understanding is concerned, one finds proof of this in the present status of the Fourteenth Amendment itself. That Amendment, as mystified Van Winkle[12] reminded us, has been a part of our Constitution

---

12. Once briefed, however, Van Winkle proved sharp indeed. The following fragment, found among his papers with the abbreviated title, "Reargt. School Seg. Cases?," suggests that he even for a time toyed with the notion of appearing *amicus curiae* opposite his eminent fellow-New Yorker, John W. Davis, Counsel for the State of South Carolina, and dean of the American corporate bar. From the references to Roscoe Conkling's argument it is plain the old libertarian took a sardonic layman's view of some matters not heretofore lightly treated either by judges or historians:

"Were we called upon to appear before your Honors in the role of counsel for corporations seeking protection as persons under Section One, challenging what even corporations apparently at times can feel to be 'invidious and discriminating legislation,' we should be obliged to make an embarrassing admission. We should have to admit that not one word ever has been found, either in the speeches of the framers, the debates of the 39th Congress, or the proceedings of the ratifying legislatures, which expressly declares, or otherwise clearly indicates, that even *one individual*, of all that extensive group, then 'contemplated or understood' corporate 'persons' to be embraced within the protection of Section One. An impenetrable barrier of silence—absolute and inscrutable—prevails here. To maintain the corporate proposition, therefore, we perhaps should be obliged to rest our case, as did that famous advocate and upstate New Yorker, Roscoe Conkling, when he appeared before this Court in 1882, wholly upon circumstantial grounds. We might be obliged to use, as was he, the Journal of the Joint Committee of Fifteen that drafted the Amendment,—and perhaps also some inference and conjecture [See Graham, *The 'Conspiracy Theory' of the Fourteenth Amendment*, 47 YALE L. J. 371, 375-385 (1938)] to show that corporations had come within the purview of the framers. We might well despair of that task—as might even our distinguished adversary, Mr. Davis himself, at this date. [See *Conn. Gen. Life Ins. Co. v. Johnson*, 303 U. S. 77, 83 (1938) ; *Wheeling Steel Corp. v. Glander*, 337 U. S. 562, 576-581 (1949).]

"But we all know that this corporate point, happily, has been foreclosed now for nearly 67 years. Not merely foreclosed, but substantially waived: In 1886, Conkling and his associate counsel were again prepared to make their extremely circumstantial argument, in a second series of *Railroad Tax Cases* involving the issues earlier left undecided when the first series had been withdrawn. At the outset of this second series of arguments, Chief Justice Waite announced from the bench, *in the only statement ever made by the full Court in deciding this crucial matter:* 'The court does not wish to hear argument on the question whether the provision in the Fourteenth Amendment to the Constitution, which forbids a State to deny to any person within its jurisdiction the equal protection of the laws, applies to these Corporations. We are all of the opinion that it does.'

Footnote continued on following page

4

eighty-five years. That it was adopted and ratified to remove all doubt about national power to protect the freedmen and to assure progressive removal of the discriminations, denials and abridgments in rights that had been a part of the slave system is generally conceded. Such has been the affirmed judicial view since 1873.[13] In 1908, moreover, Flack published his monograph, *The Adoption of the Fourteenth Amendment,* summarizing the debates in Congress and in the ratifying legislatures. Numerous works have recovered much of the ground since.[14] All agree regarding the racial motivation of the Amendment. In the meantime, however, certain collateral and secondary problems have become points of controversy. Two in particular have persisted at the judicial level: One, what framers and ratifiers contemplated or

---

Footnote continued from preceding page

"We today are beset by no difficulties or handicaps of evidence in these *School Cases.* The Congressional debates are almost too voluminous. . . .

"We will show, as predecessor counsel and historians have shown many times the past 85 years, that the Fourteenth Amendment was designed to be a bulwark for the rights of the Negro race; that it was designed to prohibit *all public* discriminations based upon race and color alone: that it was designed to wipe out what the Civil War generation rightly called the 'badges and indicia' of slavery, its hateful 'vestiges and appendages.' School Segregation, we submit, comes in this category.

"On these points, happily, our evidence is abundant; and the authorities are virtually unanimous. The ante-bellum history, the Congressional debates, the researches and writings of Flack, Fairman, Frank, Graham, Boudin, tenBroeck, and Crosskey, whatever their different emphases, and whatever the doubts or disagreements on secondary details, clearly and unanimously support our position."

The notes break off abruptly at this point. Close reading shows of course that although militantly anti-separate-but-equal, the orientation here is not anti-corporate. As some of his other memoranda made clear, Van Winkle felt that " 'Due process' and 'equal protection', not 'person', are the key words." "Query: Aren't they ample enough for anybody?" To renege on corporate personality at this date was by his view "Pretty close to infanticide. . . . Remorse inevitable, then perhaps another brood—or at least another *brood of fictions.*" See the pre-Civil War history of the diversity of citizenship clause, and McGovney thereon, *A Supreme Court Fiction,* 56 HARV. L. REV. 853 (1943). Finally, he concluded with the observation, "Calvinists haven't always thought so highly of legislatures, or had such occasion to, as people 1932-195?"

Elsewhere, Van Winkle gave hearty endorsement of the punched card project, proudly noting that IBM had made itself right at home in his native Catskills. The writer wishes to express his indebtedness to Dr. Van Winkle for numerous insights and suggestions.

13. The calamitous effects of a caste system which really was established and constitutionally condoned a full generation after Reconstruction (see WOODWARD, *op. cit supra* note 9, at 209-212 and Graham, *supra* note 4) have too long obscured this fact, as has the lush economic use made of the Amendment. Yet Justice Miller's majority opinion in the *Slaughter-House Cases, supra* note 5 and Justice Bradley's majority opinion in the *Civil Rights Cases,* 109 U. S. 3 (1883) both are strong expositions of the Negro Race motivation of the Amendment. It often is overlooked in this regard that Justice Bradley himself nominally accepted the "badges and incidents" thesis of Trumbull and Harlan. See also the strong Negro Race statements in *Shelley v. Kraemer,* 334 U. S. 1, 21 (1948) : *Buchanan v. Warley,* 245 U. S. 60, 76-77 (1917) ; *Strauder v. West Virginia,* 100 U. S. 303, 306-7 (1880). Our fears and sextants, not stars, have thrown us off course. Corrective action is a simple matter.

14. See note 3 *supra.*

5

understood with regard to corporate persons;[15] the other, whether Section One was intended to incorporate the Bill of Rights to the extent of making *all* the first eight Amendments binding upon the States.[16] Significantly, both of these controversies resulted in combing and recombing of debates for evidence to support two sets of diametrically opposed positions.[17] Research of this type necessarily has been piecemeal, with attention focused on the one narrow point, and to the neglect or subordination of larger purposes.

The upshot is that after nearly a half-century of research and debate judges and historians are still unagreed about two fundamental questions concerning the Amendment's purposes. Dismayed or not, the Court meantime, by its first two questions in the *School* cases,[18] directed that another minute search be made—on another narrow point—and again in a manner that tends to lose sight of the Amendment's broader objectives.

Furthermore, framer-intent, as a criterion in these matters, obviously has had a distinctly hit-and-miss application. So much so, indeed, that one wonders whether, in asking Negro counsel to search for and present evidence of framer-intent on this specific issue of school segregation the Court remembered that no such request ever had been made—or ever could have been made—with regard to countless matters and fields over which it previously had extended the Amendment's protection. Absolutely nothing, for example, is found in the debates on whether sound trucks[19] or picketing[20] are to be regarded as constitutionally privileged free speech. There is nothing on "reasonable" rates of return for public service companies.[21] In fact, no one ever has found a single word in the main debates suggesting that framers and ratifiers "contemplated or understood" corporations to be "persons" under the due process and equal protection clauses. Yet this last, most vital point was conceded by the Court, without formal

---

15. *Connecticut General Life Insurance Co. v. Johnson,* 303 U. S. 77, 83 (1938); *Wheeling Steel Corp. v. Glander,* 337 U. S. 562, 576 (1949).

16. *Adamson v. California,* 332 U. S. 46 (1947).

17. On the corporate personality issue, see Graham, *Conspiracy Theory of the Fourteenth Amendment,* 47 YALE L. J. 371 (1938), 48 YALE L. J. 171 (1938); and as an example of the diverse interpretations drawn therefrom, see HACKER, THE TRIUMPH OF AMERICAN CAPITALISM 388-392 (1940), and FAIRMAN, MR. JUSTICE MILLER AND THE SUPREME COURT 187-189 (1939). On the incorporation of the Bill of Rights problem, see Justice Black's historical appendix, *Adamson v. California,* 332 U. S. 46, 68, 92-123 (1947) and Fairman, *supra* note 3, and the companion article by Morrison, *Does the Fourteenth Amendment Incorporate the Bill of Rights?* 2 STAN. L. REV. 140 (1949).

18. See notes 1 and 2 *supra.*

19. *Saia v. New York,* 334 U. S. 558 (1948). *Kovacs v. Cooper,* 336 U. S. 77 (1949). See also *Railway Express Agency v. New York,* 336 U. S. 106 (1949).

20. *Thornhill v. Alabama,* 310 U. S. 88 (1940).

21. *Smyth v. Ames,* 169 U. S. 466 (1897).

6

opinion, and with the matter of framer-intent substantially waived, exactly 67 years ago![22]

On the other hand, the evidence in the debates is overwhelming that racial discrimination *very broadly conceived* was the framers' target.[23] Added *constitutional* power thus was tapped for this very reason and an attempt at a minute (or even broad) taxonomy of discriminations was understandably avoided.[24] As Bingham put it, "You do not prohibit murder in the Constitution; you guarantee life in the Constitution."[25] And so, it was with "liberty" and "protection," and above all, *equal* protection."

No doubt these are matters to which the Justices are now devoting serious consideration. It is appropriate therefore, before turning to the central difficulty that bedevilled draftmanship and early interpretation of the Fourteenth Amendment—to say nothing of our own ability to perceive and fully comprehend the framers' purposes—to call attention to one vital objection to this whole prevailing approach. Manifestly, the trend at both the judicial and historical levels has been toward a narrow antiquarianism. Facts are being determined and treated in isolation, one at a time, and virtually out of their contexts. Where we should now be synthesizing our knowledge of the Fourteenth Amendment, we go on fragmentizing it, pulverizing it, compartmentalizing it. This obviously can get us nowhere. The orbits of inquiry are too restricted; the purposes too narrow, too disconnected. Results naturally are indecisive; and can only be increasingly so. Law office history and search—and *re*-search!—of this type could go on forever to no clear result—could become as sterile and negative as medieval scholasticism. Indeed, "constitutional scholasticism" would seem an excellent name for the trend. For even if applied evenhandedly this method is open to serious objection. It tends to make 1866 the decisive date in American history; it gives rise to innumerable searches of records for guidance that simply isn't there; it leads to obscurantism and conjecture; almost inevitably it transforms the humble "argument from silence" into both a murderous and a suicidal weapon.[26]

---

22. *Santa Clara County v. Southern Pacific Ry. Co.*, 118 U. S. 394, 396 (1886) (equal protection clause); *Minneapolis and St. L. Ry. Co. v. Beckwith*, 129 U. S. 26, 28 (1889) (due process clause).
23. See TENBROEK, *op. cit. supra* note 3; Graham, *Early Antislavery Backgrounds of the Fourteenth Amendment*, [1950] WIS. L. REV. 479 and 610; Frank and Munro, cited *supra* note 3; also Graham, *supra* note 4.
24. Graham, *supra* note 4.
25. CONG. GLOBE, 39th Cong., 1st Sess. 432 (1866).
26. A national conference, or an hour of professional soul-searching on "The Use and Misuse of the Argument from Silence" might have beneficial results. Fifteen years
Footnote continued on following page

7

If we are interested in arriving at the purpose and meaning of our Fourteenth Amendment, in so far as that meaning can be determined from what was said by those who sponsored and ratified it, 1866-68, there is a simple and decisive way of doing so. The debates are extensive, but not unlimited; they simply call for systematic analysis and for *complete, detailed tabulation* of findings rather than for mere *reading, summary,* and *selective quotation.* Above all, the speakers' positions and remarks ought to be correlated with various background data, and the whole coded and analyzed with reference to all significant points and relationships.[27]

The modern, efficient way to do this is by coordinate or punched card analysis. If the eyesight and energy expended in the course of the reading and searches on each successive narrow point that has arisen had been directed along these lines, we today should have a complete permanent index covering every major issue and problem included in the debates, and one that would point up significant interrelationships, not only of the framers' ideas and objectives, but of the influences and affiliations responsible for them. With the Fourteenth Amendment today the constitutional cornerstone of civil liberties in the States,[28] and with hundreds of thousands of dollars to be expended in the next few years by the Fund for the Republic,[29] on studies of their definition and enforcement, it would seem that this long overdue project must presently be undertaken.

It is interesting to note in this respect that exploration of antislavery backgrounds[30] meanwhile has begun to afford a clearer picture of what framers of the Fourteenth Amendment were driving at, and why they employed the phraseology they did. How the equal protection-due process-privileges-immunities trilogy crystallized from primitive natural rights theories and from earlier constitutional forms; how, during the long antislavery crusade, it became a form of shorthand for, and spearhead of, the Federal Bill of Rights; how at last in 1866 it won full-fledged con-

---

Footnote continued from preceding page

ago in 47 YALE L. J. 386-387 the writer probed this problem and won numerous converts. Backsliding however has been frequent, and at times the writer himself has been sorely tempted. Resolution in these matters would be effectively aided by a truly comprehensive, multi-dimensional analysis of the debates.

27. The writer has prepared a draft schedule of a number of points and issues which in his judgment should be covered in such an analysis. He will welcome the views and suggestions of others on these matters.

28. See works cited note 3 *supra;* REPPY, CIVIL RIGHTS IN THE UNITED STATES 103 ff. (1951) and especially c. VI "Group Discrimination and the Constitution."

29. Newsweek, June 8, 1953, p. 60, col. 1.

30. See especially Graham, *supra* note 23, and TENBROEK, *op. cit. supra* note 3.

8

stitutional status as a kind of universal common denominator, is a thrilling story that need not be repeated here. The heart of it is that the framers' three-clause system represented a thirty-year winnowing and synthesis of the antislavery, anti-race discrimination argument. Religious, ethical, historical appeals constituted its original forms. At the outset, the Lockean philosophy of antecedant and inalienable rights (which colonial leaders had employed so effectively in the Revolution) simply had been given a new twist. Americans, it was argued, had to live up to their Declaration. "All men" had to mean *all men;* "Governments . . . instituted to secure these rights" of "life, liberty and the pursuit of happiness"; and governments "deriving their *just* powers from the *consent* of the governed" had to bestow protection, and to bestow it equally, irrespective of race and color, or the "self-evident truths" became self-evident mockery.

Thus, from the very beginning the antislavery movement was fundamentally a quest for *protection* of the laws. Slavery was ethically repugnant, not simply because it chattelized man, but because it repudiated the very purpose of government and arbitrarily denied to some humans its protections solely on the basis of skin color.

This double-headed concept and standard of equal protection of the laws, ethically derived from Lockean theory, from the Declaration and from the comity clauses of the Articles of Confederation and Constitution, as well as from the State and Federal Bills of Rights, was already well synthesized by the 1830s.[31] It was spelled out fully and given its most persuasive statement in two of the early documents of the organized antislavery movement: first, in the Ellsworth-Goddard argument in the *Crandall Case,*[32] wherein local Black Laws in Connecticut denying out-of-state Negro children rights of education were successfully challenged; then in repeated attacks by the newly-formed Ohio Antislavery Society on similar Ohio laws which denied free Negroes rights of residence, livelihood, court testimony and education.[33] In both of these instances strong use was made of the federal comity clause, and of a nascent concept of a "general" or paramount "American" or "national" citizenship. In the Ohio attacks, moreover, the due course of law clause of the State Constitution also was employed. Thus by 1835 all three elements of our modern Fourteenth Amendment trinity are found linked together

---

31. Graham, *supra* note 23 *passim.*
32. 10 Conn. 339, 341-348 (1834) ; see Graham *supra* note 23, at 498-506, especially n. 65.
33. *Id.* at 494-498.

9

and used actively against racial discrimination and in behalf of the rights of the free Negroes of the North.[34]

This, however, is barely half the story. The most fascinating part of it is how this primitive constitutional argument got broadcast[35] over the land—reiterated, expanded, winnowed, and clarified —until by 1866 it served the Civil War generation as a form of constitutional shorthand—an ethico-legal common denominator designed to accomplish *within* the Constitution and through the courts, precisely what, for the past thirty years, it had accomplished as a "higher law", *above* the Constitution, and *in the minds of those* who had crusaded so long against slavery and against racial discrimination. One can sense immediately the hazards and the obstacles to this sort of constitutional transsubstantiation, and these are being treated at length in another article.[36] The point here is that this powerful "antislavery impulse" radiated outward from central and western New York in the early and mid-thirties.[37] It was a part of a "revival of religion" led by Charles G. Finney, an able lawyer turned evangelist, and by Theodore Weld, then still a student at Oneida Institute and ultimately one of the most remarkable, influential men of his generation. Backed by New York philanthropists who in 1833 organized the American Antislavery Society, and aided by dedicated groups of students attracted by his leadership and personality, Weld and his "Oneidas" moved westward. During the mid- and late-thirties they converted thousands in Ohio, west Pennsylvania and New York to their "benevolent reforms"—temperance, women's and Negroes' rights, and above all, to "immediate emancipation"— i. e., emancipation *immediately begun.* By means of revivals, pamphlets, newspapers; by "declarations," resolutions, petitions, they broadcast their ethico-moral-religious-constitutional argument, abolitionizing whole communities.[38]

Such success however, soon generated reaction, and reaction brought about reorientation.[39] Denied access to the Southern and border States; maligned and attacked as subversives and sedition-

---

34. It is impossible to overstress the fact that the antislavery movement merely was the largest part of an anti-race discrimination movement. The discriminations against free Negroes, and those against Indians for example, were as vigorously attacked as slavery, and for the same reason: race and color were arbitrary, irrational bases for distinctions in men's rights. This fact obviously has tremendous bearing on the scope and purpose of both the Thirteenth and Fourteenth Amendments. Yet our tendency, almost from the first in construing the Amendments has been to think of slavery simply as chattelization, and to ignore the broader motivations.
35. See note 30 *supra*.
36. Graham, *supra* note 4.
37. See BARNES, THE ANTISLAVERY IMPULSE (1933).
38. *Ibid.;* also DUMOND, THE ANTISLAVERY ORIGINS OF THE CIVIL WAR (1938).
39. *Ibid.;* BARNES, *op. cit. supra* note 37.

10

ists by proslave forces fearful both of emancipation and of slave insurrections, obliged to defend even their own rights to discuss and to proselytize, the American Antislavery Society leaders and their movement soon were left with no alternative but political action. This alternative they at first accepted reluctantly, then exploited brilliantly. First in the Liberty Party of 1840-44,[40] then in the Free Soil Party of 1848,[41] and the Free Democracy of 1852,[42] leaders like Salmon P. Chase[43]—original converts of the Weld group—wrote into their platforms and speeches and resolutions these very concepts of protection and of equal protection derived from the Declaration of Independence and guaranteed by the paramount national citizenship of the comity clause and by state and federal due process. Such arguments of course were now no longer limited merely to proving the expediency and justice of abolition, but were turned against slavery and all its works. At length, after repeal of the Missouri Compromise by the Kansas-Nebraska Act, the new Republican Party, taking its stand now against *extension* of slavery, appropriated *in toto* and repeated in its own platforms and in countless speeches of its members and leaders, 1854-60,[44] this identical rhetoric and theory. Old texts thus were refurbished and given rebirth. So, at long last, the rejected stones came to stand at the head of the corner.

Nothing better ties all these developments together, or better reveals their true character and significance, than a speech made in the House in 1859 by John A. Bingham.[45] Bingham of course was the Ohio representative who just seven years later was destined to draft Sections One and Five of the Fourteenth Amendment. At this date he represented the 21st District which had been thoroughly abolitionized by the antislavery evangelists in 1835-37 while he himself was attending Franklin College near Cadiz. Franklin then had been second only to Oberlin as an antislavery stronghold. Indeed, we find records of petitions and resolutions of the Cadiz antislavery societies couched in the very phraseology for which Bingham, now in 1859, and later, manifests his preference. Moreover, his speech is made against a provision

---

40. The relevant planks are quoted in TEN BROEK, *op. cit. supra* note 3, at 119-121; see also STANWOOD, HISTORY OF THE PRESIDENCY 218 (1904).

41. *Id.* at 240.

42. *Id.* at 253-254.

43. See HART, SALMON P. CHASE 51-52 (1899). A thorough study of Chase's role in the antislavery movement would itself do much to set the War Amendments in clearer perspective.

44. See STANWOOD, *op. cit. supra* note 40, at 271-272, 291-294 for the due process and other antislavery constitutional theory in the Republican Platforms of 1856 and 1860. Note Planks 2, 8, and 14 of 1860.

45. See DICT. AM. BIOG.; BRENNAN, BIOG. ENCYCL. . . . OF OHIO 312 (1880); Graham, *supra* note 23 at 623, 655, n. 149, 150, 255.

11

in the Oregon Constitution of 1857[46] which was almost a repetition of the hateful Ohio Black laws: "No free Negro or mulatto not residing in the State at the time of the adoption of this Constitution, shall ever come, reside or be within this State, or hold any real estate, or make any contract or maintain any suit therein . . ."

Bingham first contended[47] that these provisions violated the Federal comity clause and the rights of "citizens of the United States." "Who are citizens of the United States? They are those, and those only, who owe allegience to the Government of the United States . . . [They are] all free persons born or domiciled within the jurisdiction of the United States, and aliens naturalized under the laws of Congress."

> I invite attention to the significant fact that natural or inherent rights, which belong to all men, irrespective of all conventional regulations, are by this Constitution guaranteed by the broad and comprehensive word "person," as contradistinguished from the limited term citizen—as in the fifth article of amendments, guarding those *sacred rights* which *are* as *universal* and *indestructible* as the human race, that "no person shall be deprived of life, liberty, or property, but by due process of law, nor shall private property be taken without just compensation." And this guarantee *applies* to all citizens within the United States. [Italics supplied.]

Against infringement of "these wise and beneficent guarantees of political rights to the citizens of the United States as such, and of natural rights to all persons, whether citizens or strangers," stood the supremacy clause.

> There, sir, is the limitation upon State sovereignty— simple, clear, and strong. No State may *rightfully,* by Constitution or statute law, impair any of these guaranteed rights either political or natural. They may not *rightfully or lawfully* declare that the strong citizens may deprive the weak citizens of their rights, natural or political . . .
>
> This provision [excluding free Negroes and mulattoes] seems to me . . . injustice and oppression incarnate. This provision, sir, excludes from the State of Oregon eight hundred thousand of the native born citizens of the other States, who are, therefore, *citizens of the United States.* I grant you that a State may restrict the exercise of the elective franchise to certain classes of citizens of the United States, to the exclusion of others; but I deny that any State may exclude a law-abiding

---

46. Art. I, § 35.
47. CONG. GLOBE, 35th Cong., 2d Sess. 981-985 (1859).

12

citizen of the United States from coming within its territory, or abiding therein, or acquiring and enjoying property therein, or from the enjoyment therein of the "privileges and immunities" of a *citizen of the United States.* What says the Constitution:

"The citizens of each State shall be entitled to all privileges and immunities of citizens in the several States." Art. 4, Section 2.

Here is no qualification . . . The citizens of each State, all the citizens of each State, *being citizens of the United States,* shall be entitled to "all privileges and immunities of citizens of the several States." Not to the rights and immunities of the several States; not to those constitutional rights and immunities which result exclusively from State authority or State legislation; but to "all privileges and immunities" of citizens of the United States in the several States. *There is an ellipsis in the language employed in the Constitution, but its meaning is self-evident,* that it is "the privileges and immunities of citizens of the United States" that it guarantees . . .

[S]ir, I maintain that the persons thus excluded from the State by this section of the Oregon Constitution, are citizens by birth of the several States, and therefore *are citizens of the United States,* and as such are entitled to all the privileges and immunities of citizens of the United States, amongst which *are* the rights of life and liberty and property, and their due protection in the enjoyment thereof by law; . . .

Who, sir, are citizens of the United States? First, all free persons born and domiciled within the United States—not all free white persons, but all free persons. You will search in vain, in the Constitution of the United States, for that word white; it is not there. You will look in vain for it in that first form of National Government—the Articles of Confederation; it is not there. The omission of this word—this phrase of caste —from our national charter, was not accidental, but intentional. . . .

This Government rests upon the absolute equality of natural rights amongst men. . . .

Who, . . . will be bold enough to deny that all persons *are equally entitled to the enjoyment of the rights of life and liberty and property, and that no one should be deprived of life or liberty,* but as punishment for crime; nor of his property, against his consent and without due compensation? . . .

The equality of all to the right to live; *to the right to know;* to argue and to utter, according to conscience; to work, and enjoy the product of their toil, is the rock on which that Constitution rests— . . . The charm of that Constitution lies in

13

the great democratic idea which it embodies, that *all men, before the law, are equal in respect to those rights of person which God gives,* and *no man or State may rightfully take away,* except as a forfeiture for crime. Before your Constitution, sir, *as it is,* as I trust it ever will be, all men are sacred, whether white or black. . . . [Italics supplied throughout.]

Surely, this speech alone is enough to put Sections One and Five in clearer perspective. All the clauses and concepts that Bingham and the Joint Committee were to employ seven years later are employed here. Protection and equal protection, due process of law, and a paramount national citizenship attained by removing the "ellipsis" from the comity clause, are all expressly relied on. They are relied on, moreover, to combat the type of racial classification, and racial discrimination, that were incidents of slavery, and which had been attacked by these forms repeatedly in the quarter century since their use in the *Crandall* arguments and in the Ohio Antislavery Society report on the state's Black Laws. (Indeed, use of the comity clause in this manner extended back to similar use in the debates over Missouri's admission to the Union, 1819-21,[48] and even to use, in 1778, of the comity clause of the still-unratified Articles of Confederation.)[49] It is interesting to note, furthermore, that although this speech was made two years after the *Dred Scott* decision, Bingham not only does not follow that decision, he does not even acknowledge or mention it; he simply disavows any color line as a basis for citizenship of the United States; he regards Milton's rights of communication and conscience, including the right *to know—to education*—as one of the great fundamental natural "rights of person which God gives and no man or state may *rightfully* take away," and which hence are "embodied," also, within, and secured by, "the great democratic idea that all men before the law are equal." In short, the concept and guarantee of the equal protection of the laws is already "embodied" in the Federal Constitution of 1859, notwithstanding the *Dred Scott* decision; this same concept, moreover, embraces "the equality of all . . . to the right to know"; and above all, there is no color line even in the Constitution of 1859!

It is the bearing and significance of this inherent and inalienable rights argument—("fundamental rights of person which God gives and no man or state may rightfully take away")—that calls for consideration. Patently, what we are witnessing in this speech of Bingham's—so typical of thousands in the two decades 1819-

---

48. See McLaughlin, *op. cit. supra* note 10, c. 29; Burgess, The Middle Period, 1817-58 c. 4 (1897).
49. Graham, *supra* note 23 at 616, n. 103.

14

66[50]—is a gradual constitutionalization of an ethico-moral argument or ideal. Slavery—with its theories of racial damnation, racial inferiority and racial discrimination—was inherently repugnant to the American Creed and the Christian ethic. This fact was being rapidly and increasingly sensed. As men sensed it, they fit it into the only political theory they knew: Governments existed, not to *give*, but to *protect* human rights; allegiance and protection were reciprocal—i. e., *ought to be reciprocal;* rights and duties were correlative—i. e., *had to be correlative* if Americans ever were to live with their consciences and to justify their declared political faith.[51]

Let us note well this point, for it is precisely the problem we still are faced with, and it is one of the keys to understanding the Fourteenth Amendment: Ethical and religious opinions were here molding and remolding constitutional doctrine. Moral premises were being translated into legal and constitutional premises—i. e., *enforceable rights.* This was being done by a "due processing" and an "equal protecting" of the Law of Nature. It was going on, as yet, largely in the public, rather than in the judicial mind, but let us not condemn it on that account. (Paraphrasing the familiar: "Is not every human a judge?") What these men were doing was using the sanctions of a "higher"—i. e., ethico-moral law—to defeat and override the claims of an arbitrary, barbarous, positive law. Now in doing this they of course got themselves into some logical and semantic difficulties. Bootstrap arguments often tend —or end— so! Yet without bootstrap arguments to give scope to men's conscience and idealism, and to their sense of justice or injustice, surely the law would have remained poor and barbarous indeed.[52]

It is strange and unfortunate so little attention has been paid to this phase of the antislavery conflict. It perhaps is the classic example of moral and ethical revision of the law and of creative

---

50. The report and pamphlet documentation of the American Antislavery Society crusade alone is huge; add to it items broadcasting the constitutional argument, the repetition by speeches, petitions, resolutions, editorials, literary society debates, etc., *over a period of two generations, throughout all the non-slave States,* and one perceives that the three-clause system of Section One was no spontaneous or fortuitous creation.

51. See Graham, *supra* note 23 at 614-617, 638-643 for characteristic statements and evidence showing the evolution of this ethical interpretation of American origins and destiny.

52. For interesting recent discussions of the relations of the "is" and "ought" in law, cf. FULLER, THE LAW QUEST OF ITSELF (1940); CAHN, THE SENSE OF INJUSTICE (1949); STONE, PROVINCE AND FUNCTION OF LAW (1946) c. VIII "Natural Law," especially pp. 227-238; COHEN, ETHICAL SYSTEMS AND LEGAL IDEALS (1933). PATTERSON, JURISPRUDENCE: MEN AND IDEAS OF THE LAW 230-243 (1953) has a useful hornbook discussion and bibliography of the "Principles of Morality as Sources" of law. See also, *id.* at 358-375, §§ 4.15-4.17 on "Natural Law."

15

popular jurisprudence and constitution making[53]—at least in the nineteenth century. "Hearthstone opinions"[54] in this process obviously were far more vital and determinative than judicial opinions.[55] Constitutional Law here was growing at the base rather than at the top. The change in the *ethos* determined the change in the *leges*, and the continuous interactions run to the heart of both history and politics. Furthermore, our own generation is now bedevilled by similar problems, and is nervously groping toward affirmative re-declarations of human rights with a view toward eventual sanctions at the international level. It would seem very much worthwhile, therefore, to re-examine this experience and learn from it all we can.

Despite this high relevance, our attitude toward those responsible for the Civil War changes has tended toward indifference and hyper-criticism. In part, this is a natural result of the Reconstruction debacle—(though certainly the worst failures of that period arose not from constitutional idealism, but from the lack or the loss of it). Hence, we still are more inclined to criticize the framers' "miserable draftsmanship",[56] or speculate on their possible cunning, or even ulterior purposes,[57] than to consider exactly what it was they had to contend with. Another factor undoubtedly has been that natural rights-higher law thinking is no

---

53. A great deal has been written about the Higher Law and Natural Law content of American constitutional decisions—cf. the familiar of Corwin, Haines, Wright, Grant, and Commager—but the fascinating and elusive relations between the popular matrix and the judicial impress are almost untouched. See however, POUND, THE FORMATIVE ERA OF AMERICAN LAW 16 (1938); and note 51 *supra*.

54. This happy phrase was discovered in a speech made by Rep. James F. Wilson during debates on the Thirteenth Amendment. The tenacious hold and blight of slavery, he said, extended "From hearthstone opinions to decisions of the Supreme Court of the United States . . ." CONG. GLOBE, 38th Cong., 1st Sess. 1201 (1864).

55. On the role of antislavery "hearthstone opinions" in expanding due process, see Graham, *Procedure to Substance, Extra Judicial Rise of Due Process, 1830-1860*, 40 CALIF. L. REV. 483 (1953).

56. For one example among many, see Grant, *The Natural Law Background of Due Process*, 31 COL. L. REV. 56, 66 (1931); or witness almost any modern law students' class discussion. Such criticism originated in the widening gap between known intent and judicial interpretation after the *Slaughter-House* decision; it has persisted and increased in recent years as our capacity to appreciate the formerly-powerful hold of natural law theories has inevitably declined.

A related astigmatism is the view, well expressed by MOTT, DUE PROCESS OF LAW 166 (1926), ". . . there seems to have been a subconscious attempt on the part of the framers and ratifiers of the Fourteenth Amendment to make it as vague as possible." The writer submits that this is hindsight with a vengeance. Possibly the shift from positive to negative form—*i. e.* moving the phrase "Congress shall have power . . ." from Section One to Section Five was dictated in part by fancied cleverness, but the antislavery backgrounds, wholly ignored by Flack and only recently rediscovered, certainly explain the rest of the draft, and incidentally expose our own long-fallacious approach to the Amendment (*i. e.* the mistaken older view that it was simply a fortuitous combination of restraint clauses plus a redundant grant of power to enforce rights already entrusted to the judiciary).

57. Cf. the perennial fascinations of the "Conspiracy Theory"; see note 3 *supra*, the articles of Graham, Boudin, McLaughlin, and references therein cited.

16

longer in vogue today.[58] Indeed, it is a red flag to a law school-drilled generation. Admittedly, old imprecisions and manifest preferences for clumsy "universals"[59] in place of today's sharp analysis have been further barriers to interest and understanding.

All we need to do, however, to purge ourselves of this bemused superciliousness toward those responsible for the Civil War constitutional changes is to consider for a moment exactly what these men had been up against. One perceives immediately that they had had to contend with one of the most difficult and confusing problems in politics and jurisprudence—the problem of the "irresolvable" conflict between the moral and the positive law— the political-legal equivalent of the scholastics' irresistible force and immovable body! In the extreme form and terms, such a problem obviously is unsolvable, except verbally. Yet in practice it rarely is so. Solution depends ultimately upon a fact situation, and hence upon the extent to which the irresistible force does move the unmovable body—or vice versa. Politics and government are essentially accommodation and compromise. It is only the most fiercely and intensely held moral convictions that ever approach the uncompromisable, or rise Phoenix-like from repeated defeats, as did the Abolitionists. Positive law itself has a dual nature. It is *both* printed texts and human behaviour. When irreconcilable opinion intervenes as a third force, polarizing the two, arraying one against the other, we have trouble. Representative government is a means of minimizing this danger. The slavery conflict marks the one utter failure in American history—the

---

58. This statement obviously needs some qualification. The rapid decline of naked natural rights thinking was made possible. and perhaps inevitable, by the Fourteenth Amendment. No one officially has deplored this development. What we too often fail to appreciate is that only these thin cloaks of substantive due process and equal protection conceal and disguise our own nakedness. Our new enthusiasm for Constitutional positivism, therefore, is at times pretty smug. This was another thing that irked Van Winkle. "Intellectual prudery", he called it. "What we need now in this School Segregation business is some 'Mote and beam jurisprudence.' For seventy years everyone else has *benefited by this ambiguity and free-wheeling discretion. Must only the Negroes continue to be victims of it?"*

59. For an interesting use of sweeping Blackstonian "absolute rights of personal security, personal liberty and personal property," followed by embarrassing attempts to delimit them by muddled distinctions, see the speech of Rep. James F. Wilson, House sponsor of the Civil Rights Act of 1866, CONG. GLOBE, 39th Cong. 1st Sess. 1115-1119 (1866). Wilson was a conscientious and able leader, but the law he had learned out of Blackstone and Kent as a harness-maker's apprentice from the age of thirteen, simply was inadequate for the purposes at hand. The writer submits that it is either snobbery or lack of imagination to conclude from such difficulties that these men had no clear idea of what they were trying to do. The trouble is simply that our greater sophistication in the complexities of a federal system tends to distract us from their perfectly clearcut anti-race discrimination purposes. Nearly any modern law student is better equipped than these men were to deal with many phases of such a problem. But the beginning of wisdom here is to stop judging men and intent by reading history backward to 1866 and to start reading it forward to that date. The Reconstruction and post-Reconstruction shambles of the Fourteenth Amendment necessarily are poor aids for its interpretation.

17

unique case where ethico-moral opinions ultimately proved uncompromisable; or, to speak more accurately, where sectional interests and taboos so rigidified, stratified, and hamstrung the federal system as to render articulated compromise and reform impossible.

From the first, of course, both sides regarded the slavery struggle as one *of, by,* and *for* Law. The difficulty was over the nature and sources of law. Was slavery *legal,* or was it not? All hands agreed slavery to be supported in each of the slave States by a body of statutes and decisions. But that did not satisfy antislavery men. Nor would it have satisfied many of us. Slavery was wrong: Ethically, morally, outrageously wrong—the wrongest, most barbarous, anachronistic institution in the civilized world.[60] Hope originally lay for its peaceful eradiction—for progressive change and attrition of the positive law through education and moral suasion. Christianity and patriotism were both powerful potential levers and solvents. Their efficacy, however, presumed and required open channels of discussion and appeal—appeal to reason and to conscience.[61]

Now in contrast, consider what actually occurred: cotton profits and politics, combining with morbid fears of slave insurrection, first had introverted, then isolated the South, withdrawing the institution from discussion and criticism, and at length—in abolitionists' eyes—blasphemously apotheosizing it, declaring it constitutionally sacred and beyond reach, a "positive good."[62] Such claims were depressing and offensive enough, even when made solely with reference to slavery *in the States.* When eventually expanded (through repeal of the Missouri Compromise and by the *Dred Scott*[63] decision) to remove all limits upon slavery in the Territories, they became intolerable. The impasse now was complete. Slavery, wrong as ever, had been put beyond reach, made unassailable, impregnable.

Now the point is that the "higher law" always had afforded the one psychological and doctrinal escape from such an impasse. It was essentially an ethical draft on the future for the benefit of the present—an unconscious borrowing from men's ideals to

---

60. See NEVINS' lucid Chapter 5, "Slavery in a World Setting". 2 THE EMERGENCE OF LINCOLN (1950), (also his earlier discussions in Chapters 13-15 in his ORDEAL OF THE UNION (1947)), for an account and view of the institution on the eve of the War. Nevins' conclusion merits pondering today (with reference to slavery's *vestiges*): "But the time had come when the country, however reluctantly, must face a plain fact: if the United States was really to be the last, best hope of mankind, it could not much longer remain a slaveholding republic." (p. 168).

61. See Dumond, *op. cit. supra* note 38; NYE, FETTERED FREEDOM (1949).

62. See Graham *supra* note 23, especially pp. 631-638. JENKINS, PROSLAVERY THOUGHT IN THE OLD SOUTH (1935).

63. 19 How. 393 (U. S. 1856).

18

civilize their law and humanize their politics. It was the one means of reconciling facts and ideals abstractly in the hope of doing so prospectively. Slavery and race discrimination were unconstitutional by a "higher law" than the Constitution. *Ergo,* the higher law ought to *become* the Constitution.[64]

To modern-trained positivists who are inclined to reject this solution, and to dismiss it as logically "naive and unsound," it is only fair to issue this challenge: How would we, believing slavery to be morally wrong and ethically indefensible, have attacked it and attempted its overthrow *by peaceful means within a federal system so effectively controlled by pro-slave forces as to remove the institution from reach and even from constructive discussion?*

How indeed! The silence soon is shattering, and it is shattering simply because the alternatives—for antislavery Whigs and Democrats particularly—are seen to have been surrender and condonation on the one hand and resort to this unsatisfactory higher law-"court of last appeal" on the other. To be candid about it, then, the higher law was a forensic and educative device; it was the safety valve that prevented antislavery men from "blowing their tops." Our generation has been unduly smug about the matter largely because we have lacked the insight to see that—fortunately—we have escaped any such intense and irreconcilable positive law-moral law conflict in our own times. (Prohibition of course compares here as a grim joke to high tragedy. Moreover, it was so susceptible to repeal by mass evasion that the example itself underscores the differences.) War crimes undoubtedly are the nearest modern approach, and indeed a very significant one: For here again, conscience leavened and innovated the positive law, rather than confess its own impotence.[65]

We can epitomize the matter by saying that ordinarily law grows interstitially and metabolically. Yet it always is a product of men's higher faculties and social challenges. When these challenges are increased to inordinate levels, responses are apt to be likewise increased. And when the challenge is an ethico-moral challenge, the law itself ultimately must grow in ethical and moral content; it will do so creatively if it is unable to do so metabolically.

---

64. The research of Professors Dumond, Nye, Jenkins, and Eaton *op cit. supra* notes 38, 61, and 62, points up the fact that the fatal blunder in the slavery struggle was the proscription of persuasion and conversion.

65. See CAHN, *op. cit. supra* note 52, at p. 30, citing R. H. Jackson, Trial of War Criminals, Dept. of State Pub. #2420 (1945) p. 7. ". . . the test of what legally is crime gives recognition to those things which fundamentally outraged the conscience of the American People and brought them finally to the conviction that their own liberty and civilization could not persist in the same world with Nazi Power."

19

If this view be taken, it is plain that the trouble throughout the long struggle over slavery was not so much that there was this inevitable dualism between moral and civil rights, but that the necessities of the case demanded that men speak these two jurisprudential languages in the same breath. That is, *forensically*, rights needed to be—and were—interchangeably regarded as preexistent ideals and as socially implemented and enforceable privileges or immunities. On the one plane stood the parchment constitution, given effect by statutes and precedents; on the other, the subjective instrument which "guaranteed" and "declared" certain antecedent natural rights. The document thus was alternately shadow and substance—an amendable legal instrument, and one which, "correctly interpreted" or "declared," required no amendment.

Now this dualism is inherent and inevitable in natural law theory. Indeed, Professor Fuller[66] has defined natural law as a body of thought that tolerates just such confusion for the sake of its ethical advantages. Hence the dualism persisted, and it reached its climax in 1866. From our present viewpoint, it would have helped, surely, if men had perceived then, as clearly as we do today, that when *amending the Constitution* it is best to eschew declaratory theories. To do otherwise, is to put an impossible strain upon the legal vocabulary: for definitions break down and overlap, and communication and straight thinking become almost impossible.[67] The point is that these men did not, and the Civil War generation could not eschew such theories, because until after 1865 that generation rarely had known nor used any other! Thus the antislaveryites' dualism—or if one wishes to be snobbish about it, confusion—really was inherent in their necessary job of "due processing" the Law of Nature and in "protecting" and *"equal* protecting" the rights of *all* human beings without regard for race or color.

It thus can be said that moral and ethical opinions were the matrix of the War Amendments. The texts and forms themselves, however, evolved under tremendous counter pressures. These identifying facts alone stamp the three amendments as unique parts of our Constitution. In geological terms, the three amendments are the "youngest," grandest parts of the document. The forces that produced them,[68] moreover, still are growing today, both by accretion and through deep seated internal changes and pressures. We must remember, too, that these "peaks"

---

66. See *op. cit. supra* note 52, at 5.
67. See Graham, *supra* note 4.
68. *Id.* and the works of Graham and tenBroek, cited note 3, *supra*.

20

arose cataclysmically in the Sixties because misguided men so misjudged their relation to these very facts and forces.

May it not be laid down as axiomatic, even, that the concept of equal protection of the laws, in racial matters, can no more be held today to its mid-nineteenth century bounds than due process of law could be held—perhaps we had better say here, *returned*— to that curiously imperfect understanding of it had by King John and his Barons at Runnymede. Indeed, what happened to old *"per legum terrae,"* 1215-1953,[69] would seem to be the answer absolute to those who now are offering us their depressing pictures of a cold, sterile, static equal protection—one cast forever in an 1866 mold;[70] just as what happened to that classic and carefully fitted volcanic plug of due process, after *Dred Scott*,[71] ought to be warning enough to the self-styled "militants" who again are bravely trucking up their cement and mixers for another filling of these same craters. Law and ethics, these men bluntly tell us, are separate fields. So indeed they are. But spare America the day again when both together do not determine the meaning of equal protection of the laws.[72]

Equal protection of the laws, as we can see, and as Dr. tenBroek[73] has shown at much greater length, meant first of all the *full* protection of the laws. Mind: not *"separate but equal,"*

---

69. See Graham, *supra* note 55 for a bibliography and noting up.

70. There were many reasons why men's understanding of equal protection, as applied to educational matters, was imperfect in 1866. There were few Negro schools of any kind at that date. Slave codes for generations had denied education to slaves. After 1835, in most slave states, it was a crime to teach *any* Negro—slave or free—to read or write. (See HURD, LAW OF FREEDOM AND BONDAGE (1862)). Negroes were barred from public schools of the North, and still widely regarded as "racially inferior" and "incapable of education." Even comparatively enlightened leaders then accepted segregation in schools. To argue that this means we today are bound by that understanding and practice is to transform the *mores* and laws of slave code days into constitutional sanctions, impossible to be cast off or even moderated.

71. See note 63 *supra*.

72. It is an unpleasant fact to remember that the constitutional protection accorded the Negro Race was vitiated and progress in race relations delayed a full two generations (1897-ca. 1930) because overburdened, poorly prepared, and at times negligent or incompetent counsel, *fighting single-handedly and at random a discrimination against an individual client*, proved no match for a battery of railroad, steamship or associated State counsel in the crucial cases 1875-1896. This situation, fortunately unique in our law, obviously is a powerful argument for reopening many of these issues and for accelerating revisionism. "Jim Crow" too often gained entrance by something very close to default or left-handed social favoritism.

73. *Op. cit. supra* note 3, at 176-180, 222. Both the Freedmen's Bureau and Civil Rights Bills of 1866 secured the Freedmen "full and equal benefit of all laws," the former in Section 7, and the latter in Section 8. The Civil Rights bill was of course passed over President Johnson's veto; and the Fourteenth Amendment was drafted and adopted to remove all doubt about Congress's power in the premises. Virtually every speaker in the debates on the Fourteenth Amendments—Republicans and Democrats alike—said or agreed that the Amendment was designed to embody or incorporate the Civil Rights Act. *"Full and equal"* therefore is strictly the canonical reading. See Graham, *supra* note 4.

21

therefore, but *"full and* equal" was the protection conceived and accorded. It was only by one of the strangest perversions of the English language on record that the word "separate" was warped into use as a synonym for "full" and the disjunctive substituted for the conjunctive.[74] That "but" alone is the giveaway—a thorn in the mind and conscience of every American to whom it is not also an insult.

No Americans today ask or expect segregated Court systems or legislatures. If a state Constitution provided for such, including a "separate but equal" Supreme Court, no man would venture to suggest that Negroes and whites were thereby "equally protected." Why? Because the very concept is odious. Yet the main reason it is more odious in this one instance than in the others is that 85 years of toleration[75] and 57 of pretense[76] have blunted our sensibilities to "separate but equal" in these other areas. The racial standard is the sole basis for the distinction in either case.

Suppose that we grant for sake of argument, what no one is obliged nor disposed to grant—that an outright majority of the framers and ratifiers *of 1866-68* did regard race segregation, in *their* public schools, as a peculiar form of race discrimination— as one which *in their* judgment, would remain unaffected by the Fourteenth Amendment. Does it follow—dare it follow—we *today* are bound by that imperfect understanding of *equal protection* of the laws? Must we, and our children, obliged to live in a world, and assume moral leadership in a world, only one-third of whose population is white, where racism daily is becoming more menacing and hateful, and a stain upon our national honor, must we accept that understanding? Must we *enforce* that understanding? For all time? Regardless? Can one generation fetter all that come after it? Freeze standards of ethics? Rigidify law? Did the generation that struck shackles from slaves, somehow shackle our minds? Our conscience? Our common sense?

To ask such questions, is to answer them. The Doctrine of Changed Conditions, applicable in constitutional cases, certainly has special force and validity in this type of situation. Law can-

74. *Plessy v. Ferguson, supra* note 6.
75 Early post-ratification interpretation of the Thirteenth and Fourteenth Amendments was quite in harmony with their purposes. See not only the Bradley-Woods decision at Circuit in the *Slaughter-House Cases,* 4 Fed. Cas. 891, No. 2,234 (C. C. D. La. 1870), but also Judge Woods' decision in *U. S. v. Hall,* 22 Fed. Cas. 79, No. 15,282 (C. C. S. D. Ala. 1871) holding even that Congress had power to reach state *inaction.* See also the Thirteenth Amendment-Civil Rights Act cases: *U. S. v. Rhodes,* 27 Fed. Cas. 785, No. 16,151 (C. C. D. Ky. 1866); *Matter of Elizabeth Turner,* 24 Fed. Cas. 337, No. 14,247 (C. C. D. Md. 1867). For the factors that deflected interpretation, see Graham, *supra* note 4.
76. See *id.* for *Plessy v. Ferguson, supra* note 6, in historical perspective.

22

not exist in a vacuum. The *equal* protection of the laws must always be, in part, an ethical and moral concept. It must grow in relevance and fulfillment with "the felt necessities of the times, . . . prevalent moral and political theories, intuitions of public policy"[77]—*ours* and our childrens'; as well as our ancestors'.

Law office history, willy-nilly, is a confining, proscriptive enterprise. One never would suspect, for example, from the State briefs and arguments in the present *School Segregation Cases,* that our Fourteenth Amendment had any ethical or moral content at all. Still less, that the spirit and text must sometimes determine intent. Much of the current pro-segregation argument reduces simply to this: that because the Civil War generation still practiced discrimination, it could never have intended to abolish it. Here again, Van Winkle's research stands us in good stead. Such a demoralized, emasculated equal protection, he pointed out, certainly was not the brand originally offered to the Supreme Court. Roscoe Conkling, indeed, was most emphatic on these matters. The determinative point, Conkling declared, when arguing for extension of the Amendment to corporations *regardless of framer intent,* was the plain meaning and spirit of these words. "The true question, in exploring the meanings of the Fourteenth Amendment, is not, in a given case, whether the framers foresaw that particular case and acted in reference to it—the inquiry is, does the case fall within the expressed intention of the Amendment. All the cases compassed by the letter of the language, must be included, unless obviously repugnant or foreign to its spirit and purpose."[78]

After quoting the celebrated declaration to this effect, made by Chief Justice Marshall in the *Dartmouth College Case,*[79] Conkling developed the point at some length, then concluded:[80]

> Man being human, and his vision finite, it is well that saving ordinances need not be shrunken in their uses or duration to the measure of what the framers foresaw. . . .

> Truths and principles do not die with occasions; nor do they apply only to events which have cast their shadows before.

> The statesman has no horoscope which maps the measureless spaces of a nation's life, and lays down in advance all the bearings of its career. . . .

---

77. HOLMES, THE COMMON LAW 1 (1881).
78. *Oral Argument of Roscoe Conkling* [in *San Mateo County v. Southern Pacific Railroad,* 116 U. S. 138 (1882)] pp. 31-32.
79. 4 Wheaton 518. 644-645 (U. S. 1819).
80. *Supra* note 78 at 33-34.

23

All that wisdom and science in legislation can do, is to establish just principles and laws; this done, every case which afterwards falls within them, is a case for which they were established. . . .

Those who devised the Fourteenth Amendment . . . builded not for a day, but for all time; not for a few, or *for a race;* [emphasis added] but for man. They planted in the Constitution a monumental truth. . . . That truth is but the golden rule, so entrenched as to curb the many who would do to the few as they would not have the few do to them.

May this persuasive eloquence, honored by a unanimous Supreme Court in 1886,[81] soon take on new lustre and significance.

---

81. *Santa Clara County v. Southern Pacific Ry. Co.,* 118 U. S. 394, 396 (1886).

24

VOLUME 69 NOVEMBER 1955 NUMBER 1

HARVARD LAW REVIEW

THE ORIGINAL UNDERSTANDING AND THE SEGREGATION DECISION†

Alexander M. Bickel *

BEFORE setting out on the direct and noble march to the Court's conclusion in the *Segregation Cases*,[1] Chief Justice Warren took care to post a rear guard. The history of the adoption of the fourteenth amendment, to which reargument in these cases had been largely addressed, though casting some light, was, the Chief Justice said, "inconclusive" at best. "The most avid proponents of the post-War Amendments undoubtedly intended them to remove all legal distinctions among 'all persons born or naturalized in the United States.' Their opponents, just as certainly, were antagonistic to both the letter and the spirit of the Amendments and wished them to have the most limited effect. What others in Congress and the state legislatures had in mind cannot be determined with any degree of certainty."[2] Three pages later, as befits a commander in mid-advance, the Chief Justice, having made his dispositions, had no further thought for the rear: "In approaching this problem, we cannot turn the clock back to 1868 when the Amendment was adopted, or even to 1896 when *Plessy v. Ferguson* was written. We must consider public education in the light of its full development and its present place in American life throughout the Nation. Only in this way can it

---

† The writer was one of two law clerks to Mr. Justice Frankfurter during the October Term, 1952. At that term, the Court heard the first argument in the *Segregation Cases* and handed down the order for reargument; the cases were reargued and decided at the following term. The writer's interest in pursuing an investigation into the original understanding of the fourteenth amendment was prompted by the events which took place during his service at the Court.

* Research Associate in Law, Harvard Law School. B.S., C.C.N.Y., 1947; LL.B., Harvard, 1949.

[1] Brown v. Board of Educ., 347 U.S. 483 (1954).

[2] *Id.* at 489.

I

be determined if segregation in public schools deprives these plaintiffs of the equal protection of the laws." [3]

The *Segregation Cases* were extensively briefed and argued at two terms of Court. Their importance, judged by every criterion relevant to the Court's work, is difficult to overestimate, and it is perfectly plain that the Court itself did not underestimate it. Yet the cases were disposed of in the end by a relatively brief opinion which hit only the high spots of issues necessarily involved.[4] The Court knew, of course, that its judgment would have an unparalleled impact on the daily lives of a very substantial portion of the population, and that the response of many of those affected would be in varying degrees hostile. It was necessary, therefore, if ever it had been, to exert to the utmost the prestige, the oracular authority of the institution. To this end, it was desirable that the Court speak unanimously, with one voice from the deep. And the less said, the less chance of internal disagreement. By the same token, it was wise to present as small a target as possible to marksmen on the outside. In sum, without imputing to the Court aspirations to a form of art it does not profess to practice, one may be entitled to surmise that here was a decision which, like a poem, "should not mean / But be," and that the Court saw this and acted on it. Considerations of this order, applicable only to so extraordinary a case, are sufficient, in any event, to explain the brevity of the reference to the history of the fourteenth amendment's adoption and the briskness of the transition from an apparent assumption of that history's relevance to the statement that the clock cannot be turned back.

Beneath the brevity and beneath the briskness lies the pervasive problem of the weight to be accorded in constitutional adjudications to evidence of the framers' original understanding.[5] Reliance on such evidence is subject to caveats applicable to the use of legislative history as an aid in statutory construction.[6] What is

---

[3] *Id.* at 492–93.

[4] The Court's deliberate approach to these cases, clearly reflecting its awareness of their unique importance, is indicated in Sacks, Foreword to *The Supreme Court, 1953 Term*, 68 HARV. L. REV. 96 (1954). For a survey of some of the issues necessarily involved, see Leflar & Davis, *Segregation in the Public Schools — 1953*, 67 HARV. L. REV. 377 (1954). This article was published in January, some four months before the decision came down.

[5] See tenBroek, *Admissibility and Use by the United States Supreme Court of Extrinsic Aids in Constitutional Construction*, 26 CALIF. L. REV. 287, 437, 664 (1938), 27 CALIF. L. REV. 157, 399 (1939).

[6] See Curtis, *A Better Theory of Legal Interpretation*, 3 VAND. L. REV. 407

more important, it may raise a fundamental question concerning the Court's function in construing the Constitution. This difficulty is best posed by quotation of two extreme judicial utterances, both advocating meticulous adherence to original intent, so-called:

1. No one, we presume, supposes that any change in public opinion or feeling, in relation to this unfortunate race, in the civilized nations of Europe or in this country, should induce the court to give to the words of the Constitution a more liberal construction in their favor than they were intended to bear when the instrument was framed and adopted. Such an argument would be altogether inadmissible in any tribunal called on to interpret it. If any of its provisions are deemed unjust, there is a mode prescribed in the instrument itself by which it may be amended; but while it remains unaltered, it must be construed now as it was understood at the time of its adoption. . . . Any other rule of construction would abrogate the judicial character of this court, and make it the mere reflex of the popular opinion or passion of the day.

2. The whole aim of construction, as applied to a provision of the Constitution, is to discover the meaning, to ascertain and give effect to the intent, of its framers and the people who adopted it. . . . As nearly as possible we should place ourselves in the condition of those who framed and adopted it.

Of course, such views, when they prevail, threaten disaster to government under a written constitution. No further proof need be adduced than that the first quotation — could anything contrast more strikingly with the opinion of the Court in the *Segregation Cases?* — comes from the judgment of Chief Justice Taney in *Dred Scott v. Sandford*,[7] and the second from Mr. Justice Sutherland's dissent in 1934 in *Home Bldg. & Loan Ass'n v. Blaisdell.*[8] But it is a long way from rejection of the Taney-Sutherland doctrine to the proposition that the original understanding is simply not relevant.[9] For arguments based on that understanding

---

(1950); Frankfurter, *Some Reflections on the Reading of Statutes,* 47 COLUM. L. REV. 527, 543 (1947).

[7] 60 U.S. (19 How.) 393, 426 (1856).

[8] 290 U.S. 398, 453 (1934).

[9] Chief Justice Hughes, for the majority in the *Blaisdell* case, made his rejection quite explicit: "If by the statement that what the Constitution meant at the time of its adoption it means to-day, it is intended to say that the great clauses of the Constitution must be confined to the interpretation which the framers, with the conditions and outlook of their time, would have placed upon them, the statement

have a strong pull. They have decided cases for judges who held the views represented by the passages quoted.[10] But the Court has also employed them without intentionally connoting, indeed while disavowing, such views.[11] And they have been relied on by judges well aware that it was *a constitution* they were expounding.[12]

The original understanding forms the starting link in the chain

---

carries its own refutation. It was to guard against such a narrow conception that Chief Justice Marshall uttered the memorable warning — 'we must never forget that it is *a constitution* we are expounding' (*McCulloch v. Maryland*, 4 Wheat. 316, 407) . . . ." 290 U.S. at 442–43.

[10] See, *e.g.*, Dimick v. Schiedt, 293 U.S. 474 (1935). This opinion, delivered over the dissent of Justice Stone in which Chief Justice Hughes and Justices Brandeis and Cardozo joined, was by Justice Sutherland. But the view expressed in this case and in the passages quoted in the text is very strong medicine, indeed, and truly steadfast adherence to it is more than can be asked of any judge. See Village of Euclid v. Ambler Realty Co., 272 U.S. 365 (1926) (opinion by Justice Sutherland).

[11] See, *e.g.*, District of Columbia v. Clawans, 300 U.S. 617 (1937). See also United States v. Flores, 289 U.S. 137 (1933); *Ex parte* Grossman, 267 U.S. 87 (1925).

[12] In Weems v. United States, 217 U.S. 349 (1910), the Court, per Justice McKenna, held that a punishment consisting of a fine plus lengthy imprisonment imposed under a Philippine statute for corruptly making false entries in public records was cruel and unusual within the meaning of the eighth amendment and hence also within the meaning of the Philippine Bill of Rights. Dealing with the argument that the Court was applying the eighth amendment in circumstances in which its framers might not have thought it applicable, Justice McKenna said, in a frequently quoted passage: "Time works changes, brings into existence new conditions and purposes. Therefore a principle to be vital must be capable of wider application than the mischief which gave it birth." 217 U.S. at 373. Justice White dissented. He noted that local conditions might well have made appropriate the severity of this punishment. Then he proceeded at length to demonstrate that the original understanding of the phrase "cruel and unusual punishment" was grounded in the excesses of the Stuart reigns and was restricted to inhuman bodily punishments and arbitrary imprisonment without sanction of statute. Justice White argued that the original understanding should not be departed from. In this opinion he was joined by Justice Holmes. 217 U.S. at 382, 413.

In National Mut. Ins. Co. v. Tidewater Transfer Co., 337 U.S. 582 (1949), Justice Frankfurter, in dissent, took a distinction between "great concepts" such as "Commerce . . . among the several States," "due process of law," "liberty," and "property," which, he said, "were purposely left to gather meaning from experience," and "explicit and specific" terms, such as the word "State" when used in article III in the grant of the diversity jurisdiction. That word, he stated, is governed by the original understanding and cannot be broadened to include the District of Columbia. 337 U.S. at 646. (Justice Reed joined in Justice Frankfurter's dissent. Chief Justice Vinson and Justice Douglas, dissenting separately, also agreed with this view. So did Justices Jackson, Black, and Burton of the majority, though they were of the opinion that Congress could, under its article I power, create federal jurisdiction in suits between a citizen of the District of Columbia and a citizen of one of the states.)

of continuity which is a source of the Court's authority, and it is not unnatural that appeals to it should recur as consistently as they do.[13] Happily, finding the original understanding, like applying the Constitution itself, is, at best, "not a mechanical exercise but a function of statecraft" and of historical insight.[14] And what

---

[13] This is especially true as regards the fourteenth amendment. In Maxwell v. Dow, 176 U.S. 581, 601-02 (1900), counsel, taking as his text the speech by Senator Jacob Howard of Michigan which opened debate on the fourteenth amendment in the Senate, Cong. Globe, 39th Cong., 1st Sess. 2764-65 (1866), see note 98 infra, argued that the amendment made the entire Bill of Rights applicable to the states. Proceeding from Howard's speech without more, the argument is plausible. The Court dealt with it on the basis of the plain meaning rule and a general proposition to the effect that historical materials such as debates are always ambiguous and of dubious value. Twice subsequently the same argument was rejected, though without examination of historical materials. Twining v. New Jersey, 211 U.S. 78 (1908); Palko v. Connecticut, 302 U.S. 319 (1937). But Justice Black, speaking for a four-man minority, returned to the fray in Adamson v. California, 332 U.S. 46, 70 (1947). Finally, Professor Fairman demonstrated that the argument was based on a misreading and an incomplete reading of the original understanding. Fairman, *Does the Fourteenth Amendment Incorporate the Bill of Rights?*, 2 Stan. L. Rev. 5 (1949).

Perhaps the most famous appeal to the fourteenth amendment's history came in the course of Roscoe Conkling's devious argument in San Mateo County v. Southern Pac. R.R., 116 U.S. 138 (1885). There is no doubt that Conkling overstated his case. See Graham, *The "Conspiracy Theory" of the Fourteenth Amendment*, 47 Yale L.J. 371, 48 Yale L.J. 171 (1938). The "conspiracy theory" of the amendment, according to which Conkling, John A. Bingham, and perhaps Reverdy Johnson and others, operating in a smoke-filled room, secretly contrived to extend the protection of substantive due process to corporations, has been pretty well exploded, whatever the effect it may have had on the adjudications of the Court in this field. See McLaughlin, *The Court, The Corporation, and Conkling*, 46 Am. Hist. Rev. 45 (1940). And in any event, it would be very questionable practice indeed, as Justice Black suggested, see Connecticut Gen. Life Ins. Co. v. Johnson, 303 U.S. 77, 87 (1938) (dissenting opinion), for the Court to deem itself bound by the uncommunicated, back-room purpose of a handful of men. One of the caveats applicable to the use of the legislative history of statutes is acutely relevant here. See Shapiro v. United States, 335 U.S. 1, 45-49 (1948) (Justice Frankfurter, dissenting); Curtis, *supra* note 6, at 411-12. But Justice Black, quoting some unguarded language from the opinion of the Court in the Slaughter-House Cases, 83 U.S. (16 Wall.) 36 (1873), went on to argue that it was inconsistent with the purpose of the fourteenth amendment, as revealed by its history and language, to extend the protection of the due process clause to corporations. Connecticut Gen. Life Ins. Co. v. Johnson, *supra*. See also Wheeling Steel Corp. v. Glander, 337 U.S. 562, 576 (1949) (Justice Douglas, dissenting). The historical materials give no more warrant for this view than for the so-called conspiracy theory. See pp. 30-31, 44, 60-61 *infra*; Graham, *supra* at 171. But cf. Boudin, *Truth and Fiction About the Fourteenth Amendment*, 16 N.Y.U.L.Q. Rev. 19, 67 (1938).

[14] Frankfurter, Mr. Justice Holmes and the Supreme Court 76 (1938). For a shining and enduring demonstration, see the opinion of Justice Bradley in Boyd v. United States, 116 U.S. 616, 624-32 (1886). For a nonjudicial tour de force, see Thayer, *Legal Tender*, 1 Harv. L. Rev. 73 (1887).

is relevant is not alone the origin of constitutional provisions, but also "the line of their growth," the further links in the chain of continuity.[15] This being so and our law not being given to following hard and fast theoretical formulations on questions of the scope of this one, it is possible, in the Chief Justice's words, for historical materials to cast some light although they are inconclusive and although, in any event, the clock cannot be turned back. But only an examination in some detail of the relevant materials themselves can make clear just how this has proved possible in the *Segregation Cases*.

The Thirty-Ninth Congress and the Fourteenth Amendment

The discussion, by the parties and by the United States as amicus, of the fourteenth amendment's history, which took place in response to questions propounded by the Court in its order for reargument of the *Segregation Cases*,[16] must surely have amounted to the most extensive presentation of historical materials ever made to the Court. The briefs and appendices are book-size and shelf-length. The heart of this mass of evidence is to be found in the reported debates of the first session of the 39th Congress, which convened on December 4, 1865,[17] and sent the fourteenth amendment to the country on June 13, 1866,[18] shortly before it adjourned to go home and face the electorate. Other materials have a bearing, of course. But the debates of the Congress which submitted, and the journals and documents of the legislatures which ratified, the amendment provide the most

---

[15] Justice Holmes in Gompers v. United States, 233 U.S. 604, 610 (1914).

[16] 345 U.S. 972 (1953). The questions which concern us are as follows:

1. What evidence is there that the Congress which submitted and the State legislatures and conventions which ratified the Fourteenth Amendment contemplated or did not contemplate, understood or did not understand, that it would abolish segregation in public schools?

2. If neither the Congress in submitting nor the States in ratifying the Fourteenth Amendment understood that compliance with it would require the immediate abolition of segregation in public schools, was it nevertheless the understanding of the framers of the Amendment

   (a) that future Congresses might, in the exercise of their power under section 5 of the Amendment, abolish such segregation, or

   (b) that it would be within the judicial power, in light of future conditions, to construe the Amendment as abolishing such segregation of its own force?

3. On the assumption that the answers to questions 2(a) and (b) do not dispose of the issue, is it within the judicial power, in construing the Amendment, to abolish segregation in public schools?

[17] Cong. Globe, 39th Cong., 1st Sess. 1 (1865). The Globe for this session will hereinafter be cited Globe; its Appendix, Globe, App.

[18] Globe 3149.

direct and unimpeachable indication of original purpose and understanding — to the extent, of course, that any such indication is to be found. Of these two sets of materials, the congressional debates are in this case the richer, and they rank, in any event, first in importance. It may perhaps be said that whatever they establish constitutes a rebuttable presumption. For it is not unrealistic, in the main, to assume notice of congressional purpose in the state legislatures. A showing of ratification on the basis of an understanding different from that revealed by congressional materials must carry the burden of proof. And, of course, the ratifying states are a chorus of voices; a discordant one among them proves little.

Very much the better part of the first session of the 39th Congress was devoted to discussing, in one connection or another, the subject matter of the fourteenth amendment: the governance of the South, readmission of the Southern states, loyalty to the Union, a place under the sun for the newly freed negro race, distribution of powers (in the context of these problems) between the states and the federal government. The bulk of this session-long debate may conveniently be analyzed as it related to four measures: The Freedmen's Bureau Bill, which President Johnson vetoed and which the Radicals failed to pass over his veto; the Civil Rights Act of 1866,[19] enacted over a veto; an abortive proposal for a short constitutional amendment, whose sponsor was John A. Bingham of Ohio; and the fourteenth amendment itself.

To obtain a proper understanding of the relevant congressional purpose, it is necessary to concentrate not only on statements dealing specifically with public school education of the negro race, but also on remarks going to subjects which were deemed to be closely allied — though the relationship may not have survived as clearly to this day. It will become plain that the right, if any, to an unsegregated public school education resided for most men who spoke at this session in a fringe area, where its companions were, among other less well-defined rights, suffrage, jury service, and intermarriage. The first two debates to be reviewed — those on the Freedmen's Bureau Bill and on the Civil Rights Bill — were, of course, debates looking to legislation rather than to a constitutional amendment, and they dealt with an issue of constitutionality as well as one of policy. The former arose under the thirteenth amendment, which had gone into ef-

---

[19] Act of April 9, 1866, c. 31, 14 STAT. 27.

fect not long before the 39th Congress convened. The two
issues are not always easy to separate and must often be examined
in tandem. Finally, it is important to form an impression of the
political atmosphere of the session. The Democrats were a small
and — with a few exceptions — cowed minority. The dominant
Republicans consisted of three groups: Radicals, Moderates, and
conservative supporters of President Andrew Johnson. The first
two factions were to form an alliance which was to wage in 1866
a bitter and successful campaign against the President. That
coming event cast an unmistakable and significant shadow over
the session.

The Freedmen's Bureau Bill

The bill to enlarge the powers of the Freedmen's Bureau [20] provided in its section 7:

> That whenever, in any State or district in which the ordinary
> course of judicial proceedings has been interrupted by the rebel-
> lion, and wherein, in consequence of any State or local law, ordi-
> nance, police, or other regulation, custom, or prejudice, any of the
> civil rights or immunities belonging to white persons, including
> the right to make and enforce contracts, to sue, be parties and give
> evidence; to inherit, purchase, lease, sell, hold, and convey . . .
> property, and to have full and equal benefit of all laws and pro-
> ceedings for the security of person and estate, are refused or de-
> nied to negroes . . . or wherein they . . . are subjected to any
> . . . different punishment . . . for the commission of any act . . .
> than are prescribed for white persons . . . it shall be the duty of
> the President . . . to extend military protection . . . ." [21]

On the passage of this bill (on January 25 and February 8 in
the Senate,[22] and on February 6 and 9 in the House [23]) the Republican Party, with one exception in the House,[24] and with the
notable absence in the Senate of Edgar Cowan, the Pennsylvania
Conservative, stood together. Senators Norton of Minnesota and
Van Winkle of West Virginia, who, with Cowan, later voted
against the Civil Rights Bill and against the fourteenth amendment, were recorded for this bill. So was Senator Doolittle of Wis-

---

[20] The Bureau had been created by Act of March 3, 1865, c. 90, 13 STAT. 507.

[21] GLOBE 318.

[22] GLOBE 421, 742, 748.

[23] GLOBE 688, 775.

[24] Lovell H. Rousseau of Kentucky.

consin, who was absent for the vote on the Civil Rights Bill but who voted against the fourteenth amendment. These votes for the Freedmen's Bureau Bill may seem inconsistent with Conservative actions later in the session. For the enumeration in section 7 of "civil rights and immunities" was not exclusive. The bill's coverage depended, therefore, on the meaning of those terms. In the subsequent debate on the Civil Rights Bill, Conservatives and others attacked similar general language as susceptible of a "latitudinarian" construction, and the leadership deemed it wise to strike it. But there are a number of explanations for these Conservative Republican votes in favor of the Freedmen's Bureau Bill. For one thing, this bill drew constitutional validity from a source — the war power — not open to the later Civil Rights Bill, which applied throughout the country. Constitutional scruples to the side, the fact that the Freedmen's Bureau Bill did not apply in the North meant that there was no occasion to worry about federal interference with practices in that part of the country, which was where constituents lived. Finally, it was not until after the vote on this bill — certainly not until after the Senate vote on January 25 — that the struggle between President and Radical Congress was publicly joined. Conservative Republicans who later sided with the President, and many Moderates as well, still entertained at this time some hope of averting the conflict. They felt that if they gave in to Radical opinion on the Freedmen's Bureau Bill their hand would be strengthened in attempts to find common ground with the Radicals, and they had reason to believe that the President would pursue the same strategy. It was for a time commonly expected that Johnson would sign the Freedmen's Bureau Bill.[25] The President, however, vetoed it on February 19, and the Senate, on the following day, failed to override.[26] The President's supporters — the party whip and illness were to deplete their ranks later — rallied around him.

In the course of debate on the Freedmen's Bureau Bill and on a predecessor proposal which was briefly before the Senate,[27] Charles Sumner and Henry Wilson of Massachusetts, Radicals of abolitionist antecedents, as well as John Sherman of Ohio and

---

[25] See R. HENRY, THE STORY OF RECONSTRUCTION 159 (1938); H. WHITE, THE LIFE OF LYMAN TRUMBULL 260 (1913); HYMAN, ERA OF THE OATH 90–91 (1954).

[26] GLOBE 915–17, 943.

[27] S. 9, 39th Cong., 1st Sess. (1865), introduced by Senator Wilson of Massachusetts. GLOBE 2, 39.

Lyman Trumbull of Illinois, Moderates, spoke in general terms of measures that would have to be taken and existing practices that would have to be eliminated, both now and in the long run, in order to better the condition of the Negro in the South. They referred, among other things, to the Negro's need for, and right to, education. In the House, Ignatius Donnelly of Minnesota moved an amendment to empower the Bureau to offer to refugees and freedmen "a common-school education." [28] These remarks and the Donnelly amendment are evidence of a real concern in Congress with education of the Southern Negro, of which we shall see more. But, except perhaps for Sumner's speech, none of them can be read as advocating unsegregated schools, or as assuming that the bill would lead to their establishment.[29] Nor, apart from a broadside

---

[28] GLOBE 513. The amendment was never voted on directly. It was lost together with a substitute bill, in which it was incorporated and which proposed other changes not here relevant. GLOBE 654, 655, 688. Section 6 of the bill, as it then stood and as finally passed, see McPHERSON, HISTORY OF THE RECONSTRUCTION 73 (1871), in any event empowered the Bureau to provide or cause to be built suitable buildings for asylums and schools. GLOBE 210.

[29] Wilson enumerated the rights listed in the bill and added the freedman's right to "go into the schools and educate himself and his children." GLOBE 111. But he was speaking of rights which would obtain if Southern Black Codes, denying, as he believed, any schooling at all, were annulled by passage of this bill. And he was speaking against the background of a report on conditions in the South by a Republican politician and Union major general, the former German revolutionary Carl Schurz, which the Senate had requested from the President and had had printed. GLOBE 30, 78–80. This report dealt with "Education of the Freedmen" and discussed the opposition to it of Southern whites. It recommended education for the Negro "as an integral part of the educational systems of the States," but spoke throughout of "negro education," "colored schools," "school-houses in which colored children were taught," and the desirability only of supporting schools for freedmen out of general tax funds to which Negroes contributed and from which white schools benefited. There were no references to unsegregated schools, even as an ultimate objective, in the Schurz Report. S. EXEC. DOC. No. 2, 39th Cong., 1st Sess. 2, 25–27 (1865). The problem to which Wilson was addressing himself was the establishment and maintenance of segregated schools for freedmen, which he believed to be a matter of some difficulty in the South of that day. The same is true of a reference by Sherman to "the right to be educated," GLOBE 42, and by Trumbull to the need "to educate, improve, enlighten, and Christianize the negro," GLOBE 322. Donnelly, arguing for his amendment, spoke of the value of education for both the white and colored races. Conceiving, obviously, of the separate education of the Negro, he said it would "shame the whites into an effort to educate themselves." He noted that Tennessee excluded Negroes from white schools, "while it makes no provision for their education in separate schools," that, evidently, being what he found objectionable. GLOBE 586, 587, 589.

There is no doubt that Charles Sumner favored unsegregated schools. See his argument in Roberts v. Boston, 59 Mass. (5 Cush.) 198, 201 (1849), and his draft of what, in amended form, became the Civil Rights Act of 1875, CONG. GLOBE,

Democratic attack in the House aimed more at future Radical objectives than at this particular bill, did the opposition so assume or argue.[30]

The Civil Rights Bill

On January 29, 1866, before passage in the House of the Freedmen's Bureau Bill, Lyman Trumbull of Illinois brought up in the Senate the Civil Rights Bill. Section 1 of the bill contained, as had section 7 of the Freedmen's Bureau Bill, a general prohibition of "discrimination in civil rights or immunities," which preceded a specific enumeration of such rights. Section 1, after conferring citizenship on native-born Negroes, provided:

> That there shall be no discrimination in civil rights or immunities among the inhabitants of any State or Territory of the United States on account of race, color, or previous condition of slavery; but the inhabitants of every race and color, without regard to any previous condition of slavery or involuntary servitude, except as a punishment for crime whereof the party shall have been duly convicted, shall have the same right to make and enforce contracts, to sue, be parties, and give evidence, to inherit, purchase, lease, sell, hold, and convey real and personal property, and to

---

42d Cong., 2d Sess. 383–84 (1872). His general remarks on this occasion may indicate that he would have liked to see unsegregated schools started in the South at this time. However, speaking specifically of the bill before the Senate, he used more guarded language. It proposed, he said, "nothing less than to establish Equality before the Law, at least so far as civil rights are concerned, in the rebel States." GLOBE 91.

[30] Lovell Rousseau of Kentucky, the Conservative Republican who was to vote against the bill, criticized the Freedmen's Bureau for having taken over schoolhouses in Charleston for the benefit of colored children. The white children were thus deprived of instruction, unless — and this was put as a preposterous proposition — "they mix up white children with black." GLOBE, App. 71. This same action of the Bureau was denounced also by John W. Chanler, Democrat of New York. GLOBE, App. 82.

The Democratic broadside was by John L. Dawson of Pennsylvania. He accused the Radicals who sponsored this bill of hugging to their bosoms "the phantom of negro equality." The Radicals, he said,

hold that the white and black races are equal. This they maintain involves and demands social equality; that negroes should be received on an equality in white families, should be admitted to the same tables at hotels, should be permitted to occupy the same seats in railroad cars and the same pews in churches; that they should be allowed to hold offices, to sit on juries, to vote, to be eligible to seats in the State and national Legislatures, and to be judges, or to make and expound laws for the government of white men. Their children are to attend the same schools with white children, and to sit side by side with them. Following close upon this will, of course, be marriages between the races . . . .

GLOBE 541.

full and equal benefit of all laws and proceedings for the security
of person and property, and shall be subject to like punishment,
pains, and penalties, and to none other, any law, statute, ordinance, regulation, or custom to the contrary notwithstanding.

Section 2 provided, by way of enforcement power:

> That any person who under color of any law . . . or custom,
> shall subject . . . any inhabitant of any State or Territory to the
> deprivation of any right secured or protected by this act . . .
> shall be deemed guilty of a misdemeanor, and on conviction shall
> be punished by fine not exceeding $1,000, or imprisonment not
> exceeding one year, or both . . . .[31]

In opening debate, Trumbull, who was no Radical, said that
the bill was intended to "secure to all persons within the United
States practical freedom." It was, he said, a question of securing
"privileges which are essential to freemen." He reviewed the
Slave Codes which had fallen with the proclamation of the thirteenth amendment. They restricted the movements of Negroes;
they forbade them to own firearms; they punished the exercise
by them of the functions of a minister of the Gospel; they excluded them from other occupations; and they made it "a
highly penal offense for any person, white or colored, to teach
slaves . . . ." In lieu of Slave Codes, Trumbull said, the South
now had Black Codes and these "still impose upon [Negroes] . . .
the very restrictions which were imposed upon them in consequence of the existence of slavery, and before it was abolished.
The purpose of the bill under consideration is to destroy all these
discriminations . . . ." Section 1, Trumbull continued, was the
heart of the bill; it was there that "civil liberty" was secured to
the Negro, "civil liberty" being what was left of "natural liberty"
after the latter had, necessarily, been circumscribed to make
possible life in society. It was of the essence of civil liberty that
laws be brought to bear on all persons equally, "or as much so
as the nature of things will admit."

Trumbull concluded his remarks on section 1 by repeating
that it would ensure for the Negro "the rights of citizens . . . .
The great fundamental rights set forth in this bill: the right to
acquire property, the right to go and come at pleasure, the right
to enforce rights in the courts, to make contracts, and to inherit
and dispose of property. These are the very rights that are set

---

[31] GLOBE 474, 475.

forth in this bill as appertaining to every freeman." When Trumbull had finished, James A. McDougall of California, a Democrat, asked him to return to section 1. What, again, was meant by "civil rights"? Trumbull answered by reading the enumeration of rights in section 1. That was the definition. Was there any reference to political rights, McDougall pursued? No, said Trumbull.[32]

With the single exception of Lot M. Morrill of Maine, a Radical who, looking beyond the bill at hand, expounded a theory of the equality of the races,[33] others — Radicals and Moderates alike — who spoke in favor of the bill were content to rest on the points Trumbull had made. The rights to be secured by the bill were those specifically enumerated in section 1, and the necessity for extending the protection so defined was demonstrated by the Black Codes enacted by Southern legislatures.[34] On its merits, this argument had one or two weaknesses. It disregarded the general civil rights guaranty which preceded the enumeration of rights in section 1, and, in directing attention only to evils existing in the South, it ignored the fact that the bill was to apply throughout the nation. These weaknesses were to be skillfully seized upon. The argument probably had another, which the opposition let pass, and which does not affect the search for congressional purpose. It is very likely that Trumbull and his fellows exaggerated the severity of the Black Codes. The picture — of which this exaggeration was a feature — of a willful reign of terror instituted or threatened by fire-eating Southerners who had learned nothing and were unreconciled to defeat and to all its consequences served Radical purposes and was, with varying degrees of sincerity and of unwitting assistance from some Southern politicians, being spread broadcast by the Radical leadership. This educational campaign, as the Radicals called it, was to con-

---

[32] GLOBE 474–75, 476.

[33] GLOBE 570.

[34] See the remarks of Henry Wilson, the Massachusetts Radical, who was to be Grant's Vice-President. GLOBE 603. Trumbull, who closed, again and in the same terms laid stress on the bill's relatively narrow purpose. GLOBE 605. John Sherman of Ohio, a Moderate, speaking on February 8 in justification of his votes in favor both of the Freedmen's Bureau and Civil Rights Bills, read section 1 of the latter bill as defining "what are the incidents of freedom, and [saying] that these men must be protected in certain rights, and so careful is it in its language that it goes on and defines those rights, the right to sue and be sued, to plead and be impleaded, to acquire and hold property, and other universal incidents of freedom." GLOBE 744.

tinue throughout the session and beyond. But no one maintains that the impression of conditions in the South fostered by the Radicals was completely unjustified. And, in any event, what is important here is the fact of its existence and of its effectiveness, not the truth of the matter asserted. This impression is incorporated by reference into congressional statements of objectives; it plays a large part in defining those objectives, regardless of the extent to which it was founded in reality and regardless of the motives which underlay its creation.[35]

Of the remarks in opposition in the Senate, those of three men — two of them Democrats, the other a nominal Republican, but an avowed supporter of the President — must be noted.[36] Willard Saulsbury of Delaware, a Democrat who had once described himself wistfully as perhaps the last slaveholder in the nation, declared that the bill was "one of the most dangerous that was ever introduced into the Senate of the United States." He attacked its constitutionality, then asked whether the bill conferred the right to vote. Certainly, he said, Trumbull might have no intention of conferring that right. But:

> The question is not what the senator means, but what is the
> legitimate meaning and import of the terms employed in the

---

[35] A number of Black Codes are collected in 1 Fleming, Documentary History of Reconstruction 273–312 (1906), and in McPherson, *op. cit. supra* note 28, at 29–44. The worst of them were vagrancy statutes and laws minutely regulating the master-servant relationship, which was taking the place of slavery but appeared in some respects to bear a striking resemblance to it. But there were also enactments such as an Alabama statute of December 9, 1865, permitting Negro testimony in court and a Florida statute of January 16, 1866, setting up schools of a sort for freedmen. Both of these are cited by Fleming. They are to be distinguished from an Arkansas statute of February 6, 1867, printed in the same place, which was passed after the Civil Rights Act had become effective, and which more or less followed its pattern. One of the principal instruments used to popularize the Radical picture of the South, especially in Congress, was the Schurz Report. See note 29 *supra*. In the election campaign of 1866, much use was made of records of hearings before subcommittees of the Joint Committee on Reconstruction. These, however, were not in print before Congress passed the fourteenth amendment. See notes 61, 77, 83, 97 *infra*. See also Henry, *op. cit. supra* note 25, at 108–10, 115–16.

[36] There were in addition two violent harangues by Garrett Davis of Kentucky, a Democrat and a thoroughly unreconstructed one. The first was not unfairly characterized in an interruption by Senator Clark (Rep., N.H.). Said Mr. Clark: "[I]t only comes back to this, that a nigger is a nigger." Said Mr. Davis: "That is the whole of it." Globe 529. In the second, Davis argued that the bill discriminated against whites by creating special rights for Negroes. He drew from Trumbull the reply that "this bill applies to white men as well as black men. It declares that all persons in the United States shall be entitled to the same civil rights . . . . The bill is applicable exclusively to civil rights." Globe 599.

bill. . . . What are civil rights? What are the rights which you, I, or any citizen of this country enjoy? . . . [H]ere you use a generic term which in its most comprehensive signification includes every species of right that man can enjoy other than those the foundation of which rests exclusively in nature and in the law of nature.[37]

Edgar Cowan, Republican of Pennsylvania, who was wholly at odds with the Radical leadership, also took a broad view of the effect of the bill. He said:

> Now, as I understand the meaning and intent of this bill, it is that there shall be no discrimination made between the inhabitants of the several States of this Union, none in any way. In Pennsylvania, for the greater convenience of the people, and for the greater convenience, I may say, of both classes of the people, in certain districts the Legislature has provided schools for colored children, has discriminated as between the two classes of children. We put the African children in this school-house, . . . and educate them there as best we can. Is this amendment [the thirteenth; the proponents of the Civil Rights Bill argued that it implemented this amendment] to the Constitution of the United States abolishing slavery to break up that system which Pennsylvania has adopted for the education of her white and colored children? Are the school directors who carry out that law and who make this distinction between these classes of children to be punished for a violation of this statute of the United States? To me it is monstrous.[38]

It was quite a different thing, Cowan continued, to grant to everyone "the right to life, the right to liberty, the right to property." This he was willing to do. But it had to be by amendment to the Constitution.

Reverdy Johnson, Democrat of Maryland, one of the great lawyers of his time, offered an analysis of the bill which came to the same point Saulsbury had made. The states, in the exercise

---

[37] GLOBE 476–77.

[38] GLOBE 500. Presumably the dire consequences Cowan feared would come about because the bill forbade discrimination in civil rights, and in Cowan's mind, as in Saulsbury's, and as in Reverdy Johnson's, see note 39 *infra*, that term was susceptible of a broad interpretation. But when, in closing, Trumbull turned on him asking whether, everything else being equal, Cowan was not in favor of extending "equal civil rights" to the Negro, Cowan, who had already said much and was to say yet more as the session progressed about the inferior place of the Negro in a society governed for and by the Caucasian race, replied, "Certainly." GLOBE 605. In this instance, he evidently accepted the narrow meaning attributed to the phrase by the majority.

of their police power, had always, and had, in Johnson's opinion, properly taken account of the prejudices of the people. When legislators failed to do that, they created the sort of situation which had resulted from the passage of the Fugitive Slave Act; they passed unenforceable legislation. "I mention that," said Johnson, "for the purpose of applying it to one of the provisions of this bill." Most states had legislated against miscegenation. Yet this bill, Johnson believed, would wipe all such legislation off the books. Trumbull, and William Pitt Fessenden of Maine, like Trumbull a Moderate, interrupted to dispute this interpretation. Negroes could not marry whites and whites could not marry Negroes, they argued; hence there could be no discrimination in an antimiscegenation statute. But neither Fessenden nor Trumbull answered Johnson's broader point, which was that even if his interpretation was wrong, the error was not "so gross a one that the courts may not fall into it." [39]

The vote on the passage of the Civil Rights Bill in the Senate, on February 2, was 33 ayes, 12 nays. Three Republicans, Cowan, Norton of Minnesota, and Van Winkle of West Virginia, were recorded against.[40]

James F. Wilson of Iowa, from the House Committee on the Judiciary, managing the bill in the House, brought it up there on March 1. This was after the President's veto of the Freedmen's Bureau Bill had been upheld. Wilson addressed himself to Section 1:

> This part of the bill . . . . provides for the equality of citizens of the United States in the enjoyment of "civil rights and immunities." What do these terms mean? Do they mean that in all things civil, social, political, all citizens without distinction of race or color, shall be equal? By no means can they be so construed. Do they mean that all citizens shall vote in the several States? No . . . . Nor do they mean that all citizens shall sit on the juries, or that their children shall attend the same schools. These are not

---

[39] GLOBE 505–06.

[40] GLOBE 606–07. Reverdy Johnson was absent. So was James R. Doolittle of Wisconsin, a Republican but a close friend of the President. The veto of the Freedmen's Bureau Bill and the definitive public breach between President and Radical Congress, which it signified, were still some two weeks away. But Thaddeus Stevens in the House already spoke of the President in ominous tones. GLOBE 536–37; see note 61 *infra*. And Conservative Republicans who considered the Freedmen's Bureau Bill an appropriate concession to offer to the Radicals, evidently felt quite differently about a statute which might be applied in their constituencies.

civil rights or immunities. Well, what is the meaning? What are
civil rights? I understand civil rights to be simply the absolute
rights of individuals, such as —

> "The right of personal security, the right of personal liberty,
> and the right to acquire and enjoy property." "Right itself, in
> civil society, is that which any man is entitled to have, or to
> do, or to require from others, within the limits of prescribed
> law." *Kent's Commentaries*, vol. 1, p. 199.

> .   .   .   .

> But what of the term "immunities"? . . . It merely secures to
> citizens of the United States equality in the exemptions of the law.
> A colored citizen shall not, because he is colored, be subjected to
> obligations, duties, pains . . . . This is the spirit and scope of the
> bill, and it goes not one step beyond.

> .   .   .   .

> . . . . Laws barbaric and treatment inhuman are the rewards
> meted out by our white enemies to our colored friends. We should
> put a stop to this at once and forever.[41]

Wilson thus presented the Civil Rights Bill to the House as a
measure of limited and definite objectives. In this he followed the
lead of the majority in the Senate. Indeed, his disclaimers of
wider coverage were more specific than those made in the Senate.
And the line he laid down was followed by others who spoke for
the bill in the House. Again, the Black Codes were referred to,
and again the point was made that the term civil rights was defined by section 1, which enumerated the rights in question.[42]

The Democratic assault on the bill commenced when George
S. Shanklin of Kentucky asked Wilson to allow an amendment
stating explicitly that nothing in the bill conferred the right to
vote. Wilson, though he was soon to give in, refused to agree to

---

[41] GLOBE 1117, 1118.

[42] The Black Codes were the evil to which the bill was directed in the view of
Burton C. Cook of Illinois, Russell Thayer of Pennsylvania, and William Windom
of Minnesota, Radicals all. GLOBE 1123–25, 1151, 1160. Thayer added that the
bill simply declared "that all men born upon the soil of the United States shall
enjoy the fundamental rights of citizenship. What rights are these? Why, sir, in
order to avoid any misapprehension they are stated in the bill." And the bill
could not possibly be read to confer suffrage. GLOBE 1151. Windom pointed out
that the bill did not confer either political or social rights. GLOBE 1159. And
John M. Broomall of Pennsylvania, another Radical, said the bill secured rights
denied to the Negro in the South; he named these rights: speech, transit, domicil,
to sue, to petition, and habeas corpus. GLOBE 1263.

such a provision, "as it is in the bill now." [43] Next came Andrew Jackson Rogers of New Jersey, a member, as we shall see, of the Joint Committee on Reconstruction, and, though under forty, a very prominent figure in the 39th Congress. Because his views were sometimes extreme and his language frequently vehement, some of the House Democrats resisted Rogers' leadership, and the Radicals, on the other hand, were often pleased to act on the bland assumption that Rogers was the official Democratic leader in the House, though he held no such position.[44] A few days previously, Rogers had had occasion to take note of the Civil Rights Bill as passed in the Senate. At that time he had seemed to favor most of what he took to be the objectives of section 1. His attack had been constitutional:

> Negroes should have the channels of education opened to them by the States, and by the States they should be protected in life, liberty, and property, and by the States should be allowed all the rights of being witnesses, of suing and being sued . . . .
>
> . . . .
>
> Who gave the Senate the constitutional power to pass that bill guarantying equal rights to all . . . ?

In this debate he made the same constitutional point. But he took a broader and less benign view of the effect of section 1:

> In the State of Pennsylvania there is a discrimination made between the schools for white children and the schools for black.

---

[43] GLOBE 1120.

[44] *E.g.:* "Mr. Windom [a Radical]. . . . I was somewhat surprised yesterday in listening to the argument of the gentleman who, I believe, is the recognized leader of the Democratic party of the House — the gentleman from New Jersey . . . .

"Mr. Rogers. Mr. Speaker —

"Mr. Windom. Have I done him too much honor?

"Mr. Rogers. Mr. Speaker, I hope nobody . . . will make that assertion again. The object . . . is only to create dissatisfaction on this side of the House.

" . . . .

"Mr. Marshall. I wish merely to say that we do not recognize him as our leader.

" . . . .

"Mr. Windom. . . . I think every member upon this side of the House and every modest member upon the other side accords to the gentleman from New Jersey the position I assign him. [Laughter.]

" . . . .

"Mr. Niblack. I desire simply to say that we on this side do not need any 'leader'. There are not enough of us. [Laughter.] Therefore every man carries on a kind of guerrilla fight." GLOBE 1157–58.

The laws there provide that certain schools shall be set apart for black persons, and certain schools shall be set apart for white persons. . . . [T]here is nothing in the letter of the Constitution which gives . . . authority to Congress [to interfere] . . . .

. . . .

. . . . As a white man is by law authorized to marry a white woman, so does this bill compel the State to grant to the negro the same right of marrying a white woman . . . .

. . . .

All the rights that we enjoy, except our natural rights, are derived from Government. Therefore, there are really but two kinds of rights, natural rights and civil rights. This bill, then, would prevent a State from refusing negro suffrage under the broad acceptation of the term "civil rights and immunities." [45]

These charges, with particular reference to suffrage, were pressed home for the Democrats by Anthony Thornton of Illinois:

It is said that the words "civil rights" do not include the right of suffrage, because that is a political right. . . . I do not assume . . . that [they] do . . . but with the loose and liberal mode of construction adopted in this age, who can tell what rights may not be conferred by virtue of the terms as used in this bill? Where is it to end? Who can tell how it may be defined, how it may be construed? Why not, then, if it is not intended to confer the right of suffrage upon this class, accept a proviso that no such design is entertained? [46]

The leadership, which was to be unsure of its majority, and hence sensitive on the issue of suffrage throughout the session, had had enough of this. Wilson moved to amend by adding a new section, as follows:

That nothing in this act shall be so construed as to affect the laws of any State concerning the right of suffrage.

He said:

Mr. Speaker, I wish to say [that] . . . that section will not change my construction of the bill. I do not believe the term civil rights includes the right of suffrage. Some gentlemen seem to have some fear on that point.

---

[45] GLOBE, App. 134; GLOBE 1121–22.
[46] GLOBE 1157.

The House adopted the amendment by voice vote.[47]

The Democrats were, of course, not pacified by this concession. Their concluding shot was fired by Michael C. Kerr of Indiana. Power to enact this bill was sought, he said, in the amendment abolishing slavery. But:

> Is it slavery or involuntary servitude to forbid a free negro, on account of race or color, to testify against a white man? Is it either to deny to free negroes, on the same account, the privilege of engaging in certain kinds of business . . . such as retailing spirituous liquors? Is it either to deny to children of free negroes or mulattoes, on the like account, the privilege of attending the common schools of a State with the children of white men?

These were all matters, apparently, in Kerr's mind, with which the bill might be thought to deal. He himself favored letting Negroes testify and "providing facilities for the education of their children." But he thought Congress was powerless to attain these ends. And the construction which might in practice be given to the term "civil rights" was quite unpredictable and would not be controlled by disclaimers made on the floor of the House.[48]

Despite its vigor, this Democratic attack might well have gone unheeded, as had the similar one in the Senate, and changes in the Senate draft might have ended with the suffrage amendment accepted by Wilson, had it not been for misgivings in the regular Republican ranks in the House as well. These came from three fairly distinct quarters. Henry J. Raymond of New York, publisher of the New York Times, and not a Radical, favored extend-

---

[47] GLOBE 1162.

[48] GLOBE 1268. It is not at all clear that the reference in the full paragraph quoted in the text to attendance at common schools "with the children of white men" means that Kerr thought the bill would require establishment of unsegregated schools rather than separate Negro schools, forming part of a state's educational system. Kerr's further remark can be read to imply that he took the educational objective of the bill to be segregated Negro schools, and that he favored it, subject to his constitutional scruples. But he did go on to express general apprehension concerning the meaning of the term "civil rights": "What are [civil] rights? One writer says civil rights are those which have no relation to the establishment, support, or management of the Government. Another says they are the rights of a citizen; rights due from one citizen to another, the privation of which is a *civil injury* for which redress may be sought by a *civil action*. Other authors define all these terms in different ways . . . . Who shall define these terms? Their definition here by gentlemen on this floor is one thing; their definition after this bill shall have become law will be quite another thing." GLOBE 1270-71.

ing to Negroes the "rights and privileges" of citizens. By that he understood the right of free passage, to bear arms, to testify, "all those rights that tend to elevate [the Negro] and educate him for still higher reaches in the process of elevation." Giving the Negro the rights of citizenship "will teach all others of his fellow-citizens of all races to respect him more, and to aid him in his steps for constant progress and advancement in the rights and duties that belong to citizenship." [49] But Raymond thought that the bill's penal enforcement provisions rendered it unconstitutional, and he therefore opposed it as a whole, though he did not seem to subscribe to the alarmist view of the scope of section 1. Perhaps it was simply that the position he took made a close analysis of that section unnecessary.

Columbus Delano of Ohio, a Moderate, shared Raymond's constitutional difficulties. He inclined to the belief that these might be removed if the general civil rights language at the head of section 1 and the penal provisions further on were struck. But, unlike Raymond, Delano feared that the bill might be construed to outlaw a wide variety of practices prevalent in the North as well as in the South. This was a question of policy, and Delano was concerned about the entire first section, not just the sentence at the beginning. He asked Wilson whether the provision in the body of section 1 entitling Negroes "to full and equal benefit of all laws and proceedings for the security of person and property *as is enjoyed by white citizens*" (the italicized phrase was not in the bill as passed by the Senate but was added in committee in the House and appears in the statute as enacted) would not confer "upon the emancipated race the right of being jurors." Wilson thought not.

> Mr. Delano. I have no doubt of the sincerity of the gentleman, and . . . I have great confidence in his legal opinions . . . .
>
> But, with all this, I must confess that it does seem to me that this bill necessarily confers the right of being jurors . . . .
>
> . . . .
>
> Now, sir . . . I presume that the gentleman himself will shrink from the idea of conferring upon this race now, at this particular moment, the right of being jurors, or from so wording this bill as

---

[49] GLOBE 1120, 1266. To the same general effect, see remarks of Thomas T. Davis of New York. GLOBE 1265. But Davis, in the end, voted for the bill and to override the veto.

to leave it a serious question and render it debatable hereafter in the courts or elsewhere.

Moreover:

[W]e once had in the State of Ohio a law excluding the black population from any participation in the public schools . . . . That law did not, of course, place the black population upon an equal footing with the white, and would, therefore, under the terms of this bill be void . . . . [50]

Here Wilson broke in with "I desire to ask the gentleman," but Delano had no further time for interruptions, and so there was no argument on this point. It is to be noted that Delano was not suggesting that Ohio would be forced to provide unsegregated schools; he was predicting only the fall of laws which excluded Negroes from schools of any sort. Despite these views, which were not met by amendment insofar as they related to provisions in the body of section 1, Delano ended up voting for the bill and to override the President's veto.

The final expression of Republican misgivings was the most formidable, and it was decisive. It came from John A. Bingham of Ohio, a Radical, and one of the most influential men in the 39th Congress. Bingham was speaking in support of a motion he had offered to recommit with instructions to strike the sentence at the head of section 1 which forbade all "discrimination in civil rights or immunities," and to substitute for the penal enforcement provisions of the bill language permitting a civil action by aggrieved parties.[51] He tried at the start to meet an argument which he knew would be advanced against him, as indeed it was:

Mr. Speaker . . . I beg leave . . . to say, that although the objections which I urge against the bill must, in the very nature of the case, apply to the proposed instructions, I venture to say no candid man, no rightminded man, will deny that by amending as proposed the bill will be less oppressive, and therefore less objectionable. Doubting, as I do, the power of Congress to pass the bill, I urge the instructions with a view to take from the bill what seems to me its oppressive and I might say its unjust provisions.

Bingham then proceeded to examine the civil rights provision

---

[50] GLOBE, App. 156–58.
[51] GLOBE 1266, 1271–72.

which he proposed to delete. "What are civil rights?" he asked.
It seemed that,

> the term civil rights includes every right that pertains to the citizen
> under the Constitution, laws, and Government of this country. . . .
> [A]re not political rights all embraced in the term "civil rights,"
> and must it not of necessity be so interpreted?
> . . . . [T]here is scarcely a State in this Union which does not,
> by its constitution or by its statute laws, make some discrimination
> on account of race or color between citizens of the United States
> in respect of civil rights.
>
> . . . .
>
> By the Constitution of my own State neither the right of the
> elective franchise nor the franchise of office can be conferred . . .
> save upon a white citizen of the United States.

Coming to the specific rights enumerated in that part of section 1
which his motion would have left untouched, Bingham noted that
they had been denied by many states, and said: "I should remedy
that not by an arbitrary assumption of power, but by amending
the Constitution of the United States, expressly prohibiting the
States from any such abuse of power in the future." He had
made no such statement about civil rights in general. He went
on then to attack the penal enforcement provisions as unwise
as well as unconstitutional. The federal government, by constitutional amendment, could protect the rights of life, liberty,
and property in the manner Bingham had just described. State
officials would then take an oath to observe such a prohibition as
he envisioned, and Congress could somehow enforce the oath.
But Congress had never, it could not, and it should not, employ
"the terrors of the penal code within organized States." The
Freedmen's Bureau Bill had been carefully worded to apply only
in territories under military occupation. Bingham quoted de
Tocqueville: " 'centralized government, decentralized administration.' That, sir, coupled with your declared purpose of equal
justice, is the secret of your strength and power." That should be
the rule in peacetime. He quoted also from Chancellor Kent on
the powers that properly belong to the states. Then occurred
these passages:

> Now what does this bill propose? To reform the whole civil and
> criminal code of every State government by declaring that there
> shall be no discrimination between citizens on account of race or

color in civil rights or in the penalties prescribed by their laws. I humbly bow before the majesty of justice, as I bow before the majesty of that God whose attribute it is, and therefore declare there should be no such inequality or discrimination even in the penalties for crime; but what power have you to correct it? . . . You further say that . . . there shall, as to qualification of witnesses, be no discrimination on account of race or color. I agree that . . . there should be no such discrimination.

But whence do you derive power to cure it by a congressional enactment? There should be no discrimination among citizens of the United States in the several States, of like sex, age, and condition, in regard to the franchises of office. But such a discrimination does exist in nearly every State. How do you propose to cure all this? By a congressional enactment? How? Not by saying, in so many words, which would be the bold and direct way of meeting this issue, that every discrimination of this kind . . . is hereby abolished. You propose to make it a penal offense for the judges of the States to obey the constitution and laws of their States . . . . I deny your power to do this. You cannot make an official act, done under color of law . . . and from a sense of public duty, a crime.[52]

Such was Bingham's position, and it is not lacking in ambiguity. Like Raymond, he thought the bill was unconstitutional, but he did not take the narrow ground of section 2 only; the bill for him was unconstitutional from top to bottom. Hence, unlike Delano, he made no pretense that his motion would cure the constitutional defect. With Delano, apparently unlike Raymond, and certainly unlike Wilson and his supporters, he read the general term "civil rights" broadly, or at any rate thought it was of uncertain reach. In the first half of his speech, it is perfectly clear that Bingham, while committing himself to the need for safeguarding by constitutional amendment the specific rights enumerated in the body of section 1, was anything but willing to make a similar commitment with respect to "civil rights" in general. The second half of the speech, in which Bingham bore down heavily on penal sanctions as provided in section 2, ends in some ambiguity. Bingham said first that he wanted no such sanctions applied to violations of rights which he was ready to enshrine in the Constitution. He mentioned the rights of life, liberty, and property, and the ideal of equal justice: the sort of thing enumerated in the body of

---

[52] GLOBE 1290–93.

section 1. Then, in the last two paragraphs, while still pressing his fight against penal sanctions, he referred both to rights specifically listed in section 1 and to at least one other which in his view was covered by the term "civil rights." And he went on record as opposed on principle to discriminations with respect to all these rights. But was he, in these two final paragraphs, spoken just before the hammer fell, hastening to say something he had rather carefully and gingerly refrained from saying before, namely that he was prepared to write what he considered to be the substance of a general "civil rights" provision into the Constitution? On their face, and following as they do a lecture on federalism, these remarks are quite consistent with a belief that some discriminations, practiced in the North as well as in the South, though objectionable on moral principle, to be sure, should be cured by state rather than federal action. Bingham's professions here are high-flown. They call on God and the majesty of justice, and they differ rather markedly from his earlier flat and specific declaration concerning the evils he would remedy by amending the Constitution. Are these not the sort of soothing but vague and vacuous concessions Bingham was likely to offer to his Radical colleagues while trying to induce them to rebel against at least one feature of a leadership bill? Similarly, in denouncing criminal sanctions imposed, as he thought, against state officials for denying the franchise to Negroes, Bingham may seem in this passage to suggest that he would have approved a "bold and direct" congressional enactment declaring "that every discrimination of this kind . . . is hereby abolished." Yet if his speech as an entirety means anything at all, it means that he would have considered such a "bold and direct" congressional enactment unconstitutional.

These are words spoken in debate by a man not normally distinguished for precision of thought and statement. Perhaps judgments may differ about them, though they must not be taken out of context. One makes out their meaning as best one can. They are important because of Bingham's role in drafting section 1 of the fourteenth amendment and his avoidance in all his drafts of the term "civil rights." Whatever the ambiguities of his speech, one thing is certain. Unless one concludes that Bingham entertained apprehensions about the breadth of the term "civil rights" and was unwilling at this stage, as a matter of policy, not constitutional law, to extend a federal guaranty covering all that

49

might be included in that term, there is no rational explanation for his motion to strike it. There was no illusion in Bingham's mind of removing a constitutional infirmity in this fashion. He was endeavoring merely to make the bill less "oppressive," less "unjust." Constitutional scruples to the side, he wanted a bill that would at least be satisfactory on policy grounds. That was the object of his attempt to remove the penal provisions. What other object could he have had in mind in trying also to eliminate the comprehensive civil rights guaranty, which in his opinion would force a change in the law of his own state?

Wilson, the manager of the bill, who rose to answer Bingham, had understood the latter as objecting to the breadth of the "civil rights" provision. He defended the term "civil rights" in accordance with the line he had laid down at the beginning of debate. Bingham, he said,

> tells the House that civil rights involve all the rights that citizens have under the Government . . . that this bill is not intended merely to enforce equality of rights, so far as they relate to citizens of the United States, but invades the States to enforce equality of rights in respect to those things which properly and rightfully depend on State regulations and laws. My friend . . . . knows, as every man knows, that this bill refers to those rights which belong to men as citizens of the United States and none other; and when he talks of setting aside the school laws and jury laws and franchise laws of the States by the bill . . . he steps beyond what he must know to be the rule of construction which must apply here, and as a result of which this bill can only relate to matters within the control of Congress.

This misrepresented Bingham's statement in that it had him referring specifically to school and jury laws, which Bingham had not done. Wilson also implied that Bingham had argued, as Bingham had not, that his motion would remove the constitutional infirmity he saw in the bill. It could not, said Wilson. If any part of section 1 was unconstitutional, all of it had to be.[53]

---

[53] Wilson also said:

I find in the bill of rights . . . that "no person shall be deprived of life, liberty, or property without due process of law." I understand that these constitute the civil rights belonging to the citizens in connection with those which are necessary for the protection and maintenance and perfect enjoyment of the rights thus specifically named, and these are the rights to which this bill relates, having nothing to do with subjects submitted to the control of the several States.

GLOBE 1294–95.

Bingham complained generally, in one sentence, that "the gentleman from Iowa has taken advantage of me by misstating my position." [54] The voting then began. Wilson asked whether

---

[54] GLOBE 1295. Commentators who have looked into the matter have tended to oversimplify Bingham's position. In the first work on the subject, he is represented as objecting to the bill "entirely upon constitutional grounds." See FLACK, THE ADOPTION OF THE FOURTEENTH AMENDMENT 35 (1908). Similarly, in a recent article, Mr. Howard Jay Graham leaves the reader with the impression that the debate on the Civil Rights Bill in the House turned wholly on the issue of constitutionality, dealt, that is, entirely with means, not ends. The implication is that Wilson on the one hand and Bingham and those Republicans who held views similar to his on the other, were all along in agreement concerning the ends which the Civil Rights Bill would attain and concerning their desirability. See Graham, *Our "Declaratory" Fourteenth Amendment,* 7 STAN. L. REV. 3, 12–18 (1954). This may be true as applied to Raymond. It is true insofar as it indicates that Bingham and Wilson were at one in their understanding of the specific ends aimed at by section 1 in its final form, and that Bingham regarded the attainment of these ends by appropriate federal action as desirable. An assertion so limited is supported by a passage from Bingham's speech which, as quoted by Mr. Graham, starts as follows: "I say, with all my heart, that [the First Section] . . . should be the law of every State . . . ." *Id.* at 15. The reference in Mr. Graham's context is to "the First Section" as enacted. In the speech itself, it was to the first section as it came from the Senate, but shorn of its first sentence. Bingham, who had just been urging the elimination of the civil rights provision in that first sentence, read the section to the House without it, and immediately thereafter declared himself as quoted. "I say, with all my heart that that should be the law of every State," he said with all his heart. GLOBE 1291. This is a poor foundation for the theory Mr. Graham erects on it. Mr. Graham ignores the form in which the bill came from the Senate, Bingham's motion, the rest of Bingham's remarks, and what happened to the bill.

Messrs. John P. Frank and Robert F. Munro state that Bingham "opposed the Civil Rights Act solely because he thought it should await passage of the Fourteenth Amendment," and attribute to him also the opinion that "appropriate language should eliminate 'all discrimination between citizens on account of race or color in civil rights.'" Frank & Munro, *The Original Understanding of "Equal Protection of the Laws,"* 50 COLUM. L. REV. 131, 142 n.51 (1950). The brief quotation used by Messrs. Frank and Munro is from the next to last paragraph of Bingham's speech, quoted and discussed in the text above. He does not in that passage in so many words express the opinion attributed to him, nor does he do so anywhere else, and in light of the full text of his speech and of his motion, it is doubtful that he held it.

Mr. Charles Fairman understands Bingham to have believed that his motion to recommit with instructions to strike the guarantee of civil rights in section 1 and to change the enforcement provision would, if adopted, have cured the bill's constitutional defect. Fairman, *supra* note 13, at 39–40. This was Delano's view and Wilson accused Bingham of holding it. Wilson must have made the same accusation in the cloakroom as well, for, as shown in the text, Bingham started right off by entering a disclaimer. His remarks calling for a constitutional amendment to embody that part of section 1 which he did not hesitate to say he approved reinforce the point.

51

it was in order for him to accept Bingham's motion to recommit with instructions. He was told that he could do so only by unanimous consent. "Mr. Stevens and others objected." Bingham's motion was then defeated by a large majority. But the House voted to recommit the bill without instructions. This vote was close: 82–70. Bingham, of course, voted to recommit. So did the Democrats; also Raymond, Delano, and Thomas T. Davis of New York, a Republican who shared Raymond's view. So did a good many Radicals such as Justin Morrill of Vermont, member of the Joint Committee on Reconstruction, and even one of the leaders of the House, Robert C. Schenck of Ohio. Thaddeus Stevens voted against and Wilson followed him, as did most Radicals.[55]

Wilson brought the bill back four days later, on March 13. He reported a committee amendment striking from section 1 the civil rights provision Bingham had objected to. Wilson said:

> Mr. Speaker, the amendment which has just been read proposes to strike out the general terms relating to civil rights. I do not think it materially changes the bill; but some gentlemen were apprehensive that the words we propose to strike out might give warrant for a latitudinarian construction not intended.

The House concurred by voice vote. Wilson noted, in response to a question, that the bill as it now stood contained no proviso excluding suffrage from its application; but he thought the committee amendment just reported should take care of any apprehensions on that score. He then pressed for a vote. Bingham and others asked that the bill be printed and allowed to lay over so gentlemen could read it again. Wilson would not give in, however, and the vote was taken. The majority for passage was large. Bingham and five other Republicans were recorded against. Raymond and a few others did not vote.[56]

Two days later the Senate concurred in the House amendments.[57] The President vetoed the bill on March 27. In discussing section 1, he conceded that the only rights safeguarded by it were those enumerated. He did not attack the section on the basis of any alarmist "latitudinarian" construction. His objections were

---

[55] GLOBE 1296.

[56] GLOBE 1366–67.

[57] But not without hearing one more violent speech by Garrett Davis, Kentucky's furious Democrat. GLOBE 1413–16; see note 36 *supra*.

constitutional.[58] The Senate took up the veto on April 4, having had a recess on account of the death of Senator Solomon Foot of Vermont. There were speeches by Trumbull, Reverdy Johnson, Cowan, and Garrett Davis, Democrat of Kentucky, who was still maintaining that the bill would abolish antimiscegenation statutes and mark the end of segregation in hotels and railroad cars and churches. Finally the Senate overrode the veto, five Republicans voting to uphold.[59] On April 9 the House also overrode, without debate. Seven Republicans, including Henry J. Raymond, voted to uphold the President. Bingham was paired in support of the veto.[60]

The Bingham Amendment

While the Senate was passing the Freedmen's Bureau and Civil Rights Bills, but before the President had vetoed the former and before the House had taken up the latter, the Joint Committee on Reconstruction [61] worked out and reported a proposed constitutional amendment dealing with the "privileges and immunities of

---

[58] GLOBE 1679–81.

[59] GLOBE 1775–80, 1782–85, 1809; GLOBE, App. 181–85.

[60] GLOBE 1861.

[61] The Committee, known popularly as the Committee of Fifteen, came into being under the Joint Resolution of December 13, 1865. GLOBE 6, 30, 46–47. The father of the Committee was Thaddeus Stevens, one of the most powerful congressional leaders in our history, who, if he were making headlines today, would doubtless be billed in them as "Mr. Radical." Stevens possessed, as he once understated it to the House, "some will of my own," and he was at no time animated by a desire to compromise with the new President. Conservatives and Moderates in his party were. But not Stevens. He would either rule the President or fight him. He conceived of the Joint Committee as a sort of Politburo, governing the South with, or without, or against the President. KENDRICK, THE JOURNAL OF THE JOINT COMMITTEE OF FIFTEEN ON RECONSTRUCTION 133–54 (1914); HENRY, *op. cit. supra* note 25, at 133–42. But, as its journal shows, the Committee was never entirely Stevens' creature.

The resolution creating the Committee was a veiled reflection of Stevens' purpose. It struck the dominant political note which, on the whole, was to characterize the work of the session. And it was to some extent a poor forecast of the business with which the Committee was to deal. It instructed the Committee to "inquire into the condition of the States which formed the so-called confederate States of America, and report whether they, or any of them, are entitled to be represented in either House of Congress, with leave to report at any time, by bill or otherwise." There were nine members from the House and six from the Senate, three of the total being Democrats: Representatives Stevens, Washburne of Illinois, Morrill of Vermont, Bingham, Conkling of New York, Boutwell of Massachusetts, and Blow of Missouri, Republicans, and Grider of Kentucky and Rogers, Democrats; Senators Fessenden of Maine, Grimes of Iowa, Harris of New York, Howard of Michigan, and Williams of Oregon, Republicans, and Reverdy Johnson, Democrat.

citizens" and with "equal protection." The principal author of this proposal, and its manager in debate, was John A. Bingham of Ohio.

The Joint Committee convened on January 6, 1866, and discussed the basis upon which the former Confederate states might again be given representation in the federal government, and the related question of negro suffrage. At the third meeting, on January 12, a subcommittee was appointed and charged with reporting on the basis of representation. It consisted of William Pitt Fessenden, the Moderate Senator from Maine, Thaddeus Stevens, Senator Jacob Howard of Michigan, a Radical, Roscoe Conkling of New York, then in the House, who generally acted with the leadership but was not a doctrinaire Radical, and Bingham. Into the hopper of the Subcommittee went the following draft, proposed by Bingham as an amendment to the Constitution:

> The Congress shall have power to make all laws necessary and proper to secure to all persons in every state within this Union equal protection in their rights of life, liberty and property.

Stevens, in addition to a proposal on the basis of representation, submitted the following:

> All laws, state and national, shall operate impartially and equally on all persons without regard to race or color.

On January 20, Fessenden, reporting to the full Committee from the Subcommittee, brought forth three proposed articles of amendment to the Constitution,

> the first two as alternative propositions, one of which, with the third proposition, to be recommended to Congress for adoption:
>
> . . . .
>
> Article A.
> Representatives and direct taxes shall be apportioned among the several States within this Union, according to the respective numbers of citizens of the United States in each State; and all provisions in the Constitution or laws of any State, whereby any distinction is made in political or civil rights or privileges, on account of race, creed or color, shall be inoperative and void.
>
> Or the following:
>
> Article B.
> Representatives and direct taxes shall be apportioned among the several States which may be included within this Union, accord-

ing to their respective numbers, counting the whole number of citizens of the United States in each State; provided that, whenever the elective franchise shall be denied or abridged in any State on account of race, creed or color, all persons of such race, creed or color, shall be excluded from the basis of representation.

Article C.

Congress shall have power to make all laws necessary and proper to secure to all citizens of the United States, in every State, the same political rights and privileges; and to all persons in every State equal protection in the enjoyment of life, liberty and property.

As is apparent, the combination of articles A and C amounted to an immediate grant of negro suffrage, while that of articles B and C was a prospective grant, to be realized when and if Congress felt so inclined, probably later than sooner, since an interim scheme was provided. As regards other rights, article A again acted directly and immediately, but negatively, on the states, with a reserve implementing power being lodged in Congress by article C, whereas article B made no provision but rather left the whole matter to Congress through article C. Articles A and C differed in that the latter struck at discriminations, in suffrage and other rights, whether or not based on color; that is, article C covered all classes of "citizens" and "persons," whereas article A did not. As regards the extent of the rights protected, the two articles were coterminous in the matter of suffrage, both using the words, "political rights and [or] privileges." But were they intended to be otherwise coterminous also? That is to say, in the view of the Subcommittee, did the power to protect the enjoyment of "life, liberty and property" granted by article C go the same length as the prohibition of distinctions in "civil rights or privileges" written into article A? If so, the Subcommittee's draftsmanship was, of course, terrible. This is not conclusive against the hypothesis, but it gives pause. Moreover, reasoning from the position Bingham, the author of the "life, liberty and property" language, took on the Civil Rights Bill, it is fair to conclude that he for one saw a difference between the term "civil rights" and his own formula. On the assumption that the Subcommittee understood civil rights protection to reach further than the Bingham proposal, articles A and C taken together reveal a rational purpose rather than monumentally bad draftsmanship, the purpose being to strike broadly and immediately at discriminations based on color, leaving to Congress the less urgent problem of other unequal laws, and at the same time to make the affirmative function of Congress to take over legislative powers hitherto reserved to the states narrower than a negative provision, limiting state power, but substituting no other. Again, comparing the two packages, one would expect the proposal which went the whole way on suffrage to protect a greater range of other rights, and the one which embodied the more conservative approach to the suffrage question to be satisfied with the grant of narrower — and prospective — additional protection. On this hypothesis, the alternative proposals presented the full Committee with a real choice all the way down the line.

It is more than likely that Thaddeus Stevens personally favored the alternative which included article A. But the old gentleman was a confirmed practitioner of the art of the possible. And so he moved that article C be severed from the other two, and then that article B be considered in preference to article A. This was done. Article B, with minor changes, was reported out as the Committee's first product. It was doomed to defeat, largely because it was unacceptable to Charles Sumner, who was at this time unable to abandon the principle of immediate suffrage, though he eventually saw the light.[62]

At the Committee's next meeting, on January 24, article C was tackled. A couple of unsuccessful attempts were made to tinker with the provision concerning political rights. Finally, by a vote of 7 to 5, it was decided to refer the proposal to a select committee consisting of Bingham, Representative George S. Boutwell of Massachusetts, a Radical, and Andrew Jackson Rogers, for redrafting. Three days later, Bingham reported it back in this form:

> Congress shall have power to make all laws which shall be necessary and proper to secure all persons in every state full protection in the enjoyment of life, liberty and property; and to all citizens of the United States in any State the same immunities and also equal political rights and privileges.

The two parts of the article had been turned around; equal pro-

---

[62] The idea embodied in article B had been first suggested by James G. Blaine of Maine. GLOBE 136, 141–42. The House passed the proposal as reported by Stevens from the Joint Committee. GLOBE 538. Sumner attacked it heavily in the Senate, GLOBE 673–87, 1224–32, 1281–82, and the addition of his vote, and the votes of one or two other Radicals, to those of the Democrats and Conservative Republicans ensured its defeat there. GLOBE 1289.

tection had become full; the same political rights had become equal; and the word "immunities" appears for the first time. These would seem to be largely matters of style, though it may be remarked that "full" is presumably something different than "equal." Stevens tried to get this proposal reported out, but could not do it. Four Republicans were absent and three voted nay. When consideration was resumed on February 3, Bingham proposed the following substitute:

> The Congress shall have power to make all laws which shall be necessary and proper to secure to the citizens of each State all privileges and immunities of citizens in the several States (Art. 4, Sec. 2); and to all persons in the several States equal protection in the rights of life, liberty and property (5th Amendment).

Protection in this draft had reverted back to "equal." The more notable change, however, is the elimination of any reference to political rights. The substitution was agreed to by a vote of 7 to 6, Stevens and Fessenden voting against. On February 10 it was decided, 9 to 5, to report this proposal out. Senator Ira Harris of New York, an inconspicuous Moderate, and Conkling were the only Republicans who voted nay.[63]

Debate began in the House on February 26. Bingham in a brief opening aired the notion indicated by the parenthetical references to the Constitution. He said:

> Every word of the proposed amendment is to-day in the Constitution of our country, save the words conferring the express grant of power upon the Congress of the United States.
>
> . . . .
>
> Sir, it has been the want of the Republic that there was not an express grant of power in the Constitution to enable the whole people of every State, by congressional enactment, to enforce obedience to these requirements of the Constitution.[64]

A number of Radicals who spoke in support of Bingham also gave vent to the idea that the proposal was in some way declarative, merely enabling Congress to enforce rights already guaranteed by the Constitution as it stood.[65] William D. "Pig-Iron" Kelley of

---

[63] KENDRICK, op. cit. supra note 61, at 39, 45–47, 50–53, 55–58, 61–63. These citations cover the entire course of the Committee's deliberations so far described in the text.

[64] GLOBE 1034.

[65] Thus William Higby of California thought the amendment would simply

Pennsylvania even expressed the opinion that the amendment would add no new powers whatever to those Congress already possessed, though he recognized that reasonable men might have doubts on this score which it was worthwhile to remove. Kelley at the same time appeared to think that the proposal dealt with suffrage.[66] Aside from him, however, and from Bingham, later, when he was responding to attacks, the supporters of the amendment had little if anything specific to say about the kind of state action to which it was directed. This contrasts with the speeches made in behalf of the Civil Rights Bill. The opposition was bipartisan, as in the case of the Senate draft of the Civil Rights Bill, and it was to prove effective.

For the Democrats, Rogers, having noted that the need which Bingham professed for his amendment proved that the Civil Rights Bill — then about to come up in the House — was unconstitutional, addressed himself to the equal protection clause. He for one evidently saw no difference between this formula and the comprehensive civil rights provision in the Senate draft of the Civil Rights Bill. Under this clause, he said,

> Congress can pass . . . a law compelling South Carolina to grant to negroes every right accorded to white people there; and as white men there have the right to marry white women, negroes, under this amendment, would be entitled to the same right . . . .

Further:

> In the State of Pennsylvania there are laws which make a distinction with regard to the schooling of white children and the schooling of black children. . . . Under this amendment, Congress would have power to compel the State to provide for white children and black children to attend the same school, upon the principle that all the people in the several States shall have equal protection in all the rights of life, liberty, and property, and all the privileges and immunities of citizens in the several States.
>
>   . . . .
>
> Sir, I defy any man upon the other side of the House to name to me any right of the citizen which is not included in the words "life,

give effect to parts of the Constitution which "probably were intended from the beginning to have life and vitality . . . ." GLOBE 1054. Frederick E. Woodbridge of Vermont said the amendment would enable Congress to "give to a citizen of the United States, in whatever State he may be, those privileges and immunities which are guarantied to him under the constitution . . . ." GLOBE 1088.

[66] GLOBE 1057, 1062–63.

liberty, property, privileges, and immunities," unless it should be the right of suffrage . . . .[67]

The speech which was very likely decisive against the Bingham amendment was delivered by Robert S. Hale of New York, a lawyer and former judge, and a man who was able to make the House sit up and listen. Hale was a regular Republican. Though he was to be recorded absent for the vote on passage of the Civil Rights Bill, he was to vote to override the veto of that bill, and eventually for the fourteenth amendment. This proposal seemed to him, however, to entrust Congress with the most extraordinary powers. To begin with, Hale paid his respects to Bingham:

> Listening to the remarks of the distinguished member of the committee who reported this joint resolution to the House, one would be led to think that this amendment was a subject of the most trivial consequence. He tells us, and tells us with an air of gravity that I could not but admire, that the words of the resolution are all in the Constitution as it stands, with the single exception of the power given to Congress to legislate. A very important exception, it strikes me . . . .
>
>   . . . .
>
> What is the effect of the amendment . . . ? I submit that it is in effect a provision under which all State legislation, in its codes of civil and criminal jurisprudence and procedure, affecting the individual citizen, may be overridden . . . and the law of Congress established instead.

This roused Thaddeus Stevens. He asked:

> Does the gentleman mean to say that, under this provision, Congress could interfere in any case where the legislation of a State was equal, impartial to all? Or is it not simply to provide that, where any State makes a distinction in the same law between different classes of individuals, Congress shall have power to correct such discrimination and inequality?

The first proposition stated by Stevens was, of course, what Hale

---

[67] GLOBE, App. 133, 134, 135. Much of the rest of Rogers' time was taken up with the kind of political small talk — the Radicals loved to bait him — into which so many of his speeches were wont to degenerate. This, of course, cannot but detract from the weight of his remarks. Thus, Samuel J. Randall, Democrat of Pennsylvania and a future Speaker of the House, felt constrained, after Rogers had finished, to state: "I wish it to be understood that the gentleman from New Jersey does not speak for me." The House reacted with laughter. Rogers modestly said, "I speak for myself." GLOBE 1034; *cf.* note 44 *supra*.

had meant, and he said so. This was much more than just a "provision for the equality of individual citizens before the laws of
the several States." Moreover, it was important to realize the
reach of this language. For example, said Hale, all states distinguished between the property rights of married women on the one
hand, and of *"femmes sole"* and men on the other. Such distinctions would be outlawed by this proposal. No, said Stevens, pro-
pounding a theory of reasonable classification under the equal
protection clause:

> When a distinction is made between two married people or two
> *femmes sole*, then it is unequal legislation; but where all of the
> same class are dealt with in the same way then there is no pre-
> tense of inequality.

Hale disagreed. The proposal, he said, "gives to *all persons* equal
protection." If what Stevens had said were the correct construction it would be sufficient also to extend the same rights to one
Negro as to another in order to satisfy the amendment. There was
no further reply from Stevens. Hale next drew Bingham's fire.
The latter put up to him the fact that property rights and procedural rights in courts of law had been denied by some states.
(Here at last we return to the Black Codes.) Was not some protection needed? This was weak ground for Hale. The states
should provide it, he said, and if Bingham found that the state of
Ohio could not protect its citizens, he ought to come to New York,
where things were different. Bingham pursued the matter:

> I do not cast any imputation upon the State of New York. The
> gentleman knows full well, from conversations I have had with him,
> that so far as I understand this power, under no possible inter-
> pretation can it ever be made to operate in the State of New York
> while she occupies her present proud position.
>
>   . . . .
>
>   . . . . It is to apply to other States [than those which seceded]
> . . . that have in their constitutions and laws to-day provisions in
> direct violation of every principle of our Constitution.
>   Mr. Rogers. I suppose the gentleman refers to the State of
> Indiana?
>   Mr. Bingham. I do not know; it may be so. It applies unques-
> tionably to the State of Oregon.[68]

This is an interesting passage. Bingham here specified state

---

[68] GLOBE 1063–65.

enactments which his proposal would strike down. He refused to commit himself on Indiana. The reference there, as Professor Fairman has pointed out, was probably to the provision of the Indiana constitution denying suffrage to Negroes and mulattoes.[69] His own state, as Bingham remarked in the Civil Rights Bill debate, made a similar discrimination. The Oregon constitution at this time, as has also been pointed out, forbade free Negroes or mulattoes not residing in the state at the time of its adoption to come into the state, reside there, hold real estate, contract, or sue.[70] This sort of thing Bingham wanted to strike down. As for the State of New York in her then proud position, whether or not Bingham knew it, her laws permitted the establishment of separate but equal schools for colored children in the discretion of local districts. Segregated schools in fact existed at least until the year 1900. And it seems quite possible, on the face of her statutes, that New York maintained her proud position in respect of permissive segregation in rural districts till 1938.[71]

---

[69] IND. CONST. art. II, §§ 2, 5 (1851) ; see Fairman, *supra* note 13, at 31 n.57.

[70] ORE. CONST. art. I, § 35 (1857) ; see Fairman, *supra* note 13, at 32 n.58; Boudin, *supra* note 13, at 35 n.13.

[71] N.Y. Sess. Laws 1864, c. 555, tit. 10, provided: "Section 1. The school authorities of any city or incorporated village . . . may, when they shall deem it expedient, establish a separate school or separate schools for the instruction of children and youth of African descent, resident therein . . . and such school or schools shall be supported in the same manner and to the same extent as the school or schools supported therein for white children, and they shall be subject to the same rules and regulations, and be furnished with facilities for instruction equal to those furnished to the white schools therein.

"Section 2. The trustees of any union school district, or of any school district organized under a special act, may, when the inhabitants of any such district shall so determine . . . establish . . . separate schools for the instruction of such colored children . . . and such schools shall be supported in the same manner, and receive the same care, and be furnished with the same facilities for instruction as the white schools therein."

N.Y. Sess. Laws 1894, c. 556, tit. 15, art. 11, §§ 28, 29, reenacted the two sections of the 1864 statute quoted above. In 1900, segregation in Queens was upheld in People *ex rel.* Cisco v. School Bd., 161 N.Y. 598, 56 N.E. 81. Following this decision, the legislature passed an act "to secure equal rights to colored children." It did so by providing that "no person shall be refused admission into or be excluded from any public school in the state of New York on account of race or color," and by repealing § 28 of the Act of 1894 (§ 1 of the Act of 1864), which permitted segregation in cities and incorporated villages. But it left undisturbed § 29 of the same Act of 1894 (§ 2 of the Act of 1864), which was the corresponding provision applicable to union school districts and districts organized under special acts, and which differed in that it permitted segregation only after a vote by the district's inhabitants. N.Y. Sess. Laws 1900, c. 492.

One hesitates to pass judgment with any feeling of confidence on this state of

The next day, Thomas T. Davis, another New York Republican, took up where Hale had left off. He, too, thought that this was an extraordinary grant of power to Congress, and he feared that the power would be used "in the establishment of perfect political equality between the colored and the white race of the South." The Negroes, he said,

> must be made equal before the law, and be permitted to enjoy life, liberty, and the pursuit of happiness. I am pledged to my own conscience to favor every measure of legislation which shall be found essential to the protection of their just rights [Davis was to vote for the Civil Rights Bill], and shall most cheerfully aid in any plan for their education and elevation which may reasonably be adopted.
>
> . . . .
>
> Give them protection, teachers, education, and hold out to them inducements to self-improvement . . . .

But this amendment meant "centralization of power in Congress" and very likely political rights — and that was going too far.[72]

The proposal was clearly in trouble, and Bingham, in a long speech, attempted a rescue operation. Among other things, he said:

> The proposition pending before the House is simply a proposition to arm the Congress . . . with the power to enforce the bill of rights as it stands in the Constitution today. It "hath that extent — no more."
>
> . . . .

---

the New York law. But the legislative action of 1900 cannot simply be attributed to an oversight. In the face of this partial repealer, would the declaration that no person should be refused admission to "any school" on account of color have been given effect in school districts to which the unrepealed § 29 was applicable? It is noteworthy that while all of the Act of 1864 was on the books, the legislature passed a civil rights act prohibiting trustees and other officers of "public institutions of learning" from excluding anyone on account of color "from full and equal enjoyment of any accommodation, advantage, facility or privilege." N.Y. Sess. Laws 1873, c. 186, § 1. Nevertheless, the New York Court of Appeals had no difficulty avoiding this statute and upholding school segregation in Brooklyn as provided for in the Act of 1864. People *ex rel.* King v. Gallagher, 93 N.Y. 438, 455–56 (1883). Perhaps by 1900 segregation outside cities and incorporated villages was not a problem. Perhaps it never had been much of one. Yet here was a section dealing with it, and there just is no satisfactory explanation for what looks like a deliberate failure to repeal it. *But cf.* Sutherland, *Segregation by Race in Public Schools Retrospect and Prospect*, 20 LAW & CONTEMP. PROB. 169, 171 (1955). The section was at last stricken from the books by N.Y. Sess. Laws 1938, c. 134.

[72] GLOBE 1085, 1087.

. . . . [R]equirements of our Constitution have been broken; they are disregarded to-day in Oregon; they are disregarded to-day, and have been disregarded for the last five, ten, or twenty years in every one of the eleven States recently in insurrection.

. . . .

. . . . Gentlemen who oppose this amendment oppose the grant of power to enforce the bill of rights. Gentlemen who oppose this amendment simply declare to these rebel States, go on with your confiscation statutes, your statutes of banishment, your statutes of unjust imprisonment, your statutes of murder and death against men because of their loyalty to . . . the United States.[73]

Bingham, though with singular lack of clarity, was suggesting to those of the members who were alarmed that he had some definite evils in mind, limited and distinct in their nature. His peroration pulled out all stops in an appeal to due process, "law in its highest sense."[74] But the assurances, the magic of somewhat windy eloquence, and even a political rallying cry, which Bingham also employed — all failed. Hale's argument had sunk in and was going to prevail. Bingham was followed by another New Yorker, Giles W. Hotchkiss, a Radical, who read the proposal as had his colleague Hale, and who, according to his own lights, also feared "the caprice" of future Congresses:

As I understand it, . . . [Bingham's] object in offering this resolution . . . is to provide that no State shall discriminate between its citizens and give one class of citizens greater rights than it confers upon another. If this amendment secured that, I should vote very cheerfully for it to-day; but . . . I do not regard it as permanently securing those rights . . . .

. . . . I am unwilling that Congress shall have [the] power [this amendment confers]. . . . The object of a Constitution is not only to confer power upon the majority, but to restrict the power of the majority . . . . It is not indulging in imagination to any great stretch to suppose that we may have a Congress here who would establish such rules in my State as I should be unwilling to be governed by.

. . . .

Mr. Speaker, I make these remarks because I do not wish to be placed in the wrong upon this question. I think the gentleman from Ohio [Mr. Bingham] is not sufficiently radical in his views upon

---

[73] GLOBE 1088, 1090–91.
[74] GLOBE 1094.

this subject. I think he is a conservative. [Laughter.] I do not make the remark in any offensive sense. But I want him to go to the root of this matter.

. . . .

. . . . Why not provide by an amendment to the Constitution that no State shall discriminate against any class of its citizens; and let that amendment stand as part of the organic law of the land, subject only to be defeated by another . . . .[75]

Roscoe Conkling, who had voted against reporting this proposal out of the Joint Committee, was quick to point out that he was against it for reasons "very different . . . from, if not entirely opposite to" those given by Hotchkiss. Conkling certainly thought the proposal went far enough and was sufficiently radical. He moved to postpone consideration of it to a day certain, the second Tuesday of April. A vote was first taken on a Democratic motion to postpone indefinitely. This was defeated by a party line-up, with, however, somewhat more than normal defections. Thus Davis and Hale voted with the Democrats. The Conkling motion, taken up next, carried 110–37. The Republican leadership was solidly behind it. Bingham himself voted for it. Six Republicans voted consistently against any kind of postponement — Democratic or Republican. Davis decided that if he could not have indefinite postponement, he wanted none, no doubt expressing the judgment, indicated also by the position of the leadership, that the proposal could be beaten then and there. The date of this vote was February 28.[76] The second Tuesday in April came and went with no further mention of the Bingham amendment. It was never brought up in the Senate, nor ever again in the House.

The Fourteenth Amendment

Having reported out Bingham's draft, the Joint Committee on Reconstruction did not resume consideration of proposed constitutional amendments till April 16.[77] On that day the Committee heard Senator Stewart, Republican of Nevada, expound a reconstruction plan which he and other Moderates had hoped might yet

---

[75] GLOBE 1095.

[76] *Ibid.*

[77] The Committee considered a measure for the readmission of Tennessee, which was controlled by anti-Johnson forces and had a special claim to Radical favor. For over a month, it did not meet. Subcommittees, however, were taking evidence on conditions in the South. KENDRICK, *op. cit. supra* note 61, at 63–81, 221–27.

provide a basis for peaceful coexistence between the Radicals and the President. The Stewart plan turned on a constitutional amendment granting equal "civil rights" to Negroes, as well as limited suffrage. The South was offered, among other things, an amnesty and the power to restrict negro suffrage so long as it did so without using race as a sole or explicit criterion.[78] Stewart and his hopes got a hearing, but nothing more, from the Joint Committee. At its next meeting on April 21,

> Mr. Stevens said he had a plan of reconstruction, one not of his own framing, but which he should support, and which he submitted to the Committee for consideration.
>
> It was read as follows:
>
> . . . .
>
> *Whereas,* It is expedient that the States lately in insurrection should . . . be restored to full participation in all political rights; therefore,
>
> *Be it resolved* . . . that the following Article be proposed . . . as an amendment to the Constitution . . . :
>
> Article —
>
> Section 1. No discrimination shall be made by any state, nor by the United States, as to civil rights of persons because of race, color, or previous condition of servitude.
>
> Sec. 2. From and after the fourth day of July, in the year one thousand eight hundred and seventy-six, no discrimination shall be made by any state, nor by the United States, as to the enjoyment . . . of the right of suffrage . . . .
>
> Sec. 3. [Excluded all persons who were denied suffrage from the basis of representation, till 1876.]
>
> Sec. 4. [Confederate debt and compensation for slaves.]
>
> Sec. 5. Congress shall have power to enforce by appropriate legislation, the provisions of this article.
>
> *And be it further resolved,* [former Confederate states which ratified this amendment and enacted legislation in compliance with it, to be readmitted to the Union, when ratification of the amendment was complete.]
>
> *Provided,* [that certain "rebels" be excluded from office till 1876.][79]

---

[78] *Id.* at 82, 252–55. Section 1 of Stewart's proposed amendment read: "All discriminations among the people because of race, color or previous condition of servitude, either in civil rights or the right of suffrage, are prohibited; but the States may exempt persons now voters from restrictions on suffrage hereafter imposed." GLOBE 1906.

[79] KENDRICK, *op. cit. supra* note 61, 83–84.

As Stevens said, this proposal was not his own. It had been placed before him in March by Robert Dale Owen, reformer son of a reformer father. Owen, some nine years later, described his meeting with Stevens. The latter objected to prospective suffrage, as provided in section 2. This was a frank recognition, said Owen, of the fact that the Negro was not yet ready to vote or hold office. "I hate to delay full justice so long," said Stevens. But suffrage was not now the Negro's immediate need, the younger man answered. "He thirsts after education, and will have it if we but give him a chance, and if we don't call him away from the school-room to take a seat which he is unfitted to fill in a legislative chamber." Stevens then made a quick decision in favor of the proposal. He said there was not a majority for immediate suffrage, and this could pass. Owen, as he recalled, also took his amendment around to other members of the Joint Committee. Fessenden; Representative Elihu Washburne of Illinois, Grant's friend, who was briefly to be his Secretary of State; Roscoe Conkling; Senator Jacob Howard of Michigan and Representative George S. Boutwell of Massachusetts, two Radicals — all approved with various degrees of enthusiasm, though none with the decisiveness of Stevens. "So, qualifiedly [these are Owen's words], did Bingham, observing, however, that he thought the first section ought to specify, in detail, the civil rights which we proposed to assure; he had a favorite section of his own on that subject." [80]

The Committee went at the Owen proposal section by section. Bingham moved that section 1 be amended by adding the following:

> nor shall any state deny to any person within its jurisdiction the equal protection of the laws, nor take private property for public use without just compensation.

This motion was lost, 7 to 5. Stevens voted with Bingham. So did Rogers and Reverdy Johnson, though not Grider, the other Democrat. The Committee then voted 10 to 2 (Grider and Rogers) to adopt section 1 as it stood. Sections 2, 3, and 4 were also adopted. When the Committee reached section 5, Bingham moved the following as a substitute:

> Sec. 5. No state shall make or enforce any law which shall abridge the privileges or immunities of citizens of the United States;

---

[80] Owen, *Political Results From the Varioloid*, 35 ATLANTIC MONTHLY 660, 662–64 (1875).

nor shall any state deprive any person of life, liberty or property
without due process of law, nor deny to any person within its jurisdiction the equal protection of the laws.

This is, of course, language which now appears unchanged in the
fourteenth amendment. The Committee adopted it, 10 to 2 (Grider
and Rogers). Section 5 of the original proposal was renumbered
and also accepted. Throughout this meeting Fessenden and Conkling as well as Senator Ira Harris of New York were absent.

Two days later, the Committee, Fessenden still absent, modified
the final provisions of the proposal following the numbered articles, which it severed, intending to report them out separately. At
the next meeting, on April 25, Senator George H. Williams of
Oregon, a Radical, moved to strike section 5, that is, the substitute
which Bingham had got accepted at the meeting before last. Williams had voted for the substitution. His present motion carried,
7 to 5. Stevens was with Bingham in opposition. So was Rogers,
who had voted with Bingham for equal protection language in
section 1, a vote Bingham had lost, but against the substitution
of the section he was now supporting. So far Rogers favored equal ·
protection only as a losing cause. Harris, Howard, Johnson, Williams, Grider, Conkling, and Boutwell voted to strike the section.
Fessenden was still absent. The Committee then voted, 7 to 6, to
report the entire package. Conkling, Boutwell, and Representative Henry T. Blow of Missouri were the Republicans voting nay.
Bingham, nothing daunted, promptly moved the adoption of his
deleted section 5 as a separate proposed amendment to the Constitution. He was again defeated, 8 to 4, even Stevens leaving him
on this one. The three Democrats were with Bingham. Williams
then moved that the vote to report out the package be reconsidered. This carried 10 to 2, the only nays being Howard and
Stevens. With that the Committee adjourned.

The Committee was in session again on April 28, three days
later, with Fessenden now present. This time the entire proposal
was reported out, but with major changes. Instead of granting
suffrage prospectively, it was now decided to write a new section
2, simply eliminating from the basis of representation persons to
whom the vote was denied, and a new section 3 disenfranchising,
for purposes of federal elections, large numbers of Southerners till
the year 1870. That done, Bingham, still trying, moved to substitute for section 1 (the civil rights section) his privileges and
immunities, due process, and equal protection language, which

had once been substituted for section 5 and then been struck. This motion carried 10 to 3. All three Democrats voted for it, as did Stevens and Roscoe Conkling. The opposition consisted of Howard and Representative Justin Morrill of Vermont, both stout Radicals, and Senator James W. Grimes of Iowa, a moderate Republican of the Fessenden sort. Fessenden himself and Harris abstained. On the vote to report the resulting amendment out, only three Democrats were opposed. The Committee also reported a bill readmitting, upon the ratification of the amendment, states which had voted to ratify it, and a bill excluding from office certain Confederate officials.[81]

One of the puzzles to which this course of events in the Joint Committee gives rise is solved by the recollections of Robert Dale Owen. As Thaddeus Stevens told Owen, it was Fessenden's absence at the meetings of April 21, 23, and 25 which caused the Committee not to report out the draft it had approved, including a civil rights provision in section 1 and a grant of prospective suffrage in section 2, and excluding Bingham's formula. Fessenden, who was sick of the varioloid, a mild and euphonious form of smallpox which no longer distracts our politics, was chairman of the Committee on the part of the Senate. It seemed to most members (but not to Stevens and Howard, as we have seen) a lack of courtesy to report out the Committee's most important and final product in his absence. Hence the decision to do so was left in abeyance for three days. That gave a chance to the New York, Illinois, and Indiana congressional delegations to caucus and to decide that it was politically inadvisable to go to the country in 1866 on a platform having anything to do with negro suffrage, immediate or prospective. On that issue, these delegations felt, the Republicans might lose the election. This view was communicated to the Committee. As a result, when it met again, the Committee fell to rewriting section 2.[82] Why it proceeded to redo section 1 as well, Owen was, however, unable to explain. Nor did he explain the on-again-off-again attitude toward the Bingham formula.

Section 1, as originally proposed by Owen and Stevens, was framed in terms of the sentence the House had struck from the Civil Rights Bill to avoid a "latitudinarian" construction. The language Bingham at first proposed to add to section 1 had two

---

[81] KENDRICK, *op. cit. supra* note 61, at 85–120.

[82] Owen, *supra* note 80, at 665–66.

apparent effects: it protected, as his own defeated amendment had done, against discriminations other than just those based on color, and it added a special property safeguard not dependent on discrimination. As regards negro rights, there is no internal indication whether the "equal protection of the laws" formula (*nota bene* — "of the laws," not "in the rights of life, liberty and property," as in the earlier Bingham amendment) was thought by the Committee to imply greater or lesser coverage than the term "civil rights." In either event, it must have been realized that the two provisions overlapped. Yet Bingham at first seemed to want both in, and the Committee, when at one point it accepted Bingham's substitute for section 5, might seem to have been prepared to submit them together. The answer to this oddity may lie in the mechanics of committee drafting. Inconsistencies, redundancies, and the vestiges of tactical maneuvers appear at some stages and remain to be combed out later. The Committee never actually gave final approval to both the civil rights provision and the Bingham proposal as parts of the same measure.

On April 30, 1866, Fessenden in the Senate and Stevens in the House introduced the Committee draft. They both announced that a report as well as testimony taken before the Committee would soon be printed and distributed.[83] Debate started in the House first, on May 8, under a thirty-minute rule.[84] Stevens opened. The founders, he said, had not been able to build on the uncompromising foundation of the Declaration of Independence. They had decided to wait for "a more propitious time. That time ought to be present now." Now should have been the time to build "upon the firm foundation of eternal justice." But "the public mind has been educated in error for a century. How difficult in a day to unlearn it." The new constitutional structure the Committee was erecting, Stevens said, was defective still, but it made it possible to "trust to the advancing progress of a higher morality and a purer and more intelligent principle . . . ." The proposition "falls far short of my wishes, but it fulfills my hopes. I believe it is all that can be obtained in the present state of public opinion. . . . I will take all I can get in the cause of humanity and leave it to be perfected by better men in better times. It may be that that time will not come while I am here to enjoy the glorious

---

[83] GLOBE 2265, 2286.
[84] GLOBE 2433–34.

triumph; but that it will come is as certain as that there is a just God."

In all probability, the disappointment of Thaddeus Stevens centered on the failure to make any provision for negro suffrage, immediate or prospective. It was for this reason that he had called the final Committee draft a "shilly-shally, bungling thing" in conversation with Robert Dale Owen.[85] On the other hand, while he supported Bingham's formula at various drafting stages in committee, Stevens had himself proposed language (directed specifically at racial distinctions) which he might well have regarded as more sweeping, and which, as he had early had occasion to tell the House, was "the genuine proposition," "the one I love."[86] And he spoke his disappointment to the same House now in general terms. He went on then to "refer to the provisions of the proposed amendment":

> The first section prohibits the States from abridging the privileges and immunities of citizens of the United States, or unlawfully depriving them of life, liberty, or property, or of denying to any person within their jurisdiction the "equal" protection of the laws.
>
> I can hardly believe that any person can be found who will not admit that every one of these provisions is just. They are all asserted, in some form or other, in our Declaration or organic law. But the Constitution limits only the action of Congress, and is not a limitation on the States. This amendment supplies that defect, and allows Congress to correct the unjust legislation of the States, so far that the law which operates upon one man shall operate *equally* upon all. Whatever law punishes a white man for a crime shall punish the black man precisely in the same way . . . . Whatever law protects the white man shall afford "equal" protection to the black man. Whatever means of redress is afforded to one shall be afforded to all. Whatever law allows the white man to testify in court shall allow the man of color to do the same. These are great advantages over their present codes. . . . I need not enumerate these partial and oppressive laws. Unless the Constitution should restrain them those States will . . . crush to death the hated freedmen. Some answer, "Your civil rights bill secures the same things." That is partly true, but a law is repealable by a majority.[87]

It will be noted that Stevens, in passing, suggested the argument

---

[85] Owen, *supra* note 80, at 665.
[86] GLOBE 537. See pp. 30, 41 *supra*.
[87] GLOBE 2459.

with which Bingham had supported his earlier amendment, that
is, that the provisions now proposed were "asserted" elsewhere in
the Constitution. But he went on to mention evils to which the
proposal was directed, harking back to those which had been
pointed to in support of the Civil Rights Bill. In the debate which
followed, many members were heard from. But only two on either
side of the aisle devoted more than the briefest sort of generality
to section 1. These two were Bingham, whose generalities were
not brief, and Rogers, who specified his objections. For the rest,
speakers on both sides identified section 1 with the Civil Rights
Act. Republicans added, following Stevens' lead, that that great
enactment would now be placed beyond the power of future Congresses to repeal,[88] or remarked on the self-evident justice of the
proposal, the better part of which was in the Constitution as it
stood anyway.[89] One or two regretted that suffrage was not conferred.[90] Democrats jibed that in bringing forth this proposal the
Radical leadership had admitted the unconstitutionality of the
Civil Rights Act,[91] or charged rather vaguely that the Radicals
had far-reaching ultimate aims, including political equality for the

---

[88] M. Russell Thayer of Pennsylvania: "As I understand it, it is but incorporating in the Constitution . . . the principle of the civil rights bill . . . [so that
it] shall be forever incorporated . . . ." GLOBE 2465. To the same effect, John M.
Broomall of Pennsylvania, GLOBE 2498, and Thomas D. Eliot of Massachusetts,
GLOBE 2511. Henry J. Raymond, who was going to vote for this amendment, also
thought the "principle" of this proposal was that embodied in the Civil Rights
Bill, which he had opposed on constitutional grounds. He was further of the
opinion that the same "principle" had been expressed by the Bingham amendment,
concerning which Raymond had been silent and remained so now. GLOBE 2502.

[89] William D. Kelley of Pennsylvania: "There is not a man in Montgomery or
Lehigh county [the constituency of a Pennsylvania Democrat, Benjamin M.
Boyer] that will not say those provisions ought to be in the Constitution if they
are not already there." GLOBE 2468. George F. Miller of Pennsylvania: "As to the
first, it is so just . . . and so clearly within the spirit of the Declaration of
Independence of the 4th of July, 1776, that no member of this House can
seriously object to it." GLOBE 2510. John F. Farnsworth of Illinois: "This is so
self-evident and just that no man whose soul is not too cramped and dwarfed to
hold the smallest germ of justice can fail to see and appreciate it." GLOBE 2539.
James A. Garfield, who discussed other parts of the amendment with his usual
acuity, merely referred to "this first section here which proposes to hold over
every American citizen, without regard to color, the protecting shield of law."
GLOBE 2462.

[90] *E.g.*, Eliot of Massachusetts, GLOBE 2511; Farnsworth of Illinois, GLOBE 2539.

[91] William E. Finck of Ohio: "Well, all I have to say about this section is,
that if it is necessary to adopt it . . . then the civil rights bill . . . was passed
without authority, and is clearly unconstitutional." GLOBE 2461. To the same
effect, Charles A. Eldridge of Wisconsin, GLOBE 2506.

Negro.[92] But the bulk of the debate turned on other sections, principally section 3. A number of the Republicans who spoke failed even to mention section 1.[93]

To Andrew Jackson Rogers, who at least in this respect saw farther than most, section 1 was the heart of the matter. He said:

> Now sir, I have examined these propositions . . . and I have come to the conclusion different to what some others have come, that the first section of this programme of disunion is the most dangerous to liberty. It saps the foundation of the Government . . . it consolidates everything . . . .
>
> This section . . . is no more nor less than an attempt to embody in the Constitution . . . that outrageous and miserable civil rights bill . . . .
>
> . . . .
>
> . . . . What are privileges and immunities? Why, sir, all the rights we have under the laws of the country are embraced under the definition of privileges and immunities. The right to vote is a privilege. The right to marry is a privilege. The right to contract is a privilege. The right to be a juror is a privilege. The right to be a judge or President of the United States is a privilege. I hold if that ever becomes a part of the fundamental law of the land it will prevent any State from refusing to allow anything to anybody embraced under this term of privileges and immunities. . . . It will result in a revolution worse than that through which we have just passed.

Rogers did not deal specifically with the equal protection clause. He proceeded to attack section 2, which, he said, was intended to exert indirect pressure on the South to grant negro suffrage. Then:

---

[92] Boyer of Pennsylvania: "The first section embodies the principles of the civil rights bill, and is intended to secure ultimately, and to some extent indirectly, the political equality of the negro race. It is objectionable also in its phraseology, being open to ambiguity and admitting of conflicting constructions." GLOBE 2467. Samuel J. Randall of Pennsylvania: "The first section proposes to make an equality in every respect between the two races, notwithstanding the policy of discrimination which has heretofore been exclusively exercised by the States . . . . If you have the right to interfere in behalf of one character of rights — I may say of every character of rights, save the suffrage — how soon will you be ready to tear down every barrier? It is only because you fear the people that you do not now do it." GLOBE 2530. See also remarks by George S. Shanklin of Kentucky and Myer Strouse of Pennsylvania, GLOBE 2500, 2531.

[93] Thus, James G. Blaine, Robert C. Schenck of Ohio, Green Clay Smith of Kentucky, a Conservative, Samuel McKee of Kentucky, Boutwell, Rufus P. Spalding of Ohio, John W. Longyear of Michigan, and Fernando C. Beaman of Michigan. GLOBE 2460, 2469–73, 2504–05, 2507–10, 2536–37.

Sir, I want it distinctly understood that the American people believe that this Government was made for white men and white women. They do not believe, nor can you make them believe — the edict of God Almighty is stamped against it — that there is social equality between the black race and the white.

I have no fault to find with the colored race. . . . I wish them well, and if I were in a State where they exist in large numbers I would vote to give them every right enjoyed by the white people except the right of a negro man to marry a white woman and the right to vote. But, sir this . . . . [is an] indirect way to inflict upon the people of the South negro suffrage.[94]

Bingham spoke just before some few final remarks by Stevens, which, in turn, immediately preceded a vote. Bingham said:

The necessity for the first section . . . is one of the lessons that have been taught . . . by the history of the past four years . . . . There . . . remains a want now, in the Constitution . . . which the proposed amendment will supply. . . . It is the power in the people . . . to protect by national law the privileges and immunities of all the citizens of the Republic and the inborn rights of every person within its jurisdiction whenever the same shall be abridged or denied by the unconstitutional acts of any State.

. . . . [T]his amendment takes from no State any right that ever pertained to it. No State ever had the right . . . to deny to any freeman the equal protection of the laws or to abridge the privileges and immunities of any citizen of the Republic, although many of them have assumed and exercised the power, and that without remedy. The amendment does not give, as the second section shows, the power to Congress of regulating suffrage . . . .

. . . . But, sir, it has been suggested, not here, but elsewhere, if this section does not confer suffrage the need of it is not perceived. To all such I beg leave again to say, that many instances of State injustice and oppression have already occurred in the State legislation of this Union, of flagrant violations of the guarantied privileges of citizens of the United States, for which the national Government furnished and could furnish by law no remedy whatever. Contrary to the express letter of your Constitution, "cruel and unusual punishments" have been inflicted under State laws . . . not only for crimes committed, but for sacred duty done . . . .

. . . .

. . . . That great want of the citizen and stranger, protection by national law from unconstitutional State enactments, is supplied

---

[94] Globe 2538.

by the first section of this amendment. That is the extent that it hath, no more; and let gentlemen answer to God and their country who oppose its incorporation into the organic law of the land.[95]

Bingham went on to discuss section 3, about which he was more lucid and less enthusiastic.

It was to section 3 that Thaddeus Stevens addressed his closing remarks. He noted dissension about it, and pleaded for its adoption, to save the Republican party and through it the country. Unless section 3 was passed Stevens could see "that side of the House . . . filled with yelling secessionists and hissing copperheads." Section 3 was actually "too lenient for my hard heart. Not only to 1870, but to 18070, every rebel who shed the blood of loyal men should be prevented from exercising any power in this Government." Stevens conjured up the scene in the House before the war when "the men that you propose to admit" through a milder section 3 occupied the other side, among them "the mighty Toombs, with his shaggy locks . . . . when weapons were drawn, and Barksdale's bowie-knife gleamed before our eyes. Would you have these men back again so soon to reënact those scenes? Wait until I am gone, I pray you. I want not to go through it again. It will be but a short time for my colleague to wait." With these searing words in its ears, the House, though by a close vote (84–79) in which some Democrats, who sought to keep the proposal as obnoxious as possible, provided the winning margin, obeyed Stevens and cut off amendments. (James A. Garfield had one changing section 3). By a vote of 128 to 37 the House then adopted the draft as reported by the Joint Committee. Lovell Rousseau of Kentucky and a few other Conservatives were in the opposition.[96] This was the afternoon of May 10. The final vote in committee had been had twelve days before.

The proposal was brought up in the Senate on May 23. Before debate started Charles Sumner made a point which had also been raised by a Democrat in the House. The testimony taken before the Joint Committee, he said, had not been published as a whole, and no report drawing the Committee's conclusions had been submitted. He thought it was a "mistake that we are asked to proceed . . . under such circumstances." Fessenden answered saying there was nothing to be gained by waiting longer.[97] Debate

[95] GLOBE 2542–43.

[96] GLOBE 2544–45.

[97] GLOBE 2763. The House Democrat who had made a complaint similar to

itself was opened by Jacob Howard, the Michigan Radical. Fessenden, victim of the varioloid, was not feeling well enough to speak at length. Howard paid due and reasonably loyal attention to section 1, whose inclusion in its present form he had opposed in committee:

> To these privileges and immunities, whatever they may be — for they are not and cannot be fully defined in their entire extent and precise nature — to these should be added the personal rights guarantied and secured by the first eight amendments of the Constitution . . . .

As for the equal protection clause:

> This abolishes all class legislation in the States and does away with the injustice of subjecting one caste of persons to a code not applicable to another. It prohibits the hanging of a black man for a crime for which the white man is not to be hanged. It protects the black man in his fundamental rights as a citizen with the same shield which it throws over the white man. . . .
>
> But, sir, the first section of the proposed amendment does not give . . . the right of voting. The right of suffrage . . . is merely the creature of law. It [is] . . . not regarded as one of those fundamental rights lying at the basis of all society and without which a people cannot exist except as slaves . . . .[98]

Speakers who followed Howard did not address themselves to section 1, except that Benjamin F. Wade, the Ohio Radical, and one or two others wondered whether section 1 should not define national citizenship. Stewart of Nevada made a last extended plea

---

Sumner's was Charles A. Eldridge of Wisconsin. GLOBE 2506. A majority report was submitted by Fessenden in the Senate and Stevens in the House on June 8, and ordered to be printed. GLOBE 3038, 3051. This was a political document written by Fessenden, though evidently strongly influenced by Stevens. It did not deal with § 1. Its conclusion stated that "your committee submit it [the fourteenth amendment] to Congress as the best they could agree upon, in the hope that its imperfections may be cured, and its deficiencies supplied, by legislative wisdom . . . ." See McPHERSON, *op. cit. supra* note 28, at 84–93; KENDRICK, *op. cit. supra* note 61, at 320–26. A minority report, written by Reverdy Johnson and signed as well by Rogers and Henry Grider, was also submitted, and received and printed after an unedifying partisan hassle. GLOBE 3275, 3349–50, 3646–49, 3749–50, 3766–67. This report was rather an imposing paper, arguing for the reinstatement of the Southern states in their rights of representation in Congress. It made no mention of § 1. See McPHERSON, *op. cit. supra* note 28, at 93–101.

[98] GLOBE 2765, 2766. This speech by Howard, together with a few less explicit remarks by Bingham, constitutes the principal reliance of those who purport to find an intention to incorporate the entire Bill of Rights in the fourteenth amendment. See note 13 *supra*; Fairman, *supra* note 13, at 65–68, 78–81.

for the plan he had advocated before the Joint Committee and elsewhere.[99] Further debate was then postponed. It had so far gone on for parts of two days. It was not resumed till four days later, on May 29, when Howard, "after consultation with some of the friends of this measure," presented some amendments which, "it has been thought . . . will be acceptable to both Houses of Congress and to the country . . . ."[100] In other words, a Republican caucus had been in session and had straightened out differences among the Republicans, which, as debate had revealed, centered around section 3. It was agreed to forego disenfranchising Southern whites. Instead a provision was inserted disqualifying certain Southerners for federal office; section 2, though modified, remained essentially the same; and United States citizenship was defined in section 1. Thus the amendment assumed its present form. The proceedings of the caucus were, as Thomas A. Hendricks, Democrat of Indiana, charged, so secret that "no outside Senators, not even the sharp-eyed men of the press, have been able to learn one word that was spoken, or one vote given." [101] They have remained secret to this day.

The Senate now engaged in a debate which lasted for several days. But, as had been the case in the House and earlier in the Senate itself, proportionately little was said about section 1 by either Democrats or Republicans. It was charged that the section gave citizenship to "savage" Indians and Gypsies and that it embodied the Civil Rights Act.[102] Luke Poland, Republican from Vermont and a former Chief Justice of that state, drew attention to state laws, "some of them of very recent enactment," at which the Civil Rights Act had struck. This amendment, he implied, was also directed at the Black Codes.[103] The same implication was left with the Senate by John B. Henderson of Missouri, a Republican who enjoyed much respect, and who was no doctrinaire Radical. It would be "a loss of time," he said, "to discuss the remaining provisions of the section [other than the citizenship clause, which he held to be simply declaratory of existing law], for they merely secure the rights that attach to citizenship in all free Governments." Nevertheless, Henderson did mention the Black Codes, which formed a "system of oppression" rendering

---

[99] GLOBE 2768–69, 2798–803; see note 78 *supra.*

[100] GLOBE 2869.

[101] GLOBE 2939; see KENDRICK, *op. cit. supra* note 61, at 316.

[102] GLOBE 2896, 2939, 2891–93.

[103] GLOBE 2961.

the Negro a "degraded outcast" deprived of the "commonest rights of human nature," the right to hold property, to sue, to confront witnesses, to have the process of the courts. The Freedmen's Bureau and Civil Rights Bills and, Henderson implied, section 1 of this amendment, were all intended to cure this situation.[104] Timothy O. Howe of Wisconsin, a Radical, spoke in the same vein, but in richer detail. Negroes, he said, had been denied elementary rights:

> The right to hold land . . . the right to collect their wages by the processes of the law . . . the right to appear in the courts as suitors . . . the right to give testimony . . . .
>
> . . . . [B]ut, sir, these are not the only rights that can be denied . . . . I have taken considerable pains to look over the actual legislation [in the South] . . . . I read not long since a statute enacted by the Legislature of Florida for the education of her colored people. . . . They make provision for the education of their white children also, and everybody who has any property there is taxed for the education of the white children. Black and white are taxed alike for that purpose; but for the education of colored children a fund is raised only from colored men.

Howe described the colored school system in Florida, which was, of course, segregated, without pointing out that fact; what he stressed was the inadequacy of the poorly supported colored schools. He implied that section 1 would render this legislation illegal, but he gave no indication that he believed its vice to lie in segregation.[105]

Aside from a parting shot by Reverdy Johnson, nothing else was said in the Senate about section 1, and it is perhaps noteworthy that conservative Republicans like Cowan and Doolittle, Democrats like Johnson, and even Democrats of the stripe of Garrett Davis of Kentucky spoke at some length, but refrained from raising alarms concerning the reach of section 1 and the sort of local practices it would outlaw.[106] This contrasts with Senate and House debates on the Civil Rights Act, and with Rogers' and even some of his colleagues' more recent statements in the House.

---

[104] GLOBE 3031, 3034–35.

[105] GLOBE, App. 219. The Florida statute which Howe must have had in mind is the Act of January 16, 1866, Fla. Laws 1865, c. 1475. It is printed in part in 1 FLEMING, DOCUMENTARY HISTORY OF RECONSTRUCTION 277–79 (1906).

[106] GLOBE 2896, 2939, 2891–93; GLOBE, App. 240. The same may be said of McDougall of California, also a Democrat, though not of the utterly unreconstructible Davis type. GLOBE 3030–31.

But the absence of purported alarm must be understood in the light of the paucity of attention generally devoted to section 1, which in turn is doubtless attributable to the evident greater political vulnerability of the Republicans with respect to other sections of the amendment. Just before the vote, Reverdy Johnson, who had spoken at length on the basis of representation,[107] remarked that while he saw no objection to the due process clause, he simply did not understand what would be the effect of the privileges and immunities clause, and wished it might be deleted. No one made a closing speech for the proponents. The vote followed immediately. It was 33 to 11; the date, June 8. Four Republicans — Cowan, Doolittle, Norton of Minnesota, and Van Winkle of West Virginia, the hard core of Conservatives — voted nay.[108]

On June 13 the House, under a fifteen-minute rule, took up the amendment as returned from the Senate.[109] Rogers spoke first. The burden of his remarks was a complaint that the amendment had been ill-considered by a Congress cringing under the party whip. He referred in passing to section 1, repeating that it "simply embodied the gist of the civil rights bill." His heavy artillery was concentrated on the manner in which the amendment had been pushed through the Senate by command of the secret Radical caucus.[110] A few others spoke without mentioning section 1. Then Thaddeus Stevens moved the previous question, thus bringing on the vote. But first he had a few words to say, which are worth quoting extensively, both for their characteristic bite and because they were the launching words, the last spoken before the fourteenth amendment slid down the ways. The implacable old man was not happy:

> In my youth, in my manhood, in my old age, I had fondly dreamed that when any fortunate chance should have broken up for awhile the foundation of our institutions, and released us from obligations the most tyrannical that ever man imposed in the name of freedom, that the intelligent, pure and just men of this Republic, true to their professions and their consciences, would have so remodeled all our institutions as to have freed them from every vestige of human oppression, of inequality of rights, of the recognized

---

[107] GLOBE 3026–30.
[108] GLOBE 3041–42.
[109] GLOBE 3144.
[110] GLOBE, App. 229.

degradation of the poor, and the superior caste of the rich. In short, that no distinction would be tolerated in this purified Republic but what arose from merit and conduct. This bright dream has vanished "like the baseless fabric of a vision." I find that we shall be obliged to be content with patching up the worst portions of the ancient edifice, and leaving it, in many of its parts, to be swept through by the tempests, the frosts, and the storms of despotism.

Do you inquire why, holding these views and possessing some will of my own, I accept so imperfect a proposition? I answer, because I live among men and not among angels . . . .

Perhaps more strenuous effort might have resulted in a better plan. But Congress had had to face the hostility of the President, and this proposal met in some measure the danger of "tyranny" emanating from the White House, "the danger arising from the unscrupulous use of patronage and from the oily orations of false prophets, famous for sixty-day obligations and for protested political promises . . . ." Stevens lightly reviewed some of the changes made in the Senate. The principal one was, of course, section 3, and he disapproved. He ended by urging speedy adoption of the imperfect product. "I dread delay," he said. Then:

> The danger is that before any constitutional guards shall have been adopted Congress will be flooded by rebels and rebel sympathizers. . . . Whoever has watched the feelings of this House during the tedious months of this session, listened to the impatient whispering of some and the open declarations of others; especially when able and sincere men propose to gratify personal predilections by breaking the ranks of the Union forces and presenting to the enemy a ragged front of stragglers, must be anxious to hasten the result and prevent the demoralization of our friends. Hence, I say, let us no longer delay; take what we can get now, and hope for better things in further legislation; in enabling acts or other provisions.
>
> I now, sir, ask for the question.

The vote which followed immediately and which sent the fourteenth amendment to the country was 120 yeas, 32 nays. There were no Republican votes against. Rousseau of Kentucky and a few other Conservatives were recorded absent. Eldridge, the Democrat, said: "I desire to state that if Messrs. Brooks and Voorhees had not been expelled, they would have voted against this proposition. [Great laughter.]" And Schenck, of the Radical leadership, retorted: "And I desire to say that if Jeff. Davis were here, he would probably also have voted the same way. [Renewed laughter.]" [111]

Summary and Conclusions

As we have seen, the first approach made by the 39th Congress toward dealing with racial discrimination turned on the "civil rights" formula. The Senate Moderates, led by Trumbull and Fessenden, who sponsored this formula, assigned a limited and well-defined meaning to it. In their view it covered the right to contract, sue, give evidence in court, and inherit, hold, and dispose of real and personal property; also a right to equal protection in the literal sense of benefiting equally from laws for the security of person and property, including presumably laws permitting ownership of firearms, and to equality in the penalties and burdens provided by law. Certainly able men such as Trumbull and Fessenden realized that each of the seemingly well-bounded rights they enumerated carried about it, like an upper atmosphere, an area in which its force was uncertain. Thus it is clear that the Moderates wished also to protect rights of free movement, and a right to engage in occupations of one's choice. They doubtless considered that their enumeration somehow accomplished this purpose. Similarly, the Moderates often argued that one of the imperative needs of the time was to educate, to "elevate," to "Christianize" the Negro; indeed, this was almost universally-held doctrine, from which even Conservatives like Cowan and Democrats like Rogers did not dissent. Hence one may surmise that the Moderates believed they were guaranteeing a right to equal benefits from state educational systems supported by general tax funds. But there is no evidence whatever showing that for its sponsors the civil rights formula had anything to do with unsegregated public schools; Wilson, its sponsor in the House, specifically disclaimed any such notion. Similarly, it is plain that the Moderates did not intend to confer any right of intermarriage, the right to sit on juries, or the right to vote.

Civil rights protection was first extended by the Freedmen's Bureau Bill. This was not a closely debated measure, because it was limited in duration and territorial applicability. The Conservative votes cast in its favor mark it as a sacrificial offering on the altar of Radicalism, not seriously considered on its own merits.

---

[111] GLOBE 3148–49.

When the same formula was next brought forth in the Civil Rights Bill, it evoked warnings from the Democratic and Conservative opposition in the Senate, which argued that the phrase "civil rights" might well be construed to include more rights than its sponsors intended to affect. One of the warnings related to segregation. The Moderates were unmoved, and the bill was carried in the Senate.

The Joint Committee in the meantime was dealing with the same problem. It elected not to use the civil rights formula and offered instead, in the Bingham amendment, equal protection "in the rights of life, liberty and property," plus a privileges and immunities clause. Given the evils represented by the Black Codes, which were foremost in the minds of all men, it must be supposed that this language was deemed to protect all the rights specifically enumerated in the Civil Rights Bill. But it is difficult to interpret the deliberate choice against using the term "civil rights" as anything but a rejection of what were deemed its wider implications.

The Bingham amendment did not act directly on the states. It was an unconditional grant of power to Congress, like the older grants of legislative power; and like them it was bolstered by a necessary and proper clause. This feature made it unacceptable to Moderates like Hale. The fact that the amendment itself gave no assurance of permanent protection cost the support of some Radicals. On these grounds the proposal went down to defeat. There were some questions raised also concerning the kind of rights covered, and Bingham rather clumsily responded by suggesting the Moderate position on the Civil Rights Bill, but this was completely secondary. Only Rogers, a partisan given to extreme accusations, spoke of this proposal as if there had been no difference between it and a "civil rights" guaranty.

The Civil Rights Bill itself, as brought from the Senate to the House, split the alliance of various shades of Moderates and Radicals which constituted the Republican majority. The bill was presented to the House as a measure of limited objectives, following Trumbull's views. But a substantial number of Republicans were troubled by the issue of constitutionality. Others were uneasy on policy grounds about the reach of section 1, but inclined to believe that the bill could be rendered constitutional by amendment, and, in any event, out of mixed motives at which one can only guess, conquered their apprehensions and voted for it in the end. Bingham, whose position was in this instance entirely self-

consistent, thought the bill incurably unconstitutional, its enforcement provisions monstrous, and the civil rights guaranty of very
broad application and unwise. The concession these Republicans
wrung from the leadership was the elimination of the civil rights
formula and thus the avoidance of possible "latitudinarian" construction. The Moderate position that the bill dealt only with a
distinct and limited set of rights was conclusively validated.

Against this backdrop, the Joint Committee on Reconstruction
began framing the fourteenth amendment. In drafting section 1,
it vacillated between the civil rights formula and language proposed by Bingham, finally adopting the latter. Stevens' speech
opening debate on the amendment in the House presented section
1 in terms quite similar to the Moderate position on the Civil
Rights Bill, though there was a rather notable absence of the disclaimers of wider coverage which usually accompanied the Moderates' statements of objectives. A few remarks made in the Senate sounded in the same vein. For the rest, however, section 1 was
not really debated. Rogers, whose remarks are always subject to
heavy discount, considering his shaky position in the affections of
his own party colleagues, raised "latitudinarian" alarms. One or
two other Democrats in the House did so also. But more and
more, debate turned on section 3 and not much else. The focus
of attention is well indicated by Stevens' brief address immediately
before the first vote in the House. In this atmosphere, section 1
became the subject of a stock generalization: it was dismissed as
embodying and, in one sense for the Republicans, in another for
the Democrats and Conservatives, "constitutionalizing" the Civil
Rights Act.

The obvious conclusion to which the evidence, thus summarized, easily leads is that section 1 of the fourteenth amendment,
like section 1 of the Civil Rights Act of 1866, carried out the relatively narrow objectives of the Moderates, and hence, as originally
understood, was meant to apply neither to jury service, nor suffrage, nor antimiscegenation statutes, nor segregation. This conclusion is supported by the blunt expression of disappointment to
which Thaddeus Stevens gave vent in the House. Nothing in the
election campaign of 1866 or in the ratification proceedings nega-
tives it. Section 1 received in both about the attention it had received in Congress, and in about the same terms.[112] One or two

---

[112] On the issues of the campaign of 1866, see BEALE, THE CRITICAL YEAR
(1930); with specific reference to § 1 of the fourteenth amendment, see Fairman,

"reconstructed" Southern legislatures took what turned out, of course, to be temporary measures to abolish segregation.[113] There is little if any indication of an impression prevailing elsewhere that the amendment required such action.

If the fourteenth amendment were a statute, a court might very well hold, on the basis of what has been said so far, that it was foreclosed from applying it to segregation in public schools. The evidence of congressional purpose is as clear as such evidence is likely to be, and no language barrier stands in the way of construing the section in conformity with it. But we are dealing with a constitutional amendment, not a statute. The tradition of a broadly worded organic law not frequently or lightly amended was well-established by 1866, and, despite the somewhat revolutionary fervor with which the Radicals were pressing their changes, it cannot be assumed that they or anyone else expected or wished the future role of the Constitution in the scheme of American government to differ from the past. Should not the search for congressional purpose, therefore, properly be twofold? One inquiry should be directed at the congressional understanding of the immediate effect of the enactment on conditions then present. Another should aim to discover what if any thought was given to the long-range effect, under future circumstances, of provisions necessarily intended for permanence.

That the Court saw the need for two such inquiries with respect to the original understanding on segregation is clearly indicated by the questions it propounded at the 1952 Term.[114] The Court asked first whether Congress and the state legislatures contemplated that the fourteenth amendment would abolish segregation in public schools. It next asked whether, assuming that the immediate abolition of segregation was not contemplated, the framers nevertheless understood that Congress acting under section 5, or the Court in the exercise of the judicial function would, in light of future conditions, have power to abolish segregation.

With this double aspect of the inquiry in mind, certain other

---

supra note 13, at 69–78. For a survey of ratification materials, see *id.* at 84–126. The state materials are most thoroughly reviewed in the appendix to the Government's brief as amicus in the *Segregation Cases*. Appendix to the Supplemental Brief for the United States on Reargument, Nos. 1, 2, 4, 8, 10, at 160–393, Brown v. Board of Educ., 347 U.S. 483 (1954).

[113] La. Const. art. 135 (1868); *cf.* La. Const. art. 224 (1879); La. Const. art. 248 (1898). S.C. Const. art. X (1868) (*semble*); *cf.* S.C. Const. art. XI (1895).

[114] See note 16 *supra*.

features of the legislative history — not inconsistent with the conclusion earlier stated, but complementary to it — became significant. Thus, section 1 of the fourteenth amendment, on its face,
deals not only with racial discrimination, but also with discrimination whether or not based on color. This cannot have been accidental, since the alternative considered by the Joint Committee,
the civil rights formula, did apply only to racial discrimination.
Everyone's immediate preoccupation in the 39th Congress — insofar as it did not go to partisan questions — was, of course, with
hardships being visited on the colored race. Yet the fact that the
proposed constitutional amendment was couched in more general
terms could not have escaped those who voted for it. And this
feature of it could not have been deemed to be included in the
standard identification of section 1 with the Civil Rights Act.
Again, when it rejected the civil rights formula in reporting out
the abortive Bingham amendment, the Joint Committee elected to
submit an equal protection clause limited to the rights of life, liberty, and property, supplemented by a necessary and proper clause.
Now the choice was in favor of a due process clause limited the
way the equal protection clause had been in the earlier draft, but
of an equal protection clause not so limited: equal protection "of
the laws." Presumably the lesson taught by the defeat of the
Bingham amendment had been learned. Congress was not to have
unlimited discretion, and it was not to have the leeway represented by "necessary and proper" power.[115] One would have to*
assume a lack of familiarity with the English language to conclude that a further difference between the Bingham amendment
and the new proposal was not also perceived, namely, the difference between equal protection in the rights of life, liberty, and
property, a phrase which so aptly evoked the evils uppermost in
men's minds at the time, and equal protection of the laws, a clause

---

[115] In 1871, in the course of the debate on the Act of April 20, 1871 (Ku Klux
Act), c. 22, 17 STAT. 13, Bingham argued the contrary. He contended that Congress had no less power to legislate under the fourteenth amendment than it would
have had under his own earlier, rejected proposal. In other words, he attached
no significance whatever to the defeat of that proposal. That is, of course, a
rather arbitrary way to deal with the materials. As James A. Garfield had occasion
to tell Bingham, "my colleague can make but he cannot unmake history." CONG.
GLOBE, APP., 42d Cong., 1st Sess. 83–86, 113–17, 151 (1871); see Fairman, *supra*
note 13, at 136–37; FLACK, *op. cit. supra* note 54, at 226–49. Bingham's view
evidently prevailed in Congress, but the Supreme Court, without reference to the
legislative history and dealing simply with the language of the fourteenth amendment on its face, saw it otherwise. United States v. Harris, 106 U.S. 629 (1883).

which is plainly capable of being applied to all subjects of state legislation. Could the comparison have failed to leave the implication that the new phrase, while it did not necessarily, and certainly not expressly, carry greater coverage than the old, was nevertheless roomier, more receptive to "latitudinarian" construction? No one made the point with regard to this particular clause. But in opening debate in the Senate, Jacob Howard was frank to say that only the future could tell just what application the privileges and immunities provision might have. And before the vote in the Senate, Reverdy Johnson, a Democrat, to be sure, but a respected constitutional lawyer and no rabid partisan, confessed his puzzlement about the same clause. Finally, it is noteworthy that the shorthand argument characterizing the fourteenth amendment as the constitutional embodiment of the Civil Rights Act was often accompanied on the Republican side by generalities about the self-evident demands of justice and the natural rights of man. This was true both in Congress and in the course of the election which followed.[116] To all this should be added the fact that while the Joint Committee's rejection of the civil rights formula is quite manifest, there is implicit also in its choice of language a rejection — presumably as inappropriate in a constitutional provision — of such a specific and exclusive enumeration of rights as appeared in section 1 of the Civil Rights Act.

These bits and pieces of additional evidence do not contradict and could not in any event override the direct proof showing the specific evils at which the great body of congressional opinion thought it was striking. But perhaps they provide sufficient basis for the formulation of an additional hypothesis. It remains true that an explicit provision going further than the Civil Rights Act could not have been carried in the 39th Congress; also that a plenary grant of legislative power such as the Bingham amendment would not have mustered the necessary majority. But may it not be that the Moderates and the Radicals reached a compromise permitting them to go to the country with language which they could, where necessary, defend against damaging alarms raised by the opposition, but which at the same time was sufficiently elastic to permit reasonable future advances? This is thoroughly consistent with rejection of the civil rights formula and its implications. That formula could not serve the purpose of

---

[116] See note 112 *supra.*

such a compromise. It had been under heavy attack at this session, and among those who had expressed fears concerning its reach were Republicans who would have to go forth and stand on the platform of the fourteenth amendment. Bingham, of course, was one of these men, and he could not be required to go on the hustings and risk being made to eat his own words. If the party was to unite behind a compromise which consisted neither of an exclusive listing of a limited series of rights, nor of a formulation dangerously vulnerable to attacks pandering to the prejudices of the people, new language had to be found. Bingham himself supplied it. It had both sweep and the appearance of a careful enumeration of rights, and it had a ring to echo in the national memory of libertarian beginnings. To put it another way, the Moderates, with a bit of timely assistance from Fessenden's varioloid, consolidated the victory they had achieved in the Civil Rights Act debate. They could go forth and honestly defend themselves against charges that on the day after ratification Negroes were going to become white men's "social equals," marry their daughters, vote in their elections, sit on their juries, and attend schools with their children. The Radicals (though they had to compromise once more on section 3) obtained what early in the session had seemed a very uncertain prize indeed: a firm alliance, under Radical leadership, with the Moderates in the struggle against the President, and thus a good, clear chance at increasing and prolonging their political power. In the future, the Radicals could, in one way or another, put through such further civil rights provisions as they thought the country would take, without being subject to the sort of effective constitutional objections which haunted them when they were forced to operate under the thirteenth amendment.

It is, of course, giving the men of the 39th Congress much more than their due to ennoble them by a comparison of their proceedings with the deliberations of the Philadelphia Convention. Yet if this was the compromise that was struck, then these men emulated the technique of the original framers, who were also responsible to an electorate only partly receptive to the fullness of their principles, and who similarly avoided the explicit grant of some powers without foreclosing their future assumption.[117] Whatever other support this hypothesis may have, it has behind it the very authoritative voice of Thaddeus Stevens, who held it, and twice

---

[117] See Thayer, *supra* note 14, at 75–78, and especially at 78 n.2.

gave notice of it in speaking on the fourteenth amendment. It was Stevens who dutifully defined section 1 more or less in the narrow terms a Trumbull or a Fessenden would have used; it fell short of his wishes. And it was Stevens, his hopes fulfilled, who powerfully and candidly emphasized the political opportunities which the amendment gained for the Radicals, and who looked to the future for better things "in further legislation, in enabling acts or other provisions." Similarly, when it at last emerged, though too late to influence debate, the report of the Joint Committee submitted the amendment "in the hope that its imperfections may be cured and its deficiencies supplied, by legislative wisdom . . . ." [118] It need hardly be added that in view of Stevens' remarks, and in view also of the nature of the other evidence which supports it, this hypothesis cannot be disparaged as putting forth an undisclosed, conspiratorial purpose such as has been imputed to Bingham and others with regard to protection of corporations.[119] Indeed, no specific purpose going beyond the coverage of the Civil Rights Act is suggested; rather an awareness on the part of these framers that it was *a constitution* they were writing, which led to a choice of language capable of growth.

It is such a reading as this of the original understanding, in response to the second of the questions propounded by the Court, that the Chief Justice must have had in mind when he termed the materials "inconclusive." For up to this point they tell a clear story and are anything but inconclusive. From this point on the word is apt, since the interpretation of the evidence just set out comes only to this, that the question of giving greater protection than was extended by the Civil Rights Act was deferred, was left open, to be decided another day under a constitutional provision with more scope than the unserviceable thirteenth amendment. Some no doubt felt more certain than others that the new amendment would make possible further strides toward the ideal of equality. That remained to be decided, and there is no indication of the way in which anyone thought the decision would go on any given specific issue.[120] It depended a good deal on the trend in

---

[118] See note 97 *supra*.

[119] See note 13 *supra*.

[120] Much has been made of the abolitionist antecedents of a number of men prominent in the 39th Congress, among them Stevens, and — a little more dubiously — Bingham. And it has been contended that terms similar to those used by Bingham in § 1 of the fourteenth amendment had been widely advertised abolitionist cliches, which were well understood by the country as embodying the

public opinion. Actually, one of the things the Radicals had contended for throughout the session, and doubtless considered that they gained by the final compromise, was time and the chance to educate the public. Such expectations as the Radicals had were centered quite clearly on legislative action. At least this holds true for Stevens. These men were aware of the power the Court could exercise. They were for the most part bitterly aware of it, having long fought such decisions as the *Dred Scott* case. Most probably they had little hope that the Court would play a role in furthering their long-range objectives. But the relevant point is that the Radical leadership succeeded in obtaining a provision whose future effect was left to future determination. The fact that they themselves expected such a future determination to be made in Congress is not controlling. It merely reflects their estimate that men of their view were more likely to prevail in the legislature than in other branches of the government. It indicates no judgment about the powers and functions properly to be exercised by the other branches.

Had the Court in the *Segregation Cases* stopped short of the inconclusive answer to the second of its questions handed down at the previous term, it would have been faced with one of two unfortunate choices. It could have deemed itself bound by the legislative history showing the immediate objectives to which section 1 of the fourteenth amendment was addressed, and rather clearly demonstrating that it was not expected in 1866 to apply to segregation. The Court would in that event also have repudiated much of the provision's "line of growth." For it is as clear that section 1 was not deemed in 1866 to deal with jury service and other matters "implicit in . . . ordered liberty" [121] to which the Court has since

---

fullness of the abolitionist doctrine. See TENBROEK, THE ANTISLAVERY ORIGINS OF THE FOURTEENTH AMENDMENT (1951); Graham, *The Early Antislavery Backgrounds of the Fourteenth Amendment*, 1950 WIS. L. REV. 479, 610. Yet even among the abolitionists there were differences of view concerning the extent to which uncompromising egalitarian principles should be applied — suddenly and indiscriminately — to the Negro. See NYE, FETTERED FREEDOM: CIVIL LIBERTIES AND THE SLAVERY CONTROVERSY 1830–1860 (1949). And it is always dangerous to assume that men — especially men of a revolutionary persuasion — who have achieved power act on principles they espoused while in violent opposition. Be that as it may, the abolitionist past of some Radicals can, in view of all the evidence, be relevant to only one facet of the compromise they accepted; it helps to indicate not what they believed they were achieving immediately, but what they hoped was open to future achievement.

[121] Justice Cardozo in Palko v. Connecticut, 302 U.S. 319, 325 (1937).

applied it.[122] Secondly, the Court could have faced the embarrassment of going counter to what it took to be the original understanding, and of formulating, as it has not often needed to do in the past, an explicit theory rationalizing such a course. The Court, of course, made neither choice. It was able to avoid the dilemma because the record of history, properly understood, left the way open to, in fact invited, a decision based on the moral and material state of the nation in 1954, not 1866.

---

[122] *E.g.*, Strauder v. West Virginia, 100 U.S. 303 (1880); Norris v. Alabama, 294 U.S. 587 (1935) (jury service). The Court has also, in the changed circumstances created by the fifteenth amendment, applied the equal protection clause of the fourteenth to the right to vote. Nixon v. Herndon, 273 U.S. 536 (1927); *cf.* Smith v. Allwright, 321 U.S. 649 (1944).

VOLUME 73   NOVEMBER 1959   NUMBER 1

HARVARD LAW REVIEW

TOWARD NEUTRAL PRINCIPLES OF CONSTITUTIONAL LAW †

Herbert Wechsler *

Professor Wechsler, disagreeing with Judge Learned Hand as to the justification for judicial review of legislative action, argues that courts have the power, and duty, to decide all constitutional cases in which the jurisdictional and procedural requirements are met. The author concludes that in these cases decisions must rest on reasoning and analysis which transcend the immediate result, and discusses instances in which he believes the Supreme Court has not been faithful to this principle.

ON three occasions in the last few years Harvard has been hospitable to the discussion of that most abiding problem of our public law: the role of courts in general and the Supreme Court in particular in our constitutional tradition; their special function in the maintenance, interpretation and development of the organic charter that provides the framework of our government, the charter that declares itself the "supreme law."

I have in mind, of course, Mr. Justice Jackson's undelivered Godkin lectures,[1] the papers and comments at the Marshall conference,[2] and Judge Learned Hand's addresses from this very rostrum but a year ago.[3] It does not depreciate these major contributions if I add that they comprise only a fragment of the

---

† This paper was delivered on April 7, 1959, as the Oliver Wendell Holmes Lecture at the Harvard Law School. It is reproduced without substantial change, except for the addition of the footnotes. The reader is asked to bear in mind that it was written for the ear and not the eye.

* Harlan Fiske Stone Professor of Constitutional Law, Columbia University School of Law. A.B., College of the City of New York, 1928; LL.B., Columbia, 1931.

[1] JACKSON, THE SUPREME COURT IN THE AMERICAN SYSTEM OF GOVERNMENT (1955).

[2] GOVERNMENT UNDER LAW (Sutherland ed. 1956).

[3] HAND, THE BILL OF RIGHTS (1958).

I

serious, continuous attention that the subject is receiving here as well as elsewhere in the nation, not to speak of that less serious attention that is not without importance to a university community, however uninstructive it may be.

I should regard another venture on a theme so fully ventilated as a poor expression of appreciation for the hospitality accorded me, were I not persuaded that there is a point to make and an exercise to be performed that will not constitute mere reiteration; and that the point and exercise have special relevancy to the most important of our current controversies. Before I put my point and undertake the exercise it is appropriate, however, that I make clear where I stand upon the larger, underlying questions that have been considered on the previous occasions I have noted, particularly by Judge Hand last year. They have a bearing, as will be apparent, on the thesis that I mean to put before you later on.

I. The Basis of Judicial Review

Let me begin by stating that I have not the slightest doubt respecting the legitimacy of judicial review, whether the action called in question in a case which otherwise is proper for adjudication is legislative or executive, federal or state. I must address myself to this because the question was so seriously mooted by Judge Hand; and though he answered it in favor of the courts' assumption of the power of review, his answer has overtones quite different from those of the answer I would give.

Judge Hand's position was that "when the Constitution emerged from the Convention in September, 1787, the structure of the proposed government, if one looked to the text, gave no ground for inferring that the decisions of the Supreme Court, and *a fortiori* of the lower courts, were to be authoritative upon the Executive and the Legislature"; that "on the other hand it was probable, if indeed it was not certain, that without some arbiter whose decision should be final the whole system would have collapsed, for it was extremely unlikely that the Executive or the Legislature, having once decided, would yield to the contrary holding of another 'Department,' even of the courts"; that "for centuries it has been an accepted canon in interpretation of documents to interpolate into the text such provisions, though not expressed, as are essential to prevent the defeat of the venture at hand"; that it was therefore "altogether in keeping with established practice for the Supreme Court to assume an authority to keep the states, Congress, and the President within their prescribed powers"; and, finally and explicitly, that for the reason stated "it was not a lawless act to import into the Constitution such a grant of power." [4]

Though I have learned from past experience that disagreement with Judge Hand is usually nothing but the sheerest folly, I must make clear why I believe the power of the courts is grounded in the language of the Constitution and is not a mere interpolation. To do this you must let me quote the supremacy clause,[5] which is mercifully short:

> This Constitution, and the Laws of the United States which shall be made in Pursuance thereof; and all Treaties made, or which shall be made, under the Authority of the United States, shall be the supreme Law of the Land; and the Judges in every State shall be bound thereby, any Thing in the Constitution or Laws of any State to the Contrary notwithstanding.

Judge Hand concedes that under this clause "state courts would at times have to decide whether state laws and constitutions, or even a federal statute, were in conflict with the federal constitution" but he adds that "the fact that this jurisdiction was confined to such occasions, and that it was thought necessary specifically to provide such a limited jurisdiction, looks rather against than in favor of a general jurisdiction." [6]

Are you satisfied, however, to view the supremacy clause in this way, as a grant of jurisdiction to state courts, implying a denial of the power and the duty to all others? This certainly is not its necessary meaning; it may be construed as a mandate to all of officialdom including courts, with a special and emphatic admonition that it binds the judges of the previously independent states. That the latter is the proper reading seems to me persuasive when the other relevant provisions of the Constitution are brought into view.

Article III, section 1 declares that the federal judicial power "shall be vested in one supreme Court, and in such inferior Courts as the Congress may from time to time ordain and establish."

---

[4] *Id.* at 27, 29, 14, 15, 29.
[5] U.S. CONST. art. VI, § 2.
[6] HAND, *op. cit. supra* note 3, at 28.

This represented, as you know, one of the major compromises of the Constitutional Convention and relegated the establishment *vel non* of lower federal courts to the discretion of the Congress.[7] None might have been established, with the consequence that, as in other federalisms, judicial work of first instance would all have been remitted to state courts.[8] Article III, section 2 goes on, however, to delineate the scope of the federal judicial power, providing that it "shall extend [*inter alia*] to all Cases, in Law and Equity, arising under this Constitution . . ." and, further, that the Supreme Court "shall have appellate jurisdiction" in such cases "with such Exceptions, and under such Regulations as the Congress shall make." Surely this means, as section 25 of the Judiciary Act of 1789 [9] took it to mean, that if a state court passes on a constitutional issue, as the supremacy clause provides that it should, its judgment is reviewable, subject to congressional exceptions, by the Supreme Court, in which event that Court must have no less authority and duty to accord priority to constitutional provisions than the court that it reviews.[10] And such state cases might have encompassed every case in which a constitutional issue could possibly arise, since, as I have said, Congress need not and might not have exerted its authority to establish "inferior" federal courts.

If you abide with me thus far, I doubt that you will hesitate upon the final step. Is it a possible construction of the Constitution, measured strictly as Judge Hand admonishes by the test of "general purpose," [11] that if Congress opts, as it has opted, to create a set of lower courts, those courts in cases falling within their respective jurisdictions and the Supreme Court when it passes on their judgments are less or differently constrained by the supremacy clause than are the state courts, and the Supreme

---

[7] See 1 FARRAND, THE RECORDS OF THE FEDERAL CONVENTION 104–05, 119, 124–25 (1911), summarized in HART & WECHSLER, THE FEDERAL COURTS AND THE FEDERAL SYSTEM 17 (1953).

[8] See, *e.g.*, the position in Australia, described in Bailey, *The Federal Jurisdiction of State Courts*, 2 RES JUDICATAE 109 (1940); WHEARE, FEDERAL GOVERNMENT 68–72 (2d ed. 1951). The slow statutory development of federal-question jurisdiction in our lower federal courts is traced in HART & WECHSLER, *op. cit. supra* note 7, at 727–33, 1019–21, 1107–08, 1140–50.

[9] Act of Sept. 24, 1789, ch. 20, § 25, 1 Stat. 85.

[10] This too I think Judge Hand does not deny, though this concession appears only in the course of his description of the Jeffersonian position. See HAND, *op. cit. supra* note 3, at 5.

[11] *Id.* at 19.

Court when it reviews their judgments? Yet I cannot escape, what is for me the most astonishing conclusion, that this is the precise result of Judge Hand's reading of the text, as distinct from the interpolation he approves on other grounds.

It is true that Hamilton in the seventy-eighth *Federalist* does not mention the supremacy clause in his argument but rather urges the conclusion as implicit in the concept of a written constitution as a fundamental law and the accepted function of the courts as law interpreters. Marshall in *Marbury. v. Madison* echoes these general considerations, though he also calls attention to the text, including the judiciary article, pointing only at the end to the language about supremacy, concerning which he says that it "confirms and strengthens the principle, supposed to be essential to all written constitutions, that a law repugnant to the constitution is void; and that *courts*, as well as other departments, are bound by that instrument." [12] Much might be said on this as to the style of reasoning that was deemed most persuasive when these documents were written but this would be irrelevant to my concern about the meaning that Judge Hand insists he cannot find within the words or structure of the Constitution, even with the aid of the historical material that surely points in the direction I suggest.[13]

You will not wonder now why I should be concerned about the way Judge Hand has read the text, despite his view that the judicial power was a valid importation to preserve the governmental plan. Here as elsewhere a position cannot be divorced from its supporting reasons; the reasons are, indeed, a part and most important part of the position. To demonstrate I quote Judge Hand:

> [S]ince this power is not a logical deduction from the structure of the Constitution but only a practical condition upon its successful operation, it need not be exercised whenever a court sees, or thinks that it sees, an invasion of the Constitution. It is always a preliminary question how importantly the occasion demands an answer. It may be better to leave the issue to be worked out without authoritative solution; or perhaps the only solution available is one that the court has no adequate means to enforce.[14]

---

[12] Marbury v. Madison, 5 U.S. (1 Cranch) 137, 180 (1803). (Emphasis in original.)

[13] See HART & WECHSLER, *op. cit. supra* note 7, at 14–16; Hart, Book Review, *Professor Crosskey and Judicial Review,* 67 HARV. L. REV. 1456 (1954).

[14] HAND, *op. cit. supra* note 3, at 15.

If this means that a court, in a case properly before it, is free — or should be free on any fresh view of its duty — either to adjudicate a constitutional objection to an otherwise determinative action of the legislature or executive, national or state, or to decline to do so, depending on "how importunately" it considers the occasion to demand an answer, could anything have more enormous import for the theory and the practice of review? What showing would be needed to elicit a decision? Would anything suffice short of a demonstration that judicial intervention is essential to prevent the government from foundering — the reason, you recall, for the interpolation of the power to decide? For me, as for anyone who finds the judicial power anchored in the Constitution, there is no such escape from the judicial obligation; the duty cannot be attenuated in this way.

The duty, to be sure, is not that of policing or advising legislatures or executives, nor even, as the uninstructed think, of standing as an ever-open forum for the ventilation of all grievances that draw upon the Constitution for support. It is the duty to decide the litigated case and to decide it in accordance with the law, with all that that implies as to a rigorous insistence on the satisfaction of procedural and jurisdictional requirements; the concept that Professor Freund reminds us was so fundamental in the thought and work of Mr. Justice Brandeis.[15] Only when the standing law, decisional or statutory, provides a remedy to vindicate the interest that demands protection against an infringement of the kind that is alleged, a law of remedies that ordinarily at least is framed in reference to rights and wrongs in general, do courts have any business asking what the Constitution may require or forbid, and only then when it is necessary for decision of the case that is at hand. How was it Marshall put the questions to be faced in *Marbury*?

> 1st. Has the applicant a right to the commission he demands?
>
> 2dly. If he has a right, and that right has been violated, do the laws of his country afford him a remedy?
>
> 3dly. If they do afford him a remedy, is it a *mandamus* issuing from this court? [16]

---

[15] See Freund, On Understanding the Supreme Court 64–65 (1949); Freund, *Mr. Justice Brandeis: A Centennial Memoir*, 70 Harv. L. Rev. 769, 787–88 (1957). See also Bickel, The Unpublished Opinions of Mr. Justice Brandeis 1–20 (1957).

[16] 5 U.S. (1 Cranch) at 154.

It was because he thought, as his opponents also thought,[17] that the Constitution had a bearing on the answers to these questions, that he claimed the right and duty to examine its commands.

As a legal system grows, the remedies that it affords substantially proliferate, a development to which the courts contribute but in which the legislature has an even larger hand.[18] There has been major growth of this kind in our system [19] and I dare say there will be more, increasing correspondingly the number and variety of the occasions when a constitutional adjudication may be sought and must be made. Am I not right, however, in believing that the underlying theory of the courts' participation has not changed and that, indeed, the very multiplicity of remedies and grievances makes it increasingly important that the theory and its implications be maintained?

It is true, and I do not mean to ignore it, that the courts themselves regard some questions as "political," meaning thereby that they are not to be resolved judicially, although they involve constitutional interpretation and arise in the course of litigation. Judge Hand alluded to this doctrine which, insofar as its scope is undefined, he labeled a "stench in the nostrils of strict constructionists." [20] And Mr. Justice Frankfurter, in his great paper at the Marshall conference, avowed "disquietude that the line is often very thin between the cases in which the Court felt compelled to abstain from adjudication because of their 'political' nature, and the cases that so frequently arise in applying the concepts of 'liberty' and 'equality'." [21]

The line is thin, indeed, but I suggest that it is thinner than it needs to be or ought to be; that all the doctrine can defensibly imply is that the courts are called upon to judge whether the

---

[17] It will be remembered that the Jeffersonian objections to the issuance of a mandamus to the Secretary rested on constitutional submissions with respect to the separation of judicial and executive authority. See 1 WARREN, THE SUPREME COURT IN UNITED STATES HISTORY 232 (1937); Kendall v. United States, 37 U.S. (12 Pet.) 524, 610 (1838); Lee, *The Origins of Judicial Control of Federal Executive Action*, 36 GEO. L.J. 287 (1948).

[18] See, *e.g.*, *Developments in the Law — Remedies Against the United States and Its Officials*, 70 HARV. L. REV. 827 (1957).

[19] Decisions that entail such growth do not always confront the underlying problem. See, *e.g.*, Harmon v. Brucker, 355 U.S. 579 (1958). Compare the opinion of Judge Prettyman below, 243 F.2d 613 (D.C. Cir. 1957).

[20] HAND, *op. cit. supra* note 3, at 15.

[21] Frankfurter, *John Marshall and the Judicial Function*, 69 HARV. L. REV. 217, 227-28 (1955), in GOVERNMENT UNDER LAW 6, 19 (Sutherland ed. 1956).

Constitution has committed to another agency of government the autonomous determination of the issue raised, a finding that itself requires an interpretation. Who, for example, would contend that the civil courts may properly review a judgment of impeachment when article I, section 3 declares that the "sole Power to try" is in the Senate? That any proper trial of an impeachment may present issues of the most important constitutional dimension, as Senator Kennedy reminds us in his moving story of the Senator whose vote saved Andrew Johnson,[22] is simply immaterial in this connection.

What is explicit in the trial of an impeachment or, to take another case, the seating or expulsion of a Senator or Representative [23] may well be found to be implicit in others. So it was held,[24] and rightly it appears to me, respecting the provision that the "United States shall guarantee to every State in this Union a Republican Form of Government . . . ." This guarantee appears, you will recall, in the same clause as does the duty to protect the states against invasion; [25] it envisages the possible employment of the military force and bears an obvious relationship to the autonomous authority of the Houses of Congress in seating their respective members.[26]

It also may be reasonable to conclude, or so it seems to me, though there are arguments the other way,[27] that the power of Congress to "make or alter" state regulations of the "Manner of

---

[22] See KENNEDY, PROFILES IN COURAGE 126 (1956).

[23] U.S. CONST. art. I, § 5 provides, "Each House shall be the Judge of the Elections, Returns and Qualifications of its own Members . . . . Each House may determine the Rules of its Proceedings, punish its Members for disorderly Behaviour, and, with the Concurrence of two thirds, expel a Member."

For a constitutional challenge to the sufficiency of primary irregularities as ground for the refusal to seat a United States Senator, see BECK, MAY IT PLEASE THE COURT 265 (1930).

[24] Pacific States Tel. & Tel. Co. v. Oregon, 223 U.S. 118 (1912); Luther v. Borden, 48 U.S. (7 How.) 1, 42 (1849).

[25] U.S. CONST. art. IV, § 4: "The United States shall guarantee to every State in this Union a Republican Form of Government, and shall protect each of them against Invasion; and on Application of the Legislature, or of the Executive (when the Legislature cannot be convened) against domestic Violence."

[26] Cf. Luther v. Borden, 48 U.S. (7 How.) 1, 42 (1849): "And when the senators and representatives of a State are admitted into the councils of the Union, the authority of the government under which they are appointed, as well as its republican character, is recognized by the proper constitutional authority."

[27] See, e.g., Lewis, Legislative Apportionment and the Federal Courts, 71 HARV. L. REV. 1057 (1958).

holding Elections for Senators and Representatives," [28] implying
as it does a power to draw district lines or to prescribe the standards to be followed in defining them, excludes the courts from
passing on a constitutional objection to state gerrymanders,[29] even
if the Constitution can be thought to speak to this kind of inequality and the law of remedies gives disadvantaged voters legal
standing to complain, which are both separate questions to be
faced.[30]

If I may put my point again, I submit that in cases of the kind
that I have mentioned, as in others that I do not pause to state,[31]
the only proper judgment that may lead to an abstention from decision is that the Constitution has committed the determination of
the issue to another agency of government than the courts. Difficult as it may be to make that judgment wisely, whatever factors
may be rightly weighed in situations where the answer is not
clear, what is involved is in itself an act of constitutional interpretation, to be made and judged by standards that should govern
the interpretive process generally. That, I submit, is *toto caelo*
different from a broad discretion to abstain or intervene.

The Supreme Court does have a discretion, to be sure, to grant
or to deny review of judgments of the lower courts in situations
in which the jurisdictional statute permits certiorari but does not
provide for an appeal.[32] I need not say that this is an entirely different matter. The system rests upon the power that the Constitution vests in Congress to make exceptions to and regulate the
Court's appellate jurisdiction; it is addressed not to the measure
of judicial duty in adjudication of a case but rather to the right to
a determination by the highest as distinguished from the lower
courts. Even here, however, it is well worth noting that the Court
by rule has defined standards for the exercise of its discretion,[33]
standards framed in neutral terms, like the importance of the

---

[28] U.S. Const. art. I, § 4.

[29] See Colegrove v. Green, 328 U.S. 549, 554 (1946) (Frankfurter, J.); Professor Freund's comment in Supreme Court and Supreme Law 46–47 (Cahn ed.
1954).

[30] For an effort to face these questions, see Lewis, *supra* note 27, at 1071–98.

[31] See Hart & Wechsler, *op. cit. supra* note 7, at 192–97, 207–09; Post, The
Supreme Court and Political Questions (1936).

[32] 28 U.S.C. §§ 1254–57 (1952). The major steps in the statutory substitution
of discretionary for obligatory Supreme Court review are traced in Hart & Wechsler, *op. cit. supra* note 7, at 400–03, 1313–21. The classic detailed account appears in Frankfurter & Landis, The Business of the Supreme Court (1927).

[33] U.S. Sup. Ct. R. 19.

question or a conflict of decisions. Only the maintenance and the improvement of such standards [34] and, of course, their faithful application [35] can, I say with deference, protect the Court against the danger of the imputation of a bias favoring claims of one kind or another in the granting or denial of review.

Indeed, I will go further and assert that, necessary as it is that the Court's docket be confined to manageable size, much would be gained if the governing statutes could be revised to play a larger part in the delineation of the causes that make rightful call upon the time and energy of the Supreme Court.[36] Think of the protection it gave Marshall's court that there was no discretionary jurisdiction, with the consequence that he could say in *Cohens v. Virginia*: [37]

> It is most true that this Court will not take jurisdiction if it should not: but it is equally true, that it must take jurisdiction if it should. The judiciary cannot, as the legislature may, avoid a measure because it approaches the confines of the constitution. We cannot pass it by because it is doubtful. With whatever doubts, with whatever difficulties, a case may be attended, we must decide it, if it be brought before us. We have no more right to decline the exercise of jurisdiction which is given, than to usurp that which is not given. The one or the other would be treason to the constitution.

II. The Standards of Review

If courts cannot escape the duty of deciding whether actions of the other branches of the government are consistent with the Constitution, when a case is properly before them in the sense I have attempted to describe, you will not doubt the relevancy and importance of demanding what, if any, are the standards to be fol-

---

[34] It is regrettable, in my view, that when the Court revised its rules in 1954 it determined not to attempt an improved articulation of the statement of "considerations governing review on certiorari." *But see* Wiener, *The Supreme Court's New Rules*, 68 HARV. L. REV. 20, 60–63 (1954).

[35] See, *e.g.*, Note, *Supreme Court Certiorari Policy in Cases Arising Under the FELA*, 69 HARV. L. REV. 1441 (1956).

[36] The present distribution of obligatory and discretionary jurisdiction derives largely, though not entirely, from the Judiciary Act of 1925, ch. 229, 43 Stat. 936, the architects of which were a committee of the Court. See Taft, *The Jurisdiction of the Supreme Court Under the Act of February 13, 1925*, 35 YALE L.J. 1 (1925); FRANKFURTER & LANDIS, *op. cit. supra* note 32, at 255–94. For major changes since 1925, see HART & WECHSLER, *op. cit. supra* note 7, at 1317.

[37] 19 U.S. (6 Wheat.) 264, 404 (1821).

lowed in interpretation. Are there, indeed, any criteria that both the Supreme Court and those who undertake to praise or to condemn its judgments are morally and intellectually obligated to support?

Whatever you may think to be the answer, surely you agree with me that I am right to state the question as the same one for the Court and for its critics. An attack upon a judgment involves an assertion that a court should have decided otherwise than as it did. Is it not clear that the validity of an assertion of this kind depends upon assigning reasons that should have prevailed with the tribunal; and that any other reasons are irrelevant? That is, of course, not only true of a critique of a decision of the courts; it applies whenever a determination is in question, a determination that it is essential to make either way. Is it the irritation of advancing years that leads me to lament that our culture is not rich with critics who respect these limitations of the enterprise in which they are engaged?

You may remind me that, as someone in the ancient world observed — perhaps it was Josephus — history has little tolerance for any of those reasonable judgments that have turned out to be wrong. But history, in this sense, is inscrutable, concealing all its verdicts in the bosom of the future; it is never a contemporary critic.

I revert then to the problem of criteria as it arises for both courts and critics — by which I mean criteria that can be framed and tested as an exercise of reason and not merely as an act of willfulness or will. Even to put the problem is, of course, to raise an issue no less old than our culture. Those who perceive in law only the element of fiat, in whose conception of the legal cosmos reason has no meaning or no place, will not join gladly in the search for standards of the kind I have in mind. I must, in short, expect dissent *in limine* from anyone whose view of the judicial process leaves no room for the antinomy Professor Fuller has so gracefully explored.[38] So too must I anticipate dissent from those more numerous among us who, vouching no philosophy to warranty, frankly or covertly make the test of virtue in interpretation whether its result in the immediate decision seems to hinder or advance the interests or the values they support.

I shall not try to overcome the philosophic doubt that I have

---

[38] See Fuller, *Reason and Fiat in Case Law*, 59 HARV. L. REV. 376 (1946).

mentioned, although to use a phrase that Holmes so often used —
"it hits me where I live." That battle must be fought on wider
fronts than that of constitutional interpretation; and I do not
delude myself that I can qualify for a command, great as is my
wish to render service. The man who simply lets his judgment
turn on the immediate result may not, however, realize that his
position implies that the courts are free to function as a naked
power organ, that it is an empty affirmation to regard them, as
ambivalently he so often does, as courts of law. If he may know
he disapproves of a decision when all he knows is that it has sustained a claim put forward by a labor union or a taxpayer, a Negro
or a segregationist, a corporation or a Communist — he acquiesces
in the proposition that a man of different sympathy but equal information may no less properly conclude that he approves.

You will not charge me with exaggeration if I say that this type
of *ad hoc* evaluation is, as it has always been, the deepest problem
of our constitutionalism, not only with respect to judgments of
the courts but also in the wider realm in which conflicting constitutional positions have played a part in our politics.

Did not New England challenge the embargo that the South
supported on the very ground on which the South was to resist
New England's demand for a protective tariff? [39] Was not Jefferson in the Louisiana Purchase forced to rest on an expansive
reading of the clauses granting national authority of the very kind
that he had steadfastly opposed in his attacks upon the Bank? [40]
Can you square his disappointment about Burr's acquittal on the
treason charge and his subsequent request for legislation [41] with

---

[39] See 4 ADAMS, HISTORY OF THE UNITED STATES OF AMERICA DURING THE SEC-
OND ADMINISTRATION OF THOMAS JEFFERSON 267 (1890): "If Congress had the right
to regulate commerce for such a purpose in 1808, South Carolina seemed to have
no excuse for questioning, twenty years later, the constitutionality of a protective
system."

[40] See 2 ADAMS, HISTORY OF THE UNITED STATES OF AMERICA DURING THE FIRST
ADMINISTRATION OF THOMAS JEFFERSON 90 (1889): "[T]he Louisiana treaty gave
a fatal wound to 'strict construction,' and the Jeffersonian theories never again
received general support. In thus giving them up, Jefferson did not lead the way,
but he allowed his friends to drag him in the path they chose." See also 3 WILSON,
A HISTORY OF THE AMERICAN PEOPLE 182–83 (1902).

[41] In his annual message of October 27, 1807, Jefferson said:
I shall think it my duty to lay before you the proceedings and the evidence
publicly exhibited on the arraignment of the principal offenders before the circuit court of Virginia. You will be enabled to judge whether the defect was in
the testimony, in the law, or in the administration of the law; and wherever
it shall be found, the Legislature alone can apply or originate the remedy.
The framers of our Constitution certainly supposed that they had guarded as

the attitude towards freedom and repression most enduringly associated with his name? Were the abolitionists who rescued fugitives and were acquitted in defiance of the evidence able to distinguish their view of the compulsion of a law of the United States from that advanced by South Carolina in the ordinance that they despised? [42]

To bring the matter even more directly home, what shall we think of the Harvard records of the Class of 1829, the class of Mr. Justice Curtis, which, we are told,[43] praised at length the Justice's dissent in the *Dred Scott* case but then added, "Again, *and seemingly adverse to the above,* in October, 1862, he prepared a legal opinion and argument, which was published in Boston in pamphlet form, to the effect that President Lincoln's Proclamation of prospective emancipation of the slaves in the rebellious States is *unconstitutional.*"

Of course, a man who thought and, as a Justice, voted and maintained [44] that a free Negro could be a citizen of the United States and therefore of a state, within the meaning of the constitutional and statutory clauses defining the diversity jurisdiction; that Congress had authority to forbid slavery within a territory, even one acquired after the formation of the Union; and that such a pro-

---

well their Government against destruction by treason as their citizens against oppression under pretense of it, and if these ends are not attained it is of importance to inquire by what means more effectual they may be secured.

1 RICHARDSON, MESSAGES AND PAPERS OF THE PRESIDENT 429 (1896). The trial proceedings were transmitted to the Senate on November 23, 1807. See 17 ANNALS OF CONG. APP. 385–778 (1807).

Jefferson's conception of the "remedy" not only involved legislation overcoming Marshall's strict construction of the treason clause but also a provision for the removal of judges on the address of both Houses of Congress. See 3 RANDALL, THE LIFE OF THOMAS JEFFERSON 246–47 (1865); 1 WARREN, THE SUPREME COURT IN UNITED STATES HISTORY 311–15 (1937).

On the former point, different bills were introduced in the Senate and the House. The Senate bill by Giles undertook to define "levying war" for purposes of treason. The proposed definition included "assembling themselves together with intent forcibly to overturn or change the Government of the United States, or any one of the Territories thereof . . . or forcibly to resist the general execution of any public law thereof . . . or if any person or persons shall traitorously aid or assist in the doing any of the acts aforesaid, although not personally present when any such act is done . . . ." 17 ANNALS OF CONG. 108–09 (1808). For discussion of the measure in the Senate, see 17 *id.* at 109–27, 135–49. The House bill by Randolph defined a separate offense, "conspiracy to commit treason against the United States . . . ." 18 *id.* at 1717–18.

[42] See South Carolina Ordinance of Nullification, 1 S.C. Stat. 329 (1832).

[43] See 1 CURTIS, A MEMOIR OF BENJAMIN ROBBINS CURTIS 354–55 n.1 (1879).

[44] See Scott v. Sandford, 60 U.S. (19 How.) 393, 564–633 (1857).

hibition worked emancipation of a slave whose owner brought him to reside in such a territory — a man who thought all these things detracted obviously from the force of his positions if he also thought the President without authority to abrogate a form of property established and protected by state law within the states where it was located, states which the President and his critic alike maintained had not effectively seceded from the Union and were not a foreign enemy at war.

How simple the class historian could make it all by treating as the only thing that mattered whether Mr. Justice Curtis had, on the occasions noted, helped or hindered the attainment of the freedom of the slaves.

I have cited these examples from the early years of our history since time has bred aloofness that may give them added force. What a wealth of illustration is at hand today! How many of the constitutional attacks upon congressional investigations of suspected Communists have their authors felt obliged to launch against the inquiries respecting the activities of Goldfine or of Hoffa or of others I might name? How often have those who think the Smith Act, as construed, inconsistent with the first amendment made clear that they also stand for constitutional immunity for racial agitators fanning flames of prejudice and discontent? Turning the case around, are those who in relation to the Smith Act see no virtue in distinguishing between advocacy of merely abstract doctrine and advocacy which is planned to instigate unlawful action,[45] equally unable to see virtue in the same distinction in relation, let us say, to advocacy of resistance to the judgments of the courts, especially perhaps to judgments vindicating claims that equal protection of the laws has been denied? I may live a uniquely sheltered life but am I wrong in thinking I discerned in some extremely warm enthusiasts for jury trial a certain diminution of enthusiasm as the issue was presented in the course of the debate in 1957 on the bill to extend federal protection of our civil rights?

All I have said, you may reply, is something no one will deny, that principles are largely instrumental as they are employed in politics, instrumental in relation to results that a controlling sentiment demands at any given time. Politicians recognize this fact of life and are obliged to trim and shape their speech and votes ac-

---

[45] See Yates v. United States, 354 U.S. 298, 318 (1957).

cordingly, unless perchance they are prepared to step aside; and the example that John Quincy Adams set somehow is rarely followed.

That is, indeed, all I have said but I now add that whether you are tolerant, perhaps more tolerant than I, of the *ad hoc* in politics, with principle reduced to a manipulative tool, are you not also ready to agree that something else is called for from the courts? I put it to you that the main constituent of the judicial process is precisely that it must be genuinely principled, resting with respect to every step that is involved in reaching judgment on analysis and reasons quite transcending the immediate result that is achieved. To be sure, the courts decide, or should decide, only the case they have before them. But must they not decide on grounds of adequate neutrality and generality, tested not only by the instant application but by others that the principles imply? Is it not the very essence of judicial method to insist upon attending to such other cases, preferably those involving an opposing interest, in evaluating any principle avowed?

Here too I do not think that I am stating any novel or momentous insight. But now, as Holmes said long ago in speaking of "the unrest which seems to wonder vaguely whether law and order pay," we "need education in the obvious." [46] We need it more particularly now respecting constitutional interpretation, since it has become a commonplace to grant what many for so long denied: that courts in constitutional determinations face issues that are inescapably "political" — political in the third sense that I have used that word — in that they involve a choice among competing values or desires, a choice reflected in the legislative or executive action in question, which the court must either condemn or condone.

I should be the last to argue otherwise or to protest the emphasis upon the point in Mr. Justice Jackson's book, throughout the Marshall conference, and in the lectures by Judge Hand. I have, indeed, insisted on the point myself.[47] But what is crucial, I submit, is not the nature of the question but the nature of the answer that may validly be given by the courts. No legislature or executive is obligated by the nature of its function to support its choice of values by the type of reasoned explanation that I

---

[46] HOLMES, *Law and the Court*, in COLLECTED LEGAL PAPERS 291, 292 (1920).

[47] See, *e.g.*, Wechsler, *Comment* on Snee, *Leviathan at the Bar of Justice*, in GOVERNMENT UNDER LAW 134, 136–37 (Sutherland ed. 1956).

have suggested is intrinsic to judicial action — however much we may admire such a reasoned exposition when we find it in those other realms.

Does not the special duty of the courts to judge by neutral principles addressed to all the issues make it inapposite to contend, as Judge Hand does, that no court can review the legislative choice — by any standard other than a fixed "historical meaning" of constitutional provisions [48] — without becoming "a third legislative chamber"? [49] Is there not, in short, a vital difference between legislative freedom to appraise the gains and losses in projected measures and the kind of principled appraisal, in respect of values that can reasonably be asserted to have constitutional dimension, that alone is in the province of the courts? Does not the difference yield a middle ground between a judicial House of Lords and the abandonment of any limitation on the other branches — a middle ground consisting of judicial action that embodies what are surely the main qualities of law, its generality and its neutrality? This must, it seems to me, have been in Mr. Justice Jackson's mind when in his chapter on the Supreme Court "as a political institution" he wrote [50] in words that I find stirring, "Liberty is not the mere absence of restraint, it is not a spontaneous product of majority rule, it is not achieved merely by lifting underprivileged classes to power, nor is it the inevitable by-product of technological expansion. It is achieved only by a rule of law." Is it not also what Mr. Justice Frankfurter must mean in calling upon judges for "allegiance to nothing except the effort, amid tangled words and limited insights, to find the path through precedent, through policy, through history, to the best judgment that fallible creatures can reach in that most difficult of all tasks: the achievement of justice between man and man, between man and state, through reason called law"? [51]

You will not understand my emphasis upon the role of reason and of principle in the judicial, as distinguished from the legislative or executive, appraisal of conflicting values to imply that I depreciate the duty of fidelity to the text of the Constitution, when its words may be decisive — though I would certainly remind you

---

[48] HAND, *op. cit. supra* note 3, at 65.

[49] *Id.* at 42.

[50] JACKSON, THE SUPREME COURT IN THE AMERICAN SYSTEM OF GOVERNMENT 76 (1955).

[51] FRANKFURTER, *Chief Justices I Have Known*, in OF LAW AND MEN 138 (Elman ed. 1956).

of the caution stated by Chief Justice Hughes: "Behind the words of the constitutional provisions are postulates which limit and control." [52] Nor will you take me to deny that history has weight in the elucidation of the text, though it is surely subtle business to appraise it as a guide. Nor will you even think that I deem precedent without importance, for we surely must agree with Holmes that "imitation of the past, until we have a clear reason for change, no more needs justification than appetite." [53] But after all, it was Chief Justice Taney who declared his willingness "that it be regarded hereafter as the law of this court, that its opinion upon the construction of the Constitution is always open to discussion when it is supposed to have been founded in error, and that its judicial authority should hereafter depend altogether on the force of the reasoning by which it is supported." [54] Would any of us have it otherwise, given the nature of the problems that confront the courts?

At all events, is not the relative compulsion of the language of the Constitution, of history and precedent — where they do not combine to make an answer clear — itself a matter to be judged, so far as possible, by neutral principles — by standards that transcend the case at hand? I know, of course, that it is common to distinguish, as Judge Hand did, clauses like "due process," cast "in such sweeping terms that their history does not elucidate their contents," [55] from other provisions of the Bill of Rights addressed to more specific problems. But the contrast, as it seems to me, often implies an overstatement of the specificity or the immutability these other clauses really have — at least when problems under them arise.

No one would argue, for example, that there need not be indictment and a jury trial in prosecutions for a felony in district courts. What made a question of some difficulty was the issue whether service wives charged with the murders of their husbands overseas could be tried there before a military court. [56] Does the language of the double-jeopardy clause or its preconstitutional history actually help to decide whether a defendant tried for

---

[52] Principality of Monaco v. Mississippi, 292 U.S. 313, 322 (1934).

[53] HOLMES, *Holdsworth's English Law,* in COLLECTED LEGAL PAPERS 285, 290 (1920).

[54] Passenger Cases, 48 U.S. (7 How.) 283, 470 (1849).

[55] HAND, *op. cit. supra* note 3, at 30.

[56] See Reid v. Covert, 354 U.S. 1 (1957), *reversing on rehearing* 351 U.S. 487 (1956).

107

murder in the first degree and convicted of murder in the second, who wins a reversal of the judgment on appeal, may be tried again for murder in the first or only murder in the second? [57] Is there significance in the fact that it is "jeopardy of life or limb" that is forbidden, now that no one is in jeopardy of limb but only of imprisonment or fine? The right to "have the assistance of counsel" was considered, I am sure, when the sixth amendment was proposed, a right to defend by counsel if you have one, contrary to what was then the English law.[58] That does not seem to me sufficient to avert extension of its meaning to imply a right to court-appointed counsel when the defendant is too poor to find such aid [59] — though I admit that I once urged the point sincerely as a lawyer for the Government.[60] It is difficult for me to think the fourth amendment freezes for all time the common law of search and of arrest as it prevailed when the amendment was adopted, whatever the exigencies of police problems may now be or may become. Nor should we, in my view, lament the fact that "the" freedom of speech or press that Congress is forbidden by the first amendment to impair is not determined only by the scope such freedom had in the late eighteenth century, though the word "the" might have been taken to impose a limitation to the concept of that time — a time when, President Wright has recently reminded us, there was remarkable consensus about matters of this kind.[61]

Even "due process," on the other hand, might have been confined, as Mr. Justice Brandeis urged originally,[62] to a guarantee of fair procedure, coupled perhaps with prohibition of executive displacement of established law — the analogue for us of what

---

[57] See Green v. United States, 355 U.S. 184 (1957).

[58] "Throughout the eighteenth century counsel were allowed to speak in cases of treason and misdemeanour only." 1 STEPHEN, A HISTORY OF THE CRIMINAL LAW OF ENGLAND 453 (1883). See also ASSOCIATION OF THE BAR OF THE CITY OF NEW YORK & NATIONAL LEGAL AID & DEFENDERS ASS'N, EQUAL JUSTICE FOR THE ACCUSED 40–42 (1959).

[59] See Johnson v. Zerbst, 304 U.S. 458 (1938).

[60] Walker v. Johnston, 312 U.S. 275 (1941).

[61] WRIGHT, CONSENSUS AND CONTINUITY, 1776–1787 *passim* (1958). See also CHAFEE, HOW HUMAN RIGHTS GOT INTO THE CONSTITUTION (1952). For the suggestion that political consensus has been the abiding characteristic of American democracy, see HARTZ, THE LIBERAL TRADITION IN AMERICA 139–42 (1955).

[62] "Despite arguments to the contrary which had seemed to me persuasive, it is settled that the due process clause of the Fourteenth Amendment applies to matters of substantive law as well as to matters of procedure." Whitney v. California, 274 U.S. 357, 373 (1927) (concurring opinion).

the barons meant in Magna Carta. Equal protection could be taken as no more than an assurance that no one may be placed beyond the safeguards of the law, outlawing, as it were, the possibility of outlawry, but nothing else. Here too I cannot find it in my heart to regret that interpretation did not ground itself in ancient history but rather has perceived in these provisions a compendious affirmation of the basic values of a free society, values that must be given weight in legislation and administration at the risk of courting trouble in the courts.

So far as possible, to finish with my point, I argue that we should prefer to see the other clauses of the Bill of Rights read as an affirmation of the special values they embody rather than as statements of a finite rule of law, its limits fixed by the consensus of a century long past, with problems very different from our own. To read them in the former way is to leave room for adaptation and adjustment if and when competing values, also having constitutional dimension, enter on the scene.

Let me repeat what I have thus far tried to say. The courts have both the title and the duty when a case is properly before them to review the actions of the other branches in the light of constitutional provisions, even though the action involves value choices, as invariably action does. In doing so, however, they are bound to function otherwise than as a naked power organ; they participate as courts of law. This calls for facing how determinations of this kind can be asserted to have any legal quality. The answer, I suggest, inheres primarily in that they are — or are obliged to be — entirely principled. A principled decision, in the sense I have in mind, is one that rests on reasons with respect to all the issues in the case, reasons that in their generality and their neutrality transcend any immediate result that is involved. When no sufficient reasons of this kind can be assigned for overturning value choices of the other branches of the Government or of a state, those choices must, of course, survive. Otherwise, as Holmes said in his first opinion for the Court, "a constitution, instead of embodying only relatively fundamental rules of right, as generally understood by all English-speaking communities, would become the partisan of a particular set of ethical or economical opinions . . . ."[63]

The virtue or demerit of a judgment turns, therefore, entirely

---

[63] Otis v. Parker, 187 U.S. 606, 609 (1903).

on the reasons that support it and their adequacy to maintain any choice of values it decrees, or, it is vital that we add, to maintain the rejection of a claim that any given choice should be decreed. The critic's role, as T. R. Powell showed throughout so many fruitful years, is the sustained, disinterested, merciless examination of the reasons that the courts advance, measured by standards of the kind I have attempted to describe. I wish that more of us today could imitate his dedication to that task.

III. Some Appraisals of Review

One who has ventured to advance such generalities about the courts and constitutional interpretation is surely challenged to apply them to some concrete problems — if only to make clear that he believes in what he says. A lecture, to be sure, is a poor medium for such an undertaking, for the statement and analysis of cases inescapably takes time. Nonetheless, I feel obliged to make the effort and I trust that I can do so without trespassing on the indulgence you already have displayed.

Needless to say, I must rely on you to understand that in alluding to some areas of constitutional interpretation, selected for their relevancy to my thesis, I do not mean to add another capsulated estimate of the performance of our highest court to those that now are in such full supply. The Court in constitutional adjudications faces what must surely be the largest and the hardest task of principled decision-making faced by any group of men in the entire world. There is a difference worthy of articulation between purported evaluations of the Court and comments on decisions or opinions.

(1). — I start by noting two important fields of present interest in which the Court has been decreeing value choices in a way that makes it quite impossible to speak of principled determinations or the statement and evaluation of judicial reasons, since the Court has not disclosed the grounds on which its judgments rest.

The first of these involves the sequel to the *Burstyn* case,[64] in which, as you recall, the Court decided that the motion picture is a medium of expression included in the "speech" and "press" to which the safeguards of the first amendment, made applicable to the states by the fourteenth, apply. But *Burstyn* left open, as it was of course obliged to do, the extent of the protection that the

---

[64] Joseph Burstyn, Inc. v. Wilson, 343 U.S. 495 (1952).

movies are accorded, and even the question whether any censorship is valid, involving as it does prior restraint. The judgment rested, and quite properly, upon the vice inherent in suppression based upon a finding that the film involved was "sacrilegious" — with the breadth and vagueness that that term had been accorded in New York. "[W]hether a state may censor motion pictures under a clearly drawn statute designed and applied to prevent the showing of obscene films" was said to be "a very different question" not decided by the Court.[65] In five succeeding cases, decisions sustaining censorship of different films under standards variously framed have been reversed, but only by per curiam decisions. In one of these,[66] in which I should avow I was of counsel, the standard was undoubtedly too vague for any argument upon the merits. I find it hard to think that this was clearly so in all the others.[67] Given the subtlety and difficulty of the problem, the need and opportunity for clarifying explanation, are such unexplained decisions in a new domain of constitutional interpretation consonant with standards of judicial action that the Court or we can possibly defend? I realize that nine men often find it easier to reach agreement on result than upon reasons and that such a difficulty may be posed within this field. Is it not preferable, however, indeed essential, that if this is so the variations of position be disclosed? [68]

---

[65] *Id.* at 506.

[66] Gelling v. Texas, 343 U.S. 960, *reversing per curiam* 157 Tex. Crim. 516, 247 S.W.2d 95 (1952) (ordinance prohibited exhibition of picture deemed by Censorship Board "of such character as to be prejudicial to the best interests of the people" of Marshall, Texas, "if publicly shown").

[67] See Times Film Corp. v. City of Chicago, 355 U.S. 35, *reversing per curiam* 244 F.2d 432 (7th Cir. 1957); Holmby Prods., Inc. v. Vaughn, 350 U.S. 870, *reversing per curiam* 177 Kan. 728, 282 P.2d 412 (1955); Superior Films, Inc. v. Department of Educ., 346 U.S. 587 (1954), *reversing per curiam* 159 Ohio St. 315, 112 N.E.2d 311 (1953); Superior Films, Inc. v. Department of Educ., *supra*, *reversing per curiam* Commercial Pictures Corp. v. Board of Regents of the Univ. of N.Y., 305 N.Y. 336, 113 N.E.2d 502 (1953).

[68] Attention should be called to Kingsley Int'l Pictures Corp. v. Regents of the Univ. of N.Y., 360 U.S. 684 (1959), decided with full opinions since the present paper was delivered. The Court was unanimous in holding invalid New York's refusal to license the exhibition of a film based on D. H. Lawrence's *Lady Chatterley's Lover*. The opinion of the Court by Mr. Justice Stewart, deeming the censorship order to rest solely on the ground that the picture portrays an adulterous relationship as an acceptable pattern of behavior, held the statute so construed an unconstitutional impairment of freedom to disseminate ideas. Justices Black and Douglas joined in the opinion but in brief concurrences expressed their view that any prior restraint on motion pictures is as vulnerable as the censorship of

The second group of cases to which I shall call attention involves what may be called the progeny of the school-segregation ruling of 1954. Here again the Court has written on the merits of the constitutional issue posed by state segregation only once; [69] its subsequent opinions on the form of the decree [70] and the defiance in Arkansas [71] deal, of course, with other matters. The original opinion, you recall, was firmly focused on state segregation in the public schools, its reasoning accorded import to the nature of the educational process, and its conclusion was that separate educational facilities are "inherently unequal."

What shall we think then of the Court's extension of the ruling to other public facilities, such as public transportation, parks, golf courses, bath houses, and beaches, which no one is obliged to use — all by per curiam decisions? [72] That these situations present a weaker case against state segregation is not, of course, what I am saying. I am saying that the question whether it is stronger, weaker, or of equal weight appears to me to call for principled decision. I do not know, and I submit you cannot know, whether the per curiam affirmance in the *Dawson* case, involving public bath houses and beaches, embraced the broad opinion of the circuit court that all state-enforced racial segregation is invalid or approved only its immediate result and, if the latter, on what ground. Is this "process of law," to borrow the words Professor Brown has used so pointedly in writing of such unexplained decisions upon matters far more technical [73] — the process that

---

newspapers or books. Mr. Justice Frankfurter in one opinion and Mr. Justice Harlan in another, joined by Justices Frankfurter and Whittaker, conceived of the New York statute as demanding some showing of obscenity or of incitement to immorality and thought, therefore, that it escaped the condemnation of the majority opinion. In their view, however, the film could not be held to have embodied either obscenity or incitement. Hence, the statute was invalid as applied.

[69] Brown v. Board of Educ., 347 U.S. 483 (1954). See also Bolling v. Sharpe, 347 U.S. 497 (1954), dealing with segregation in the District of Columbia.

[70] Brown v. Board of Educ., 349 U.S. 294 (1955).

[71] Cooper v. Aaron, 358 U.S. 1 (1958).

[72] New Orleans City Park Improvement Ass'n v. Detiege, 358 U.S. 54, *affirming per curiam* 252 F.2d 122 (5th Cir. 1958); Gayle v. Browder, 352 U.S. 903, *affirming per curiam* 142 F. Supp. 707 (M.D. Ala. 1956); Holmes v. City of Atlanta, 350 U.S. 879, *reversing per curiam* 223 F.2d 93 (5th Cir. 1955); Mayor & City Council v. Dawson, 350 U.S. 877, *affirming per curiam* 220 F.2d 386 (4th Cir. 1955); Muir v. Louisville Park Theatrical Ass'n, 347 U.S. 971 (1954), *reversing per curiam* 202 F.2d 275 (6th Cir. 1953).

[73] Brown, *Foreword: Process of Law, The Supreme Court, 1957 Term*, 72 HARV. L. REV. 77 (1958).

alone affords the Court its title and its duty to adjudicate a claim that state action is repugnant to the Constitution?

Were I a prudent man I would, no doubt, confine myself to problems of this order, involving not the substance but the method of decision — for other illustrations might be cited in the same domain. I shall, however, pass beyond this to some areas of substantive interpretation which appear to me to illustrate my theme.

(2). — The phase of our modern constitutional development that I conceive we can most confidently deem successful inheres in the broad reading of the commerce, taxing, and related powers of the Congress, achieved with so much difficulty little more than twenty years ago — against restrictions in the name of state autonomy to which the Court had for a time turned such a sympathetic ear.

Why is it that the Court failed so completely in the effort to contain the scope of national authority and that today one reads decisions like *Hammer v. Dagenhart*,[74] or *Carter Coal*,[75] or the invalidation of the Agricultural Adjustment Act [76] with eyes that disbelieve? No doubt the answer inheres partly in the simple facts of life and the consensus they have generated on the powers that a modern nation needs. But is it not a feature of the case as well — a feature that has real importance — that the Court could not articulate an adequate analysis of the restrictions it imposed on Congress in favor of the states, whose representatives — upon an equal footing in the Senate — controlled the legislative process and had broadly acquiesced in the enactments that were subject to review?

Is it not also true and of importance that some of the principles the Court affirmed were strikingly deficient in neutrality, sustaining, for example, national authority when it impinged adversely upon labor, as in the application of the Sherman Act, but not when it was sought to be employed in labor's aid? On this score, the contrast in today's position certainly is striking. The power that sustained the Wagner Act is the same power that sustains Taft-Hartley — with its even greater inroads upon state autonomy but with restraints on labor that the Wagner Act did not impose.

One of the speculations that I must confess I find intriguing is upon the question whether there are any neutral principles that

---

[74] 247 U.S. 251 (1918).
[75] Carter v. Carter Coal Co., 298 U.S. 238 (1936).
[76] United States v. Butler, 297 U.S. 1 (1936).

might have been employed to mark the limits of the commerce power of the Congress in terms more circumscribed than the virtual abandonment of limits in the principle that has prevailed. Given the readiness of President Roosevelt to compromise on any basis that allowed achievement of the substance of his program, might not the formulae of coverage employed in the legislation of the Thirties have quite readily embraced any such principles the Court had then been able to devise before the crisis became so intense — principles sustaining action fairly equal to the need? I do not say we would or should be happier if that had happened and the Court still played a larger part within this area of our federalism, given the attention to state interests that is so inherent in the Congress and the constitutional provisions governing the selection and the composition of the Houses, which make that attention very likely to endure.[77]   I say only that I find such speculation interesting. You will recall that it was Holmes who deprecated argument of counsel the logic of which left "no part of the conduct of life with which on similar principles Congress might not interfere." [78]

(3). — The poverty of principled articulation of the limits put on Congress as against the states before the doctrinal reversal of the Thirties was surely also true of the decisions, dealing with the very different problem of the relationship between the individual and government, which invoked due process to maintain *laissez faire*. Did not the power of the great dissents inhere precisely in their demonstrations that the Court could not present an adequate analysis, in terms of neutral principles, to support the value choices it decreed? Holmes, to be sure, saw limits beyond which "the contract and due process clauses are gone"; and his insistence on the need for compensation to sustain a Pennsylvania prohibition of the exploitation of subsurface coal, threatening subsidence of a dwelling belonging to the owner of the surface land, indicates the kind of limit he perceived.[79] Am I simply voicing my own sympathies in saying that his analysis of those limits has a thrust entirely lacking in the old and now forgotten

---

[77] See Wechsler, *The Political Safeguards of Federalism: The Role of the States in the Composition and Selection of the National Government*, 54 COLUM. L. REV. 543 (1954), in FEDERALISM MATURE AND EMERGENT 97 (MacMahon ed. 1955).

[78] Northern Sec. Co. v. United States, 193 U.S. 197, 403 (1904) (dissenting opinion).

[79] Pennsylvania Coal Co. v. Mahon, 260 U.S. 393, 412 (1922).

judgments striking down minimum-wage and maximum-hour laws?

If I am right in this it helps to make a further point that has more bearing upon current issues, that I believe it misconceives the problem of the Court to state it as the question of the proper measure of judicial self-restraint, with the resulting issue whether such restraint is only proper in relation to protection of a purely economic interest or also in relation to an interest like freedom of speech or of religion, privacy, or discrimination (at least if it is based on race, origin, or creed). Of course, the courts ought to be cautious to impose a choice of values on the other branches or a state, based upon the Constitution, only when they are persuaded, on an adequate and principled analysis, that the choice is clear. That I suggest is all that self-restraint can mean and in that sense it always is essential, whatever issue may be posed. The real test inheres, as I have tried to argue, in the force of the analysis. Surely a stronger analysis may be advanced against a particular uncompensated taking as a violation of the fifth amendment than against a particular limitation of freedom of speech or press as a violation of the first.

In this view, the "preferred position" controversy hardly has a point — indeed, it never has been really clear what is asserted or denied to have a preference and over what.[80] Certainly the concept is pernicious if it implies that there is any simple, almost mechanistic basis for determining priorities of values having constitutional dimension, as when there is an inescapable conflict between claims to free press and a fair trial. It has a virtue, on the other hand, insofar as it recognizes that some ordering of social values is essential; that all cannot be given equal weight, if the Bill of Rights is to be maintained.

Did Holmes mean any less than this when he lamented the tendency "toward underrating or forgetting the safeguards in bills of rights that had to be fought for in their day and that still are worth fighting for"?[81] Only in that view could he have dissented in the *Abrams* and the *Gitlow* cases[82] and have struggled so intensely to develop a principled delineation of the freedom that he

---

[80] See, *e.g.*, Kovacs v. Cooper, 336 U.S. 77, 88 (1949).

[81] 2 HOLMES-POLLOCK LETTERS 25 (Howe ed. 1941); see 1 HOLMES-LASKI LETTERS 203, 529–30 (Howe ed. 1953); *cf.* 2 *id.* at 888.

[82] Abrams v. United States, 250 U.S. 616, 624 (1919); Gitlow v. New York, 268 U.S. 652, 672 (1925).

voted to sustain. Even if one thinks, as I confess I do, that his analysis does not succeed if it requires that an utterance designed to stimulate unlawful action must be accorded an immunity unless it is intended to achieve or creates substantial danger of *immediate* results,[83] can anyone deny it his respect? Is not the force of a position framed in terms of principles of the neutrality and generality that Holmes achieved entirely different from that of the main opinion, for example, in the *Sweezy* case,[84] resting at bottom as it does, on principles of power separation among the branches of state government that never heretofore have been conceived to be a federal requirement and that, we safely may predict, the Court will not apply to any other field?[85]

(4). — Finally, I turn to the decisions that for me provide the hardest test of my belief in principled adjudication, those in which the Court in recent years has vindicated claims that deprivations based on race deny the equality before the law that the fourteenth amendment guarantees. The crucial cases are, of course, those involving the white primary,[86] the enforcement of racially restrictive covenants,[87] and the segregated schools.[88]

The more I think about the past the more skeptical I find myself about predictions of the future. Viewed a priori would you not have thought that the invention of the cotton gin in 1792 should have reduced the need for slave labor and hence diminished the attractiveness of slavery? Brooks Adams tells us that its consequences were precisely the reverse; that the demand for slaves increased as cotton planting became highly lucrative, increased

---

[83] "I do not doubt for a moment that by the same reasoning that would justify punishing persuasion to murder, the United States constitutionally may punish speech that produces or is intended to produce a clear and imminent danger that it will bring about forthwith certain substantive evils that the United States constitutionally may seek to prevent." Abrams v. United States, 250 U.S. 616, 627 (1919). Is it possible, however, that persuasion to murder is only punishable constitutionally if the design is that the murder be committed "forthwith"? *Cf.* HAND, *op. cit. supra* note 3, at 58–59.

[84] Sweezy v. New Hampshire, 354 U.S. 234 (1957).

[85] See Uphaus v. Wyman, 360 U.S. 72, 77 (1959), decided after the present paper was delivered: "[S]ince questions concerning the authority of the committee to act as it did are questions of state law, . . . we accept as controlling the New Hampshire Supreme Court's conclusion that '[t]he legislative history makes it clear beyond a reasonable doubt that it [the Legislature] did and does desire an answer to these questions'."

[86] Smith v. Allwright, 321 U.S. 649 (1944).

[87] Shelley v. Kraemer, 334 U.S. 1 (1948); Barrows v. Jackson, 346 U.S. 249 (1953).

[88] Brown v. Board of Educ., 347 U.S. 483 (1954).

so greatly that Virginia turned from coal and iron, which George Washington envisaged as its future, into an enormous farm for breeding slaves — forty thousand of whom it exported annually to the rest of the South.[89] Only the other day I read that the Japanese evacuation, which I thought an abomination when it happened, though in the line of duty as a lawyer I participated in the effort to sustain it in the Court,[90] is now believed by many to have been a blessing to its victims, breaking down forever the ghettos in which they had previously lived.[91] But skeptical about predictions as I am, I still believe that the decisions I have mentioned — dealing with the primary, the covenant, and schools — have the best chance of making an enduring contribution to the quality of our society of any that I know in recent years. It is in this perspective that I ask how far they rest on neutral principles and are entitled to approval in the only terms that I acknowledge to be relevant to a decision of the courts.

The primary and covenant cases present two different aspects of a single problem — that it is a state alone that is forbidden by the fourteenth amendment to deny equal protection of the laws, as only a state or the United States is precluded by the fifteenth amendment from denying or abridging on the ground of race or color the right of citizens of the United States to vote. It has, of course, been held for years that the prohibition of action by the state reaches not only an explicit deprivation by a statute but also action of the courts or of subordinate officials, purporting to exert authority derived from public office.[92]

I deal first with the primary. So long as the Democratic Party in the South excluded Negroes from participation, in the exercise of an authority conferred by statute regulating political parties, it was entirely clear that the amendment was infringed; the exclusion involved an application of the statute.[93] The problem became difficult only when the states, responding to these judgments, repealed the statutes, leaving parties free to define their membership as private associations, protected by the state but not directed

[89] See B. Adams, *The Heritage of Henry Adams*, in H. Adams, The Degradation of the Democratic Dogma 22, 31 (1919).

[90] Korematsu v. United States, 323 U.S. 214 (1944).

[91] See Newsweek, Dec. 29, 1958, p. 23.

[92] See, *e.g.*, *Ex parte* Virginia, 100 U.S. 339, 347 (1880); Hale, Freedom Through Law ch. xi (1952).

[93] See Nixon v. Condon, 286 U.S. 73 (1932); Nixon v. Herndon, 273 U.S. 536 (1927).

or controlled or authorized by law. In this position the Court held in 1935 that an exclusion by the party was untouched by the amendment, being action of the individuals involved, not of the state or its officialdom.[94]

Then came the *Classic* case [95] in 1941, which I perhaps should say I argued for the Government. *Classic* involved a prosecution of election officials for depriving a voter of a right secured by the Constitution in willfully failing to count his vote as it was cast in a Louisiana Democratic primary. In holding that the right of a qualified voter to participate in choosing Representatives in Congress, a right conferred by article I, section 2,[96] extended to participating in a primary which influenced the ultimate selection, the Court did not, of course, deal with the scope of party freedom to select its members. The victim of the fraud in *Classic* was a member of the Democratic Party, voting in a primary in which he was entitled to participate, and the only one in which he could.[97] Yet three years later *Classic* was declared in *Smith v. Allwright* [98] to have determined in effect that primaries are a part of the election, with the consequence that parties can no more defend racial exclusion from their primaries than can the state, a result reaffirmed in 1953.[99] This is no doubt a settled proposition in the

---

[94] Grovey v. Townsend, 295 U.S. 45 (1935).

[95] United States v. Classic, 313 U.S. 299 (1941).

[96] "The House of Representatives shall be composed of Members chosen every second Year by the People of the several States, and the Electors in each State shall have the Qualifications requisite for Electors of the most numerous Branch of the State Legislature."

The seventeenth amendment contains similar provisions for the choice of Senators.

[97] The Government brief in *Classic* stated with respect to *Grovey*:

Moreover, what Article I, Section 2 secures is the right to choose. The implicit premise of the *Grovey* decision is that the negroes excluded from the Democratic primary were legally free to record their choice by joining an opposition party or by organizing themselves. In the present case the voters exercised the right to choose in accordance with the contemplated method; and the wrong alleged deprived them of an opportunity to express their choice in any other way.

Brief for the United States, pp. 34–35, United States v. Classic, 313 U.S. 299 (1941).

[98] 321 U.S. 649 (1944). Mr. Justice Frankfurter concurred only in the result. Mr. Justice Roberts alone dissented.

[99] Terry v. Adams, 345 U.S. 461 (1953). See also Rice v. Elmore, 165 F.2d 387 (4th Cir. 1947), *cert. denied*, 333 U.S. 875 (1948). There is no opinion of the Court in *Terry*. Justices Douglas and Burton joined in an opinion by Justice Black. Justice Frankfurter, saying that he found the case "by no means free of difficulty," wrote for himself. Chief Justice Vinson and Justices Reed and Jackson joined in an opinion by Justice Clark. Justice Minton dissented.

Court. But what it means is not, as sometimes has been thought, that a state may not escape the limitations of the Constitution merely by transferring public functions into private hands. It means rather that the constitutional guarantee against deprivation of the franchise on the ground of race or color has become a prohibition of party organization upon racial lines, at least where the party has achieved political hegemony. I ask with all sincerity if you are able to discover in the opinions thus far written in support of this result — a result I say again that I approve — neutral principles that satisfy the mind. I should suppose that a denial of the franchise on religious grounds is certainly forbidden by the Constitution. Are religious parties, therefore, to be taken as proscribed? I should regard this result too as one plainly to be desired but is there a constitutional analysis on which it can be validly decreed? Is it, indeed, not easier to project an analysis establishing that such a proscription would infringe rights protected by the first amendment?

The case of the restrictive covenant presents for me an even harder problem. Assuming that the Constitution speaks to state discrimination on the ground of race but not to such discrimination by an individual even in the use or distribution of his property, although his freedom may no doubt be limited by common law or statute, why is the enforcement of the private covenant a state discrimination rather than a legal recognition of the freedom of the individual? That the action of the state court is action of the state, the point Mr. Chief Justice Vinson emphasizes in the Court's opinion [100] is, of course, entirely obvious. What is not obvious, and is the crucial step, is that the state may properly be charged with the discrimination when it does no more than give effect to an agreement that the individual involved is, by hypothesis, entirely free to make. Again, one is obliged to ask: What is the principle involved? Is the state forbidden to effectuate a will that draws a racial line, a will that can accomplish any disposition only through the aid of law, or is it a sufficient answer there that the discrimination was the testator's and not the state's? [101] May not the state employ its law to vindicate the privacy of property against a trespasser, regardless of the grounds of his ex-

---

[100] See Shelley v. Kraemer, 334 U.S. 1, 14–23 (1948).

[101] *Cf.* Gordon v. Gordon, 332 Mass. 197, 210, 124 N.E.2d 228, 236, *cert. denied*, 349 U.S. 947 (1955).

clusion, or does it embrace the owner's reasons for excluding if it buttresses his power by the law? Would a declaratory judgment that a fee is determinable if a racially restrictive limitation should be violated represent discrimination by the state upon the racial ground? [102] Would a judgment of ejectment?

None of these questions has been answered by the Court nor are the problems faced in the opinions.[103] Philadelphia, to be sure, has been told that it may not continue to administer the school for "poor male white orphans," established by the city as trustee under the will of Stephen Girard, in accordance with that racial limitation.[104] All the Supreme Court said, however, was the following: "The Board which operates Girard College is an agency of the State of Pennsylvania. Therefore, even though the Board was acting as a trustee, its refusal to admit Foust and Felder to the college because they were Negroes was discrimination by the State. Such discrimination is forbidden by the Fourteenth Amendment." When the Orphans' Court thereafter dismissed the city as trustee, appointing individuals in substitution, its action was sustained in Pennsylvania.[105] Further review by certiorari was denied.[106]

One other case in the Supreme Court has afforded opportunity for reconsidering the basis and scope of the *Shelley* principle, *Black v. Cutter Labs.*[107] Here a collective-bargaining agreement was so construed that Communist Party membership was "just cause" for a discharge. In this view, California held that a worker was lawfully dismissed upon that ground. A Supreme Court majority concluded that this judgment involved nothing but interpretation of a contract, making irrelevant the standards that would govern the validity of a state statute that required the discharge. Only Mr. Chief Justice Warren and Justices Douglas and Black, dissenting, thought the principle of *Shelley v. Kraemer* was involved when the state court sustained the discharge.[108]

---

[102] See Charlotte Park & Recreation Comm'n v. Barringer, 242 N.C. 311, 88 S.E.2d 114 (1955), *cert. denied*, 350 U.S. 983 (1956).

[103] Mr. Chief Justice Vinson, dissenting in Barrows v. Jackson, 346 U.S. 249, 260 (1953), urged a distinction between enforcement of the covenant by injunction, the problem in *Shelley*, and an action for damages against a defaulting covenantor by a co-covenantor. He was alone in his dissent.

[104] Pennsylvania v. Board of Directors, 353 U.S. 230, 231 (1957).

[105] Girard College Trusteeship, 391 Pa. 434, 441-42, 138 A.2d 844, 846 (1958).

[106] Pennsylvania v. Board of Directors, 357 U.S. 570 (1958).

[107] 351 U.S. 292 (1956).

[108] Attention also should be called to Dorsey v. Stuyvesant Town Corp., 299

Many understandably would like to perceive in the primary and covenant decisions a principle susceptible of broad extension, applying to the other power aggregates in our society limitations of the kind the Constitution has imposed on government.[109] My colleague A. A. Berle, Jr., has, indeed, pointed to the large business corporation, which after all is chartered by the state and wields in many areas more power than the government, as uniquely suitable for choice as the next subject of such application.[110] I doubt that the courts will yield to such temptations; and I do not hesitate to say that I prefer to see the issues faced through legislation, where there is room for drawing lines that courts are not equipped to draw. If this is right the two decisions I have mentioned will remain, as they now are, *ad hoc* determinations of their narrow problems, yielding no neutral principles for their extension or support.

Lastly, I come to the school decision, which for one of my persuasion stirs the deepest conflict I experience in testing the thesis I propose. Yet I would surely be engaged in playing Hamlet without Hamlet if I did not try to state the problems that appear to me to be involved.

The problem for me, I hardly need to say, is not that the Court departed from its earlier decisions holding or implying that the equality of public educational facilities demanded by the Constitution could be met by separate schools. I stand with the long tradition of the Court that previous decisions must be subject to reexamination when a case against their reasoning is made. Nor is the problem that the Court disturbed the settled patterns of a portion of the country; even that must be accepted as a lesser evil than nullification of the Constitution. Nor is it that history does not confirm that an agreed purpose of the fourteenth amendment was to forbid separate schools or that there is important evidence

---

N.Y. 512, 87 N.E.2d 541 (1949), holding state action not involved in racial discrimination in the selection of tenants by the owner corporation, although the housing development involved had been constructed with the aid of New York City which, pursuant to a contract authorized by statute, had condemned the land for the corporation and granted substantial tax exemptions. Certiorari was denied, 339 U.S. 981 (1950), Justices Black and Douglas noting their dissent.

[109] See, *e.g.*, Ming, *Racial Restrictions and the Fourteenth Amendment: The Restrictive Covenant Cases*, 16 U. CHI. L. REV. 203, 235–38 (1949).

[110] See, *e.g.*, Berle, *Constitutional Limitations on Corporate Activity — Protection of Personal Rights From Invasion Through Economic Power*, 100 U. PA. L. REV. 933, 948–51 (1952); BERLE, ECONOMIC POWER AND THE FREE SOCIETY 17–18 (Fund for the Republic 1957).

that many thought the contrary; [111] the words are general and leave room for expanding content as time passes and conditions change. Nor is it that the Court may have miscalculated the extent to which its judgment would be honored or accepted; it is not a prophet of the strength of our national commitment to respect the judgments of the courts. Nor is it even that the Court did not remit the issue to the Congress, acting under the enforcement clause of the amendment. That was a possible solution, to be sure, but certainly Professor Freund is right [112] that it would merely have evaded the claims made.

The problem inheres strictly in the reasoning of the opinion, an opinion which is often read with less fidelity by those who praise it than by those by whom it is condemned. The Court did not declare, as many wish it had, that the fourteenth amendment forbids all racial lines in legislation, though subsequent per curiam decisions may, as I have said, now go that far. Rather, as Judge Hand observed,[113] the separate-but-equal formula was not overruled "in form" but was held to have "no place" in public education on the ground that segregated schools are "inherently unequal," with deleterious effects upon the colored children in implying their inferiority, effects which retard their educational and mental development. So, indeed, the district court had found as a fact in the Kansas case, a finding which the Supreme Court embraced, citing some further "modern authority" in its support.[114]

Does the validity of the decision turn then on the sufficiency of evidence or of judicial notice to sustain a finding that the separation harms the Negro children who may be involved? There were, indeed, some witnesses who expressed that opinion in the Kansas case,[115] as there were also witnesses in the companion Virginia case, including Professor Garrett of Columbia,[116] whose

---

[111] See Bickel, *The Original Understanding and the Segregation Decision*, 69 HARV. L. REV. 1 (1955).

[112] See Freund, *Storm Over the American Supreme Court*, 21 MODERN L. REV. 345, 351 (1958).

[113] HAND, *op. cit. supra* note 3, at 54.

[114] For a detailed account of the character and quality of research in this field, see Note, *Grade School Segregation: The Latest Attack on Racial Discrimination*, 61 YALE L.J. 730 (1952).

[115] See Record, pp. 125–26, 132 (Hugh W. Speer), Brown v. Board of Educ., 347 U.S. 483 (1954); *id.* at 164–65 (Wilbur B. Brookover); *id.* at 170–71 (Louisa Holt); *id.* at 176–79 (John J. Kane).

[116] See Record, pp. 548–55, 568–72 (Henry E. Garrett), Davis v. County Bd. of Educ., 347 U.S. 483 (1954).

view was to the contrary. Much depended on the question that the witness had in mind, which rarely was explicit. Was he comparing the position of the Negro child in a segregated school with his position in an integrated school where he was happily accepted and regarded by the whites; or was he comparing his position under separation with that under integration where the whites were hostile to his presence and found ways to make their feelings known? And if the harm that segregation worked was relevant, what of the benefits that it entailed: sense of security, the absence of hostility? Were they irrelevant? Moreover, was the finding in Topeka applicable without more to Clarendon County, South Carolina, with 2,799 colored students and only 295 whites? Suppose that more Negroes in a community preferred separation than opposed it? Would that be relevant to whether they were hurt or aided by segregation as opposed to integration? Their fates would be governed by the change of system quite as fully as those of the students who complained.

I find it hard to think the judgment really turned upon the facts. Rather, it seems to me, it must have rested on the view that racial segregation is, in principle, a denial of equality to the minority against whom it is directed; that is, the group that is not dominant politically and, therefore, does not make the choice involved. For many who support the Court's decision this assuredly is the decisive ground. But this position also presents problems. Does it not involve an inquiry into the motive of the legislature, which is generally foreclosed to the courts? [117] Is it alternatively defensible to make the measure of validity of legislation the way it is interpreted by those who are affected by it? In the context of a charge that segregation *with equal facilities* is a denial of equality, is there not a point in *Plessy* in the statement that if "enforced separation stamps the colored race with a badge of inferiority" it is solely because its members choose "to put that construction upon it"? [118] Does enforced separation of the sexes discriminate against females merely because it may be the females who resent it and it is imposed by judgments predominantly male?

---

[117] Motive is open to examination when executive action is challenged as discriminatory, but there the purpose is to show that an admitted inequality of treatment was not inadvertent. See, *e.g.*, Snowden v. Hughes, 321 U.S. 1 (1944). Even in such a case, invidious motivation alone has not been held to establish the inequality.

[118] Plessy v. Ferguson, 163 U.S. 537, 551 (1896).

Is a prohibition of miscegenation a discrimination against the colored member of the couple who would like to marry?

For me, assuming equal facilities, the question posed by state-enforced segregation is not one of discrimination at all. Its human and its constitutional dimensions lie entirely elsewhere, in the denial by the state of freedom to associate, a denial that impinges in the same way on any groups or races that may be involved. I think, and I hope not without foundation, that the Southern white also pays heavily for segregation, not only in the sense of guilt that he must carry but also in the benefits he is denied. In the days when I was joined with Charles H. Houston in a litigation in the Supreme Court, before the present building was constructed, he did not suffer more than I in knowing that we had to go to Union Station to lunch together during the recess. Does not the problem of miscegenation show most clearly that it is the freedom of association that at bottom is involved, the only case, I may add, where it is implicit in the situation that association is desired by the only individuals involved? I take no pride in knowing that in 1956 the Supreme Court dismissed an appeal in a case in which Virginia nullified a marriage on this ground, a case in which the statute had been squarely challenged by the defendant, and the Court, after remanding once, dismissed per curiam on procedural grounds that I make bold to say are wholly without basis in the law.[119]

But if the freedom of association is denied by segregation, integration forces an association upon those for whom it is unpleasant or repugnant. Is this not the heart of the issue involved, a conflict in human claims of high dimension, not unlike many others that involve the highest freedoms — conflicts that Professor Sutherland has recently described.[120] Given a situation where the state must practically choose between denying the association to those individuals who wish it or imposing it on those who would avoid it, is there a basis in neutral principles for holding that the Constitution demands that the claims for association should prevail? I should like to think there is, but I confess that I have not yet written the opinion. To write it is for me the challenge of the school-segregation cases.

---

[119] See Ham Say Naim v. Naim, 197 Va. 80, 87 S.E.2d 749, *vacated*, 350 U.S. 891 (1955), *on remand*, 197 Va. 734, 90 S.E.2d 849, *appeal dismissed*, 350 U.S. 985 (1956).

[120] See SUTHERLAND, THE LAW AND ONE MAN AMONG MANY 35–62 (1956).

Having said what I have said, I certainly should add that I offer no comfort to anyone who claims legitimacy in defiance of the courts. This is the ultimate negation of all neutral principles, to take the benefits accorded by the constitutional system, including the national market and common defense, while denying it allegiance when a special burden is imposed. That certainly is the antithesis of law.

———————————

I am confident I have said much with which you disagree — both in my basic premises and in conclusions I have drawn. The most that I can hope is that the effort be considered worthy of a rostrum dedicated to the memory of Mr. Justice Holmes. Transcending all the lessons that he teaches through the years, the most important one for me has come to this: Those of us to whom it is not given to "live greatly in the law" are surely called upon to fail in the attempt.

University of Pennsylvania Law Review

FOUNDED 1852

Formerly

American Law Register

| VOL. 108 | NOVEMBER, 1959 | No. 1 |

RACIAL DISCRIMINATION AND JUDICIAL INTEGRITY: A REPLY TO PROFESSOR WECHSLER [*]

LOUIS H. POLLAK [†]

To the great and on-going public debate on the proper scope of judicial review, notable contributions have been forthcoming from two distinguished students of the Supreme Court who have, last year and this, delivered the annual Holmes Lecture at Harvard. The first of these contributions is Learned Hand's eloquent essay "The Bill of Rights." [1] The second, partly responsive to Judge Hand and partly building upon him, is Herbert Wechsler's characteristically provocative and thoughtful paper, "Toward Neutral Principles of Constitutional Law." [2] In insisting on neutral constitutional adjudication, Professor

[*] This Article was largely written during the past summer, when the writer was privileged to participate in a Seminar on Legal Sanctions in Desegregation Cases, conducted by the University of Wisconsin Law School, with the support of the Ford Foundation. The seminar dealt, at least tangentially, with a number of the problems considered here, and some of the thinking which underlies this essay was shaped by the provocative and friendly interchange among the members of the seminar: G. W. Foster, Jr., Professor of Law at the University of Wisconsin and skillful ringmaster of the seminar; Harry Ball, Professor of Sociology at Pomona; Paul Mishkin, Professor of Law at the University of Pennsylvania; Paul Sanders, Professor of Law at Vanderbilt; George Simpson, Professor of Anthropology and Sociology at Oberlin; and Melvin Tunin, Professor of Sociology at Princeton. This Article also draws upon extremely rewarding conversations with J. Willard Hurst and Samuel Mermin, Professors of Law at the University of Wisconsin, and with several of the writer's colleagues at Yale.

[†] Associate Professor of Law, Yale University Law School. A.B., 1943, Harvard University; LL.B. 1948, Yale University.

[1] Printed in book form as HAND, THE BILL OF RIGHTS (1958) (hereinafter cited as HAND).

[2] Printed in the current issue of the Harvard Law Review at 73 HARV. L. REV. 1 (1959) (hereinafter cited as *Wechsler*).

(1)

Wechsler blueprints a sound theoretical structure of reasoned and dispassionate judicial review. But he singles out as prime examples of judicial unneutrality the major recent Supreme Court decisions in the field of race discrimination, culminating in the Court's consideration of segregation in the public schools. Because the decisions Professor Wechsler challenges doubtless comprise the most significant judicial restatement of our national policy in the past century, it seems important to consider whether the decisions are not in fact valid exercises of the power of judicial review.

Professor Wechsler begins his paper by delineating the differences between his position and that of Judge Hand. Judge Hand, it will be recalled, expounds the thesis that the Supreme Court's power to review the constitutionality of acts of other branches of national and state government is not one which can be found in or fairly inferred from the words of the Constitution. But the power of keeping government officials within their prescribed limits was one which, Judge Hand believes, the Court had to assume nonetheless: the absence of such a power would have invited anarchy, and "in construing written documents it has always been thought proper to engraft upon the text such provisions as are necessary to prevent the failure of the undertaking." [3] What this doctrine implies, however, is merely an authority, to be exercised as sparingly as possible, to confine officials to actions within their realms of assigned responsibility, but *never* an authority to review the substance of such actions. In arrogating to itself the latter authority —especially in measuring federal and state laws against the broad strictures of the fifth and fourteenth amendments—the Supreme Court has illicitly and undemocratically assumed the role of a "third legislative chamber." [4]

With Judge Hand's view of the propriety and scope of the Supreme Court's power of judicial review, Professor Wechsler takes profound issue. Like Marshall in *Marbury v. Madison*,[5] Professor Wechsler sees the power of judicial review as one authenticated, and indeed required, by the supremacy clause of the Constitution.[6] Judge Hand found the supremacy clause an insufficient source of power, arguing indeed that the specific mandate to *state* courts to defer to supreme federal law in the event of conflict "looks rather against than in favor of a general

---

[3] HAND 29.

[4] *Id.* at 55.

[5] 5 U.S. (1 Cranch) 137 (1803).

[6] U.S. CONST. art. VI, § 2: "This Constitution, and the Laws of the United States which shall be made in Pursuance thereof; and all Treaties made, or which shall be made, under the Authority of the United States, shall be the supreme Law of the Land; and the Judges in every State shall be bound thereby, any Thing in the Constitution or Laws of any State to the Contrary notwithstanding."

jurisdiction." [7] But Professor Wechsler pointedly demonstrates that the logic of this particular negative pregnant has most uncomfortable implications: it either denies to the Supreme Court, when processing appeals from state courts, the right to re-examine the constitutional determinations made by the state courts at the behest of the supremacy clause, or, perhaps even more paradoxically, it affirms the power of judicial review as an ingredient of the Supreme Court's appellate jurisdiction over state courts while denying it in appeals from the lower federal courts and in those lower federal courts themselves. [8]

Positing the clear propriety of the power of judicial review—rather than giving it, after Judge Hand's fashion, a left-handed welcome as the twilight child of a doctrine of necessity—Professor Wechsler asserts that its full exercise in cases within the Supreme Court's jurisdiction is not dependent, as Judge Hand would have it, on "how importunately the occasion demands an answer," [9] but is a matter of obligation. [10]

From all this it follows that the power of judicial review cannot be confined, as Judge Hand none too hopefully seems to urge, to the job of charting "the frontiers of another 'Department's' authority" rather than reviewing "the propriety of its choices within those frontiers." [11] Professor Wechsler's acceptance of the full sweep of judicial review carries with it acquiescence in the Supreme Court's scrutiny of the substantive acts challenged as in conflict with constitutional limita-

---

[7] HAND 28.

[8] At this point in the argument, one who agrees with Professor Wechsler that the Constitution does imply a system of judicial review is impelled, nevertheless, to enter a partial demurrer to an analysis which overpowers but does not fully persuade. Indeed, it is an analysis so virulent as, by inversion, to undermine the Supreme Court's asserted power to review state courts: if it is anachronistic to posit a supreme federal tribunal sitting in review of state courts whose power to review federal questions is not as broad as the obligation of the state courts to consider such questions below, the anachronism casts as much doubt on the appellate relationship—which is not spelled out in the Constitution—as on the claimed disparity of power to consider certain federal questions. The essential difficulty is that Professor Wechsler's quasi-textual construct implies a purposive symmetry in the minds of the framers which might better have expressed itself in some explicit avowal of the powerful role to be played by the federal courts. Such avowal of the power of judicial review does not appear in the text of the Constitution. But, as Professor Wechsler indeed seems to acknowledge, the public expectation of Hamilton and others that the courts would utter the last word on constitutional questions seems an adequate basis for sustaining the authenticity of judicial review. Certainly it is a less taxing, if less ingenious, basis than Professor Wechsler's potent syllogism.

[9] HAND 15.

[10] *Wechsler* 6. Professor Wechsler of course takes careful note of limitations on the exercise of this obligation: *e.g.*, the "political question" doctrine, which he sees as part of the Constitution's basic distribution of authority; and the discretion, embodied in certiorari practice, deliberately confided to the Court to allow it largely to determine the character and sequence of the great public questions it adjudicates.

[11] HAND 29-30.

tions. But Professor Wechsler insists, and properly so, that this revisory power does not make the Supreme Court a "third legislative chamber" if the Court employs appropriately dispassionate standards. For judges charged with the task of judicial review must take their value spectrum from the Constitution and eschew the multitudinous and far more transient personal policy preferences which legislators can and should act upon.

Here indeed lies the heart of Professor Wechsler's thesis—insistence on the rational and disinterested application of constitutional norms to all comparable controversies. This is the recipe for a

> "principled decision . . . one that rests on reasons with respect to all the issues in the case, reasons that in their generality and then neutrality transcend any immediate result that is involved. When no sufficient reasons of this kind can be assigned for overturning value choices of the other branches of the Government or of a state, those choices must, of course, survive. Otherwise, as Holmes said in his first opinion for the Court, 'a constitution, instead of embodying only relatively fundamental rules of right, as generally understood by all English-speaking communities, would become the partisan of a particular set of ethical or economical opinions. . . .' " [12]

With this central thesis no quarrel should be forthcoming. No quarrel, that is, except from those whose legal litmus paper is sensitive to the identity of the litigant rather than the merits of his cause. But for those whose Constitution is grounded in accepted canons of judicial integrity, acquiescence in Professor Wechsler's neutral principles would seem automatic. As Justice Frankfurter observed a decade ago in *Terminiello,* when chastising his brethren of the majority for making a federal case out of a sow's ear: "This is a court of review, not a tribunal unbounded by rules. We do not sit like a kadi under a tree dispensing justice according to considerations of individual expediency." [13]

With insistence on adjudication by neutral principle as his point of departure, Professor Wechsler turns to the formulation of a bill of particulars—asserted failures by the Court in the recent past to do its job of principled adjudication. And for a time he is on firm ground. Thus, the Court certainly seems to merit censure when it summarily disposes of important and difficult questions—for example, *Gayle v.*

---

[12] *Wechsler* 19.

[13] Terminiello v. Chicago, 337 U.S. 1, 11 (1949). The Court there by-passed an extremely difficult free-speech issue—found a very tractable one—by pouncing on an "error" never urged by petitioner in the state courts or in the Supreme Court. See BERNS, FREEDOM, VIRTUE AND THE FIRST AMENDMENT 113-15 (1957); Pollak, *Mr. Justice Frankfurter—Judgment and the Fourteenth Amendment,* 68 YALE L.J. 304, 310 (1958).

Browder,[14] invalidating segregation on intrastate buses—via the inscrutable per curiam. This is a method of adjudication which, as Professor Wechsler succinctly puts it, "makes it quite impossible to speak of principled determinations or the statement and evaluation of judicial reasons, since the Court has not disclosed the grounds on which its judgments rest."[15]   And Ernest Brown has made persuasive demonstration that the method is one to which the Court is showing signs of addiction.[16]

The point at which Professor Wechsler invites serious controversy is when he shifts from the Court's sins of omission to what he regards as its sins of commission.   Here he singles out three crucial instances in which the Court has recently found race discrimination incompatible with the Constitution—the white primary, the restrictive covenant, and segregated public schools—and contends that none of these is based "on neutral principles and . . . entitled to approval in the only terms . . . relevant to a decision of the courts."[17]   Plainly enough all of these milestone judgments have elicited in certain quarters the most vigorous kind of public criticism.   But very little criticism has been forthcoming from those who believe, with Professor Wechsler, that these cases "have the best chance of making an enduring contribution to the quality of our society of any . . . in recent years."[18]   His undisguised hostility to the discriminations there uprooted lends impressive weight to his doubts that the decisions are supportable. Conversely, the purity of his doubts imposes on those who have thought the decisions proper a special burden of reappraisal.

To make such a reappraisal is the main purpose of this essay. No attempt is here made to dissect Professor Wechsler's concept of neutrality of constitutional adjudication.   Quite the contrary: this essay accepts that concept on the assumption that what Professor Wechsler has in mind is exorcising, once and for all, "the kadi . . . dispensing justice according to considerations of individual expediency." But it may be, as is suggested at the close of this paper, that Professor Wechsler is really hunting larger game.   In that event, the careful scrutiny his theme of neutrality deserves must be undertaken elsewhere. It does not lend itself easily to the immediate objective, which is to review the momentous decisions Professor Wechsler is doubtful of.

---

[14] 352 U.S. 903, *affirming* 142 F. Supp. 707 (D. Ala. 1956).
[15] *Wechsler* 20.
[16] Brown, *Process of Law*, 72 Harv. L. Rev. 77 (1958); *cf.* Bickel & Wellington, *Legislative Purpose and the Judicial Process: The Lincoln Mills Case*, 71 Harv. L. Rev. 1 (1957).   Comment, 26 U. Chi. L. Rev. 279 (1959).
[17] *Wechsler* 27.
[18] *Ibid.*

RESTRICTIVE COVENANTS

In *Shelley v. Kraemer,*[19] the question was whether state courts could, consistently with the equal protection clause, compel Negro purchasers to vacate homes sold to them in contravention of racially restrictive covenants. The Court acknowledged that the fourteenth amendment curbs state authority as such, not private bigotry, and hence neither "the restrictive agreements standing alone" nor "voluntary adherence to their terms" presented any constitutional question.[20] The constitutional vice lay in judicial enforcement of the covenants; through their courts "the States have made available to . . . individuals the full coercive power of government to deny to petitioners, on the grounds of race or color, the enjoyment of property rights . . . ."[21]

Imputing Private Prejudice to the States

Professor Wechsler has no difficulty with the thought that court action is "state action" for fourteenth amendment purposes. What troubles him is the logic underlying "the crucial step . . . that the state may properly be charged with the discrimination when it does no more than give effect to an agreement that the individual involved is, by hypothesis, entirely free to make."[22]

So formulated, the query posed by Professor Wechsler seems reasonable enough, and it assuredly is not put to rest by anything said in Chief Justice Vinson's opinion for the unanimous Court. But the very simplicity of the words in which the query is phrased may obscure the point at which analysis of the problem can profitably begin.

To say that the state, through one of its agencies, "does no more than give effect to an agreement," carries with it the pleasing sense of automation; asked to enforce a hypothetically valid private arrangement, a court has no option but to respond. And thus the state is insulated from responsibility for a course of action it has no hand in initiating.

A few moments' reflection should serve to clarify the reasons for attributing to the state responsibility for the private policies its courts elect to implement. A question posed by Professor Wechsler may serve as a convenient point of departure:

"Is the state forbidden to effectuate a will that draws a racial line, a will that can accomplish any disposition only through the aid of

---

[19] 334 U.S. 1 (1948); *cf.* Hurd v. Hodge, 334 U.S. 24 (1948).
[20] 334 U.S. at 13.
[21] *Id.* at 19.
[22] *Wechsler* 29.

law, or is it a sufficient answer there that the discrimination was the testator's and not the state's? [Citing *Gordon v. Gordon*]." [23]

The *Gordon* case was one of those unhappy internecine struggles to which our testamentary structure so often lends itself—an action by four sisters to terminate their brother's interest in the paternal estate because the brother, in contravention of father's will, had married a young lady so improvident as to be the issue of Catholic parents and hence "a person not born in the Hebrew faith." By way of defense, young Gordon urged, *inter alia*, that to enforce the limitation contained in his father's will was a restraint on religious freedom and inconsistent with other guarantees implicit and explicit in the fourteenth amendment. Cited in support of the argument were the restrictive covenant cases and the school segregation cases. But the Massachusetts Supreme Judicial Court concluded that those cases "involve quite different considerations from the right to dispose of property by will." [24]   And the Supreme Court denied certiorari. [25]

But before reaching the constitutional issue the Massachusetts court had dwelt at rather great length on the "contention . . . that a restriction conditioned upon the religious faith of the parents of the prospective wife at the time of her birth is unreasonable." [26]   The issue was regarded as a new one in Massachusetts, but in reliance on foreign jurisdictions, particularly a line of New York decisions, the court concluded that the provision was a valid one. "The question is not whether the testator used good judgment . . . in his will or whether we should approve or disapprove his action. What we have to decide is whether he was prevented from doing as he did by a rule of law. We are unable to discover that he was." [27]

The New York cases relied on had indeed uniformly sustained provisions of the kind at issue in *Gordon*—although (as the Massachusetts court observed but did not embroider on) "in each case . . . the court found a way to prevent the forfeiture of the estate." [28]   As summarized by Judge Lehman twenty years ago, the New York rule is as follows:

"A condition calculated to induce a beneficiary to marry, even to marry in a manner desired by the testator, is not against public policy. A condition calculated to induce a beneficiary to live in

---

[23] *Ibid. Gordon v. Gordon* may be found in 332 Mass. 197, 124 N.E.2d 228, *cert. denied,* 349 U.S. 947 (1955).
[24] 332 Mass. at 208, 124 N.E.2d at 235.
[25] 349 U.S. 947 (1955).
[26] 332 Mass. at 207, 124 N.E.2d at 234.
[27] 332 Mass. at 207-8, 124 N.E.2d at 234.
[28] 332 Mass. at 207, 124 N.E.2d at 234.

celibacy or adultery is against public policy. . . . Conditions in partial restraint of marriage, which merely impose reasonable restrictions upon marriage, are not against public policy." [29]

Thus, in the recent *Rosenthal* litigation, Surrogate Collins bowed to the ineluctable New York rule:

"The petitioner's situation commands the court's sympathy. It is unfortunate that she cannot have both a marriage with the man of her choice *and* the inheritance. Present are considerations which tug at the heart but do not resolve the legal queries propounded by the petition. Undeniably, Article Twelfth is discriminatory but to discriminate in the disposition of property is frequently the motivation of a will. A testator 'may exclude a child or other descendant from any participation in his estate for sound reason, or because of whim or prejudice which might seem unreasonable to others' . . . . The court is compelled to uphold the manifest intent of the testator's will. The determination was written into that will and is binding on the petitioner." [30]

As it turned out, Surrogate Collins did have some flexibility as to how to construe Mr. Rosenthal's will—or so, at least, a divided Appellate Division and a divided Court of Appeals concluded, parsing the document with a generosity adequate to permit petitioner to "have both a marriage with the man of her choice *and* the inheritance." [31] Surrogate Collins was right, however, in his view that as a trial judge he had no leeway to reject or modify the law of New York framed for him by the Court of Appeals. But the strictures which bind Surrogate Collins did not inhibit Judge Lehman and do not inhibit those who today compose New York's—or Massachusetts'—highest tribunal. As Judge Lehman made plain, the reasonableness—and hence the validity —of challenged testamentary limitations turns on the "public policy" of the state as that policy is fashioned and refashioned by its appellate judges. When the New York Court of Appeals decides that it will enforce a will designed to encourage Jew to marry Jew, or Catholic to marry Catholic, but that it will turn its stony judicial face against a testamentary provision "calculated to induce a beneficiary to live in celibacy" (a lawful and honorable status in most jurisdictions), the

---

[29] Matter of Liberman, 279 N.Y. 458, 464, 18 N.E.2d 658, 660 (1939).

[30] *In re* Rosenthal's Estate, 204 Misc. 432, 440, 123 N.Y.S.2d 326, 335 (Surr. Ct. 1953). *But cf.* Cardozo: "Judges march at times to pitiless conclusions under the prod of remorseless logic which is supposed to leave them no alternative. They deplore the sacrificial rite. They perform it, none the less, with averted gaze, convinced as they plunge the knife that they obey the bidding of their office. The victim is offered up to the gods of jurisprudence on the altar of regularity." CARDOZO, THE GROWTH OF THE LAW 66 (1924).

[31] 283 App. Div. 316, 127 N.Y.S.2d 778, *aff'd,* 307 N.Y. 715, 121 N.E.2d 539 (1954).

court is choosing a policy and acting upon it. Moreover, frequent expressions of judicial distaste for the discriminatory arrangements reluctantly sustained do nothing to lessen their impact. "[T]he undertones of the opinion . . . seem utterly discordant with its conclusion. . . . The case which irresistibly comes to mind as the most fitting precedent is that of Julia, who, according to Byron's reports, 'whispering "I will ne'er consent,"—consented.' " [32]

What has been said has of course no claim to novelty. But, at the risk of laboring the obvious, the nature of judicial choice—of sovereign choice voiced by the courts—has been rehearsed as a reminder of what Holmes observed half a century ago: "Law is a statement of the circumstances in which the public force will be brought to bear upon men through the courts." [33]   It is the disposition of this "public force" which is really at issue when a court propounds the misleading neutralism, "What we have to decide is whether he was prevented from doing as he did by any rule of law." [34]   What the court has to decide is whether to *enforce*—to bring the "public force" to bear in behalf of—the testament or covenant which the draftsman was entirely free to commit to paper and which those within range of the instrument were entirely free to adhere to of their own volition. And when the arrangements contemplated by the instrument will fail but for the intervention of "public force"—when "it becomes not respondent's voluntary choice but the State's choice that she observe her covenant or suffer damages" [35] —the limitations of the fourteenth amendment come into play.

From Buchanan v. Warley to Shelley v. Kraemer

Of course, a finding of the requisite state action does not doom the challenged discrimination. The existence of state action is a threshold problem, and with "this hurdle cleared" there remains "the ultimate substantive question, whether in the circumstances of this case the action complained of was condemned by the Fourteenth Amendment. . . ." [36]   But in the case of the racial covenant, that "ultimate substantive question"—the absence of governmental power to put Negroes in one part of town and whites in another—had been determined by the Supreme Court long before in *Buchanan v. Warley.*[37]   To be sure, the unanimous decision voiding the Louisville zoning ordinance

---

[32] Everson v. Board of Education, 330 U.S. 1, 19 (1946) (dissenting opinion of Jackson, J.).

[33] American Banana Co. v. United Fruit Co., 213 U.S. 347, 356 (1909).

[34] Gordon v. Gordon, 332 Mass. 197, 207-08, 124 N.E.2d 228, 234 (1955).

[35] Barrows v. Jackson, 346 U.S. 249, 254 (1953).

[36] Rice v. Sioux City Memorial Park Cemetery, 349 U.S. 70, 72 (1955).

[37] 245 U.S. 60 (1917).

was apparently put upon due process grounds [38] rather than upon equal protection to which the Court turned in *Shelley v. Kraemer.* Why the opinion in *Buchanan v. Warley* took the shape it did is not hard to conjecture; for one thing, the equal protection clause still bore the relatively fresh gloss of the "separate but equal" doctrine [39] which might have been thought to support the even-handed injustice of the ordinance; for another, the protagonist of the fourteenth amendment was the white seller disabled from selling to a Negro, and arguably he lacked standing to talk in equal protection terms.[40] Also, it bears remembering that *Buchanan,* decided in 1917, was the product of a judicial climate quite receptive to the conclusion that a challenged economic regulation "was not a legitimate exercise of the police power of the state." [41] Surely an equal protection approach would have been more apposite, and, indeed, would have been the approach actually employed had the case arisen a generation later. Passing the question which section of the fourteenth amendment *Buchanan* should have turned on, the point vital to the validity of *Buchanan* (and, derivatively, of *Shelley*) is that the elimination of racial criteria in land acquisition and tenure was one of the few relatively clear purposes of the proponents of the fourteenth amendment. So much Justice Day made abundantly plain in *Buchanan,* relying on a statute of 1866,—the year the amendment was adopted by Congress—giving all "citizens, of every race and color . . . the same right in every State and Territory . . . to make and enforce contracts, to sue, be parties, and give evidence, to inherit, purchase, lease, sell, hold and convey real and personal property . . . as is enjoyed by white citizens. . . ." [42] The fourteenth amendment has come to the aid of many—from corporations to Communists—whom its framers may have had no special interest in; certainly in those instances where the framers' protective purpose is

---

[38] See Bolling v. Sharpe, 347 U.S. 497, 499 (1954).

[39] Plessy v. Ferguson, 163 U.S. 537 (1896).

[40] *But cf.* Barrows v. Jackson, 346 U.S. 249 (1953).

[41] Buchanan v. Warley, 245 U.S. 60, 82 (1917). *Cf.* Bolling v. Sharpe, 347 U.S. 497, 500 (1954): "Segregation in public education is not reasonably related to any proper governmental objective. . . ."

[42] Civil Rights Act of 1866, ch. 31, 14 Stat. 27. The statute, which was § 1 of the Civil Rights Act of 1866, also declared all persons other than untaxed Indians born in the United States "to be citizens of the United States." The statute was re-enacted as part of the Civil Rights Act of 1870, ch. 114, 16 Stat. 140, two years after the amendment's ratification, lending point to the Court's observation in Oyama v. California, 332 U.S. 633, 640 (1948), that it was "enacted before the Fourteenth Amendment but vindicated by it." Today the statute is to be found divided among two separate but companion code provisions, Rev. Stat. §§ 1977-78 (1875), 42 U.S.C. §§ 1981-82 (1952).

The phrasing of the statute in terms of rights of citizenship is suggestive of a kinship with the privileges and immunities clause of the fourteenth amendment, rather than with the much more vigorously applied due process and equal protection clauses. Of course the emasculation of the privileges and immunities clause long antedated *Buchanan v. Warley.*

tolerably clear, there is, in the hallowed phrase, both "reason and authority" for giving it effect.

So much for *Buchanan v. Warley*. For perhaps the wrong reasons it rightly decided that the fourteenth amendment barred states from establishing Negro ghettos. It is familiar history that *Buchanan* and subsequent decisions [43] "caused white supporters of residential segregation to rely upon the judicial enforcement of racial covenants." [44] A generation elapsed in which, encouraged by dicta in *Corrigan v. Buckley*,[45] courts sustained the covenants with regularity. But if *Buchanan* was right, the result at last reached in *Shelley* was foreordained; for it had long been clear that whether a challenged discrimination is legislative or judicial is a matter of no consequence in finding the state action on which the fourteenth amendment operates.[46] The distribution of state power among the three branches of government "is for the determination of the State. And its determination one way or the other cannot be an element in the inquiry whether the due process of law prescribed by the Fourteenth Amendment has been respected by the State or its representatives when dealing with matters involving life or liberty." [47] Thus, it was that *Shelley* at last correctly ratified the conclusion arrived at by an unsung federal trial judge in 1892 that the enforcement of a racial covenant was a denial of the equal protection of the laws.[48]

The Limits of the Logic

What has been said thus far comes simply to this: *Shelley v. Kraemer*, like *Gordon v. Gordon*, was a case in which the courts were called on to get people to do things they might have done—but also might not have done—voluntarily. The racial covenant in *Shelley* was unenforceable judicially because the state lacks power to limit land tenure and occupancy by race.

It would seem to follow that the enforceability of the testamentary limitation in *Gordon v. Gordon* should depend on the substantive ques-

---

[43] Harmon v. Tyler, 273 U.S. 668 (1927); Richmond v. Dean, 281 U.S. 704 (1930).

[44] VOSE, CAUCASIANS ONLY 52 (1959).

[45] 271 U.S. 323 (1926).

[46] Democratic theory suggests that the distinction is not unimportant at the ultimate point of testing substantive constitutionality. The United States in its Brief Amicus Curiae, pp. 83-85, Shelley v. Kraemer, 334 U.S. 1 (1948), suggests that presumptions of validity attendant on legislation do not work so powerfully to sustain judicial law-making.

[47] Dreyer v. Illinois, 187 U.S. 71, 84 (1902).

[48] Gandolfo v. Hartman, 49 Fed. 181 (S.D. Cal. 1892). Properly speaking, the federal court's inability to enforce the covenant should have been articulated in fifth amendment terms. See Hurd v. Hodge, 334 U.S. 24 (1948). Especially so in the era before Erie R.R. v. Tompkins, 304 U.S. 64 (1938).

tion whether the state has power to inhibit—perhaps to prohibit altogether—miscegenation of Jews and others. If it has not—and one may infer from Professor Wechsler's criticism of *Naim v. Naim*,[49] where the Court clumsily retreated from passing on Virginia's anti-miscegenation statute,[50] that he reads the Constitution adversely to the power [51] —then enforcement should have been denied.

But it would be idle to suggest that an analysis which sustains *Shelley v. Kraemer*, or undercuts *Gordon v. Gordon*, sufficiently answers further questions which Professor Wechsler properly sees latent in *Shelley*:

> "What is the principle involved? . . . Can the state, indeed, employ its law to vindicate the privacy of property against a trespasser, regardless of the grounds of his exclusion, or does it embrace the owner's reasons for excluding if it buttresses his power by the law? Would a declaratory judgment that a fee is determinable if a racially restrictive limitation should be violated represent discrimination by the state upon the racial ground? . . . Would a judgment of ejectment?"[52]

In short, Professor Wechsler is asking whether every instance of judicial cognition of private discrimination is state action prohibited by the fourteenth (or fifth) amendment. The answer is "No." But the answer calls for amplification and for some indication of the categories of situations to which these constitutional prohibitions should and should not apply.

As a starting point, it may be useful to revert to the *Gordon* case, and to Professor Wechsler's query whether the state is "forbidden to effectuate a will that draws a racial line." Reflection suggests that the hypothesized "will that draws a racial line" really embraces two quite different kinds of situations—and the difference between them may have vital implications.

In one of these situations the state power is exerted—or, if not exerted, waits in the wings—to induce compliance by others with the

---

[49] 350 U.S. 891 (1955), 350 U.S. 985 (1956).

[50] The Virginia Supreme Court of Appeals sustained the annulment of the marriage of a white woman and a man of Chinese ancestry, apparently resident in Virginia. 197 Va. 80, 87 S.E.2d 749 (1955). On appeal, the Supreme Court remanded the case for amplification of a record whose "inadequacy . . . as to the relationship of the parties to the Commonwealth of Virginia at the time of the marriage in North Carolina and upon their return to Virginia" was thought to interfere with resolution of the constitutional issues. 350 U.S. 891 (1955). The Virginia court's stated inability to arrange for an ampler record, 197 Va. 734, 90 S.E.2d 849 (1956), left the case "devoid of a properly presented federal question" and necessitated dismissal of the appeal. 350 U.S. 985 (1956).

[51] *Wechsler* 34. Some day, hopefully, the Court will feel itself able forthrightly to invalidate such laws. See Perez v. Sharp, 32 Cal. 2d 711, 198 P.2d 17 (1948).

[52] *Wechsler* 29-30.

discriminatory behavior patterns favored by the testator. This was what happened in *Gordon,* where the state power to terminate the son's interest in his father's estate was utilized as a means of restraining the son from marrying a non-Jew.

In the second situation the state's acquiescence in the testator's prejudices extends only to the point of learning his purpose—not to the point of using state power to compel conformity by others with the discriminatory pattern. Thus, let us suppose that in *Gordon* the testamentary limitation barred any share in the estate to a child who had, before learning the terms of his father's will, married a non-Jew. Under these circumstances, the probate court's necessary inquiry would be confined to identifying which of the children were the intended beneficiaries of the testator's prejudice. A determination that the son had previously married a Catholic and thereby disqualified himself would. not be coercive of the son's or anyone else's present or future behavior. Here judicial enforcement of the limitation would no more adopt the testator's prejudices than would enforcement of a will dividing the testator's property among three named persons all of whom are Jews and selected for that reason—an exercise of private prejudice the fourteenth amendment can hardly be thought to interfere with.

What marks the line between these cases? The line sought to be drawn is that beyond which the state assists a private person in seeing to it that others behave in a fashion which the state could not itself have ordained. The principle underlying the distinction is this: the fourteenth amendment permits each his personal prejudices and guarantees him free speech and press and worship, together with a degree of free economic enterprise, as instruments with which to persuade others to adopt his prejudices; but access to state aid to induce others to conform is barred.

What does this view of the amendment mean in concrete terms? It means that an employer may freely contract with a union to maintain a lily-white shop, but that the provision is one which fails whenever the employer's self-interest so dictates: the union cannot coerce compliance through an injunction or an award of damages. Conversely, however, a court need not—at the behest of Negro third-party maleficiaries—compel abandonment of the provision.[53] Judicial refusal

---

[53] Compare *Black· v. Cutter Laboratories,* 351 U.S. 292 (1956). An employee of Cutter Laboratories was discharged on the stated grounds of Communist Party membership and misrepresentation of her pre-employment history. The collective bargaining agreement permitted discharge for "just cause," and a board of arbitration held, on the union's petition for reinstatement, that the employee had actually been fired for union activity which was of course held not to be "just cause." On petition for enforcement of the award the lower California courts affirmed the board's order of reinstatement, but the state supreme court reversed. 43 Cal. 2d 788, 278 P.2d

to interfere is entirely analogous to legislative disinclination to enact a fair employment practices act—a sovereign decision to leave private prejudice alone. (Conversely, of course, the fourteenth amendment would be no barrier if the courts or the legislature were to insist that private hiring proceed on a non-racial basis.) [54]

To take a very different example, this view of the amendment means that the homeowner can continue to turn others off his premises, no matter how outrageous his standards of exclusion, and may call on the police to enforce the laws of trespass on his behalf. So too—as lawyers have supposed ever since the Court in the *Civil Rights Cases* [55] held it beyond Congress' power under the fourteenth amendment to bar the exclusion of Negroes from private "inns, public conveyances . . . and other places of amusement"—with the proprietor of an ice cream

---

905 (1955). The Supreme Court granted certiorari, 350 U.S. 816 (1956), and then, after briefs and argument, dismissed the writ. 351 U.S. 292 (1956).

The majority of the Court found that the California Supreme Court had held that "just cause" included Communist Party membership, and that this holding disposed of the case on non-federal grounds. Justice Douglas, joined by Chief Justice Warren and Justice Black, dissented. The dissenters were less certain of the state supreme court's rationale, but felt that if that court had refused enforcement on the ground that "just cause" included Communist Party membership, this was judicial action of the same character condemned in *Shelley v. Kraemer.*

The analysis proposed in the text suggests that both the majority and the dissenting opinions were wrong: the dissenters were wrong in characterizing what happened as one in which California's "courts [were] implicated in . . . a discriminatory scheme." 351 U.S. at 302. Assuming the union and the employer did agree that Communist Party membership was a bar to employment or an appropriate ground for discharge, all that the California courts did was to leave the situation alone—*i.e.,* not interfere with the employer's exercise of a right it and the union agreed the employer should possess. On the other hand, if the employer had failed to discharge an employee for a reason—*e.g.,* Communist Party membership, or being a Negro—that it had promised the union would disqualify an employee from continued service, the union's resort to the courts to compel discharge in conformity with the agreement would have meant that the "courts [were] implicated in . . . a discriminatory scheme."

Conversely, the too-broad reasoning of the majority concluding that construction of the term "just cause" in the bargaining agreement to include Communist Party membership was a matter of "local law" presenting no federal question must be regarded as unsound. There was in fact no federal question in the case the Court decided, because the California courts simply left the employer free to act or fail to act in the fashion the employer and the union had mutually agreed upon. But a federal question of major proportion would have been presented if the California courts had been called on to compel the employer, against its wishes, to discharge an employee in conformity with the judicial interpretation of a contractual obligation to fire a class of worker whose delineation was construed as embracing such criteria as being a Communist or a Negro. (This discussion is *not* meant to suggest that the constitutional questions involved in judicially compelling the discharge of a Communist *qua* Communist and a Negro *qua* Negro are interchangeable.)

This consideration of *Black v. Cutter Laboratories* has not necessitated any classification of the arbitration proceeding as state or non-state action. Such a classification should depend on whether adherence to an arbitral award is the voluntary election of the parties or depends (as in *Black v. Cutter Laboratories*) on the availability of a court order enforcing the award.

[54] See Railway Mail Ass'n v. Corsi, 326 U.S. 88 (1945), and *cf.* Williams v. International Bhd., 27 Cal. 2d 586, 165 P.2d 903 (1946).

[55] 109 U.S. 3 (1883).

parlor.[56]   So, too, with the board of directors of a private cemetery.[57] When the employees and the union, or the private homeowner and the petty merchant, are aggregated many times into a comprehensive social entity such as a company town, *Marsh v. Alabama* [58] of course suggests that exclusion or refusal to hire by reason of color or faith or political persuasion is inadmissible.   But this is precisely because the fourteenth amendment is directed at community arrangements, and its mandates cannot be circumvented by local concepts of property which purport to make a private barony of a social organism having "all the characteristics of any other American town." [59]   To be sure, it is relatively easy to put the one-family dwelling, the cemetery and the ice cream parlor on one side of a line and the company town on the other side; charting closer cases will be harder, but the process will be one of those measurements of subtle but decisive differences in degree which are the familiar province of constitutional adjudication.

Thus, it is suggested, the individual may select his guests at will. And he may—again, in the absence of limitations imposed by local law —hire only elderly Negro women to wait upon his table and refuse to sell or lease his home to any but militant vegetarians.   But if he gives his home to Harvard to be a residence for Negro graduate students, that limitation is one that the members of the Harvard Corporation should be free to observe or refrain from observing as they choose, without judicial or other state intervention—assuming the limitation is

---

[56] See State v. Clyburn, 247 N.C. 455, 101 S.E.2d 295 (1958). Simply licensing someone to do business does not make him a state agent; indeed extending tax exemptions or powers of eminent domain or both may not be sufficient. See Dorsey v. Stuyvesant Town Corp., 299 N.Y. 512, 87 N.E.2d 541 (1949), *cert. denied*, 339 U.S. 981 (1950). But compare the limitations assumed by one who operates a governmentally conferred monopoly. See Pollak v. Public Util. Comm'rs, 342 U.S. 848 (1951); *cf.* Brotherhood of R.R. Trainmen v. Howard, 343 U.S. 768 (1952).

[57] In Rice v. Sioux City Memorial Park Cemetery, 348 U.S. 880 (1954), the Court affirmed by an equally divided vote the lower courts' dismissal of a damage suit brought by a widow against a private cemetery which had refused to bury her Indian husband in a lot she had purchased, the refusal being predicated on a limitation of interment to non-Caucasians contained in the deed of sale of the burial lot. When apprised, on petition for rehearing, of an Iowa statute (provoked by the notoriety of the case) designed to prevent racial discrimination in interment in the future, the Court vacated its original affirmance and dismissed the writ of certiorari as improvidently granted; three justices dissented from dismissal of the writ.   349 U.S. 70 (1955).

In terms of the analysis proposed here, the private cemetery was entitled to refrain from according interment for any arbitrary reason, and the fourteenth amendment did not impose on the Iowa courts an obligation to compel the cemetery to abandon its perversity at the instance of Mrs. Rice. Under Iowa law she had an enforceable contract right to have the cemetery inter qualified Caucasians—but not her husband—in the lot she purchased. The fourteenth amendment gives her no greater right.

[58] 326 U.S. 501 (1946), reversing the trespass conviction of a Jehovah's Witness who distributed religious tracts on the streets of a company town; see Tucker v. Texas, 326 U.S. 517 (1946). Compare Dorsey v. Stuyvesant Town Corp., 299 N.Y. 512, 87 N.E.2d 541 (1949), *cert. denied*, 339 U.S. 981 (1950).

[59] Marsh v. Alabama, 326 U.S. 501, 502 (1946).

one which is itself a preference proscribed by the fourteenth amendment. And, it would seem to follow, a reversionary clause to take effect on failure of the limitation could not be enforced by a declaratory judgment, by ejectment, or otherwise.[60]

Of course it must be acknowledged that no pure logical line can be drawn between, on the one hand, permitting the members of the Harvard Corporation to observe the limitation in their discretion and, on the other, denying access to the courts to enforce the limitation. As Elias Clark has made abundantly clear in his extremely perceptive study of the implications of the *Girard College Case*,[61] the law touches the modern charitable trust at so many points that its "administration . . . must ultimately be characterized as state action." [62]   But it is also true, as Professor Clark observes, that, "in the last analysis, all human activity is controlled by law." [63]   In short, we are again faced with the ineluctable duty of making distinctions of degree. And distinctions between more formal and less formal manifestations of state authority are defensible until the essentially experiential process of constitutional litigation demonstrates their inadequacy. Certainly one would be ill-advised to launch a permanent and categorical demarcation exempting the discretion of the administrators of charitable trusts from constitutional scrutiny. "Were the Ford Foundation to disperse its millions on a discriminatory basis, society would find the result intolerable." [64]   So too, perhaps, with the powers exercised by vast industrial and financial entities pursuant to state charters of incorporation.[65] Yet there is much wisdom in Professor Wechsler's preference that "the issues [be] faced through legislation, where there is room for drawing lines that courts are not equipped to draw." [66]   In practical terms this is presumably the answer, for the hypothesized discriminations of the Ford Foundation or the steel industry would be met by corrective legislation long before a proper case had lumbered its way past the paper curtain of certiorari into its final resting place in the U. S. Reports.

---

[60] See Capital Fed. Sav. & Loan Ass'n v. Smith, 136 Colo. 265, 316 P.2d 252 (1957) ; *but cf.* Charlotte Park & Recreation Comm'n v. Barringer, 242 N.C. 311, 88 S.E.2d 114 (1955), *cert. denied,* 350 U.S. 983 (1956).

[61] Pennsylvania v. Board of Directors, 353 U.S. 230 (1957), discussed at text accompanying note 68 *infra.*

[62] Clark, *Charitable Trusts, the Fourteenth Amendment, and the Will of Stephen Girard,* 66 YALE L.J. 979, 1008 (1957).

[63] *Id.* at 1009.

[64] *Ibid.*

[65] Compare Berle, *Constitutional Limitations on Corporate Activity—Protection of Personal Rights from Invasion through Economic Power,* 100 U. PA. L. REV. 933 (1952).

[66] *Wechsler* 31.

But one who essays to tinker with constitutional theory may not properly take refuge in the likelihood of less-than-constitutional solutions to bail him out of following the limits of his logic. He must face the fact that the distinction between judgments of the Massachusetts Supreme Judicial Court and decisions of the members of the Harvard Corporation cannot permanently be sanctified in terms of state versus private action. What is offered is tentative, a beginning point, premised on the avowed value judgment that in 1959 it is consistent with the democratic theory embodied in the fourteenth amendment to let the members of the Harvard Corporation choose if they will to prefer Negroes—or whites, or Christian Scientists—in order to assure a further flow of endowment, or for any other reason. Conversely, it is submitted, for the Massachusetts Supreme Judicial Court to compel adherence to a discriminatory standard is not consistent with that democratic theory.

Very likely the conventional conceptualisms of state versus private power underlying the supposed distinction between judicial enforcement and trustee discretion will trouble many lawyers habituated to the more searching inquiries of legal realism. And properly so. Yet the distinction is one which at least in retrospect seems to account for the result in the case which implicitly "posed a threat to every charitable trust" [67] —the *Girard College Case.* There the City of Philadelphia, acting through an official board as trustee pursuant to the will of Stephen Girard, had since long before the fourteenth amendment utilized the fortune left by Girard to operate a school for "poor, male white orphan children." In 1957, at the behest of two Negro boys who had vainly sought admission, the Supreme Court held (without hearing argument) that "even though the Board was acting as a trustee, its refusal to admit Foust and Felder to the college because they were Negroes was discrimination by the State. Such discrimination is forbidden by the Fourteenth Amendment." [68] On remand the Pennsylvania courts replaced the City of Philadelphia with private trustees so that Girard's dominant discriminatory purpose might continue to be fulfilled; [69] and the Supreme Court declined to review the new arrangement. [70] A private

---

[67] Clark, *supra* note 62, at 1002.

[68] Pennsylvania v. Board of Directors, 353 U.S. 230, 231 (1957).

[69] *In re* Girard College Trusteeship, 391 Pa. 434, 138 A.2d 844 (1958).

[70] 357 U.S. 570 (1958). Passing the possibility that the denial of certiorari betokens no approval of the Pennsylvania judgment authorizing the substitution of private trustees capable of discriminating, the *Girard College Case* also raises special questions about the validity of state action (substitution of trustees) precisely calculated to perpetuate a theretofore unlawful racial ban. But these questions are tangential to the present discussion. Moreover it is perhaps inappropriate for the writer, who was of counsel, to relitigate the *Girard College Case* in this forum.

undertaking had been remitted to private hands, and the structure of charitable discrimination appeared secure. Yet if the thesis advanced in the preceding discussion has validity, the perpetuation of Stephen Girard's discriminatory plan may not be permanent. For a change of heart among the private trustees could lead to an abandonment of the exclusionary scheme with which the Pennsylvania courts should be held powerless to interfere.

The concern generated by the *Girard College Case* in some legal circles mainly stemmed from the feeling that a fundamental right to make arbitrary testamentary dispositions was in jeopardy. It is surely appropriate to recognize the high premium Anglo-American traditions put upon testamentary freedom. But other values also come into play. Every community imposes limits of some sort on how far the decedent may project his idiosyncracies into the future. And the appropriateness of setting these limits is not open to question because, in the quaint phrase, "the right to take property by devise or descent is the creature of the law, and not a natural right. . . ."[71] But it is precisely those enterprises that are "creature[s] of the law" to which the fourteenth amendment is addressed.

Reappraisal in fourteenth amendment terms of those nominally private arrangements which are "creature[s] of the law" is only beginning. Without torturing the prevailing syllogism, which is our heritage from the *Civil Rights Cases,* that the fourteenth amendment speaks only to state action, the frontiers of state action could be pushed forward to embrace much—*e.g.,* trustee discretion—not presently included. Alternatively there is ground for arguing that preservation of fourteenth amendment rights may necessarily and properly require national restraints—perhaps only by Congress, perhaps by the courts as well—upon private action which tends to undermine the oportunity to enjoy those rights. The principles which support national regulation of intrastate commerce where necessary to the protection of interstate commerce[72] may have some transferability.[73] But for many—and perhaps most—present purposes there has been no compelling demonstration of the need to push the fourteenth amendment to the ultimate limits of its logic. We are at a way station. Case by case—as in other realms of constitutional adjudication—experience will push us forward.

---

[71] Magoun v. Illinois Trust & Sav. Bank, 170 U.S. 283, 288 (1898). See Knowlton v. Moore, 178 U.S. 41, 55 (1900).

[72] See Houston E. & W. Tex. Ry. v. United States, 234 U.S. 342 (1914); Southern Ry. v. United States, 222 U.S. 20 (1911). *Cf.* the concurring opinion of Justice Pitney in Newberry v. United States, 256 U.S. 232, 275, 285-90 (1921).

[73] See Marsh v. Alabama, 326 U.S. 501, 506-7 (1946); *but cf.* the concurring opinion of Justice Frankfurter, *id.* at 510.

White Primaries

A closely related area of adjudication in which experience has already pushed us forward is the group of cases testing the validity of the white primary. From the turn of the century to World War II the white primary was the principal device by which the white South barred Negroes from participating in the political process. When the exclusion of Negroes from the primary was a formal state requirement, its invalidity was pretty clear. It was widely assumed that relinquishment of formal state controls of the primary would effectively and constitutionally permit the dominant Democratic Party to perpetuate the exclusion as a private venture. For a time this worked. But in 1944, in *Smith v. Allwright*,[74] the Court changed its mind, imposing on the Texas Democratic Party standards of equal treatment derived from the fifteenth amendment which, like the fourteenth, is directed in terms only at state action.

The result in *Smith v. Allwright* seems inconsistent with the result ultimately reached in the *Girard·College Case*, where state disengagement apparently sufficed to authenticate continued racial exclusion. Is there an explanation for the apparent inconsistency? Are there, despite Professor Wechsler's doubts, "neutral principles that satisfy the mind" [75] which support *Smith v. Allwright*? To answer these queries a closer scrutiny of the primary cases seems in order.

The first of the white primary cases was *Nixon v. Herndon*,[76] in which Holmes for a unanimous Court held that a Texas statute barring Negroes from voting in the Democratic primary violated the fourteenth amendment. The next Texas statute vested in the State Executive Committee of the Democratic Party power to set criteria for admission to the primary—and Nixon returned to court when the committee exercised its power so as to bar Negroes. Again Nixon prevailed, Cardozo in *Nixon v. Condon* [77] holding for a divided Court that the committee was acting on behalf of the state. Invalidation of the second statute left authority to determine admission to the Democratic primary in the hands of the Democratic state convention, where, Cardozo had indicated, it inherently belonged. The convention's refusal to let Negroes vote in the primary precipitated *Grovey v. Townsend*,[78] which unanimously sustained the exclusion as a private discrimination untouched by the fourteenth and fifteenth amendments.

---

[74] 321 U.S. 649 (1944).

[75] *Wechsler* 29.

[76] 273 U.S. 536 (1927).

[77] 286 U.S. 73 (1932).

[78] 295 U.S. 45 (1935).

The *Classic* case [79]—ratifying federal authority to protect the integrity of Louisiana primaries for candidates for federal office—served to instruct the Supreme Court that in most Southern states the Democratic primary is effectively the election. With this in mind the Supreme Court in *Smith v. Allwright* decided to reconsider the issue posed in *Grovey v. Townsend*. Specifically what concerned the Court was whether the presence in *Nixon v. Condon* and the absence in *Grovey v. Townsend* of a statute vesting discretion in an organ of the Democratic Party to determine admissibility to the primary was really a matter of constitutional dimension—whether, in short, the Court could sanction "a variation in the result from so slight a change in form." [80] The answer was in the negative. "The United States is a constitutional democracy. Its organic law grants to all citizens a right to participate in the choice of elected officials without restriction by any State because of race. This grant . . . is not to be nullified by a State through casting its electoral process in a form which permits a private organization to practice racial discrimination in the election." [81] And in *Terry v. Adams*,[82] in 1953, the Court reaffirmed the holding of *Smith v. Allwright* in even more extreme circumstances. For there Negroes were barred not from the county primary as such but from a pre-primary plebiscite conducted by the Jaybird Democratic Association. Justice Black wrote:

> "The only election that has counted in this Texas county for more than fifty years has been that held by the Jaybirds from which Negroes were excluded. The Democratic primary and the general election have become no more than the perfunctory ratifiers of the choice that has already been made in Jaybird elections from which Negroes have been excluded. It is immaterial that the state does not control that part of this elective process which it leaves for the Jaybirds to manage. . . . The effect of the whole procedure, Jaybird primary plus Democratic primary plus general election, is to do precisely that which the . . . Amendment forbids—strip Negroes of every vestige of influence in selecting the officials who control the local county matters that intimately touch the daily lives of citizens." [83]

From a doctrinal point of view the issue these cases present is that of finding the state action on which the Constitution imposes limitations when all the state has done, as in the *Girard College Case*, is to withdraw from the arena—"casting its electoral process in a form which

---

[79] United States v. Classic, 313 U.S. 299 (1941).
[80] Smith v. Allwright, 321 U.S. 649, 661 (1944).
[81] *Id.* at 664.
[82] 345 U.S. 461 (1953).
[83] *Id.* at 469-70.

permits a private organization to practice racial discrimination. . . ." [84]
Is failure to restrain private prejudice equatable with active state discrimination? A bald affirmative answer sounds destructive of principles regarded as settled ever since the *Civil Rights Cases*. But even there, it is well to remember, the Court's conclusion that Congress could not penalize "the act of a mere individual, the owner of the inn, the public conveyance or place of amusement, refusing the accommodation," [85] involved a pertinent judicial assumption. The assumption was that such refusal constituted "an ordinary civil injury, properly cognizable by the laws of the State, and presumably subject to redress by those laws until the contrary appears." [86] Is there an intimation that if the contrary were made to appear, if it were demonstrable that a state afforded a Negro no remedy for such a discrimination, one might then establish a basis for invoking a federal remedy fashioned by Congress or the courts? Perhaps. At all events, long after the *Civil Rights Cases*, Chief Justice Taft—in the very different context of labor relations—articulated for the Court a federal right of protection from state withdrawal of a pre-existing civil remedy:

> "It is true that no one has a vested right in any particular rule of the common law, but it is also true that the legislative power of a State can only be exerted in subordination to the fundamental principles of right and justice which the guaranty of due process in the Fourteenth Amendment is intended to preserve, and that a purely arbitrary or capricious exercise of that power whereby a wrongful and highly injurious invasion of property rights, as here, is practically sanctioned and the owner stripped of all real remedy, is wholly at variance with those principles." [87]

Finally, note should be taken of the Court's recent opinion in *Railway Employes' Dept. v. Hanson*.[88] This was an action brought by nonunion employees of the Union Pacific Railroad to enjoin enforcement as against them of the union shop provisions of a collective bargaining agreement entered into between a railway brotherhood and the carrier: being required to pay union dues as the price of holding their jobs was said by plaintiffs to breach various constitutional liberties. But wherein lay the governmental action subject to constitutional limitation? Nebraska, in whose courts the action was brought, had a "right to work law" which made union shop provisions unenforceable.

---

[84] Smith v. Allwright, 321 U.S. 649, 664 (1944).
[85] 109 U.S. 3, 24 (1883).
[86] *Ibid.*
[87] Truax v. Corrigan, 257 U.S. 312, 329-30 (1921).
[88] 351 U.S. 225 (1956).

From 1934 to 1951 the Federal Railway Labor Act had contained a similar provision governing collective bargaining agreements in the railroad industry. But in 1951 Congress reversed its policy and amended the Railway Labor Act so as to *permit* the negotiation of such agreements, the laws of "any state" to the contrary notwithstanding. Plaintiffs argued that this pre-emptive act subjected the resultant union shop provision, which the contracting parties were then free to adopt or not as they chose, to fifth amendment limitations. Numerous *amici* attorneys general—including Attorney General Almond of Virginia and Attorney General Shepperd of Texas—filed briefs endorsing this view.[89] And the Court agreed, citing *Smith v. Allwright*: "If private rights are being invaded, it is by force of an agreement made pursuant to federal law which expressly declares that state law is superseded. . . . In other words, the federal statute is the source of the power and authority by which any private rights are lost or sacrificed."[90]

What has been said above puts the emphasis in the white primary cases on the shift from state regulation to formal state neutrality, with the suggestion that doctrinally the state is still responsible for abandoning a situation "in a form which permits a private organization to practice racial discrimination."[91] This, it is submitted, is an inadequate basis for supporting the results reached in *Smith v. Allwright* and *Terry v. Adams,* for it suggests that a different result would and should have been reached if the state had never played a formal role and *Nixon v. Herndon* and *Nixon v. Condon* had not been litigated. Fortunately, *Smith v. Allwright* and *Terry v. Adams* need not and they in fact do not depend on imputing to the state continued responsibility for an activity which the state once regulated. If this were their rationale, the fourteenth amendment would have been dispositive of these cases, as it was of *Nixon v. Herndon* and *Nixon v. Condon*. *Smith v. Allwright* and *Terry v. Adams* actually stand on narrower and firmer ground—the fifteenth amendment, which expressly protects "the right to vote" against abridgement "on account of race, color, or previous condition of servitude."

Yet how can the fifteenth amendment apply where the fourteenth does not, since both are addressed to state action? The question generates its own answer: with respect to the particular problem to

---

[89] Attorney General Cook of Georgia filed a statement supporting the brief filed by Attorney General Shepperd. It is notable that the AFL-CIO, in an *amicus* brief supporting the union shop agreements, likewise urged that they be tested against constitutional limitations.

[90] 351 U.S. at 232. The Court went on to hold the union shop constitutional. See also Allen v. Southern Ry., 43 L.R.R.M. 2652 (N.C. Sup. Ct. 1959); Looper v. Georgia S. & F. Ry., 213 Ga. 279, 99 S.E.2d 101 (1957).

[91] Smith v. Allwright, 321 U.S. 649, 664 (1944).

which the fifteenth amendment is addressed—protecting the right of Negroes not to be discriminated against at the polls—the amendment must impose on the states a heavier affirmative duty to assure an equal franchise than does the fourteenth. If this were not so, the fifteenth amendment would be a redundancy, having no scope for separate and effective application.

Construing the fifteenth amendment to be an independently meaningful guarantee is in harmony with its framers' comprehensive purposes. "It was . . . well understood in Congress at the time the Amendment was under consideration that it applied to any election, from that of presidential elector down to the most petty election for a justice of the peace or a fence-viewer." [92] But the Court had learned in *Classic* that in the deep South the only opportunity to exercise the constitutionally protected right to vote arises at the primary (or, as in *Terry v. Adams,* the pre-primary) balloting. Thus, to find no state duty to prevent the exclusion of Negroes from the only elections which matter would be to delete the fifteenth amendment from the Constitution.

Smith v. Allwright and *Terry v. Adams* do not mean, as Professor Wechsler suggests they mean,[93] that the Constitution would prevent a dominant political party from excluding from its primary the members of a disfavored faith. For the fifteenth amendment speaks only to racial distinctions, not to religious distinctions or any of the other arbitrary classifications interdicted by the equal protection clause.

In short what Professor Wechsler sees as a cognate form of exclusion could be reached only through the fourteenth amendment. Imposing fourteenth amendment restraints on a southern Democratic primary would have to be predicated on a judgment that managing the electoral process is an inalienable sovereign function, and that whoever does that managing acts on the state's behalf. Perhaps such a judgment is supportable. "Only a State can own a Statehouse; only a State can get income by taxing." [94] So too, it may be plausibly urged, only a state can conduct elections—especially so where the state is one in which, under the Constitution, a republican form of government is perpetually guaranteed.[95] But the argument, whatever its validity, is one which goes far beyond the limited guarantee of racial equality in the political process embodied in the fifteenth amendment and properly vindicated in *Smith v. Allwright* and *Terry v. Adams.*

[92] MATHEWS, LEGISLATIVE AND JUDICIAL HISTORY OF THE FIFTEENTH AMENDMENT 38 (1909).

[93] *Wechsler* 29.

[94] Frankfurter, J., in New York v. United States, 326 U.S. 572, 582 (1946).

[95] U.S. CONST. art. IV, § 4.

THE SCHOOL SEGREGATION CASES

Of the cases which trouble Professor Wechsler, the one which causes him the greatest concern is the initial decision in *Brown v. Board of Education*,[96] decreeing the invalidity of state-imposed segregation in public schools. If Professor Wechsler's criticisms were simply addressed to the form of the Court's opinion in *Brown*, one would be hard put to dispute them. Certainly the opinion is most obscure in its crucial elements—*e.g.*, is inequality a "fact"? Whatever it is, how do judges determine it? Moreover, the opinion does not appear to articulate any grounds for disposing of the arguably quite different issues—segregated beaches,[97] golf courses,[98] buses,[99] and parks [100]—subsequently resolved per curiam in apparent reliance on *Brown*.

But Professor Wechsler goes further. He suggests that the problem in *Brown* is not one of discrimination at all, for both races are disadvantaged and the burden of guilt surely falls more heavily on whites than on Negroes. The real legal issue, Professor Wechsler believes, is a claim of right of association balanced against an equal and opposite claim of right of nonassociation. Seeing the issue this way, he seems to suggest that no supportable opinion could have been written in *Brown*—or at least that writing such an opinion is a "challenge" not yet successfully met.[101] Faced with this challenge, perhaps one who supports the judgment but confesses dissatisfaction with the opinion rendered has some obligation to draft what he regards as an adequate opinion:

> "These four consolidated cases, which come to us from three federal district courts and one state supreme court, present a single question: the compatibility with the Fourteenth Amendment's equal protection clause of state laws which require, or permit local authorities to require, segregation of white and Negro school children in compulsory public schools. The courts below all sustained the challenged laws; but there was division among them on the subsidiary issue whether it is harmful to Negro children, in whose behalf these class actions were brought, to shunt them off on racial grounds to schools which are the equivalent in every non-racial dimension of the white schools

---

[96] 347 U.S. 483 (1954).
[97] Baltimore v. Dawson, 350 U.S. 877 (1955).
[98] Holmes v. Atlanta, 350 U.S. 879 (1955).
[99] Gayle v. Browder, 352 U.S. 903 (1956).
[100] New Orleans Parks Ass'n v. Detiege, 358 U.S. 54 (1958).
[101] *Wechsler* 34.

from which they are barred.   (In the Delaware case, the
state supreme court found that, quite apart from racial
separation, the Negro school was not the equivalent of the
white schools.)

"At the outset we are strongly urged to affirm without
further ado on the ground that educational policy is beyond the purview of federal power.   As a general proposition this is of course true.   The management of American
schools is one of the most cherished and vital local prerogatives, and the enormous success of American public education doubtless owes much to the diversity born of our
federal structure.   But public education, like all other
publicly regulated enterprises, must conform to the comprehensive standards which the Fourteenth Amendment
imposes on all state activity.   *West Virginia v. Barnette,*
319 U.S. 624; *cf. Pierce v. Society of Sisters,* 268 U.S. 510.

"It is also urged upon us that the extensive research
into the history of the Fourteenth Amendment's adoption,
so diligently conducted by counsel at our request, fails to
disclose any intent on the part of the framers to end
segregation in public schools.   We think it is true, but not
of itself dispositive.   For one thing, it is familiar constitutional history that this Court has progressively brought
within the ambit of the Fourteenth Amendment many
issues and many litigants probably not contemplated by
those who framed and ratified the Amendment.   Moreover—and of more immediate moment—we read the history
of the Amendment as contemplating an essentially dynamic
development by Congress and this Court of the liberties
outlined in such generalized terms in the Amendment.

"Next it is argued that the precise question at issue
has already been disposed of by this Court in *Plessy v.
Ferguson,* 163 U.S. 537.   In response it is said that *Plessy*
dealt with segregation on intrastate railways, and is dis-
tinguishable.   We think it is not possible to ignore this
Court's heavy reliance, in sustaining the segregation challenged in *Plessy,* on what it regarded as the manifest
validity of segregated public schools.   But we do not doubt
our power, or indeed our obligation, to re-examine grave
constitutional questions in a proper case.   Given the finality
of constitutional determinations, they must always be 'open

to reconsideration, in the light of new experience and greater knowledge and wisdom.' 317 U.S. XLII, XLVII (Remarks of Chief Justice Stone on the death of Justice Brandeis). And this is especially true when the constitutional provisions at issue are themselves of an evolutionary generality.

"*Plessy v. Ferguson* essentially rests on three interconnected propositions. The first is that the equal protection clause was intended to secure equality of 'civil and political rights' but was not intended to affect social relationships. The second is that 'Jim Crow laws'—laws requiring segregation of whites and Negroes—operate only in the social arena. The third is that such laws—providing as they commonly do 'separate but equal' facilities—neither impose nor imply inequality except as such inequality lies in the eye of the beholder.

"We think that on re-examination these propositions cannot be sustained. Nothing in the equal protection clause suggests a dichotomy between laws affecting civil and political rights and those affecting social relationships. That clause proscribes *all* laws which impose special disabilities on particular persons or groups without any reasoned basis for the differential treatment. Therefore we must decide (1) whether there is a demonstrable state need for the racial divisions imposed by the Jim Crow laws here involved, and (2) whether these racial divisions work significant harm to the segregated Negro.

"On the issue of the reasonableness of governmentally imposed distinctions between whites and Negroes, as well as on the issue of whether harm accrues to either group through enforced separation, we have been deluged with scholarly writings. These writings supplement extensive testimony which is of record in some, but not all, of the cases before us. Learned and impressive authority is deeply engaged on both sides of these twin issues. Were it our function to assess what has been put before us, we would find ourselves unpersuaded that there are demonstrable differences other than those of pigment between whites and Negroes, or that any state policy other than the impermissible one of nourishing race prejudice (see *Hirabayashi v. United States*, 320 U.S. 81) underlies the requirement that the races be separated. Moreover, we would be inclined to surmise that governmental separation of the races sets in motion grievous consequences for whites and Negroes alike.

"But, assuming we were competent to make such judgments, we do not think we are called on to do so in order to determine the issues presently tendered. For we start from the base point that in the United States 'all legal restrictions which curtail the civil rights of a single racial group are immediately suspect.' *Korematsu v. United States,* 323 U.S. 214, 216. Certainly legislation cast in such terms is not entitled to the ordinary presumptions of validity. On the contrary there is special need for 'a searching judicial inquiry into the legislative judgment in situations where prejudice against discrete and insular minorities may tend to curtail the operation of those political processes ordinarily to be relied on to protect minorities.' Justice Stone dissenting in *Minersville School District v. Gobitis,* 310 U.S. 586, 606. See *United States v. Carolene Products,* 304 U.S. 144, 152, n.4. We could not, therefore, sustain the reasonableness of these racial distinctions and the absence of harm said to flow from them, unless we were prepared to say that no factual case can be made the other way. As indicated above, we are not prepared to say this.

"We have said that we do not think it incumbent upon us, at least for present purposes, to resolve controversies as to the justification for and impact of Jim Crow legislation. But we would be less than candid if we failed to acknowledge that denial of the degrading effects of such legislation seems to us to border on the disingenuous:

> '[T]he Jim Crow laws applied to *all* Negroes—not merely to the rowdy, or drunken, or surly, or ignorant ones. The new laws did not countenance the old conservative tendency to distinguish between classes of the race, to encourage the "better" element, and to draw it into a white alliance. Those laws backed up the Alabamian who told the disfranchising convention of his state that no Negro in the world was the equal of "the least, poorest, lowest-down white

man I ever knew." . . . The Jim Crow laws put the authority of the state or city in the voice of the street-car conductor, the railway brakeman, the bus driver, the theater usher, and also into the voice of the hoodlum of the public parks and playgrounds. They gave free rein and the majesty of the law to mass aggressions that might otherwise have been curbed, blunted, or deflected.

'The Jim Crow laws, unlike feudal laws, did not assign the subordinate group a fixed status in society. They were constantly pushing the Negro farther down.' C. VANN WOODWARD, THE STRANGE CAREER OF JIM CROW, p. 93.

'All others can see and understand this. How can we properly shut our minds to it?' Bailey v. Drexel Furniture Co., 259 U.S. 20, 37. We see little room for doubt that it is the function of Jim Crow laws to make identification as a Negro a matter of stigma. Such governmental denigration is a form of injury the Constitution recognizes and will protect against. See Joint Anti-Fascist Refugee Comm. v. McGrath, 341 U.S. 123.

"We have ventured to disclose our intuitions about issues hotly controverted by those social scientists professionally entitled to have opinions. We would think it corrosive of the judicial function were we to translate our amateur wisdom into constitutional imperatives. Fortunately, disposition of these cases does not require us to pursue such a ruinous course. Suffice it here to conclude that the constitutional doubts instantly generated by statutes drawing racial lines have not been allayed. We have never demanded proof that a Negro tried, or merely indicted, by a jury from which Negroes are systematically excluded was subjected to actual discrimination because of his race. Yet we have reversed criminal convictions prefaced by such racial exclusion ever since Strauder v. West Virginia, 100 U.S. 303. As there made plain, it was 'the apprehended existence of prejudice' by whites against Negroes that led to adoption of the equal protection clause. We are not persuaded that the prejudice apprehended by the framers does not infect the bluntly racial laws before us. Therefore they cannot be sustained.

"The 'separate but equal' doctrine announced in *Plessy v. Ferguson* was the product of sophistication. At an earlier day it was apparent to this Court that mere separation by reason of race was discriminatory. In 1873, in *Railroad Co. v. Brown*, 17 Wall. 445, this Court recognized that a federal statute of 1866 prohibiting a railroad from excluding persons 'on account of color,' was not met by the use of separate cars for Negroes. This Court read the statute as a direction 'that this discrimination must cease, and the colored and white races, in the use of the cars, be placed on an equality.' It was in such a natural sense that this Court first understood the generous ambit of the equal protection clause. 'What is this but declaring that the law in the States shall be the same for the black as for the white; that all persons, whether colored or white, shall stand equal before the laws of the states and, in regard to the colored race, for whose protection the Amendment was primarily designed, that no discrimination shall be made against them by law because of their color?' *Strauder v. West Virginia, supra*, at 307. It is to this original understanding that we return.

"In support of what we deem to be the well-founded contention that governmentally imposed segregation carries with it a stigma directed at the segregated group, plaintiffs have placed great emphasis on the aggravated onus of segregation imposed in facilities—such as public schools here at issue—which the segregated group is *required* to utilize. We do not find it necessary to make a present determination whether segregation by law could be sustained in state facilities made available for the voluntary use of its citizens—public parks, for example. That case is not now before us. It may, however, be appropriate to observe that where facilities are voluntary the community's asserted need to ordain segregation seems even less weighty than in the cases before us: for under such circumstances those for whom racial mingling is obnoxious are under no obligation to attend. What deserves present mention, however, is that defendants likewise take comfort from the compulsory character of school attendance laws. This factor is said to constitute a special ground for sustaining state imposed segregation. We are told that invalidation of required segregation in public schools arbitrarily elevates plaintiffs' claim of right not to be separated on racial lines above an equally weighty claim of right of others, both white and Negro, not to be compelled to mingle. But we think the contention fails. To the extent that implementation of this decision forces racial mingling on school children against their will, or against the will of their parents, this consequence follows because the community through its political processes has chosen and may continue to choose compulsory education—just as, from time to time, the nation has, through federal legislation, adopted the principle of coerced association implicit in a draft army. In neither instance can the coercion be said to emanate from this Court or from the Constitution. In any event, parents sufficiently disturbed at the prospect of having their children educated in democratic fashion in company with their peers are presumably entitled to fulfill their educational responsibilities in other ways. *Cf. Pierce v. Society of Sisters*, 268 U.S. 510.

"Finally, we are warned that a departure from *Plessy v. Ferguson* will be accompanied by vast social unrest—that the principle of mandatory racial separation is so ingrained in southern life that relaxation of it will promote widespread discord between and within the races. Nevertheless, 'important as is the preservation of the public peace, this aim cannot be accomplished by laws or ordinances which deny rights created or protected by the federal Constitution.' *Buchanan v. Warley*, 245 U.S. 60.

"Accordingly the judgments below, except for that in the Delaware case, must be reversed. But the form and timing of the mandates appropriate in these cases present problems of such magnitude that we will for the present withhold the entry of judgments and continue the cases on our docket to permit further argument relating to these procedural questions. . . ."

A draft opinion, prepared in hindsight by one who has no responsibility to decide, is only an academic exercise designed to prove a point. The fateful national consequences of *Brown v. Board of Education* flow from the opinion and judgment actually rendered. Professor Wechsler, sympathetic to the result but skeptical of the rationale, is frankly uncertain of history's verdict: "Who will be bold enough to say whether the judgment in the segregation cases will be judged fifty years from now to have advanced the cause of brotherhood or to have illustrated Bagehot's dictum that the 'courage which strengthens an enemy, and which so loses, not only the present battle, but many after battles, is a heavy curse to men and nations'." [102]   But some are bold enough— or fool-hardy enough—to make the prophecy Professor Wechsler eschews: the judgment in the segregation cases will as the decades pass give ever deeper meaning to our national life.   It will endure as long as our Constitution and our democratic faith endure.

NEUTRAL PRINCIPLES AND RACIAL DISCRIMINATION

If the judgments in the covenant cases, the white primary cases, and the school cases are not supportable on the basis of neutral constitutional principles, they deserve to be jettisoned.   Indeed, if the integrity of our judicial institutions means anything it means that irresponsible decisions will at last generally find their way to the oblivion of *Dred Scott*,[103] *Hammer v. Dagenhart*, [104] *United States v. Butler* [105] and comparable cases.   Surely to conclude that bad decisions are as negotiable as good in democratic currency would be to rob of all significance the judicial authority and the judicial self-restraint so painfully and prayerfully developed.

The thesis articulated above is that neutral constitutional principles do sustain the three great groups of cases.   But in any final assessment of these cases it cannot be too much stressed that the decisive constitutional principles here relevant are in a vital sense not neutral. The three post-Civil War Amendments were fashioned to one major end—an end to which we are only now making substantial strides— the full emancipation of the Negro:

> "We repeat, then, in the light of this recapitulation of events, almost too recent to be called history, but which are familiar to us all; and on the most casual examination of the language of these amendments, no one can fail to be impressed with the one pervading purpose found in them all, lying at the foundation of each, and without which none of them would have been even suggested; we mean the freedom of the slave race, the security and firm establishment of that freedom, and the protection of the newly-made freeman and citizen from the oppressions of those who had formerly exercised unlimited dominion over him.   It is true that only the fifteenth amendment, in terms, mentions the negro by

---

[102] Wechsler, *Reflections on the Conference,* Col. L. Alumni Bull. Dec. 1958, p. 1, 2.

[103] Scott v. Sandford, 60 U.S. (19 How.) 691 (1857).

[104] 247 U.S. 251 (1918).

[105] 297 U.S. 1 (1936).

speaking of his color and his slavery. But it is just as true that each of the other articles was addressed to the grievances of that race, and designed to remedy them as the fifteenth.

"We do not say that no one else but the negro can share in this protection. Both the language and spirit of these articles are to have their fair and just weight in any question of construction. Undoubtedly while negro slavery alone was in the mind of the Congress which proposed the thirteenth article, it forbids any other kind of slavery, now or hereafter. If Mexican peonage or the Chinese coolie labor system shall develop slavery of the Mexican or Chinese race within our territory, this amendment may safely be trusted to make it void. And so if other rights are assailed by the States which properly and necessarily fall within the protection of these articles, that protection will apply, though the party interested may not be of African descent. But what we do say, and what we wish to be understood is, that in any fair and just construction of any section or phrase of these amendments, it is necessary to look to the purpose which we have said was the pervading spirit of them all, the evil which they were designed to remedy, and the process of continued addition to the Constitution, until that purpose was supposed to be accomplished, as far as constitutional law can accomplish it." [106]

NEUTRAL PRINCIPLES AND THE JUDICIAL PROCESS

The central purpose of this paper has been to reappraise the several landmark cases in the field of race discrimination which Professor Wechsler has called into question. Intentionally, therefore, its principal focus has been upon those cases, not upon Professor Wechsler's insistence on the disposition of constitutional cases pursuant to neutral principles. It was hoped, indeed, that acquiescence in Professor Wechsler's thesis of neutrality would not only serve as an acceptable point of departure for study of the discrimination cases, but would also obviate controversy about jurisprudential issues which bear only tangentially on the cases themselves.

To accomplish this pacific purpose, the assumption was indulged that what Professor Wechsler chiefly seeks is a method of adjudication which is disinterested, reasoned, and comprehensive of the full range of like constitutional issues, coupled with a method of judicial exposition which plainly and fully articulates the real bases of decision. So stated, the proferred creed is hard to resist, and few are likely to be counted in opposition. To be sure, there may be no "positive law which binds the judges . . . to give a reasoned opinion from the bench, in support of their judgment upon matters that are stated before

---

[106] Slaughter-House Cases, 83 U.S. (16 Wall.) 36, 71-72 (1873).

them. But the course hath prevailed from the oldest times. It hath been so general and so uniform, that it must be considered as the law of the land." [107]

But perhaps this free-hand effort to intuit Professor Wechsler's meaning has been unfair. Perhaps, instead of fulfilling the purpose of seating everyone at the same jurisprudential table, all that has been done is to take Professor Wechsler's vintage wine and water it down to grape juice. If this is so, it was an act of hospitable ignorance, not of malice.

Unfortunately, it is not so easy to reverse the alchemy and reconstruct Professor Wechsler's true meaning. Very likely the idea of neutral constitutional adjudication does have implications broader than those notions of dispassionate judging which have here been ascribed to it. But if so, Professor Wechsler is best situated to illuminate the motto emblazoned on his flag. Short of that, it remains for this writer to state that the judicial neutrality he himself espouses does not preclude the disciplined exercise by a Supreme Court Justice of that Justice's individual and strongly held philosophy. Surely our Constitution is stronger because Cardozo—probing the "liberty" guaranteed by the fifth and fourteenth amendments—persuaded the Court that "freedom of thought, and speech . . . is the matrix, the indispensable condition, of nearly every other form of freedom." [108] It would have been stronger still had the Court believed, with Brandeis, that "the right to be let alone [is] the most comprehensive of rights and the right most valued by civilized men." [109]

If one is right in guessing that Professor Wechsler would not demur to the method by which Cardozo and Brandeis found constitutional equivalents for these deeply felt convictions, one is forced to speculate on what it is that makes their method palatable. Very likely Justice Frankfurter, who has thought long and deeply about constitutional adjudication, has put the matter best:

> "In dealing not with the machinery of government but with human rights, the absence of formal exactitude, or want of fixity of meaning, is not an unusual or even regrettable attribute of constitutional provisions. Words being symbols do not speak without a gloss. On the one hand the gloss may be the deposit of his-

---

[107] The language is Burke's in the *Report of the Committee of Managers on the Causes of the Duration of Mr. Hasting's Trial* in 4 SPEECHES OF EDMUND BURKE 200-01 (1816) ; it is quoted by Justice Frankfurter in a footnote to his opinion for the Court in Rochin v. California, 342 U.S. 165, 170 n.4 (1952). Actually there is a certain amount of "positive law" imposing on judges some obligation to explain their judgments. See, *e.g.*, FED. R. CIV. P. 52(a) ; compare OHIO REV. CODE ANN. § 2503.20 (Page 1954), the predecessor of which caused the Supreme Court some confusion in Perkins v. Benguet Mining Co., 342 U.S. 437, 441-42 (1952).

[108] Palko v. Connecticut, 302 U.S. 319, 326 (1937).

[109] Olmstead v. United States, 277 U.S. 438, 478 (1928) (dissenting opinion).

tory, whereby a term gains technical content. . . . On the other hand, the gloss of some of the verbal symbols of the Constitution does not give them a fixed technical content. It exacts a continuing process of application. When the gloss has thus not been fixed but is a function of the process of judgment, the judgment is bound to fall differently at different times and differently at the same time through different judges. . . . We may not draw on our merely personal and private notions and disregard the limits that bind judges in their judicial function. . . . To practice the requisite detachment and to achieve sufficient objectivity no doubt demands of judges the habit of self-discipline and self-criticism, incertitude that one's own views are incontestable and alert tolerance toward views not shared. But these are precisely the presuppositions of our judicial process. They are precisely the qualities society has a right to expect from those entrusted with ultimate judicial power." [110]

If Professor Wechsler means what Justice Frankfurter meant, the issue need not be pursued. But if Professor Wechsler's neutrality inhabits a more spacious domain, present efforts to capture and tame the concept are plainly unavailing. Suffice it to say, as Myres Mc-Dougal has recently said in another context,

> "The essence of a reasoned decision by the authority of the secular values of a public order of human dignity is a disciplined appraisal of alternative choices of immediate consequences in terms of preferred long-term effects, and not in either the timid fore-swearing of concern for immediate consequences or in the quixotic search for criteria of decision that transcend the world of men and values in metaphysical fantasy. The reference of legal principles must be either to their internal—logical—arrangement or to the external consequences of their application. It remains mysterious what criteria for decision a 'neutral' system could offer." [111]

---

[110] Rochin v. California, 342 U.S. 165, 169-72 (1952). See Freund, *Mr. Justice Frankfurter*, 26 U. Chi. L. Rev. 205, 210, 214-15 (1959).

[111] McDougal, *Perspectives for an International Law of Human Dignity*, 1959 Am. Soc'y Int'l L. Proceedings 107, 121 (1959).

THE LAWFULNESS OF THE SEGREGATION DECISIONS

CHARLES L. BLACK, JR.†

IF the cases outlawing segregation [1] were wrongly decided, then they ought to be overruled. One can go further: if dominant professional opinion ever forms and settles on the belief that they were wrongly decided, then they will be overruled, slowly or all at once, openly or silently. The insignificant error, however palpable, can stand, because the convenience of settlement outweighs the discomfort of error. But the hugely consequential error cannot stand and does not stand.[2]

There is pragmatic meaning then, there is call for action, in the suggestion that the segregation cases cannot be justified.[3] In the long run, as a corollary, there is practical and not merely intellectual significance in the question whether these cases were rightly decided. I think they were rightly decided, by overwhelming weight of reason, and I intend here to say why I hold this belief.

My liminal difficulty is rhetorical—or, perhaps more accurately, one of fashion. Simplicity is out of fashion, and the basic scheme of reasoning on which these cases can be justified is awkwardly simple. First, the equal protection clause of the fourteenth amendment should be read as saying that the Negro race, as such, is not to be significantly disadvantaged by the laws of the states. Secondly, segregation is a massive intentional disadvantaging of the Negro race, as such, by state law. No subtlety at all. Yet I cannot disabuse myself of the idea that that is really all there is to the segregation cases. If both these propositions can be supported by the preponderance of argument, the cases were rightly decided. If they cannot be so supported, the cases are in perilous condition.

As a general thing, the first of these propositions has so far as I know never been controverted in a holding of the Supreme Court. I rest here on

---

†Henry R. Luce Professor of Jurisprudence, Yale Law School.

1. Brown v. Board of Educ. (The School Segregation Cases), 347 U.S. 483 (1954); Bolling v. Sharpe, 347 U.S. 497 (1954); New Orleans' City Park Improvement Ass'n v. Detiege, 358 U.S. 54 (1959); Gayle v. Browder, 352 U.S. 903 (1956); Holmes v. Atlanta, 350 U.S. 879 (1955); Mayor & City Council v. Dawson, 350 U.S. 877 (1955); Muir v. Louisville Park Theatrical Ass'n, 347 U.S. 971 (1954).

2. *Cf.* Pollak, *Racial Discrimination and Judicial Integrity: A Reply to Professor Wechsler*, 108 U. PA. L. REV. 1, 31 (1959). I am indebted throughout to this Article, though the rationale I offer in support of the decisions differs from Professor Pollak's. His, however, seems to me a sound alternative ground for the desegregation holdings.

3. See Wechsler, *Toward Neutral Principles of Constitutional Law*, 73 HARV. L. REV. 1, 34 (1959). The present Article was immediately suggested by Professor Wechsler's questionings. It is not, however, to be looked on as formal "reply," since I cover here only one part of the ground he goes over, and since my lines of thought are only partly responsive in terms to the questions as he sees them.

161

the solid sense of *The Slaughterhouse Cases*[4] and of *Strauder v. West Virginia*,[5] where Mr. Justice Strong said of the fourteenth amendment:

> It ordains that no State shall make or enforce any laws which shall abridge the privileges or immunities of citizens of the United States (evidently referring to the newly made citizens, who, being citizens of the United States, are declared to be also citizens of the State in which they reside). It ordains that no State shall deprive any person of life, liberty, or property, without due process of law, or deny to any person within its jurisdiction the equal protection of the laws. What is this but declaring that the law in the States shall be the same for the black as for the white; that all persons, whether colored or white, shall stand equal before the laws of the States, and, in regard to the colored race, for whose protection the amendment was primarily designed, that no discrimination shall be made against them by law because of their color? The words of the amendment, it is true, are prohibitory, but they contain a necessary implication of a positive immunity, or right, most valuable to the colored race,—the right to exemption from unfriendly legislation against them distinctively as colored,—exemption from legal discriminations, implying inferiority in civil society, lessening the security of their enjoyment of the rights which others enjoy, and discriminations which are steps towards reducing them to the condition of a subject race.[6]

If *Plessy v. Ferguson*[7] be thought a faltering from this principle, I step back to the principle itself. But the *Plessy* Court clearly conceived it to be its task to show that segregation did not really disadvantage the Negro, except through his own choice.[8] There is in this no denial of the *Slaughterhouse* and *Strauder* principle; the fault of *Plessy* is in the psychology and sociology of its minor premise.

The lurking difficulty lies not in "racial" cases but in the total philosophy of "equal protection" in the wide sense. "Equal protection," as it applies to the whole of state law, must be consistent with the imposition of disadvantage on some, for all law imposes disadvantage on some; to give driver's licences only to good drivers is to disadvantage bad drivers. Thus the word "reasonable" necessarily finds its way into "equal protection," in the application of the latter concept to law in general. And it is inevitable, and right, that "reasonable," in this broader context, should be given its older sense of "supportable by reasoned considerations."[9] "Equal" thereby comes to mean not really "equal," but "equal unless a fairly tenable reason exists for inequality."

---

4. 83 U.S. (16 Wall.) 36 (1873).
5. 100 U.S. 303 (1880).
6. *Id.* at 307-08.
7. 163 U.S. 537 (1896).
8. "We consider the underlying fallacy of the plaintiff's argument to consist in the assumption that the enforced separation of the two races stamps the colored race with a badge of inferiority. *If this be so, it is not by reason of anything found in the act, but solely because the colored race chooses to put that construction upon it.*" *Id.* at 551. (Emphasis added.) The curves of callousness and stupidity intersect at their respective maxima.
9. See Lindsley v. Natural Carbonic Gas Co., 220 U.S. 61 (1911).

But the whole tragic background of the fourteenth amendment forbids the feedback infection of its central purpose with the necessary qualifications that have attached themselves to its broader and so largely accidental radiations. It may have been intended that "equal protection" go forth into wider fields than the racial. But history puts it entirely out of doubt that the chief and all-dominating purpose was to ensure equal protection for the Negro. And this intent can hardly be given the self-defeating qualification that necessity has written on equal protection as applied to carbonic gas. If it is, then "equal protection" for the Negro means "equality until a tenable reason for inequality is proferred." On this view, Negroes may hold property, sign wills, marry, testify in court, walk the streets, go to (even segregated) school, ride public transportation, and so on, only in the event that no reason, not clearly untenable, can be assigned by a state legislature for their not being permitted to do these things. That cannot have been what all the noise was about in 1866.

What the fourteenth amendment, in its historical setting, must be read to say is that the Negro is to enjoy equal protection of the laws, and that the fact of his being a Negro is not to be taken to be a good enough reason for denying him this equality, however "reasonable" that might seem to some people. All possible arguments, however convincing, for discriminating against the Negro, were finally rejected by the fourteenth amendment.

It is sometimes urged that a special qualification was written on the concept of "equality" by the history of the adoption of the amendment—that an intent can be made out to exclude segregation from those legal discriminations invalidated by the requirement of equality, whether or not it actually works inequality. This point has been discussed and documented by Professor Alexander Bickel,[10] who, though he finds convincing arguments for the conclusion that school segregation was not among the evils the framers of the amendment intended for immediate correction,[11] suggests that they intended at the same time to set up a general concept for later concrete application.[12] Other recent writers take somewhat similar views.[13] The data brought forward by Professor Bickel do not seem to me as persuasive, on his first point, as they do to him.[14]

---

10. Bickel, *The Original Understanding and the Segregation Decision*, 69 HARV. L. REV. 1 (1955).
11. *Id.* at 58.
12. *Id.* at 61-65.
13. Wechsler, *supra* note 3, at 31-32; Pollak, *supra* note 2, at 25.
14. Actually, the question of my dissent from Professor Bickel's conclusions depends on their exact meaning. In his data I find, to be sure, a case for concluding that the relevant people did not "intend" to abolish segregation, in the sense that they had no positive and consciously formed intention of doing so. That conclusion means little when one is dealing with general language. I am not convinced that a sufficient equivalency is made out between the Civil Rights Bill and the fourteenth amendment (there being no relevant legislative history whatever on the amendment as such) to justify attaching the bill's history to the amendment for the purpose of establishing a definitely formed intent to exclude segregation from the prohibitive ambit of the amendment's general words—a totally different meaning of the predicate "did not intend." The motive for insertion of

But in supporting his second point he develops a line of thought tending to establish that the legislative history does not render the segregation decisions improper, and I am glad to join him in that practical conclusion. I would add only one point: The question of the "intent" of the men of 1866 on segregation *as we know it* calls for a far chancier guess than is commonly supposed, for they were unacquainted with the institution as it prevails in the American South today. To guess their verdict upon the institution as it functions in the midtwentieth century supposes an imaginary hypothesis which grows more preposterous as it is sought to be made more vivid. They can in the nature of the case have bequeathed us only their generalities; the specifics lay unborn as they disbanded. I do not understand Professor Bickel to hold a crucially different view.

Then does segregation offend against equality? Equality, like all general concepts, has marginal areas where philosophic difficulties are encountered. But if a whole race of people finds itself confined within a system which is set up and continued for the very purpose of keeping it in an inferior station, and if the question is then solemnly propounded whether such a race is being treated "equally," I think we ought to exercise one of the sovereign prerogatives of philosophers—that of laughter. The only question remaining (after we get our laughter under control) is whether the segregation system answers to this description.

Here I must confess to a tendency to start laughing all over again. I was raised in the South, in a Texas city where the pattern of segregation was firmly fixed. I am sure it never occurred to anyone, white or colored, to question its meaning. The fiction of "equality" is just about on a level with the fiction of "finding" in the action of trover. I think few candid southerners deny this. Northern people may be misled by the entirely sincere protestations of many southerners that segregation is "better" for the Negroes, is not intended to hurt them. But I think a little probing would demonstrate that what is meant is that it is better for the Negroes to accept a position of inferiority, at least for the indefinite future.

But the subjectively obvious, if queried, must be backed up by more public materials. What public materials assure me that my reading of the social meaning of segregation is not a mere idiosyncracy?

First, of course, is history. Segregation in the South comes down in apostolic succession from slavery and the *Dred Scott* case. The South fought to keep slavery, and lost. Then it tried the Black Codes, and lost. Then it looked around for something else and found segregation. The movement for segregation was an integral part of the movement to maintain and further

---

the present equal protection clause seems to me, on Professor Bickel's evidence, simply mysterious. *Cf.* Fairman, *Does the Fourteenth Amendment Incorporate the Bill of Rights?*, 2 STAN. L. REV. 5, 41 (1949). Obviously, the development, qualification, and support of these points would call for more discussion than is warrantable in the present context, given the practical agreement in which Professor Bickel and I (as I believe) find ourselves.

"white supremacy"; its triumph (as Professor Woodward has shown) represented a triumph of extreme racialist over moderate sentiment about the Negro.[15] It is now defended very largely on the ground that the Negro as such is not fit to associate with the white.

History, too, tells us that segregation was imposed on one race by the other race; consent was not invited or required. Segregation in the South grew up and is kept going because and only because the white race has wanted it that way—an incontrovertible fact which in itself hardly consorts with equality. This fact perhaps more than any other confirms the picture which a casual or deep observer is likely to form of the life of a southern community—a picture not of mutual separation of whites and Negroes, but of one in-group enjoying full normal communal life and one out-group that is barred from this life and forced into an inferior life of its own. When a white southern writer refers to the woes of "the South," do you not know, does not context commonly make it clear, that he means "white southerners"? When you are in Leeville and hear someone say "Leeville High," you know he has reference to the white high school; the Negro school will be called something else—Carver High, perhaps, or Lincoln High to our shame. That is what you would expect when one race forces a segregated position on another, and that is what you get.

Segregation is historically and contemporaneously associated in a functioning complex with practices which are indisputably and grossly discriminatory. I have in mind especially the long-continued and still largely effective exclusion of Negroes from voting. Here we have two things. First, a certain group of people is "segregated." Secondly, at about the same time, the very same group of people, down to the last man and woman, is barred, or sought to be barred, from the common political life of the community—from all political power. Then we are solemnly told that segregation is not intended to harm the segregated race, or to stamp it with the mark of inferiority. How long must we keep a straight face?

Here it may be added that, generally speaking, segregation is the pattern of law in communities where the extralegal patterns of discrimination against Negroes are the tightest, where Negroes are subjected to the strictest codes of "unwritten law" as to job opportunities, social intercourse, patterns of housing, going to the back door, being called by the first name, saying "Sir," and all the rest of the whole sorry business. Of course these things, in themselves, need not and usually do not involve "state action," and hence the fourteenth amendment cannot apply to them. But they can assist us in understanding the meaning and assessing the impact of state action.

"Separate but equal" facilities are almost never really equal. . Sometimes this concerns small things—if the "white" men's room has mixing hot and cold taps, the "colored" men's room will likely have separate taps; it is

---

15. WOODWARD, THE STRANGE CAREER OF JIM CROW ch. II *Capitulation to Racism*, at 49-95 (1957). See generally *id. passim.*

always the back of the bus for the Negroes; "Lincoln Beach" will rarely if ever be as good as the regular beach. Sometimes it concerns the most vital matters—through the whole history of segregation, colored schools have been so disgracefully inferior to white schools that only ignorance can excuse those who have remained acquiescent members of a community that lived the Molochian child-destroying lie that put them forward as "equal."

Attention is usually focused on these inequalities as things in themselves, correctible by detailed decrees. I am more interested in their very clear character as *evidence* of what segregation means to the people who impose it and to the people who are subjected to it. This evidentiary character cannot be erased by one-step-ahead-of-the-marshal correction. Can a system which, in all that can be measured, has practiced the grossest inequality, actually have been "equal" in intent, in total social meaning and impact? "Thy speech maketh thee manifest . . ."; segregation, in all visible things, speaks only haltingly any dialect but that of inequality.

Further arguments could be piled on top of one another, for we have here to do with the most conspicuous characteristic of a whole regional culture. It is actionable defamation in the South to call a white man a Negro.[16] A small proportion of Negro "blood" puts one in the inferior race for segregation purposes;[17] this is the way in which one deals with a taint, such as a carcinogene in cranberries.

The various items I have mentioned differ in weight; not every one would suffice in itself to establish the character of segregation. Taken together they are of irrefragable strength. The society that has just lost the Negro as a slave, that has just lost out in an attempt to put him under quasi-servile "Codes," the society that views his blood as a contamination and his name as an insult, the society that extralegally imposes on him every humiliating mark of low caste and that until yesterday kept him in line by lynching—this society, careless of his consent, moves by law, first to exclude him from voting, and secondly to cut him off from mixing in the general public life of the community. The Court that refused to see inequality in this cutting off would be making the only kind of law that can be warranted outrageous in advance —law based on self-induced blindness, on flagrant contradiction of known fact.

I have stated all these points shortly because they are matters of common notoriety, matters not so much for judicial notice as for the background knowledge of educated men who live in the world. A court may advise itself of them as it advises itself of the facts that we are a "religious people," that the country is more industrialized than in Jefferson's day, that children are the natural objects of fathers' bounty, that criminal sanctions are commonly thought to deter, that steel is a basic commodity in our economy, that the imputation of unchastity is harmful to a woman. Such judgments, made on

---

16. See MANGUM, LEGAL STATUS OF THE NEGRO ch. II *Libel and Slander* (1940), citing and discussing cases.
17. *Id.* ch. I.

such a basis, are in the foundations of all law, decisional as well as statutory; it would be the most unneutral of principles, improvised *ad hoc*, to require that a court faced with the present problem refuse to note a plain fact about the society of the United States—the fact that the social meaning of segregation is the putting of the Negro in a position of walled-off inferiority—or the other equally plain fact that such treatment is hurtful to human beings. Southern courts, on the basis of just such a judgment, have held that the placing of a white person in a Negro railroad car is an actionable humiliation;[18] must a court pretend not to know that the Negro's situation there is humiliating?

I think that some of the artificial mist of puzzlement called into being around this question originates in a single fundamental mistake. The issue is seen in terms of what might be called the metaphysics of sociology: "Must Segregation Amount to Discrimination?" That is an interesting question; someday the methods of sociology may be adequate to answering it. But it is not our question. Our question is whether discrimination inheres in that segregation which is imposed by law in the twentieth century in certain specific states in the American Union. And that question has meaning and can find an answer only on the ground of history and of common knowledge about the facts of life in the times and places aforesaid.

Now I need not and do not maintain that the evidence is all one way; it never is on issues of burning, fighting concern. Let us not question here the good faith of those who assert that segregation represents no more than an attempt to furnish a wholesome opportunity for parallel development of the races; let us rejoice at the few scattered instances they can bring forward to support their view of the matter. But let us then ask which balance-pan flies upward.[19]

The case seems so onesided that it is hard to make out what is being protested against when it is asked, rhetorically, how the Court can possibly advise itself of the real character of the segregation system. It seems that what is being said is that, while no actual doubt exists as to what segregation is for and what kind of societal pattern it supports and implements, there is no ritually sanctioned way in which the Court, as a Court, can permissibly learn what is obvious to everybody else and to the Justices as individuals. But surely,

---

18. See *id.* at 209-10, 219-20.

19. Professor Wechsler, in the Article to which I am in several points responding, says: "The virtue or demerit of a judgment turns . . . entirely on the reasons that support it and their adequacy to maintain any choice of values it decrees, *or, it is vital to add, to maintain the rejection of a claim that any given choice should be decreed.*" Wechsler, *supra* note 3, at 19-20. (Emphasis added.) Unless it chose to rely without reexamination on the sociology of *Plessy v. Ferguson*, or to follow the evasive, futile, and novel procedure of leaving the matter to Congress (see *id.* at 31-32, rejecting both these nonsolutions, and on the latter point, see my forthcoming *The People and the Court*, at 137-39), what kind of an opinion could the Court have written sustaining the affirmative thesis that segregation as we know it *really is equal*—especially in view of the fact, which I suppose would be conceded, that the very least one can possibly say is that no strong presumption of validity supports racially classificatory state laws?

confronted with such a problem, legal acumen has only one proper task—that of developing ways to make it permissible for the Court to use what it knows; any other counsel is of despair. And, equally surely, the fact that the Court has assumed as true a matter of common knowledge in regard to broad societal patterns, is (to say the very least) pretty far down the list of things to protest against.

I conclude, then, that the Court had the soundest reasons for judging that segregation violates the fourteenth amendment. These reasons make up the simple syllogism with which I began: The fourteenth amendment commands equality, and segregation as we know it is inequality.

Let me take up a few peripheral points. It is true that the specifically hurtful character of segregation, as a net matter in the life of each segregated individual, may be hard to establish.[20] It seems enough to say of this, as Professor Pollak has suggested,[21] that no such demand is made as to other constitutional rights. To have a confession beaten out of one might in some particular case be the beginning of a new and better life. To be subjected to a racially differentiated curfew might be the best thing in the world for some individual boy. A man might ten years later go back to thank the policeman who made him get off the platform and stop making a fool of himself. Religious persecution proverbially strengthens faith. We do not ordinarily go that far, or look so narrowly into the matter. That a practice, on massive historical evidence and in common sense, has the designed and generally apprehended effect of putting its victims at a disadvantage, is enough for law. At least it always has been enough.

I can heartily concur in the judgment that segregation harms the white as much as it does the Negro.[22] Sadism rots the policeman; the suppressor of thought loses light; the community that forms into a mob, and goes down and dominates a trial, may wound itself beyond healing. Can this reciprocity of hurt, this fated mutuality that inheres in all inflicted wrong, serve to validate the wrong itself?

Finally it is doubtless true that the *School Segregation Cases*, and perhaps others of the cases on segregation, represented a choice between two kinds of freedom of association. Freedom from the massive wrong of segregation entails a corresponding loss of freedom on the part of the whites who must now associate with Negroes on public occasions, as we all must on such occasions associate with many persons we had rather not associate with. It is possible to state the competing claims in symmetry, and to ask whether there are constitutional reasons for preferring the Negroes' desire for merged participation in public life to the white man's desire to live a public life without Negroes in proximity.[23]

---

20. See Wechsler, *supra* note 3, at 32-33.
21. Pollak, *supra* note 2, at 28.
22. See Wechsler, *supra* note 3, at 34.
23. *Ibid.*

The question must be answered, but I would approach it in a way which seems to me more normal—the way in which we more usually approach comparable symmetries that might be stated as to all other asserted rights. The fourteenth amendment forbids inequality, forbids the disadvantaging of the Negro race by law. It was surely anticipated that the following of this directive would entail some disagreeableness for some white southerners. The disagreeableness might take many forms; the white man, for example, might dislike having a Negro neighbor in the exercise of the latter's equal right to own a home, or dislike serving on a jury with a Negro, or dislike having Negroes on the streets with him after ten o'clock.[24] When the directive of equality cannot be followed without displeasing the white, then something that can be called a "freedom" of the white must be impaired. If the fourteenth amendment commands equality, and if segregation violates equality, then the status of the reciprocal "freedom" is automatically settled.

I find reinforcement here, at least as a matter of spirit, in the fourteenth amendment command that Negroes shall be "citizens" of their States. It is hard for me to imagine in what operative sense a man could be a "citizen" without his fellow citizens' once in a while having to associate with him. If, for example, his "citizenship" results in his election to the School Board, the white members may (as recently in Houston) put him off to one side of the room, but there is still some impairment of their freedom "not to associate." That freedom, in fact, exists only at home; in public, we have to associate with anybody who has a right to be there. The question of our right not to associate with him is concluded when we decide whether he has a right to be there.

I am not really apologetic for the simplicity of my ideas on the segregation cases. The decisions call for mighty diastrophic change. We ought to call for such change only in the name of a solid reasoned simplicity that takes law out of artfulness into art. Only such grounds can support the nation in its resolve to uphold the law declared by its Court; only such grounds can reconcile the white South to what must be. *Elegantia juris* and conceptual algebra have here no place. Without pretending either to completeness or to definitiveness of statement, I have tried here to show reasons for believing that we as lawyers can without fake or apology present to the lay community, and to ourselves, a rationale of the segregation decisions that rises to the height of the great argument.

These judgments, like all judgments, must rest on the rightness of their law and the truth of their fact. Their law is right if the equal protection clause in the fourteenth amendment is to be taken as stating, without arbitrary exceptions, a broad principle of practical equality for the Negro race, inconsistent with any device that in fact relegates the Negro race to a position of

---

24. The white inhabitants of Mobile in their corporate capacity moved to protect this particular "freedom not to associate" in 1909. See WOODWARD, *op. cit. supra* note 14, at 86-87.

inferiority. Their facts are true if it is true that the segregation system is actually conceived and does actually function as a means of keeping the Negro in a status of inferiority. I dare say at this time that in the end the decisions will be accepted by the profession on just that basis. Opinions composed under painful stresses may leave much to be desired;[25] it may be that the per curiam device has been unwisely used. But the judgments, in law and in fact, are as right and true as any that ever was uttered.

---

25. I do not mean here to join the hue and cry against the *Brown* opinion. The charge that it is "sociological" is either a truism or a canard—a truism if it means that the Court, precisely like the *Plessy* Court, and like innumerable other courts facing innumerable other issues of law, had to resolve and did resolve a question about social fact; a canard if it means that anything like principal reliance was placed on the formally "scientific" authorities, which are relegated to a footnote and treated as merely corroboratory of common sense. It seems to me that the venial fault of the opinion consists in its not spelling out that segregation, for reasons of the kind I have brought forward in this Article, is perceptibly a means of ghettoizing the imputedly inferior race. (I would conjecture that the motive for this omission was reluctance to go into the distasteful details of the southern caste system.) That such treatment is generally not good for children needs less talk than the Court gives it.

COMMENT

BROWN v. BOARD OF EDUCATION AND THE INTEREST-CONVERGENCE DILEMMA

Derrick A. Bell, Jr.[*]

After Brown v. *Board of Education was decided, Professor Herbert Wechsler questioned whether the Supreme Court's decision could be justified on the basis of "neutral" principles. To him* Brown *arbitrarily traded the rights of whites not to associate with blacks in favor of the rights of blacks to associate with whites. In this Comment, Prof. Derrick Bell suggests that no conflict of interest actually existed; for a brief period, the interests of the races converged to make the* Brown *decision inevitable. More recent Supreme Court decisions, however, suggest to Professor Bell a growing divergence of interests that makes integration less feasible. He suggests the interest of blacks in quality education might now be better served by concentration on improving the quality of existing schools, whether desegregated or all-black.*

IN 1954, the Supreme Court handed down the landmark decision *Brown v. Board of Education*,[1] in which the Court ordered the end of state-mandated racial segregation of public schools. Now, more than twenty-five years after that dramatic decision, it is clear that *Brown* will not be forgotten. It has triggered a revolution in civil rights law and in the political leverage available to blacks in and out of court. As Judge Robert L. Carter put it, *Brown* transformed blacks from beggars pleading for decent treatment to citizens demanding equal treatment under the law as their constitutionally recognized right.[2]

Yet today, most black children attend public schools that are both racially isolated and inferior.[3] Demographic patterns, white flight, and the inability of the courts to effect the necessary degree of social reform render further progress in implementing *Brown* almost impossible. The late Professor Alex-

---

[*] Professor of Law, Harvard University. This Comment is a later version of a paper presented at a Harvard Law School symposium held in October 1978, to commemorate the 25th anniversary of Brown v. Board of Educ., 347 U.S. 483 (1954). I wish to thank Professors Owen Fiss, Karl Klare, Charles Lawrence, and David Shapiro for their advice and encouragement on this piece.

[1] 347 U.S. 483 (1954).

[2] Carter, *The Warren Court and Desegregation*, in RACE, RACISM AND AMERICAN LAW 456–61 (D. Bell ed. 1973).

[3] *See* Bell, Book Review, 92 HARV. L. REV. 1826, 1826 n.6 (1979). *See also* C. JENCKS, INEQUALITY 27–28 (1972).

518

ander Bickel warned that *Brown* would not be overturned but, for a whole array of reasons, "may be headed for — dread word — irrelevance."[4] Bickel's prediction is premature in law where the *Brown* decision remains viable, but it may be an accurate assessment of its current practical value to millions of black children who have not experienced the decision's promise of equal educational opportunity.

Shortly after *Brown*, Professor Herbert Wechsler rendered a sharp and nagging criticism of the decision.[5] Though he welcomed its result, he criticized its lack of a principled basis. Professor Wechsler's views have since been persuasively refuted,[6] yet within them lie ideas which may help to explain the disappointment of *Brown* and what can be done to renew its promise.

In this Comment, I plan to take a new look at Wechsler within the context of the subsequent desegregation campaign. By doing so, I hope to offer an explanation of why school desegregation has in large part failed and what can be done to bring about change.

I. PROFESSOR WECHSLER'S SEARCH FOR NEUTRAL PRINCIPLES IN BROWN

The year was 1959, five years after the Supreme Court's decision in *Brown*. If there was anything the hard-pressed partisans of the case did not need, it was more criticism of a decision ignored by the President, condemned by much of Congress, and resisted wherever it was sought to be enforced.[7] Certainly, civil rights adherents did not welcome adding to the growing list of critics the name of Professor Herbert Wechsler, an outstanding lawyer, a frequent advocate for civil rights causes, and a scholar of prestige and influence.[8] Nevertheless,

---

[4] A. BICKEL, THE SUPREME COURT AND THE IDEA OF PROGRESS 151 (1970).

[5] Wechsler, *Toward Neutral Principles of Constitutional Law*, 73 HARV. L. REV. 1 (1959). The lecture was later published in a collection of selected essays. H. WECHSLER, PRINCIPLES, POLITICS, AND FUNDAMENTAL LAW 3 (1961).

[6] *See, e.g.*, Black, *The Lawfulness of the Segregation Decisions*, 69 YALE L.J. 421 (1960); Heyman, *The Chief Justice, Racial Segregation, and the Friendly Critics*, 49 CALIF. L. REV. 104 (1961); Pollak, *Racial Discrimination and Judicial Integrity: A Reply to Professor Wechsler*, 108 U. PA. L. REV. 1 (1959).

[7] The legal campaign that culminated in the *Brown* decision is discussed in great depth in R. KLUGER, SIMPLE JUSTICE (1976). The subsequent 15 years is reviewed in S. WASBY, A. D'AMATO & R. METRAILER, DESEGREGATION FROM BROWN TO ALEXANDER (1977).

[8] Professor Wechsler is the Harlan Fiske Stone Professor of Constitutional Law Emeritus at the Columbia University Law School. His work is reviewed in 78 COLUM. L. REV. 969 (1978) (issue dedicated in Professor Wechsler's honor upon his retirement).

Professor Wechsler chose that time and an invitation to deliver Harvard Law School's Oliver Wendell Holmes Lecture as the occasion to raise new questions about the legal appropriateness and principled shortcomings of *Brown* and several other major civil rights decisions.[9]

Here was an attack that could not be dismissed as after-the-fact faultfinding by a conservative academician using his intellect to further a preference for keeping blacks in their "separate-but-equal" place. Professor Wechsler began by saying that he had welcomed the result in *Brown*; he noted that he had joined with the NAACP's Charles Houston in litigating civil rights cases in the Supreme Court.[10] He added that he was not offended because the Court failed to uphold earlier decisions approving segregated schools. Nor was he persuaded by the argument that the issue should have been left to Congress because the Court's judgment might not be honored.[11]

Wechsler did not align himself with the "realists," who "perceive in law only the element of fiat, in whose conception of the legal cosmos reason has no meaning or no place,"[12] nor with the "formalists," who "frankly or covertly make the test of virtue in interpretation whether its result in the immediate decision seems to hinder or advance the interests or the values they support."[13] Wechsler instead saw the need for criteria of decision that could be framed and tested as an exercise of reason and not merely adopted as an act of willfulness or will. He believed, in short, that courts could engage in a "principled appraisal" of legislative actions that exceeded a fixed "historical meaning" of constitutional provisions without, as Judge Learned Hand feared, becoming "a third legislative chamber."[14] Courts, Wechsler argued, "must be genuinely principled, resting with respect to every step that is involved in reaching judgment on analysis and reasons quite transcending the immediate result that is achieved."[15] Applying these standards, which included constitutional and statutory interpretation, the subtle guidance provided by history, and appropriate but not slavish fidelity to precedent, Wechsler found difficulty with Supreme Court decisions where principled reasoning was in his view either deficient or, in some instances,

---

[9] *See* Wechsler, *supra* note 5, at 31–35.

[10] Wechsler recalled that Houston, who was black, "did not suffer more than I in knowing that we had to go to Union Station to lunch together during the recess." *Id.* at 34.

[11] *Id.* at 31–32.

[12] *Id.* at 11.

[13] *Id.*

[14] *Id.* at 16.

[15] *Id.* at 15.

nonexistent.[16] He included the *Brown* opinion in the latter category.

Wechsler reviewed and rejected the possibility that *Brown* was based on a declaration that the fourteenth amendment barred all racial lines in legislation.[17] He also doubted that the opinion relied upon a factual determination that segregation caused injury to black children, since evidence as to such harm was both inadequate and conflicting.[18] Rather, Wechsler concluded, the Court in *Brown* must have rested its holding on the view that "racial segregation is, *in principle*, a denial of equality to the minority against whom it is directed; that is, the group that is not dominant politically and, therefore, does not make the choice involved."[19] Yet, Wechsler found this argument untenable as well, because, among other difficulties, it seemed to require an inquiry into the motives of the legislature, a practice generally foreclosed to the courts.[20]

After dismissing these arguments, Wechsler then asserted that the legal issue in state-imposed segregation cases was not one of discrimination at all, but rather of associational rights: "the denial by the state of freedom to associate, a denial that impinges in the same way on any groups or races that may be involved."[21] Wechsler reasoned that "if the freedom of association is denied by segregation, integration forces an association upon those for whom it is unpleasant or repugnant."[22] And concluding with a question that has challenged legal scholars, Wechsler asked:

> Given a situation where the state must practically choose between denying the association to those individuals who wish it or imposing it on those who would avoid it, is there a basis in neutral principles for holding that the Constitution demands that the claims for association should prevail?[23]

In suggesting that there was a basis in neutral principles for holding that the Constitution supports a claim by blacks for an associational right, Professor Wechsler confessed that he had not yet written an opinion supporting such a holding. "To write it is for me the challenge of the school-segregation cases."[24]

---

[16] *Id.* at 19.
[17] *Id.* at 32.
[18] *Id.* at 32–33.
[19] *Id.* at 33 (emphasis added).
[20] *Id.* at 33–34.
[21] *Id.* at 34.
[22] *Id.*
[23] *Id.*
[24] *Id.*

II. THE SEARCH FOR A NEUTRAL PRINCIPLE: RACIAL EQUALITY AND INTEREST CONVERGENCE

Scholars who accepted Professor Wechsler's challenge had little difficulty finding a neutral principle on which the *Brown* decision could be based. Indeed, from the hindsight of a quarter century of the greatest racial consciousness-raising the country has ever known, much of Professor Wechsler's concern seems hard to imagine. To doubt that racial segregation is harmful to blacks, and to suggest that what blacks really sought was the right to associate with whites, is to believe in a world that does not exist now and could not possibly have existed then. Professor Charles Black, therefore, correctly viewed racial equality as the neutral principle which underlay the *Brown* opinion.[25] In Black's view, Wechsler's question "is awkwardly simple,"[26] and he states his response in the form of a syllogism. Black's major premise is that "the equal protection clause of the fourteenth amendment should be read as saying that the Negro race, as such, is not to be significantly disadvantaged by the laws of the states."[27] His minor premise is that "segregation is a massive intentional disadvantaging of the Negro race, as such, by state law."[28] The conclusion, then, is that the equal protection clause clearly bars racial segregation because segregation harms blacks and benefits whites in ways too numerous and obvious to require citation.[29]

Logically, the argument is persuasive, and Black has no trouble urging that "[w]hen the directive of equality cannot be followed without displeasing the white[s], then something that can be called a 'freedom' of the white[s] must be impaired."[30] It is precisely here, though, that many whites part company with Professor Black. Whites may agree in the abstract that blacks are citizens and are entitled to constitutional protection against racial discrimination, but few are willing to recognize that racial segregation is much more than a series of quaint customs that can be remedied effectively without altering the status of whites. The extent of this unwillingness is illustrated by the controversy over affirmative action programs, particularly those where identifiable whites must step aside for blacks they deem less qualified or less deserving. Whites simply cannot envision the personal responsibility and the potential sacrifice inherent in Professor Black's conclusion that true equality

---

[25] *See* Black, *supra* note 6, at 428–29.
[26] *Id*. at 421.
[27] *Id*.
[28] *Id*.
[29] *Id*. at 425–26.
[30] *Id*. at 429.

for blacks will require the surrender of racism-granted privileges for whites.

This sober assessment of reality raises concern about the ultimate import of Black's theory. On a normative level, as a description of how the world *ought* to be, the notion of racial equality appears to be the proper basis on which *Brown* rests, and Wechsler's framing of the problem in terms of associational rights thus seems misplaced. Yet, on a positivistic level — how the world *is* — it is clear that racial equality is not deemed legitimate by large segments of the American people, at least to the extent it threatens to impair the societal status of whites. Hence, Wechsler's search for a guiding principle in the context of associational rights retains merit in the positivistic sphere, because it suggests a deeper truth about the subordination of law to interest-group politics with a racial configuration.

Although no such subordination is apparent in *Brown*, it is possible to discern in more recent school decisions the outline of a principle, applied without direct acknowledgment, that could serve as the positivistic expression of the neutral statement of general applicability sought by Professor Wechsler. Its elements rely as much on political history as legal precedent and emphasize the world as it is rather than how we might want it to be. Translated from judicial activity in racial cases both before and after *Brown*, this principle of "interest convergence" provides: The interest of blacks in achieving racial equality will be accommodated only when it converges with the interests of whites. However, the fourteenth amendment, standing alone, will not authorize a judicial remedy providing effective racial equality for blacks where the remedy sought threatens the superior societal status of middle and upper class whites.

It follows that the availability of fourteenth amendment protection in racial cases may not actually be determined by the character of harm suffered by blacks or the quantum of liability proved against whites. Racial remedies may instead be the outward manifestations of unspoken and perhaps subconscious judicial conclusions that the remedies, if granted, will secure, advance, or at least not harm societal interests deemed important by middle and upper class whites. Racial justice — or its appearance — may, from time to time, be counted among the interests deemed important by the courts and by society's policymakers.

In assessing how this principle can accommodate both the *Brown* decision and the subsequent development of school desegregation law, it is necessary to remember that the issue of school segregation and the harm it inflicted on black children did not first come to the Court's attention in the *Brown* litigation: blacks had been attacking the validity of these policies for 100 years.[31] Yet, prior to *Brown*, black claims that segregated public schools were inferior had been met by orders requiring merely that facilities be made equal.[32] What accounted, then, for the sudden shift in 1954 away from the separate but equal doctrine and towards a commitment to desegregation?

I contend that the decision in *Brown* to break with the Court's long-held position on these issues cannot be understood without some consideration of the decision's value to whites, not simply those concerned about the immorality of racial inequality, but also those whites in policymaking positions able to see the economic and political advances at home and abroad that would follow abandonment of segregation. First, the decision helped to provide immediate credibility to America's struggle with Communist countries to win the hearts and minds of emerging third world peoples. At least this argument was advanced by lawyers for both the NAACP and the federal government.[33] And the point was not lost on the news media. *Time* magazine, for example, predicted that the international impact of *Brown* would be scarcely less important than its effect on the education of black children: "In many countries, where U.S. prestige and leadership have been damaged by the fact of U.S. segregation, it will come as a timely reassertion of the basic American principle that 'all men are created equal.'"[34]

Second, *Brown* offered much needed reassurance to American blacks that the precepts of equality and freedom so heralded during World War II might yet be given meaning at home. Returning black veterans faced not only continuing discrimination, but also violent attacks in the South which rivalled those that took place at the conclusion of World War I.[35] Their disillusionment and anger were poignantly expressed by the black actor, Paul Robeson, who in 1949 declared: "It is unthinkable . . . that American Negroes would

---

[31] *See, e.g.*, Roberts v. City of Boston, 59 Mass. (5 Cush.) 198 (1850).

[32] The cases are collected in Larson, *The New Law of Race Relations*, 1969 WIS. L. REV. 470, 482, 483 n.27; Leflar & Davis, *Segregation in the Public Schools — 1953*, 67 HARV. L. REV. 377, 430–35 (1954).

[33] *See* Bell, *Racial Remediation: An Historical Perspective on Current Conditions*, 52 NOTRE DAME LAW. 5, 12 (1976).

[34] *Id.* at 12 n.31.

[35] C. VANN WOODWARD, THE STRANGE CAREER OF JIM CROW 114 (3d rev. ed. 1974); J. FRANKLIN, FROM SLAVERY TO FREEDOM 478–86 (3d ed. 1967).

go to war on behalf of those who have oppressed us for generations . . . against a country [the Soviet Union] which in one generation has raised our people to the full human dignity of mankind."[36] It is not impossible to imagine that fear of the spread of such sentiment influenced subsequent racial decisions made by the courts.

Finally, there were whites who realized that the South could make the transition from a rural, plantation society to the sunbelt with all its potential and profit only when it ended its struggle to remain divided by state-sponsored segregation.[37] Thus, segregation was viewed as a barrier to further industrialization in the South.

These points may seem insufficient proof of self-interest leverage to produce a decision as important as *Brown*. They are cited, however, to help assess and not to diminish the Supreme Court's most important statement on the principle of racial equality. Here, as in the abolition of slavery, there were whites for whom recognition of the racial equality principle was sufficient motivation. But, as with abolition, the number who would act on morality alone was insufficient to bring about the desired racial reform.[38]

Thus, for those whites who sought an end to desegregation on moral grounds or for the pragmatic reasons outlined above, *Brown* appeared to be a welcome break with the past. When segregation was finally condemned by the Supreme Court, however, the outcry was nevertheless great, especially among poorer whites who feared loss of control over their public schools and other facilities. Their fear of loss was intensified by the sense that they had been betrayed. They relied, as had generations before them, on the expectation that white elites would maintain lower class whites in a societal status superior

---

[36] D. BUTLER, PAUL ROBESON 137 (1976) (unwritten speech before the Partisans of Peace, World Peace Congress in Paris).

[37] Professor Robert Higgs argued that the "region's economic development increasingly undermined the foundations of its traditional racial relations." Higgs, *Race and Economy in the South, 1890–1950*, in THE AGE OF SEGREGATION 89–90 (R. Haws ed. 1978). Sociologists Frances Piven and Richard Cloward have also drawn a connection between this economic growth and the support for the civil rights movement in the 1940's and 1950's, when various white elites in business, philanthropy, and government began to speak out against racial discrimination. F. PIVEN & R. CLOWARD, REGULATING THE POOR 229–30 (1971). *See also* F. PIVEN & R. CLOWARD, POOR PEOPLE'S MOVEMENTS 189–94 (1977).

[38] President Lincoln, for example, acknowledged the moral evil in slavery. In his famous letter to publisher Horace Greeley, however, he promised to free all, some, or none of the slaves, depending on which policy would most help save the Union. SPEECHES AND LETTERS OF ABRAHAM LINCOLN, 1832–65, at 194–95 (M. Roe ed. 1907).

to that designated for blacks.[39] In fact, there is evidence that segregated schools and facilities were initially established by legislatures at the insistence of the white working class.[40] Today, little has changed. Many poorer whites oppose social reform as "welfare programs for blacks" although, ironically, they have employment, education, and social service needs that differ from those of poor blacks by a margin that, without a racial scorecard, is difficult to measure.[41]

Unfortunately, poorer whites are now not alone in their opposition to school desegregation and to other attempts to improve the societal status of blacks: recent decisions, most notably by the Supreme Court, indicate that the convergence of black and white interests that led to *Brown* in 1954 and influenced the character of its enforcement has begun to fade. In *Swann v. Charlotte-Mecklenburg Board of Education*,[42] Chief Justice Burger spoke of the "reconciliation of competing values" in desegregation cases.[43] If there was any doubt that "competing values" referred to the conflicting interests of blacks seeking desegregation and whites who prefer to retain existing school policies, then the uncertainty was dispelled by *Milliken v. Bradley*,[44] and by *Dayton Board of Education v. Brinkman (Dayton I)*.[45] In both cases, the Court elevated the concept of "local autonomy" to a "vital national tradition":[46] "No single tradition in public education is more deeply rooted than local control over the operation of schools; local autonomy has long been thought essential both to the maintenance of community concern and support for public schools and to quality of the educational process."[47] Local con-

---

[39] *See* F. PIVEN & R. CLOWARD, POOR PEOPLE'S MOVEMENTS 187 (1977). *See generally* Bell, *supra* note 33.

[40] *See* C. VANN WOODWARD, *supra* note 35, at 6.

[41] Robert Heilbruner suggests that this country's failure to address social issues including poverty, public health, housing, and prison reform as effectively as many European countries is due to the tendency of whites to view reform efforts as "programs to 'subsidize' Negroes. . . . In such cases the fear and resentment of the Negro takes precedence over the social problem itself. The result, unfortunately, is that the entire society suffers from the results of a failure to correct social evils whose ill effects refuse to obey the rules of segregation." Heilbruner, *The Roots of Social Neglect in the United States*, in IS LAW DEAD? 288, 296 (E. Rostow ed. 1971).

[42] 402 U.S. 1 (1971).

[43] *Id.* at 31.

[44] 418 U.S. 717 (1974) (limits power of federal courts to treat a primarily black urban school district and largely white suburban districts as a single unit in mandating desegregation).

[45] 433 U.S. 406 (1977) (desegregation orders affecting pupil assignments should seek only the racial mix that would have existed absent the constitutional violation).

[46] *Id.* at 410; 418 U.S. at 741–42.

[47] 418 U.S. at 741.

trol, however, may result in the maintenance of a status quo that will preserve superior educational opportunities and facilities for whites at the expense of blacks. As one commentator has suggested, "It is implausible to assume that school boards guilty of substantial violations in the past will take the interests of black school children to heart."[48]

As a result of its change in attitudes, the Court has increasingly erected barriers to achieving the forms of racial balance relief it earlier had approved.[49] Plaintiffs must now prove that the complained-of segregation was the result of discriminatory actions intentionally and invidiously conducted or authorized by school officials.[50] It is not enough that segregation was the "natural and foreseeable" consequence of their policies.[51] And even when this difficult standard of proof is met, courts must carefully limit the relief granted to the harm actually proved.[52] Judicial second thoughts about racial balance plans with broad-range busing components, the very plans which civil rights lawyers have come to rely on, is clearly evident in these new proof standards.

There is, however, continuing if unpredictable concern in the Supreme Court about school boards whose policies reveal long-term adherence to overt racial discrimination. In many cases, trial courts exposed to exhaustive testimony regarding the failure of school officials to either desegregate or provide substantial equality of schooling for minority children, become convinced that school boards are violating *Brown*. Thus far, unstable Supreme Court majorities have upheld broad desegregation plans ordered by these judges,[53] but the reservations expressed by concurring Justices[54] and the vigor of those Justices who dissent[55] caution against optimism in this still controversial area of civil rights law.[56]

---

[48] *The Supreme Court, 1978 Term*, 93 HARV. L. REV. 60, 130 (1979).

[49] *See generally* Fiss, *School Desegregation: The Uncertain Path of the Law*, 4 PHILOSOPHY & PUB. AFF. 3 (1974); Kanner, *From Denver to Dayton: The Development of a Theory of Equal Protection Remedies*, 72 Nw. U.L. REV. 382 (1977).

[50] Dayton Bd. of Educ. v. Brinkman (Dayton I), 433 U.S. 406 (1977).

[51] Columbus Bd. of Educ. v. Penick, 99 S. Ct. 2941, 2950 (1979).

[52] Austin Independent School Dist. v. United States, 429 U.S. 990, 991 (1976) (Powell, J., concurring).

[53] Dayton Bd. of Educ. v. Brinkman (Dayton II), 99 S. Ct. 2971 (1979); Columbus Bd. of Educ. v. Penick, 99 S. Ct. 2941 (1979).

[54] *See* Columbus Bd. of Educ. v. Penick, 99 S. Ct. 2941, 2952 (1979) (Burger, C.J., concurring); *id.* at 2983 (Stewart, J., concurring).

[55] *See id.* at 2952 (Rehnquist, J., dissenting); *id.* at 2988 (Powell, J., dissenting). *See also* Dayton Bd. of Educ. v. Brinkman (Dayton II), 99 S. Ct. 2971, 2983 (1979) (Stewart, J., dissenting).

[56] The Court faces another difficult challenge in the 1979 Term when it reviews whether the racial balance plan in Dallas, Texas, goes far enough in eliminating one

At the very least, these decisions reflect a substantial and growing divergence in the interests of whites and blacks. The result could prove to be the realization of Professor Wechsler's legitimate fear that, if there is not a change of course, the purported entitlement of whites not to associate with blacks in public schools may yet eclipse the hope and the promise of *Brown*.

III. INTEREST-CONVERGENCE REMEDIES UNDER BROWN

Further progress to fulfill the mandate of *Brown* is possible to the extent that the divergence of racial interests can be avoided or minimized. Whites in policymaking positions, including those who sit on federal courts, can take no comfort in the conditions of dozens of inner-city school systems where the great majority of nonwhite children attend classes as segregated and ineffective as those so roundly condemned by Chief Justice Warren in the *Brown* opinion. Nor do poorer whites gain from their opposition to the improvement of educational opportunities for blacks: as noted earlier, the needs of the two groups differ little.[57] Hence, over time, all will reap the benefits from a concerted effort towards achieving racial equality.

The question still remains as to the surest way to reach the goal of educational effectiveness for both blacks and whites. I believe that the most widely used programs mandated by the courts — "antidefiance, racial balance" plans — may in some cases be inferior to plans focusing on "educational components," including the creation and development of "model" all-black schools. A short history of the use of the antidefiance strategy would be helpful at this point.

By the end of the 1950's, it was apparent that compliance with the *Brown* mandate to desegregate the public schools would not come easily or soon. In the seventeen border states and the District of Columbia, fewer than 200 thousand blacks were actually attending classes with white children.[58] The states in the deep South had not begun even token desegregation,[59] and it would take Supreme Court action to reverse

---

race schools in a large district that is now 65% black and Hispanic. Tasby v. Estes, 572 F.2d 1010 (5th Cir. 1978), *cert. granted sub nom.* Estes v. Metropolitan Branches of Dallas NAACP, 440 U.S. 906 (1979).

[57] *See* p. 526 *supra.*

[58] P. BERGMAN, THE CHRONOLOGICAL HISTORY OF THE NEGRO IN AMERICA 561 (1969).

[59] *Id.* at 561–62.

the years-long effort of the Prince Edward County School Board in Virginia to abolish rather than desegregate its public schools.[60] Supreme Court orders[61] and presidential action had already been required to enable a handful of black students to attend Central High School in Little Rock, Arkansas.[62] Opposition to *Brown* was clearly increasing. Its supporters were clearly on the defensive, as was the Supreme Court itself.

For blacks, the goal in school desegregation suits remained the effective use of the *Brown* mandate to eliminate state-sanctioned segregation. These efforts received unexpected help from the excesses of the massive resistance movement that led courts to justify relief under *Brown* as a reaffirmance of the supremacy of the judiciary on issues of constitutional interpretation. *Brown*, in the view of many, might not have been a wise or proper decision, but violent and prolonged opposition to its implementation posed an even greater danger to the federal system.

The Supreme Court quickly recognized this additional basis on which to ground school desegregation orders. "As this case reaches us," the Court began its dramatic opinion in *Cooper v. Aaron*,[63] "it raises questions of the highest importance to the maintenance of our federal system of government."[64] Reaching back to *Marbury v. Madison*,[65] the Court reaffirmed Chief Justice Marshall's statement that "[i]t is emphatically the province and duty of the judicial department to say what the law is."[66] There were few opponents to this stand, and Professor Wechsler was emphatically not one of them. His criticism of *Brown* concluded with a denial that he intended to offer "comfort to anyone who claims legitimacy in defiance of the courts."[67] Those who accept the benefits of our constitutional system, Wechsler felt, cannot deny its allegiance when a special burden is imposed. Defiance of court orders, he asserted, constituted the "ultimate negation of all neutral principles."[68]

For some time, then, the danger to federalism posed by the secessionist-oriented resistance of Southern state and local of-

---

[60] Griffin v. County School Bd., 377 U.S. 218 (1964).

[61] Cooper v. Aaron, 358 U.S. 1 (1958).

[62] P. BERGMAN, *supra* note 58, at 555–56, 561–62.

[63] 358 U.S. 1 (1958).

[64] *Id.* at 4.

[65] 5 U.S. (1 Cranch) 137, 177 (1803).

[66] 358 U.S. at 18.

[67] Wechsler, *supra* note 5, at 35.

[68] *Id.*

ficials provided courts with an independent basis for supporting school desegregation efforts.[69] In the lower federal courts, the perceived threat to judicial status was often quite personal. Surely, I was not the only civil rights attorney who received a favorable decision in a school desegregation case less by legal precedent than because a federal judge, initially hostile to those precedents, my clients and their lawyer, became incensed with school board litigation tactics that exhibited as little respect for the court as they did for the constitutional rights of black children.

There was a problem with school desegregation decisions framed in this antidefiance form that was less discernible then than now. While a prerequisite to the provision of equal educational opportunity, condemnation of school board evasion was far from synonymous with that long-promised goal. Certainly, it was cause for celebration when the Court recognized that some pupil assignment schemes,[70] "freedom-of-choice" plans,[71] and similar "desegregation plans," were in fact designed to retain constitutionally condemned dual school systems. And, when the Court, in obvious frustration with the slow pace of school desegregation, announced in 1968 what Justice Powell later termed "the *Green/Swann* doctrine of 'affirmative duty,'"[72] which placed on school boards the duty to disestablish their dual school systems, the decisions were welcomed as substantial victories by civil rights lawyers. Yet, the remedies set forth in the major school cases following *Brown* — balancing the student and teacher populations by race in each school, eliminating one-race schools, redrawing school attendance lines, and transporting students to achieve racial balance[73] — have not in themselves guaranteed black children

---

[69] *See, e.g.*, Goss v. Board of Educ., 373 U.S. 683 (1963) (struck down "minority to majority" transfer plans enabling resegregation of schools); Bush v. New Orleans Parish School Bd., 188 F. Supp. 916 (E.D. La.), *aff'd*, 365 U.S. 569 (1961) (invalidation of state "interposition acts"); Poindexter v. Louisiana Financial Comm'n, 275 F. Supp. 833 (E.D. La. 1967), *aff'd per curiam*, 389 U.S. 215 (1968) ("tuition grants" for children attending private segregated schools voided).

[70] These plans, requiring black children to run a gauntlet of administrative proceedings to obtain assignment to a white school, were at first judicially approved. *See* Covington v. Edwards, 264 F.2d 780 (4th Cir.), *cert. denied*, 361 U.S. 840 (1959); Shuttlesworth v. Birmingham Bd. of Educ., 162 F. Supp. 372 (N.D. Ala.), *aff'd*, 358 U.S. 101 (1958).

[71] Green v. County School Bd., 391 U.S. 430 (1968) (practice of "free choice" — enabling each student to choose whether to attend a black or white school — struck down).

[72] Keyes v. School Dist. No. 1, 413 U.S. 189, 224 (1973) (Powell, J., concurring in part and dissenting in part).

[73] *See, e.g.*, Swann v. Charlotte-Mecklenburg Bd. of Educ., 402 U.S. 1 (1971); Green v. County School Bd., 391 U.S. 430 (1968).

better schooling than they received in the pre-*Brown* era. Such racial balance measures have often altered the racial appearance of dual school systems without eliminating racial discrimination. Plans relying on racial balance to foreclose evasion have not eliminated the need for further orders protecting black children against discriminatory policies, including resegregation within desegregated schools,[74] the loss of black faculty and administrators,[75] suspensions and expulsions at much higher rates than white students,[76] and varying forms of racial harassment ranging from exclusion from extracurricular activities[77] to physical violence.[78] Antidefiance remedies, then, while effective in forcing alterations in school system structure, often encourage and seldom shield black children from discriminatory retaliation.

The educational benefits that have resulted from the mandatory assignment of black and white children to the same schools are also debatable.[79] If benefits did exist, they have begun to dissipate as whites flee in alarming numbers from school districts ordered to implement mandatory reassignment plans.[80] In response, civil rights lawyers sought to include entire metropolitan areas within mandatory reassignment plans in order to encompass mainly white suburban school districts

---

[74] *See, e.g.*, Jackson v. Marvell School Dist. No. 22, 425 F.2d 211 (8th Cir. 1970). There were also efforts to segregate students within desegregated schools by the use of standardized tests and achievement scores. *See* Singleton v. Jackson Mun. Separate School Dist., 419 F.2d 1211 (5th Cir.), *rev'd per curiam*, 396 U.S. 290 (1970); Hobson v. Hansen, 269 F. Supp. 401 (D.D.C. 1967), *aff'd sub nom.* Smuck v. Hobson, 408 F.2d 175 (D.C. Cir. 1969).

[75] *See, e.g.*, Chambers v. Hendersonville City Bd. of Educ., 364 F.2d 189 (4th Cir. 1966). For a discussion of the wholesale dismissal and demotion of black teachers in the wake of school desegregation orders, see materials compiled in 2 N. DORSEN, P. BENDER, B. NEUBORNE & S. LAW, ENERSON, HABER, AND DORSEN'S POLITICAL AND CIVIL RIGHTS IN THE UNITED STATES 679–80 (4th ed. 1979).

[76] Hawkins v. Coleman, 376 F. Supp. 1330 (N.D. Tex. 1974); Dunn v. Tyler Independent School Dist., 327 F. Supp. 528 (E.D. Tex. 1971), *aff'd in part and rev'd in part*, 460 F.2d 137 (5th Cir. 1972).

[77] Floyd v. Trice, 490 F.2d 1154 (8th Cir. 1974); Augustus v. School Bd., 361 F. Supp. 383 (N.D. Fla. 1973), *modified*, 507 F.2d 152 (5th Cir. 1975).

[78] For a recent example, see the account of racial violence resulting from desegregation in Boston in Husoch, *Boston: The Problem That Won't Go Away*, N.Y. Times, Nov. 25, 1979, § 6 (Magazine), at 32.

[79] *See* N. ST. JOHN, SCHOOL DESEGREGATION 16–41 (1975).

[80] *See* D. Armor, White Flight, Demographic Transition, and the Future of School Desegregation (1978) (Rand Paper Series, The Rand Corp.); J. Coleman, S. Kelly & J. Moore, Trends in School Segregation, 1968–73 (1975) (Urban Institute Paper). *But see* Pettigrew & Green, *School Desegregation in Large Cities: A Critique of the Coleman "White Flight" Thesis*, 46 HARV. EDUC. REV. 1 (1976); Rossell, *School Desegregation and White Flight*, 90 POL. SCI. Q. 675 (1975); R. Farley, School Integration and White Flight (1975) (Population Studies Center, U. Mich.).

where so many white parents sought sanctuary for their children.[81]

Thus, the antidefiance strategy was brought full circle from a mechanism for preventing evasion by school officials of *Brown's* antisegregation mandate to one aimed at creating a discrimination-free environment. This approach to the implementation of *Brown*, however, has become increasingly ineffective; indeed, it has in some cases been educationally destructive. A preferable method is to focus on obtaining real educational effectiveness which may entail the improvement of presently desegregated schools as well as the creation or preservation of model black schools.

Civil rights lawyers do not oppose such relief, but they clearly consider it secondary to the racial balance remedies authorized in the *Swann*[82] and *Keyes*[83] cases. Those who espouse alternative remedies are deemed to act out of suspect motives. *Brown* is the law, and racial balance plans are the only means of complying with the decision. The position reflects courage, but it ignores the frequent and often complete failure of programs which concentrate solely on achieving a racial balance.

Desegregation remedies that do not integrate may seem a step backward toward the *Plessy* "separate but equal" era. Some black educators, however, see major educational benefits in schools where black children, parents, and teachers can utilize the real cultural strengths of the black community to overcome the many barriers to educational achievement.[84] As Professor Laurence Tribe argued, "[J]udicial rejection of the 'separate but equal' talisman seems to have been accompanied by a potentially troublesome lack of sympathy for racial separateness as a possible expression of group solidarity."[85]

This is not to suggest that educationally oriented remedies can be developed and adopted without resistance. Policies necessary to obtain effective schools threaten the self-interest of teacher unions and others with vested interests in the status quo. But successful magnet schools may provide a lesson that

---

[81] *See, e.g.*, Milliken v. Bradley, 418 U.S. 717 (1974). In Los Angeles, where the court ordered reassignment of 65,000 students in grades four through eight, 30–50% of the 22,000 white students scheduled for mandatory busing boycotted the public schools or enrolled elsewhere. U.S. COMM'N ON CIVIL RIGHTS, DESEGREGATION OF THE NATION'S PUBLIC SCHOOLS: A STATUS REPORT 51 (1979).

[82] Swann v. Charlotte-Mecklenburg Bd. of Educ., 402 U.S. 1 (1971).

[83] Keyes v. School Dist. No. 1, 413 U.S. 189 (1973).

[84] S. LIGHTFOOT, WORLDS APART 172 (1978). For a discussion of the Lightfoot theory, see Bell, *supra* note 3, at 1838.

[85] L. TRIBE, AMERICAN CONSTITUTIONAL LAW § 16-15, at 1022 (1978) (footnote omitted).

effective schools for blacks must be a primary goal rather than a secondary result of integration. Many white parents recognize a value in integrated schooling for their children but they quite properly view integration as merely one component of an effective education. To the extent that civil rights advocates also accept this reasonable sense of priority, some greater racial interest conformity should be possible.

*   *   *

Is this what the *Brown* opinion meant by "equal educational opportunity"? Chief Justice Warren said the Court could not "turn the clock back to 1868 when the [fourteenth] Amendment was adopted, or even to 1896 when *Plessy v. Ferguson* was written."[86] The change in racial circumstances since 1954 rivals or surpasses all that occurred during the period that preceded it. If the decision that was at least a catalyst for that change is to remain viable, those who rely on it must exhibit the dynamic awareness of all the legal and political considerations that influenced those who wrote it.

Professor Wechsler warned us early on that there was more to *Brown* than met the eye. At one point, he observed that the opinion is "often read with less fidelity by those who praise it than by those by whom it is condemned."[87] Most of us ignored that observation openly and quietly raised a question about the sincerity of the observer. Criticism, as we in the movement for minority rights have every reason to learn, is a synonym for neither cowardice nor capitulation. It may instead bring awareness, always the first step toward overcoming still another barrier in the struggle for racial equality.

---

[86] Brown v. Board of Educ., 347 U.S. 483, 492 (1954).

[87] Wechsler, *supra* note 5, at 32.

Mississippi Law Journal

VOLUME XXXVIII   MARCH 1967   NUMBER 2

DE FACTO AND DE JURE SCHOOL SEGREGATION: SOME REFLECTED LIGHT ON THE FOURTEENTH AMENDMENT FROM THE CIVIL RIGHTS ACT OF 1875.

*by Alfred Avins**

I. INTRODUCTION

More than ten years after *Brown v. Board of Educ.*[1] race relations and schools are still very much in the news. The continuing number of cases on de facto and de jure school segregation[2] has continued public interest in this area. A review of the original understanding of the framers of the fourteenth amendment as applied to school segregation is clearly appropriate at this time.

Ten years ago, an article reviewing the original intent as reflected in the debates on the fourteenth amendment itself concluded that direct light on the subject was quite scanty.[3] However, there is abundant reflected light from the debates on the proposed school clause of the bill which ultimately became the Civil Rights Act of 1875.[4] The fact that the school clause was ultimately stricken from the bill has no doubt discouraged research in this area. Yet the debates thereon are illuminating for the reflected light they cast on the intent of the fourteenth amendment as it relates to schools. This article will analyze that debate.

II. SUMNER AND THE AMNESTY BILL AMENDMENT

On May 13, 1870, Senator Charles Sumner, the ultra-equalitarian

---

*Professor of Law, Memphis State University Law School. B.A., 1954, Hunter College; LL.B., 1956, Columbia University; LL.M., 1957, New York University; M.L., 1961, J.S.D., 1962, University of Chicago; Ph.D., 1965, University of Cambridge (England).

[1]Brown v. Board of Educ., 347 U.S. 483 (1954).

[2]Many recent cases and articles are referred to in Dowell v. School Bd., 244 F. Supp. 971 (W.D. Okla. 1965).

[3]Bickel, *The Original Understanding and the Segregation Decision*, 69 HARV. L. REV. 1, 56-59 (1959).

[4]18 Stat. 335 (1875).

Radical Republican from Massachusetts, introduced in the Senate a bill to supplement the Civil Rights Act of 1866.[5] The first section of this bill covered a variety of matters, including common carriers, inns, places of amusement, churches, cemeteries, and benevolent institutions. In pertinent part, it read as follows:

> That all citizens of the United States, without distinction of race, color or previous condition of servitude, are entitled to the equal and impartial enjoyment of any accommodation advantage, facility, or privilege furnished . . . by trustees, commissioners, superintendents, teachers, or other officers of common schools and other public institutions of learning, the same being supported or authorized by law . . . and this right shall not be denied or abridged on any pretense of race, color, or previous condition of servitude.[6]

The bill died after being sent to the Senate Judiciary Committee and reported adversely by its chairman, Senator Lyman Trumbull of Illinois, for the committee.[7] In the next session, Sumner once again introduced his bill,[8] and once more it was referred to the Judiciary Committee from which Trumbull reported it adversely, and again it died.[9] In both cases, the adverse report, although not written, was unanimous. Some members thought that Sumner's bill was unconstitutional, and others thought that it was unnecessary.[10] For a third time, in the First Session of the Forty-Second Congress, Sumner introduced his bill. Again no other senator evinced much interest, and again the bill expired of its own accord.[11]

In the face of these rebuffs, Sumner moved, in the next session of Congress, on December 20, 1871, to tack his proposal on as a rider to the Amnesty Bill, a proposal authorized by the third section of the fourteenth amendment to lift the remaining political disabilities imposed by that section on many prominent confederates.[12]

When Sumner declared that his bill was designed to secure "equal

---

[5] 14 Stat. 27 (1866).

[6] CONG. GLOBE, 42d Cong., 2d Sess. 244 (1871). See also CONG. GLOBE, 41st Cong., 2d Sess. 3434 (1870); CONG. GLOBE, 42d Cong., 2d Sess. 821 (1872).

[7] CONG. GLOBE, 41st Cong., 2d Sess. 5314 (1870). See also CONG. GLOBE, 42d Cong., 2d Sess. 821 (1872).

[8] CONG. GLOBE, 41st Cong., 3d Sess. 616 (1871).

[9] Id. at 1263. See also CONG. GLOBE, 42d Cong., 2d Sess. 822 (1872).

[10] CONG. GLOBE, 42d Cong., 2d Sess. 493, 731 (1872).

[11] CONG. GLOBE, 42d Cong., 1st Sess. 21 (1871). See also CONG. GLOBE, 42d Cong., 2d Sess. 822 (1872).

[12] CONG. GLOBE, 42d Cong., 2d Sess. 237, 240 (1871). The political machinations over amnesty are described in Kelly, *The Congressional Controversy over School Segregation 1867-1875*, 64 AMER. HIST. REV. 537, 550-52 (1959).

rights," Senator Joshua Hill, a Georgia Republican, rose to deny this. He declared: "Nor do I hold that if you have public schools, and you give all the advantages of education to one class as you do to another, but keep them separate and apart, there is any denial of a civil right in that."[13]

Sumner denied that separation was equality, and maintained that both races were forced into inequality by being separated. He asserted that "Equality is where all are alike. A substitute can never take the place of equality." Although discussion was principally centered on railroads, Sumner also applied the rule to schools. He observed:

> Show me, therefore, a legal institution, anything created or regulated by law, and I show you what must be opened equally to all without distinction of color . . . .[N]otoriously, schools are public institutions created and maintained by law; and now I simply insist that in the enjoyment of those institutions there shall be no exclusion on account of color.[14]

Sumner then started reading letters from Negroes. One of them suggested that "In our public schools is the place to commence to break down caste."[15] A resident of West Virginia protested that the local insane asylum would not accept her son, but Senator Arthur I. Boreman, a West Virginia Republican, replied that this was due to overcrowding and not racial discrimination.[16] Ultimately, Sumner's bill was ruled out of order.

The next day, Sumner again moved his amendment in the Committee of the Whole.[17] Debate centered around contentions that Sumner's amendment would destroy any chance for passage of the amnesty bill.[18] Sumner modified the school clause to include those "being supported by monies derived from general taxation." A vote was then taken, and Sumner's proposal lost by 30 to 29.[19]

Sumner renewed his amendment in the whole Senate.[20] When Congress returned from its Christmas holiday, he made a long speech urging his amendment on January 15, 1872. He first protested that "among us little children are turned away and forbidden at the door of the common school, because of the skin."[21] He also declared that "Equality

---

13*Id.* at 241.
14*Id.* at 242.
15*Id.* at 244.
16*Id.* at 245.
17*Id.* at 263.
18*Id.* at 272.
19*Id.* at 274.
20*Id.* at 278.
21*Id.* at 381 (1872).

in all institutions created or regulated by law, is . . . [not] a question of society," and therefore "no question of social equality" exists.[22]

Sumner decried separate schools and institutions of learning and science. He declared:

> It is easy to see that the separate school founded on an odious discrimination and sometimes offered as an equivalent for the common school, is an ill-disguised violation of the principle of Equality, while as a pretended equivalent it is an utter failure. . . .
>
> A slight illustration will show how it fails, and here I mention an incident occurring in Washington, but which must repeat itself wherever separation is attempted. Colored children, living near what is called the common school, are driven from its doors, and compelled to walk a considerable distance, often troublesome and in certain conditions of the weather difficult, to attend the separate school. One of these children has suffered from this exposure, and I have myself witnessed the emotion of the parent. This could not have occurred had the child been received at the common school in the neighborhood. Now, it is idle to assert that children compelled to this exceptional journeying to and fro, are in the enjoyment of equal rights. The superadded pedestrianism and its attendent discomfort furnish the measure of inequality in one of its forms, increased by the weakness or ill health of the child. What must be the feelings of a colored father or mother daily witnessing this sacrifice to the demon of Caste?
>
> . . . The indignity offered to the colored child is worse than any compulsory exposure, and here not only the child suffers, but the race to which he belongs is blasted and the whole community is hardened in wrong.
>
> The separate school wants the first requisite of the common school, inasmuch as it is not equally open to all; and since this is inconsistent with the declared rule of republican institutions, such a school is not republican in character. Therefore it is not a preparation for the duties of life. The child is not trained in the way he should go; for he is trained under the ban of inequality. How can he grow up to the stature of equal citizenship? He is pinched and dwarfed while the stigma of color is stamped upon him. This is plain oppression, which you, sir, would feel keenly were it directed against you or your child. . . .
>
> Nor is separation without evil to the whites. The prejudice of color is nursed when it should be stifled. . . . the school itself must practice the lesson [of equality]. Children learn by example more than by precept. How precious the example which teaches that all are equal in rights. But this can be only where all commingle in the common school as in common citizenship. . . . There should be no separate school. It is not enough that all should be taught alike; they must all be taught

[22]*Id.* at 382.

together. . . . nor can they receive equal quantities of knowledge in the same way, except at the common school.

. . . But even where a separate school is planted it is inferior in character. No matter what the temporary disposition, the separate school will not flourish as the common school. . . . That the two must differ is seen at once, and that this difference is adverse to the colored child is equally apparent. For him there is no assurance of education except in the common school, where he will be under the safeguard of all. White parents will take care not only that the common school is not neglected, but that its teachers and means of instruction are the best possible, and the colored child will have the benefit of this watchfulness. This decisive consideration completes the irresistible argument for the common school as the equal parent of all without distinction of color.[23]

Sumner analogized other institutions of learning or science, churches and cemeteries, "public in character and organized by law," to schools. He declared that separation would be insulting to Negroes.[24] He also scorned two Ohio decisions which held that a mulatto child would be entitled to go to school only if he had a sufficient amount of white blood in him to be generally recognized as white.[25] Sumner concluded with an extensive peroration on the Declaration of Independence and color prejudice. He reasoned that since the original Constitution did not mention color, "Equality is the supreme law of the land, 'and the judges in every State shall be bound thereby, anything in the constitution or laws of any State to the contrary notwithstanding.'" This he derived from "the original text of the Constitution, in presence of which you might as well undertake to make a king as to degrade a fellow-citizen on account of his skin."[26] Not once in his lengthy discourse did Sumner mention the fourteenth amendment.

Two days later, Sumner was again engaged in advocating his bill by reading letters from Negroes and others supporting it. One letter from a school controller in Reading, Pennsylvania stated that the colored school was situated away from the populated part of the city, and the children had to walk several miles through inclement winter weather to go to school. The controller stated that he had ordered four colored

---

[23]*Id.* at 384. Senator Sumner also stated:
There can be no substitute for equality; nothing but itself. Even if accommodations are the same, as notoriously they are not, there is no Equality. In the process of substitution the vital elixir exhales and escapes.
Id. at 383.   .
[24]*Id.* at 384.
[25]*Id.* at 385, discussing Lane v. Baker, 12 Ohio 237 (1843) and Van Camp v. Board of Educ. 9 Ohio St. 406 (1859).
[26]CONG. GLOBE, 42d Cong., 2d Sess. 385 (1872).

children admitted to a neighborhood white school, but the school board threatened him with impeachment, and return of the colored children to their school. Sumner declared that this letter was evidence that separate schools were not equivalent, and placed a hardship on Negroes.[27] Likewise an article was read which described the burning of colored school houses in Texas. Sumner added: "A separate school becomes at once an indignity to the race, and also a mark and target for the arrows of their enemies."[28] He also read a letter from a Negro lawyer who was a professor at Howard University, which stated that no matter how good the educational facilities were, a Negro could not be properly educated "if he is not made to feel in the common school, the academy, the college, and the professional school, that his manhood . . . [is] recognized and respected."[29] Sumner read yet another resolution demanding equal treatment in public schools and other places of learning drawn up by professors and students at Howard University, which denied that this had any relation to social equality. He declared that the "separate school has for its badge inequality," and urged that this was contrary "to the promises of the Declaration of Independence." Sumner concluded by reading with approval from a report of the trustees of the colored schools in the District of Columbia, as follows:

> It is our judgment that the best interests of the colored people of this capital, and not theirs alone, but those of all classes, require the abrogation of all laws and institutions creating or tending to perpetuate distinctions based on color, and the enactment in their stead of such provisions as shall secure equal privileges to all classes of citizens. The laws creating the present system of separate schools for colored children in this District were enacted as a temporary expedient to meet a condition of things which has now passed away. That they recognize and tend to perpetuate a cruel, unreasonable, and unchristian prejudice, which has been and is the source of untold wrong and injustice to that class of the community which we represent, is ample reason for their modification. The experience of this community for the last few years has fully demonstrated that the association of different races in their daily occupations and civic duties is as consistent with the general convenience as it is with justice. . . . Yet while the fathers may sit together . . . the children are required by law to be educated apart. We see neither reason nor justice in this discrimination. . . .
>
> Children, naturally, are not affected by this prejudice of race or color. To educate them in separate schools tends to beget and intensify it in their young minds, and so to perpetuate

---

[27]*Id.* at 432.
[28]*Id.* at 433.
[29]*Ibid.*

it to future generations. If it is the intention of the United States that these children shall become citizens in fact, equal before the law with all others, why train them to recognize these unjust and impolitic distinctions? To do so is not only contrary to reason, but also to the injunction of Scripture, which says, "Train up a child in the way he should go, and when he is old he will not depart from it."[30]

Senator Frederick T. Frelinghuysen, a New Jersey Republican lawyer and a former attorney-general of that state, next arose to suggest that many colored people had saved money and purchased churches, schools, and colleges for their use. He objected that Sumner's bill might allow the more numerous white population "to wrest this property from the colored people." On the other hand, Frelinghuysen noted that Sumner could not "make the amendment I propose without falling into the absurdity of discriminating against whites while attempting to abolish the distinction of races." Frelinghuysen therefore suggested the following exemption to "perpetuate to the colored people their own institutions. . . ."

> *Provided*, That churches, schools, cemeteries, and institutions of learning established exclusively for either the white or the colored race, shall not be taken from the control of those who established them, but shall remain devoted to their use.[31]

Several days later, Sumner added the substance of this proviso to his bill, namely:

> But churches, schools, cemeteries, and institutions of learning established exclusively for white or colored persons, and maintained respectively by the contributions of such persons, shall remain according to the terms of the original establishment.[32]

When Senator Allen G. Thurman, an Ohio Democrat and a former chief justice of the state supreme court, declared that the whole bill was unconstitutional, Senator James W. Nye, a Nevada Republican lawyer, belittled these objections. To this Thurman replied that "I am not accustomed to attempt impossibilities . . . and therefore I would never attempt to make the Senator from Nevada understand a constitutional argument. (Laughter)"[33]

---

[30]*Id.* at 434.

[31]*Id.* at 435.

[32]*Id.* at 487. The senators may have had Girard College in Philadelphia in mind. For an extensive account of the litigation concerning the Girard will and Girard College, see *In re* Girard's Estate, 386 Pa. 548, 127 A.2d 287 (1956).

[33]Conc. Globe, 42d Cong., 2d Sess. 495 (1872). See also *id.* at 530-31.

On January 25, 1872, Sumner's position received a grievous blow from an erstwhile ally, Senator Lot M. Morrill of Maine, a Radical Republican lawyer who had played a prominent part in anti-slavery measures during the Civil War,[34] and who had voted in favor of the fourteenth amendment in the Senate. [35] Morrill condemned the whole proposal as being in excess of Congress' power under the fourteenth amendment. Adverting to the school clause, Morrill declared:

> Sir, is it a right of the Government of the United States to take the direction of the education of the people? . . . But can they . . . [take] the direction of the common schools of the States? That is the proposition. That is invading a province, I repeat, which lies outside of the domain of this Government. That is invading a province which is within that domain which is provided for in the Constitution of the United States, when it says that the powers not herein delegated are reserved to the people or to the States. That is a province which you cannot invade.[36]

Senator Eli Saulsbury, a Delaware Democrat, also attacked the bill saying:

> If a man . . . of his own motion sends his children to the same school to be educated in the same class, . . . then he chooses social equality with negroes for himself and his children. . . . But, if, on the other hand, he is compelled to . . . send his children to the same school, then it is enforced social equality . . . .[37]

Saulsbury condemned compulsory school integration, and pointed out:

> [T]he Senator from Massachusetts proposes to compel the white people of the country, who are dependent upon common schools for the education of their children, to send them there to associate with colored children, or to keep them at home without the advantages of acquiring an education.
>
> The rich man is not dependent upon common schools for the education of his children; even men in moderate circumstances may be able to send their children to select schools or colleges; but the poor man who labors from day to day for the maintenance of his family, with scarcely a dollar to spare for any other purpose, must educate his children at the common

---

[34]Avins, *Freedom of Choice in Personal Service Occupations: Thirteenth Amendment Limitations on Anti-Discrimination Legislation*, 49 CORNELL L.Q. 228, 233 (1964).

[35]CONG. GLOBE, 39th Cong., 1st Sess. 3042 (1866).

[36]CONG. GLOBE, 42d Cong., 2d Sess. app. 4 (1872).

[37]*Id.* at 9. See also CONG. GLOBE, 42d Cong., 2d Sess. 913 (1872): "[T]he Federal Government shall, through United States courts, coerce social equality between the races in public schools. . . ."

schools or they must go without an education. It is that class of men against whom this legislation is directed. The children of the poor men of the country must be educated with Negroes, while the children of the rich are to be placed in schools of a higher grade.[38]

Saulsbury then declared that none of the Senators voting with Sumner would send his child to a mixed school in the south where there was a large number of Negroes. He pointed out that poor whites had just as much a desire to educate their children as did rich ones, and that they ought not to be deprived of the ability to obtain a segregated education for their children because of lack of funds. He predicted that southern and border-state whites would boycott the mixed schools and that the school system would be destroyed there.[39]

Sumner could afford to ignore Saulsbury's protests, but Morrill's thrust, if unrebutted, might change votes in a closely divided Senate. Sumner's reply to Morrill's constitutional challenge was characteristic. He read more letters from Negroes asking that the bill be passed and complaining about discrimination.[40] Ultimately when Sumner came to constitutionality, he declared:

> [T]he Constitution is full of power; it is overrunning with power. I find it not in one place or in two places or three places, but I find it almost everywhere, from the preamble to the last line of the last amendment.[41]

Sumner urged Morrill to "read between the lines" and to interpret the Constitution by the Declaration of Independence. He rested in addition on the thirteenth amendment. The fourteenth amendment was thrown in as an afterthought because Sumner was "profoundly convinced that the conclusion founded on the thirteenth amendment was unanswerable, so as to make further discussion surplusage . . . .[42] Sumner concluded by reading a constitutional rebuttal to Morrill in a letter written by a Negro whose analysis was as imprecise as Sumner's own thinking, and, by threatening the Republicans with a loss of colored votes at the next election.[43]

Morrill was offended by the threat of withdrawal of colored votes, and unimpressed by Sumner's constitutional rebuttal. He ridiculed the arguments based on the Declaration of Independence and the thirteenth amendment. But Sumner stuck to the Declaration as a source of au-

---

38CONG. GLOBE, 42d Cong., 2d Sess. app. 10 (1872).
39Id. at 10-11.
40CONG. GLOBE, 42d Cong., 2d Sess. 726-27 (1872).
41Id. at 727.
42Id. at 728.
43Id. at 729.

thority,[44] even when this theory was once again derided by Senator Matthew H. Carpenter, a Wisconsin Republican lawyer.[45]

Under questioning by Thurman, Carpenter supported the bill in respect to public schools. He said:

> I have no doubt of the power of this Government under the fourteenth amendment . . . to say that a colored man shall have his right in the common school . . . . The distinction seems to me to be broad and clear and well-founded between those voluntary institutions, whether incorporated or not, which we ought not to interfere with, and those great institutions which are supported by law and maintained by general taxation. . . . Now, to say that the children of one class of citizens shall not have the benefit of a common school supported at the public expense by general taxation . . . is a thing which I never will countenance or give the slightest support to.[46]

Thurman answered that this was not the question, that no one suggested that colored children be excluded from school. He said that the issue was whether the federal government could proscribe state regulation and require integrated schools. Carpenter replied that the bill did not interfere with state power to regulate schools except in the one instance authorized by the Constitution, namely, to prevent exclusion of colored children from school.[47]

On February 5, Carpenter proposed an amendment designed to limit the bill to schools maintained at public expense or endowed for public use,[48] and not merely those incorporated by state law.[49] The next day,

---

[44] *Id.* at 730.

[45] *Id.* at 761. See also *id.* at 823-27.

[46] *Id.* at 763.

[47] *Ibid.* But see *id.* at 819: "You propose . . . to put the children together in the schools."

[48] *Id.* at 818. The following colloquy occurred with Senator John Scott, a Pennsylvania Republican lawyer:

Mr. SCOTT. . . . It applies to schools or colleges which are "supported by endowment for public use." Is the language such as to make it applicable to schools and colleges which have been endowed by private benefactions for the use of the public of any particular class that may be enumerated?

Mr. CARPENTER. That is the intention of it, and I think it does. If the endowment is for public use, then the public are entitled to the benefit of it.

Mr. SCOTT. Do I understand, then, that the proposed substitute would control the intention of the benefactor, if he, in making the endowment, has made it applicable only to certain classes and conditions?

Mr. CARPENTER. No, Sir, I should not understand that to be an endowment for a public use, but for a particular and specified use; and this would not override it.

[49] *Id.* at 843. See CONG. GLOBE, 42d Cong., 2d Sess. app. 28 (1872).

Senator John Sherman, an Ohio Republican lawyer who had voted for the fourteenth amendment, defended the constitutionality of Sumner's bill, *inter alia*, to give to Negroes "the right to participate in your school fund, which is collected alike of black and white . . . ."[50] Sherman pointed to the privileges and immunities clause as the basis for Congress' power, and then said that one of the privileges was the right to equal protection of the law. He confused the subject even more when he came to the school clause, saying:

> It is the privilege of every person born in this country, of every inhabitant of the country whether born here or not, of a certain age, to attend our public schools which by law are set aside for the public benefit. Boys and girls go to the schools. It is the privilege of all, and declared to be so. All contribute to the taxes for their support; all are benefited by the education given to the rising generation; and therefore all are entitled to equal privileges in the public schools.[51]

Considering the fact that Sherman did not limit his discussion to citizens, and also considering the fact that the privileges and immunities clause is limited not only to privileges of citizens, but privileges of national citizenship, it is clear that Sherman was talking in very imprecise terms about the fourteenth amendment.

Sherman's colleague, Thurman, then arose. After identifying the privileges and immunities protected by the fourteenth amendment as those found in the original Constitution and the Bill of Rights, Thurman declared that no "such right guaranteed to a citizen [existed] as that he shall go into a common school in company with every other child that goes to that common school." Senator George F. Edmunds, a Republican lawyer from Vermont, who voted for the fourteenth amendment, replied that the equal protection clause of the fourteenth amendment is violated "when the law of the State. . . declares that a man of one color of hair or of skin may send his children, and the man of another color of hair may not send his."[52] The following then ensued:

> Mr. THURMAN. . . . The substance of the Senator's position is simply this: that although a State may give to every child in it equal advantages of education, it shall have no power of regulation over its schools. That is what it comes to.
> Mr. EDMUNDS. Oh no.
> Mr. THURMAN. It does; let the Senator hear me and he will see. Let me turn the argument of the Senator. Is not a female child a citizen? Is she not entitled to equal rights?

[50]CONG. GLOBE, 42d Cong., 2d Sess. 843 (1872).

[51]*Id.* at 844.

[52]CONG. GLOBE, 42d Cong., 2d Sess. app. 26 (1872).

Why, then, do you allow your school directors to provide a school for her separate from a school for the male? Why do you not force them into the same school? Why do you allow the States to separate the sexes in the schools if every school that is set up and supported by public money is necessarily thrown open to every citizen of the United States? Will the Senator say that all the laws of the States providing for a division of the schools by sexes are unconstitutional and infringe the fourteenth amendment? He cannot say that; and if he cannot say that, his argument falls to the ground. Does not the separation exist by virtue of the power of regulation, which belongs to the State? All that can be claimed is this, that in regard to schools supported by the public money, that money shall be so applied as that each citizen shall have an equal advantage from its application. Therefore, preserving that equality, the State in the exercise of its power of regulation may apply a part of it to support a school for boys, a part of it to support a school for girls, a part of it to support a school for white children, a part of it to support a school for colored children. That is not denying them the equal protection of the laws in any sense whatsoever. In no wise is it denying them the equal protection of the laws. In no sense is it denying their equality before the law.[53]

Thurman also said that the bill denied people "the liberty to choose their own associates . . . in the school," and that "if the supreme power in a State, in the exercise of a wise judgment and discretion, and for the interest of education and of its youth sees fit to make a regulation that white children shall be in one school and colored children in another, I am not in favor of depriving them of that right, of denying them that liberty." Thurman endorsed Saulsbury's argument that the bill was actually aimed at poor whites. He noted that even in Ohio, which had separate Negro and white schools, rich men sent their children to private schools. Thurman observed:

When, therefore, you shall force colored children into the common school, you will not force them into an association with the children of the rich, (the children of the rich will not be there,) but you will force them into social intercourse with the children of the poor whites; and the tendency of your law, instead of being to elevate the colored race to the level of the white, will be to pull down the poor white child to the level of the black. . . . Instead of elevating the negro, it is to depress the white. The rich man's child goes to some seminary of learning supported by wealth and the contributions of the rich; he associates with no colored child. . . . but the poor man's child must have that social equality thrust upon him, or he must go

---

53 *Id.* at 26-27.

without education. . . . I say from experience, first, that there is no necessity for this admixture in the schools; and, in the second place, that the worst enemy of the common-school system could not devise a worse thrust at it than this very amendment of the Senator from Massachusetts.[54]

Senator Orris S. Ferry, a Connecticut Republican lawyer, attacked the school clause on other grounds. He stated that the bill did not affect his state, which always had integrated schools, but he opposed any federal interference in state control of its schools.[55] He declared that the legislation as a whole went beyond the equal protection clause of the fourteenth amendment.[56] Senator James K. Kelly, an Oregon Democratic lawyer, added that "Most of the States have schools for colored children and separate schools for white children."[57]

Senator George Vickers, a Maryland Democratic lawyer, also spoke against the constitutionality of the school clause. He said it was not a privilege or immunity of national citizenship to attend school. He asked: "Because he has a right to study a profession at his own expense, pursue an avocation at his own cost, does that give him the right to go into your public schools or into any of your schools and acquire information and education at the expense of the State or of other people?" Vickers said that Negroes paid very little school taxes, and that mixed schools would destroy the usefulness of schools. He reiterated Thurman's argument that public school integration would affect only poor whites, and that if the federal government had the power to interfere with a regulation requiring racial segregation, it could interfere with all other regulations. Vickers concluded:

> If you can legislate for the purpose of obtaining an education for the negro by the side of the white, you can do so also for the purpose of securing an equal proportion of the teachers, because it may be said that colored persons have not equal advantages unless they are taught by persons of their own hue.

---

[54]Id. at 27.

[55]Cong. Globe, 42d Cong., 2d Sess. 892 (1872). Senator Ferry said:
It is because this amendment of the Senator from Massachusetts exerts Federal authority over the schools and the school officers of the States that the provision which the Senator has placed in it is most objectionable. . . . [I]f you give to the Federal Government power to interfere in the regulation of the schools of the different States upon one subject, I do not see how you are to restrain that power in reference to other topics relating to education; and so we see and hear how continually more and more of efforts made to bring the Federal Government into direct control of the school systems of the States.

[56]Id. at 893.

[57]Id. at 894.

And if you can do it in reference to teachers, you can do it in reference to books, you may do it in relation to the subjects to be taught. It is, I repeat, a question of power. Once invade the sanctuary of the school, and you can assume entire control over the system and all its details.[58]

Vickers also declared that the states could better run the schools than the federal government since they were closer to the people.[59]

Senator Lyman Trumbull, the veteran Illinois lawyer and legislator who, as Republican Chairman of the Senate Judiciary Committee, had shepherded to passage the Civil Rights Act of 1866, the forerunner of the equal protection clause of the fourteenth amendment, and had frequently acted as spokesman and leader of the Senate Republicans in the Thirty-Ninth Congress, spoke next. He confined civil rights to those enumerated in the 1866 statute, and defended segregation by railroads. He opposed the whole of Sumner's amendment.[60] At length, a vote was taken on Sumner's rider to the amnesty bill, and it resulted in a tie, 28 to 28. All the Democrats, the liberal Republicans, and almost half of the southern Republicans, opposed the amendment. The Radicals and half of the southern Republicans were with him. The vice-president then broke the tie in Sumner's favor.[61]

Senator Henry Wilson, Sumner's Massachusetts Republican colleague, warmly endorsed the combined bill, as "settling the question of equality in the primary schools of the country where so much is to be done to educate the rising generation of the country to forget caste and

---

[58]CONG. GLOBE, 42d Cong., 2d Sess. app. 42 (1872), where Senator Vickers also stated:

The children of the rich, of the middle classes, of all who have the ability to set up and sustain schools for their children, will not be affected, for they will not submit to the degradation which this amendment proposes; and the necessary result will be that the children of the poor, as dear to their parents as the children of the rich are to them, will be obliged to be educated side by side with the negro and mulatto or be reared in ignorance and vice. The friends of this measure are unwilling that separate schools for the races shall be provided, and "equality" being their motto, they seem determined to force it upon the community, at the hazard of producing intense feeling and opposition, and the destruction of the school system.

• • • •

Suppose it be thought proper to separate the sexes on the ground that the pupils will progress more rapidly and efficiently, that it will be more to their interest and advantage that this order or arrangement shall obtain; if the principle of this bill is sustained you have the power to change that regulation as well as any other.

[59]*Id.* at 43.

[60]CONG. GLOBE, 42d Cong., 2d Sess. 901 (1872).

[61]*Id.* at 919.

believe in the equality of our common humanity."[62] But a number of the strongest supporters of amnesty stated they would vote against the combined bill because they regarded Sumner's bill as unconstitutional.[63] Saulsbury also predicted it would break up the Delaware school system.[64] The vote on the combined measure was 33 to 19, less than the necessary two-thirds required to pass the amnesty bill.[65]

On February 19, a bill similar to Sumner's was introduced in the House.[66] Congressman James G. Blair, a Missouri Republican lawyer, attacked the bill as unconstitutional,[67] and particularly excoriated the school clause as one enforcing social equality. He noted that his state had segregated schools, and that since the facilities, books, and instruction were free and equal, Negroes lacked no rights possessed by whites, and the provision "to force Negro social equality upon the white children of the country" was obnoxious. He declared:

> As long as the white children are opposed to having negro children associate with them in our schools I will never force or coerce them* to it, especially when the negro children can get the same education in separate schools. Nor would I . . . force the white children upon the negro children contrary to their will.
>
> The time never was, and I hope never will be, when any man, white or black, or any race or nation of people, will have the legal right to my society or the society of my children. The black and the white man alike, whether under the natural, civil, or common law, have ever had the Heaven-born privilege of choosing their own society, and I hope it may ever continue so.[68]

Blair predicted that white children would be driven to private schools if the schools were integrated, the school system would be abolished, and Negroes would be without education. He said that Negroes were not demanding integrated schools.[69]

Congressman Henry D. McHenry, a Kentucky Democratic lawyer, also decried the bill for "compulsory social equality and association with those whose company is distasteful to. . . ."[70] He observed that since a "rich man can educate his children in private schools, . . . this law will

---

[62]*Id.* at 921.

[63]*Id.* at 926-28.

[64]*Id.* at 928.

[65]*Id.* at 928-29.

[66]*Id.* at 1116.

[67]CONG. GLOBE, 42d Cong., 2d Sess. app. 142 (1872).

[68]*Id.* at 143. Congressman Blair also said: "[I]t is not depriving the colored children of any legal right by sending them to separate schools. . . ." *Id.* at 144.

[69]*Id.* at 143-44. See also *id.* at 18.

[70]*Id.* at 217.

be no great hardship upon him; but the poor man's child must look to the common schools or go without education, and this bill forces that child to sit on the same seat with the negro, and to be raised up in fellowship with him."[71] McHenry predicted that the people would abolish the school system rather than submit to integrated schools. He added:

> It would not be right for a State to tax negroes to educate the whites unless they had the privilege of the schools, and in every State where they are so taxed they have that privilege. In my State we do not tax them for school purposes, nor have we undertaken to educate them, and we do not propose to be forced to do so by despotic laws. For many years we had no common-school system at all, and it is only of recent date that our system has become efficient, and after we have paid the enormous taxes imposed on us [to] educate the white children, it is unreasonable to ask us to tax ourselves further to educate the negroes who pay no tax, comparatively speaking.[72]

Somewhat later, Congressman James C. Harper, a North Carolina Democrat, condemned the school clause. He read from a Virginia Republican newspaper predicting that integration would destroy the school system. He decried the harsh penalties against school officials,[73] and predicted: "Nor will the northern States be exempt from similar afflictions." He said that Negroes would try to force themselves into northern schools and colleges. He concluded that not even Negroes wanted mixed schools in the South, and that compulsory integration would destroy the school system.[74] Congressman John M. Rice, a Kentucky Democratic lawyer, also predicted that the school clause would destroy the school system in many states, and that people would use private schools.[75]

On May 4, 1872, Senator Thomas F. Bayard, a Democratic lawyer from Delaware, made a lengthy attack on proposed school integration in the District of Columbia. He first noted that colored schools in the District had been generously provided for out of taxes largely raised from whites, and that if colored schools were inferior with such a generous provision for their support, it was but "an admission [of colored] inferiority, an absolute inferiority, a confession of some great defects which must exist by the law of nature, and against which these puny efforts of human legislation will prove utterly and absurdly fruit-

---

[71]*Id.* at 218.
[72]*Ibid.*
[73]*Id.* at 370.
[74]*Id.* at 371.
[75]*Id.* at 597-98. See also *id.* at 383.

less."[76] After detailing the money spent on accommodations for colored schools, Bayard went on to urge the Senate to take into consideration the prejudices of the people. He stated that there was a division of opinion among the Negroes about school integration, and that the whites were overwhelmingly opposed to it. He added that the senators who intended to vote for this measure would not send their own children to integrated schools, although they intended to consign the children of poor whites to such schools.[77] Bayard also predicted that the rich would withdraw their children to private schools, and that school integration would drive white children out of the public schools of the District and would discourage skilled white workers from moving into the District. He closed with an attack on Sumner's proposal as one calculated to result in miscegenation by breaking down race prejudice in children while they were still young.[78]

Three days later, there was some further debate on Sumner's bill to desegregate schools in the District. Trumbull took a dim view of it, while Sumner and Edmunds strongly urged it.[79] Ferry urged a local referendum on school desegregation, calling Sumner's bill "a tyrannical rule from without."[80]

On May 8, the Senate returned to the amnesty question, [81] and Sumner immediately moved to annex his civil rights bill to the amnesty bill which the House had passed[82] During the ensuing debate and parliamentary maneuvering, Trumbull criticized his fellow Republicans with some warmth for saddling the amnesty bill with Sumner's measure. The following colloquy then occurred:

---

[76]Id. at 353.

[77]Id. at 353-55. He said:

Senators, there is not a Senator on this floor who expects his children, . . . ever to go to those schools and to be subjected to this contact, who will vote for this bill; not one; not one. . . . [T]hey may condemn the children of their brother white men, whose poverty compels them to send their children to public schools, they may seek to compel them to this contact, but they will be very careful that they are not personally the sharers in such results.

No, sir, no blue-eyed, fair-haired child of any Senator on this floor, no little grandchild at that time of life when children are so open to mere impression, and especially to evil impression, will ever be permitted to suffer by this proposed contact. They may condemn others who are poorer, but they will be careful to save their own.

Id. at 355.

[78]Id. at 355-57.

[79]CONG. GLOBE, 42d Cong., 2d Sess. 3123 (1872).

[80]Id. at 3124-25.

[81]Id. at 3179.

[82]Id. at 3181.

Mr. EDMUNDS. How about the right to go to a public school?

Mr. TRUMBULL. The right to go to school is not a civil right and never was.

Mr. EDMUNDS. What kind of a right is it?

Mr. TRUMBULL. It is not a right.

Mr. EDMUNDS. What is it?

Mr. TRUMBULL. It is a privilege that you may have to go to school. Does the Senator from Vermont mean to force everybody to go to school?

Mr. EDMUNDS. No, but I mean to force everybody to let anybody go to school who is a citizen of this country who wants to go.

Mr. TRUMBULL. Well, I think you cannot do any such thing. . . . I deny his right as a member of Congress to force anybody into a school, or to force anybody to take anybody into a school. . . . The Senator . . . is not speaking of the District of Columbia; he is speaking of a bill for the country.[83]

Ferry then chimed in to say that Negroes were not denied any rights in the District of Columbia, and that it was "precisely the same for blacks as for whites in this District." Trumbull re-echoed this point and thanked Ferry for his remark, and pointed out "that there is no discrimination" in the District schools. Ferry added:

The same facilities, the same advantages, the same op-portunities of education are given to the white child and the black child in the District of Columbia to-day. The only dif-ference is that they do not receive those equal facilities and advantages in the same school-room; and you might as well deny that equal facilities and equal advantages exist in the northern States to the two sexes where the sexes are by the action of the authorities taught in different school-rooms or school buildings, as to deny it here.[84]

Edmunds asked Ferry whether colored children could go to as high a grade of school as white children could, and the latter answered in the affirmative. Edmunds then asserted that it was no more equality before the law to segregate students by law than it would be to require Negroes to use one street and whites to use another street. Ferry then asked Edmunds whether segregation in schools by sex in New England was a denial of right, and the latter replied that he did not know, but analogized racial segregation to segregation by color of hair or nativity, which he declared was a denial of right. Ferry then asserted "that it is not a denial of equality of right" to "have different rooms for

---

[83]*Id.* at 3189.
[84]*Id.* at 3190.

the education of the races."[85]

Trumbull then reiterated that "going to school was not a civil right, and that so far as I know the colored people of this country had all the civil rights that the whites had, and it is a misnomer to call this a civil rights bill." Trumbull declared that Edmund's "position about the schools was indefensible. . . ." He added:

> I do say, in reply to the Senator from Vermont, that the right to go to school is not a civil right, and that the schools are regulated all over the land, and must be, for the advancement of education. We have graded schools. Boys of one class are kept in one room; of another class in another; the girls are confined to one room and the boys to another; but this is not a denial of civil rights to either. If the facilities for education are the same nobody has a right to complain. This which the Senator speaks of as a civil right is no civil right at all.[86]

Senator Oliver P. Morton, an Indiana Republican lawyer, then asked Trumbull what kind of a right it was to go to school if not a civil right. Trumbull replied that it was "not any right at all" but a matter "to be regulated by the localities." Trumbull said that the states could abolish schools. He repeated that civil rights were only those protected by the Civil Rights Act of 1866.[87]

Morton then replied that Sumner's amendment did not require free schools to be maintained by the states, but where such schools were "supported by taxes levied upon everybody without regard to color . . . there shall be an equal right to participate in the benefit of those schools created by common taxation. That is the point. . . ." Morton added: "If a right to participate in these schools is to be governed by color or any other distinction, I say that is a fraud upon those who pay taxes." Morton concluded that it made no difference whether the right to go to school was deemed a civil right or not, but where taxes were raised from all persons for schools, "there is a civil right that there shall be equal participation in those schools."[88]

---

[85] Ibid.

[86] Ibid.

[87] Id. at 3190-91. He said: "We have colleges in the country, and a student who applies there and pays his tuition fees, you may say, has certain rights there; but they are not what I understand to be embraced in the general broad term 'civil rights.'" Id. at 3191.

[88] Id. at 3191. The following colloquy then occurred:

Mr. MORTON. . . . The proposition that I made was that where schools were supported by taxation upon everybody, there must be equal rights to everybody in those schools. . . . Now, the substance of the Senator's position is this, and it needs but to be stated to be understood, and I think universally execrated, that there exists a right to levy a tax upon everybody, white and black, for

Senator John Sherman, the Ohio Republican lawyer who had voted with Trumbull for the fourteenth amendment, reminded the latter that he was author of and leader in the passage of the Civil Rights Act of 1866, and that the fourteenth amendment added to Congress' power since then.[89] Sherman pointed to the need to allow Negroes to share equally in school funds, and declared that Sumner's bill simply carried out the purposes of the 1866 act.[90] Sherman went on to point out that the bill permitted private schools to discriminate, but only required "that the children of negroes shall have an equal and fair share in the enjoyment of that which is collected by public taxation." Sherman then said:

The supreme court of the State of Ohio have recently passed upon our own law in that State, which does in certain cases provide for separate schools for colored children, and have held it to be constitutional, and I believe they are right. There, in certain cases defined by the law, the colored peole may have, when they are of a certain number, separate schools, and provision is made in such cases as that for a distribution *pro rata* of the funds. In ordinary cases, by the common consent and custom of every one there since the war was over, the whites and the blacks go to the same schools.[91]

We may pause here to note that Sherman was undoubtedly referring to the decision in *State v. McCann*[92] of the previous day. He had been a member of the Ohio bar for almost thirty years at this time, and had been in Congress for a total of seventeen years. He was a regular, if not a Radical Republican. He had voted with the majority for all of its reconstruction measures, and even voted to impeach and remove President Andrew Johnson. He had participated actively in the debates on the fourteenth amendment, and voted for it on its passage. He had just been speaking about the constitutionality of Sumner's bill under the first section of the fourteenth amendment and defending it from Trumbull's attacks. Hence, when this veteran lawyer

---

the support of common schools, and at the same time to deny to everybody an equal right to participate in the benefit of those schools. . . .
Mr. TRUMBULL. I never made any such statement.
[89]*Id.* at 3191-92.
[90]*Id.* at 3192. He said that the 1866 act
does not protect them in their right to the enjoyment of money collected from them and from other citizens of the United States for the education of their children, but that discriminations are made on account of race, color and previous condition of servitude . . . in the right to have one's children educated at the common school.
[91]*Id.* at 3193.
[92]State v. McCann, 21 Ohio St. 198 (1872).

and legislator affirmed the correctness of the *McCann* decision, it adds the strongest possible weight to the case. In other words, Sherman affirmed the constitutionality of having local school boards set up segregated schools or desegregated schools, under authority of law, in accordance with local sentiment in the area.

Sherman reinforced this position by pointing out that in many Ohio communities there were integrated schools and that no problems resulted, as the white and Negro children got along well together. He said that in "northern States . . . not the social distinction but the distinction of rights" soon disappears. He added:

> In the southern State my opinion would be that for a time it might be a matter of municipal regulation, it might be a matter of convenience assented to both by whites and blacks to keep them in separate schools.[93]

Senator Arthur I. Boreman, a West Virginia Republican and former state judge, also denied that school segregation violated equal rights.[94] Senator Francis P. Blair, a Missouri Democratic lawyer, likewise advocated separate schools for Negroes.[95] Trumbull once again called Sumner's bill a "social equality bill," just what the Democrats were calling it.[96]

Ferry then moved to amend Sumner's bill by striking out the school clause. He first advocated local control over the schools.[97] He then noted

---

[93]CONG. GLOBE, 42d Cong., 2d Sess. 3193 (1872).

[94]*Id.* at 3195. He said:
It is said here we are denying equal rights to the colored and white people in the schools. I deny it. The same provision in regard to schools exists in reference to the white and colored children of the country in most of the States. It is so in my State. It is true that there are separate schools, schools for white children and schools for the colored; but nevertheless the provisions of the school laws from beginning to end apply precisely to the one as they do to the other; and it is just as much a violation of the right of a white child to keep him out of a black school as it is of a black child to keep him out of a white school, if we are narrowed down to such a proposition as that. The time will come, I have no doubt, when these distinctions will pass away in all the States, when school laws will be passed without this question appearing upon the face of those laws; but it is not so now, and for the present I am willing to allow the laws of the State to remain as they are where they provide schools for both classes.

[95]*Id.* at 3251. See also *id.* at 3253.

[96]*Id.* at 3254.

[97]*Id.* at 3257. He declared:
And hence, when an effort is made directly by Federal legislation to dictate to the local communities what is most expedient as to the management of the particular schools under their care, you are commencing a species of

that the Negro population of the District of Columbia was rapidly increasing, and that if schools there were integrated it would drive the whites out of the District. He referred to the law of Ohio, which permitted each district to have mixed or separate schools, and read from a newspaper account of the *McCann* decision. He said that the Ohio Supreme Court, a majority of whose members were Republican, had upheld separate schools under the fourteenth amendment, and added:

> I believe that that decision of the supreme court of Ohio is good law. There is nothing, then, in the establishment by different communities, as each may think it expedient for itself, of separate schools, in conflict with the fourteenth amendment; and the proposition with respect to schools therefore is simply by legislation by Congress, without any constitutional provision demanding it, acting compulsorily upon all the school districts in the United States.[98]

The Ferry amendment lost by the narrow margin of 26 to 25. Those for the motion included thirteen Democrats, three southern Republicans, and nine other Republicans, two from Connecticut and one each from Illinois, Indiana, Iowa, Nebraska, New York, Pennsylvania, and West Virginia. Trumbull probably cast the most significant affirmative vote. Eight southern Republicans voted in the negative, joined by eighteen northern Republicans. Ten of these had voted for the fourteenth amendment as a member of the Senate, and three as a member of the House of Representatives. Probably the most significant vote to retain the school clause was cast by Sherman, who had just affirmed the constitutionality of segregated schools.[99] Blair then offered the following amendment: "the people of every city, county, or State shall decide for themselves, at an election to be held for that purpose, the question of mixed or separate schools for the white or black people."[100]

Senator James L. Alcorn, a Mississippi Republican lawyer, then spoke in favor of local control over schools. He stated that the legislature of Mississippi, controlled by colored people, had provided for segregated schools, which was satisfactory to both whites and Negroes. He added that separate white and Negro universities were established with equal endowments and concluded that the question had been settled by the legislature and he wanted no more trouble about it. Sumner replied to him by reading from a paper by Frederick Douglass which rejected

---

legislation whose principle is, in my judgment, fatal to the school system of the country.

[98]*Id.* at 3258.

[99]*Ibid.*

[100]*Ibid.*

the right of the people of the District of Columbia to vote on whether schools should be desegregated.[101] Sumner added:

> You are called on to decide whether you will give your sanction to a system of caste which so long as it endures will render your school system a nursery of wrong and injustice, when it ought to be of right. How can you expect the colored child or the white child to grow up to those relations which they are to have together at the ballot-box if you begin by degrading the colored child at the school and by exalting the white child at the school? Train up the child in the way he should go. There are Senators here who would train children in the way they should not go.[102]

Sumner then read from another paper by Douglass, as follows:

> Throughout the South all the schools should be mixed. . . . Educate the poor white children and the colored children together, let them grow up to know that color makes no difference as to the rights of a man, that both the black man and the white man are at home, that the country is as much the country of one as of the other. . . . Now, in the South the poor white man is taught that he is better than the black man. . . .[103]

Blair answered Sumner by saying that he favored upholding the right of local self-government and the right of the people of the states who pay taxes to decide how their schools should be managed. He endorsed Alcorn's argument that Congress should not override state laws. He observed: "The associations of our children are to be dictated by a central oligarchy seated here in Washington." Blair said that most of the school funds were collected from taxes paid by whites, and that the rich people could send their children to private schools, while the poor whites would be deprived of any schooling because the schools would be closed if Sumner's amendment passed. Blair concluded that the school clause was unconstitutional anyway.[104]

Senator Timothy O. Howe, a Radical Republican from Wisconsin, replied to Blair by first agreeing with Sumner's caste argument, and then by saying that segregated schools would require a double system of schools which would be more expensive than a single system. Howe concluded that authority to pass the provision was to be found in one of the

---

[101]*Ibid.* Douglass said: "Why should it [Congress] not abolish the teaching of caste . . . whether the people of the District would have it done or not?"

[102]*Id.* at 3259.

[103]*Ibid.*

[104]*Ibid.* Senator Hill of Georgia added that most Negroes were content with separate schools.

three recently ratified amendments, but he did not say which one.[105] Edmunds also rose to answer Blair. He said that if it was proper to segregate children by race it would be proper to segregate native-born children from foreign-born children, children of Catholic parents from those of Protestant parents, children of Methodist parents from those of Congregationalist parents, and children of Democrats from those of Republicans. He emphasized that "if color is a distinction which is fit to be left to the States and the communities to decide upon as the test of rights, then we ought not to interfere." But Edmunds added in reference to religious, nativity, and political segregation:

> [T]he sense of all mankind would cry shame at such a thing, and yet this is precisely the same principle, unless you can maintain that this old notion of race . . . is one in which it is fit, under the constitutional principles of a free country, to base a distinction upon. The notion of sex or age, which the Senator from Connecticut alluded to, has nothing at all to do with the question; that depends upon questions of fitness and decency, as to cleanliness and good order and degree of education, and all that. That is a test which everybody can understand, and which you must leave to the local jurisdiction; but this is a matter of inherent right, unless you adopt the slave doctrine that color and race are reasons for distinction among citizens.[106]

Bayard then arose to denounce the bill as an unconstitutional usurpation of local self-government. Senator Eugene Casserly, a California Democratic lawyer who had once been Corporation Counsel of New York City, made the same assertion. To answer Sumner's argument about caste, Casserly read from the opinion of the Massachusetts Supreme Judicial Court in *Roberts v. City of Boston*,[107] which he said had first brought Sumner to public notice, and in which the court had rejected Sumner's argument and sustained public school segregation. Senator John P. Stockton, a New Jersey Democratic lawyer, whose expulsion or exclusion from the Senate in 1866 made possible Republican control of the Senate by the two-thirds majority necessary to override President Andrew Johnson's vetoes and pass the fourteenth amendment, contented himself by urging popular referenda and denouncing the bill for violating personal liberty.[108]

A vote was then taken and Blair's amendment lost by 30 to 23. One Pennsylvania Republican changed from his previous stand and voted negative, and three previously absent northern Republicans re-

---

[105]*Ibid.*
[106]*Id.* at 3260.
[107]Roberts v. City of Boston, 59 Mass. (5 Cush.) 198, 209-10 (1849).
[108]CONG. GLOBE, 42d Cong., 2d Sess. 3261 (1872).

turned to vote with the majority. Three minority Republicans were now absent, but two previously absent Republicans returned to vote with the minority. One of them, Senator William Sprague of Rhode Island, was a Radical who had voted for the fourteenth amendment and to impeach and convict President Andrew Johnson. The votes of Trumbull and Sherman remained unchanged.[109]

Alcorn then warned once again that Sumner's bill would destroy the Mississippi school system, and the Republican Party's majority as well.[110] Trumbull also disapproved of Sumner's bill for "forcing white and colored children into the same schools. . . ."[111] A vote was then taken on annexing the civil rights bill to the amnesty bill, and a 29 to 29 tie resulted. The vice-president then voted in favor of Sumner's amendment.[112]

At the urging of Senator Roscoe Conkling, the property-rights minded New York Republican lawyer, Sumner accepted an amendment and eliminated all private schools merely because they were incorporated, leaving only tax-supported schools or those "authorized by law." Vickers, a Democrat, and Senator John Scott, a Pennsylvania Republican lawyer, suggested eliminating those "authorized by law." Sumner objected, and Boreman supported him on the ground that all persons were invited to use institutions of learning authorized by law. Sumner added that Harvard College and Amherst College in Massachusetts were not tax-supported, but since they were authorized by law, Sumner wanted to prevent them from discriminating.[113] Thereafter, a second vote on annexing Sumner's bill to the amnesty bill was taken. Again, a 28 to 28 tie resulted, and the vice-president voted in Sumner's favor.[114] But once again, the supporters of the amnesty bill, including Trumbull, who felt that Sumner's bill was unconstitutional, voted against the combined measure, and the vote of 32 yea to 22 nay was less than the requisite two-thirds.[115]

---

[109]*Id.* at 3262.

[110]*Ibid.*

[111]*Id.* at 3263. Senator Edmunds also declared:

The real trouble is, as is evinced by this debate, that the honorable Senator from Illinois does not believe that the right to go to a State school or to a District of Columbia school is a right that belongs to a citizen of the United States independent of color.

Id. at 3264.

[112]*Id.* at 3264-65.

[113]*Id.* at 3266-67. *But see,* Am. Historical Ass'n Ann. Rep. 156 (1889), wherein it was stated that "the appropriations by the State to Harvard have amounted to $784,793, in addition to 46,000 acres of land. The state has also given $157,500 to Williams, and $52,500 to Amherst."

[114]*Id.* at 3268.

[115]*Id.* at 3270.

Several days later, Trumbull declared that "I want amnesty so much that I will vote for almost anything that is not unconstitutional to get it." But he added that Sumner's bill "has been misnamed a civil rights bill, proposing to establish social rights which is unconstitutional in its provisions, and which I shall not vote for."[116] Sumner replied to Trumbull by reading a speech by Frederick Douglass saying that Negroes wanted equal school rights but not social equality. Trumbull replied by reading a report of a speech by a Negro professor saying that he wanted social equality.[117]

Sumner then moved to tack his bill to another piece of legislation, and Boreman moved to strike out the school clause.[118] The latter protested that "here it is proposed to require that all laws in the several States providing for common schools and separating the races shall be nullified; that all shall be allowed to associate together in the same schools." Boreman said that his home State of West Virginia had segregated schools, and that these were as good or better than mixed ones. Sumner answered, urging defeat of Boreman's amendment "to expel caste from the common schools of the country." Ferry, in reply, ridiculed the argument that segregated facilities denied equality.[119] Thurman re-entered the discussion to say that Sumner had never pointed to any constitutional provision giving Congress power to enact the school clause. He pointed out that in the *McCann* Case the Ohio Supreme Court, composed of five Republican judges, had unanimously upheld the constitutionality of a school segregation law. He concluded that "of its soundness I do not think any good lawyer can doubt for a moment, [and] there is an end of all pretense of constitutional foundation for this bill."[120]

Edmunds next accused University of Georgia officials of refusing to let colored students get the benefit of an agricultural college education under the federal land grant act, and said that Negroes should be entitled to equal rights to obtain a federally-financed education. Hill replied that the university had no time yet to use the fund.[121] Alcorn once again protested that Mississippi had segregated schools, and that

---

116*Id.* at 3361.
117*Id.* at 3362. Senator Trumbull also called it a "social equality bill" the next day. *Id.* at 3418, 3421.
118*Id.* at 3421.
119*Id.* at 3422. Senator Ferry said:
It is nonsense, sir, to talk of the necessity of educating youth in the same building in order to give them equal facilities, advantages, immunities, rights. What matter whether they be in the same building or in different buildings, so that the educational facilities bestowed upon them are identical?
120*Id.* at 3423.
121*Id.* at 3424.

the colored university was getting more money than the white university at Oxford (University of Mississippi), while Blair added another dire warning about school closing.[122] Trumbull and Edmunds then got into a dispute as to whether Georgia was giving white students education in a university while Negroes were deprived of such education. Trumbull also reiterated that going to school was not a civil right. He added:

> I think all persons should have the benefit of our appropriation, and I think, too, in regard to money raised for schools by taxation, colored people should have it as well as white people. I have always thought so. I entertain no different view about that. But I do not believe in legislation forcing them into the same schools, or in our undertaking to control how they shall go to school by act of Congress. I believe myself that you should not tax the colored people for schools to educate white persons exclusively. I have no such idea as that.[123]

Edmunds replied that if the states could "establish separate schools you can establish separate courts . . . for colored men so that they should not disturb the pride or the prejudice . . . of white people who choose to attend other courts as suitors."[124]

Carpenter of Wisconsin finally decided to break the deadlock by bringing up an independent civil rights bill during an evening session while Sumner was away from the Senate chamber and while barely a quorum was present.[125] He moved an amendment which eliminated the school clause.[126] Several Republicans objected. One considered Carpenter's amendment "emasculating the bill entirely." Frelinghuysen specifically disapproved of eliminating the school clause. But Senator John A. Logan, an Illinois Republican lawyer, endorsed Carpenter's amendment and argued for elimination of the school clause because "it interfered with state laws." The Carpenter substitute was ultimately adopted by a vote of 22 to 20. The majority included thirteen Democrats, one southern Republican, and eight northern Republicans, including one from California, Illinois, Iowa, Kansas, Maine, Oregon, Pennsylvania, and Wisconsin. Probably the most significant vote to eliminate the school clause was cast by Morrill of Maine. The minority were all Republicans.[127] The Carpenter bill was then passed by a strict party-line vote of 28 to 14.[128]

---

[122]*Id.* at 3425.
[123]*Id.* at 3426. See also Saulsbury's remark. *Id.* at 3428.
[124]*Id.* at 3427.
[125]*Id.* at 3727.
[126]*Id.* at 3730, 3734.
[127]*Id.* at 3735.
[128]*Id.* at 3736.

The Senate then took up the amnesty provision, and debated it until the next morning, when Sumner arrived. He moved to tack his original bill to the amnesty bill, protesting the "emasculated civil rights bill" adopted the previous night in his absence. He protested that "the spirit of caste will receive new sanction in the education of children."[129] But Sumner's entreaties were in vain. The Senate rejected his amendment by the lop-sided vote of 29 to 13, and went on to pass the amnesty bill by a vote of 38 to 2, with only Sumner and a western Radical voting in the negative.[130]

Sumner's disappointment knew no bounds, and he insisted that the rights of the Negroes had been sacrificed by his colleagues. But they told him that the limited bill "is all that can be accomplished at this session,"[131] and his strictures achieved no more than to irk his colleagues.[132] Thus, Sumner's bill died for that session of Congress.

III. Sumner's Legacy

When the first session of the Forty-Third Congress opened on December 1, 1873, President Grant had been re-elected the previous year. The Supreme Court had also decided the *Slaughter-House Cases*,[133] which reminded the lawyers in Congress that the fourteenth amendment, and particularly the privileges and immunities clause, did not radically expand the powers of the federal government. Since the civil rights bill depended for enforcement on the judiciary, it would have to run the gauntlet of Supreme Court review. A better constitutional basis would have to be found than the Declaration of Independence.

When the session opened, Sumner once again introduced his bill. Ferry of Connecticut and Morrill of Maine renewed a general attack on it as being unconstitutional.[134] Debate commenced in the House, where a copy of Sumner's bill had previously been introduced.[135] Congressmen Clarkson N. Potter, a New York Democratic lawyer, and Thomas Whitehead, a conservative Virginia lawyer who voted with the Democrats, both moved to strike out the school clause, while Congressman Charles A. Eldridgo, a veteran legislator, moved to allow separate accommodations for white persons.[136]

129*Id.* at 3737-38. He added: "I ask the Senate to set its face against that spirit of caste now prevailing in the common schools. . . ." *Id.* at 3738.

130*Id.* at 3738.

131*Id.* at 3739.

132*Ibid.* See *id.* at 3740-41.

133Slaughter House Cases, 83 U.S. (16 Wall.) 36 (1873).

1342 Cong. Rec. 10-11 (1873).

135*Id.* at 97, 337-38.

136*Id.* at 339.

Congressman Benjamin F. Butler, Republican Chairman of the Judiciary Committee, commenced his advocacy of the bill by noting that it gave nobody any rights he did not already have by common law, in which he included the right to go to a school supported at public expense or endowed for public use. He referred specifically to the common law of New England, England, and the United States generally, and said that the object of the bill was to abrogate state laws which discriminated against any class in exercising these rights.[137]

We may pause here to note that Butler's position as to the common law was not accurate. In England, at common law, no obligation existed for a parent to give his child an education,[138] and it was not until the twentieth century that it was finally held that a local school authority had a duty to admit children resident in the area.[139] In Canada, the obligation of local school authorities to admit children seems to have been recognized earlier.[140] In Ontario it had been held that separate schools might be established for colored children, in which case they would have no right to attend the common schools,[141] but if no segregated schools were set up, they would be entitled to go to the common schools.[142]

In the United States, there was never any general right apart from statute to attend school. The right to go to school was always restricted by such factors as residence.[143] In fact, at one time in some northern states free Negroes were not entitled to go to any school.[144] The

---

[137]Id. at 340. See also id. at 412 (1874).

[138]Hodges v. Hodges, Peake Add. Cas. 79, 170 Eng. Rep. 201 (N. P. 1796).

[139]Gateshead Union v. Durham County Council, [1918] 1 Ch. 146 (C.A.).

[140]See Ex parte Miller, 34 N.B. 318 (1897); Ex parte Gallagher, 31 N.B. 472 (1892); Dunn v. Windsor Bd. of Educ., 6 Ont. 125 (1883).

[141]Hill v. Camden, 11 U.C. Rep. 573 (1854); but cf. Hutchison v. St. Catharines School Trustees, 31 U.C. Rep. 274 (1871).

[142]Re Stewart & Sandwich East School Trustees, 23 U.C. Rep. 634 (1864). In Washington v. Charlotteville School Trustees, 11 U.C. Rep. 569, 573 (1854), it was held:

> The Legislature does seem to have meant, though reluctantly, to give way so far to any prejudices that may exist in the minds of the white inhabitants, as to allow of the establishment of separate schools for the coloured people, if thought expedient, but not so far as to consent to shut them out from the only public schools that do exist, by leaving it discretionary in the school trustees to deny admission to them arbitrarily, where they have no other school to go to.

[143]See Wheeler v. Burrow, 18 Ind. 14 (1862); Inhabitants of Haverhill v. Gale, 103 Mass. 104 (1869); Opinion of Justices, 42 Mass. (1 Met.) 580 (1841); School Dist. v. Bragdon, 23 N.H. 507 (1851).

[144]Draper v. Cambridge, 20 Ind. 268 (1863); Van Camp v. Board of Educ., 9 Ohio St. 406 (1859); cf. Crandall v. State, 10 Conn. 339 (1834).

217

school directors were deemed to have broad powers of deciding what students should be admitted to which schools,[145] including the right to segregate them by race.[146] In fact, that very year the Supreme Judicial Court of Massachusetts, Butler's home state, had held that the right to attend school was a "political right" and not a private or civil right.[147] This was precisely the distinction which Trumbull had repeatedly insisted on.[148] By way of contrast, although free Negroes had no common-law right to attend school, even in the slave states before the Civil War, the courts had unanimously held that they had a right to obtain, hold, and dispose of property.[149]

Congressman James B. Beck, a Kentucky Democratic lawyer, opened the opposition attack by decrying compulsory school desegregation and asserting that, under the decision in the *Slaughter-House Cases,* Congress lacked power to legislate respecting state schools.[150] He, too, observed that racial segregation was no different in principle from segregation by sex, that rich children could be sent to private school so that the bill would only affect poor whites, and that compulsory desegregation would destroy the public school system.[151] Congressman John T. Harris, an unreconstructed Virginia Democratic lawyer, added to a similar argument about the bill's lack of constitutional foundation a long paean on the segregated public schools of Virginia and how integration would ruin them. He also read from letters by administrators that integration in insane asylums would aggrevate the mental illnesses of people there, and that it would ruin the school for the deaf, dumb and blind. He concluded that it would even break up the University of Virginia.[152]

Another Democratic attack came from Congressman Alexander H. Stephens, a Georgia Democrat and the distinguished former Vice-President of the Confederacy. In addition to asserting the constitutional argument derived from the *Slaughter-House Cases,* he stated that Georgia Negroes were content with segregated schools and a segregated

---

[145]Grove v. School Inspectors, 20 Ill. 532 (1858); People v. Easton, 13 Abb. Pr. (n.s.) 159 (N.Y. Sup. Ct. 1872).

[146]State v. Duffy, 7 Nev. 342, 8 Am. Rep. 713 (1872); Dallas v. Fosdick, 40 How. Pr. 249 (N.Y. Sup. Ct. 1869).

[147]Learock v. Putnam, 111 Mass. 499 (1873).

[148]CONG. GLOBE, 42d Cong., 2d Sess. 901 (1872). See also notes 83, 86 and 87 *supra.*

[149]Tannis v. Doe, 21 Ala. 449 (1852); Ewell v. Tidwell, 20 Ark. 136 (1859); Davis v. Fitchett, 5 Fla. 261 (1853); Beall v. Drane, 25 Ga. 430 (1858); Bowers v. Newman, 27 S.C.L. 472 (1842); Winnard v. Robbins, 22 Tenn. 613 (1842); Hepburn v. Dundas, 54 Va. (13 Gratt.) 219 (1856).

[150]2 CONG. REC. 342 (1873).

[151]Id. at 343.

[152]Id. at 375-77 (1874). See also id. at 405.

university.[153] He was answered by a South Carolina Negro Republican, Congressman Alonzo J. Ransier, who advocated the bill because "negro-haters would not open school-houses . . . to the colored people upon equal terms. . . ."[154] Representative Roger Q. Mills, a Texas Democratic lawyer, added an argument on the limited scope of the privileges and immunities clause of the fourteenth amendment and Congress' lack of power to legislate regarding schools under it. He, too, issued due warnings about school closing if the bill was enacted.[155]

The next day, Beck offered an amendment permitting segregation.[156] His colleague from Kentucky, Congressman Milton J. Durham, also a Democrat, after a stock *Slaughter-House Cases* argument, also warned that the school system there would be destroyed by integration. He noted that thousands of poor white children were for the first time being educated by a tax levied on white taxpayers. Since Negroes paid no school taxes, he urged that they should not go to white schools. Taxes levied on Kentucky Negroes were used exclusively to support colored paupers in many counties. He expressed the hope that eventually there would be colored schools in every part of the state, and offered a segregation amendment also.[157] Still a third school segregation amendment was offered by Congressman Lloyd Lowndes, a Maryland Republican lawyer.[158] Congressman James H. Blount, a Georgia Democratic lawyer, after stating that in his state Negroes had equal school facilities, added the usual warning about school closing if integration were required.[159]

Congressman William Lawrence, a former Ohio state judge and a Republican who had voted for the fourteenth amendment, was the next to speak. He read what was actually a legal brief in support of the bill, complete with citations to cases and other authorities supporting its constitutionality. He said:

> When it is said 'no State shall deny to any person the equal protection' of these laws, the word 'protection' must not be understood in any restricted sense, but must include every benefit to be derived from laws. . . . When the States by law create and protect, and by taxation on the property of all support, benevolent institutions designed to care for those who need their benefits, the dictates of humanity require that equal provision should be made for all. Those who share these benefits

---

[153]*Id.* at 379-81.
[154]*Id.* at 382.
[155]*Id.* at 384-85. See also *id*, at 414-15 for a similar argument.
[156]*Id.* at 405.
[157]*Id.* at 406.
[158]*Id.* at 407.
[159]*Id.* at 411.

enjoy in them and by them "the protection of the laws," the benefit of all that results from the laws which create, protect, and support them. And by the fourteenth amendment, no State shall deny to any the equal benefit of these laws, and Congress is charged with the duty of enforcing this equality of benefits or protection.....[160]

Lawrence went on to point out that the "design of the fourteenth amendment was to confer upon Congress the power to enforce civil rights." He quoted extensively from the debates in 1866 to show that the first section of the fourteenth amendment was proposed by Congress because of doubts about its constitutional power to enact the Civil Rights Act of 1866, and cited cases and commentary on the constitutional right of Congress to re-enact the 1866 act in 1871, which it did. He concluded that under the fourteenth amendment the "power to secure equal civil rights by 'appropriate legislation' is an express power...."[161]

An exhortation from Congressman Josiah R. Walls, a Florida Republican Negro farmer, contained a potpourri of constitutional tidbits followed by a plea for the bill to "open up the common schools...."[162] Next, Congressman William S. Herndon, a Texas Democratic lawyer, again read copiously from the *Slaughter-House Cases* to show that the bill was unconstitutional, and likewise predicted the end of southern school systems. He noted that the whites paid the taxes for both colored and white schools, and that they would refuse to levy taxes if the schools were integrated.[163]

In the course of a long harangue, Congressman William J. Purman, a Florida Republican lawyer, gave the following hypothetical example of "conditions of inequality" imposed by a "states-rights legislature" which Congress could legislate to prevent: "An act to exclude all children not clothed in velvet and such as have blue eyes from admission into any public school supported by public taxation."[164] Congressman William H. H. Stowell, a Virginia Republican carpetbagger, urged defiance of the threats to close the schools if the bill were enacted. He said that half of Virginia's population was illiterate, that schools were only open for five months a year, and that only fifteen per cent of the colored population attended school. He advocated the bill because "Our State constitution also provides for the education of all the children in

---

160[Id.](Id.) at 412.
161[Id.](Id.) at 412-14. Congressman James Monroe, an Ohio Republican but not a lawyer, also urged an equal protection argument well mixed with declamation. *Id.* at 414.
162[Id.](Id.) at 417.
163[Id.](Id.) at 419-22.
164[Id.](Id.) at 423-24.

the old Commonwealth, and yet a democratic Legislature has practically excluded them from this privilege."[165] In reply, two Democrats read from Virginia Republican newspapers approving school integration and predicting elimination of public education as a consequence.[166] One of them also pointed out that it was no more a violation of equality to segregate by race than by sex, that the bill was actually designed to impose social equality, and that under the *Slaughter-House Cases* Congress had no power to pass it.[167]

The next day, when House debate closed, Congressman Milton I. Southard, an Ohio Democratic lawyer, read from the *McCann* case, noted that many states had school segregation laws, and pronounced the bill unconstitutional.[168] A Georgia Democrat declared that Negroes were being treated absolutely equally by school segregation laws, exhorted the House against forcing social equality, and issued the usual warnings about abandonment of public schools if the bill should pass.[169] A Missouri Democrat also defended school segregation, and added:

> When has President Grant chosen to take his children from a white school and send them to a colored school? . . . Why have we never witnessed the 'civil rights' advocates setting one solitary example of the propriety, the advantage, and the excellence of a law which they propose to enforce against their remonstrating countrymen with fire and sword? . . . Why do we not see them, by a delicious choice, . . . sending their children to negro schools? Why, sir, do they not do what they say is all right and proper, before they attempt to coerce us into compliance with an act most monstrous. . . .[170]

Butler closed the debate in his usual sarcastic manner. He said:

> Again, we are told that if we do pass this bill we shall break up the common-school system of the South. I assume this is intended as a threat. If so, to that I answer as Napoleon did, "France never negotiates under a threat." I regret the argument, if it was one, was put forward in that form. "Break up the common-school system of the South." Why, sir, until we

---

[165]*Id.* at 426.

[166]*Id.* at 427, 429.

[167]*Id.* at 428.

[168]2 Cong. Rec. app. 1-3 (1874).

[169]*Id.* at 3-4 (remarks of Congressman Hiram P. Bell). See also 2 Cong. Rec. 4053-55 (1874) (remarks of Congressman John D. C. Atkins) and *id.* at 726 (remarks of Congressman Henry R. Harris).

[170]2 Cong. Rec. app. 5 (1874).

sent the carpet-baggers down there you had not in fact a common-school system in the South. (Laughter.).[171]

Butler then scorned the inadequacies of the southern school systems,
and facetiously warned the southerners not to retaliate against Negroes
because the latter did the labor in the South and if they left the
southerners would be poverty-stricken. However, he remarked that retaining school segregation should be carefully considered because
colored children were so eager for school that white truants might retard
them in mixed classes.[172] The bill was then returned to the Judiciary
Committee.[173]

Several days later, Congressman Robert Vance, a prominent
Democratic ex-confederate, renewed the debate. He observed that the
whites in his state of North Carolina had cheerfully taxed themselves
for separate colored schools, and that this bill was a social rights bill
which would break up the school system for both races. He stated that
since the University of South Carolina had been integrated it had only
six to nine students, and advocated school segregation.[174]

Congressman Richard H. Cain, a South Carolina Negro Republican,
answered him. He said that although students had left the University
of South Carolina, the buildings were still there and the professors still
remained and taught the few who were there, so that the university was
not destroyed. He added that integrated schools were being operated in
a number of northern cities without problems. However, he chiefly
wanted the retention of the school clause because without it Negroes
in many areas were being deprived of any schooling whatever.[175]

Several days later, Congressman Samuel S. Cox, a New York

---

[171] 2 CONG. REC. 456 (1874).
[172] Id. at 456-57.
[173] Id. at 457-58.
[174] Id. at 555-56.
[175] Id. at 565-66. He also said:
I know that, indeed, some of our republican friends are even a little weak on
the school clause of this bill; but sir, the education of the race, the education of the nation, is paramount to all other considerations. . . . Sir, if you
look over the reports of superintendents of schools in the several States, you
will find, I think, evidences sufficient to warrant Congress in passing the civil-
rights bill as it now stands. The report of the commissioner of education of
California show that, under the operation of law and of prejudice, the colored
children of that State are practically excluded from schooling. Here is a
case where a large class of children are growing up in our midst in a state
of ignorance and semi-barbarism. . . . In Illinois, too, the superintendent of
education makes this statement: that, while the law guarantees education to
every child, yet such are the operations among the school trustees that they
almost ignore, in some places, the education of colored children.
Id. at 566.

Tammany Democrat, opposed federal aid to education because it would be a lever for integrated schools.[176] He predicted that no matter what other rights were given to Negroes they would never be satisfied until they had this one.[177] He said that they wanted to educate white students against race prejudice.[178] Congressman William M. Robbins, a North Carolina Democrat, added that not only would the school clause destroy the southern school systems, but it would eliminate southern white Republicans as well. He added that Negroes did not want mixed schools.[179] Cain answered him by pointing out that it was a penal offense to educate slaves before the Civil War, and demanded that the school question be settled.[180] Ransier, his colleague, also answered the prior Democratic arguments that mixed schools would destroy the school system by pointing out that northern colleges, such as Yale, Harvard,

---

[176]*Id.* at 614-18. These same arguments had been made in the previous session. See Conc. Globe, 42d Cong., 2d Sess. app. 15-16, 18 (1872).

[177]2 Cong. Rec. 616 (1874). He said:

But . . . if the civil-rights bill does come back with mixed schools out, the colored members here, and colored voters elsewhere, will not be satisfied. The battle will rage again. You may give them the freedom of the inn, the railroad, and the theater; you may bury them side by side with the white in the cemetery; you may go further, and provide that we shall all rise together out of the same mold in the resurrection, irrespective of race, of color, or of previous condition; but the broadvoweled Africanese tongue will talk, and . . . will still make its music of agitation. Gentlemen of white persuasion may tender the forty acres, but the inquiry still will be "Where's your mule?"

[178]*Id.* at 618. He quoted a prominent advocate of equality as follows:

Having this regard, you will not consent to have the clause securing us from proscription in public schools in the several States stricken from the civil-rights bill now before you. It is to us the clause of primary import. Public schools inculcate ideas, teach the rising generation. If the rising generation is taught by the State to look on the color of a citizen, and (as the arrangement setting them apart implies) to despise them, to regard the class as inferior, one that may be outraged, they not only, in thus educating them, unfit the despised as well as the despising class to sit on the juries, but the arrangement wars with the Constitution, which forbids any State from making or enforcing any law abridging the right of citizens. . . .

[179]*Id.* at 900.

[180]*Id.* at 902. Congressman Cain said:

The gentleman says that he does not desire that the colored people shall be crowded into the schools of the white people. Well, I do not think that they would be harmed by it; some few of them might be. But experience has taught us that it is not true that great harm will come from any such measure. I think, therefore, that if we pass this bill we will be doing a great act of justice, we will settle for all time the question of the rights of all people. And that until that question is settled there can not be that peace and harmony in the country that is necessary to its success.

Wilberforce, Cornell, and Oberlin, and Berea College in Kentucky all admitted colored students without ill effects. He noted that when colored students were admitted to Berea College, a number of white students left, but soon they returned. He quoted a report saying: "There is nothing like such a school as this to teach mutual respect . . . and to take away some of the arrogant superciliousness of caste and race." He concluded by quoting another writer, as follows:

> In times past the negro race has been the exponent of labor at the South; and it is, for many years to come, to be closely associated with it. If, therefore, this race is to be separated from all others in the public schools, and even the youngest children are made to feel that the race is set apart for its special mission and destiny in society, how can we hope to make labor respectable? The old badge of servile degradation will attach to it not only for the black man but for the white man. To place blacks and whites in the same school is not to say that the races are equal or unequal. It is to animate all the individuals with a common purpose, with reference to which color or nationality has nothing to do. If color or nationality has anything to do with social affinities, non-proscriptive schools will not affect their natural and healthy influences. . . .
> The class distinctions perpetuated and taught by class schools infuse a detrimental influence into politics. Black men, no less than white men, should differ on public questions. But such difference cannot show itself in political action to any great extent as long as there is perpetuated a distinction so fundamental between the white man and the black as that the children of the latter cannot go to school with those of the former. In such a case class interests will predominate over those interests which are more general and less personal.[181]

Debate began in the Senate on Sumner's bill on January 27, 1874. A number of Senators had doubts about the constitutionality of various provisions. Ferry of Connecticut and Morrill of Maine once again reiterated their belief that the bill was unconstitutional, before it was referred to the Judiciary Committee.[182] On March 11, 1874, while the bill was under consideration, Sumner died. His last wish was the passage of his civil rights bill.[183]

Frelinghuysen reported the bill for the Judiciary Committee, and narrowed its constitutional basis to the equal protection clause of the fourteenth amendment. He thrice stated that the "bill therefore properly

---

[181]*Id.* at 1313-14.
[182]*Id.* at 945-51. See also Senator Thurman's assertion that the bill was unconstitutional. *Id.* at 3455.
[183]*Id.* at 4786. See also 3 CONG. REC. 952 (1875) (remarks of Congressman Thomas Whitehead).

secures equal rights to the white as well as the colored race."[184] When Frelinghuysen turned to the school clause, he supported it on the ground that institutions "which are supported by the taxation of all, should be subject to the equal use of all.' Subjecting to taxation is a guarantee of the right to use." He added:

> Uniform discrimination may be made in schools and institutions of learning and benevolence on account of age, sex, morals, preparatory qualifications, health, and the like. But the son of the poorest Irishman in the land . . . shall have as good a place in our schools as the son of the chief man of the parish. The old blind Italian, who comes otherwise within the regulations of an asylum for the blind supported by taxation, shall have as good a right to its relief as if he were an American born. There is but one idea in the bill and that is: The equality of races before the law.[185]

Frelinghuysen then turned to the question of "whether this bill admits of the classification of races in the common-school system; that is, having one school for white and another for colored children." He first read to the Senate from the decision in *Clark v. Board of Directors.*[186] In this case, a Negro child had demanded the right to attend a neighborhood school, and the local school board said that it had discretion to refuse admission thereto, and to require her to go to a central separate colored school in accordance with local sentiment. However, the Iowa Supreme Court held that the board had no such discretion under Iowa law, and had to admit her to the neighborhood school. He then quoted from the decision in *State v. McCann,*[187] in which the Ohio Supreme Court had held that state school segregation statutes do not violate the fourteenth amendment. Frelinghuysen then explained:

> The constitution and laws of Iowa provide for the "education of all the youths of the State without distinction of color." In Ohio the statute expressly provided for separate schools for white and colored children. Therefore the decisions of those courts afford no precedent for the construction of this bill when enacted. The language of this bill secures full and equal privi-

---

[184]2 Cong. Rec. 3451 (1874).

[185]*Id.* at 3452. However, shortly thereafter Frelinghuysen inconsistently moved to restrict the benefits of the bill to citizens because 'I do not think that a person merely landing in this country is entitled, as a matter of right, to the benefit of our schools, which are supported by taxation" although the Equal Protection Clause covers all "persons," and not merely citizens, who are covered by the Privileges and Immunities Clause. See *id.* at 4081.

[186]Clark v. Board of Directors, 24 Iowa 266 (1868).

[187]State v. McCann, 21 Ohio St. 198 (1872).

leges in the schools, subject to laws which do not discriminate as to color. . . .

. . . .

The bill does not permit the exclusion of one from a public school on account of his nationality alone.

The object of the bill is to destroy, not to recognize, the distinctions of race.

When in a school district there are two schools, and the white children choose to go to one and the colored to the other, there is nothing in this bill that prevents their doing so.

And this bill being a law, such a voluntary division would not in any way invalidate an assessment for taxes to support such schools.

And let me say that from statements made to me by colored Representatives in the other House, I believe that this voluntary division into separate schools would often be the solution of difficulty in communities where there still lingers a prejudice against a colored boy, . . . because of his blood.

The colored race have in the last ten years manifested such noble and amiable qualities, judiciously adapting themselves to the demands of their peculiar position, that we should not hesitate to believe that they will in the future conciliate and remove rather than provoke unworthy prejudices; and there is nothing in this law which would affect the legality of schools which were voluntarily thus arranged, one for the white and the other for the colored children. . . .

. . . .

If it be asked what is the objection to classification by race, separate schools for colored children, I reply, that question can best be answered by the person who proposes it asking himself what would be the objection in his mind to his children being excluded from the public schools that he was taxed to support on account of their supposed inferiority of race.

The objection to such a law in its effect on the subjects of it is that it is an enactment of personal degradation.

The objection to such a law on our part is that it would be legislation in violation of the fundamental principles of the nation.

The objection to the law in its effect on society is that "a community is seldom more just than its laws;" and it would be perpetuating that lingering prejudice growing out of a race having been slaves which it is as much our duty to remove as it was to abolish slavery.

Then, too, we know that if we establish separate schools for colored people, those schools will be inferior to those for the whites. The whites are and will be the dominant race and rule society. The value of the principle of equality in government is that thereby the strength of the strong inures to the benefit of the weak, the wealth of the rich to the relief of the poor, and the influence of the great to the protection of the lowly. It makes the fabric of society a unit, so that the humbler portions cannot suffer without the more splendid parts being injured and defaced. This is protection to those who need it.[188]

Frelinghuysen then went on to justify the constitutionality of school regulation by Congress under (1) the principles of the three reconstruction amendments lumped together with recent history, (2) the privileges and immunities clause of the fourteenth amendment, and (3) the equal protection clause.[189] He conceded that "it is not one of the privileges of a citizen of the United States to have any education in a State; that a State may abolish all its schools." However, he contended that it was one of the privileges of national citizenship "not to be discriminated against on account of race or color by the law of a State relating to . . . schools. . . ." He asserted that excluding a child from school solely because he was of German or African descent "would violate his privileges as a citizen of the United States." Frelinghuysen also contended that the privileges and immunities clause went further than the old interstate privileges and immunities clause of article IV, section 2,[190] although Congressman John A. Bingham, the Radical Republican lawyer from Ohio who drafted the clause, stated that the fourteenth amendment clause did not go any further and was solely designed to give Congress power to enforce the original constitutional provision.[191] Frelinghuysen also failed to notice that his construction of the privileges and immunities clause would have invalidated the widespread and long-standing school laws requiring residence of children in the district.[192]

Several days later, Senator Thomas M. Norwood, a Georgia Democrat, delivered a long harangue during which he, too, raised the point that the rich children could be sent to private schools while poor children, under the bill, must choose either integration or ignorance.[193] He sarcastically identified the war power as the source of Congress' power to "declare war between white children and black children in the public schools," and since "the power to make war necessarily carries with it the power to destroy, Congress can go further and even

---

[188]2 CONG. REC. 3452 (1874).
[189]*Id.* at 3453.
[190]*Id.* at 3454.
[191]H.R. Rep. No. 22, 41st Cong., 3d Sess. 1 (1871):
The clause of the fourteenth amendment, "No State shall make or enforce any law which shall abridge the privileges or immunities of citizens of the United States," does not, in the opinion of the committee, refer to privileges and immunities of citizens of the United States other than those privileges and immunities embraced in the original text of the Constitution, article 4, section 2.
[192]See cases cited note 143 *supra.*
[193]2 CONG. REC. app. 237 (1874).

destroy the public schools!"[194] Ultimately, he became serious and made a long argument that the right to go to school was not protected under the privileges and immunities clause.[195]

On May 20, when the Senate resumed consideration of the civil rights bill, Senator Daniel W. Pratt, a Republican lawyer from Indiana, explained his support of the school clause as follows:

> But the chief objection is to allowing what are called mixed schools. In the first place, this bill does not necessarily lead to that, especially in the large cities, where colored people abound. In this city, for example, the schools are kept separate and will continue to be, though this bill become a law. Where the colored people are numerous enough to have separate schools of their own, they would probably prefer their children should be educated by themselves, and there is nothing in this bill which prohibits this. But in the villages and country separate schools will be impracticable, and the colored children, if educated at all in public schools, must necessarily be where the great majority of the children are white. There may be but one or two colored families in the district, and I admit that here the question must be fairly met whether they shall share or be excluded from the benefits of the public schools.
>
> In the first place, if not allowed, they must remain uneducated; a thing to be avoided, since these children will one day be voters, and policy requires they should be intelligent voters. In the next place, there is no more reason or justice why they should be excluded than an equal number of white children, for their father as a citizen has been taxed to build the school-house and to maintain the school. And, lastly, there is precisely the same reason his children should receive a rudimentary education at the common school that there is for white children. Beyond all this, what becomes of the colored man's rights as a citizen if this discrimination shall operate against him in a point where a parent's heart is most sensitive, to exclude his children from drinking at the common fount of knowledge.[196]

Pratt added that opposition to school integration would evaporate when the law was passed.[197]

---

[194]*Id.* at 238.

[195]*Id.* at 239-44.

[196]2 CONG. REC. 4082 (1874).

[197]*Id.* at 4033. He said:

It is said such a law as this bill enacts will be so odious that it cannot be executed. The objection assumes what I deny is true, that it will be generally odious. . . . It will be odious only in particular sections of the country, for in many parts their rights and privileges as set out in this bill are now recognized. In one State the practice of mixed schools has always been the rule, and in several of the Southern States the rule has been established by

Thurman, an implacable Democratic foe of the bill, arose to answer Pratt. After an extensive analysis of the privileges and immunities clause designed to demonstrate that the bill was unconstitutional,[198] he asserted that if Pratt "has understood this first section as allowing the State of Indiana to provide by law that the children of colored people and of white people shall be educated in different schools, [he] is entirely mistaken." Thurman then quoted extensively from the *McCann* decision of the Ohio Supreme Court, "composed of five eminent republicans," to the effect that school segregation laws did not violate the fourteenth amendment. He added that since "the exclusion of colored children from white schools is not a violation of the fourteenth amendment, then you have no right to punish such exclusion." He concluded by observing that whites paid almost all of the school taxes, and issued the stock dire warning about school closing if the bill were passed.[199] The next day, Senator John W. Johnston, a Virginia Democratic lawyer, told the Senate of the great progress the Democratic administration of his state had made in building up a school system, that colored school facilities were equal to those of white schools, that neither party wanted school integration, and if it came the school system would be destroyed.[200]

Morton spoke next. He first stated that the words "the equal protection of the laws" in the fourteenth amendment "means to the equal benefit of the laws" because the "whole body of the law is for protection in some form—the definition and protection of the rights of person and property. . . ."[201] He then got into a colloquy with Senator Augustus S. Merrimon, a North Carolina Democratic lawyer, who asked him whether a person, by virtue of United States citizenship, had the "right to attend a particular class of schools," and whether a state could require that females be educated separately from males:

> Mr. MORTON. . . . [T]his phrase, "nor shall any State deny to any person within its jurisdiction the equal protection of the laws," denies to any State the power to make a discrimination against any class of men as a class. . . . it denies the power to exclude them from schools because they are negroes . . . . The question of separating males and females into different schools does not come within the principle at all. The great object of

State laws. Pass this bill and all opposition will cease in a few months, when it is known that the question is settled; for people will come to see that the law is supported by reason and justice, and that free government demands the abolition of all distinctions founded on color and race.

198 *Id.* at 4085–88.
199 *Id.* at 4088–90.
200 *Id.* at 4114–15.
201 2 Cong. Rec. app. 358 (1874).

the fourteenth amendment was to establish the equality of races, equality before the law. The separation of the sexes, putting male children into one school and females into another, does not violate that principle, provided it extends to all races. . . . The power of the States to establish different grades of schools . . . remains just as it was, with this difference, that the power to discriminate between races is taken away. The States are not bound to establish common schools; but if the States do establish common schools to be supported at public expense, they cannot exclude the children of any race from those schools. . . . They may say if they please—perhaps that is an extreme case—that none but male children shall attend; but they must be the males of all races. I will not go that far, but the law may say that no child shall attend a common school, if you please, over sixteen years of age.

    Mr. MERRIMON. Why do you use the word "races?" . . . The point I make is this: the Constitution does not say anything about "races" except in certain respects. . . . there is no such expression touching distinctions as to race in any other respect whatsoever.

    Mr. MORTON. The Constitution in effect does say so. It says that no person shall be denied the equal protection of the laws; and if common schools are established and the children of colored men are excluded from those schools, I ask my friend—and he cannot deny it for a moment—if they are not denied the equal protection of the laws?

    Mr. MERRIMON. I say they are not, if like provision is made for the education of colored children that is made for white children."[202]

Merrimon then pressed Morton as to whether segregation of Chinese or Indian students was constitutional. Morton replied that it is a violation of the fourteenth amendment to exclude colored children from schools entirely. Merrimon said that he admitted this, but reiterated that states could provide separate and equal facilities and segregate by race or sex. Morton answered that when Merrimon "concedes that the exclusion of colored children from schools is a violation of the fourteenth amendment, it occurs to me that he has conceded all that we can ask." Merrimon continued to press his segregation point as follows:

    Mr. MERRIMON. . . . I say that the State Legislature cannot pass a law providing that white children should be educated and that colored children should not be, because that would deny the equal protection of the laws. But when it affords the same provision, the same measure, the same character for the colored race that it afforded for the white race, there is no

202*Id.* at 359.

more discrimination against one race than there is against the other; and therefore it is competent for the Legislature to do it, there being no restriction on such a power in the Constitution of the United States.

Mr. MORTON. My friend's argument then comes to this, that under the fourteenth amendment the State must make equal provision for the children of both races, and if there be any inequality in the benefits, then it is a violation of the fourteenth amendment. It brings him down then to the possibility of making separate and distinct schools precisely equal in point of benefit.[203]

Morton then completely ignored the segregation question and reiterated that colored children could not be denied the equal benefits of the school system. In spite of Merrimon's persistent questioning on the point, he studiously avoided discussing segregation at all.[204]

Senator George S. Boutwell, a Massachusetts Radical Republican, then offered an amendment to strike from the Judiciary Committee draft the provision that all persons "shall be entitled to the full and equal enjoyment . . . of common schools," and insert "of every common school and public institution of learning or benevolence . . . that may hereafter be endowed by any State, or supported . . . by public taxation."[205] He supported the school clause based on the privileges and immunities clause, and disagreed with the decision in the *Slaughter-House Cases*. He also said he was offering his amendment because the committee draft left it in doubt as to how far school segregation was permitted. He wanted to forbid it entirely, saying:

A system of public instruction supported by general taxation is security, first, for the prevalence and continuance of those ideas of equality which lead every human being to recognize every other human being as an equal in all natural and political rights; and the only way by which those ideas can be made universal is to bring together in public schools, during the forming period of life, the children of all classes, and educate them together.

The public school is an epitome of life, and in it children are taught so that they understand those relations and conditions of life which, if not acquired in childhood and youth, are not likely afterward to be gained. To say, as is the construction placed upon so much of this bill as I propose to strike out, that equal facilities shall be given in different schools, is to rob your system of public instruction of that quality by which our people, without regard to race or color, shall be assimilated in ideas,

---

[203] *Ibid.*

[204] *Id.* at 359-61.

[205] 2 Cong. Rec. 4115 (1874). See also *id.* at 3570.

personal, political, and public, so that when they arrive at the period of manhood they shall act together upon public questions with ideas formed under the same influences and directed to the same general results; and therefore, I say, if it were possible, as in the large cities it is possible, to establish separate schools for black children and for white children, it is in the highest degree inexpedient to either establish or tolerate such schools.

The theory of human equality cannot be taught in families; . . . but in the public school, where children of all classes and conditions are brought together, this doctrine of human equality can be taught, and it is the chief means of securing the perpetuity of republican institutions. And inasmuch as we have in this country four million colored people, I assume that it is a public duty that they and the white people of the country, with whom they are to be associated in political and public affairs, shall be assimilated and made one in the fundamental idea of human equality. Therefore, where it would be possible to establish distinct schools, I am against it as a matter of public policy.

But throughout the larger part of the South it is not possible to establish separate schools for black children and for white children, that will furnish means of education suited to the wants of either class; and therefore in all that region of country it is a necessity that the schools shall be mixed, in order that they shall be of sufficient size to make them useful in the highest degree; and it is also important that they should be mixed schools in order that, when the prejudice which now pervades portions of our people shall be rooted out by the power of general taxation, they will be able to accumulate in every district those educational forces by which the public schools shall be made useful to the highest degree for which there is capacity in the public will with the power of general taxation.[206]

Senator John P. Stockton, a New Jersey Democratic lawyer whose expulsion or exclusion from the 39th Congress gave the Republicans the necessary two-thirds majority to override President Andrew Johnson's vetoes, ended the day's proceedings with a plea for local control over schools. He told his colleague, Frelinghuysen, to go to the New Jersey legislature if he wanted to regulate schools, and added that the state legislature would never pass a bill like this.[207]

The next day, May 22, was the last day of Senate debate. Stockton finished his speech by reading from a statement by Senator William G. Brownlow, a Tennessee Republican, attacking school integration. He added that Boutwell's speech contained the same ideas as those urged by Sumner and by sundry Negro conventions, that Negroes were entitled not merely to equal schools but to go to the same schools as

---

[206]*Id.* at 4116.
[207]*Id.* at 4117.

white children in order "that this miserable prejudice that existed should be rooted out of the hearts of the young as they grow up."[208] He, too, warned that the bill would destroy the school system.[209]

Howe then commenced a speech in support of the bill. Like Boutwell, he differed with the Supreme Court's restricted interpretation of the privileges and immunities clause of the fourteenth amendment in the *Slaughter-House Cases*.[210] He asserted that, in Georgia, school districts could give Negroes inferior schooling or none at all,[211] and spurned the threats of school-closing.[212] But he declared:

> Mr. President, we are not providing in this bill for mixing colors at all. If you are resolved that the two colors shall not mingle in your school-houses, . . . they need not mingle, in spite of anything in this bill. I do not agree with my honorable friend from Massachusetts, [Mr. Boutwell] who said yesterday that it was necessary to mingle them, if I understood him, in the school-houses, in order that they might there unlearn this prejudice which separates one color from the other. I do not believe in that doctrine at all. I do not believe that it belongs to education to unteach this prejudice. . . .
>
> Mr. President, I say if you insist upon it that the colors shall never be mingled in your school-houses, this bill will not force them together. If you choose to build two school houses on every acre in every district, and to give the two colors the privilege of choosing between the two, each color will go to that where they feel the most at home and where their education is most advanced. Open two school-houses wherever you please; furnish in them equal accommodations and equal instruction, and the whites will for a time go by themselves, and the colored children will go by themselves for the same reason, because each will feel more at home by themselves than at present either can feel with the other; and the child who should separate from his own color to go into the white school for mere social reasons would feel and would be treated by his own color as a rebel against his race. But, on the contrary, let your law say that they shall not be educated together, and then the subordinate

---

208 *Id.* at 4144.

209 *Id.* at 4145.

210 *Id.* at 4148.

211 *Id.* at 4150.

212 *Id.* at 4151. Senator Howe said:

But Senators say, "Let us be careful; do not go too far; . . . do not you dare to say that the colors in those schools be mixed; say that and the schools fall; there shall be none." I hear the threat, and I admit I am afraid. I do not know but they will do it. . . . This [threat] is one that comes very near me. I do not know but the schools will fall if we do not stay our course; but when peril threatens of any kind I can meet it but in one way. Let justice be done though the common schools and the very heavens fall.

color must take just such accommodations as are provided, let them be poor or good. Let the law speak, then; offer equal inducements to each of the races, and each will in the schoolhouse continue to keep by themselves. But let the individuals and not the superintendent of schools judge of the comparative merits of the schools; that is the point. They will know where they are best taken care of. I would rather trust them than to trust any municipal officer.[213]

Howe also asserted that little children are not prejudiced, and that they are color-blind until taught prejudice.[214]

Alcorn, who had consistently spoke and voted against Sumner's bill in the prior Congress,[215] now advocated it. He said that "I am not in favor of mixing [schools] and I contend that this bill does not mix them." He explained that in Mississippi the Negroes controlled the whole government, "Yet there is not a mixed school in the State of Mississippi, and we have civil rights there." He added that the colored people "believe the interests of both races will be promoted by keeping the schools separate," and that a satisfactory segregated school system was in operation which gave every citizen "a right to send your child to any school you choose," but that children of both races were, by the choice of their parents, sent to segregated schools. He urged the bill because in some states Negroes had no right to go to any school.[216] Alcorn concluded by accusing Boutwell of hypocrisy in a proposed amendment limiting schools covered to those "hereafter" established, contending that he wanted to bar them from the old Massachusetts colleges. He said that Negroes demanded the right of admission to all schools, and if refused on constitutional grounds they will "trample down constitutions." His conclusion made it clear that he had changed his position because his colored constituents demanded it.[217]

Boutwell replied to this that a college, such as Dartmouth College,

---

[213]*Ibid.*

[214]*Ibid.* He said:

They are not the laws of nature. Nature gives the lie to the assertion everywhere. There is not in Washington a white child, until politics gets possession of the unfortunate to some extent, that makes the slightest discrimination between the black and the white race; not one. Politicians teach that prejudice. It is not a law of nature; it is one of the worst and most degrading lessons we learn, and one of the most mischievous.

[215]CONG. GLOBE, 42d Cong., 2d Sess. 274, 3264, 3268, 3270 (1872).

[216]2 CONG. REC. app. 305 (1874).

[217]*Id.* at 307. He said: "The colored people of my State demand the passage of this bill. I yield to that demand. My refusal would excite them to anger; they would keenly feel the injustice and wrong. I bend gracefully to their will." His mind may have been changed by the fact that he was an unsuccessful candidate for governor in 1873, in between the last Congress and this one.

which was founded by a private person, could not be required to integrate even if it later received gifts from the state, citing *Dartmouth College v. Woodward*,[218] because it "takes its law from the founder of the institution . . . and all subsequent gifts and bequests are upon that foundation, and, as a matter of law, follow the will of the founder, even though the subsequent gifts may greatly exceed the original one." He said that Congress could only reach institutions originally endowed from state money, or subsequently endowed or supported out of tax money. Boutwell concluded:

> To say that an institution private in its foundation and receiving its law from the founder, though it may have afterwards received a donation or a gift from a State, shall be open to every citizen for the purposes of education, is going further than I think we can go under the principles of law and according to the decisions of the Supreme Court.[219]

But Alcorn was not satisfied. He said that the United States Constitution could impair state contracts and charters, and demanded admission to Dartmouth College for Negroes.[220]

Senator Lewis Bogy, a Missouri Democratic lawyer, likewise referred to Boutwell's amendment as an illustration or northern hypocrisy.[221] He, too, predicted that his state would repeal its school laws if the bill were passed, that the school system would be destroyed, and that rich white children would be sent to private school while poor whites and Negroes would go without education.[222] But Senator Henry R. Pease, Alcorn's Republican colleague from Mississippi, told the Senate that none of the southern states would abolish their school system if the bill passed because labor would leave without a school system and this was against their interests.[223] He noted that by law in Mississippi Negroes could enter any school but chose to have segregated schools. He said that not a single Negro had applied to Oxford University (now the University of Mississippi) although entitled to do so, but instead

---

218 Dartmouth College v. Woodward, 17 U.S. (4 Wheat.) 518 (1819).
219 2 Cong. Rec. 4152 (1874).
220 Id. at 4152-53.
221 2 Cong. Rec. app. 320-21 (1874). He said:
While northern Senators are determined that the southern people shall associate with their colored neighbors, and that the blacks shall be admitted to the schools of the country, . . . on an equal footing with the whites they are unwilling that they should enter the halls of learning at the North; they are unwilling to do that for them at home which they compel us to do for them in our homes.
222 Id. at 321-22.
223 2 Cong. Rec. 4153 (1874).

asked to have a colored university set up, which was done. He also stated that he opposed Boutwell's amendment because he wanted Negroes to have the right to go to Harvard and Dartmouth. He added:

> Gentlemen say that if equal advantages in separate schools are provided the law is met so far as privileges and immunities are concerned. I say that whenever a State shall legislate that the races shall be separated, and that legislation is based upon color or race, there is a distinction made; it is a distinction the intent of which is to foster a concomitant of slavery and to degrade him. The colored man understands and appreciates his former condition; and when laws are passed that say that "because you are a black man you shall have a separate school," he looks upon that, and justly, as tending to degrade him. There is no equality in that.[224]

Senator Henry Cooper, a Tennessee Democratic lawyer, also attacked the school clause. He said that the committee draft, unlike the original bill, was ambiguous on whether the states could maintain a system of segregated schools. He urged that no benefit was gained by Negroes in forcing themselves into white schools where there would be prejudice against them. He, too, concluded that Tennessee would close its schools if the bill were passed.[225]

Saulsbury of Delaware made the next assault on the school clause. After attacking Boutwell's view that segregated schools should be abolished to root out prejudice, and "that children are to be forced into the same school in order that their ideas and views and opinions may become one," he declared:

> [E]very Senator on this floor who favors the bill knows, that the only effect and operation of it is to be had upon the poorer classes in this country, who are dependent upon common schools. While that Senator and the Senators who support this bill advocate mixed schools, and insist that it is the right of the colored man to send his children to the same school with the white man, there is not one of them—I repeat in the presence of Senators, there is not one of them—who will send his children to any such mixed school. . . . Ah, sir, fortune has favored them, and they are able to select their schools and send their children to them and pay for their tuition; but the humble poor man . . . it is against them and their children that the provisions of this bill are directed. We had as well deal frankly with this question. I know full well that in no section of this country are mixed common schools patronized by gentlemen of fortune. They select their schools, and Senators know full well that if

---

²²⁴*Id.* at 4154.
²²⁵*Id.* at 4154-55.

this bill goes into operation it will not affect their children, while
they are avowing their purpose to force the mixed schools
whereby the children of the poor white men may be compelled
to be educated in associations with the colored children or not
educated at all.[226]

Saulsbury predicted that school integration would produce miscegenation,[227] and the destruction of southern and border-state school systems,
which would intensify white prejudice against Negroes rather than
alleviate it.[228]

    With the Senate going into an all-night session to force passage of
the bill, Senator James K. Kelly, an Oregon Democratic lawyer, attacked
it on constitutional grounds. Once again, he explained the limited
nature of the privileges and immunities clause, and prophesied that
"if the States should abolish the common schools, the Federal Government would undertake to coerce the people of the States, to levy taxes
to support common schools."[229] Merrimon's contribution to the Democratic filibuster consisted of a rambling discourse which ended with
a lengthy analysis of the limited scope of the privileges and immunities
and equal protection clauses.[230] He returned to his analogy between
segregation by race and segregation by sex in the schools, and noted
that Morton was unable to say why one was permitted and the other
forbidden. He contended that equal protection was preserved when
separate schools were provided for both classes, and that the fourteenth
amendment did not mention race any more than sex, and either
permitted both types of segregation or neither.[231] He added:

> Will it be said the Negro child has not the right to go to a
> white school? Then I answer, the white child has no right to
> go to the Negro school. It is as broad one way as it is the other,

---

[226]*Id.* at 4158.

[227]*Id.* at 4160.

[228]*Id.* at 4161. See also 3 CONG. REC. app. 105 (1875) (remarks of Senator
Thomas F. Bayard).

[229]2 CONG. REC. 4162-64 (1874).

[230]2 CONG. REC. app. 311-13 (1874).

[231]*Id.* at 313. He said:
Will it be said that because the difference is on account of color it will not
do? That objection is unfounded, it seems to me. There is no provision
in the Constitution of the United States which protects color any more than
sex or age. If there was any purpose to protect *color* against the exercise
of the police power of the States, and prevent the States from exercising their
powers to regulate right and society, why was it not so provided? Are the
States to be deprived of the absolute right to exercise the important power
of police upon the merest speculative inference? Surely not. That it was
not contemplated that any such restriction on the States was thought of,

and the principle in this case does not differ from the principle
in the case where a law provides that males shall be educated
only in male schools and females only in female schools. I cannot understand or comprehend a distinction in point of principle between the power to educate the sexes in separate
schools and that to require the races to be educated in separate
schools. Like equal legal provision must be made for each
race, and this is the equality of right and protection required
by the Constitution. The State may exercise the power to
distinguish on the ground of race, so as to provide for the education of the races in separate schools equally provided for in all
material respects. But, even apart from the police powers, I
cannot see wherein one man is injured and deprived of any
right in the one case more than he is in the other.[232]

Merrimon, too, accused the Republican majority of hypocrisy.[233] He

intended, or provided, appears in the provision contained in the fifteenth
amendment, that no person shall be deprived by the United States, or any
State of his right *to vote* on account of *race, color, or previous condition of
servitude.* Why was this provision limited to the right to *vote* alone? . . . .
It was easy to have provided that no distinction for any cause should ever
be made because of *race, color, or previous condition of servitude,* but no
such provision was made.
[232]*Ibid.* He also observed:
But it is said that these police powers may be exercised in many respects,
but it cannot be done in the matter of color. Why not in the matter of color?
If the Legislature of a State, in their judgment founded on the experience of
the people, think and determine that the black race and the white race
should be educated separately, why is it not competent for them so to provide by statute? It is said it is a discrimination against the black race. It is
just as much a discrimination, in point of principle, against the white race.
If there are separate schools, the black man has the same right to deny my
child admission to the school where his children go as I have to deny his
children admission to the schools where my children go; so that we are upon
a perfect equality of right in principle.
The Senator from Wisconsin [Mr. Howe] to-day declaimed loudly against
the proposition of the minority here and of the people in certain States, as
tending to deprive the colored people of education. He talked about shutting
the door in their faces, keeping them locked up in ignorance indefinitely or
forever. Nobody has made any such uncharitable proposition. . . . The
proposition is to allow the colored people of the country to have their own
school-house; to allow the white people to have their own school-house, and
that neither race shall interfere with the other. . . .
Id. at 315.
[233]*Id.* at 317. He said:
I venture to say that any one may go to the Senators who expect to vote for
this bill and put the plain, practical question to them . . . "Are you willing
your daughter shall attend a school with the negro children in my town?"
And if he would give you a sincere answer he would tell you "nay," and
yet he would have his fellow-countrymen do what he would not do himself.

ended his declamation with a warning against miscegenation and school closing.[234]

With the Republicans still refusing to adjourn at 1:30 a.m.,[235] Senator William T. Hamilton, a Maryland Democratic lawyer, began a lengthy discussion of the bill. He first asserted that its constitutionality could not be justified under the fourteenth amendment, since that amendment said nothing about race, and if Congress could forbid racial discrimination thereunder, it could forbid other kinds of discrimination as well.[236] He advocated segregated schools, and declared that mixed schools would lead to racial strife. He, too, predicted that Maryland would close its schools rather than submit to integration.[237]

At this point, Senator Aaron A. Sargent, a California Republican lawyer, moved the following amendment:

> *Provided,* That nothing herein contained shall be construed to prohibit any State or school district from providing separate schools for persons of different sex or color, where such separate schools are equal in all respects to others of the same grade established by such authority, and supported by an equal *pro rata* expenditure of school funds.[238]

A vote was taken on this amendment and it lost, 26 nay to 21 yea. The armative votes were cast by 13 Democrats, 1 southern Republican, and 7 northern Republicans, from California, Illinois, Iowa, Maine, Nevada, Pennsylvania, and West Virginia. Included in the affirmative votes were those of Morrill of Maine, who had always voted against Sumner's bill, Senator William M. Stewart, a Nevada Republican lawyer who had voted for the fourteenth amendment and who was a prominent Radical throughout the whole reconstruction period, and Senator William B. Allison, an Iowa Republican lawyer who, as a member of the House in the 39th Congress, had voted for the fourteenth amendment on its

---

[234]*Id.* at 316-18.

[235]2 Cong. Rec. 4166 (1874).

[236]2 Cong. Rec. app. 362 (1874).

[237]*Id.* at 367-69. He said:

I do not want the sentiments and principles enunciated by the Senator from Massachusetts [Mr. Boutwell] to be applied to our people and forced upon us. The policy of forcing mixed schools upon us, of forcing our children into schools with colored children, is publicly avowed. There is to be no choice. If desired by neither race it must still be done, says the Senator, to perpetuate or establish a principle. I care not whether it be right or wrong in sentiment, whether it should or should not be done as a matter of principle; I say as a matter of policy and or philosophy the men who would do this are blind to the intent of both races.

Id. at 368.

[238]2 Cong. Rec. 4167 (1874). See also *id.* at 4153.

passage. The negative votes were cast by 19 northern Republicans and 7 southern Republicans. Three of these had voted for the fourteenth amendment as members of the Senate and 5 as members of the House. Frelinghuysen, Howe, and Pratt, all of whom said that a dual school system and voluntary segregation were permissible at the least voted in the negative, so apparently Sargent's amendment must have been construed as permitting compulsory segregation by law.[239]

Boutwell then moved his amendment, and Stewart opposed it. He said that now that Negroes could vote, they could look out for themselves, and pointed to the votes for the civil rights bill in the Senate as the effect of Negro suffrage. He said that while Congress could constitutionally compel the states to repeal their segregation laws, it was inexpedient to do so because some of them had fledgling school systems which might be ruined by the bill. Frelinghuysen then said that he would vote against Boutwell's amendment because the Judiciary Committee draft, without the defeated amendment of Sargent, "leaves the schools, colored schools or white schools, as they are." Frelinghuysen explained that "it is perfectly competent to have one school for the whites to go to, another school for the colored children to go to; and I suppose by the law as it stands a colored child has a right to go to a white school, or a white child to go to a colored school," and that "it would not be a violation of the law [to provide separate school systems]."[240]

Boutwell then explained his amendment as follows:

> What e [sic] feared is just exactly that condition of things which the honorablI [sic] chairman of the Committee on the Judiciary intimates may happen. I wish to break down the prejudice in the public mind by which it is possible in some cities and sections of the country to make separate schools and give to children, who when they become men are bound by the same political bonds to a government based upon the doctrine of equality, ideas which are inconsistent with the existence of such institutions; for it is only by instilling into the minds of the children and the youth of the country the idea that there is no difference by nature or birth or race or color or caste, that we can take security for the continuance of the institutions under which we live; and every system which tolerates, encourages, or lays the foundation for the dissemination of different ideas, is a system hostile to republican government. Inasmuch as these four million colored people are made, by the Constitution, citizens of the country, as they and their posterity through all time are to have a lot and part with us as citizens, I say now . . . let us do that thing which is right in

[239]*Id.* at 4167.
[240]*Id.* at 4167-68.

the eye of the Constitution; and nothing is right but absolute equality of rights.[241]

Frelinghuysen then asked Boutwell whether "he proposes by his amendment to compel colored children to go to white schools." The latter replied that he could not do this, but that he intended to eliminate a dual school system. Stewart rebutted Boutwell's assertion "that it is necessary now, in order to preserve the Republic, to require the children of colored people and white people to go to the same school, whether they desire it or not, and that we should not leave it optional even with them to separate themselves, but must force them into the same school, and this for accomplishing of a great moral idea." Stewart warned his Republican colleagues that in many of the states a free school system was not firmly established, and that integration might create so much opposition as to destroy it. He concluded that he was not going to surrender to the Negro vote at the expense of education.[242]

Under questioning by Stockton, Boutwell reiterated that the purpose of his amendment was not to eliminate all distinctions of race and color "but to remove the prejudices which exist between persons of different races and different colors, and substitute the idea of human equality." Frelinghuysen said that he disagreed with this. A vote was then taken on Boutwell's amendment. Five votes were cast in its favor, 1 by Boutwell and 4 by Republican Senators from Alabama, Louisiana, Mississippi, and South Carolina. Each of these states had heavy Negro voting populations. Forty-two votes were cast against the amendment. Thirteen were Democrats, 4 were southern Republicans, and 25 were northern Republicans. This last group included five Republicans who had voted for the fourteenth amendment as members of the Senate, and five as members of the House, including Senator Roscoe Conkling, an erstwhile colleague of Boutwell on the Joint Committee on Reconstruction which had reported out the fourteenth amendment. Even Senator William B. Washburn, a Republican colleague of Boutwell from Mas-

---

[241]*Id.* at 4168.

[242]*Id.* at 4168-69. Senator Stewart said:
My friend from Massachusetts knows how our ranks have been augmented since that event [fifteenth amendment] for he acted a conspicuous part in giving the ballot to the negro. He knows very well how the forces that advocate these rights have been augmented by the ballot. He hears that potent voice. Eight hundred thousand votes in America are calculated to make the politicians tremble. . . . If for education, then the amendment of the Senator from California is right; if to conciliate eight hundred thousand voters at the expense of the loss of education in many States, then the amendment of the Senator from Massachusetts is right. . . . I do not believe that but for these eight hundred thousand votes there would be ten votes, or even five votes, in this Chamber for this particular clause.

sachusetts who had, as a member of the House, voted for the fourteenth amendment on its pasage there, voted against his proposal to abolish a dual school system.[243]

A vote was then taken to strike out the whole school clause, and it lost by a strict party-line vote of 30 to 14, with only Boreman voting with the minority.[244] Next, Alcorn moved to amend the committee draft to include colleges which had received state endowments. This provision was opposed by Frelinghuysen because a state, "by making an endowment to an institution . . . [could not] change it from a private to a public institution."[245] Nine Republican senators voted for this—7 from the south and 2 from the north. Thirty-seven senators voted against it— 13 Democrats, 2 southern Republicans, and 22 northern Republicans, including Boutwell. All of the Republicans who had voted for the fourteenth amendment to the Senate or House voted against this.[246]

Sargent then proposed an amendment to give Negroes the equal benefit of the school system, and the following colloquy occurred:

> Mr. EDMUNDS. . . . The whole effect of this proposition is to authorize States on account of color to deny the right . . . to go to a particular common school. If there is anything in the bill, it is exactly contrary to that. If there is anything in the fourteenth amendment it is exactly opposite to that. The fourteenth amendment does not authorize us to make any trades with States either way on the subject, or regulate the action of States. What the Constitution authorizes us to do is to enforce equality; and it is not half-equality, for there is no such thing as half-equality. It is entire equality or nothing at all. . . . To put in these words here or in any part of the bill is merely to say in substance and effect that this bill shall have no force in asserting the equality that the fourteenth amendment to the Constitution asserts, if that asserts any equality at all; and, of course the bill goes on the theory that it does. . . .
>
> Mr. SARGENT. I do not know that the fourteenth amendment enjoins upon us that we shall have mixed schools. I do not know that the fourteenth amendment performs any of the offices the Senator speaks of. . . . I doubt if the fourteenth amendment provides that females shall be intruded into male schools or males into female schools; and yet this would be the office of the fourteenth amendment under the logic of the Senator from Vermont.[247]

Sargent next said that a powerful and wealthy religious organization

---

[243]*Id.* at 4169.
[244]*Id.* at 4170.
[245]*Id.* at 4168.
[246]*Id.* at 4171.
[247]*Id.* at 4171-72.

was at work to undermine the public school systems of the states, and that this bill would help them do it. He accused his Republican colleagues of surrendering educational welfare to the Negro vote.[248] He concluded:

> If you say that the fourteenth amendment absolutely levels all distinctions and justifies you in putting heavy penalties to prevent a system of separate schools, then I say you cannot separate your sexes; you must put them all into the same school, and the boy who demands to enter a female school has just as much right to do it under the fourteenth amendment. Following your principle, lauded here, you are required to enforce this by a law and penalties just as much as you are that a person of a particular color shall be allowed to enter into schools of another color. I would give all the full benefit of the school system, and I would do no more.[249]

Edmunds then said that Sargent had adopted the Democratic position that the fourteenth amendment does not forbid all distinctions in state laws based on race or color or religion. He emphasized: "But the Senator's argument results in exactly this: that the fourteenth amendment does not, as it respects common schools, level a distinction which a State may have a right to make on account of race and color."[250] Edmunds then stated that the bill proceeded on the theory that the fourteenth amendment does make a state blind to race, color, or origin. He added:

> [T]he Senator's argument is the democratic argument, inasmuch as he says the State has the right to regulate this business of common schools and to exclude people on account of their color one way or the other. If the State has that right, we cannot interfere with it. If the State has not that right, we cannot confer it by an act of Congress, because such an act of Congress would be in violation of the fourteenth amendment itself. The Senator's amendment proposes to recognize the right in a State to discriminate on account of color, and if it does recognize that right, it recognizes it as a right inherent in the State and which the fourteenth amendment does not

---

[248]*Id.* at 4172. He said:
But by the effect of this legislation, which is insisted on here for political purposes, in order to gain the eye of the colored people and encourage them to adhere to the republican party—for that is what it amounts to, for political purposes—we are sacrificing the higher interest of the county. . . . I consider that these are more important considerations than the question whether the republican party shall have more or less of the colored vote of this country.
[249]*Ibid.*
[250]*Ibid.*

touch. If it does not touch it, then there is not a right in your bill that is constitutional. On the other hand, if the fourteenth amendment does touch it, and this right to discriminate on account of color is not in the State, then I repeat, the Congress of the United States has no power to confer such a right upon a State to make discriminations between its citizens on account of color.[251]

Edmunds then deplored Sargent's reference to the alleged Roman Catholic Church opposition to public schools, and praised it for never having made racial discriminations. He went on to quote various statistics designed to show that southern Negroes had inferior school opportunities to those of whites, and urged the Senate to run the risk of any disturbances in the school systems which the bill might engender.[252] Three Democrats—Johnston of Virginia, Norwood of Georgia, and Merrimon of North Carolina—rebutted Edmund's assertion about inferior Negro schooling in the South.[253] Sargent replied that, as a consistent Republican, he believed that segregation by race was no more a violation of the fourteenth amendment than segregation by sex.[254] However, his amendment lost by 28 to 16. Two Republicans switched sides from the prior vote and several were absent who had originally voted with Sargent. However, Stewart continued to vote with Sargent although this amendment was less favorable to Negro claims than the prior one.[255] The bill then passed 29 to 16, with only three Republicans voting with the Democrats in the negative.[256]

The House took no action on the bill during this session. Several Democrats attacked it for requiring social equality and race mixing, asserted that Negroes themselves wanted separate schools, and issued the usual dire warnings about destruction of the school system or inevitable miscegenation.[257] A Tennessee Republican stated that almost all Negroes were satisfied with segregated schools except a few "smarties" or "would-be leaders," and questioned the constitutionality of the law.[258] Congressman James T. Rapier, an Alabama Negro Republican lawyer, charged that the Democrats were using the civil rights bill to gain

---

[251]*Id.* at 4173.

[252]*Ibid.*

[253]*Id.* at 4173-75.

[254]*Id.* at 4174-75.

[255]*Id.* at 4175.

[256]*Id.* at 4176.

[257]2 CONG. REC. app. 341-44 (1874) (remarks of Congressman William B. Read); *id.* at 417-21 (remarks of Congressman Ephraim K. Wilson); *id.* at 481 (remarks of Congressman John J. Davis).

[258]2 CONG. REC. 4592-93 (1874) (remarks of Congressman Roderick R. Butler).

votes.[259] He denied any desire for social equality, and complained that whites wanted to shut Negroes out of schools completely.[260]

Congressman Chester B. Darrall, a Louisiana Republican, read a section of that state's constitution giving every child in the state the right to attend any public school without distinction of race or color. He noted that this provision was put into force in New Orleans over a good deal of white opposition, and opponents urged white parents to withdraw their children from school. He read a report by the president of the city board of school directors that no unfavorable results which had been freely predicted had occurred. Most students attended school with members of their own race, but in some instances where schools became mixed there was no difficulty. In one school, where white students were withdrawn in protest, they soon returned. Representative Darrall declared that since the law had gone into effect, the school system of Louisiana had increased and flourished and that many prominent white people now endorsed the non-discriminatory school system. He concluded that the prophesies that schools would be closed if the bill should pass were groundless.[261] He declared:

> As to the threat in regard to the school clause that we will destroy the schools of some of the States, I have only to say that it is rather late in the day to be making threats of any kind, and we are all tired of these continual threats of what will be done if we do not quit legislating to protect our citizens in their rights. But there is no danger whatever that these threats will ever be carried into effect, or if they are, if the Legislature of Virginia or of Tennessee should fail to appropriate for one year, they would find their people were wiser than they were, and it would not be repeated. But should the worst come, should the schools fall, let them fall, but let justice be done.[262]

IV. THE HIGH-WATER MARK

In the elections of 1874 the Republican Party suffered a political hemorrhage. The hold-overs in the Senate kept it Republican by a much reduced margin. The policy of the equalitarians, who had passed the fourteenth amendment, to admit sparsely populated western states with more trees than people as soon as two staunch Republicans could be found to give them equal Senate representation paid handsome party dividends. But in the House, where more nearly "one-man, one vote" obtained, a party line-up of 194 Republicans, 92 Democrats, and

---

[259]*Id.* at 4782.

[260]*Id.* at 4782-83, 4785.

[261]2 CONG. REC. app. 478-79 (1874).

[262]*Id.* at 479.

14 others, in the 43d Congress, became 109 Republicans, 169 Democrats, and 14 others, in the 44th Congress.[263] Massachusetts, that bastion of Republicanism, was swept by the Democratic tidal wave; even Butler's own seat could not be saved from the holocaust.[264] The depression, fraud, corruption, and sundry scandals were major Democratic assets, but the "party of the rebellion" also made the civil rights bill, and especially race-mixing in schools, pay handsome dividends in the election.[265]

When the "lame-duck" second session of the 43d Congress met in the early part of 1875, Congressman Alexander White, an Alabama Republican lawyer, moved to amend the Senate bill by specifically permitting school segregation, while Congressman John Cessna, a Pennsylvania Republican lawyer, moved to retain the Senate bill intact, and Congressman Stephen W. Kellogg, a Connecticut Republican lawyer, moved to strike all reference to schools.[266] Congressman John R. Lynch, a Mississippi Republican Negro photographer, then launched into a defense of the Senate school clause. He said:

> I regard this school clause as the most harmless provision in the bill. If it were true that the passage of this bill with the school clause in it would tolerate the existence of none but a system of mixed free schools, then I would question very seriously the propriety of retaining such a clause; but such is not the case. . . . [I]t simply confers upon all citizens [the right] . . . to send their children to any public free school that is supported in whole or in part by taxation, the exercise of the right to remain a matter of option as it now is—nothing compulsory about it. That the passage of this bill can result in breaking up the public school system in any State is absurd. The men who make these reckless assertions are very well aware of the fact, or else they are guilty of unpardonable ignorance, that every right and privilege that is enumerated in this bill has already been conferred upon all citizens alike in at least one-half of the States of this Union by State legislation. In every Southern State where the Republican Party is in power a civil rights bill is in force that is more severe in its penalties than are the penalties in this bill. We find mixed-school clauses in some of their State constitutions. If, then, the passage of this bill, which does not confer upon the colored people of such States any rights that they do not possess already, will result in breaking up the public-school system in their respective States, why is it that State legislation has not broken them up? This

263U.S. Bureau of the Census, Historical Statistics of the United States, Colonial Times to 1957, 691 (1960).

264Trefousse, Ben Butler 230 (1957).

2653 Cong. Rec. 951, 952, 978, 982, 1001, app. 17, 20, 113 (1875).

2663 Cong. Rec. 938-39 (1875).

proves very conclusively, I think, that there is nothing in the argument whatever. . . . My opinion is that the passage of this bill just as it passed the Senate will bring about mixed schools practically only in localities where one or the other of the two races is small in numbers, and that in localities where both races are large in numbers separate schools and separate institutions of learning will continue to exist, for a number of years at least.[267]

Lynch then read an editorial from the Jackson *Clarion,* a Democratic newspaper, that the pending bill would have no effect on the Mississippi school system. He concluded that although Negroes did not want mixed schools, they did not want to be separated by law instead of individual choice, and declared that if the bill were passed, "there will be nothing more for the colored people to ask or expect in the way of civil rights."[268]

Congressman William E. Finck, an Ohio Democratic lawyer who had voted against the fourteenth amendment in the 39th Congress, stated that it did not give the federal government power to regulate admission to schools. He quoted copiously from the *McCann* case to support this proposition.[269] Congressman John B. Storm, a Pennsylvania Democratic lawyer, also urged that segregated schools conferred equal rights.[270] Cain, a South Carolina Negro Republican, added that he thought

---

[267]*Id.* at 945.

[268]*Ibid.* He said:

[I]t is contrary to our system of government to discriminate by law between persons on account of their race, their color, their religion, or the place of their birth. It is just as wrong and just as contrary to republicanism to provide by law for the education of children who may be identified with a certain race in separate schools to themselves, as to provide by law for the education of children who may be identified with a certain religious denomination in separate schools to themselves. The duty of the law-maker is to know no race, no color, no religion, no nationality, except to prevent distinctions in any of these grounds, so far as the law is concerned.

The colored people in asking the passage of this bill just as it passed the Senate do not thereby admit that their children can be better educated in white than in colored schools; nor that white teachers because they are white are better qualified to teach than colored ones. But they recognize the fact that the distinction when made and tolerated by law is an unjust and odious proscription; that you make their color a ground of objection, and consequently a crime. This is what we most earnestly protest against. Let us confer upon all citizens, then, the rights to which they are entitled under the Constitution; and then if they choose to have their children educated in separate schools, as they do in my own State, then both races will be satisfied, because they will know that the separation is their own voluntary act and not legislative compulsion.

[269]*Id.* at 948.

[270]*Id.* at 951.

Negroes "shall not lose anything if it [the school clause] is struck out." He said that they "could afford for the sake of peace in the Republican ranks, if for nothing else—not as a matter of principle—to except the school clause."[271] A Virginia Democrat praised the state's school system and warned that the bill would deliver a fatal blow to it,[272] a view which a Republican colleague of his endorsed.[273]

The next day, February 4, 1875, was the last day of House debate. Congressman James B. Sener, a Virginia Republican lawyer who had been defeated for re-election, told the House that not only would the school clause demolish the southern school systems, but also it would drag down the Republican Party in the South.[274] Congressman Ellis H. Roberts, a Republican newspaper editor from New York, opposed the complete elimination of the school clause because he wanted to give Negroes the right to go to school, but favored the segregation provision so that the South would not be antagonized.[275] A Missouri Republican, who also had been defeated, extolled the segregated schools of St. Louis and opposed the bill.[276]

Cain arose, despairing of the school clause, which he called the most important part of the bill. He said:

> As a republican, and for the sake of the welfare of the republican party, I am willing, if we cannot rally our friends to those higher conceptions entertained by Mr. Sumner—if we cannot bring up the republican party to that high standard with regard to the rights of man as seen by those who laid the foundation of this Government—then I am willing to agree to a compromise. If the school clause is objectionable to our friends, and they think they cannot sustain it, then let it be struck out entirely. We want no invidious discrimination in the laws of this country. Either give us that provision in its entirety or else leave it out altogether, and thus settle the question.[277]

Under questioning, Cain averred that the southern Negroes did not want mixed schools, and said that the only mixed institution in South Carolina was the state college. He further declared that if Congress would force people to accept mixed schools, they would obey without trouble. But he once again concluded that he would prefer the school

---

[271]*Id.* at 957.
[272]3 CONG. REC. app. 119-20 (1875) (remarks of Congressman Eppa Hunton).
[273]*Id.* at 158-59 (remarks of Congressman Ambler Smith).
[274]3 CONG. REC. 978-79 (1875). He said: "in this effort they are crippling the great republican party in eight of the [southern] states . . . which . . . cast their electoral vote for . . . Grant. . . ."
[275]*Id.* at 980-81.
[276]*Id.* at 981 (remarks of Congressman Edwin O. Stanard).
[277]*Ibid.*

clause striken rather than have a segregation provision therein.[278]

Congressman Simeon B. Chittenden, a New York Republican, then explained why he was going to vote against the bill:

> I do not want to go down with my party quite so deep as the bill would sink it if it becomes the law, and that is the reason why I speak. . . . I am a practical man, and believe it impolitic unnecessarily to vex white men, North and South, by passing this bill now.[279]

White of Alabama then made a major speech in favor of the segregation amendment. He attacked fellow Republican extremists and counseled "moderation on this subject." He said that the evil "to be remedied by this bill is that the people of color in many of the States are denied the privilege of admission to public schools." He added that neither Negroes or whites in the South desired race-mixing and adverted to the action of the House Judiciary Committee in reporting a school segregation amendment, commenting as follows:

> This is a question of expediency, not a matter of right. Your committee concede this by providing in their bill for separate schools. Had it been a matter of right or of principle, they could not have provided in their bill for separate schools; but as it was neither, but only a question of expediency, they could do so, and acted wisely and well in so doing.[280]

White then made a lengthy political analysis, in which he pointed out that the civil rights bill was changing so many white votes that it would cost the Republican Party every southern state.[281] Speaking of the Republican mountain areas, he warned:

> No earthly power could have loosed your hold upon them but the republican party itself. But when you proposed to put the Senate bill upon them; when, as they were told, you proposed to invade the sanctity of their homes and to force social equality

---

[278]*Id.* at 981-82.

[279]*Id.* at 982.

[280]3 CONG. REC. app. 15 (1875).

[281]*Id.* at 16-24. He said:

But it is to the effects of this measure upon the people of the Southern States I wish to call attention. The elections there have swept nearly every republican Representative from the States of Virginia, West Virginia, North Carolina, Tennessee, Georgia, Alabama, and Arkansas . . . while in the State Legislatures there has been a corresponding diminution of power. Falling bodies move with accelerated rapidity and cumulative force, and unless this downward movement is speedily checked, in a brief time the republicans in the South will have no Representative here, and no power or influence in

upon them; when you proposed to force their children into schools with colored children or deprive them of the benefits of the common schools, the blood of the Anglo-Saxon rebelled, and they turned away from you. You may say that this is a prejudice but they say it is not, that it is a sentiment; but whether the one or the other it is a fact, and a stubborn fact— one that will not yield to force. If the civil-rights bill which is on your table becomes the law, you will drive these men, whose fidelity to republican principles has been proven by sacrifices and trials to which no northern republican has been subjected, permanently away from you, and you obliterate in a brief time the republican party South.[282]

Kellogg then explained that he was moving to strike out the school clause because schools should be under local control, because the school clause might injure the school systems, and because national legislation should not provide for segregation by law. Congressman James Monroe, an Ohio Republican, added that although he preferred the Senate bill, he would rather have the school clause striken out than to take the House Judiciary Committee's provision providing for segregated schools. He explained that Negroes and radicals were opposed to any statutory racial distinctions, and would prefer to take their chances for obtaining an education for colored students under the Constitution without a statute, than to accept segregated education under federal law.[283] Congressman Barbour Lewis, a Tennessee Republican, warned about sentiment against school-mixing in the South.[284]

Congressman Julius C. Burrows, a Michigan Radical Republican, arose to warmly endorse the Senate bill. He pointed to the widespread illiteracy among Negroes as the reason why they needed schools more than anything else. He further protested against the school segregation provision as "entering upon that course of legislation which draws a line of demarcation between [A]merican citizens who by your laws and your Constitution stand in absolute equality. . . ."[285] He added that the

---

a Legislative Assembly in the South. . . . These consequences have followed from the proposal to pass the civil rights bill of last session, and will be multiplied and it may be made irreparable by its passage. The result then will be to lose you the entire South, and to break and dissipate your political power there for all time to come. Looking at it as a mere question of party tactics, where in the North and West can you expect to gain, by the passage of this bill, States or voters to compensate you for the loss of nine hundred thousands voters and seven or eight States in the South?

Id. at 17.
[282]*Id.* at 20.
[283]3 CONG. REC. 997-98 (1875).
[284]*Id.* at 998-99.
[285]*Id.* at 999.

provision permitting states to establish school segregation "is to establish by Federal law separate schools in the majority of the States of this Union." To this, objection came on several grounds. First, he said that it would create racial prejudice in small children where none had existed before. Second, he urged that a segregated school system would double the expense for schools. Finally, he said that the federal law would reopen the contest about school segregation in those states which had already eliminated it by local law. He named Connecticut, Illinois, Iowa, Massachusetts, Minnesota, and Michigan as states where school segregation had been abolished.[286] Rapier, the Negro Republican colleague of White, also rejected any compromise and made an emotional appeal for the Senate bill.[287]

Congressman William W. Phelps, a New Jersey Republican lawyer, opposed the bill as unconstitutional and destructive of the budding southern school systems. But his main argument was political. He said that the two parties had divided in the last election on the bill, and that the people voted against it emphatically.[288] But Congressman Charles G. Williams, a Wisconsin Republican, opposed school segregation, "thereby nurturing a prejudice they never knew, and preparing these classes for mutual hatred hereafter, though they are the ones . . . upon whose action the peace and tranquility of the nation must depend."[289] Finally, two Republicans appealed for Democratic votes to let Negroes go to school, based on God and the 1872 Democratic platform.[290] Butler of Massachusetts, who concluded the debate, also expressed a preference for no school provision rather than for one with segregated schools.[291]

A vote was then taken on Kellogg's motion, striking out the entire school clause, including its section permitting states to maintain segregated schools. This vote carried by 128 to 48. A vote to restore the school clause, and providing for segregation in schools and other public accommodation, on White's motion, lost by 114 to 91. In neither case were the yeas and nays taken.[292]

Federal compulsion of school desegregation then reached what would be its high water mark for over three-quarters of a century. A vote was taken on restoring the school clause as it passed the Senate.

[286]*Id.* at 1000.

[287]*Id.* at 1001.

[288]*Id.* at 1001-02.

[289]*Id.* at 1002.

[290]*Id.* at 1003 (remarks of Congressman William A. Phillips and Congressman John P. Shanks).

[291]*Id.* at 1005.

[292]*Id.* at 1010.

This vote lost by 114 yeas to 148 nays.[293] The affirmative votes were all cast by Republicans. Of the negative votes, 61 were cast by Republicans and 87 by Democrats. All the few remaining Democrats who had served in the 39th Congress, Charles Eldredge of Wisconsin, William E. Finck of Ohio, William E. Niblack of Indiana, and Samuel J. Randall of Pennsylvania, all of whom had voted against the fourteenth amendment in the House, and James W. Nesmith of Oregon, who as Senator was absent when the vote was taken on it in 1866, voted nay, as could be expected.

The Republican vote is of more interest. The school clause split off about one-third of the Republican party. This split was not based on North-South lines. Of the Republicans voting for the school clause, 98 came from the North, 1 came from a border state (Maryland), and 15 came from the South. Of the Republicans voting against the school clause, 37 came from the North, 7 from the border states of Delaware, Maryland, West Virginia, and Missouri, and 17 came from the South. To further show the nature of the split, all five Republicans from Louisiana, all three from Mississippi, and all four from South Carolina voted for the school clause, while four out of five from Alabama, all five from Tennessee, and four out of five from Virginia voted against it. Seven out of nine Michigan Republicans voted for it, but all three Minnesota Republicans voted against it. The New Jersey Republican delegation was split three to three, while the Pennsylvania delegation was split, twelve for and nine against. There was a somewhat heavier vote against the clause by Republicans in marginal seats. About one-third of the Republicans who voted for the school clause had been defeated in 1874, while one-half who had voted against it had been defeated. However, this does not seem to be such undue proportion as to lead to the conclusion that the defeats in 1874 were the sole factors for voting against the clause, although doubtless they were an important cause.

By this time only a handful of Republicans sat in the House who had been in the 39th Congress and voted for the fourteenth amendment. The following of that group voted for the school clause: Godlove S. Orth of Indiana, John A. Kasson of Kansas, Henry L. Dawes and Samuel Hooper of Massachusetts, James A. Garfield and William Lawrence of Ohio, William D. Kelley, Leonard Myers, and Charles O'Neill of Pennsylvania, and Philetus Sawyer of Wisconsin, all of whom but Hooper and Sawyer were lawyers. Four Republicans who had voted for the fourteenth amendment voted against the school clause. They were Hezekiah S. Bundy, an Ohio Republican lawyer, Robert S. Hale, a former New York State judge whose speech against the original draft of the four-

---

[293]*Id.* at 1011.

teenth amendment had resulted in the substantial rewording of the first section,[294] Glenni W. Scofield of Pennsylvania, a former state judge, who had several years before spoken against railroad segregation,[295] and Luke P. Poland, a former Chief Justice of the Vermont Supreme Court who had likewise taken a prominent part in urging passage of the fourteenth amendment, as a senator from that state.[296]

The House vote for the fourteenth amendment was 128 to 37.[297] The party line-up in the 39th Congress of 149 Republicans and 42 Democrats[298] is not very dissimilar to the total vote on the school clause of 142 Republicans and 58 Democrats, if the southern and Nebraska delegations, which were unrepresented in the 39th Congress when the fourteenth amendment was proposed, is eliminated from both party totals. Thus, if the third of the Republicans in the House which had defected on the school clause at the end of the reconstruction in 1875, were presented with a school clause by the Radicals in 1866, and likewise defected then, as they probably would have, it would have meant a swing of 40 Republican votes. The vote on the fourteenth amendment with a school desegregation provision would have been about 88 to 77, far less than the two-thirds necessary for passage. A school desegregation provision on the fourteenth amendment would have blocked that amendment in the House, without considering the more narrowly divided Senate.

V. SUMMARY AND CONCLUSIONS.

In contrast to the scanty debates in 1866 on schools, those on the Civil Rights Act of 1875 were voluminous and exhaustive. These debates have been set forth at some length above to demonstrate that virtually every possible position that is espoused today was known and advocated by 1875 in regard to race relations and schools. Moreover, every substantial argument for or against school segregation or integration was known and advocated at that time. The only difference today is that partisans of these positions are using longer words and bigger footnotes to say the same thing. One must flatter oneself to believe that

---

294See CONG. GLOBE, 39th Cong. 1st Sess. 1063-66 (1866).

295CONG. GLOBE, 40th Cong., 2d Sess. 1965 (1868).

296CONG. GLOBE, 39th Cong., 1st Sess. 2961-64 (1866). Poland was also a member of the House Judiciary Committee which drafted the committee's school segregation provision, and was one of the three Republican committee members to vote against the Senate school clause, four of them voting for it.

297Id. at 2545.

298U.S. BUREAU OF THE CENSUS, HISTORICAL STATISTICS OF THE UNITED STATES, COLONIAL TIMES TO 1957, 691 (1960).

one has something really new to say on the subject which was not said almost a century ago.[299]

The views expressed ranged the entire spectrum. The unreconstructed Democrats from Delaware and Kentucky expressed the *antebellum* view that Negroes paid so little in taxes that they ought to be exempted from taxes for schools and should not go to any kind of school at all. We need not concern ourselves with what they thought of the fourteenth amendment. More progressive Democrats such as Thurman and Merrimon thought that the fourteenth amendment had nothing to do with schools, or at least school segregation, and that Negroes in schools should be rigidly segregated by law. However, as all Democrats and conservatives voted against the fourteenth amendment, their views are not too significant.

The "swing" group of Republican moderates, who made possible the fourteenth amendment, led by Trumbull of Illinois, believed that the right to go to school was not a civil right protected by the fourteenth amendment, over which Congress could legislate. As for the District of Columbia, this group advocated or acquiesced in separate and equal facilities by law for Negroes. This group included not only the moderates of 1866, but also such erstwhile regulars and Radicals as Morrill of Maine, Poland of Vermont, and Sprague of Rhode Island. It constituted at all relevant times about a third of the Republican strength in both Houses of Congress.

There was also a handful of regulars, such as Pratt of Indiana and Sherman of Ohio, who believed that the *McCann* case was correctly decided but that Congress could abolish at least state-wide school segregation laws. Apparently, they believed that the local school boards should decide whether schools should be segregated or integrated. Their view would probably also require the overruling of *Berea College v. Kentucky*.[300]

The Radical view, as illustrated by the speeches of Edmunds of Vermont, Frelinghuysen of New Jersey, and Howe of Wisconsin, was that the fourteenth amendment prohibited state or local laws which segregated students by race, but that school boards could maintain a dual

---

[299]See 3 CONG. REC. 950 (1875), where Congressman John B. Storm, a Pennsylvania Democrat stated:

I believed that this subject had been talked threadbare both before the House and the country. Since 1870 it has been discussed in all its various phases, so that it is impossible for the ingenuity of man to say anything either new or original upon it.

Congressman Eppa Hunton a Virginia Democrat also said: "So much has been said on the civil rights bill that but little can be uttered now either new or interesting." 3 CONG. REC. app. 117 (1875).

[300]Berea College v. Kentucky, 211 U.S. 45 (1908).

system of schools and do everything to encourage racial segregation short of compelling it. This view would sustain *Brown v. Board of Educ.*,[301] if read very narrowly, far more narrowly than the Supreme Court has ever read it. It would certainly not support the gloss placed on it by *Goss v. Board of Educ.*,[302] or by the later decisions of the lower federal courts.[303]

Finally, the Sumner-Boutwell view was that there should be a single school system with everybody going to his neighborhood school. This is the way the Supreme Court has so far viewed the fourteenth amendment. Nobody suggested that the school authorities had an obligation to transport students around the city to eliminate "de facto" segregation because of neighborhood population patterns.

A determination of which of these views the fourteenth amendment embodied is a matter of simple arithmetic. Boutwell's proposal received not a single additional vote from a northern Republican, so obviously the fourteenth amendment could not have embodied this. The Radical ideas, as embodied in the Senate bill, never obtained a two-thirds vote in either House, which would have been necessary to embody it in a constitutional amendment. The Republicans who voted against the school clause did not do so, as has been suggested, because of the stock warnings that southerners would dismantle their school systems.[304] This was simply a makeweight argument that those against the school clause used, with those for it either claiming that it would not occur or willing to take their chances. Those Republicans who opposed the school clause either did so because of fear of voter reaction, personal belief that the fourteenth amendment did not require school desegregation, or personal hostility to school desegregation, or a combination of these views. Insofar as such action was based on fear of voter antipathy, it constitutes a strong argument against the possibility that the fourteenth amendment requires school desegregation. The amendment was proposed as a platform for the Republican Party to run on in the key fall 1866 elections,[305] and the party was forced to forego its far more moderate and ardently desired objective of Negro suffrage for this reason. Indeed,

---

[301]347 U.S. 483 (1954).

[302]Goss v. Board of Educ., 373 U.S. 683 (1963).

[303]A number of these are collected in Dowell v. School Bd., 244 F. Supp. 971 (W.D. Okla. 1965).

[304]Frank & Munro, *The Original Understanding of "Equal Protection of the Laws,"* 50 COLUM. L. REV. 131, 161-62 (1950). Professor Kelley has indicated that threats of school closing were important, but even he has recognized that political considerations were decisive. Kelly, *The Congressional Controversy Over School Segregation 1867-1875*, 64 AMER. HIST. REV. 537, 554-61 (1959).

[305]JAMES, THE FRAMING OF THE FOURTEENTH AMENDMENT 110-20, 123-24, 134-35, 145 (1956).

Sherman had warned his colleagues to be "moderate" and "to waive extreme opinions,"[306] and Democrats twitted the majority on its surrender to the voters.[307] In light of the fact that the House at the beginning of the reconstruction period had given District of Columbia Negroes the ballot,[308] even before the fourteenth amendment was proposed, but never, even by 1875, had desegregated District schools, it is inconceivable that the fourteenth amendment would have been loaded down with a proposition so likely to defeat both it and the Republican Party.[309]

In 1866, as in 1875, the Republicans could not have afforded to lose a third, or indeed, any significant number of their party ,and still muster a two-thirds vote in the Congress. The moderates held the balance of power in 1866. Their views must therefore be deemed decisive, since without them nothing could have been accomplished. This group emphatically and consistently demonstrated that it considered that the fourteenth amendment neither compelled of itself nor gave Congress the power to compel school desegregation.

The conclusion is inevitable. The rule of *Brown v. Board of Educ.* is not now, nor has it ever been, the supreme law of the land. Rather, it is an unwarranted exercise of non-existent authority which, being illegitimate in its origin, cannot be made legitimate by the lapse of time, nor by compliance, voluntary, purchased, or coerced. As for so-called "de facto" segregation, to believe that the fourteenth amendment mandated elimination of this requires a complete hallucination. The short answer to the array who urge the contrary was given by Mr. Justice Field, a contemporary of the amendment, in another context as follows:

> But notwithstanding the great names which may be cited in favor of the doctrine, and notwithstanding the frequency with which the doctrine has been reiterated, there stands, as a perpetual protest against its repetition, the constitution of the United States, which recognizes and preserves the autonomy and independence of the states. . . . Supervision over either the legislative or the judicial action of the states is in no case permissible except as to matters by the constitution specifically authorized or delegated to the United States. Any interference with either, except as thus permitted, is an invasion of the

---

[306]Cong. Globe, 39th Cong., 1st Sess. app. 132 (1866).

[307]Cong. Globe, 39th Cong., 1st Sess. 2530 (1866) (remarks of Congressman Randall).

[308]*Id.* at 311.

[309]See 3 Cong. Rec. 1001 (1875), where Congressman William W. Philps, a Republican opponent of the civil rights bill from New Jersey, declared that in the form of the bill Sumner left "the [Republican] party which he created and led, a legacy so full of the seeds of disintegration and decay. . . ."

authority of the state, and, to that extent, a denial of its independence.[310]

If a synthesis of radical and moderate views on schools were attempted, it would result in a doctrine that it is the parent and not the State who must control the educational atmosphere of the child. In such a synthesis, the duty of each school board is to create, consistently with efficient school administration, such a number of schools, both segregated and integrated, by race or otherwise, as will afford to the parents an opportunity to place their children in the educational atmosphere which they desire. Such a scheme would give the fullest opportunity for freedom of choice and association, but yet guard any child against unwanted association. To the extent that it is administratively feasible, the local school board should run a variety of schools and classes to suit the desires of all segments of the community. To the extent that the fourteenth amendment has anything to do with school segregation, it merely guarantees individual freedom of choice, consistent with the choice of all other individuals. Anyone who thinks he has a right to force himself on others is not asserting his fourteenth amendment rights but trampling on the rights of others.

---

[310]Baltimore & Ohio R.R. Co. v. Baugh, 149 U.S. 368, 401 (1893) (dissenting opinion) quoted in Erie R.R. Co. v. Tompkins, 304 U.S. 64, 78-79 (1938).

SCHOOL SEGREGATION AND PROFESSOR AVINS' HISTORY: A DEFENSE OF BROWN v. BOARD OF EDUCATION

*Walter E. Dellinger, III**

For Professor Avins the conclusion is inevitable: "The rule of *Brown v. Board of Educ.* is not now, nor has it ever been, the supreme law of the land."[1] He is not the first to express this view and, unfortunately, he will not be the last.[2] His article commands attention, however, because it is the product of historical research by a scholar with impressive credentials. His evidence and his reasoning are nonetheless unconvincing: they simply do not lead to the conclusion that the school segregation cases were wrongly decided.

Professor Avins' article is an attempt to reduce the broad guarantees of the fourteenth amendment to a series of fixed, mechanical rules.[3] He finds it unnecessary even to consider the basic judgment of the *Brown* decision that a state denies Negro children equal treatment by compelling them to attend segregated schools. For in his view the command of the fourteenth amendment that "No state shall . . . deny to any person . . . the equal protection of the laws" does not apply to school segregation even if such segregation in fact constitutes unequal treatment. His reason: despite its seemingly broad language, the amendment, as originally understood by the Congress that sent the amendment to the states, was not intended to apply to school segregation. Therefore, a judicial decision in 1954, purporting to rest upon the fourteenth amendment and

---

* Associate Professor of Law, University of Mississippi. B.A. 1963, University of North Carolina at Chapel Hill; LL.B. 1966, Yale University.

[1] Because of the publication schedule, it will not be possible for the author to cite by page or footnote to Professor Avins' article which immediately preceeds this reply. Uncited quotations are to that article.

[2] I do not mean to imply that all criticism of the Court's decision is irresponsible. Legal scholarship is quite fortunate, for example, to have such a provocative, critical assessment of the Court's opinion as Professor Wechsler's *Toward Neutral Principles of Constitutional Law*, 73 HARV. L. REV. 1, 31-34 (1959).

But there is a difference, to my ear at least, between the statement that a case was incorrectly decided and Avins' assertion that *Brown* is "not the supreme law of the land." One might believe, of course, that an incorrect decision by the Supreme Court is not "law" in some theoretical sense. In the context in which it is offered, however, Avins' statement will lead some to think that he believes that a citizen has no obligation to comply with the holding. While I do not read him as urging citizens or officials to disobey the law, I think that his choice of language is, at best, unfortunate. See *Cooper v. Aaron*, 358 U.S. 1 (1958).

[3] A further exposition of Professor Avins' views on the interpretation of the

248

holding segregated public school systems unconstitutional, is an "unwarranted exercise of non-existent authority . . . ."

The first problem with Avins' thesis is that the evidence he presents concerning the "intention" of Congress is implausible. He states first that the 1866 Congressional debates on the fourteenth amendment offer only scanty and inconclusive evidence of the amendment's intended impact on segregation in public schools. He claims, however, that abundant "reflected" evidence of Congress' intention can be found in proceedings that occurred *eight years after the fourteenth amendment was promulgated,* when a later Congress considered, as a part of the Civil Rights Act of 1875, a proposed clause providing for desegregated public schools. How do the actions of the 43d Congress reflect upon the intention of the 39th Congress that passed the fourteenth amendment? Avins argues as follows. Congress failed to enact the school desegregation clause in 1874 because the Moderate Republicans in Congress declined, for various reasons, to support such a provision. He therefore assumes that had the fourteenth amendment, when it was considered in 1866, contained a specific school desegregation clause, Moderate Republicans would not have supported the amendment. Without the support of the Moderates the fourteenth amendment would not have received the two-thirds vote necessary for passage. Thus, (in Avins' words) "as a matter of simple arithmetic" the amendment does not apply to school segregation.

For several reasons, this 1874 "evidence" is virtually worthless as an indicator of the intention of the Congress that promulgated the fourteenth amendment in 1866. In the first place the membership of Congress and of the Moderate block changed substantially between 1866 and 1874.[4] To the extent that different people are involved, it is highly questionable to assume that the views of the "Moderates" of 1874 can be read back as being the views of the "Moderates" of 1866.

Even more troublesome is the problem of ascertaining the meaning of the Moderates' opposition to the 1874 school clause. At one point Avins asserts that by their 1874 statements and votes against the proposed school clause the Republican Moderates demonstrated their constitutional judgment that "the fourteenth amendment neither compelled of itself

---

fourteenth amendment may be found in recent articles dealing with other aspects of racial discrimination. See Avins, *The Civil Rights Act of 1875: Some Reflected Light on the Fourteenth Amendment and Public Accommodations,* 66 COLUM. L. REV. 873 (1966); Avins, *Anti-Miscegenation and the Fourteenth Amendment: The Original Intent,* 52 VA. L. REV. 1224 (1966).

[4] In the instant article Avins states that in 1874 "only a handful of Republicans sat in the House who had been in the 39th Congress and voted for the fourteenth amendment." In his related article in the *Columbia Law Review* Avins states that sixteen of the thirty-three Senators who voted for the fourteenth amendment participated in the debates on the Civil Rights Act of 1875. Avins, *supra* note 3, at 875.

nor gave Congress the power to compel school desegregation." Neither the debates recounted nor the votes recorded are adequate to support Avins' claim.

Granted, the proposed school clause of 1874 attracted insufficient support to be enacted. One should hesitate, however, before relying upon that naked fact. To give affirmative content to the failure of Congress to pass proposed legislation is often misleading. A legislature does not enact a principle by failing to enact its opposite. In this particular instance, the fact that a given congressman voted against the desegregation clause does not necessarily mean that he approved (even in 1874) of segregated schools or that he thought such segregation constitutional. More than one congressman, for example, is quoted as having decried the harsh penalties incorporated into the school clause of the 1874 bill. One might very well believe that segregated schools violate the fourteenth amendment and yet shrink from a bill that would enforce desegregation (as this one would have) by subjecting school board members, principals, and teachers to the criminal sanctions of fine and imprisonment.[5]

Nor do the debates on the school clause justify the assumption that the Moderates cast their negative votes for constitutional reasons. Admittedly, some Moderates who had voted for the fourteenth amendment expressed the retrospective view that the amendment "neither compelled of itself nor gave Congress the power to compel school desegregation." Avins' article itself, however, is replete with other reasons for the votes against the clause. Frequently, the statement was made that passage of the clause would result in the destruction of the public school system in the South. (This argument was made so often that it is referred to as the "stock argument about school closing.") Avins, in fact, states that those Republicans who opposed the school clause did so either because of "personal belief that the fourteenth amendment did not require school desegregation" *or* because of fear of voter reaction, personal hostility to desegregation, or a combination of these views.

His own admission seriously undercuts his thesis. Had he shown most of the Republican Moderates stating unequivocally that they were voting against the school clause because they believed school segregation outside the proscriptions of the fourteenth amendment, and that this had been their understanding eight years earlier when they had supplied the votes necessary for the passage of that amendment, his point would

---

[5] See CONG. GLOBE, 42 Cong., 2d Sess. app. 142 (1872).

[6] Even if the 1874 evidence had established unmistakably the constitutional point he sought to draw from it, such evidence still would not have foreclosed the *Brown* decision. The drastic changes that have occurred in the role of public education over the last century negate any attempt to find an explicit intention regarding the

have been stronger.[6] As it stands, the record indicates that many of the votes cast against the clause were motivated by reasons completely unrelated to the arguments over the constitutionality of segregated schools. It is perfectly possible that a congressman could have voted for the fourteenth amendment with the understanding that the amendment was capable of supporting congressional or judicial action against segregation and then found eight years later that it was politically unfeasible for him to vote for a bill enforcing immediate desegregation of the public schools.

Apart from the inadequacy of his evidence, Avins' thesis is subject to a more fundamental objection. He fails to examine the possibility that the fourteenth amendment was intended to have both immediate and long-range consequences. In his landmark study, *The Original Understanding and The Segregation Decision*,[7] Alexander Bickel concludes that the amendment was intended to carry out immediately only the limited objectives that had been embodied in the Civil Rights Act of 1866. That bill covered basic areas such as the right to sue and to

---

segregated schools of our time. The point has been made most sharply by Charles L. Black, Jr.:

> The question of the "intent" of the men of 1866 on segregation *as we know it* calls for a far chancier guess than is commonly supposed, for they were unacquainted with the institution as it functions in the American South today. To guess their verdict upon the institution as it functions in the midtwentieth century supposes an imaginary hypothesis which grows more preposterous as it is sought to be made more vivid.

Black, *The Lawfulness of the Segregation Decisions*, 69 YALE L.J. 421, 424 (1960).

The use of legislative evidence—however persuasive—gleaned from debates that took place eight years after the passage of a constitutional amendment also raises serious theoretical problems. In his provocative discussion, *The Blinding Light: The Uses of History in Constitutional Interpretation*, 31 U. CHI. L. REV. 502 (1964), John Wofford argues that the law-giver whose intention should be consulted with regard to the meaning of a constitutional provision is not only Congress, but the state conventions or legislatures that must ratify the amendment. After including the states in the calculus of intention, the search becomes virtually impossible. One answer to Wofford is that whatever the congressional debates establish should constitute a rebuttable presumption, since "it is not unrealistic, in the main, to assume notice of congressional purpose in the state legislatures." Bickel, *The Original Understanding and the Segregation Decison*, 69 HARV. L. REV. 1, 7 (1955). This answer, however, does not apply to legislative history supplied in Congress *after* an amendment has been ratified by the states. The states could not, in the nature of things, have had any notice of the "intention" that Avins purports to uncover from the records of 1874.

In addition to the problems of theory mentioned above, other obvious considerations should restrain a doctrine that would allow constitutional provisions, or statutes, to be restricted or "repealed" by post-enactment declarations of a few men whose votes had been essential to passage.

make contracts but was not directed at such problems as jury service, sufferage or school segregation. Bickel goes on to conclude, however, that Congress did not limit the amendment to these few immediate objectives but established a general standard of equality that could be applied in the future to other problems. The important fact is that the Joint Committee on Reconstruction rejected, as a draft for the fourteenth amendment, a specific and exclusive enumeration of the limited rights embodied in the 1866 Act. They chose instead to write a broad, organic provision. They chose language dealing not only with the immediate concern of racial discrimination, but with any discrimination that deprives "any person" of equal protection, whether or not based on race; they chose, instead of a provision limited to equal protection of life, liberty and property, one expanded to insure equal protection "of the laws." While finding no specific purpose going beyond the limited protections afforded under the 1866 Act, Bickel does find "an awareness on the part of the framers that it was *a constitution* they were writing, which led to a choice of language capable of growth."[8] Through this choice of language the amendment fulfilled a dual purpose: it provided for the immediate correction of a certain set of specific, pressing evils (a set which perhaps did not include segregation) *and* it established a general anti-discrimination standard capable of later concrete application to other problems. The question of affording greater liberty in constitutional form to the Negro than would have been encompassed in a specific enumeration of the limited guarantees of the 1866 Civil Rights Act was thus deferred, and the way left open for future Congresses (by legislation) and future courts (by the principled, evolutionary techniques of the judicial process) to draw from the equal protection clause a source of authority for measures insuring full equality.[9]

Avins' 1874 evidence in no way undermines the findings that Professor Bickel made ten years ago. All that Avins' article tells us is that Congress and the nation were not yet ready in 1874 to apply in full measure the equalitarian principle of 1866. The principle remained unimpaired, however, awaiting another day for its full vindication.[10]

In short, it is Professor Avins, and not the Supreme Court, who

---

[7] 69 HARV. L. REV. 1 (1955).

[8] *Id.* at 63.

[9] *Ibid.*

[10] This brief article is intended only as a reply to Professor Avins. I do not presume to answer all possible criticisms of the *Brown* decision. There is no doubt in my mind, however, that the case was correctly decided. The best affirmative argument for the decision is found in Black, *The Lawfulness of the Segregation Decisions*, 69 YALE L.J. 421 (1960).

seeks to rewrite the fourteenth amendment. In place of the broad guarantee of equal protection of the laws, Avins would substitute a detailed list of the rights included and excluded in the amendment. He would have the Court enforce only those rights to equality that would have been included had Congress chosen to promulgate such a detailed list. The short answer is that Congress did not so choose.

Black Teachers' Salaries and the Federal Courts Before Brown v. Board of Education: One Beginning for Equity

Bruce Beezer, *School of Education, North Carolina State University*

The elimination of racial discrimination in employment has been a long and continuing struggle for blacks in the United States. History and the enactment of numerous civil rights laws affirm this fact.[1] Public education also was not immune from using concepts about race and equality in employment practices that were conceived in inequity and born in infamy.[2]

This article explains how one racially discriminatory employment practice, unequal salary schedules for black and white teachers with similar qualifications, was eliminated in the public schools. The defeat of such a discriminatory condition took place primarily in the federal courts through the leadership of the newly appointed assistant special council for the National Association for the Advancement of Colored People (NAACP), Thurgood Marshall,[3] whose personal commitment and legal talents were essential to the successful outcome. Besides the often cited higher education cases that raised equal protection issues,[4] the teacher salary schedule cases also extended blacks' equal protection rights under the U.S. Constitution.

---

[1]See 42 U.S.C. Sec. 1983 (no person under color of state law may racially discriminate); 42 U.S.C. Sec. 2000 (d) et seq. (no racial discrimination in federal funded programs); 42 U.S.C. Sec. 2000 (e) et seq. (no racial discrimination in employment).

[2]See, for a general discussion: Horace Mann Bond, *The Education of the Negro in the American Social Order* (New York: Prentice-Hall, Inc., 1934), pp. 263–283.

[3]Now a U.S. Supreme Court Justice.

[4]*McLaurin v. Oklahoma State Regents for Higher Education*, 339 U.S. 637 (1950); *Sipuel v. Oklahoma State Board of Regents*, 33 U.S. 631 (1948); *Sweatt v. Painter*, 339 U.S. 629 (1950); *Missouri ex rel Gaines v. Canada*, 305 U.S. 337 (1938).

Journal of Negro Education, Vol. 55, No. 2 (1986)
Copyright © 1986, Howard University

The following points are to be considered in this article to show how the discriminatory salary schedules were successfully challenged: (1) to review pertinent federal court cases, (2) to discuss the legal principles developed by the courts, (3) to consider legal arguments raised against the black teachers' challenges, (4) to indicate how adopted salary schedules in contrast to "merit" based salary schedules affected court decisions, (5) to explain the reason for multiple court cases, and (6) to show the effect the court decisions had on racially discriminatory salary schedules.

BACKGROUND

Historical evidence is clear that black and white teachers were paid different salaries, particularly in those states that had segregated schools. By way of evidence, Table I shows in aggregate figures the differences in salaries for eleven southern states.

While the salary data in Table I show the average salary for white teachers was $910 and for black teachers $510, it was also informative to calculate the ratio difference for each state. The ratio ranges from 1.0 in Oklahoma to 3.5 in Mississippi, with a median ratio for the eleven states at approximately 1.8. This means, on the average, a white teacher's salary was 80 percent greater than that of a black teacher.

There were reasons for the aggregate salary difference. Many school districts used salary schedules that determined salary by education level attained, years of experience, and grade level taught. Black teachers, on the average, had fewer years of education than white teachers. Fewer blacks than whites taught at the secondary level, which paid higher salaries, because southern states had established fewer black secondary schools. Irrespective of these neutral criteria, most segregated school districts discriminated against black teachers by maintaining a dual salary schedule, a practice that paid blacks less than similarly qualified whites. A common explanation given by school authorities for such a practice was that, in contrast to white teachers, black teachers had fewer employment options, and were willing to teach for less.[5]

It was in 1936 that the NAACP began its legal efforts to equalize the salaries of black and white teachers in those states that maintained segregated schools. Between 1914 and 1936, the NAACP had centered its legal activity on the four areas of black suffrage, residential segregation ordinances, restrictive covenants, and due process and equal protection in criminal cases. Why did the NAACP

[5]Bond, *The Education of the Negro*, p. 271.

TABLE I

Comparative Salaries of White and Negro Public School Teachers, 1939–1940

Annual Salaries				Difference between Salaries	
White Teachers		**Negro Teachers**			
State	Amount (in descending order)	State	Amount (in descending order)	State	Amount (in ascending order)
Louisiana	$1,193	Oklahoma	$971	Oklahoma	$ 27
Texas	1,153	Texas	667	Arkansas	263
Florida	1,147	N. Carolina	645	N. Carolina	265
Oklahoma	998	Virginia	608	Virginia	300
South Carolina	953	Florida	583	Alabama	466
North Carolina	910	Louisiana	504	Texas	486
Virginia	908	Alabama	408	Georgia	498
Georgia	901	Georgia	403	S. Carolina	562
Alabama	874	S. Carolina	391	Florida	564
Mississippi	821	Arkansas	375	Mississippi	586
Arkansas	638	Mississippi	235	Louisiana	689
Median State	910	Median State	504	Median State	486

Source: Data in Report of Southern States Work-Conference on School Administrative Problems, 1941.

begin to emphasize education-related legal action? One reason was to fulfill a long-held conviction that equal educational opportunity was central to any effort by blacks to break down employment discrimination. A second reason, regarded as strategically feasible given southern racism, was that the forcing of equal treatment in segregated schools was a "benign" enough thrust for whites to accept by the mid-1930s.

There was also a practical reason for the inclusion of education-related legal action by the NAACP. In 1922, Charles Garland, a Harvard undergraduate from Boston, inherited a large share of his millionaire father's estate. He chose not to accept the inheritance because he believed it was wrong for anyone to gain such wealth without earning it. He therefore contributed some $800,000 toward the establishment of a foundation for the support of liberal and radical causes. The American Fund for Public Service, as the foundation was named, was administered by a group of liberal activists which included James W. Johnson, then General Secretary of the NAACP. Through Johnson's efforts a grant of $100,000 was proposed for the NAACP to carry out a legal campaign in education. The money was to finance taxpayers' suits to assure "separate but equal" schools in seven southern states whose school allocations were clearly a violation of the "separate but equal" standard.[6] The grant was approved, and some $8,000 was initially used to pay for the development of a specific legal plan. The person chosen to prepare the plan was Nathan Ross Margold, a white New York lawyer well known for his legal work associated with liberal causes.

After studying the school segregation laws of the various states, Margold developed a plan. He found that the states with the worst records in terms of unequal school allocations were not required to provide equal funds under their state statutes. The heart of Margold's plan was to bring suits in those states where it could be shown that school officials were under no statutory obligation to provide separate but equal schools for blacks. He contended that such practices were unconstitutional because they violated U.S. Supreme Court rulings in Plessy v. Ferguson,[7] which required separate but equal treatment, and Yick Wo v. Hopkins[8] which held that laws administered in a discriminatory manner were a denial of equal protection rights. What Margold proposed in his 1931 report was not to attack separate but equal schools but to challenge segregated

---

[6]The seven states were: Alabama, Arkansas, Florida, Georgia, Louisiana, Mississippi, and South Carolina.
[7]163 U.S. 537 (1896).
[8]118 U.S. 356 (1886).

education as actually provided and administered.[9] The NAACP adopted this cautious and conservative strategy by beginning legal actions to require school districts to pay similarly qualified black and white teachers the same salary.

There is one final note on the background regarding the NAACP's legal efforts related to teacher salaries. Thurgood Marshall faced a number of challenges as he undertook a leadership role in prosecuting teacher salary cases. The NAACP was not able to provide sufficient funds to cover the costs associated with such cases; therefore, Marshall had to travel extensively to encourage local black teacher groups to raise funds for the cases.[10] He also had to persuade individual black teachers to bring suit since the NAACP did not have legal standing to sue. This was a difficult task because many black teachers hesitated to be plaintiffs for fear of losing their jobs or having to face harsh white retaliation. Compounding these challenges was the fact that the suits were to require states and school districts to spend more money at a time when they were faced with cutbacks due to the Depression. There also existed the racism of whites who fought to prevent any change in race related practices.

CHALLENGES TO SEPARATE SALARY SCHEDULES

Marshall began his efforts to equalize teacher salaries in Maryland, a state that maintained racially discriminatory salary schedules by statute.[11] Black teachers, however, were eligible for tenure after several years of satisfactory performance. Here then was a discriminatory state law violating the separate but equal standard and black teachers who could sue without fear of losing their jobs.

With Marshall's encouragement, the black teachers in Montgomery County, Maryland, in 1936, asked the NAACP to help them take legal action against the discriminatory salary schedule used by their school district. William Gibbs, a black teacher and principal, filed suit in a Maryland court requiring the Board of Education of Montgomery County to equalize his salary with those of white employees with similar qualifications and performing the same type of work. The evidence in the case showed that white high school teachers received maximum salaries of $1,574 compared to $859 for black teachers. White elementary teachers earned a maximum salary of $1,362 in contrast to $631 for black teachers. The case was

---

[9]See, for a detailed discussion, Richard Kluger, *Simple Justice* (New York: Vintage Books, 1977), pp. 132–138.

[10]See "Along the N.A.A.C.P. Battlefront," *Crisis*, 45 (January, 1938), 21; ibid., 46 (January, 1939), 22; ibid., 46 (May, 1939), 149.

[11]See "Along the N.A.A.C.P. Battlefront," *Crisis*, 45 (February, 1938), 56.

settled by a consent decree wherein the school board promised to equalize salaries by 1939.[12]

A second effort was made in Calvert County, Maryland, in November 1937 when Elizabeth Brown, an elementary teacher, sued in state court to equalize her salary with white teachers. She claimed that she was receiving $600 while white teachers with similar qualifications and duties were earning $1,100. This case was also settled by a consent decree in favor of black teachers.[13]

Marshall decided that filing suits in Maryland state courts would require too much time and expense. He therefore decided to sue Maryland's State Board of Education in the federal district court in an attempt to get a favorable decision that had statewide significance.[14] He alleged in *Mills* v. *Lowndes*[15] that Maryland taxes were being used to supplement county education expenditures and were thereby perpetuating the grossly unequal salary schedules between black and white teachers. The federal district court ruled against Walter Mills on a jurisdictional point of law. The court said Mills was not entitled to his requested injunction enjoining enforcement of Maryland's salaries relating to white and black teachers since he had not shown he would sustain any injury by distribution of the state funds. The funds were for equalization and their sole purpose was to aid poor school districts with inadequate tax bases. The court did say, however, that Mills had constitutional grounds to bring a suit against the local school district because it was the local district that determined the salary schedule.

With this encouragement, Marshall returned to the same federal district court in *Mills* v. *Board of Education of Anne Arundel County.*[16] This time, the court's ruling was favorable. The wisdom of Margold's strategy was affirmed by what the court regarded as the controlling issue. It was not "whether the statutes are unconstitutional on their face, but whether in their practical application they constitute an unconstitutional discrimination on account of race and color prejudicial to the plaintiff."[17] The court found that the evidence showed that because Mills was black he received less salary than similarly qualified whites. The court concluded that the practice violated the equal protection clause. The immediate effect of the *Mills* decision was that all cases pending in the Maryland

[12]See "Along the N.A.A.C.P. Battlefront," *Crisis*, 44 (February, 1937), 53–54; ibid., 45 (February, 1938), 56.
[13]See "Along the N.A.A.C.P. Battlefront," *Crisis*, 45 (February, 1938), 56.
[14]Kluger, *Simple Justice*, p. 214.
[15]25 F. Supp. 792 (D. Md. 1939).
[16]30 F. Supp. 245 (D. Md. 1939).
[17]Ibid., p. 248.

state courts were dismissed with the stipulation that salaries would be equalized for all teachers by the 1940–41 school year.

The struggle for equal salary schedules shifted next to Virginia where success was much slower. It was difficult to find a plaintiff among black teachers in Virginia, for there was no teacher tenure in that state. Hence, as soon as a black teacher brought a suit, he/she was dismissed. For example, a suit against the School Board of the City of Norfolk was denied in a Virginia state court. As an appeal was being prepared, the teacher was fired; thereby the case became moot since the teacher was no longer an employee of the school district.[18]

Marshall immediately filed a new suit on behalf of a Melvin Alston, a high school teacher in Norfolk. To prevent this case from becoming moot, Marshall joined as plaintiff the Norfolk Teachers' Association, a black teachers' group. The suit sought to obtain a declaratory judgment to the effect that the Board's policy in maintaining a salary schedule which fixed black teachers' salaries at a lower rate than that of white teachers of equal qualifications and experience, and performing the same duties and services, on the sole basis of race, was a violation of the equal protection clause.[19] The suit, however, was dismissed on the grounds that Alston and the School Board were the only necessary parties to the cause of action, and that Alston had waived his constitutional rights when he voluntarily entered into a written contract to teach for a year at the salary fixed in the contract.

Alston won an appeal to the U.S. Court of Appeals for the Fourth Circuit.[20] The court refuted the Board's argument that only a teacher holding a contract had any interest in the salary rate paid him/her and that a teacher cannot sue because he/she has waived the alleged unconstitutional discrimination by freely entering into the contract. The court reasoned that a state:

> may not impose conditions which require the relinquishment of constitutional rights. If the state may compel the surrender of one constitutional right as a condition of its favor, it may, in like manner, compel a surrender of all. It is inconceivable that guarantees embedded in the Constitution of the United States may thus be manipulated out of existence.[21]

In essence, the School Board's use of a racially discriminatory salary schedule was a "condition" that violated black teachers' rights under the equal protection clause.

---

[18]Jessie Parkhurst Guzman, ed., *Negro Yearbook: A Review of Events Affecting Negro Life, 1941–1946* (Tuskegee Institute, Ala.: Department of Records and Research, 1947), p. 63.

[19]This was the same argument that was used in the *Mills* case.

[20]*Alston v. School Board of City of Norfolk*, 112 F.2d 992 (4th Cir.); *cert. denied*, 311 U.S. 693 (1940).

[21]Ibid., p. 997.

The *Alston* decision, while strictly applicable only in Norfolk, did encourage Virginia's black teachers to demand equal pay. Litigation in Virginia continued for some five years as school boards resisted compliance with the *Alston* ruling. Finally, in 1945, a contempt of court order issued against the School Board of Newport News brought an end, for all practical purposes, to racially discriminatory dual salary schedules.[22]

Spurred by success in Maryland and Virginia, the NAACP helped black teachers in other southern states to challenge salary schedules. Two of these cases were of special significance. The decision in *McDaniel* v. *Board of Public Instruction for Escembia County, Florida,*[23] ruled on two key issues. The first issue was whether Vernon McDaniel, a high school principal, could sustain a class action suit for all black educators. The court held that he could because principals and teachers were members of the same profession. This ruling in effect broadened the class of black educators who could bring a suit. The second issue was whether the State of Florida could be sued along with the local school board. Florida officials argued that the state constitution provided for a county school system, and if there was any discrimination between the salaries paid to white and those paid to black teachers it was an act of the county school system and not of the state. The argument was refuted by the court on the grounds that the county boards of education were administrative agencies of the state, and the prohibitions of the Fourteenth Amendment applied to the acts of such agencies. The *McDaniel* decision, while applicable only in northern Florida, did give the NAACP precedent for arguing in other jurisdictions and thereby reduced the need to bring numerous suits against individual school districts.

A Tennessee federal district court denied an argument that had been used by many southern districts to justify the difference between black and white teachers' salaries. The Board of Education of the City of Nashville, in *Thomas* v. *Hibbitts,* argued that the salary difference was the effect of an economic condition.[24] It was that black teachers were more numerous than white teachers, their living standards were less expensive, and they could be employed at a lower salary. Unable to reconcile such a position, the court found that,

> the studied and consistent policy of the Board . . . is to pay its colored teachers salaries which are considerably lower than the salaries paid to the

[22]Henry A. Bullock, *A History of Negro Education in the South* (Cambridge, Mass.: Harvard University Press, 1967), p. 219.
[23]39 F. Supp. 638 (N.D. Fla. 1941).
[24]46 F. Supp. 368 (M.D. Tenn. 1942).

white teachers, although the eligibility qualifications and experience . . . [are] the same for both white and colored teachers, and that the sole reason for this difference is because of the race and color of the colored teachers.[25]

This finding, the court ruled, was a denial of the equal protection clause.

EFFECT OF SEPARATE SALARY SUITS

Within four to five years following the *Mills* and *Alston* decisions, numerous court decisions and stipulation orders favorable to black educators were decided in eleven southern states. Most local boards of education attempted to obey the court decisions to equalize salaries; however, the transition was gradual even in those districts directly involved. The courts usually allowed the districts and states time, because the cost of implementing equal salary schedules was in excess of current tax income.

There were also political effects of the salary equalization suits. Governor Henry Nice of Maryland announced in December, 1937, that he would initiate the necessary steps to equalize the salaries paid black teachers and white teachers. He estimated the cost to be approximately $486,000.[26]

North Carolina's Advisory Budget Commission, in fall 1942, when preparing the 1943–44 appropriations bill, recommended wiping out the salary differential between black and white teachers. The final step was taken by the State Board of Education in 1944 when it adopted a plan to equalize salaries by using surplus funds available for the 1944–45 school year.[27] These actions were taken without a suit being brought in North Carolina on teacher salaries. Yet, officials were certainly aware of court decisions in neighboring states.

There were also negative political reactions. The South Carolina legislature developed plans to revoke all existing teacher certificates. The new system proposed to permit local boards to determine a teacher's certification level and, thereby, salary. Its purpose was to allow local boards to continue racially-discriminatory salaries between races. The plan was defeated.[28]

State officials and school districts also attempted to intimidate black educators who supported salary equalization efforts and punish those who filed suits. At a conference in October, 1943, Mississippi's black principals were warned by State Superintendent of

---

[25]Ibid., p. 371.
[26]See "Along the N.A.A.C.P. Battlefront," *Crisis*, 45 (February, 1938), 56.
[27]Guzman, *Negro Yearbook*, p. 67.
[28]Bullock, *A History of Negro Education*, p. 218.

208   *The Journal of Negro Education*

Education J. S. Candiver, not to bring suits for salary equalization. He said resorting to court action would result in the loss of whites sympathetic to black education.[29] Charles Stubbins, plaintiff in a teacher salary case in Palm Beach, Florida, was fired after he won a favorable consent decree in 1943.[30]

SALARY BASED ON "VALUE AND WORTH"

The *Mills* and *Alston* decisions and their progeny did reduce the use of separate salary schedules that discriminated against black educators. Judge Chestnut, however, in the *Mills* decision had stated:

> The court is not determining what particular amounts of salaries must be paid in Anne Arundel County either to white or colored teachers individually; nor is the Board in any way to be prohibited by the injunction in this case from exercising its judgment as to the respective amounts to be paid to individual teachers based on their individual qualifications, capacities and abilities. . . .[31]

In essence, Judge Chestnut had opened the door to "merit pay" salary schedules, and local boards began to implement them.

The use of a "merit pay" schedule was challenged by a Florida black teacher in *Turner* v. *Keefe*.[32] The school board had adopted a salary schedule in 1942 that paid teachers in one of three classifications. The classification was determined by the rating a teacher received on twenty-nine characteristics grouped under three general headings: (1) physical health, personality, and character; (2) scholarship and attitude; and (3) instructional skill and performance. A rating committee composed of two principals, two assistant directors of instruction, and the superintendent classified all the teachers and principals by means of the new evaluation system. There were two major results of the rating evaluations. The first result was that all black teachers and principals received a salary increase while some white teachers and principals were given salary decreases. The second result was not as favorable to black employees. The majority (84 percent) of the white teachers were classified in the highest salary rank while the majority (80 percent) of the black teachers were placed in the lowest salary rank. A similar pattern was also followed when a majority of white principals got a higher classification than black principals.[33]

The court ruled in the *Turner* case that the rating system was

[29]Guzman, *Negro Yearbook*, p. 64.
[30]Bullock, *A History of Negro Education*, pp. 218–19.
[31]*Mills*, p. 251.
[32]50 F. Supp. 647 (S.D. Fla. 1943).
[33]Ibid., pp. 650–51.

not unconstitutional on its face and there was no evidence of racial discrimination in its implementation. Particular mention was made by the court of the Rating Committee members' excellent qualifications and their sincere efforts to apply the criteria in an objective manner. As to the marked disparity between black and white salary classifications, the court said the differences may have significance, but there also must be proof that the rating criteria was applied in a discriminatory manner, and none was evident.[34]

A second Florida case, *Reynolds v. Board of Public Instruction for Dade County*,[35] considered a rating procedure and classification schedule similar to that ruled in *Turner*. The results of rating were that white teachers, as a group, received higher salaries than blacks. The U.S. Court of Appeals for the Fifth Circuit affirmed the district court's judgment that unless evidence showed racial discrimination, the salary classification based on a teacher's "value and worth" to a school district was not unconstitutional under the equal protection clause.[36]

The *Turner* and *Reynolds* decisions marked a setback for Thurgood Marshall and the NAACP. They were very aware that the determination of salaries based on either a teacher's "value and worth" to a district or a subjective evaluation of a teacher's effectiveness would continue to leave open the door for discrimination against blacks. Their position was that salary schedules should be based on only two criteria: extent of preparation and experience.

This position was eventually acknowledged in *Thompson v. Gibbs*,[37] which was a suit against Reckland County Board of Education in South Carolina. It alleged that the Board fixed teacher salaries on a basis that resulted in blacks receiving less than whites, and the only reason for the difference was racial discrimination. The Board argued that since the *Alston* decision it had been attempting to equalize salary differences and, further, it was adopting the criteria recently mandated by the South Carolina legislature to be used by the state for classifying applicants for teacher certification. The state plan classified applicants by the use of three criteria: (1) amount of education, (2) length of experience, and (3) score received on an examination prepared by the National Education Board.[38] The court,

---

[34]Ibid., p. 652.
[35]148 F.2d 754 (5th Cir.); *cert. denied*, 326 U.S. 746 (1945).
[36]Ibid., p. 755.
[37]60 F. Supp. 872 (E.D.S.C. 1945).
[38]The criteria on amount of education was broken down into those having: (1) master's degree, (2) partial graduate work, (3) college degree, (4) two years of college, and (5) less than two years of college.

however, postponed its decision for one year to allow the Board time to equalize salaries under the new salary plan.

The *Turner* and *Thompson* decisions, however, did not stop Marshall and black educators from obtaining a decision that would stop school districts from using salary schedules that classified teachers on their *worth* to the school system. The evidence was clear that this type of salary classification had in practice resulted in a disproportionate number of blacks, compared to whites, receiving low salaries. A favorable decision was rendered in *Davis* v. *Cook*.[39]

Samuel Davis, a black teacher in Atlanta, claimed his and all black educators' equal protection rights were violated by the way the school board initially placed them on the salary schedule. The Atlanta school board had adopted a salary schedule divided into four tracts, with each tract having a series of increment steps awarded for years of service and collegiate work completed. In addition to these objective criteria, however, there were subjective criteria for placement and advancement in each salary tract. Among them were teaching efficiency, special talents or skills, and personality. Davis argued that the evidence showed a pattern and practice of placing blacks on the lowest tract and increment level based on the subjective criteria.

The court first noted that the subjective criteria, when applied in a fair and nondiscriminatory manner, were not only permissible but important and commendable. The competency of teachers could not be determined by scholastic degrees and experience alone, said the court, because teaching ability varied a great deal among those having equal training and experience. Good teaching was also an outcome of those intangible factors used in the salary schedule, the court contended.[40]

The court then said, however, if statistical evidence showed that a higher proportion of black teachers were placed in a lower salary tract than would randomly be expected, racial discrimination would be evident. After reviewing an extensive statistical study on the placement of black and white teachers, the court found that the evidence showed a greater differential between the salaries white and black teachers received, in favor of the former, and placement on the salary schedule was uniformly and decidedly more favorable to white teachers, far beyond what objective qualifications would justify.[41] The court then ruled that the comparative salaries of black

---

[39]80 F. Supp. 443 (N.D. Ga. 1948); See, for an earlier case, *Morris* v. *Williams*, 59 F. Supp. 508 (E.D. Ark. 1944) p; *rev'd and remanded*, 149 F.2d 703 (8th Cir. 1945).
[40]Ibid., p. 447.
[41]Ibid., p. 451.

and white teachers were attributable to racial discrimination. The *Davis* decision was a significant victory against racial discrimination in salary allocations, for it put school boards on notice that the pattern and practice of their actions could be used as evidence.

CONCLUDING REMARKS

Black educators by the late 1940s, through lawsuits filed by Thurgood Marshall and other NAACP attorneys, had successfully challenged the use of dual salary schedules that discriminated against black teachers. The use of merit-based salary schedules, while ruled constitutional, was also under close legal scrutiny when statistical evidence showed the existence of racial discrimination in practice and pattern. The acceptance of the NAACP's position that salaries should be based on the objective criteria of academic attainment and length of employment was not entirely supported by the courts. However, in 1945, for example, North Carolina and South Carolina, did adopt these criteria for all teacher salaries paid from state funds. One reason for doing so was to avoid possible legal challenges to teacher salary schedules.

The salary schedule cases also attest to the success of the Margold Plan which had been to force states to at least abide by the constitutional mandate to provide "separate but equal" treatment. The overall hope was that the states with segregated education would find the resulting costs to be so prohibitive they would cease segregation of the races. The Margold Plan, however, failed to realize the extent to which racism was engrained in those states. By the early 1950s, Marshall decided that the "separate but equal" standard must be eliminated in public education. The salary schedule cases had not argued against the standard, and therefore were of little significance as legal precedent in the new legal challenge to racism. The challenge proved successful in the *Brown* decision.[42]

The achievements of the salary cases, nevertheless, were a significant step toward racial equity in public school employment practices, especially when considered in their time frame. The initial suits were brought during the 1930s, a time when the country was suffering a major economic depression. Subsequent suits were tried in the early 1940s when the United States was engaged in World War II. Yet, the NAACP never ceased to challenge long established racially discriminatory practices in the workplace. By doing so, the

---

[42]*Brown* v. *Board of Education*, 347 U.S. 483 (1954).

NAACP kept before the American public, during those crucial times, the rights of black citizens. The salary schedule cases were one beginning for racial equity in an institution that should have manifested equality of opportunity—the public schools.

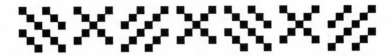

The Dilemma of School Integration in the North: Gary, Indiana, 1945-1960

*Ronald D. Cohen**

On August 27, 1946, the Gary, Indiana, school board adopted a perhaps unprecedented policy: that children shall not be discriminated against "in the school district in which they live, or within the schools which they attend, because of race, color or religion." Integration leader Reuben Olsen was particularly ecstatic. "Last night the Board of Education, in solemn session, enacted the non-discrimination policy long fought over, and much feared," he reported to the National Urban League. "History was written last night." The future for civil rights looked bright indeed. Sixteen years later, however, in a law suit filed against the Gary school board, the plaintiffs charged that the city's schools, now over 50 percent black, were rigidly and systematically segregated. Whether by intent or accident, by 1961, 90 percent of the schools were segregated. What had happened to dash the high hopes of Reuben Olsen and his civil rights colleagues? Why were their dreams blighted?[1]

Public school integration has been one of the cornerstones of the civil rights movement in the United States since World War II. The 1954 *Brown* v. *Board of Education* decision marked

* Ronald D. Cohen is professor of history at Indiana University Northwest, Gary, Indiana. An initial draft of this paper was presented at the annual meeting of the Organization of American Historians, Cincinnati, April, 1983. The author is indebted to William Reese, Edward McClellan, and Michael Homel for their astute comments.

[1] Gary *Post-Tribune*, August 28, 1946; Reuben Olsen to Manet Fowler, August 29, 1946, Container 24, Gary, Indiana, Research File VI, C (National Urban League Papers, Library of Congress, Washington, D.C.); cited hereafter as NUL Papers; Max Wolff, "Segregation in the Schools of Gary, Indiana," *Journal of Educational Sociology*, XXXVI (February, 1963), 251-61. On the lawsuit *Bell* v. *School City of Gary* (1962), see John Kaplan, "Segregation Litigation and the Schools—Part III: The Gary Litigation," *Northwestern University Law Review*, LIX (May-June, 1964), 121-70.

the beginning of a new era in the struggle for racial equality by undermining Jim Crow and insisting that separate schools meant inherently unequal schools. The prime battleground between segregationists and integrationists was initially in the South; conflict in the North was muted until the 1960s. Northern segregation, however, was more subtle and elusive, and perhaps more insidious. It was clearly more persistent. An examination of school segregation and integration in Gary, Indiana, between the war and the beginnings of a national civil rights struggle enables us to comprehend more readily the historical forces that both promoted and resisted the expansion of civil rights to all citizens in the North and across the nation.

There is no general study of postwar northern school segregation, but bits and pieces of the story have begun to appear. In Chicago, for example, public schools became increasingly segregated during and after the 1920s. Michael Homel found that, "In 1965, 89 percent of Chicago's black pupils were enrolled at schools with 90-100 percent black enrollments, a figure slightly above the level of the 1930s." The *Brown* decision had seemingly little influence. Vincent Franklin, in his study of black education in Philadelphia, concluded that "many northern school boards revealed that through various quasilegal maneuvers, such as the shifting of school boundaries within the districts, school officials were able to create separate [and inferior] black and other minority public schools." What frustrated any attempt to change conditions, however—and there were scattered active and passive protests—was the essentially *de facto* nature of northern segregation. In many cities school boards did indeed pursue a policy of separating black and white children. But with or without these efforts—and the lack of interventionist measures, such as busing—school segregation would have occurred, for neighborhoods, more than deliberate policies, fostered separate schools. Such was certainly the case in Gary.[2]

---

[2] Michael Homel, *Down from Equality: Black Chicagoans and the Public Schools, 1920-1941* (Urbana, Ill., 1984), 187; Vincent Franklin, *The Education of Black Philadelphia: The Social and Educational History of a Minority Community, 1900-1950* (Philadelphia, 1979), 199-200. See also David Kirp, *Just Schools: The Idea of Racial Equality in American Education* (Berkeley, Calif., 1982); August Meier and Elliott Rudwick, *Along the Color Line: Explorations in the Black Experience* (Urbana, Ill., 1976), 359-63. For a general overview of race and education which slights the North, see Diane Ravitch, *The Troubled Crusade: American Education, 1945-1980* (New York, 1983), 114-44. For the *Brown* case, see Richard Kluger, *Simple Justice: The History of Brown v. Board of Education and Black America's Struggle for Equality* (New York, 1975). In general, see Harvard Sitkoff, *The Struggle for Equality* (New York, 1981), chap. 1. For increasing segregation in Chicago, see Arnold R. Hirsch, *Making the Second Ghetto: Race and Housing in Chicago, 1940-1960* (Cambridge, England, 1983).

The first northern city to champion school integration publicly was an unlikely choice for the honor. The public school system of Gary began in 1906 when the city was founded on the southern shore of Lake Michigan by the United States Steel Corporation. Within a few years the city would boast the world's largest integrated steel mill and a multiethnic, multiracial population; by 1960 the population would reach 178,000, 40 percent of whom would be non-white. Its school system, once considered one of the most innovative and "progressive" in the country, would drop from the limelight by the eve of World War II, although it still maintained much of its original organization and program. By 1960 these, too, would be in shambles. The enrollment would be 22,000 in 1950 and over 41,000 in 1960, of whom half would be black.[3]

Gary's schools always had been essentially segregated by residential boundaries and school board policy. In 1927, responding to a strike by white students at the Emerson school, the board decided to reinforce the existing *de facto* segregation by transferring the few black students out of the Emerson school and deciding to build the all-black Roosevelt school. Only the Froebel school, in the midst of the city's crowded ethnic and black south side, thereafter had a racially mixed student body. While about 40 percent of the school's more than 2,000 students in grades K-12 were black in 1945, there was only one black teacher. Social and recreational activities were routinely segregated.[4]

White community leaders and school officials had taken little notice of the segregated nature of the schools until the Detroit race riots of 1943, which frightened the Chamber of Commerce into appointing a fifteen member committee to study the city's pervasive segregation. Composed of the mayor, the editor of the local newspaper, the superintendent of the U.S. Steel plant, the school superintendent, and six blacks, the committee

---

[3] Ronald D. Cohen and Raymond A. Mohl, *The Paradox of Progressive Education: The Gary Plan and Urban Schooling* (Port Washington, N.Y., 1979); Ronald D. Cohen, "World War II and the Travail of Progressive Schooling: Gary, Indiana, 1940-1946," in Ronald K. Goodenow and Diane Ravitch, eds., *Schools in Cities: Consensus and Conflict in American Educational History* (New York, 1983), 263-86; James B. Lane, *"City of the Century": A History of Gary, Indiana* (Bloomington, Ind., 1978); Raymond A. Mohl and Neil Betten, *Steel City: Urban and Ethnic Patterns in Gary, Indiana, 1906-1950* (New York, 1986), especially 55-59.

[4] Theodore Brameld, *Minority Problems in the Public Schools* (New York, 1946), chap. 7; National Urban League, "A Study of the Social and Economic Conditions of the Negro Population of Gary, Indiana," mimeo (December, 1944), 27 (Calumet Regional Archives, Indiana University Northwest, Gary, Indiana).

drafted a code on race relations which deplored segregation and discrimination. Other organizations, including the local Congress of Industrial Organizations (CIO), supported these sentiments. In October, 1944, school officials sent representatives to a conference on intergroup education sponsored by the Rosenwald Foundation. Subsequently, the superintendent requested that the Bureau for Intercultural Education provide a consultant to the schools, and late in the year Gary became one of three cities to obtain such assistance. By August, 1945, school administrators and teachers had attended three conferences in the city which explored the use of intercultural activities in the classrooms. But talk was not enough. As Theodore Brameld of the Bureau wrote at the time, "The real task of breaking the steel ring of discrimination and segregation now gripping Copperberg [Gary] so malevolently will require all the strength of ordinary citizens as well as the finest kind of schools." The test came soon enough.[5]

"A nationwide strike consciousness manifested itself in Gary this morning as white grade and high school pupils of Froebel school walked out of class in protest against Negro pupils in that institution," the Gary *Post-Tribune* informed its readers on September 18, 1945. The Froebel strike garnered national headlines and ran sporadically for the next three months. It was a disturbing experience for all concerned, coming on the heels of the great victory over fascism and amid a national labor strike fever. From the beginning community leaders, including the superintendent and a united all-white school board, opposed any concessions to the strikers. As the local daily paper editorialized, "approximately one fifth of Gary citizens are Negroes and their needs and rights and privileges must be given equal consideration with all others."[6]

---

[5] Theodore Brameld, *Minority Problems in the Public Schools*, 218, and chap. 7 in general; National Urban League, "A Study of the Social and Economic Conditions of the Negro Population of Gary, Indiana," mimeo (December, 1944), 23 (Calumet Regional Archives). On the history of the Bureau for Intercultural Education, see Nicholas V. Montalto, *A History of the Intercultural Educational Movement, 1924-1941* (New York, 1982). See also, Harvard Sitkoff, "Racial Militancy and Interracial Violence in the Second World War," *Journal of American History*, LVIII (December, 1971), 661-81.

[6] Gary *Post-Tribune*, September 18, 21, 22, 1945; James Tipton, *Community in Crisis: The Elimination of Segregation from a Public School System* (New York, 1953). From August, 1945, to August, 1946, there were a record 4,630 strikes nationwide, with 5,000,000 strikers compiling a total of 120,000,000 days off. The Froebel strike took place in this context. See Foster Rhea Dulles and Melvyn Dubofsky, *Labor in America: A History* (4th ed., Arlington Heights, Ill., 1984), 334-41.

According to Noma Jensen of the National Association for the Advancement of Colored People (NAACP), the strike and its counterparts in schools in Chicago and New York were excellent examples "of how Fascists can use and are using our children to foment strife between our racial and religious groups." The city's recent immigrant population seemed particularly susceptible to such machinations. A report by the school system's social welfare director, Mark Roser, noted that virtually all of the strikers did not "have what might be loosely called 'An American Background.'" Moreover, they were below average academically and exhibited a *"lack of status."* In his detailed study of the strike, *Community in Crisis*, James Tipton reaffirmed that "these boys who initiated the Bartow [Froebel] strike and who chose the anti-Negro goal were ones whose lives, both at home and in school, had been largely unhappy and difficult. One or two of them were badly maladjusted, the majority were mildly so, and one or two were fairly well adjusted." He also noted that "they were driven to become attention-seekers, 'zoot-suiters,' extremists in behavior, speech, and appearance."[7]

It was easy at first to blame seemingly fascist parents and maladjusted children for starting the strike, but as it progressed the issues became more complicated. Initially the strikers, a majority of the white high school students joined by some of the younger students, demanded removal of all black students and the school's principal. On October 1 the strikers returned to classes upon the school board's promise to investigate "charges of maladministration" by the principal. In late October, with the principal exonerated by an outside review board, the strike resumed, lasting from October 29 to November 12. The students now demanded, not the transfer of blacks out of Froebel, but the integration of all of the city's schools. The strikers' new goal went to the heart of the city's and the school board's long-standing segregation policies. Slowly civic leaders recognized the depth of the problem foretold in Brameld's recent warning. The strikers and their parents, their hostility to the city's elite lying just below the surface, led the way in forging an integration plan. "We are asking that all the schools be opened to all students, both white and Negro," the Parents' Committee announced when the strike resumed. "We are asking that all the public parks and beaches be opened to all citizens of the community, both white

---

[7] Noma Jensen, "What's Behind These School Strikes?" *The Nation's Schools* (December, 1945), 24; [Mark Roser], "Some Conclusions From the Study of the Personalities in the Strike," manuscript in the Guy Wulfing Papers (Calumet Regional Archives); Tipton, *Community in Crisis*, 68-69.

and Negro. By standing behind us in these demands, the responsible members of other communities in Central City [Gary] can show unequivocably their sincerity when speaking of the 'democratic process.'" Three days later Frank Sinatra, "The King of Swoon," arrived in the city "to croon Gary bobby-soxers and their boy friends into a democratic attitude on the race relations problem." Sinatra charmed the girls, denounced the strikers, then quickly left town. Less than two weeks later the defeated strikers returned to their classes, having obtained no satisfaction.[8]

While the white establishment—business, political, civic, religious, and labor leaders—quickly rallied to oppose the strike, the black community's response was weak and divided. A central problem was the initial absence of a strong civil rights organization. The local chapter of the NAACP, founded three decades before, had become inactive. In late September National Secretary Walter White urged local chapter president Alfred Hall to contact the superintendent, "making it known to him your opposition to separate schools for Negroes." A month later, with still no action, White arrived in the city, meeting with the editor of the paper and other community leaders. They reaffirmed their commitment to integration and planned a mass rally, which never transpired, to feature Supreme Court Justice Frank Murphy and entertainer Paul Robeson. White also urged William Hastie, an attorney with the national office of the NAACP, to press the justice department concerning possible federal action, but this also produced no results. In mid-December Assistant Secretary Roy Wilkins lamented that "the recent school disturbance revealed that our branch was haplessly weak and ineffectual." The following spring Director of Branches Ella Baker was again urging Hall to do something, particularly since the National Urban League (NUL) had established a branch in Gary and was making a frontal attack on the Gary school dilemma. "That the community had to wait for a new organization to be established before the school situation was energetically attacked is a definite reflection upon the NAACP," Baker complained. And indeed it was.[9]

---

[8] Gary *Post-Tribune*, October 1, 29, November 1, 1945; Tipton, *Community in Crisis*, 109.

[9] Secretary Walter White to Alfred Hall, September 24, 1945, School Incidents, January-October, 1945, Container 501, Series A, General Office File, 1940-1955, National Association for the Advancement of Colored People Papers (Library of Congress, Washington, D.C.); cited hereafter as NAACP Papers; White to Hall, October 22, 1945, *ibid.*; [Noma Jensen], "School Strikes in Gary, Chicago, and New York," [1945], *ibid.*; Roy Wilkins to [Ella] Baker, December 12, 1945, folder 1940-1945, Gary, Indiana, Branch File 1940-1955, NAACP Papers; Baker to Hall, March 27, 1946, folder 1946-1955, *ibid.*

A highly critical 1944 study by the National Urban League of racial conditions in Gary had paved the way for the league's arrival the following year. Organized in early fall the local chapter was in no position to intervene during the strike's initial stages. In early October J. Harvey Kerns, a representative from the national office, advised the small group against "participation in the highly controversial school strike" because "the League was too new—the organization was really not a going concern and had not been given an opportunity to demonstrate its usefulness on many non-controversial issues." Kerns did meet, however, with School Superintendent Charles Lutz and representatives of the Bureau for Intercultural Education, who were still in the city. The league became more directly involved with the arrival of Joseph Chapman, its first executive secretary, later in the month. In December it joined with other organizations to form a coordinating agency on interracial problems.[10]

Although they had returned to their classes, Froebel's white students were still not satisfied and by early February they were threatening a renewal of the strike. As the school board began considering a citywide integration plan, the local NUL chapter began playing a central role in bringing Froebel whites and blacks together. Chapman informed the national office in February that "we have established a relationship, that is, the local League and these dissatisfied parents, and we are talking over very frankly racial issues. Through this same group the Executive [Chapman] has established a relationship with a small group of Negroe [sic] students and White students (former strike leaders), and through the two we believe the League is going to make a significant contribution in solving the Froebel problem and prevent a strike." He was correct. In early March six student leaders, black and white, having met in Chapman's office, issued a public statement "declaring a permanent truce" and urging the board of education to pass a general integration policy. The community was relieved. "Froebel high school is once more the scene of light-hearted bobby soxers, whose main concern these days is the chance of Froebel's thinlies in the Spring track events," the Gary *American*, the city's black weekly, announced. "The spectre of race hate, suspicion, and mutual distrust between Negro and white students, has been dissolved." Mark Roser, who had strongly opposed the strike, commented "that

---

[10] J. Harvey Kerns to Eugene Kinckle Jones, October 12, 1945, Container 25, Gary, Indiana, Research File, VI, C, NUL Papers; Gary *Post-Tribune*, December 21, 1945.

the students of Froebel school are becoming the most tolerant in the whole city." As events would demonstrate he was probably correct.[11]

By late spring pressure was mounting to integrate the schools and generally improve race relations. Organized and unorganized intercultural activities flourished. In April, when the school board created an intercultural scholarship foundation in order to send teachers to intercultural workshops, the school superintendent reluctantly confessed, "race relations is Gary's major problem." Finally, on August 27, 1946, the school board adopted an integration policy stating that children "shall not be discriminated against in the school districts in which they live, or within the school which they attend, because of race, color or religion." The Urban League's Manet Fowler later wrote that "with this step, the board not only raised a proud standard for democracy, but soundly and courageously stuck its spade against the root of all future strikes." Implementation was to begin in September, 1947, when all children, black and white, in grades K-3 (later changed to K-6) would have to attend their neighborhood school. Older children would be allowed to finish in the school they had been attending.[12]

Gary was one of the first northern cities to officially integrate its schools. Why did this happen? Foremost, the city's elite was united on the need for promoting racial harmony. They had first tried educational programs and token measures, but when faced with unruly working-class students and parents whose protests were tinged with overt racism, they decided to take a harder line. Moreover, their resolve to integrate was reinforced by the city's more progressive organizations, such as a civil liberties committee, the CIO, Anselm Forum, and the League of Women Voters. The school board's membership reflected the interests of the city's elite. Among its five members were a druggist, a U.S. Steel production planner, a Presbyterian minister, the retiring president of the Chamber of Commerce and executive of the local power company, and a civic leader who was the only female on the board. Three of the members were Democrats, one was a Republican, and one was an Independent (the minister), but all five were connected to the city's close-knit power

---

[11] Joseph Chapman to Lester B. Granger, February 20, 1946, Container 91, Gary, Indiana, Research File, VI, F, NUL Papers; Gary *Post-Tribune*, March 2, 1946; Gary *American*, March 8, 1946; Tipton, *Community in Crisis*, 87-97.

[12] Gary *Post-Tribune*, April 10, August 28, 1946; Manet Fowler, "Spotlight Still on Gary," *American Unity*, V (January, 1947), 6; Tipton, *Community in Crisis*, 97-101.

structure. Their integration plan reflected enlightened liberal thinking, yet when implemented it obviously would not seriously disrupt the community. It was safe. It also served as an important symbol of cooperation among community, business, and labor leaders who were otherwise divided along economic and political lines. James Tipton has stressed the growing national climate for integration as a general cause of integration in specific cities, but this does not seem to have been of much importance given the continued segregation in other northern cities. Also of little importance were the efforts of the black community which, aside from the belated activities of the NUL, played a minimal role throughout the controversy. Although committed to supporting equality through integration while retaining pride in the all-black schools, the black community lacked organizational unity and forceful leadership.[13]

An integration policy had finally been adopted, but implementing it would not be easy. Particularly difficult was the situation at the Emerson school, the city's second oldest, situated in a predominantly middle-class neighborhood on the north side—the area most susceptible to integration. Many believed that the Froebel strike had been partially fueled by the memory of the success of the Emerson strikers in 1927. The predominantly white neighborhood was now as opposed to integration as it had been nineteen years earlier. In November, 1946, the school board received a petition from purportedly 90 percent of the taxpayers of the district protesting enrollment of "any persons other than members of the Caucasian race" in the Emerson school. The petition was immediately "branded as undemocratic, un-American and un-Christian" by the city's establishment, according to the Gary *Post-Tribune*. School authorities, strongly supported by the teachers, moved slowly ahead to insure peaceful integration the following year. By June, 1947, it was evident that only a handful of black children, dispersed among six previously all-white schools, would be directly affected and that no white children would be transferred to any all-black schools. Hopes brightened in the spring when the antidiscrimination candidate for mayor won the Democratic primary by a slim margin against a man opposed to integration, and black doctors were finally allowed to practice in the city's Methodist and Catholic hospitals.[14]

---

[13] Tipton, *Community in Crisis*, 101-11.

[14] Gary *Post-Tribune*, November 13, 1946; Tipton, *Community in Crisis*, 112-32. Emerson, similar to Froebel and Gary's other major schools, still included grades K-12. The establishment of separate high schools would come in the late 1950s. On the 1927 Emerson strike, see Cohen and Mohl, *Paradox of Progressive Education*, 138-40. On intercultural policy in 1946 and 1947, see also Dana Philip Whitmer, "Proposed Extension in the School and Classroom Programs of Intergroup Education in the Public Schools of Gary, Indiana" (Ph.D. dissertation, Ohio State University, 1949), 31-34.

EMERSON SCHOOL STUDENTS' STRIKE, 1947

Courtesy of the Calumet Regional Archives, Gary, Indiana.

The rest of the city was apparently prepared for the inevitable. However, when school opened in September and 116 black children cautiously entered the doors of six previously all-white schools, a storm broke at Emerson as about 200 students walked out to protest the 38 newcomers to the elementary grades. The next day they were joined by another 600 or 700, mostly from the high school. School authorities, having learned their lesson, did not hesitate to threaten retaliation. Students under sixteen who did not return to classes were to be considered truants, while students sixteen and over were to be suspended and made ineligible for athletics. The strike lasted ten days. Again most of the community rallied behind school authorities, and there was no trouble at the other newly integrated schools. "What have the people of Emerson district accomplished by standing out against the democratic policy of the school board," the local paper editorialized. "They have lost a week's schooling for their children. They have stirred up a cauldron of ill-will which can become a lasting poison if it is not countered with a realization they have made a mistake. For they are trying to turn backward the democratic process in an age in which that process is being accelerated everywhere." The strikers were also condemned by the Catholic church and other religious organizations, the CIO, the Chamber of Commerce, and the Gary Bar Association, to name but a few. The black community again took a back seat, however. The NAACP national office wrote to local president Hall, "we expect that the NAACP leadership in matters of this kind would be in the thick of the fray working with various groups and with our own membership urging them to take a dynamic and aggressive part to alleviate the basic problems which confront our citizenry." But nothing happened. Similarly, the Urban League stayed in the background, confident that the white establishment would satisfactorily handle the situation.[15]

The principle, if not necessarily the substance, of integration was firmly established in the Gary schools by late 1947. Some had resisted, others had argued that more should have been accomplished (particularly the integration of the all-black schools and the high school grades), but most were satisfied. "The tremendous job of allaying tensions, of reestablishing good will and of educating the public to a proper acceptance of the Negro's rightful position in the community remains to be done," S. An-

---

[15] Gary *Post-Tribune*, September 5, 1947; Gloster B. Current to Hall, September 16, 1947, folder 1946-1955, Gary, Indiana, Branch File, 1940-1955, NAACP Papers; Joseph C. Chapman, interview with author, Gary, Indiana, December 1, 1981; Tipton, *Community in Crisis*, 133-49.

dhil Fineberg reported to the Bureau for Intercultural Education in late September. "These things can be done better, however, now that the system of segregation in Gary schools has ended." In early 1948 Mrs. Eleanor Roosevelt presented Superintendent Charles Lutz a citation from the Bureau for Intercultural Education for the Gary schools' "contribution to the democratic cause."[16]

It was now necessary for Gary leaders to build upon the gains that had been made. Representatives from the bureau temporarily remained in the city to offer advice and establish networks within and between the schools to promote intercultural activities. A City-wide Democractic Living Committee, composed of representatives from each school's Building Committee on Democratic Living, organized the previous year, discussed ways of promoting better democratic living and brought in consultants to meet with the teachers. By 1949, however, a shortage of funds forced the bureau to withdraw, and the lack of an overall strategy to promote equality by the school board and school administrators continued to produce mixed results. In his 1949 dissertation on the Gary school system, Dana Whitmer applauded how much had been accomplished, but also warned: "there has been no planned program through which the majority, or even a large number, of teachers have worked toward common ends in integroup education. The programs of intergroup education which have been developed . . . have depended largely on the individual interest, initiative, and enthusiasm of the principals and teachers in the schools." He also noted that "with the exception of two schools, pupils in Gary Schools have complete equality of opportunity in regard to school curricula, activities, and services." In the Froebel school there was full integration in the lower grades, but in grades eight through twelve discrimination persisted in athletics, the band, swimming facilities, theater, social activities, and class offices. A few black teachers had been hired, however, as well as a black school psychologist.[17]

Although disturbed by continuing inequalities, the black community focused its attention on having the mayor appoint a

---

[16] Gary *Post-Tribune*, February 21, 1948; S. Andhil Fineberg, "What Happened in Gary," September 26, 1947, American Jewish Committee Papers (Blaustein Library, New York).

[17] Whitmer, Proposed Extension in the School and Classroom Programs," 36-40, 244-45. For information on an intercultural unit at the Emerson school, see Gladys Pierce, "Intercultural Relations, Gary, Indiana" (Master's thesis, Indiana University, 1950).

black member to the school board. "Many individuals not living in the Central District are of the impression that the citizens south of the Wabash tracks are not too concerned over the present school board appointment that is to be made in the near future," the Gary *American* editorialized in August, 1948. The whites could not be more wrong. "We're quiet, but we're not asleep in the Central District." Success came the following year when, after months of delay, Mayor Eugene Swartz appointed the Reverend J. Claude Allen of the Colored Methodist Episcopal church to the school board. The Gary *American* was jubilant, commenting that this "has won the respect for the mayor of nearly every citizen in the Central District." This appointment and the passage of a statewide desegregation plan were flickers of hope as the troubled decade ended.[18]

While hope remained, conditions deteriorated. By 1951, 85 percent of the schools were segregated, and 83 percent of the 8,406 black children were attending all-black schools. Ten years later 90 percent of the schools were highly segregated, and 97 percent of the 23,055 black pupils were in eighteen predominantly or exclusively black schools, with primarily black teachers and administrators. The ever worsening problem of school overcrowding was particularly galling. All five schools in the black district were over capacity; by 1949 the Roosevelt school was bulging at the seams with 3,800 in a building built to hold no more than 2,711. Half-day classes, rented facilities, and overflowing classrooms soon became common at Roosevelt and many other schools.[19]

Gary entered the 1950s as one of the most segregated cities in the North. While a 1955 Urban League study by Warren Banner argued "that the Board of Education and school administrators [should] be lauded for their zeal in attempting to provide sufficient building facilities for the school population and for their efforts in eliminating discriminatory practices in the school system," all were not satisfied. The local Urban League, for instance, was concerned about six issues: the segregation of school districts, the integration of teaching staffs, equal access for blacks to all school facilities, the hiring of additional black employees in the school system, the expansion of vocational programs, and attention to the employment opportunities of high school graduates. Furthermore, Clifford Minton, director of the local NUL, felt that Banner had gone too far in praising school officials. "It

---

[18] Gary *American*, August 27, 1948, March 4, 1949.
[19] Wolff, "Segregation in the Schools of Gary, Indiana," 251-61.

is commonly known and generally agreed that the initiation and progress on integration in the Gary School System came as the direct result of a 'crisis,' " he wrote to Banner in New York. "Further that in the main, the gradual changes which have taken place from year to year came almost in spite of rather than because of interest and leadership on the part of top school administrators. In most cases positive changes have been effected in proportion to the extent they were warranted by expediency." Minton believed the best tactic for obtaining action on the local NUL's concerns was through "communication and negotiation with the superintendent and his staff and members of the [school] board rather than formal pronouncements and I think we got a heck of a lot more done that way." He was particularly proud of the role he played in replacing School Superintendent Lutz with Alden Blankenship in 1956. "We remained in the background," he informed Urban League Executive Director Lester Granger, "but to put it mildly, our interest and influence on this development was siginificant." A member of the advisory board to select Lutz's successor, he believed his personal knowledge of Blankenship through NUL connections was a decisive factor.[20]

Lutz was fired by the school board in September, 1955, following the publication of a very critical survey of the schools conducted by the Public Administration Service (PAS). The survey reported that the schools were overcrowded, the curriculum inadequate, finances in disarray, and "student achievement . . . low and in great need of improvement." The responsibility for these faults, the survey concluded, lay with the superintendent: Lutz's weak leadership served to "undermine completely the morale and confidence of the board and of teachers, principals, parents, and students in those persons and institutions which are supposed to provide positive and responsible leadership in public education." Although virtually complete in its examination of Lutz and the school system, the report ignored any signs of racial segregation or discrimination. It mirrored the official line that denied there were any problems. Following the Supreme Court's *Brown* ruling the previous year, the Gary *Post-Tribune* had crowed that the decision had come more than seven years after the Gary School Board had laid down

---

[20] Warren M. Banner, *A Study of the Social and Economic Conditions in Three Minority Groups, Gary, Indiana* (New York, 1955), 81; Clifford Minton, interview with author, Gary, Indiana, October 19, 1982; Minton to Warren Banner, June 3, 1955, Container 97, Gary 1955, Affiliate File D, 1 Administrative Department, NUL Papers; Minton to Granger, January 24, 1956, Container 97, Gary 1956, *ibid.*

the policy that had eliminated such segregation from the Gary school system, and quoted Superintendent Lutz's optimistic evaluation, "The program of eliminating gradually segregation in the city's schools has now been completed." Such self-deception was easy when there were the more pressing problems of overcrowding and funding. A few, however, did not share the prevalent optimism. "Local citizens have and are raising many pertinent and constructive questions about progress on carrying out the Gary school integration policy," Minton noted in May, 1955. "It seems that the consensus is that after the pressure of the incidents that lead [sic] to the '1946 Policy' subsided, that school administrators have not been consistent or given much or effective leadership to this matter."[21]

Blankenship was quickly embroiled in questions of segregation and integration. The situation at two transition schools was particularly acute, prompting Minton to inform the new superintendent in March, 1957, that there was "evidence of subtle and overt teacher-pupil resentment to the increase of Negro enrollment in the school population [that] has not and is not being met with positive leadership." Moreover, questions were "raised about evident methods by which school district boundaries are regulated and the apparent plans to maintain as high a degree of racial segregation in the schools of the area as possible through illogical or unnatural manipulation of school boundaries." In December Blankenship assured the Urban League director: "we are making progress in the schools even though we do not have all of the answers. In our school curriculum, we are emphasizing the likenesses of people of different races and creeds and the fact that it is the individual rather than his race, color or creed which is important. . . . We still have some schools with an all-white or an all-Negro population. . . . Changes will come slowly in certain areas of the community. Nevertheless, we feel that we are making progress on a sound basis." Two days later Minton informed the national office that while some progress had indeed been made, particularly in the few integrated schools, there remained many problems. "A major proportion of the new schools constructed during recent years are located in areas almost totally inhabited by Negroes," he noted. "Generally, due to the placement of these schools, they will have little, if any, influence on the integration process." He preferred, however, to stress the

21 Public Administration Service, *The Public School System of Gary, Indiana* (n.p., 1955), 17, 37; Gary *Post-Tribune*, May 18, 1954; [Clifford Minton], "Implementation of Policy on Integration Adopted by Gary School Board—9 Years Ago—August, 1946," May 25, 1955, Minton Papers.

"progress" that had been made in order to "realistically enhance our city's prestige."[22]

Segregation, so pervasive, was difficult to reduce, but more specific grievances were easier to confront, if not redress. The black community, desiring to broaden the students' opportunities, continually sought more vocational courses and counseling. In a 1949 editorial the Gary *Post-Tribune* related that the "Gary American [sic] has hammered away for years for more shops, better equipped. Maybe one day the head of the institution will see the need for teaching for the masses instead of the classes." The problem, simply, was the elitist principle. The PAS survey listed the Roosevelt school, still the largest all-black school, as having one of the three best vocational programs in the city. This, however, was within the context that the "entire industrial arts program in the Gary schools is poorly developed and has been neglected by the administration both centrally and in the individual schools." The previous year a group of black ministers had queried the school board regarding the employment opportunities for black high school graduates who did "not meet standards normally expected of individuals with high school education." They particularly lacked English, typing, and shorthand skills. In his official reply Assistant Superintendent Whitmer related that school officials were color-blind regarding vocational courses and guidance. "Our experience indicates that membership of a student in any religious, ethnic, or racial group does not determine his needs, interests, and potentialities. These are determined by factors of heredity and environment," he concluded. "Consequently, we have not set up special programs in guidance activities for Negro students." Still, complaints continued. In 1959 Minton reported to the Urban League that black youth still had difficulty obtaining clerical jobs because of inadequate school training. He echoed the old charge "that while possibly not more than 25 percent of the graduates of some Gary schools enter college, . . . high priority is placed on college preparatory training." As the decade ended the curriculum issue remained clouded.[23]

---

[22] Minton to Alden Blankenship, March 5, 1957, Gary Urban League Papers (University of Illinois at Chicago Library, Chicago, Illinois); Blankenship to Minton, December 3, 1957, *ibid.*; Minton to R. Maurice Moss, December 5, 1957, *ibid.*

[23] Gary *Post-Tribune*, November 11, 1949; Public Administration Service, *Public School System of Gary, Indiana*, 89; Reverend Ivor Moore *et al.* to Charles E. Daugherty, March 16, 1954, Minton Papers; Dana Whitmer to Ministers' Study Group, May 11, 1954, *ibid.*; Minton to Members, Gary Urban League Board of Directors and Advisory Council, January 20, 1959, Gary Urban League Papers.

Another source of friction was teacher segregation. The large year-by-year jump in school enrollments created periodic shortages and required continual recruitment and placement of new teachers. The Urban League supported integrated faculties. But in 1955 four schools had all-black teaching staffs, thirteen schools had all-white staffs, and another eight schools had integrated staffs. Eleven of the twenty-five schools had no black students. Overall, 42 percent of the pupils were nonwhite, but only 25 percent of the teachers. Minton recognized that some teachers might not be comfortable in integrated classrooms, but integration, he felt, had to be the goal. Two years later Blankenship assured Minton "we base our selection of staff members on the person best qualified for the job." The meaning of this statement became clear in November, 1959, when the league discovered that in an advertisement of current teaching vacancies certain positions were secretly designated as being for white applicants while others were for blacks. In an interview with the director of personnel, he "admitted that this was the first occasion on which 'apparent racial designations' were used to describe the location of specific vacancies." He added "that no subsequent announcements with such 'connotations' had been, or would be, used." Such a blatant policy was probably dropped, but integration remained elusive.[24]

Occasionally there were events which provided a glimmer of hope for the advancement of school staff integration. For example, when the first black supervisor was appointed in 1956 the Gary *American* believed the appointment would "mean much toward bettering race relations in the city." But in late 1959 the Midtown Citizens' Committee, an interracial group, reported that aside from supervisory personnel, there had been little progress. "There is little if any evidence to show that systematic efforts are being made to encourage or to implement a policy of teacher integration in the majority of our public schools," the committee noted. One glaring problem was "that the majority of the school principals have a passive or reactionary or negative attitude toward teacher integration," black as well as white. The committee found only six or seven schools with token teacher integration, and they were ones with predominantly black student bodies; the remainder of the thirty-six schools were either all white or all black. The superintendent and the school board, meeting with

---

[24] [Minton] to Mary Harris, May 17, 1955, Minton Papers; Blankenship to Minton, December 3, 1957, Gary Urban League Papers; Charles Graves to Minton, November 12, 1959, *ibid.*

URBAN LEAGUE DINNER, 1958

Left to right, Clifford E. Minton, executive director of the Gary Urban League; H. B. Snyder, president of the Gary Urban League and publisher of the Gary *Post-Tribune*; Winthrop Rockefeller; and Peter Mandich, mayor of Gary, Indiana

Courtesy of the Calumet Regional Archives, Gary, Indiana.

the committee, once again promised "an uneventful integration of all school personnels [sic]."[25]

Another somewhat clearer problem was school overcrowding. The rapid increase of students, particularly in black and white working-class neighborhoods, put a great strain on school buildings and finances. By mid-decade new schools were being built at a rapid rate, but this rate continued to lag behind the increase in demand. The black community continually demanded new classrooms. In 1950 hundreds of Roosevelt school students were either in rented facilities or attending half-day sessions. Two years later the Gary *Post-Tribune* boasted, "For the first time in more than 20 years Roosevelt School will operate with all children on full-time schedules." Of course, almost two hundred were still housed in the American Legion hut or in the basement of the local Lutheran church. The opening of six new elementary schools in 1958 finally allowed for the conversion of Roosevelt and three other unit (K-12) schools to upper grades only. While conditions eased somewhat at Roosevelt, elementary students at Froebel, now a predominantly black school, experienced half-day sessions or attended classes at the Galilee Baptist Church, First Hungarian Reform Church, Gary National Guard Armory, and the local branch library. Overall some 2,000 students citywide were taught in similar facilities in 1958.[26]

While new schools were greatly needed and welcomed, their location could cause controversy. In 1957, Minton wrote: "a major proportion of the new schools constructed during recent years are located in areas almost totally inhabited by Negroes. Generally, due to the placement of these schools, they will have little, if any, influence on the integration process." During the decade Minton attempted from time to time to raise the issue of grouping new schools with school officials, but, as he later admitted, "we just simply didn't have the horses—we could have made a stronger protest but that's just about what it really added up to." Finally, in 1962 the NAACP entered a lawsuit on behalf of 100 black plaintiffs. In *Bell* v. *School City of Gary* the plaintiffs made three charges: that the school board and superintendent had a "constitutional duty to provide and maintain a racially integrated school system"; that segregation was deliberate; and

---

[25] Gary *American*, August 31, 1956; "Special Factors Re: Teacher-Integration in Gary Public Schools to be Considered at the December Meeting of the Midtown Citizens' Committee," December 4, 1959, Gary Urban League Papers; F. Laurence Anderson *et al.* to Joseph Lucky *et al.*, January 8, 1960, *ibid.*; Anderson to Midtown Citizens Committee, February 12, 1960, *ibid.*

[26] Gary *Post-Tribune*, September 8, 1952.

GATHERING OF GARY SCHOOL ADMINISTRATORS AND TEACHERS, CA. EARLY 1950S. DANA WHITMER IS ON THE FAR RIGHT.

Courtesy of the Calumet Regional Archives, Gary, Indiana.

that black schools had "unequal facilities in all respects, including, but not limited to over-crowded and larger classes, and unequal recreational facilities." The suit, one of the first in the North, although lost, capped the twenty-year struggle to achieve equal schooling in Gary.[27]

In 1962, eighteen of the forty-two schools had an essentially all-black student body, twenty were all white, and only four were mixed. According to one authority 97 percent of the 23,000 black students attended segregated schools. The school board's decision in March to build another high school in the predominantly black Central District touched off a protest in the black community, which preferred a site further west to insure greater integration. A month later the board backed down. Now committed to challenging the board, the rejuvenated local NAACP decided to file a general discrimination suit against the board. School authorities, while admitting racial imbalance, denied this was intentional or that the black schools were in any way inferior. The trial in federal court began on September 10 and lasted four days. Robert Carter, chief counsel of the NAACP, orchestrated the plaintiffs' case, which hinged on the testimony of an expert witness, Dr. Max Wolff.[28]

The plaintiffs lost because they could not prove that Gary's school segregation was designed by the school board. High school boundaries essentially had not changed since 1941, a time when racial segregation was permitted under state law as well as official school board policy. While elementary school construction had continually altered attendance boundaries, these boundaries could be explained on the basis of natural barriers and conditions—railroad tracks, roads, and rivers. There was no written or oral evidence that race had been a factor in boundary selection; indeed, school authorities had plausible explanations for the building of various schools and their attendance patterns. New schools were grouped together because of population congestion and the availability of land, often land already owned by the school system. Particularly damaging to the plaintiffs' case was the testimony of the black school board president and a white prointegration member that race had never been considered in drawing district boundaries. The judge ruled that the plaintiffs had failed to prove the school board had "deliberately or pur-

---

[27] Minton to Moss, December 5, 1957, Gary Urban League Papers; interview with Minton; Kaplan, "Segregation Litigation and the Schools—Part III," 131-32.

[28] Wolff, "Segregation in the Schools of Gary, Indiana," 252. For somewhat different figures, see Kaplan, "Segregation Litigation and the Schools—Part III," 128.

posely segregated the Gary schools," although there was legal precedent for putting the burden of proof on the defendants in such cases.[29]

The absence of school board reports and inadequate board minutes, combined with a scarcity of supporting documentation, make it very difficult to corroborate either the charges of the NAACP or the findings of the court. What seems clear is that the five-member school board, composed through the 1950s of essentially middle-class businessmen, union leaders, and a black minister—eight men and one woman—gave little thought to school integration. Responding to pressures from various neighborhoods to eliminate overcrowding, their primary goal was to build new schools. They did what they thought was expedient. That their decisions encouraged segregation, and that they ignored methods of promoting integration were matters of little concern to them. Gary's persistent school segregation can be said, therefore, to have been essentially *de facto*.

As for the charge that the black schools were inferior and grossly overcrowded, and that their students displayed poorer academic achievement, the judge ruled that in building ten new schools in the Central District the school board had shown good faith in trying to cope with the population explosion. The plaintiffs could have emphasized the almost complete segregation of teachers, which did appear contrived, but "they carefully avoided implying that the Negro schools might be made in any way inferior by their predominant number of Negro teachers." Since the courts had not ruled that *de facto* segregation necessarily meant academic inferiority, the charge used by the plaintiffs was weak. Busing and its controversial justifications were still in the future. In fact, the judge argued that transferring students miles from their homes in order to promote integration "would in my opinion be indeed a violation of the equal protection clause of the Fourteenth Amendment." The judge was upheld by the Seventh Circuit Court of Appeals. It ruled that there was no legal remedy for *de facto* school segregation, which the plaintiffs had now practically admitted was the form of segregation existing in Gary schools. The Supreme Court never heard the case.[30]

Following the *Bell* case, as the city was becoming more black, there was an increasing commitment in Gary to foster school

---

[29] Kaplan, "Segregation Litigation and the Schools—Part III," 142.

[30] *Ibid.*, 155; John Kaplan, "Segregation Litigation and the Schools—Part II: The General Northern Problem," *Northwestern University Law Review*, LVIII (May-June, 1963), 191. Also see, in general, J. Harvie Wilkinson, *From Brown to Bakke: The Supreme Court and School Integration, 1954-1978* (New York, 1979).

integration. Integration had become a political and social, rather than a legal, issue per se. Although most whites remained unconvinced of the need to promote integration, most blacks felt that further integration was necessary for black academic performance to improve; this despite continuing black pride in all-black schools, Roosevelt in particular. Still, there were indications that there were troubles in the few mixed schools. In 1957 Minton alerted the superintendent to ways of preventing friction at two newly integrated white schools where there was "evidence of subtle and overt teacher-pupil resentment to the increase of Negro enrollment in the school population [which] has not and is not being met with positive leadership and planning." More serious problems erupted at the previously troubled Emerson school in 1960. Black parents charged some of the (all) white teachers and students, supported by the principal, with violence and intimidation. The superintendent reported to the school board "that he and his supervisory staff have investigated the charges and are continuing to seek a solution to the school's human relations problems." Unfortunately, such difficulties would continue as blacks moved into other previously all-white neighborhoods and schools.[31]

In the two decades following World War II Gary, with a large black population, remained one of the main battlefields in the North over school integration. The Froebel strike, the school board's integration plan, the Emerson strike, galloping *de facto* segregation, attempts to promote intercultural education and teacher integration, and finally a lawsuit kept Gary in the headlines and made it a focal point for the dreams and aspirations of those who supported civil rights. The role of the black community in this struggle was generally low-key, except in the earliest years when the Urban League was instrumental in healing the wounds at the Froebel school and bringing about an integration plan. Nevertheless, the league never abandoned the dream of educational equality and opportunity, normally working with and through the city's white power structure. A key factor was the league's long-time president H. B. Snyder, publisher of the Gary *Post-Tribune*, whom Minton attributes with much behind-the-scenes maneuvering. Minton well expressed his dilemma, "you're in the middle in the Urban League, you're suspect by many whites of being too liberal or too radical and you're right

---

[31] Minton to Blankenship, March 5, 1957, Gary Urban League Papers; Gary *Post-Tribune*, April 27, 1960.

in the middle and you have a tight line to walk." And walk it he did.[32]

Gary accomplished much on paper but little in practice. One problem was that *de facto* segregation, in the years before the relief of busing, successfully prevented substantial school integration. The black community, growing rapidly, spread outward from its base in the Central District, providing little chance for mixed neighborhoods. In the *Bell* suit the NAACP tried to prove deliberate school segregation but was unsuccessful and even dropped this line of argument in its appeals. To be sure there was white resistance, both overt and subtle. This, combined with natural demographic changes, successfully frustrated any real integration. After the Emerson strike in 1947 the battle between integrationists and segregationists was essentially muted: the former claiming victory, the latter uneasily awaiting the future. Following the *Brown* decision the city's elite congratulated themselves on solving Gary's problems and with their fellow Northerners turned their eyes to the South. They were also confident that school integration would be limited to the working-class schools, which was essentially true until the 1960s. Gary was an early leader among northern cities in recognizing the obvious dangers of blatant racism and segregation, but it chose to settle for paper solutions and token satisfaction, a northern trait of the period. Such acquiescence was directly challenged in the 1960s in Gary and elsewhere, again with mixed results. The dilemma of discrimination and segregation in the land of democracy would continue to plague everyone concerned.[33]

---

[32] Interview with Minton.

[33] On integration attempts in the 1960s, see, in addition to the works cited above, Allen Matusow, *The Unravelling of America: A History of Liberalism in the 1960s* (New York, 1984), 60-96, 180-216.

ARTICLES

CONFRONTATION AS REJOINDER TO COMPROMISE: REFLECTIONS ON THE LITTLE ROCK DESEGREGATION CRISIS*

Raymond T. Diamond**

In September 1957, soldiers of the 101st Airborne Division of the United States Army were called to duty in hostile territory. These soldiers were called to Little Rock, Arkansas, to keep safe nine Black children who, under a court order of desegregation, attended Little Rock's Central High School.[1] The Little Rock crisis is writ large in the history of the desegregation of the American South. Because many of the events of the crisis were performed before the television camera at a time when television was new, the Little Rock crisis was etched graphically in the American consciousness.[2] The camera showed in violent detail the willingness of the South to maintain segregation, and the willingness of the federal government to support federal law.

Many books have been published regarding the Little Rock crisis. Daisy Bates wrote *The Long Shadow of Little Rock, A Memoir* from her perspective as a leader of the Arkansas branch of the National Association for the Advancement of Colored People (NAACP).[3] Brooks Hays[4] and Orval Faubus[5] have provided the perspective of elected officials who influenced the event of Little Rock. Virgil Blossom wrote as a superintendent of schools who attempted to implement a "go slow" desegregation plan which would recognize the mandate of *Brown v. Board of Education*[6] but still take advantage of the

* The ideas in Part III of this essay were presented in earlier form at the July 1987 annual meeting of the American Association of Law Librarians, and comments there received are acknowledged.

** Assistant Professor, Louisiana State University Law Center. B.A. 1973, J.D. 1977 Yale University. The author acknowledges also the research assistance of Michael Colvin, J.D., L.S.U. 1986; Brett Beyer III, J.D., L.S.U. 1987; and Karen Hayne, L.S.U. Class of 1989.

1. Exec. Order No. 10,730, Sept. 24, 1957, 22 F.R. 7628 (1957). D. Eisenhower, Radio and Television Address to the American People on the Situation in Little Rock, 1957 PUBLIC PAPERS OF THE PRESIDENTS: DWIGHT D. EISENHOWER 689 (1957) (hereinafter cited as 1957 PUBLIC PAPERS). *See also* Proclamation 3,204, Sept. 24, 1957, 22 F.R. 7628 (1957).

2. The power of these television images is presented in "Fighting Back (1957-62)," *Eyes on the Prize: America's Civil Rights Years*, 1954-65 (PBS television broadcast, January 28, 1986) (videotape available through PBS Adult Learning Services). *See also* J. WILLIAMS, EYES ON THE PRIZE - AMERICA'S CIVIL RIGHTS YEARS, 1954-1965 (1987) (hereinafter cited as EYES ON THE PRIZE).

3. D. BATES, THE LONG SHADOW OF LITTLE ROCK, A MEMOIR (1982).

4. B. HAYS, POLITICS IS MY PARISH, AN AUTOBIOGRAPHY (1981), and B. HAYS, A SOUTHERN MODERATE SPEAKS (1959). Hays was a member of Congress who lost his seat because he counseled moderation.

5. O. FAUBUS, DOWN FROM THE HILLS (1980). Faubus was a governor who pioneered what came to be known as massive resistance.

6. 347 U.S. 483 (1954) (hereinafter cited as *Brown I*). *Brown I* declared "[s]eparate educational facilities are inherently unequal." *Brown I* at 347 U.S. 494.

weaknesses of *Brown's* implementation formula,[7] and who was frustrated from even this minimal attempt.[8] Elizabeth Huckaby's *Crisis at Central High* is the account of an assistant principal at Central High during the critical period, an eyewitness account of what happened not just outside the schoolhouse gates but also what happened behind the schoolhouse's closed doors.[9]

None of these authors have attempted to explain the Little Rock crisis in constitutional terms. Content to describe events and explain them as they understood them, these authors have the gift and the limitation of personal perspective. Not even Tony Freyer's *The Little Rock Crisis A Constitutional Interpretation*,[10] written from the perspective of an objective observer, fully explains the constitutional significance of Little Rock. Instead it performs the same descriptive task as the participants in this crisis, but paints a more global picture.

This Article speaks to this lacuna in our understanding of the events of Little Rock. The remainder of this Article is divided into four parts. Part I describes the events of the Little Rock crisis. Part II suggests the implications of *Brown v. Board's* implementation formula as a factor contributing to the character and the severity of the Little Rock crisis. Part III examines the constitutional basis of interposition and the concept of localism as a justification for resistance in Little Rock.

The concluding section speaks to the question which the Little Rock crisis begged and which was answered by the Supreme Court in *Cooper v. Aaron*,[11] whether the pronouncements of the Supreme Court deserve recognition as the law of the land.

I. PEOPLE AND EVENTS

The seeds of the crisis in Little Rock were planted the day after *Brown v.*

---

7. Desegregation was to take place not immediately but "with all deliberate speed" 349 U.S. 294, 300 (1955) (hereinafter cited as *Brown II*) and "as soon as practicable" *Id.* at 299.

8. V. BLOSSOM, IT HAS HAPPENED HERE (1959).

9. E. HUCKABY, CRISIS AT CENTRAL HIGH (1980).

10. T. FREYER, THE LITTLE ROCK CRISIS: A CONSTITUTIONAL INTERPRETATION (1984). The subtitle is deceiving. THE LITTLE ROCK CRISIS is not a constitutional interpretation, instead a rendering of the facts and their political/sociological explanations. Freyer's intent was to "approach the integration conflict in terms of the interplay of local politics and judicial process." *Id.* at ix. He explores through the history of the Little Rock crisis "the relationship between change imposed through law and that achieved through moral principle." *Id.* at 4. Though THE LITTLE ROCK CRISIS performs the same task as have the works of the participants who have written on the crisis, it not only benefits from a more global perspective, but it is a book with more factual depth, having the benefit of access to records of the Federal Bureau of Investigation, private records of the National Association for the Advancement of Colored People and private legal files. *Id.* at ix. I. SPITZBERG, JR., RACIAL POLITICS IN LITTLE ROCK, 1954-1967 (1987), covers the crisis as part of a more extenstive time period of examination. Other non-participants have published on the subject of the Little Rock crisis but have not had the benefit of Freyer's sources. *See, e.g.,* C. SILVERMAN, THE LITTLE ROCK STORY. Additionally they have attempted to view Little Rock not as an isolated topic of a major work but have written chapters on Little Rock in books on larger topics. *See, e.g.,* N. BARTLEY, THE RISE OF MASSIVE RESISTANCE: RACE AND POLITICS IN THE SOUTH DURING THE 1950's (1969); E. JACOWBY and D. COLBURN, SOUTHERN BUSINESSMEN AND DESEGREGATION (1982); A. BICKEL, THE LEAST DANGEROUS BRANCH (1962); J. PELTASON, FIFTY EIGHT LONELY MEN (1961); F. READ, L. MCGOUGH, LET THEM BE JUDGED (1978); O. HANDLIN, FIRE BELL IN THE NIGHT (1964); *but cf.* ARKANSAS GAZETTE, CRISIS IN THE SOUTH: THE LITTLE ROCK STORY (1958); H. ALEXANDER, THE LITTLE ROCK RECALL ELECTION (1960).

11. 358 U.S. 1 (1958).

Board[12] was rendered in 1954. On May 17, 1954, *Brown I,* as it later was called, laid to rest the constitutional doctrine of "separate but equal," recognized by *Plessy v. Ferguson,*[13] declaring instead that "[s]eparate educational facilities are inherently unequal."[14] On May 18th, the Little Rock school board instructed its superintendent, Virgil Blossom, "to develop a plan consistent with the Court's order," and by the end of the month school officials had issued a public statement committing Little Rock to desegregation.[15]

By fall of 1954, Superintendent Blossom had formed a plan under which desegregation would begin almost immediately, in two high schools as soon as construction reached completion by 1956, and in junior high schools by 1957.[16] For several months, Blossom promoted the plan before the academic community and the public at large.[17]

In May of 1955, however, the school board approved a second and less ambitious plan. It limited desegregation to but one high school, Central High School, to the extent of allowing entrance to "only a handful of black children."[18] The plan would not desegregate junior high and elementary schools until years later.[19] This, the school board and its superintendent explained, was "consistent with an absolute minimum of what the law required."[20]

Little Rock's grudging willingness to desegregate its schools went hand in hand with the Supreme Court's second decision bearing the name *Brown v. Board of Education.*[21] *Brown II,* decided May 31, 1955, provided that district courts implementing desegregation need not order immediate and full desegregation, but should take cognizance of local conditions. Desegregation, the Court said, should take place not immediately but "with all deliberate

---

12. 347 U.S. 483 (1954).
13. 163 U.S. 537 (1896).
14. *Brown I,* 347 U.S. at 494.
15. FREYER, *supra* note 10, at 15.
16. *Id.* at 16. The overall outlines of the plan were extensive:

In the eastern part of the city a new all-black junior high school was being built. According to the Blossom Plan, this would instead become an integrated high school (subsequently named Horace Mann High School), and Dunbar, the existing black high school, would become a junior high whose student body would remain black. A second high school (subsequently called Hall High School) was under construction in the western part of Little Rock; it, too, would be integrated on completion, probably in September 1956. The next year the junior high schools would be integrated. The date for integration of the elementary schools was left unclear, but Blossom expected the process to occur more slowly. Finally, the board would outline several school attendance zones throughout the city. Assignment of students to these zones was to be made without regard to race. For several months, Blossom promoted his plan before various white business organizations and Black and White parent groups.

Note that this plan did not desegregate existing high schools, that the details of junior high desegregation were left unspecified, and that the date of desegregation for elementary school was nebulous and that actual desegregation for these was expected to move even more slowly.

17. *Id.*
18. *Id.* at 16, 17.
19. A second phase would open the junior high schools of a few blacks by 1960. No specific date for integration of the elementary schools was set, but the fall of 1963 was considered a strong possibility. Children would be allowed to transfer out of districts where their race was in a minority, which virtually assured that Horace Mann High, when opened, would be all Black. Finally, the Phase Program provided for a selective screening process that made it certain that only a small number of black children would attend Central.

Id. at 17.
20. *Id.*
21. 349 U.S. 294 (1955).

speed."[22] The state of Arkansas in its amicus brief filed November 15, 1954 in *Brown II*[23] had supported this position.[24] Between fall 1954 and May 1955 the Little Rock School board revised its plan "along lines remarkably consistent" with the state's brief.[25] In effect, when the Supreme Court issued the opinion in *Brown II*, "it therefore indirectly sanctioned the [new] Blossom Plan."[26]

After a period of internal dissension within the local branch of the National Association for the Advancement of Colored People (NAACP) and the Little Rock Black community,[27] the NAACP, in order to force the pace of desegregation in Little Rock,[28] filed suit in February 1956 on behalf of thirty-three children not allowed to register at White schools. This request was rejected by the federal courts,[29] but not before the matter of school desegregation became an issue in the 1956 Arkansas gubernatorial campaign.

Orval Faubus had taken office as governor of Arkansas in 1955,[30] but because of a two-year term of office, campaigning was a constant, though not always formal activity. In September 1955, Faubus was warned that a refusal to actively support school segregation would lead to opposition in the 1956 race; Faubus' position that whatever he might do "might only aggravate the situation" was not acceptable.[31] Indeed, Faubus drew opposition based on the segregation issue in the 1956 campaign, in which he was accused of " 'pussyfooting' on the integration question and . . . wait[ing] for sentiment to develop before taking a stand . . . ."[32]

---

22. *Id.* at 300.
23. Amicus Brief of the Attorney General of Arkansas, Brown v. Board of Education, 349 U.S. 294 (1955) *reprinted in* 49A LANDMARK BRIEFS AND ARGUMENTS OF THE SUPREME COURT OF THE UNITED STATES 831 (1975) [hereinafter cited as Amicus Brief].
24. *Id.* at 7-13.
25. FREYER, *supra* note 10, at 35.
26. *Id.*
27. *Id.* at 42-45.
28. FREYER, *supra* note 10, at 45. The NAACP's reasoning was this:
    Our objective is to secure the prompt and orderly end of segregation in the public schools. We want all children, regardless of race, to have the opportunity to go to the public schools nearest their homes. We seek an end to the hazards, inconveniences and discrimination of a system which now requires little children to pass each day several schools from which they are barred because of race and to travel nearly 10 miles to racially designated schools. . . .
    We are unwilling to connive by continued silence at such blows against the welfare of our young people, and so we have entered this suit.
    The school board has announced what it calls a "three-phase" plan for desegregation. It has, however, given no fixed dates for integration at any level and not even the vaguest target dates for integration at the elementary and junior high level. Meanwhile, it proposes to allow young children to endure indefinitely unnecessary hazards of needless daily travel. Its policy continues to exclude Negro boys from the training necessary for many important trades in technical fields. School authorities have refused relief even on these points and have thus driven us to ask the courts for needed relief for the children now in school.
    Interview with J. C. Crenshaw, president of the Little Rock NAACP, as reported by the Arkansas Democrat, February 8, 1956, at 1, as excerpted in W. RECORD & J. RECORD, LITTLE ROCK U.S.A. 12 (1960).
29. Aaron v. Cooper, 143 F. Supp. 855 (E.D. Ark 1956), *aff'd* 243 F.2d 361 (8th Cir. 1957). A description of the trial and initial decision in *Aaron* may be found in FREYER, *supra* note 10, at 54-59.
30. FREYER, *supra* note 10, at 23; FAUBUS, DOWN FROM THE HILLS, *supra* note 5, at 72-74; 11 WHO'S WHO IN THE SOUTH AND SOUTHWEST 1969-70, at 325 (1969) [hereinafter cited as WHO'S WHO].
31. FREYER, *supra* note 10, at 65.
32. Southern School News, August 1956, at 3, *reprinted in* W. RECORD & J. RECORD, *supra* note 28, at 19. Faubus maintained that "segregation was a minor issue because all the candidates agreed

In particular, segregation was brought to the fore by the candidacy of James Johnson, a former state senator who in 1954 had lost a statewide race for attorney general, and who had found in segregation a new and popular issue.[33] Johnson had gained some notoriety in opposing desegregation of schools in Hoxie, Arkansas, a tiny town which had sought to voluntarily desegregate its schools — because "it was 'right in the sight of God,' necessary because of the *Brown* decisions, and 'cheaper' "[34] — only to be opposed by a statewide, even interstate network of segregationists who threatened violence, intimidated members of the school board and parents of Black children, and engenderd a boycott of Hoxie schools.[35] A federal injunction put a stop to the opposition,[36] but the opposition had already reaped a significant result in the prominence of the name of James Johnson as a vigorous and imaginative segregationist.[37]

Johnson became convinced of the sense of the doctrine of interpostion; the state, he thought, could and should interpose itself between the federal courts and the people of the state on the issue of segregation.[38] He proposed in late 1955 three measures meant to forestall desegregation. The first was a state constitutional amendment directing the legislature to "take appropriate action" to evade the *Brown* decisions. The second was an act meant to effectuate pupil assignment on grounds other than race. The third was a resolution of interposition placing the state on record against desegregation.[39] These measures met with success in the November 1956 election, but Johnson's candidacy, which the measures, in part, were meant to foster, did not.[40]

Governor Faubus had understood the need to position himself in favor of segregation,[41] and had understood that as the perceived segregationist candidate, Johnson was the candidate to beat.[42] As a result, Faubus jumped on the interposition bandwagon and, turning the issue to good advantage, won in a landslide.[43] Faubus' position had implications, however, that in Little Rock proved critical.

When the Arkansas legislature met in February 1957, it passed several statutes meant to maintain school segregation, and Governor Faubus felt constrained to support them.[44] This put Faubus and the legislature at odds with

---

on the subject," but promised there would be "no breakdown of the state's traditional segregation pattern." *Id.*

33. FREYER, *supra* note 10, at 68. Southern School News August 1956, at 3, *reprinted in* W. RECORD & J. RECORD, *supra* note 28, at 19.

34. FREYER, *supra* note 10, at 64.

35. Hoxie School District No. 46 v. Brewer, 135 F. Supp. 296, (E.D. Ark. 1955). Order for Injunction printed in 1 RACE REL. LAW REP. 43, 45 (1956).

36. *Id. See* Freyer's discussion of the *Hoxie* incident at 63-68.

37. FREYER, *supra* note 10, at 68.

38. *Id.* at 70.

39. *Id.* at 70-71, 79-80, 87-88. Southern School News December 1956, at 8, *reprinted in* W. RECORD & J. RECORD, *supra* note 28, at 27.

40. Southern School News, December 1956, at 8, *reprinted in* W. RECORD & J. RECORD, *supra* note 28, at 26. FREYER, *supra* note 10, at 81.

41. FREYER, *supra* note 10, at 75.

42. *Id.* at 78.

43. *Id.* at 81; FAUBUS DOWN FROM THE HILLS, *supra* note 5, at 141.

44. Once interposition formally became part of the state's law in November, legislators in the upcoming session of 1957 were bound to consider a number of segregation measures. One such proposal (a result of Amendment 47) would create a state sovereignty commission with extensive investigative and police powers. Newly elected state attorney general Bruce

the school board and the people of Little Rock, who in March 1957 elected two moderates to the school board over two segregationists.[45] Faubus' position was in concert with the band of segregationists who had obstructed desegregation in Hoxie and who now sought to do the same in Little Rock. As the spring and summer wore on this opposition caused concern to the school board, who were determined to let their plan go forward.[46]

In late August of 1957, the situation grew tense. On August 22nd, Governor Marvin Griffin of Georgia, a guest of Governor Faubus at the Arkansas governor's mansion in Little Rock, delivered a rabble-rousing segregationist speech. Faubus claimed that the speech changed citizen perception of desegregation, such that now the governor feared violence at Central High.[47] Whether violence was an honest concern of Faubus is not clear. Two days before Griffin's speech, Faubus had talked with a United States Justice Department official about the subject,[48] and on August 29th in a state court proceeding he had instigated to enjoin the school board from desegregating Central High School,[49] Faubus testified to his fear of violence.[50] On neither of these occasions did Faubus state the basis for his concern.[51] Moreover, Faubus' concern was belied in the state court proceeding by the testimony of Superintendent Blossom that he had no expectation of trouble,[52] and by the later finding of a federal district court that until September 2nd "no acts of violence or threats of violence in connection with the carrying out of the plan had occurred."[53] Nonetheless, as a result of Faubus' testimony, a state judge on August 22nd granted an injunction against the September 3 desegregation, an injunction which itself was enjoined by a federal judge on August 30th.[54]

Bennett sponsored other legislation requiring supporters of desegregation, particularly local NAACP branches, to register and make public reports of their activities. And, finally, Governor Faubus pushed for his own enactments: one to relieve school children of compulsory attendance in racially mixed school districts, the other to authorize school districts to hire legal counsel to defend school boards and school officials in suits involving desegregation. Although he had not sponsored them, Faubus publicly supported the Bennett and sovereignty commission measures, despite their doubtful constitutionality and threat to civil liberties.

FREYER, *supra* note 10, at 88-89 (footnotes omitted).

45. *Id.* at 92.

46. *Id.* at 93-98. The influence of the federal government on the positions of Faubus and of the board was minimal.

President Eisenhower had provided little direct public support for desegregation in general, and in a public statement in July 1957 he said that use of federal forces to enforce the prinicple was unlikely. Neither the president nor the Justice Department resisted Governor Allan Shiver's use of Rangers to reestablish segregation in several Texas communities after desegregation had resulted in disorderly crowds. Division in the president's cabinet had also prevented vigorous executive lobbying for a new civil rights bill, which enabled southern congressional leaders to significantly weaken the measure during the summer of 1957.

FREYER, *supra* note 10, at 98-99 (footnotes omitted).

47. *Id.* at 100-01.

48. *Id.* at 101.

49. *Id.*

50. *Id.* at 102.

51. *Id.* at 101-02.

52. *Id.* at 102. Moreover, when asked about Governor Faubus' statement, Little Rock's police chief responded, "Let's say I haven't heard what Governor Faubus says he hears." Southern School News September 1957, at 6 *reprinted in* W. RECORD & J. RECORD, *supra* note 28, at 33, 34.

53. Aaron v. Cooper, 156 F. Supp. 220, 225 (E.D. Ark 1957).

54. Aaron v. Cooper, (E.D. Ark. Civ. No. 3113 August 30, 1957), *reprinted in* 2 RACE REL.

In spite of this loss in federal court, Governor Faubus on September 2nd issued a proclamation calling out the Arkansas National Guard,[55] and explained that because of an "imminent danger of tumult, riot and breach of peace and the doing of violence to persons and property,"[56] he had charged the Guard to prevent, "for the time being," desegregation at Central High School.[57]

On September 3rd, the school board petitioned the federal district court for instructions,[58] and the court ordered implementation of the plan "immediately and without delay."[59] The following day, the National Guardsmen nonetheless blocked the entrance of the nine Black students, and pictures and reports of the abuse of one student appeared around the nation and the world.[60] That same day, Governor Faubus telegramed President Eisenhower, disclaiming any interest in "integration vs. segregation," and claimed that the

LAW REP. 934 (1957). FREYER, *supra* note 10, at 102. Southern School News September 1957, at 6, *reprinted in* W. RECORD & J. RECORD, *supra* note 28, at 33, 34.

55. O. Faubus, Proclamation, Sept. 2, 1957, *reprinted in* 2 RACE REL. LAW REP. 937.

56. *Id.*

57. O. Faubus, Television Address, September 2, 1957, *reprinted in* W. RECORD & J. RECORD, *supra* note 28, at 37.

58. Petition of William G. Cooper et al., Aaron v. Cooper, 156 F. Supp. 220 (E.D. Ark. 1957) *reprinted in* 2 RACE REL. LAW REP. 937.

59. Order, Aaron v. Cooper, 156 F. Supp. 220 (E.D. Ark. 1957) *reprinted in* 2 RACE REL. LAW REP. 938, 939.

60. FREYER, *supra* note 10, at 104 and sources cited therein, at 114, 68. EYES ON THE PRIZE, *supra* note 9, at 101, 102. The simple word "abuse" does not fully describe the ordeal suffered by the student, Elizabeth Eckford:

> Getting off the bus near Central High, Eckford saw a throng of white people and hundreds of armed soldiers. But the presence of the guardsmen reassured her. The superintendent had told the black students to come in through the main entrance at the front of the school, so Elizabeth headed in that direction. "I looked at all the people and thought, 'Maybe I'll be safe if I walk down the block to the front entrance behind the guards,' " she remembers. "At the corner I tried to pass through the long lines of guards around the school so as to enter the grounds behind them. One [soldier] pointed across the street . . . so I walked across the street conscious of the crowd that stood there, but they moved away from me . . . [Then] the crowd began to follow me, calling me names. I still wasn't afraid - just a little bit nervous. Then my knees started to shake all of a sudden and I wondered whether I could make it to the center entrance a block away. It was the longest block I ever walked in my whole life. Even so, I wasn't too scared, because all the time I kept thinking the [guards] would protect me.
>
> "When I got in front of the school, I went up to a guard again," she continues. "He just looked straight ahead and didn't move to let me pass. I didn't know what to do . . . Just then the guards let some white students through . . . I walked up to the guard who had let [them] in. He too didn't move. When I tried to squeeze past him, he raised his bayonet, and then the other guards moved in and raised their bayonets . . . Somebody started yelling, 'Lynch her! Lynch her!' "
>
> . . .
>
> "I tried to see a friendly face somewhere in the mob . . .," Elizabeth recalls. "I looked into the face of an old woman, and it seemed a kind face, but when I looked at her again, she spat on me."
>
> The young woman heard someone snarl, "No nigger bitch is going to get in our school. Get out of here." The guards looked on impassively; Eckford was on her own. "I looked down the block and saw a bench at the bus stop. Then I thought, 'If I can only get there, I will be safe.' " She ran to the bench and sat down, but a cluster of ruffians had followed her. "Drag her over to the tree," said one of them, calling for a lynching.
>
> Then Benjamin Fine, an education writer for the New York Times, put his arm around Elizabeth. "He raised my chin and said, 'Don't let them see you cry,' " she recalls. Finally a white woman named Grace Lorch, whose husband taught at a local black college, guided Elizabeth away from the mob. The two tried to enter a nearby drugstore to call a cab, but someone slammed the door in their faces. Then they spotted a bus coming and quickly boarded it. Lorch accompanied Elizabeth home safely, but the experience had left its mark.

issue "now is whether or not a head of a sovereign state can exercise his constitutional powers and discretion in maintaining peace and good order within his jurisdiction . . . ."[61]

Federal Judge Ronald Davies, presiding over the case, on September 5th requested that the Justice Department investigate the disruption of the desegregation plan,[62] and on September 7th turned down the school board's request to suspend the desegregation plan.[63] On September 9th, Judge Davies received the Justice Department's report and directed the department to file a petition for injunction against Governor Faubus.[64] A hearing on the matter was set for September 20.[65] Negotiations in the meantime with federal officials, including the President, resolved nothing except that Faubus would obey the decision of the federal district court.[66]

At the hearing on Friday, September 20th, no evidence was presented that showed a concern for violence before September 3rd, and as a result an order ensued enjoining the governor's actions.[67] In response Faubus withdrew the Guard but claimed that a "crucifixion" would be coming.[68] When the following Monday came, Faubus turned out to be nearly correct, for a nearly rioting crowd outside the school caused the withdrawal of the Black students before the day was finished.[69] The following day, none of the Black students

---

Afterwards, the fifteen-year-old sometimes woke in the night, terrified, screaming about the mob.
EYES ON THE PRIZE, *supra* note 2, at 101-02. The call for a lynching was not necessarily rhetorical. Barely two years before, in August 1955 a fifteen-year old Black boy was lynched in Money, Mississippi. *Id.* at 37-57. *See also* S. WHITFIELD, A DEATH IN THE DELTA: THE STORY OF EMMITT TILL (1988). One of the last recorded racial lynchings in the nation occurred two years after the Little Rock crisis, in 1959 in Lumbarton, Mississippi. *See* H. SMEAD, BLOOD JUSTICE: THE LYNCHING OF MACK CHARLES PARKER xi (1986).

61. Telegram, September 4, 1957, Orval Faubus to President Eisenhower, *printed in* Southern School News October, 1957, at 1-2, excerpted at W. RECORD & J. RECORD, *supra* note 28, at 39. FREYER, *supra* note 10, at 105.

62. *Id.*

63. *Id.* Aaron v. Cooper, Civil Action No. 3113 (E.D. Ark. Septemeber 7, 1957). Order, reprinted in 2 RACE REL. LAW REP. 941; oral statement in support thereof, *Id.* at 940. FREYER, *supra* note 10, at 105.

64. FREYER, *supra* note 10 at 106.

65. *Id.*

66. *Id.* Federal officials failed to take a strong stand against Governor Faubus. "Negotiations came to focus on finding some means for Faubus to retreat without making it seem that he was backing down willingly." *Id. See also* Governor Faubus' description of his meeting on September with President Eisenhower. FAUBUS, DOWN FROM THE HILLS *supra* note 5, at 255-58. No public pressure was put on Faubus to change his stance. President Eisenhower, for example, after meeting with Faubus stated that he was "gratified by [the Governor's] constructive and cooperative attitude. . . . [and] was pleased to hear from the Governor of the progress already made in the elimination of segregation in other activites in the State of Arkansas." D. Eisenhower, Statement September 14, 1957, 1957 PUBLIC PAPERS, *supra* note 1, at 674. Brooks Hays, a representative in Congress representing Little Rock, suggested that the President federalize the National Guard and neutralize the governor's authority, but this suggestion was disallowed by federal negotiators. FREYER, *supra* note 10, at 106.

67. FREYER, *supra* note 10 at 107. Aaron v. Cooper, 156 F. Supp. 220 (E.D. Ark. 1957).

68. FREYER, *supra* note 10, at 107.

69. *Id.* at 107, 108. *See* EYES ON THE PRIZE, *supra* note 2, at 105, 106:

The black journalists arrived at Central seconds before the students. As the four got out of their car, the 8:45 school bell rang. Suddenly, someone in the throng of hundreds of whites yelled, "Look, here they come!" The reporters had apparently been mistaken for parents escorting their children to school. About twenty whites began to chase the men down the street; others soon followed. Newsman Alex Wilson chose not to flee and was savaged. "Somebody had a brick in his hand," remembers James Hicks, another of journal-

attended, but another crowd was present at the school, bent on preventing the desegregation of Central High School.[70]

President Eisenhower took action in response to the two days' events. On September 23, 1957, he released a statement promising to use "the full power of the United States including whatever force may be necessary to prevent any obstruction of the law and to carry out the orders of the Federal Court."[71] On September 24th, Eisenhower ordered regular army troops to Little Rock to protect the students, and federalized the Arkansas National Guard as well, as much to prevent their use for any contrary purpose as to aid in the protection of the students.[72]

The soldiers of the 101st Airborne Division left Little Rock on November 27, 1957 and were replaced at Central High School by the federalized National Guard.[73] By this time opposition to desegregation was fixed, and there was still a good deal of unrest at the school.[74] As a result the school board

---

ists, "and instead of throwing the brick, 'cause he was too close, he hit Alex Wilson up the side of his head . . . Wilson was more than six feet tall, an ex-Marine—he went down like a tree."

• • •

With the students out of reach, the mob turned its anger on white journalists on the scene. *Life* magazine reporter Paul Welch and two photographers, Grey Villet and Francis Miller, were harrassed and beaten. The photographers' equipment was smashed to the ground. The crowd began to chant to the white students now staring out of Central's windows, "Don't stay in there with them."

Before noon the mob had swelled to about a thousand people, and Police Chief Gene Smith felt compelled to quell the rioting by removing the black students from the school.

70. FREYER, *supra* note 10, at 108. On September 24, "11 persons [were arrested], including two youths who appeared to be of high school age. All were white men. That brought the number of arrests for the two days to 44, including both whites and Negroes." R. Morin, Sacramento Bee, September 24, 1957, at 1, A6., *reprinted in* W. RECORD & J. RECORD, *supra* note 28, at 67, 68.

71. D. Eisenhower, Statement, September 23, 1957, 1957 PUBLIC PAPERS, *supra* note 1, at 689.

72. FREYER, *supra* note 10, at 108. Technically, Eisenhower merely directed the Secretary of Defense to take "appropriate steps" to enforce the court's order in Little Rock, and to federalize units of the Arkansas guard "as he may deem appropriate." Executive Order 10,730, *supra* note 1.

73. Cooper v. Aaron, 358 U.S. 1, 13 (1958).

74. *See, e.g.*, the notes of Arkansas Gazette reporters in Southern School News, January 1958, *reprinted in* W. RECORD & J. RECORD, *supra* note 28, at 84:

considerable amount of remarks, "Hey, nigger" when the Negroes walk around the corridors. Several have been run into "on purpose" and their books knocked out of their arms. Most of this seems to be done by sophomores and juniors, not the seniors.

• • •

Reportedly the most unpopular [Negro] is Minnie Brown—known as "The Big M" because of her size. Termed "the type who would cause a fight," Minnie, it seems, talks back (the others don't) and reportedly sometimes not in a very lady-like manner. Minnie is supposed to have asked a white boy in a classroom to move his foot. He refused. She stepped on his foot and he slapped her. She went rushing outside for her 101st guard, the teacher told him to stay outside, that that was her classroom and that she would take care of the situation. He did and she did.

Id. Minnie Brown's tendency to retaliate led to disciplinary action against her:

Shortly before Christmas, one of the Little Rock Nine decided to fight back. "For a couple of weeks there had been a number of white kids following us," recalls Ernest Green, "continuously calling us niggers. 'Nigger, nigger, nigger' —one right after the other. Minniejean Brown was in the lunch line with me, and there was this white kid who was much shorter than Minnie . . . he reminded me of a small dog yelping at somebody's leg.

"Minnie had just picked up her chili, and before I could even say . . . 'Minnie, why don't you tell him to shut up?' Minnie . . . turned around and took that chili and dumped it on the dude's head." For a moment, the cafeteria was dead silent, Green remembers, "and then the help, all black, broke into applause. And the white kids there didn't know what to do. It was the first time that anybody [there] had seen somebody black retaliate."

The incident led to Minniejean's suspension. Then, in February, she was expelled from

sought to postpone desegregation.

The Supreme Court resolved the status of desegregation in Little Rock by ruling on September 12, 1958, that desegregation would not be suspended and must proceed apace.[75] Before this event, however, several other events took place. Central High School graduated its first Black student,[76] and Orval Faubus won the nomination of the Democratic Party to a third term as governor by an unprecedented sixty-nine percent of the vote.[77] Brooks Hays, the congressman who had counseled moderation, beat a segregationist candidate in the Democratic primary, normally tantamount to election,[78] but lost in November to a segregationist write-in candidacy initiated two weeks before the election.[79] James Johnson parlayed his high profile on segregation into a seat on the Arkansas Supreme Court.[80]

In these events are two lessons. The first is that desegregation, as the law of the land, was inevitable. The second is that political success in the South often coincided with fervent opposition to desegregation. The crisis in Little Rock was not caused by constitutional theories in conflict, but rather by political surrender to racism.

II. THE PAST AS PROLOGUE

Arkansas politicians were not the only ones who surrendered to racism. The United States Supreme Court surrendered or at least compromised with racism in rendering the implementation formula of *Brown II*. While *Brown I's* 1954 pronouncement that "[s]eparate educational facilities are inherently unequal"[81] represented a major step forward, the pronouncement of *Brown II* in 1955 that desegregation of schools should be implemented "with all deliberate speed,"[82] represented at least a half step back. District judges were to implement the rule of *Brown I* "by dealing with 'varied local problems,' according to 'equitable principles' that were guided by 'practical flexibility' in 'adjusting and reconciling public and private needs.' "[83] *Brown II*, it has been correctly

---

Central after a white girl called her a "nigger bitch" and she in turn denounced the young woman as "white trash."

EYES ON THE PRIZE, *supra* note 2, at 117. Southern School News, March 1958, at 1, *reprinted in* W. RECORD & J. RECORD, *supra* note 28, at 89, reported Brown's reaction to her expulsion:

I just can't take everything they throw at me without fighting back.

I don't think people realize what goes on at Central, she said. "You just wouldn't believe it. They throw rocks, they spill ink on your clothes, they call you "nigger," they just keep bothering you every five minutes.

After Brown's expulsion, students circulated printed cards saying "One Down, Eight to Go." *Id.* EYES ON THE PRIZE, *supra* note 2, at 117.

75. Cooper v. Aaron, 358 U.S. 1 (1958).

76. EYES ON THE PRIZE, *supra* note 2, at 118. Even at this point racism disrupted the peace of the school. After the baccalaureate service a graduating senior spat in the face of a black leaving the ceremony, but was arrested for his deed. Perhaps as a result no incidents were recorded at the graduation ceremony two days later. Southern School News, June 1958, at 10, *reprinted in* W. RECORD & J. RECORD, *supra* note 28, at 95.

77. FREYER, *supra* note 10, at 147. EYES ON THE PRIZE, *supra* note 2, at 118.

78. FREYER, *supra* note 10.

79. *Id.* at 157, 158.

80. *Id.* at 147.

81. *Brown*, 347 U.S. at 494.

82. *Brown*, 349 U.S. at 300.

83. FREYER, *supra* note 10, at 9, (quoting *Brown II*, 349 U.S. at 298-99).

stated, "reflected compromise and equivocation in virtually every line."[84] *Brown II*, in effect, represented a pact between the Supreme Court and the South: desegregation would occur, but slowly and with delay ample for the South to win battles even though it had lost the war.[85]

The Supreme Court in *Brown II* failed to consider the implications of the pre-*Brown* higher education desegregation decisions, and this failure of vision had unfortunate consequences for the point the Court attempted to make clear in *Brown I*. For these decisions and other cases involving the desegregation of higher education constitute a clear suggestion that no matter how forthright and lacking in compromise and equivocation such a mandate might be, the South would find ways to avoid and otherwise minimize the effect of court mandates respecting desegregation.[86]

Missouri ex rel. Gaines v. Canada[87] alone makes this suggestion. Decided in 1938, *Gaines* was the first of a series of desegregation decisions by the Supreme Court before *Brown*. *Gaines* found if not its genesis, certainly its impetus, in the efforts of the NAACP to overcome the legacy of *Plessy v. Ferguson*.[88] While *Plessy* had dealt specifically with segregation in public accommodations, the Supreme Court approved segregation in higher education in 1908 in *Berea College v. Kentucky*,[89] and by 1927 the Supreme Court described the doctrine of separate but equal in education as "many times decided."[90] The NAACP strategy for overcoming separate but equal was to at-

---

84. Hutchinson, *Unanimity and Desegregation: Decision-making in the Supreme Court, 1948-1958.* 68 GEO. L.J. 4, 56 (1979).

85. This pact was completely at odds with the previous understanding that the constitutional right to equality of treatment "is a personal one." McCabe v. Atchison, Topeka, and Santa Fe Railway Co., 235 U.S. 151, 161 (1914). The Supreme Court had long since held that "[i]t is the individual who is entitled to equal protection of the laws . . . ." *Id.* at 161, 162. Even if the individual might still "properly complain that his constitutional privilege has been invaded[,]" *id.* at 162, under *Brown II* an individual whose right to an equal education had been violated might never come to experience desegregation. *Brown II* recognized that "the personal interest of the plaintiffs" was at stake, but stated that this interest was only in achieving an equal education "as soon as practicable." *Brown II,* 349 U.S. at 299 (emphasis added). The brief in *Brown* filed in December 1952 by the U.S. Department of Justice, was the first suggestion ever of such a position, and even its chief architect, Phillip Elman, thought it was "entirely unprincipled, it was just plain wrong as a matter of constitutional law, to suggest that someone whose personal constitutional rights were being violated should be denied relief." Elman, *The Soliciter General's Office, Justice Frankfurter, and Civil Rights Litigation, 1946-1960: An Oral History,* 100 HARV. L. REV. 817, 827 (1987). His reason for making this "unprincipled" suggestion was to assure that the Supreme Court would issue a unanimous opinion in *Brown* overruling *Plessy.* From his discussions with Justice Frankfurter, Elman viewed the issuance of a unanimous opinion as important, the alternative to which he viewed as "an incredible godawful mess: possibly nine different opinions, nine different views on the Court. It would have set back the cause of desegregation; and it would have damaged the Court." *Id.* at 828, 829.

86. This is a clear inference to be made from M. TUSHNET, THE NAACP'S LEGAL STRATEGY AGAINST SEGREGATED EDUCATION, 1925-1950 (1987).

87. 305 U.S. 337 (1938).

88. 163 U.S. 537 (1896). While Lloyd Gaines may have wanted to attend the University of Missouri, there was no guarantee that the NAACP would support him simply on this account. The NAACP took care to properly screen the applicants it supported. They had not only to be "qualified," but "of *outstanding* scholarship . . . neat, personable, and unmistakably a Negro." William Hastie, staff counsel to the NAACP, quoted in TUSHNET, *supra* note 86, at 36, 37. The attack on segregated education began with graduate and professional education; such challenges found plaintiffs more readily available and were more easily litigated since the problem to be resolved generally was not "separate but equal" but instead "separate and non-existant." *Id.* at 36, 42.

89. 211 U.S. 45 (1908).

90. Gong Lum v. Rice, 275 U.S. 78, 86 (1927).

tack the "equal" part of the separate but equal equation. In 1936, in *Pearson v. Murray*,[91] the NAACP convinced the Maryland Supreme Court that an out-of-state scholarship program did not provide for Blacks a legal education equal to that provided for Whites at the University of Maryland. In 1937, in *Gaines* the NAACP made a similar attempt before the Missouri Supreme Court, and failed.[92]

The case was appealed to the United States Supreme Court, where, in 1938, the NAACP won the case.[93] While the Supreme Court did not challenge the doctrine of separate but equal, the Court did recognize as unconstitutional the legislative scheme which allowed Whites to attend law school at the University of Missouri but forbade Blacks to do the same, in the absence of an equal law school for Blacks.[94] The fact that the legislature had provided that the state's university for Blacks, Lincoln University, had the discretion to open a law school was not adequate to overcome the constitutional objection; the mere legislative purpose to establish the separate but equal facility was not enough.[95] The case was remanded to the Missouri Supreme Court for proceedings "not inconsistent" with the United States Supreme Court opinion.[96]

The Supreme Court's opinion in *Gaines* may well have been thought by detractors of segregation as a great victory,[97] and perhaps the principle established did constitute such a victory. But the authorities in Missouri saw to it that Gaines himself never saw the fruits of that victory.

The Missouri Supreme Court rendered its decision on the remanded case in August 1939.[98] Gaines failed in his attempt to achieve entrance to the University of Missouri. The state legislature, between the United States Supreme Court opinion and the second state court opinion, had enacted into law a provision making mandatory the establishment of a law school for Blacks at Lincoln University.[99] The United States Supreme Court had ruled Gaines "entitled to be admitted to the State University *in the absence of other and proper provision for his training.*"[100] Since that absence had been redressed, the state court held that Gaines had no right to attend the University of Missouri.

Lincoln University, thus, would go on to establish a law school, a school with limited funds,[101] only a small number of books,[102] located in a building

---

91. 182 A. 595 (Md. 1936).
92. 113 S.W.2d 783 (Mo. 1937).
93. 305 U.S. 337 (1938).
94. *Id.* at 349, 350
     The basic consideraton is not as to what sort of opportunities other states provide, or whether they are as good as those in Missouri, but as to what opportunities Missouri itself furnishes to white students and denies to negroes solely on the ground of color. The admissibility of laws separating the races in the enjoyment of privileges afforded by the state rests wholly upon the equality of the privileges which the laws give to the separate groups within the state.
Id. at 349.
95. *Id.* at 346, 347.
96. *Id.* at 352.
97. The Nation, for example, carried an article which termed the decision "a milestone, epoch-making," and cause for "unlimiting rejoicing." 147 THE NATION 696 (1938).
98. 131 S.W.2d 217 (Mo. 1939).
99. 1939 Mo. Laws 635. *See* 131 S.W. 2d at 218, 219.
100. *Id.* at 218 (emphasis supplied by the Missouri Supreme Court).
101. The legislature appropriated $200,000, TUSHNET, *supra* note 86, at 73, but the university

shared with a motion picture theater whose sound system treated the law school's students each day to a distraction from study in the sounds of the latest in movie entertainment.[103] Whether Gaines might have successfully challenged the new law school's equality to the law school at the University of Missouri, as the NAACP had planned to test[104] and as the Missouri Supreme Court had suggested as Gaines' remedy,[105] is unknown. During the litigation, Lloyd Gaines had received a master's degree from the University of Michigan and sometime in 1939 had disappeared.[106] By the end of 1939, the NAACP was forced to accept a dismissal of the case.[107]

In effect, the *Gaines* case represented a formula for the frustration of attempts to desegregate educational institutions. The first element of the formula was delay. Gaines had applied to law school in 1935 and was finally denied admission in 1939, by which point he had apparently lost interest in law, at least at the institution he had chosen originally. The second element was a willingness on the part of state officials to overlook the intent of Supreme Court pronouncements on the subject of desegregation and instead to look for loopholes which might allow the choice of segregation to survive. The third element was state legislative and administrative authority responsiveness to less enlightened themes dominating the state's political will, authority determined to place every available obstacle between its people and its schools on the one hand, and desegregation on the other.

Each of these elements was at work in the crisis surrounding the desegregation of Little Rock's Central High School. The Little Rock school board initially proposed only a modest plan of desegregation, then retreated to a minimalist plan when the promise of *Brown II* was anticipated. In short, the Little Rock school authorities took what the Supreme Court gave them, and they took the good along with the bad.

While the response of the school board is not so different from that of state authorities in *Gaines*, the response of Arkansas' governor and legislature and of Arkansas' people, who sought to nullify the judicial mandate of desegregation, is. Part of this difference may well be allayed to the emotional impact of schooling for children as opposed to graduate and professional education for adults. But part of the difference also must be in an unintended effect of *Brown II*. Given suggestions by the Court itself that its own decision in *Brown I* might legally be circumvented, state authorites in Little Rock looked for excuses to believe that the mandate of desegregation was merely an unwelcome suggestion and not the law of the land.

Whether the Supreme Court should have anticipated the resistance of the South in the form of physical violence cannot be ascertained and is not suggested. Nonetheless, the Supreme Court may well have been on notice that the all deliberate speed implementation formula of *Brown II* was merely a call

---

only controlled a fraction of that amount. N. Barksdale, *The Gaines Case and Its Effect in Negro Education in Missouri*, 51 SCHOOL AND SOCIETY 309, 312 (1940).

102. Bluford, *The Lloyd Gaines Story*, 32 J. OF EDUC. SOC. 242, 244 (1958).
103. *"Jim Crow" Law School*, 14 NEWSWEEK 32 (1939); TUSHNET, *supra* note 86, at 73.
104. TUSHNET, *supra* note 86, at 74.
105. *Gaines*, 131 S.W.2d at 219.
106. Bluford, *supra* note 102, at 245, 246; TUSHNET, *supra* note 86, at 74.
107. TUSHNET, *supra* note 86, at 74.

for and an encouragement to official state opposition, even though desegregaton under *Brown I* should have been recognized to be inevitable.

Notice of the South's political will to avoid desegregation is suggested by the *Gaines* case. How much weight this suggestion should bear can only be determined by examining the entire history of pre-*Brown* higher education desegregation. If the suggestion bears the weight indicated by *Gaines*, then the riddle as to why the Little Rock crisis took place finds part of its answer in the refusal of the Supreme Court to have been more forthright in the manner of implementing the moral and constitutional precepts of *Brown I*.

III. THE SOUTHERN FAILURE OF JUSTIFICATION

Part II of this Article suggests that the implementation formula of *Brown II* gave encouragement to the White South in its die-hard enthusiasm for segregated schools and in its desire for elected officials to resist desegregation. In the Little Rock crisis, Arkansas public officials went beyond the *Gaines* opposition formula of delay, determination, and cleverness within the opportunities allowed by law, and actually defied the law. The actions of Arkansas' public officials in turn encouraged White opposition to desegregation.

This point, however, begs the question of whether there is any constitutional rather than political justification for the official actions taken by Arkansas officials. Whatever the justification, it cannot lie in the first amendment,[108] which certainly shields the speech of parties private and public who would resist or even advocate resistance to desegregation. The first amendment, in effect, guarantees the right to disagree, a not inconsiderable right; but the official state actions precipitating the Little Rock crisis went beyond disagreement with the mandate of desegregation, subsuming active frustration of that mandate instead.

A. *The Call of Localism*

The political justifiction offered by Arkansas authorities was that of localism, in effect a skewed reading of states' rights and constitutional federalism.[109] The idea that local concerns might take precedence over a national mandate was not a completely outrageous one. This in fact was the point of

---

108. Congress shall make no law respecting an establishment of religion, or prohibiting the free exercise thereof; or abridging the freedom of speech, or the press; or the right of the people peaceably to assemble, and to petition the Government for a redress of grievances. U.S. CONST. AMEND I.

109. In his inaugural speech for his second term, Governor Faubus stated his opposition " 'to any forcible integration of our public schools. These matters . . . must be left to the will of the people in the various districts. The people must decide on the basis of what is best as a whole for each particular area.' " BARTLEY, MASSIVE RESISTANCE, *supra* note 10, at 261, (quoting Faubus' inaugural address as *reprinted in* the Arkansas Gazette, January 16, 1957). In September 1957, Governor Faubus reiterated desegregation to be a "local problem . . . best . . . solved on the local level according to the peculiar circumstances and conditions of each local school district." Southern School News, October 1957, 2-5, *quoted in* FREYER, *supra* note 10, at 80. State Education Commissioner Ford thought interpositionist measures had virtue in that "it would help [local] districts which wanted to keep their segregated schools." Southern School News, December 1956, p.8, *reprinted in* W. RECORD & J. RECORD, *supra* note 26, at 27. Eight Little Rock aldermen released a statement approving the calling of the Arkansas National Guard to halt desegregation, as this was "the desire of the overwhelming majority of the citizens of Little Rock." Southern School News October 1957, at 2, *reprinted in* W. RECORD & J. RECORD, *supra* note 28, at 42.

the all deliberate speed formula of *Brown II*. But in *Brown II*, the Supreme Court had cited localism only as a factor to be considered by federal district courts when implementing the federal mandate, not as an excuse for state authorities to override the federal mandate. Localism, as the state obstructionists invoked it, was a concept in conflict with the Supremacy Clause of the Constitution, which states clearly that the "Constitution . . . shall be the supreme Law of the Land . . . anything in the Constitution or laws of any State to the contrary nontwithstanding."[110]

In the case of Little Rock, the call to localism is an ironic one, for local governmental interest in Little Rock favored desegregation, and the voices of resistance in Little Rock originated from outside Little Rock[111] and indeed, outside Arkansas.[112] The local school board had found a way to live with the mandate of desegregation, and in this was the will of the local community. Thus, for Governor Faubus and the Arkansas legislature to truly represent local interests, they would have given political and administrative support to the desegregation plan, and not argued localism while in fact frustrating it.[113]

In calling out the National Guard, the governor had not consulted with any of the local authorities in Little Rock, who, a federal district court found, "were prepared to cope with any incidents which might arise . . . ."[114] Instead of furthering local interests, the actions of Governor Faubus were quite to the contrary. The Little Rock school board expressed it well:

> The effect of [calling out of the National Guard,] was to harden the core of opposition to the Plan and cause many persons who theretofore had reluctantly accepted the Plan to believe that there was some power in the State of Arkansas which, when exerted, could nullify the Federal law and permit disobedience of the decree of [the District] Court, and from that date hostility to the Plan was increased and criticism of the officials of the [School] District has become more bitter and unrestrained.[115]

---

110. U.S. CONST. art. IV, cl. 2.

111. Segregationist spokesman and activist James Johnson, a 1957 gubernatorial candidate, hailed from Crossett in southeastern Arkansas. FREYER, *supra* note 10, at 68. For a description of his not inconsiderable influence on the Little Rock crisis, *see* FREYER, *supra* note 10, at 64-66, 68-74 & 78-82. Governor Faubus himself was from Huntsville in Madison county. FAUBUS, DOWN FROM THE HILLS, *supra* note 5, at 1, 3. Even though he resided in Little Rock as a state government official in 1949-53 and after taking office as Governor in 1955, Faubus was nonetheless a state official and not a local one. FREYER, *supra* note 10, at 23. 11 WHO'S WHO *supra* note 30, at 325. *C.f.* the desegregation of Hoxie, Arkansas. *See* FREYER, *supra* note 10, at 63-63. *See also* note 111 *infra*.

112. *E.g.*, Rev. J. A. Lovell of Dallas, Texas was a guest speaker before the Little Rock Capital Citizens' Council, FREYER, *supra* note 10, at 93. Marvin Griffin, Governor of Georgia, on August 22, 1957 delivered in Little Rock a speech which is credited by Freyer and also Governor Faubus as being responsible for generating a major change of opinion in Little Rock and as being the impetus for Faubus' dispatch of the National Guard to prevent desegregation. FREYER, *supra* note 10, at 100-01, 103. *See also* Southern School News, September 1957 at 7, *reprinted in* part in W. RECORD & J. RECORD, *supra* note 28, at at 32-33, for a report of Griffin's speech.

113. *See* FREYER, *supra* note 10, at 116 and citations therein. When the governor called out the National Guard to prevent desegregation, the mayor of Little Rock noted that "[t]he people of Little Rock recently had a school board election and elected by an overwhelming vote the school board members who advocated [gradual integration]." In exasperation he offered that "were [it] not for my own respect for due process of law, I would be tempted to issue an executive order interposing the city of Little Rock between Gov. Faubus and the Little Rock school board." Southern School News October 1957 p. 1, *reprinted in* W. RECORD & J. RECORD, *supra* note 28, at 37.

114. Cooper v. Aaron, 358 U.S. at 10, (citing Aaron v. Cooper, 156 F. Supp. 220 at 225).

115. Cooper v. Aaron, 358 U.S. at 10, (quoting the school board's petition before the district court).

In short, the call to localism was not only misplaced, but hypocritical as well. Addtionally, in Little Rock the call to localism was self-serving. Whether local interests were argued to predominate depended on the federal interests at stake. In the South, "[l]ocalism, manifested as a general distrust of outsiders and mixed with a touch of paranoia, whether anti-Communist, anti-semitic, or anti-big business, was a dynamic element in southern attitudes."[116] Similarly and yet by contrast, "at times, [southern politicians] appealed fervently to the Constitution as the touchstone of benign national strength; but on other occasions they attacked the evil of the federal octopus with all the resolutions of demogogues."[117] Where federal power brought economic benefit, it was extolled; but when federal power threatened the Southern way of life, it was villified. "In such an environment political expediency gave words such as *federal, state's rights,* and *Constitution* a manifestly symbolic meaning."[118]

This framework belies but also explains the assertion of localism as a justification for the official actions taken opposing desegregation in the Little Rock crisis. Localism, states' rights, and federalism were concepts that could not be divorced from the context in which they were raised, and thus offered no independent justification for any activity undertaken in Little Rock by official actors opposing desegregation. The bottom line is that official resistance in Little Rock was simply political. The best politics became the politics of obstruction and resistance.

B. *The Doctrine of Interposition*

To be sure, this resistance had a purportedly legal basis. The basis was the doctrine of interposition. Simply put, according to the doctrine, when the federal government or some facet thereof undertook an unconstitutional act, a state could interpose itself between its citizens and the federal government, thereby nullifying the power of the federal government to act. By the time of the Little Rock crisis, however, the doctrine had been completely scuttled as an acceptable facet of constitutional law.

The doctrine of interposition did not rise fully formed from the heads of Southern obstructionists, as did Athena rise from the head of Zeus in classical Greek mythology.[119] The classical origin of interposition lies instead in the writings of such early American giants as James Madison and John C. Calhoun. Madison saw the power of state governments in this light:

> [I]n case of a deliberate, palpable and dangerous exercise [by the federal government] of other powers not granted by the said compact, the States who are parties thereto have the right, and are in duty bound, to interpose for arresting the progress of the evil, and for maintaining, within their respective limits, the authorities, rights, and liberties appertaining to them.[120]

---

116. FREYER, *supra* note 10, at 10-11.
117. *Id.* at 11.
118. *Id.*
119. *See* E. HAMILTON, MYTHOLOGY 29-30 (1940).
120. Resolution of Dec. 24, 1798 VA. STAT. AT LARGE 192 (1806). Authored by Madison, the resolution is quoted in part in 1 RACE REL. LAW REP. 468. Thomas Jefferson authored the corresponding Kentucky resolution of 1798, dated November 16, 1798, *reprinted in* E. WARFIELD, KENTUCKY RESOLUTIONS OF 1798 75-85 (1894). K. ANDRESEN, THE THEORY OF STATE INTERPOSITION TO CONTROL FEDERAL ACTION 49 (1960) (University Microforms Inc.) (hereinafter cited as ANDRESEN, STATE INTERPOSITION). Jefferson's draft can be found at P. FORD, 7 THE

The powers of the federal judiciary were particularly suspect in Madison's view. He wrote in 1799:

> However true, therefore, it may be that the judicial department is, in all questions submitted to it by the forms of the Constitution, to decide in the last resort, this resort must necessarily be deemed the last in relation to the authorities of the other departments of the Government; not in relation to the rights of the parties to the constitutional compact, from which the judicial as well as the other departments hold their delegated trusts.
>
> On any other hypothesis the delegation of judicial power would annul the authority delegating it; and the concurrence of this department with the others in usurped powers might subvert forever, and beyond the possible reach of any rightful remedy, the very Constitution which all were instituted to preserve.[121]

Calhoun emphatically agreed. "This right of interposition . . . I conceive to be the fundamental principle of our system."[122] Yet, as Calhoun recognized, on the matter of interposition there were two sides to the tale.[123]

The contrary argument was put by Chief Justice Marshall in *McCulloch v. Maryland*:

> [T]he constitution and the laws made in pursuance thereof are supreme; . . .they control the constitutions and laws of the respective states and cannot be controlled by them. . . . It is of the very essence of supremacy, to remove all obstacles to its action within its own sphere, and so to modify every power vested in subordinate governments, as to exempt its own operations from their own influence.[124]

Since in *Marbury v. Madison* it had already been established that "the province and duty of the judicial department [is] to say what the law is,"[125] the case for those opposing interposition could with *McCulloch* be considered to have been closed.

But the arguments over interposition had preceded *Marbury* and *McCulloch*, and they continued beyond these cases as well. The first expositions of the doctrine of interposition in the nation's history under the Constitution came a scant ten years after the Constitution's ratification, with the enactment of the Alien and Sedition Acts of 1798.[126] Objecting to these acts on the ground that they violated the strictures of the first amendment, Kentucky and Virginia passed resolutions of interposition and urged other states to do the same.[127] A constitutional confrontation was spared when the Alien and Sedition Acts expired in 1801.

WRITINGS OF THOMAS JEFFERSON 289-309 (1892-99). For more on the views of Jefferson and Madison, *see* ANDRESEN, STATE INTERPOSITION 69-78.

121. Committee report to Virginia House of Delegates, Session of 1799-1800, authored by Madison, quoted at 1 RACE REL. LAW REP. 469, also *reprinted in* E. POWELL, NULLIFICATION AND SECESSION IN THE UNITED STATES 100-04 (1897).

122. J. Calhoun, Address of July 26, 1831, *printed in* 6 WORKS OF JOHN C. CALHOUN 61 (1831), *quoted in* 1 RACE REL. LAW REP. 487.

123. *Id.*

124. 17 U.S. (4 Wheat) 316, 426-27 (1819).

125. 5 U.S. (1 Cranch) 137, 177 (1803).

126. Act of June 25, 1798, ch. 58, 1 Stat. 570 (1798); Act of July 14, 1798, ch. 74, 1 Stat. 596 (1798).

127. *Supra* note 119:

> Actually, there were four sets of resolutions, each of the two state legislatures passing one set in 1798, with Kentucky passing a second set the next year, followed by virginia in 1800. . . . Copies of the first sets of resolutions were sent to the other states by Kentucky and Virginia. Nine states replied to Virginia and eight to Kentucky, all disagreeing with the

The Supreme Court first passed directly on the doctrine of interposition in the 1809 case of *United States v. Peters*.[128] In *Peters*, the Supreme Court issued a writ of mandamus to a federal judge to enforce a judgment against the state of Pennsylvania. The Pennsylvania legislature had passed an act which had defied an order of the federal circuit court requiring the governor "to demand for the use of the state of Pennsylvania, the money which [was the subject of the judgement in federal court],"[129] asserting that the federal court had had no jurisdiction to hear the case in question as a result of the eleventh amendment.

The Supreme Court in *Peters* disposed of the eleventh amendment question against the interest of the state, and in doing so rejected the legislature's resolution of interposition:

> If the legislatures of the several states may at will, annul the judgments of the courts of the United States, and destroy the rights acquired under those judgments, the constitution itself becomes a solemn mockery, and the nation is deprived of the means of enforcing its laws by the instrumentality of its own tribunals. . . . If the ultimate right to determine the jurisdiction of the courts of the Union is placed by the constitution in the several state legislatures, then this act concludes the subject; but if that power necessarily resides in the supreme judicial tribunal of the nation, then the jurisdiction of the District Court of Pennsylvania, over the case in which that jurisdiction was exercised, ought to be most deliberately examined; and the act of Pennsylvania, with whatever repect it may be considered, cannot be permitted to prejudice the question.[130]

The "Pennsylvania Rebellion" did not end, however, with the opinion in *Peters*, for the state continued in the rhetoric and the exercise of interposition. The governor sent a message to the legislature stating his intention to call out the militia to prevent enforcement of the court decree. The legislature responded with resolutions maintaining "a most exteme statement of State-rights and Nullification" and denying the power of the Supreme Court to have adjudicated the case.[131] In the end, when a federal marshal sought to serve process in connection with the case, he was met with the state militia, and the general of the militia was ultimately indicted, arrested, and convicted for his deeds, all with the support of James Madison,[132] then President of the United States. By this time, however, the troops had been withdrawn and judgment had been executed in pursuance of the decree in *Peters*, and within a month of the general's conviction, he received a pardon from President Madison.[133] The point had been made, however — the state had no power to oppose the

---

interposition ideas expressed in the interposition resolutions of the two protesting states. These replies caused the issuance of the second sets of Resolutions.
ANDRESEN, STATE INTERPOSITION, *supra* note 119, at 48, 49 (footnotes omitted). These resolutions are reprinted together in J. ELLIOT, 4 THE DEBATES IN THE SEVERAL STATE CONVENTIONS 528-29, 540-44 (1876).

128. 9 U.S. (5 Cranch) 115 (1809).
129. *Id.* at 135.
130. *Id.* at 136.
131. 1809 Pa. Laws 200, approved April 3, 1809.
132. 1 RACE REL. LAW REP. 476-77 (1956).
133. *Id.* The Pennsylvania Rebellion is discussed in ANDRESEN, STATE INTERPOSITION, *supra* note 120, at 28-30, and C. WARREN, 1 THE SUPREME COURT IN UNITED STATES HISTORY 96-101 (1926).

authority of the courts of the federal government, and the federal government was entirely capable of enforcing this position.

Each new incident of interposition following *Peters* resulted in political or constitutional rejection of interposition. In 1816, in *Martin v. Hunter's Lessee*,[134] the Supreme Court rejected the position that Virginia's highest court could refuse to obey a Supreme Court decision rendered on appeal from the Virginia court.[135] The Hartford Convention of 1814, involved New Englanders who opposed the War of 1812, resented the advantages the South accured as a result of the three fifths clause of the Constitution[136] and feared southern and westward expansion, defended interposition by the states in cases of "deliberate, dangerous and palpable" infractions of the Constitution.[137] The convention resulted in "the complete annihilation from the American political scene of the Federalist party . . . ."[138] In 1819, *McCulloch v. Maryland*[139] rejected Maryland's attempt to oppose the institution and continued operation of the Bank of the United States.

South Carolina's Ordinance of Nullification[140] declaring the federal tariffs of 1828[141] and 1832[142] void within the state met with President Jackson's quick dispatch of the navy to Charleston Harbor,[143] four companies of artillery and five thousand muskets to Fort Moultrie outside of Charleston,[144] and

---

134. 14 U.S. (1 Wheat) 304 (1816).

135. A bad idea, like bad grass, is hard to kill. This same notion that the Supreme Court was without power to override a state court was afoot when the California Supreme Court refused to allow a writ of error to the United States Supreme Court in Johnson v. Gordon, 4 Cal. 368 (1854). The California legislature responded in 1855 by making it a crime for a state judge or clerk of court not to comply with the Federal Judiciary Act of 1789. Warren, *Legislative and Judicial Attacks on the Supreme Court*, 47 AM. U.L. REV. 161, 176 (1913). Later, but over a strong dissenting opinion, the California Supreme Court acceded to the validity of the act in Ferris v. Cooper, 11 Cal. 176 (1858).

136. U.S. CONST. art I, § 2 read, in part,

Representatives and direct Taxes shall be apportioned among the several States which may be included within this Union, according to their respective Numbers, which shall be determined by adding to the whole Number of free persons, including those bound to Service for a Term of Years, excluding Indians not taxed, three-fifths of all other Persons. . .

By the terms of the three-fifths clause, all free persons, whether Black or White, would be counted. Slaves, who did not vote and who could not govern, were counted as sixty percent of a person in the state in which they resided for purposes of federal apportionment. The South primarily benefitted as the overwhelming number of slaves resided in that region of the country. In 1790, 658,000 of the nation's 698,000 slaves resided in the South; in 1800, 857,00 of 893,000; and in 1810, 1,161,000 of 1,191,000. DEPARTMENT OF COMMERCE, BUREAU OF THE CENSUS, NEGRO POPULATION, 1790-1915 at 55 (1918).

137. REPORT OF THE HARTFORD CONVENTION, printed in T. DWIGHT, HISTORY OF THE HARTFORD CONVENTION 352, 361 (1833).

138. 1 RACE REL. LAW REP. 479-80. *See* J. BANNER, JR., TO THE HARTFORD CONVENTION (1970) and D. ROBINSON, SLAVERY IN THE STRUCTURE OF AMERICAN POLITICS, 1765-1820, at 278-82 (1971).

139. 17 U.S. (4 Wheat) 316 (1819).

140. S. C. Ordinance of November 24, 1832, *reprinted in* STATE PAPERS ON NULLIFICATION 28 (1854).

141. Act of May 19, 1828, ch. 55, 4 Stat. 270 (1828).

142. Act of July 14, 1832, ch. 227, 4 Stat. 583 (1832).

143. Letter of Andrew Jackson to Joel R. Poinsett, December 2, 1832, printed in W. GOLDSMITH, 1 THE GROWTH OF PRESIDENTIAL POWER 268, 269 (1974) (hereinafter cited as PRESIDENTIAL POWER). 1 RACE REL. LAW REP. 486.

144. 1 PRESIDENTIAL POWER, *supra* note 143, at 285. Letter of Andrew Jackson to Joel R. Poinsett *supra* note 143. Jackson was determined to end the South Carolina threat. In a letter to Poinsett dated December 9, 1832, Jackson boasted that if need be, he could place 100,000 armed men

a request to Congress for the enactment of a bill allowing him to enforce the federal law by use of the military as he saw fit.[145] A compromise ensued. A less onerous tariff passed Congress on March 2, 1833,[146] simultaneous to the grant of authority Jackson sought,[147] and South Carolina withdrew the Statute of Nullification.[148]

In *Worchester v. Georgia*,[149] the Supreme Court in 1832 heard the appeal of a conviction in the Georgia courts for failure to obtain a state license to enter Cherokee Indian territory, permission for which entry had already been granted under federal authority. The state did not appear before the Supreme Court to defend the conviction, its legislature having declared any attempt by the Supreme Court at reversal of any state conviction to be "unconstitutional and arbitrary," and any appearance before the Supreme Court a compromise to the dignity of Georgia's sovereignty.[150] The men convicted were released from state custody after the Supreme Court rejected the state's position, calling it "repugnant to the constitution, laws, and treaties of the United States."[151]

The intersectional battle over slavery represented the occasion for numer-

---

in South Carolina within eighty days. 1 PRESIDENTIAL POWER 269, 270. In a January 13, 1833 letter to Vice-President Martin Van Buren, Jackson explained that with troops from North Carolina, Tennessee and the western states he could march with 40,000 men; from Pennsylvania alone he could depend on 50,000 men, and additionally from North Carolina he could depend on an entire regiment. 1 PRESIDENTIAL POWER 285, 286.

145. 1 RACE REL. LAW REP. 486. *See also* A. Jackson, *Proclamation*, December 10, 1832, in 1 PRESIDENTIAL POWER, *supra* note 143, at 271-85, in which Jackson stated in no uncertain terms the necessity and his determination to put down the nullification crisis.

146. Act of March 2, 1833, ch. 55, 4 Stat. 629 (1833).

147. Act of March 2, 1833, ch. 57, 4 Stat. 632 (1833).

148. S. C. Ordinance of March 15, 1833, *reprinted in* STATE PAPERS, *supra* note 140, at 352. This was not South Carolina's first step of conciliation and/or capitulation. Within three weeks of Jackson's December 10 proclamation, the Ways and Means Committeee of the U.S. House of Representatives proposed to reduce tariffs, and on January 21, 1833, South Carolina suspended the nullification statute. C. BOUCHER, THE NULLIFICATION CONTROVERSY IN SOUTH CAROLINA 271-275 (1916) (reprinted 1968). S. MORRISON and H. COMMAGER, THE GROWTH OF THE AMERICAN REPUBLIC 484 (1942) (hereinafter MORRISON and COMMAGER). The state was not wholly chastened by the episode. When the state repealed the statute of nullification, it also passed another nullifying the "force bill." S. C. Ordinance of March 18, 1833, *reprinted in* STATE PAPERS at 373. The need to test the new statute was not anticipated, because the state was pleased with the compromise tariff. MORRISON and COMMAGER 484.

149. 31 U.S. (6 Pet.) 515 (1832).

150. 1830 Ga. Laws 282, approved Dec. 22, 1830. The summary of arguments by counsel at 31 U.S. (6 Pet.) 534, 535 reveals no argument by the state of Georgia. *See also* 1 RACE REL. LAW REP. 490.

151. Worchester v. Georgia, 31 U.S. (6 Pet.) at 561. Andrew Jackson, then President, is reputed to have said of this decision, "Well, John Marshall has made his decision, now let him enforce it." A. MCLAUGLIN, A CONSTITUTIONAL HISTORY OF THE UNITED STATES 429 (1936). This statement may have given the state some comfort, but Jackson "did not in fact, refuse to aid in enforcing the Court's decision; and the charge . . . that Jackson actually defied the Court's decrees is clearly untrue." C. WARREN, 1 SUPREME COURT 769. Instead, Jackson negotiated a settlement of the dispute underlying the case, obtaining the release of the men who had been imprisoned for failure to obtain the state license, and in so doing secured the support of Georgia in the South Carolina nullification crisis. R. REMINI, ANDREW JACKSON 129-40 (1966). Georgia Resolution of November 29, 1832, *reprinted in* STATE PAPERS 271. *See* E. Miles, *After John Marshall's Decision: Worchester v. Georgia and the Nullification Crisis*, 39 JOURNAL OF SOUTHERN HISTORY 539 (1973). This did not resolve the state's recalcitrance on the issue of the authority of the U.S. Supreme Court. In 1854, the Georgia Supreme Court considered itself "co-equal and co-ordinate with the Supreme Court of the United States, and not inferior and subordinate to that Court." Padelford, Fay & Co. v. Mayor and Aldermen of Savannah, 14 Ga. 438, 506 (1854).

ous conflicts between the authorities of free states and the federal government,[152] which, under the Fugitive Slave Clause of the Constitution and the acts passed by Congress to enforce it, had a position on this matter in line with that of the Southern states.[153] By and large, Northern judges respected the supremacy of the federal government, even when they engaged in legal gymnastics to maintain the freedom of those who might otherwise be slaves.[154]

But *Ableman v. Booth*,[155] a case decided by the Supreme Court in 1859, represents an instance in which the Wisconsin Supreme Court, because of the political nature of a case dealing with slavery, did not so respect the federal perogative, releasing by writ of habeas corpus a federal prisoner accused of illegally freeing from federal custody a fugitive slave. The Wisconsin court directed its clerk of court to make no return to the writ of error to the United States Supreme Court.[156] Writing for the Court, Chief Justice Roger Taney rejected the Wisconsin court's position, stressing the need for one final voice to decide all federal issues. The Wisconsin legislature nonetheless passed a resolution questioning the need for a supreme judicial voice when the nation was constituted as a union of separate sovereigns.[157] The reaction in other Northern states to this resolution was approval for the position of Wisconsin.[158] By contrast, in the slave South there was approval for Justice Taney's position and criticism for that of Wisconsin.[159]

The irony of *Ableman v. Booth* is that commentators in slave states such as Virginia and Georgia, states which had previously taken strong stands in favor of interposition, were now applauding the rejection of this doctrine.[160] This irony suggests that positions on interposition develop and change in accordance with whose ox is being gored and whether the pain involved is per-

---

152. *See* P. FINKELMAN, AN IMPERFECT UNION (1981); R. COVER, JUSTICE ACCUSED (1975).
153. D. FEHRENBACHER, THE DRED SCOTT CASE 36-47 (1978).
154. R. COVER, JUSTICE ACCUSED, *supra* note 152, at 159-191.
155. 62 U.S. (21 How.) 479 (1856). *See* T. MORRIS, FREE MEN ALL: THE PERSONAL LIBERTY LAWS OF THE NORTH, 1780-1861, at 173-180 (1974) (hereinafter cited as FREE MEN ALL) for a discusssion of this case.
156. 62 U.S. (21 How.) at 512.
157. 1859 Wis. Laws Joint Resolution IV, p. 247, March 19, 1859.
158. *See* MORRIS, *supra* note 155, at 186-199.
159. *Id.* at 199-201, 203-204. *See also* 1 RACE REL. LAW REP. 495; and note 157, *infra*.
160. Consider the views of Robert Toombs, Senator from Georgia:

On January 24, 1860, Senator . . . Toombs . . . launched a vitriolic attack on the legislation of the free states and on the recent efforts to obtain laws preventing slave-hunting. On the floor of the United States Senate he taunted the "Black Republicans" who "mock at constitutional obligations, jeer at oaths." In every state where they held power the Fugitive State Law was a dead letter. It had been nullified, he explained in a later speech, by "higher-law" teachings, acts passed under the fraudulent pretense of preventing kidnapping, and "new constructions" such as with the writ of habeas corpus. He was indignant particularly about the judgments of the Wisconsin Supreme Court, and the effort to obtain a new Personal Liberty Law in New York. Wisconsin, said Toombs, "who got rotten before she got ripe, comes to us even in the first few years of her admission, with her hands all smeared with the blood of a violated Constitution, all polluted with perjury." The law introduced in New York exceeded those in other states "in iniquity, in plain, open, shameless, and profligate perfidy."

FREE MEN ALL, *supra* note 155, at 199-200 (footnotes deleted). William Smith, representing Virginia in the House of Representatives, called for a special House committee to be instructed to consider the policy of expelling from the union of states any state "which shall, by her legislation, aim to nullify an act of Congress." CONG. GLOBE, 36th Cong. 2d Sess., Dec. 17, 1860, 107 *quoted in* FREE MEN ALL, *supra* note 151, at 203, 204.

ceived to be acceptable.[161] This suggestion explains the willingness of those same states who applauded *Ableman v. Booth* barely a year later to engage in secession, the ultimate act of interposition.

In the Civil War that followed, secession was crushed. By implication, interposition was rejected, both constitutionally and in terms of national politics. As one Georgia court stated in 1890, "[a]fter the State has yielded to the federal army, it can well afford to yield to the federal judiciary. . . ."[162] The stand of interpositon by Orval Faubus and the Arkansas legislature was thusly based on grounds other than the thoroughly reprobated doctrine of interposition. Like the call to localism itself, the Arkansas claim to interposition stands as misplaced, and in the end hypocritical and self-serving.

IV. AFTERMATH: THE AVOIDANCE OF ANARCHY

A. *Cooper v. Aaron*

By the end of the 1957-58 school year, Little Rock's Central High School had seen not only the appearance of nine Black children on a previously all-White campus, but also regular army troops, National Guardsmen, shouting crowds, and scores of news personnel. The school had become the center of national attention, and what the nation saw was "chaos, bedlam and turmoil."[163] There had been "repeated incidents of more or less serious violence directed against Negro students and their property,"[164] the entire educational program had been compromised by "tension and unrest,"[165] and in short, "the situation was 'intolerable.' "[166]

This was what the Little Rock school board perceived when it petitioned the federal district court in February 1958 to postpone for two and one-half years the desegregation of Central High School. The board's position was that "because of extreme public hostility, . . . engendered largely by the official attitudes and actions of the Governor and the legislature, the maintenance of a sound educational program at Central High School, with the Negro students in attendance, would be impossible."[167] In June the district court ruled in the school board's favor, and after the Eighth Circuit reversed the district court in mid-August, the school board appealed to the Supreme Court.[168] In a fast paced and highly unusual series of moves, the Supreme Court set September 8th as the day on or before which a petition for certiorari might be filed.[169] It set September 11th as the date for argument, decided the case per curiam on September 12th,[170] and released an extended opinion on the matter on September 29, 1958, under the names of each of the nine justices.[171]

---

161. This suggestion is made further by James Madison's stand as President of the United States against interposition during the Pennsylvania rebellion as opposed to his stand in its favor during the time of the Alien and Sedition Acts. *See, supra* note 120 and text at n. 118 and 126-131.

162. Wrought Iron Fence Co. v. Johnson, 84 Ga. 754, 759, 11 S.E. 233, 235 (1890).

163. Cooper v. Aaron, 358 U.S. at 13 (quoting the district court at 163 F. Supp. 20-26).

164. *Id.*

165. *Id.*

166. *Id.*

167. *Id.* at 10.

168. *Id.* at 13-14.

169. *Id.* at 14.

170. *Id. See also* 358 U.S. at 5.

171. 358 U.S. 1 (1958).

In the September 29th opinion, under the name *Cooper v. Aaron*, the Supreme Court emphasized two main points. The first was that the implementation formula of *Brown II*, while it did not necessarily call for immediate and/or total desegregation in every circumstance, would not countenance delay on the basis of opposition engendered, allowed, implemented, and incited by state officials:[172]

> [I]n many locations, obedience to the duty of desegregation would require the immediate general admission of Negro children, otherwise qualified as students for their appropriate classes, at particular schools. On other hand, a District Court, after analysis of the relevant factors (which, of course, excludes hostility to racial desegregation), might conclude that justification existed for not requiring the present nonsegregated admission of all qualified Negro children. . . . the courts should scrutinize the program of the school authorities to make sure that they had developed arrangements pointed toward the earliest practicable completion of desegregation, and had taken appropriate steps to put their program into effective operation. . . . only a prompt start, diligently and earnestly pursued, to eliminate racial segregation from the public schools could constitute good faith compliance.[173]

Thus, three years after *Brown II*, the Supreme Court recognized the obstructionist gloss that might be put on *Brown II* and sought to overcome that interpretation. Whatever the compromise intended by the words "all deliberate speed," the Supreme Court served notice in *Cooper v. Aaron* that it intended no equivocation about the message of *Brown I*.

The Supreme Court emphasized also that *Brown I* had been reached by a unanimous court after "the most serious consideration," and even with the advent of three new justices replacing members of the *Brown I* court, the Supreme Court was yet unanimous in reaffirming *Brown I*.[174] With this emphasis, the Supreme Court reached toward its second main point in *Cooper v. Aaron*. No matter how distasteful, *Brown I*'s stricture that "separate facilities . . . are inherently unequal"[175] was not simply an unpalatable demand of the Supreme Court to be ignored by states at their pleasure and for the false protection of their citizens. It was instead part of the "supreme law of the land," binding under the supremacy clause not only on the federal government but on the states as well.[176]

The Supreme Court found a firm basis for this second point in as fundamental an opinion as *Marbury v. Madison*, wherein "Chief Justice Marshall, speaking for a unanimous court, referr[ed] to the Constitution as 'the fundamental and paramount law of the nation,' declar[ing] also that 'It is emphatically the province and duty of the judical department to say what the law is.' "[177] The Court also found support even in the words of Chief Justice Taney, a defender of the law of White supremacy,[178] when he wrote in *Ableman*

---

172. *Id.* at 6-7.
173. *Id.* at 7.
174. *Id.* at 19.
175. *Brown I, supra* note 6, at 494.
176. Cooper v. Aaron, 358 U.S. at 18.
177. *Id.* (quoting *Marbury*, 5 U.S. (1 Cranch) 137, 177 (1803)).
178. Chief Justice Taney delivered the opinion of the Supreme Court in *Dred Scott v. Sanford*, 60 U.S. (19 How.) 393 (1856), which concluded that blacks "are not included and were not intended to be included, under the word 'citizens' in the Constitution, and therefore claim none of the rights and privileges which that instrument provides for and secures to the citizens of the United States." *Id.* at 404. Historically, and by implication at the time of the decision, Blacks were "regarded as beings of

v. Booth that the supremacy of the federal government as stipulated in the Constitution "reflected the framers 'anxiety to preserve it in full force, in all its powers, and to guard against resistance to or evasion of its authority, on the part of a State.' "[179] As Chief Justice Marshall put it in *United States v. Peters*, and as the Court in *Cooper v. Aaron* quoted with approval, "If the legislatures of the several states may, at will, annul the judgments of the courts of the United States, and destroy the rights acquired under those judgments, the constitution itself becomes a solemn mockery. . . ."[180]

Thus, this second point by the Supreme Court, that its interpretation of the Constitution is supreme law, was meant to hopefully lay to final rest the moribund but undead doctrine of interposition. By exposing to the light of constitutional scrutiny the strategy of state officials in Arkansas, the Court hoped to ease the course of desegregation throughout the South, and not incidentally reiterate what *Marbury v. Madison* made clear a century and a half earlier, the duty of all to follow the law as established by the federal judiciary, in general, and the Supreme Court, in particular.

B. *A Cautionary Note*

The events which led to *Cooper v. Aaron* sound a cautionary note about the anarchy which can ensue when federal authority is treated by the states as less than what the supremacy clause says, "the supreme Law of the Land."[181] That is an anarchy that Attorney General Edwin Meese III then invited in his October 21, 1986 speech at Tulane University.[182]

Meese argued that *Cooper v. Aaron* cannot mean what it says, when it states that the Supreme Court's interpretation of the Constitution is the supreme law of the land.[183] If the *Cooper v. Aaron* court were right, Meese argues, then each decision by the Supreme Court would be immutably fixed for all time. *Plessy v. Ferguson*, for example, could not have been overruled by *Brown I*.[184] *Batson v. Kentucky*,[185] which guaranteed for each individal defendant the right to be free from racial discrimination in petit jury selection by allowing proof of discrimination in each case, could not have overruled *Swain v. Alabama*,[186] which made "peremptory challenges to persons on the basis of race virtually unreviewable under the Constitution."[187] And the position of Abraham Lincoln that the *Dred Scott*[188] decision was unconstitutional would be just as wrong as Lincoln presumed *Dred Scott* to have been decided incorrectly.[189]

---

an inferior order . . . so far inferior, that they had no rights which the white man was bound to respect. . . ." *Id.* at 407.

179. Cooper v. Aaron, 358 U.S. at 18 (quoting *Abelman*, 62 U.S. (21 How.) 506, 524 (1859)).
180. *Id.* (quoting *Peters*, 9 U.S. (5 Cranch) 115, 136 (1809)).
181. U.S. CONST., art. vi, cl. 2.
182. Meese, *The Law of the Constitution*, 61 TUL. L. REV. 979 (1987) (hereinafter cited as Meese).
183. *Id.* at 986.
184. *Id.* at 983.
185. 476 U.S. 79 (1986).
186. 380 U.S. 202 (1965).
187. Meese, *supra* note 182, at 983.
188. Dred Scott v. Sanford, 60 U.S. (19 Haw.) 393 (1856).
189. Meese, *supra* note 182, at 984, 985. Attorney General Meese has not chosen these examples by happenstance. They are meant to tug at our sense of racial equity, to emotionally predispose and manipulate his audience toward his position. This is a cheap shot on Meese's part. Conspicuous by

Professor Neuborne has summarized the Meese position better than Meese has put it himself:

> The Attorney General and his executive branch predecessors derive the executive's asserted legal right to "nonacquiesce" in settled judicial precedent from a rigid reading of *Marbury v. Madison.* In *Marbury,* Chief Justice Marshall justified the judiciary's power over both Congress and the President as a necessary incident to the process of resolving a pending judicial proceeding. According to Marshall, judicial review is merely the *ex necessitate* selection by a judge of a governing rule of law from among the competing candidates put forth by the parties. Even if *Marbury* establishes that such an *ex necissitate* selection is valid within the confines of the judicial branch, why, the Attorney General asks, should it have self-executing impact on the future activities of the executive branch as they affect non-parties? While doctrines of *stare decisis* or preclusion will often make the outcome of future judicial proceedings involving the same issues highly predictable, the Attorney General argues that strict adherence to Marshall's analysis in *Marbury* entitles the executive branch to adhere to its view of the governing law at the administrative level unless and until the matter once again reaches the courts, where the judiciary decides the issue. Of course, given the predictability of the ultimate judicial outcome, the executive might, as a matter of respect, prudence, or *real politik,* elect to recede voluntarily from its legal position, but according to the Attorney General's theory, the executive is under no legal obligation to do so.[190]

This position of Attorney General Meese is not inherently unreasonable,[191] but it is dangerous. If the Supreme Court is not the final arbiter of the Constitution, then each branch of the federal government under the Meese theory of authoritativeness can act alone and at odds with the other. This idea of a "cacaphonous constitution" lacks the virtues of clarity, finality, practicality, and the capability of guidance.[192] Only if one locks the Constitution into

---

its absence from Meese's speech and even the footnoted publication is any reference to other decisions having nothing to do with race in which the Supreme Court has overruled itself on constitutional issues. *See, e.g.,* Garcia v. San Antonio Metropolitan Transit Authority, 469 U.S. 528 (1985) (overruling National League of Cities v. Usery, 426 U.S. 833 (1976)); Brandenburg v. Ohio, 395 U.S. 444 (1969), (overruling Whitney v. California, 274 U.S. 357 (1927)); Baker v. Carr, 369 U.S. 186 (1962), (effectively overruling Colegrove v. Green, 328 U.S. 549 (1946)); Mapp v. Ohio, 367 U.S. 643 (1961), (overruling Wolf v. Colorado, 338 U.S. 25 (1949)); West Virginia State Bd. of Educ. v. Barnette, 319 U.S. 624 (1943), (overruling Minersville School Dist. v. Gobitis, 310 U.S. 586 (1940)); and Erie R.R. Co. v. Tompkins, 304 U.S. 64 (1938) (overruling Swift v. Tyson, 41 U.S. (16 Pet.) 1 (1842)).

190. Neuborne. *The Binding Quality of Supreme Court Precedent,* 61 TUL. L. REV. 991, 993-94 (1987).

191. *See, e.g.,* Levinson, *Could Meese Be Right This Time?,* 243 THE NATION 689 (1986), reprinted in 61 TUL. L. REV. 1071 (1987); Tushnet, *The Supreme Court, the Supreme Law of the Land, and Attorney General Meese: A Comment,* 61 TUL. L. REV. 1017 (1987); Colby, *Two Views on the Legitimacy of Nonacquiescence in Judicial Opinions,* 61 TUL. L. REV. 1041 (1987).

192. Neuborne, *supra* note 190, at 994. The troublesome nature of a constitution without a single authoritative voice to construe it is not merely recently considered. In Ferris v. Cooper, the California Supreme Court declared:

> That there should be a central tribunal, having power to give authoritative exposition to the Constitution, and laws, and treaties of the United States, and which should also possess the power to secure every citizen the rights to which he is entitled under them, seems to us highly expedient. The value of uniformity of decisions where the Constitution and laws of the Federal Government are to be expounded in cases of individual rights, and the importance of the principle that every citizen of the United States know the extent, and be protected by a tribunal of the highest authority and free from local prejudices or passions in the enjoyment of all the rights, exemptions, and privileges with which the Constitution and laws of the Union invest him, cannot easily be exaggerated. Indeed, in order to render the Constitution and laws of the Federal Government the same things to the people of the United

the jurisprudence of original intention does the Meese position on authoritativeness bear virtue, and then only because the Constitution is thought not to be a living document but instead shackled by the perceptions and limitations of its framers and the framers' times. By contrast, a Constitution not so shackled is susceptible of different readings over time, in accordance with changing levels of sophistication and sensibilities. Under such an interpretation of the Constitution, Lincoln might well argue for a change in the understanding of the law of the Constitution underlying the *Dred Scott* case, and *Brown I* might legitimately overrule *Plessy v. Ferguson*, all without undermining the authoritative nature of Supreme Court pronouncements.

The opposite tack which Attorney General Meese has taken ignores the danger that underlies *Cooper v. Aaron*, the very case whose statement respecting authoritativeness of Supreme Court pronouncements Meese seeks to question. If the Supreme Court is not the final arbiter of constitutional law, then the inference may be had that anyone can be an authoritative arbiter of the Constitution, the position of the Supreme Court notwithstanding. Meese's position gives comfort to those who would revive the corpse of interposition, and that specter is an ugly one, as demonstrated by the Little Rock crisis. Out of this crisis a caution is issued and a warning is sounded, one especially compelling for a document over 200 years old.

The warning is this: the Constitution must be the supreme power, and no local interest can be allowed to predominate over its mandate, no matter how important the local interest nor how stubborn its supporters. For there is no power in a law that is not obeyed, and no beauty in a Constitution whose power dissipates even as it is spoken.

States, it is necessary that they receive their ultimate construction from the same tribunal; for there is but little practical difference between two or more different Constitutions and one Constitution variously and differently construed.
11 Cal. at 180. *See also* United States v. Peters, 9 U.S. (5 Cranch) 115, at 135-36; Cohens v. Virginia, 19 U.S. (6 Wheat.) 264, 385 (1821); Ableman v. Booth, 62 U.S. (21 Haw.) 506, at 514-16 (1858).

ORAL ARGUMENT BEFORE THE
SUPREME COURT: MARSHALL *v.* DAVIS
IN THE SCHOOL SEGREGATION CASES

Milton Dickens and Ruth E. Schwartz

Because of the national importance of the issue presented and because of its importance to the State of Kansas, we request that the State present its views at oral argument. If the State does not desire to appear, we request the Attorney General to advise whether the State's default shall be construed as a concession of invalidity [of the laws and Constitution of Kansas].[1]

Thus spoke the Supreme Court in an early stage of *Brown v. Board of Education* when neither the Topeka School Board nor the State's Attorney General indicated a readiness to argue that case. And in 1954 the Court adopted Rule 45(1): "The Court looks with disfavor on the submission of cases on briefs, without oral argument, and therefore may, notwithstanding such submission, require oral argument of the parties."[2]

Despite such explicit statements by the Court, and despite the seminal influence on public discussion by landmark cases of "The Warren Court," a paucity of research on oral argument before the Supreme Court is reported in the literature of speech communication.[3] The

main reason for this research gap is probably the difficulty of securing the necessary transcripts.[4]

The dual purpose of this essay is (1) to compare and evaluate the oral argument of Thurgood Marshall and John W. Davis in the school segregation cases in 1952-1953[5] and simultaneously (2) to describe distinctive characteristics of oral argument in major cases before the Supreme Court.[6]

The school segregation cases were five in number, chosen by the Court to illuminate several facets of a single basic issue—the constitutionality of school segregation laws. The cases were argued three times—1952, 1953, and 1955. Counsel included seven attorneys for plaintiffs, eleven for defendants, and ten for

Mr. Dickens is Professor of Speech Communication and Chairman of the Graduate Program in Communication at the University of Southern California; Mrs. Schwartz is Lecturer in Theater Arts at the University of California at Los Angeles.

[1] 344 U.S. 141, 142.

[2] Robert L. Stern and Eugene Gressman, *Supreme Court Practice*, 2nd ed. (Washington, D.C., 1954), p. 482.

[3] Two related studies were found: David Boyd Strother, "Evidence, Argument and Decision in *Brown v Board of Education*" (Ph.D. dissertation, University of Illinois, 1958) and Jamye Coleman Williams, "A Rhetorical Analysis of Thurgood Marshall's Arguments Before

the Supreme Court in the Public School Segregation Controversy" (Ph.D. dissertation, Ohio State University, 1959).

[4] Such difficulties with regard to these particular cases were eliminated recently with the publication of *Argument: The Oral Argument Before the Supreme Court in Brown v. Board of Education, 1952-1955*, ed. Leon Friedman (New York, 1969). In a review of this book in QJS, LVI (October 1970), 341-342, we indicated some of the problems that still persist for researchers who may wish to secure transcripts of oral arguments before the Supreme Court in other cases.

[5] Marshall, currently Associate Justice of the Supreme Court, and Davis, former Democratic candidate for President of the United States, were described in legal literature as among the most experienced and successful constitutional lawyers of modern times.

[6] For a detailed presentation, see Ruth Evelyn Schwartz, "A Descriptive Analysis of Oral Argument Before the United States Supreme Court in the School Segregation Cases, 1952-1953" (Ph.D. dissertation, University of Southern California, 1966).

amici. The opposing chief counsel, Marshall and Davis, were pitted directly against one another in 1952 and 1953 in *Briggs v. Elliott.*

Counsel addressed at least three audiences: (1) the members of the Court; (2) a small group of spectators, including representatives of the news media;[7] and (3) the American public (indirectly through the newsmen's reports). From the standpoints of communication theory and of practical public speaking methods, the attorney had a fourth audience—himself. As Justice Jackson so delightfully described this: "I used to say that, as Solicitor General, I made three arguments of every case. First came the one that I planned—as I thought, logical, coherent, complete. Second was the one actually presented—interrupted, incoherent, disjointed, disappointing. The third was the utterly devastating argument that I thought of after going to bed that night."[8]

METHODOLOGY

The complete transcripts of all the 1952-1955 oral arguments were read and reread, applying various treatments to the data. Chief Justice Warren's personal collection of the written briefs (including his occasional marginal notes) was studied. A third source of primary data was provided by letters from eight of the counsel who participated in the cases.

Arguments were evaluated on the assumption that the Court was the primary audience. A vital methodological task was to determine major criteria by which to estimate the comparative effectiveness of oral arguments on members of this Court. What were *their* standards? The

answer was sought by going directly to the transcript.

A special feature of oral argument before the Supreme Court is that the justices may break in at any time with questions. During the ten days of argument in the three hearings there were 1,432 questions (or comments). Analysis of these interchanges indicated that the justices gave highest priority to three criteria, which were tentatively labeled *clarity, adaptability,* and *strategy.*[9]

These criteria were checked against legal literature dealing with appellate court advocacy. In other words, what the justices *did* was compared with what they and other judicial authorities *said they did.* In analyzing these materials, the procedure was to mark all words and phrases advising the attorney of what to do or avoid. As expected, variety of terminology was encountered. However, about 75 per cent of the terms fell into three main "clusters," corresponding with the labels derived from the transcript. Each cluster comprised more than 50 related terms.[10]

The above procedure may be figuratively compared with the quantitative technique of factor analysis (utilizing, please forgive, the researcher's brain as a computer). This procedure of deriving criteria from the data may be contrasted with the more common practice of adopting the criteria of previous rhetoricians, e.g., Aristotle's triad or Kenneth Burke's pentad.

The design of this study combines

---

[7] Pencil and paper notetaking is permitted but cameras, tape recorders, etc. are forbidden.

[8] Robert H. Jackson, "Advocacy Before the Supreme Court: Suggestions for Effective Case Presentations," *American Bar Association Journal,* XXXVII (November 1951), 803.

[9] The three combined suggest the corollary that an attorney's advance preparation for "his hour upon the stage" is awesome. The scope of the Court's questions included the early history of the Fourteenth Amendment, early history of the public school system, population and enrollment statistics, social science researches, some 118 previous court decisions, and so on.

[10] For example: ADAPTABILITY, flexibility, resiliency, interaction, deftness, directness, agility, dexterity, interchange, crossfire, courtesy, respect, personality impact, involvement, lawyer's clues, etc.

empirical (descriptive) and critical (evaluative) methods. One reason for this choice is that the illusion of a dynamic ongoing process—the feel or flavor—of oral argument before the Supreme Court (description) may be captured by projecting flashbacks, with commentary, showing the verbal thrust and parry between two powerful adversaries (evaluation). Another reason is that the three criteria are, with but small adaptation, also descriptions of significant characteristics of the argument. "Oral argument," as here used, involves the interrelationships between the verbal behaviors of two or more persons speaking on opposing sides of a controversial proposition. Hence, much of the description of the oral argument (e.g., contention-and-rebuttal) automatically includes comparison; the functions of reporter and critic are inextricably interwoven.

CLARITY

The importance and the difficulties of achieving clarity during argument before the Supreme Court should be compared with other types of public address and debate. In political campaigning, for example, deliberate ambiguity and opacity may be cultivated; speech organization and style may be polished by teams of ghost writers and read from manuscript by the candidate; the only interruptions may be bursts of applause from a partisan audience; answers to rebuttals by the opposing party may be delayed for days; a memorized "all purpose" speech may be delivered repeatedly. Not so, in the Supreme Court. There, the arguments must be unambiguous; opponent's rebuttals must be handled promptly; and a planned presentation may be interrupted by a justice's remarks at any time. Furthermore, Rule 44(1) says, "The Court looks with disfavor on any oral argument that is read

from a prepared text."[11] In light of these difficulties the overall clarity of both Marshall and Davis deserves praise.

Nevertheless, critics reading straight through the arguments by Marshall and Davis would almost certainly agree that Davis is much clearer and easier to read, both as to speech organization and language usage.

Davis gives early previews of his main contentions, discussing them in the promised sequence, supporting each contention with evidence and logic before going to the next, and supplying transitional words or phrases.

Marshall, on the other hand, is impossible to reduce to outline form. His basic plan gradually "emerged." When he was about two-thirds through his 1952 argument, in response to a question, he suddenly said: "But Mr. Justice Frankfurter, I was trying to make three different points. I said that the first one was peculiarly narrow, under the McLaurin and the Sweatt decisions. The second point was that on a classification basis, these statutes were bad. The third point was the broader point, that racial distinctions in and of themselves are invidious. I consider it as a three-pronged attack."[12] Marshall's wording of his three "prongs" was clear only in the context of his preceding half hour of speaking. A rereading of that half hour revealed that he had indeed adhered to his three points. However, he did not seem greatly concerned with maintaining his preplanned sequence, e.g., his listing of the three prongs did not correspond at all with the sequence in which he had been discussing them. His idea seemed to be to have an underlying set of a few key points and to develop any one of them at any time, especially as he responded to questions by the Court. This McLuhanesque progression was well suited to the

---

[11] Stern and Gressman, p. 481.
[12] Friedman, p. 45.

threat of interruptions. So perhaps Marshall deliberately sacrificed clarity for the sake of adaptability and its potential strategic gains.

Clarity is also a function of language usage. Here again, comes a study in contrasts. Davis revealed an astonishing mastery of the King's English, using words with precision, and almost without grammatical lapses. Marshall's vocabulary was more limited, his wording sometimes awkward, and he made some mistakes in grammar. Davis' language was sophisticated, sometimes formal, apparently always fluent. Marshall's was ordinary, usually informal, and occasionally suggested a fight to find the wanted words. Davis' style could be summarized as elegant; Marshall's, as earthy, e.g., Davis would refer to "infant Negro children"; Marshall called them "kids." Another comparison, regarding the testimony of psychologists:

MR. MARSHALL: Appellees, in their brief comment, say that they do not think too much of them [the psychologists].[13]

MR. DAVIS: It would be difficult for me to conceal my opinion that that evidence in and of itself is of slight weight and in conflict with the opinion of other and better informed sources.[14]

Or compare the closing words of Marshall's opening argument with the first words of Davis' reply:

JUSTICE JACKSON: Do you think that might not apply to the Indians?

MR. MARSHALL: I think it would. But I think that the biggest trouble with the Indians is that they just have not the judgment or the wherewithal to bring lawsuits.

JUSTICE JACKSON: Maybe you should bring some up.

MR. MARSHAL: I have a full load now, Mr. Justice.

THE CHIEF JUSTICE: Mr. Davis.

MR. DAVIS: May it please the Court, I think if the appellants' construction of the Fourteenth Amendment should prevail here, there is no doubt in my mind that it would catch the Indian within its grasp just as much as the Negro.[16]

Davis never suffered stylistic defeats such as the following sample of Marshall at his worst: "It is our understanding that the Fourteenth Amendment, following the Civil Rights Law, but not limited to the Civil Rights Act of 1866, in the debates, it is obvious, especially in the later debates, that left with the courts of the land was this problem of deciding as to the interpretation, so that as to power, it is our position that the Court gets specific power in addition to the regular judiciary act, in this Act of 1871, Title 8, which is not Title 8."[16]

On the other hand, perhaps Davis was *too* sophisticated, e.g., "chirography," "attar," "Serbonian," and a few others. Was the elegant image appropriate for the chief opponent of a case based on democratic egalitarianism? Argued before an egalitarian Court?

ADAPTABILITY

The requirements for adaptability during argument before the Supreme Court are more severe than for most other persuasive speeches. For instance, speeches at political rallies or revival meetings are seldom interrupted except for applause, appreciative laughter, or "amen." Even at news conferences prepared statements may be read, most of the questions are predictable, and embarrassing ones can often be avoided by humor, "no comment," or other simple devices. Not so, in the Supreme Court. Answers may not be delayed—when an attorney says he will come to the question later in his argument, the almost inevitable reply is, "Please answer it now." Attempts to dodge are seldom successful—the justice pursues his cross-

13 *Ibid.*, p. 37.
14 *Ibid.*, p. 51.

15 *Ibid.*, pp. 50-51.
16 *Ibid.*, p. 196.

examination until satisfied. The slightest hint of flippancy or discourtesy is immediately crushed. The scope of subject matter covered by questioning is too broad to be predictable. The questions are often subtle, complex, and technical. Effective adaptation requires not only fluency and resiliency but, above all, an extensive knowledge and rapid recall. Neither Marshall nor Davis blundered seriously (some of their colleagues did) when cross-examined, although both of them were severely challenged.

The data provide this unusual statistic: Marshall was interrupted 127 times by questions or comments, while Davis was interrupted only 11 times. Why this extreme discrepancy? Analysis of the interchanges showed that sometimes Marshall was questioned because his occasional oral "shorthand" (as Chief Justice Vinson once called it) puzzled someone on the bench; vice versa, a critical reading of the text indicated that Davis was usually so unmistakably clear that the justices did not need to ask him to restate an idea. But this line of explanation accounted for only a portion of the discrepancy. A more subtle variable appeared to be the differing attitudes and tactics of the two men.

The one extensive interchange between Davis and the Court occurred before he was half through his 1952 argument. Here is what happened:

Justice Burton: What is your answer, Mr. Davis, to the suggestion mentioned yesterday that at that time the conditions and relations between the two races were such that what might have been unconstitutional then would not be unconstitutional now?

Mr. Davis: My answer to that is that changed conditions may affect policy, but changed conditions cannot broaden the terminology of the Constitution, the thought is an administrative or a political question, and not a judicial one.

Justice Burton: But the Constitution is a living document that must be interpreted in relation to the facts of the time in which it is interpreted. Did we not go through with that in connection with child labor cases, and so forth?

Mr. Davis: Oh, well, of course, changed conditions may bring things within the scope of the Constitution which were not originally contemplated, and of that perhaps the aptest illustration is the interstate commerce clause. Many things have been found to be interstate commerce which at the time of the writing of the Constitution were not contemplated. . . .

Justice Frankfurter: Mr. Davis, do you think that "equal" is a less fluid term than "commerce between the states"?

Mr. Davis: Less fluid?

Justice Frankfurter: Yes.

Mr. Davis: I have not compared the two on the point of fluidity.

Justice Frankfurter: Suppose you do it now.

Mr. Davis: I am not sure that I can approach it in just that sense.

Justice Frankfurter: The problem behind my question is [the same] whatever the phrasing may be.

Mr. Davis: That what is unequal today may be equal tomorrow, or vice versa?

Justice Frankfurter: That is it.

Mr. Davis: That might be. I should not philosophize about it. But the effort in which I am now engaged is to show how those who submitted this amendment and those who adopted it conceded it to be, and what their conduct by way of interpretation has been since its ratification in 1868.

Justice Frankfurter: What you are saying is, that as a matter of history, history puts a gloss upon "equal" which does not permit elimination or admixture of white and colored in this aspect to be introduced?

Mr. Davis: Yes, I am saying that.

Justice Frankfurter: That is what you are saying?

Mr. Davis: Yes, I am saying that.[17]

With Davis, the pattern was always question-pause-answer. His answers were succinct but dogmatic. He refused to help the Court by exploring the implications of "the Constitution is a living document." He disregarded the loaded language, "history puts a gloss upon." Frankfurter's remarks might even suggest that he was annoyed by Davis' tactics. All in all, it appeared that Davis' responses discouraged questioning when

17 *Ibid.*, pp. 55-56.

the opposite should have been his goal.

Marshall's attitude toward the Court's questions and his mode of answering provided a vivid contrast. For instance, Marshall opened his 1953 argument by previewing three main points. Immediately came the following:

JUSTICE JACKSON: May I suggest, I do not believe—

MR. MARSHALL: Yes, sir.

JUSTICE JACKSON: I do not believe the Court was troubled about its own cases. It has done a good deal of reading of those cases.

MR. MARSHALL: And the first group are all from this very Court; I was just trying to relate them.

JUSTICE JACKSON: Good. Maybe the question was more nearly . . . the question of the propriety of exercising judicial power to reach this result. . . . It is a question—

MR. MARSHALL: Well, so far—if I understand you correctly, Mr. Justice Jackson—you mean power that would come from the legislative history of the Fourteenth Amendment?

JUSTICE JACKSON: Whether the Amendment, with what light you can throw on it, makes it appropriate for judicial power, after all that has intervened, to exercise this power instead of—

MR. MARSHALL: Leaving it to the Congress.

JUSTICE JACKSON: That is right. I do not like to see you waste your time on a misunderstanding, because I do not think we had any doubt about our cases. Things are so often read—

JUSTICE FRANKFURTER: And the books.

MR. MARSHALL: Believe it or not, I have read about it. I think then I should change and leave out the first group.[18]

The above excerpt illustrates two aspects of Marshall's adaptability under pressure of the Court's questions. First, Marshall and Jackson were interacting so closely as to almost "read one another's minds"; note the completing of one another's sentences. Second, the ending of the excerpt shows how Marshall radically revised his planned argument—abruptly dropping discussion of his first major point.

There were seemingly mysterious conversations between Marshall and a jus-

tice in which they would pursue an argument to a mutually satisfactory conclusion without either of them spelling out the sequence of logical steps. A simple "yes, sir" from Marshall could transmit quite a bit of information:

JUSTICE FRANKFURTER: Well, the Delaware case tests that. You are opposed to—you are in favor of the requested equality there, because I do not know whether you are—

MR. MARSHALL: Yes, sir.

JUSTICE FRANKFURTER: That is generally under your wing?

MR. MARSHALL: It is not only under our wing, sir; we are very proud of the fact that the children are going to school there, and they are demonstrating that it can be done.

JUSTICE FRANKFURTER: All I am saying is that with reference to the basis on which the Delaware decision went, you reject—

MR. MARSHALL: Yes, sir.

JUSTICE FRANKFURTER: I follow that.[19]

Analysis of the transcript suggests that Marshall's style invited questioning. He made positive use of interchanges, developing his contentions, creating personal involvements. In short, he did more adapting than Davis, and he did it better.

STRATEGY

Successful rhetorical strategy before the Supreme Court differs from most other persuasive speaking situations. Successful strategy in political campaigning may resemble commercial advertising. Strategies in legislative debates and jury trials may be loosely constructed, partly irrelevant, even contradictory. Protest rallies may be simplistic or irrational. If the issue is of deep social concern, these strategies are shaped by the interstimulation and response of large crowds or by the mass audiences of radio, television, and newspapers. Not so, in the Supreme Court. The attorneys' strategies here must be adapted to an audience of

---

18 *Ibid.*, pp. 194-195.   19 *Ibid.*, pp. 202-203.

nine black-robed justices sitting behind their high desk, listening critically to the speaker at the lectern immediately in front of the bench. The conversation is face-to-face and intimate, yet constrained by a formal set of rules and a formidable tradition. An attorney's argument must not only withstand immediate probing questions but must also withstand a lengthy period of careful analysis by this group of highly disciplined minds. The attorney's task must also be evaluated in the context of the hundreds of pages of written briefs, submitted in advance, from which he must choose a small portion for oral emphasis, realizing that almost any choice requires a calculated risk.

Marshall and Davis each chose one central contention to which all else was subordinate, and these two contentions provided a direct clash. Davis defended the legal status quo—the doctrine of "separate but equal."[20] Marshall argued that separation in and of itself is a denial of equality.

In 1952 Marshall began the proof of his central contention by reviewing the expert testimony: "Witnesses testified that segregation deterred the development of the personalities of these children. Two witnesses testified that it deprives them of equal status in the school community, that it destroys their self-respect. Two other witnesses testified that it denies them full opportunity for democratic social development. Another witness said that it stamps him with a badge of inferiority. The summation of that testimony is that the Negro children have road blocks put up in their minds."[21]

Marshall then dissected in detail the

opposition witnesses in the lower court, showing that none was an expert and concluding that they had made "no effort whatsoever" to directly refute the psychological evidence. Therefore, this evidence stood unchallenged as a finding of fact. Witnesses may not be called later during an appellate trial, so Davis was handicapped by the mistake of his predecessors in the lower court. Here is how he sought to surmount the obstacle: "Now, these learned witnesses do not have the whole field to themselves. They do not speak without contradiction from other sources. We quote in our brief—I suppose it is not testimony, but it is quotable material, and we are content to adopt it."[22]

Marshall would not permit Davis to escape so easily, saying in rebuttal: "But I think if it is true that there is a large body of scientific evidence on the other side, the place to have produced that was in the District Court."[23] Justice Frankfurter inquired if he could not take "judicial notice" of the references cited in Davis' brief, and the exchange proceeded:

JUSTICE FRANKFURTER: It is better to have witnesses, but I did not know that we could not read the works of competent writers.

MR MARSHALL: Mr. Justice Frankfurter, I did not say that it was bad. I said that it would have been better if they had produced the witnesses so that we would have had an opportunity to cross-examine and test their conclusions. For example, the authority of Hodding Carter, the particular article quoted, was a magazine article of a newspaperman answering another newspaperman, and I know of nothing further removed from scientific work than one newspaperman answering another. I am not trying—

JUSTICE FRANKFURTER: I am not going to take issue with you on that.[24]

Attacking plaintiff's psychological evidence, Davis employed ridicule. He reviewed details of one experiment in

---

[20] The strategic import of such choices may be illustrated by supposing that Davis had chosen the central contention that desegregation is legally the responsibility of Congress rather than of the Supreme Court.
[21] Friedman, p. 38.

[22] Ibid., p. 60.
[23] Ibid., p. 63.
[24] Ibid.

which 16 children were shown white dolls and colored dolls and, as he told about it, surely even a social scientist would have chuckled. Likewise he made fun of a couple of other researches. But then he turned from understatement to overstatement: "I may have been unfortunate, or I may have been careless, but it seems to me that much of that which is handed down under the name of social science is an effort on the part of the scientist to rationalize his own preconceptions. They find usually, in my limited observation, what they go out to find."[25] He concluded his rebuttal with a quoted description of social science: "Fragmentary expertise based on an examined presupposition."

Sarcasm is a risky tactic which may boomerang. But Davis was in a desperate situation because in recent cases (e.g., *Sweatt* and *McLaurin*) the Court had accepted certain "intangibles" as evidence. He may have reasoned that an orthodox rebuttal would not be strong enough; but he gambled recklessly. Would this Court agree that social science research is a laughing matter?

Let us turn now to Davis' direct argument in defense of the legal status quo. He evoked the judicial principle of *stare decisis* (i.e., abide by previous decisions) with eloquence and power in both 1952 and 1953. He summarized it in this way:

But be that doctrine [*stare decisis*] what it may, somewhere, sometime to every principle comes a moment of repose when it has been so often announced, so confidently relied upon, so long continued, that it passes the limits of judicial discretion and disturbance.

That is the opinion which we held when we filed our former brief in this case. We relied on the fact that this Court had not once but seven times, I think it is, pronounced in favor of the "separate but equal" doctrine.

We relied on the fact that the courts of last appeal of some sixteen or eighteen states have passed upon the validity of the "separate but equal" doctrine vis-a-vis the Fourteenth Amendment.

We relied on the fact that Congress has continuously since 1862 segregated its schools in the District of Columbia.

We relied on the fact that twenty-three of the ratifying states . . . had by legislative action evinced their conviction that the Fourteenth Amendment was not offended by segregation, and we said in effect that that argument—and I am bold enough to repeat it here now—that in the language of Judge Parker in his opinion below, after that had been the consistent history for over three-quarters of a century, it was late indeed in the day to disturb it on any theoretical or sociological basis. We stand on that proposition.[26]

Marshall devoted his opening argument in 1953 to attacking the validity of "separate but equal." This plea was so chopped up by the Court's questions (53 questions in about 40-45 minutes) that upon first reading, Marshall's basic plan was not clear. Laborious rereading revealed that Marshall had employed a pincers strategy, attacking both flanks simultaneously. He argued that in the earliest relevant cases, *Slaughter-House* (1873) and *Strauder* (1880) the Fourteenth Amendment was interpreted broadly to include all types of racial discrimination; in the middle period beginning with *Plessy v. Ferguson* (1896) the interpretation was narrowed to "separate but equal"; but in the latest cases, e.g., *Sweatt* (1950) and *McLaurin* (1950), the Court returned to the broad interpretation. Then he closed the pincers: "The 'separate but equal' doctrine is just out of step with the earlier decisions . . . and the recent cases in this Court."[27]

In his next appearance Davis said nothing about Marshall's flanking maneuver. He never once mentioned *Slaughter-House* or *Strauder* although Marshall cited them repeatedly. Only once did he so much as mention *Sweatt*

25 *Ibid.*, p. 59.
26 *Ibid.*, p. 215.
27 *Ibid.*, p. 201.

and *McLaurin* while Marshall referred to these cases more than twenty times. Davis' silence spoke loud.

The 1953 argument focused on five questions propounded by the Court. Two of these questions dealt with the early history of the Fourteenth Amendment; the remaining three dealt with the who and how of enforcement in the event that segregation was struck down.

Davis frequently described or implied the difficulties of enforcement. For instance, regarding the 2,799 Negro and 295 white children in the South Carolina school district under dispute, he asked: "Who is going to disturb that situation? If they were to be reassorted or comingled [*sic*], who knows how that could best be done? If it is done on the mathematical basis, with 30 children as a maximum . . . you would have 27 Negro children and 3 whites in one school room. Would that make the children any happier? Would they learn any more quickly? Would their lives be more serene?"[28]

Marshall urged prompt enforcement of desegregation. First, he proposed a vague plan of redistricting the schools but he floundered when questioned about details, and Davis stung him neatly, e.g., "He has some plan, the mathematics of which I do not entirely grasp."[29] Second, he bluntly said that "insofar as this is a tough problem, it was tough, but the solution was not to deprive people of their constitutional rights."[30] Third, he movingly described the contradictions of Negro children's status quo:

I got the feeling on hearing the discussion yesterday that when you put a white child in a school with a whole lot of colored children, the child would fall apart or something. Everybody knows that is not true. Those same kids in Virginia and South Carolina—and I have seen

them do it—they play in the streets together, they play on their farms together, they go down the road together, they separate to go to school, they come out of school and play ball together. They have to be separated in school. There is some magic to it. You can have them voting together, you can have them not restricted because of law in the houses they live in. You can have them going to the same state university and the same college, but if they go to elementary and high school, the world will fall apart.[31]

Fourth, Marshall sought to soothe the Court by predicting that if it nullified segregation, almost everybody would obey the new law.

Davis had opened his case in 1952 by praising the recent improvements in Negro schools in the South. He concluded his case in 1953 by again praising the existing school system, and he said: "I am reminded—and I hope it won't be treated as a reflection on anybody—of Aesop's fable of the dog and the meat: The dog, with a fine piece of meat in his mouth, crossed a bridge and saw the shadow in the stream and plunged for it and lost both substance and shadow. Here is equal education, not promised not prophesied, but present. Shall it be thrown away on some fancied question of racial prestige?"[32] Marshall spotted that one dangerous sentence, and here is what he did to it: "Now that is the policy that I understand them to say that it is just a little feeling on the part of the Negroes, they don't like segregation. As Mr. Davis said yesterday, the only thing the Negroes are trying to get is prestige. Exactly correct. Ever since the Emancipation Proclamation, the Negro has been trying to get . . . the same status as anybody else regardless of race."[33]

In closing his case Marshall said that "the only way that this Court can decide this case in opposition to our position . . . is to find that for some reason

28 *Ibid.*, p. 215.
29 *Ibid.*, p. 53.
30 *Ibid.*, p. 64.

31 *Ibid.*, p. 239.
32 *Ibid.*, p. 216.
33 *Ibid.*, p. 236.

Negroes are inferior to all other human beings. . . . And now is the time, we submit, that this Court should make it clear that that is not what our Constitution stands for."[34]

SUMMARY AND CONCLUSIONS

The unanimous Final Decision on the Merits was read by Chief Justice Warren.[35] The matters discussed in this decision closely parallel those discussed at oral argument. This parallelism may be coincidental or it may indicate that the oral argument strongly influenced the thinking of the Court. Oversimplified cause and effect reasoning should of course be avoided. The concept of multiple causation suggests that the decision may have been a product of the prior personal convictions of the justices, the briefs and other written materials, the reactions of the news media and the public. Nevertheless, a comparison of the oral argument with the decision, suggests that the relative weight of the oral argument may be heavier than most people suspect.

The Court ruled that the arguments concerning the early history of the Fourteenth Amendment were "indecisive." Psychological evidence was declared valid.[36] Davis' central contention failed —the "separate but equal" doctrine was struck down in a single sentence. Marshall's central contention prevailed: "Separate educational facilities are inherently unequal." The question of implementation was postponed for further argument (in 1955).

It must be concluded that Marshall's strategical choices coincided much more closely with the Court's verdict than did Davis' choices. A further conclusion seems justified—Davis made some serious mistakes. He should not have avoided *Slaughter-House* and *Strauder* nor *Sweatt* and *McLaurin;* he went too far in his use of ridicule in attacking social science research; and he should have made a more positive effort to invite questioning.[37]

The mighty struggle between Marshall and Davis shows that oral argument before the Supreme Court differs from other common persuasive speaking situations, such as political campaigns, protest rallies, legislative debates, revival meetings, and even jury trials. The peculiar rhetorical problems that confront any counselor at law who aspires to argue orally before the Supreme Court include these:

(1) In preparation for a single hour of oral argument, he must become familiar with thousands of pages of briefs, previous testimony and decisions, and other sources of fact and law.

(2) He must select for oral emphasis an extremely small portion of the voluminous relevant materials; time limits are strict.

(3) He must speak within the confines of a formal set of rules, some requiring technical (legal) training, knowledge, and experience.

(4) The traditions, atmosphere, and physical setting impose additional constraints, rendering inappropriate or ineffectual many rhetorical techniques commonly used in other types of persuasive speaking; the elements of a public spectacle are conspicuously absent.

(5) He must be ready to answer im-

---

34 *Ibid.*, pp. 239-240.
35 *Ibid.*, pp. 325-331.
36 Appended to this is the famous "footnote 11," citing seven social science sources.

37 These rather harsh criticisms of Davis may reflect the virtues of hindsight. In light of the liberal composition of this Court and the trend of the times in 1954, it is possible that Marshall began with a winning cause and Davis with a losing one; if so, they faced quite different rhetorical tasks. Marshall's task was to protect his lead; Davis was forced, as the athletic coaches say, to play the riskier game of "catch-up."

mediately and be answered by opposing counsel.

(6) He stands intellectually alone before the Court, forbidden to read his oral argument from manuscript, unable to rely on ghost writers or others for assistance.

(7) He must be able to respond in-stantly to questions or comments or commands from a highly trained, intelligent, and articulate group of justices whose verdict he is trying to influence.

(8) His oral effectiveness will be largely determined by his clarity, his adaptability, and his rhetorical strategy.

CHAPTER IV

Does the Negro Need Separate Schools?

W. E. BURGHARDT DU BOIS

There are in the United States some four million Negroes of school age, of whom two million are in school, and of these, four-fifths are taught by forty-eight thousand Negro teachers in separate schools. Less than a half million are in mixed schools in the North, where they are taught almost exclusively by white teachers. Beside this, there are seventy-nine Negro universities and colleges with one thousand colored teachers, beside a number of private secondary schools.

The question which I am discussing is: Are these separate schools and institutions needed? And the answer, to my mind, is perfectly clear. They are needed just so far as they are necessary for the proper education of the Negro race. The proper education of any people includes sympathetic touch between teacher and pupil; knowledge on the part of the teacher, not simply of the individual taught, but of his surroundings and background, and the history of his class and group; such contact between pupils, and between teacher and pupil, on the basis of perfect social equality, as will increase this sympathy and knowledge; facilities for education in equipment and housing, and the promotion of such extra-curricular activities as will tend to induct the child into life.

If this is true, and if we recognize the present attitude of white America toward black America, then the Ne-

gro not only needs the vast majority of these schools, but it is a grave question if, in the near future, he will not need more such schools, both to take care of his natural increase, and to defend him against the growing animosity of the whites. It is of course fashionable and popular to deny this; to try to deceive ourselves into thinking that race prejudice in the United States across the Color Line is gradually softening and that slowly but surely we are coming to the time when racial animosities and class lines will be so obliterated that separate schools will be anachronisms.

Certainly, I shall welcome such a time. Just as long as Negroes are taught in Negro schools and whites in white schools; the poor in the slums, and the rich in private schools; just as long as it is impracticable to welcome Negro students to Harvard, Yale and Princeton; just as long as colleges like Williams, Amherst and Wellesley tend to become the property of certain wealthy families, where Jews are not solicited; just so long we shall lack in America that sort of public education which will create the intelligent basis of a real democracy.

Much as I would like this, and hard as I have striven and shall strive to help realize it, I am no fool; and I know that race prejudice in the United States today is such that most Negroes cannot receive proper education in white institutions. If the public schools of Atlanta, Nashville, New Orleans and Jacksonville were thrown open to all races tomorrow, the education that colored children would get in them would be worse than pitiable. It would not be education. And in the same way, there are many public school systems in the North where Negroes are admitted and tolerated, but they are not educated; they are crucified. There are certain Northern universities where Negro students, no matter what their ability, desert, or accomplishment, cannot get fair recognition, either in classroom or on the campus, in dining halls and student activities, or in common human courtesy. It is well-known that in certain faculties of the University of Chicago, no Negro has yet received the doctorate and seldom can achieve the mastership in arts; at Harvard, Yale and Columbia, Negroes are admitted but not welcomed; while in other institutions, like Princeton, they cannot even enroll.

Under such circumstances, there is no room for argument as to whether the Negro needs separate schools or not. The plain fact faces us, that either he will have separate schools or he will not be educated. There may be, and there is, considerable difference of opinion as to how far this separation in schools is today necessary. There can be argument as to what our attitude toward further separation should be. Suppose, for instance, that in Montclair, New Jersey, a city of wealth and culture, the Board of Education is determined to establish separate schools for Negroes; suppose that, despite the law, separate Negro schools are already established in Philadelphia, and pressure is being steadily brought to extend this separation at least to the junior high school; what must be our attitude toward this?

Manifestly, no general and inflexible rule can be laid down. If public opinion is such in Montclair that Negro children can not receive decent and sympathetic education in the white schools, and no Negro teachers can be employed, there is for us no choice. We have got to accept Negro schools. Any agitation and action aimed at compelling a rich and powerful majority of the citizens to do what they will not do, is useless. On the other hand, we have a right and a duty to assure ourselves of the truth concerning this attitude; by careful conferences, by public meetings and by petitions, we should convince ourselves whether this demand for separate schools is merely the agitation of a prejudiced minority, or the considered and final judgment of the town.

There are undoubtedly cases where a minority of leaders force their opinions upon a majority, and induce a community to establish separate schools, when as a matter of fact, there is no general demand for it; there has been no friction in the schools; and Negro children have been decently treated. In that case, a firm and intelligent appeal to public opinion would eventually settle the matter. But the futile attempt to compel even by law a group to do what it is determined not to do, is a silly waste of money, time, and temper.

On the other hand, there are also cases where there has been no separation in schools and no movement toward it. And yet the treatment of Negro children in the schools, the kind of teaching and the kind of advice they get, is such that they ought to demand either a thorough-going revolution in the official attitude toward Negro students, or absolute separation in educational facilities. To endure bad schools and wrong education because the schools are "mixed" is a costly if not fatal mistake. I have long been convinced, for instance, that the Negroes in the public schools of Harlem are not getting an education that is in any sense comparable in efficiency, discipline, and human development with that which Negroes are getting in the separate public schools of Washington, D.C. And yet on its school situation, black Harlem is dumb and complacent, if not actually laudatory.

Recognizing the fact that for the vast majority of colored students in elementary, secondary, and collegiate education, there must be today separate educational institutions because of an attitude on the part of the white people which is not going materially to change in our time, our customary attitude toward these separate schools must be absolutely and definitely changed. As it is today, American Negroes almost universally disparage their own schools. They look down upon them; they often treat the Negro teachers in them with contempt; they refuse to work for their adequate support; and they refuse to join public movements to increase their efficiency.

The reason for this is quite clear, and may be divided into two parts: (1) the fear that any movement which implies segregation even as a tem-

porary, much less as a relatively permanent institution, in the United States, is a fatal surrender of principle, which in the end will rebound and bring more evils on the Negro than he suffers today. (2) The other reason is at bottom an utter lack of faith on the part of Negroes that their race can do anything really well. If Negroes could conceive that Negroes could establish schools quite as good as or even superior to white schools; if Negro colleges were of equal grade in accomplishment and in scientific work with white colleges; then separation would be a passing incident and not a permanent evil; but as long as American Negroes believe that their race is constitutionally and permanently inferior to white people, they necessarily disbelieve in every possible Negro Institution.

The first argument is more or less metaphysical and cannot be decided a priori for every case. There are times when one must stand up for principle at the cost of discomfort, harm, and death. But in the case of the education of the young, you must consider not simply yourself but the children and the relation of children to life. It is difficult to think of anything more important for the development of a people than proper training for their children; and yet I have repeatedly seen wise and loving colored parents take infinite pains to force their little children into schools where the white children, white teachers, and white parents despised and resented the dark child, made mock of it, neglected or bullied it, and literally rendered its life a living hell. Such parents want their child to "fight" this thing out,—but, dear God, at what a cost! Sometimes, to be sure, the child triumphs and teaches the school community a lesson; but even in such cases, the cost may be high, and the child's whole life turned into an effort to win cheap applause at the expense of healthy individuality. In other cases, the result of the experiment may be complete ruin of character, gift, and ability and ingrained hatred of schools and men. For the kind of battle thus indicated, most children are under no circumstances suited. It is the refinement of cruelty to require it of them. Therefore, in evaluating the advantage and disadvantage of accepting race hatred as a brutal but real fact, or of using a little child as a battering ram upon which its nastiness can be thrust, we must give greater value and greater emphasis to the rights of the child's own soul. We shall get a finer, better balance of spirit; an infinitely more capable and rounded personality by putting children in schools where they are wanted, and where they are happy and inspired, than in thrusting them into hells where they are ridiculed and hated.

Beyond this, lies the deeper, broader fact. If the American Negro really believed in himself; if he believed that Negro teachers can educate children according to the best standards of modern training; if he believed that Negro colleges transmit and add to science, as well as or better than other colleges, then he would bend his energies, not to escaping inescapable association with his own group, but to seeing that his group had every opportunity for its best and highest development. He would insist that his teachers be decently paid; that his

schools were properly housed and equipped; that his colleges be supplied with scholarship and research funds; and he would be far more interested in the efficiency of these institutions of learning, than in forcing himself into other institutions where he is not wanted.

As long as the Negro student wishes to graduate from Columbia, not because Columbia is an institution of learning, but because it is attended by white students; as long as a Negro student is ashamed to attend Fisk or Howard because these institutions are largely run by black folk, just so long the main problem of Negro education will not be segregation but self-knowledge and self-respect.

There are not many teachers in Negro schools who would not esteem it an unparalleled honor and boast of it to their dying day, if instead of teaching black folk, they could get a chance to teach poor-whites, Irishmen, Italians or Chinese in a "white" institution. This is not unnatural. This is to them a sort of acid test of their worth. It is but the logical result of the "white" propaganda which has swept civilization for the last thousand years, and which is now bolstered and defended by brave words, high wages, and monopoly of opportunities. But this state of mind is suicidal and must be fought, and fought doggedly and bitterly: first, by giving Negro teachers decent wages, decent schoolhouses and equipment, and reasonable chances for advancement; and then by kicking out and leaving to the mercy of the white world those who do not and cannot believe in their own.

Lack of faith in Negro enterprise

leads to singular results: Negroes will fight frenziedly to prevent segregated schools; but if segregation is forced upon them by dominant white public opinion, they will suddenly lose interest and scarcely raise a finger to see that the resultant Negro schools get a fair share of the public funds so as to have adequate equipment and housing; to see that real teachers are appointed, and that they are paid as much as white teachers doing the same work. Today, when the Negro public school system gets from half to one-tenth of the amount of money spent on white schools, and is often consequently poorly run and poorly taught, colored people tacitly if not openly join with white people in assuming that Negroes cannot run Negro enterprises, and cannot educate themselves, and that the very establishment of a Negro school means starting an inferior school.

The N.A.A.C.P. and other Negro organizations have spent thousands of dollars to prevent the establishment of segregated Negro schools, but scarcely a single cent to see that the division of funds between white and Negro schools, North and South, is carried out with some faint approximation of justice. There can be no doubt that if the Supreme Court were overwhelmed with cases where the blatant and impudent discrimination against Negro education is openly acknowledged, it would be compelled to hand down decisions which would make this discrimination impossible. We Negroes do not dare to press this point and force these decisions because, forsooth, it would acknowledge the fact of separate schools, a fact that does not need to be acknowl-

edged, and will not need to be for two centuries.

Howard, Fisk, and Atlanta are naturally unable to do the type and grade of graduate work which is done at Columbia, Chicago, and Harvard; but why attribute this to a defect in the Negro race, and not to the fact that the large white colleges have from one hundred to one thousand times the funds for equipment and research that Negro colleges can command? To this, it may logically be answered, all the more reason that Negroes should try to get into better-equipped schools, and who pray denies this? But the opportunity for such entrance is becoming more and more difficult, and the training offered less and less suited to the American Negro of today. Conceive a Negro teaching in a Southern school the economics which he learned at the Harvard Business School! Conceive a Negro teacher of history retailing to his black students the sort of history that is taught at the University of Chicago! Imagine the history of Reconstruction being handed by a colored professor from the lips of Columbia professors to the ears of the black belt! The results of this kind of thing are often fantastic, and call for Negro history and sociology, and even physical science taught by men who understand their audience, and are not afraid of the truth.

There was a time when the ability of Negro brains to do first-class work had to be proven by facts and figures, and I was a part of the movement that sought to set the accomplishments of Negro ability before the world. But the world before which I was setting this proof was a disbelieving white world. I did not need the proof for myself. I did not dream that my fellow Negroes needed it; but in the last few years, I have become curiously convinced that until American Negroes believe in their own power and ability, they are going to be helpless before the white world, and the white world, realizing this inner paralysis and lack of self-confidence, is going to persist in its insane determination to rule the universe for its own selfish advantage.

Does the Negro need separate schools? God knows he does. But what he needs more than separate schools is a firm and unshakable belief that twelve million American Negroes have the inborn capacity to accomplish just as much as any nation of twelve million anywhere in the world ever accomplished, and that this is not because they are Negroes but because they are human.

So far, I have noted chiefly negative arguments for separate Negro institutions of learning based on the fact that in the majority of cases Negroes are not welcomed in public schools and universities nor treated as fellow human beings. But beyond this, there are certain positive reasons due to the fact that American Negroes have, because of their history, group experiences and memories, a distinct entity, whose spirit and reactions demand a certain type of education for its development.

In the past, this fact has been noted and misused for selfish purposes. On the ground that Negroes needed a type of education "suited" to them, we have an attempt to train them as menials and dependents; or in the case of West Indians, an attempt to perpetuate their use as low-paid laborers by limiting their knowledge; or in the case of African natives, efforts to deprive them of modern languages and modern science in order to seal their subordination to outworn mores, reactionary native rulers, industrialization.

What I have in mind is nothing like this. It is rather an honest development of the premises from which this plea for special education starts. It is illustrated by these facts: Negroes must know the history of the Negro race in America, and this they will seldom get in white institutions. Their children ought to study textbooks like Brawley's "Short History," the first edition of Woodson's "Negro in Our History," and Cromwell, Turner and Dykes' "Readings from Negro Authors." Negroes who celebrate the birthdays of Washington and Lincoln, and the worthy, but colorless and relatively unimportant "founders" of various Negro colleges, ought not to forget the 5th of March,—that first national holiday of this country, which commemorates the martyrdom of Crispus Attucks. They ought to celebrate Negro Health Week and Negro History Week. They ought to study intelligently and from their own point of view, the slave trade, slavery, emancipation, Reconstruction, and present economic development.

Beyond this, Negro colleges ought to be studying anthropology, psychology, and the social sciences, from the point of view of the colored races. Today, the anthropology that is being taught, and the expeditions financed for archeological and ethnographical explorations, are for the most part straining every nerve to erase the history of black folk from the record. One has only to remember that the majority of anthropologists have peopled the continent of Africa itself with almost no Negroes, while men like Sayce and Reisner have even declared that the Ethiopians have no Negro blood! All this has been done by the legerdemain and metaphysics of nomenclature, and in the face of the great and important history of black blood in the world.

Recently, something has been done by colored scholars to correct the extraordinary propaganda of post-war psychology which sent men like Brigham and McDougall rushing into scientific proof of Negro congenital inferiority. But much more is necessary and demanded of Negro scholarship. In history and the social sciences the Negro school and college has an unusual opportunity and rôle. It does not consist simply in trying to parallel the history of white folk with similar boasting about black and brown folk, but rather an honest evaluation of human effort and accomplishment, without color blindness, and without transforming history into a record of dynasties and prodigies.

Here, we have in America, a working class which in our day has achieved physical freedom, and mental clarity. An economic battle has just begun. It can be studied and guided; it can teach consumers' cooperation, democracy, and socialism, and be made not simply a record and pattern for the Negro race, but a guide for the rise of the working classes throughout the world, just at the critical time when these classes are about to assume their just political domination which is destined to become the redemption of mankind.

Much has been said of the special esthetic ability of the Negro race. Naturally, it has been exaggerated. Naturally, it is not a racial characteristic in the sense of hereditary, inborn, and heritable difference; but there is no doubt but what the tremendous psychic history of the American and West Indian groups has made it possible for the present generation to accumulate a wealth of material which, with encouragement and training, could find expression in the drama, in color and form, and in music. And no where could this training better be pursued than in separate Negro schools under competent and intelligent teachers? What little has already been done in this line is scarcely a beginning of what is possible, provided the object is not simple entertainment or bizarre efforts at money raising.

In biology, the pioneering work of Carolyn Bond Day could be extended indefinitely in Negro laboratories; and in the purely physical and chemical sciences, the need of Negroes familiar with the intricate technical basis of modern civilization would not only help them to find their place in the industrial scene for their own organization, but also enable them to help Abyssinia, India, China, and the colored world, to maintain their racial integrity, and their economic independence. It could easily be the mission and duty of American Negroes to master this scientific basis of modern invention, and give it to all mankind.

Thus, instead of our schools being simply separate schools, forced on us by grim necessity, they can become centers of a new and beautiful effort at human education, which may easily lead and guide the world in many important and valuable aspects. It is for this reason that when our schools are separate, the control of the teaching force, the expenditure of money, the choice of textbooks, the discipline and other administrative matters of this sort ought, also, to come into our hands, and be incessantly demanded and guarded.

I remember once, in Texas, reading in a high-school textbook for colored students, the one anecdote given concerning Abraham Lincoln: he was pictured as chasing Negro thieves all night through the woods from his Mississippi flatboat! Children could read that history in vain to learn any word of what had been accomplished in American history by Benjamin Banneker, Jan Matseliger, Elijah McCoy, Frederick Douglass, or James Dunn. In fact, one of the peculiar tragedies of the smaller Southern colleges is that they hire as teachers of history, economics and sociology, colored men trained in Northern institutions where not a word of any information concerning these disciplines, so far as Negroes are concerned, has ever been imparted to them. I speak from experience, because I came to Atlanta University to teach history in 1897, without the slightest idea from my Harvard tuition, that Negroes ever had any history!

I know that this article will forthwith be interpreted by certain illiterate "nitwits" as a plea for segregated Negro schools and colleges. It is not. It is simply calling a spade a spade. It is saying in plain English: that a separate Negro school, where children are treated like human beings, trained by teachers of their own race, who know what it means to be black in the year of salvation 1935, is infinitely better than making our boys and girls doormats to be spit and trampled upon and lied to by ignorant social climbers, whose sole claim to superiority is ability to kick "niggers" when they are down. I say, too, that certain studies and discipline necessary to Negroes can seldom be found in white schools.

It means this, and nothing more.

To sum up this: theoretically, the Negro needs neither segregated schools nor mixed schools. What he needs is Education. What he must remember is that there is no magic, either in mixed schools or in segregated schools. A mixed school with poor and unsympathetic teachers, with hostile public opinion, and no teaching of truth concerning black folk, is bad. A segregated school with ignorant placeholders, inadequate equipment, poor salaries, and wretched housing, is equally bad. Other things being equal, the mixed school is the broader, more natural basis for the education of all youth. It gives wider contacts; it inspires greater self-confidence; and suppresses the inferiority complex. But other things seldom are equal, and in that case, Sympathy, Knowledge, and the Truth, outweigh all that the mixed school can offer.

The Limits of Good Faith: Desegregation in Topeka, Kansas, 1950–1956

Mary L. Dudziak

> . . . [T]o act against social injustice is right and noble but . . . to choose to act so does not settle all moral problems but on the contrary generates new ones of an especially difficult sort.
>
> —Lionel Trilling, 'Manners, Morals and the Novel'[1]

I. Introduction

In September of 1953, eight months before *Brown v. Board of Education of Topeka, Kansas*[2] would be decided, the Topeka Board of Education voted to abolish segregation in its schools.[3] Some Topekans thought it curious that the school board would vote to abolish segregation when its case defending segregation was pending in the U.S. Supreme Court. When Edward Goss of the Topeka Civic Club asked the board why it hadn't waited for the Court's

Mary L. Dudziak is Associate Professor of Law at the University of Iowa College of Law.

This article is dedicated to the memory of Robert Cover, who was the original director of the dissertation-in-progress on which the article is based. As a critic of his students' work, Professor Cover was as kind as he was thorough. In his passing, American legal history has lost one of its most creative scholars.

I have accumulated many debts in the course of writing this article. I am particularly grateful to E. Richard Larson for getting me interested in Topeka in the first place. Others who have offered valuable criticism and who have supported and encouraged my research include Bob Cottrol, David Bryon Davis, Davison Douglas, Paul Finkleman, Chris Hansen, Dirk Hartog, Carolyn Jones, Gigi Kunzel, Burke Marshall, Adolph Reed, Elvia Rosales, Ian Shapiro, Charlene Smith, Cathy Stock and Sarah Wolf. I would like to thank Terry Harmon of the Kansas State Historical Society for facilitating my research in Topeka, and the Topeka Board of Education for giving me access to their Minutes. Indispensable funding was provided by the Woodrow Wilson Fellowship Foundation in the form of a Charlotte W. Newcombe Fellowship for the 1985–86 academic year. I would also like to thank Ed Lynch and Ed Marks for their research assistance, and Fran Swanson for secretarial assistance with the final draft of the article.

1. Lionel Trilling, 'Manners, Morals and the Novel', in *The Liberal Imagination: Essays on Literature and Society* (New York, 1951) 219.

2. Brown v. Bd. of Educ., 347 U.S. 483 (1954).

3. Topeka Bd. of Educ. Minutes, Sept. 3, 1953.

decision, board member Harold Conrad responded: 'We feel that segregation is not an American practice.'[4]

The 'unAmerican' character of racial segregation had been identified by Gunnar Myrdal in *An American Dilemma* in 1944.[5] And as the U.S. entered the post-war period, attention was increasingly focused on the problem of racial injustice at home.[6] As racial segregation came to be identified as being at odds with what were thought of as proper American values, many looked upon the South with disdain.[7] The South, after all, with its history of slavery and lynching, offered the most stark examples of widespread racially oriented violence and subjugation in this country. However, in identifying the problem of racial injustice as a quintessentially Southern problem, nonSoutherners could deflect serious criticism from themselves. The problem posed by Myrdal's American Dilemma could be seen as a problem of cleaning up someone else's backyard.[8]

In the 1950s, the State of Kansas was not allowed the luxury of blaming somebody else, as the state and the city of Topeka found themselves on the wrong side of *Brown v. Board of Education*. Many Kansans were quite uncomfortable with the state's role in *Brown*, and wondered why Kansas the 'free state' was involved in a struggle that really concerned the South. In its policies on race, Kansas had maintained a middle ground between the

---

4. 'Segregation Is Terminated at Randolph and Southwest', *Topeka Journal*, Sept. 9, 1953.

5. Gunnar Myrdal, *An American Dilemma* (New York, 1944) [hereinafter cited as Myrdal]. While the idea that racism was unAmerican was important in the intellectual history of the post-war United States, Myrdal's articulation of the issue has been questioned by later scholars. Myrdal believed that because racism was fundamentally at odds with American democratic values, the problem of racism could be resolved through the process of democratic politics. The U.S. simply had to confront the dilemma of American racism. While solutions to the problem would not be simple, they nevertheless required no radical restructuring of the polity. See ibid. at 1021–22. Jennifer Hochschild differs from Myrdal on this point. She argues that an examination of the effectiveness of school desegregation strategies shows that 'normal democratic politics' based on incrementalism and popular control do not lead to effective school desegregation. From this she concludes that race discrimination is not an anomaly in American democracy. Rather racism is symbiotic with it. The 'new American dilemma', in her view, is the question of whether the U.S. is willing to take the stronger steps required to root out the racism that is a feature of contemporary American culture. See Jennifer Hochschild, *The New American Dilemma: Liberal Democracy and School Desegregation* (New Haven, 1984).

6. See Peter J. Kellogg, 'Civil Rights Consciousness in the 1940s', *The Historian* xlii (1979) 18. See also Thomas R. Brooks, *Walls Come Tumbling Down: A History of the Civil Rights Movement, 1940–1970* (Englewood Cliffs, 1974) 58–94.

7. Liberal white Southerners, as well as Northerners, focused on the peculiarly Southern character of segregation. See, e.g., Wilbur Cash, *The Mind of the South* (New York, 1944); Robert Penn Warren, *Segregation: The Inner Conflict in The South* (New York, 1956).

8. This was notwithstanding the fact that Myrdal considered American racial injustice and segregation to be a Northern, as well as a Southern, problem. Myrdal, supra note 5 at 44–49.

widespread enforced segregation in the South and the comparative lack of legally mandated segregation in the North.[9] For Kansas, civil rights and segregation were compatible concepts, and the state maintained laws which permitted segregation in some aspects of public life, yet prohibited it in others.[10] Granting too great a legal status to racial prejudice would conflict with the heritage of 'bleeding Kansas,' born amidst a struggle against slavery within its borders.[11]

In the early 1950s, Kansas' middle-of-the-road approach did not exempt it from the growing national controversy over racial segregation. In 1951, the NAACP brought suit against the Board of Education of Topeka, Kansas, challenging the constitutionality of the Kansas law permitting segregated schools.[12] Caught in the embarrassing position of supporting a policy which was coming into increasing disfavor in other parts of the country, state and local officials waffled on the question of whether to defend the segregation statute when the NAACP appealed a lower court judgment to the U.S. Supreme Court. Some considered Kansas a 'hapless defendant' in a suit that was really concerned with practices in the deep South.[13] The state reluctantly defended its statute, while in 1953, when the appeal was pending, the Topeka school board voted to abolish segregation in its schools.[14]

Taking what it considered to be an important and progressive step, the school board moved slowly and carefully to dismantle its system of enforced racial segregation. All along the way, it was careful to provide parents who preferred to avoid integration with the time and the means to do so. Such private choice, board members came to believe, was not for the school board to oppose, but rather to facilitate in the interests of protecting associational rights of whites as well as blacks. The school board's plan would leave formerly all-black schools exclusively black. Some formerly all-white schools were integrated to varying degrees, and five schools remained exclusively white. The remaining racial isolation was not the school board's problem, the board believed, as it was the result of private choice and residence patterns, even though the board's plan maximized the effect residential patterns might have on school segregation, and affirmatively accommodated private efforts to avoid integration. As far as the Topeka school board was concerned, once they stopped enforcing a clear color line in school attendance, segregation no longer existed.[15]

---

9. See generally Pauli Murray, *States Laws on Race and Color* (Cincinnati, 1950).

10. Ibid. at 8, 10. For example, elementary school segregation in cities with populations over 15,000 was permitted; school segregation in smaller cities was prohibited. High school segregation was only permitted in Kansas City, Kansas. See infra at 357–62.

11. See generally, Kenneth S. Davis, *Kansas* (New York, 1976) 35–71.

12. Brown v. Board of Education, 98 F. Supp. 797 (1951).

13. 'In Court Paradox', *Kansas City Star*, Nov. 29, 1953.

14. See infra at 371–73, 375–76.

15. See infra at 376–77, 379–86.

The efforts of the Topeka Board of Education and other boards of education in Kansas during the 50s did not end the phenomenon of one–race schools in the state.[16] The actions of school authorities in Kansas stood in

16. See infra note 103. The effectiveness of the Topeka school board's desegregation plan would later be questioned by federal authorities and members of the black community. In 1974, the Department of Health, Education and Welfare found that the schools remained racially segregated and that the predominately black schools were of poorer quality, and consequently the school board was in violation of the Civil Rights Act of 1964. However, HEW was enjoined by the federal district court from terminating the city's federal funding because the city was acting under a court order in *Brown*, and was therefore not subject to the enforcement provisions of the Civil Rights Act. Unified School Dist. #501 v. Weinberger, No. 74–160–C5 (D. Kan. August 23, 1974); see Brown v. Bd. of Educ., 84 F.R.D. 383, 390–91 (D. Kan. 1979); see also 'How Much Integration?' *Topeka Capital-Journal*, May 12, 1974. A group of black parents later moved to intervene in the *Brown* case. Although the suit had lain dormant for years, the district court had never relinquished jurisdiction over the case, and had never found that complete compliance with the Supreme Court's ruling had been achieved. Among the intervening plaintiffs was Linda Brown Smith, one of the original plaintiffs, now suing on behalf of her children. Intervention was granted in 1979. Brown v. Bd. of Educ., 84 F.R.D. 383, 405 (1979). The case was tried in October of 1986, and on April 8, 1987, the district court ruled in favor of the defendants. Brown v. Bd. of Educ., No. T-316, slip op. at 50 (D. Kan. April 8, 1987). Because the case was decided while this article was in the publication process, my discussion of it is necessarily brief.

As of the 1985–86 academic year the Topeka elementary school population was approximately 26% nonwhite. The schools in the district ranged in racial composition from 94% white/6% nonwhite to 38% white/62% nonwhite. Ibid. at 16. Three of the twenty-six elementary schools had a greater than 50% nonwhite student body, and five elementary schools were over 90% white. Ibid. at 8–9. Using statistics and other data, the plaintiffs argued that eight schools were racially identifiably nonwhite schools, ibid. at 16, and that several schools were racially identifiable white schools. Ibid. at 30. The district court found that '[r]acial balance does not exist in the district's schools', ibid. at 46, and that '[a]t any time, more could have been done to achieve racial balance in the schools'. Ibid. at 44. Further, '[a]s compared with many desegregation cases, relatively small changes in student and staff assignment would create the balance which plaintiffs define as desegregation'. Ibid. at 45. Nevertheless, the court held that 'the *de jure* system of segregation has been dismantled and its vestiges eliminated'. Ibid. The court found that many school attendance decisions were in keeping with 'the neighborhood school policy consistently applied by the district'. Ibid. at 25. It did not believe that, in the years since *Brown I* was decided, the actions of Topeka school officials indicated 'a desire to perpetuate segregation by foregoing opportunities to desegregate schools'. Ibid. at 43.

In essence, the court found that the schools were racially imbalanced, that the school district could have done more to reduce the racial imbalance, but that this inaction was not motivated by segregative intent. In this sense, the court's posture is reminiscent of that of the original district court panel: the question of good faith, not the conditions in the schools, is the matter upon which the case turns. While discriminatory intent is, of course, required for a fourteenth amendment violation, Washington v. Davis, 426 U.S. 229, 240 (1976), once a court has determined that a school system is segregated, school officials may not sit benignly on the sidelines. They have an 'affirmative duty to take whatever steps might be necessary to convert to a unitary system in which racial discrimination would be eliminated root and branch'. Green v. New Kent County School Board, 391 U.S. 430, 437–38 (1968). Accord Columbus Bd. of Educ. v. Penick, 443 U.S. 449, 458–461 (1979) (*Columbus II*). Good faith is not enough after *Green*. The

sharp contrast to the massive resistance to attempts at far less integration in many Southern states.[17] However, the Topeka school officials were not being forced to integrate. They were not trying to resist the Court's mandate, but rather hoped to be the first to comply, that the good name of Kansas would not be sullied through association with the misdeeds of the South.

Because the district court trusted the school board as a result of its 'good faith beginning' of desegregation, the court left the board to its own devices in completing the process.[18] As a result, desegregation in Topeka could be accomplished to the limit of the board's good faith.

This article considers what the school board sought to accomplish in desegregating its schools, as illustrated by the actions it would take and the way it would justify them. Of particular interest is the question of how it is that, once the board defined segregation as a wrong, its ideas about the actions it should take to redress the wrong came to be limited in the way they were.

The article begins with a discussion of the legal history of school segregation in Kansas, a history that is unique among states that segregated students until the *Brown* period. Kansas law allowed segregation in some areas, and prohibited it in others, so that desegregation was ordered by the Kansas courts in some cases long before *Brown*. The article then turns to the history of black education and segregation in Topeka. Topeka blacks have a long history of challenging racial segregation in their schools, with the first case against the Topeka Board of Education filed in 1902. Next, the article discusses the school board's response to its involvement in *Brown*. The emphasis here is on the point in time when the board came to question the propriety of its involvement in the case, and eventually decided to abandon segregation in its schools.[19] Of particular importance is the way the Topeka

---

question of whether desegregation has ever been achieved in Topeka should not turn on the hearts of school officials, but on their handiwork. See Dayton Bd. of Educ. v. Brinkman, 443 U.S. 526, 538 (1979) (*Dayton II*).

17. See generally Francis M. Wilhoit, *The Politics of Massive Resistance* (New York, 1973).

18. See Brown v. Bd. of Educ., No. T-316, slip op. (D. Kan. Oct. 23, 1955).

19. In *Simple Justice*, Richard Kluger tells the story of Topeka's involvement in *Brown* up to the point when the district court ruled in the school board's favor. Richard Kluger, *Simple Justice* (New York, 1977) [hereinafter cited as Kluger]. This article picks up the story from that point on.

The one scholar to examine post-*Brown* school desegregation in Topeka is Raymond Wolters. Wolters begins his discussion of the effect of *Brown* on the Topeka schools by focusing on black unrest at Topeka High School which resulted in a school boycott in 1970. Raymond Wolters, *The Burden of Brown: Thirty Years of School Desegregation* (Knoxville, Tennessee, 1984) 254–55. Wolters does not examine the source of black dissatisfaction with the schools or the interracial tension he finds. His implicit assumption seems to be that black unrest and racial tension during this period were part of the legacy of school desegregation in Topeka, even though Topeka High School was not affected by *Brown* because it has always been an integrated school. Wolters also touches on the background to the reactivation of the *Brown* litigation. Ibid. at 262–71. See supra note 16. Wolters' work does not contribute significantly to an understanding

school board developed its desegregation plan, and the manner in which it would defend the plan in district court once *Brown* II was remanded.

In the conclusion, the article seeks to explain the cognitive dissonance that would seem to occur in the context of the school board members' desire to further black rights and fully comply with *Brown*, and their concern with protecting the interests of whites who wished to avoid desegregation. The concluding essay first discusses the reconciliation of these conflicting impulses on a rhetorical level. Rather than conceptualizing the remedial questions in the *Brown* litigation in terms of the rights of blacks to attend schools that were, in fact, integrated, the board articulated the right at stake as an associational right. In so doing, the board could view both whites and blacks as having legitimate and equivalent interests at stake in the remedy. The rhetoric of freedom of association enabled the board to seek to protect the interests of whites in avoiding integration without seeming to descend from the moral high road the board believed itself to have taken. In this respect, this article illustrates an aspect of the critique of rights analysis,[20] in that it shows that there was sufficient play within the concept of the right in *Brown* that the school board members could use an interpretation of *Brown* to further both the rights of black school children and the interests of those who wished to avoid the practical realization of black rights.

Second, the conclusion attempts to reconcile the board's conflicting actions on a more fundamental level by questioning the nature of the school board's interest in desegregating. In deciding to desegregate, the Topeka school board was acting to distance itself from the South which was

---

of the effect of *Brown* on the Topeka schools because he begins his study too late in time and hence does not examine the school board's initial desegregation efforts which would set the conditions for both the patterns of continuing racial isolation, and the way Topeka's school policies would be understood within the community. Rather, Wolters seems to take the school board members' assertion that they adopted racially neutral attendance policies at face value.

20. The critique of rights analysis considers the question of how it is that rights can come to be enforced in such a way that they compromise the interests of those they are intended to benefit. See Alan Freeman, 'Legitimizing Racial Discrimination Through Antidiscrimination Law: A Critical Review of Supreme Court Doctrine', 62 *Minnesota Law Review* 1049 (1978).

While I find the critique of rights useful with regard to its identification of the indeterminacy and instability of rights, I do not agree with Mark Tushnet's assessment that the idea of rights is inherently 'affirmatively harmful'. Mark Tushnet, 'An Essay on Rights', 62 *Texas Law Review* 1363, 1384 (1984). A concept of rights can be empowering and, as Tushnet notes, politically useful. See Mark Tushnet, 'The Critique of Rights: An Historical Overview' (unpublished paper presented at the Law and Society Conference, June 1, 1986) 2. That rights can be interpreted and enforced in a manner which deprives those they purportedly benefit of an interest they purportedly protect is, in my view, made possible by the fluidity of ideas of rights, but is not determined by them. Rather, it is determined by the structures of power and domination in which claims of rights are made. An argument that a concept of rights is necessarily enforced in a negative and disempowering way due to a property inherent in the concept itself gives too much determinant content to an idea simultaneously critiqued as indeterminant.

perceived as the source of 'real' segregation. As racial segregation had come to be considered to be unAmerican, the school board attempted to bring its actions within what it considered to be proper American values. I argue that the board's action can be understood as an exercise in self-definition, as an attempt to see themselves as moral actors, and, in distancing themselves from the South, to articulate the boundaries of their moral community. In this respect, the focus of the board's reform efforts was not so much on changing the character of the schools, as in changing the character of their conceptions of themselves.

The Legal History of School Segregation in Kansas

In the years prior to *Brown*, the state of Kansas maintained an ambivalent posture toward school segregation, at least as far as its legal status was concerned.[21] In enacting its first school law in 1861, the Kansas State Legislature granted school districts the authority 'to make such orders as they deem proper for the separate education of white and colored children, securing to them equal advantages'.[22] This authority to segregate was retained for several years in varying forms.[23] However, when Kansas codified its school laws in 1876, it deleted the authority to segregate from its statutes with no recorded debate or explanation.[24] This

---

21. Ambivalence, or outright hostility toward blacks, appeared in other areas as well. Although, in the 1850s, opposition to slavery was a motivating force in the battle for control of what would become the state of Kansas, the state's first official constitution did not extend equal rights to free blacks. Suffrage was extended only to white male citizens. Kan. Const. art. 5 §1 (1859). The framers of the Kansas constitution considered and rejected a proposal to make Kansas 'not only a free state, but a free white state' by forbidding black immigration. Kan. Const. Debates at 178. The convention was divided on the question of black education. In discussing a provision regarding a system of 'common schools' for the children of the state, several delegates argued that blacks should be excluded entirely from public schooling. Their opponents argued that, since blacks would be living in Kansas, 'they should be made as intelligent and moral as education can make them'. Further, the white majority in a community could 'protect itself', from blacks, if need be, by providing racially segregated schools. Ibid. at 176. In its final form, the Kansas Constitution did not expressly address the question of black education, leaving discretion over the matter to the state legislature. Kan. Const. Art. 6 (1859).

22. 1861 Kan. Laws, ch. 76, art. III, sec. I.

23. In 1862, the Kansas legislature required separate taxation of white and non-white persons for the purpose of supporting segregated schools. All white taxes would go for the support of white schools, and non-white taxes would support non-white schools. 1862 Kan. Laws, Ch. 46, Art. IV, Sec. 18–19. This measure was repealed two years later, and discretion over school taxes was vested in boards of education. 1864 Kan. Laws, ch. 67, sec. 14–16. The 1864 school law retained for school boards the power to segregate school children, but contained no proviso that separate schools had to be equal. Ibid., sec. 4.

24. 1876 Kan. Laws, ch. 122, art. X, sec. 4.

temporary aberration apparently had no effect on the practice of segregation.[25]

In 1879, the Kansas state legislature enacted the law which would shape the course of permissible school segregation in Kansas for the next seventy-five years. The legislature distinguished between 'cities of the first class' with populations of 15,000 and over, and smaller cities of the second and third classes. First class cities were explicitly granted the authority to segregate students in the elementary grades. Such segregation was permitted, but not required, and 'no discrimination . . . on account of color' was allowed in high school.[26] The legislature was silent on the question of whether smaller cities could segregate school children.

Whether, under Kansas law, 'cities of the second class' could provide segregated schooling without legislative authorization was considered by the Kansas Supreme Court in 1881 in a case involving the schools in Ottawa, Kansas.[27] Leslie Tinnon, a black second grader, sued the Ottawa Board of Education, arguing that Kansas law requiring communities to maintain a system of 'common schools' 'free to all children residing in such city'[28] prohibited the establishment of separate schools for blacks. In addition, he claimed that school segregation violated the Fourteenth Amendment.[29]

Noting that the law on the subject was unclear, the Kansas Supreme Court did not consider the constitutionality of segregation per se. It limited its inquiry to the question of whether, in the absence of state legislation authorizing segregation, smaller 'cities of the second class' had the authority to establish separate schools. The court found that:

25. But see Kluger, supra note 19 at 371. Kluger suggests, I believe erroneously, that the process of desegregation began after passage of the 1876 law. This is unlikely as, in 1876, it was not at all clear that legislative authorization was necessary for local school officials to segregate their schools. Further, even after the illegality of certain forms of segregation was settled in 1881, a court mandate was usually required to dismantle illegally segregated schools. See infra note 42. Some, if not all, school districts were unaffected by the temporary change in the law. See Board of Education of the City of Ottawa v. Tinnon, 26 Kan. 1, 18 (1881). Kluger refers to the existence of some mixed-race schools in 1876. Most likely, these schools began as integrated schools, rather than changing their racial composition due to legislative action. Cf. Reynolds v. Bd. of Educ. of the City of Topeka, 66 Kan. 672 (1903) (elementary school integrated until 1900); Bd. of Educ. of the City of Ottawa v. Tinnon, 26 Kan. 1 (1881) (elementary school integrated until 1880).

26. 1879 Kan. Laws, ch. 81, sec. 1. This statute withstood a constitutional challenge in Reynolds v. Bd. of Educ. of the City of Topeka, 66 Kan. 672 (1903). See discussion infra at 359–61.

27. Until September of 1880 the city of Ottawa, a city of the second class, educated all city school children, grades one through twelve, in one school building. By 1880 the accommodations had become somewhat crowded, and the Board of Education moved all black children to a separate building. Bd. of Educ. of the City of Ottawa v. Tinnon, 26 Kan. 1, 3, 8–10 (1881).

28. 1879 Kan. Gen. Stat., ch. 92, sec. 151.

29. Tinnon, 26 Kan. 1 at 3, 8–10.

[t]he tendency of the times is, and has been for several years, to abolish all distinctions on account of race, or color, or previous condition of servitude, and to make all persons absolutely equal before the law. Therefore, unless it appears clear beyond all question that the legislature intended to authorize such distinctions to be made, we should not hold that any such authority has been given.[40]

Accordingly, the court strictly construed Kansas school laws on the question of whether authority to segregate had been granted. It held that boards of education did not have the power to segregate students by race unless the legislature clearly authorized such segregation, and it did not find such a clear authorization for segregation in cities of the second class. Rather, 'by the clearest implication, if not in express terms, [the legislature] has prohibited the boards from establishing any such [segregated] schools'.[31]

In 1903, in a case involving the schools in Topeka, the Kansas Supreme Court addressed the question it had reserved in *Tinnon*: whether legislatively authorized school segregation violated the state and federal constitutions. In *Reynolds v. Board of Education of the City of Topeka*,[32] which involved

---

30. 26 Kan. at 18.
    In construing the school law, the court noted that it had been passed in an era 'when the minds of all men were inclined to adopt the most cosmopolitan views of human rights, and not to adopt any narrow or contracted views founded merely upon race, or color, or clan, or kinship'. 26 Kan. at 18. According to the court, the 'tendency of the present age' was to educate all kinds of children together without classifying them on the basis of race, sex or other characteristics. Society as a whole gained from such integration, for

> [a]t the common schools, where both sexes and all kinds of children mingle together, we have the great world in miniature; there they may learn human nature. . . . But on the other hand, persons by isolation may become strangers even in their own country; and by being strangers, will be of but little benefit either to themselves or to society. As a rule, people cannot afford to be ignorant of the society which surrounds them; and as all kinds of people must live together in the same society, it would seem to be better that all should be taught in the same schools.

26 Kan. at 19.

31. 26 Kan. at 20. Justice Valentine's majority opinion prompted Justice Brewer to file the term's only dissent. Brewer found Valentine's analysis to turn on matters more properly reserved for the legislature. For him, the question was not the wisdom of segregation as an educational policy, but rather the scope of the power the legislature had conferred upon boards of education. In addition, although Valentine had reserved the question of the constitutionality of legislatively authorized segregation, Brewer 'dissent[ed] entirely from the suggestion' that school segregation might be unconstitutional. He would have held that 'free schools mean equal school advantages to every child, leaving questions of classification by territory, sex, or color, to be determined by the wisdom of the local authorities'. 26 Kan. at 25.
    Tinnon would remain good law throughout the history of legislatively authorized school segregation in Kansas. See infra at 361–62.

32. 66 Kan. 672 (1903). Topeka, Kansas segregated its elementary schools in accordance with the Kansas statute permitting such segregation. 1879 Kan. Laws, ch. 81. In the fall of 1902, William Reynolds, a black resident of Topeka, sought admission of his son to

school segregation in a city of the first class, the court first considered whether segregation violated the provision of the state constitution requiring the establishment of 'a uniform system of common schools'.[33] The court found it 'perfectly plain' that a uniform system of schools did not imply integrated schools, but rather uniform educational facilities. And in Kansas,

> [t]he system of educational opportunities, advantages, methods and accommodations is uniform, constant, and equal, whether availed of by children in a rural district or a city ward; whether by males or females; whether by blacks and whites commingling, or by them separately; and whether race classification be made in one grade, or department, or city, or county, or in many.[34]

In disposing of the state law claim, the Kansas court noted that the convention which framed the state constitution had considered the question of education for blacks, and had intended to leave the legislature free to act as it saw fit.[35]

The court then turned to the validity of the Kansas law under the U.S. Constitution, quoting at length from opinions by other state courts holding that the Fourteenth Amendment was not violated when states provided separate-but-equal schooling for blacks.[36] The court grounded its view of the Fourteenth Amendment on the U.S. Supreme Court's ruling in *Plessy v. Ferguson*,[37] which found that

> [t]he object of the amendment was undoubtedly to enforce the absolute equality of the two races before the law, but in the nature of things it could not have intended to abolish distinctions based upon color, or to enforce social, as distinguished from political equality, or a commingling of the races upon terms unsatisfactory to either.[38]

According to *Plessy*, segregation statutes did not necessarily 'imply the inferiority of either race to the other', and were generally recognized to be

---

a white school. When he was refused, Reynolds sought a Writ of Mandamus in the Kansas Supreme Court to compel the Topeka school board to admit his son to the school. Reynolds claimed that school segregation in Topeka violated state law and the federal constitution. Affidavit for Alternative Writ of Mandamus at 4, Reynolds v. Bd. of Educ. of the City of Topeka, 66 Kan. 672 (1903). See infra at 12–15 for a discussion of the historical background to the *Reynolds* case.

33. 66 Kan. at 679; Kans. Const. art. VI, sec. 2. The court also considered and rejected technical arguments that the statute permitting segregation had not been properly enacted. 66 Kan. at 673–79.

34. 66 Kan. at 679–80. The court quoted at length from decisions by the courts of Indiana, New York and Massachusetts involving similar state law issues which supported their conclusions. Cory, et al., v. Carter, 48 Ind. 327 (1847); People, ex. rel. Cisco v. School Board, 161 N.Y. 598 (1900); Roberts v. City of Boston, 5 Cush. [Mass.] 198 (1849).

35. 66 Kan. at 686.

36. 66 Kan. at 686–90, quoting The States, ex rel. Garnes v. McCann, et. al., 21 Ohio St. 198 (1871); People, ex rel. King v. Gallagher, 93 N.Y. 438 (1883); Ward v. Flood, 48 Cal. 36 (1874).

37. 163 U.S. 537 (1896).

38. Ibid. at 544.

within the police power of the states. The most common instance of such segregation was 'the establishment of separate schools for white and colored children, which has been held to be a valid exercise of the legislative power even by courts of states where the political rights of the colored race have been longest and most earnestly enforced'.[39] Following *Plessy*, the Kansas court held that the Kansas statute permitting segregation did not violate the U.S. Constitution. It further held that the educational facilities provided to blacks in Topeka were not unequal and, consequently, segregation in the Topeka schools was consistent with state and federal law.[40]

In upholding segregation in *Reynolds*, the Kansas Supreme Court validated the dichotomy in Kansas law which would remain in effect until segregation was outlawed in *Brown v. Board of Education* in 1954.[41] Segregation was lawful in larger cities where it was authorized by the legislature, and unlawful in smaller cities where it was not explicitly authorized. As the legislature would not choose to materially alter the school segregation laws in the intervening years,[42] the only legal questions between *Reynolds* and *Brown* would be concerned with the refinement and application of these principles.[43] Litigation continued even though the law was so

---

39. 163 U.S. at 543–44, quoted in 66 Kan. at 691.

40. 66 Kan. at 692. See infra at 363–64 regarding the disparity in school facilities.

41. 347 U.S. 483 (1954).

42. The only change in the segregation statutes between 1903 and 1954 was a 1905 law permitting high school segregation, but only in Kansas City, Kansas. 1905 Kan. Laws, ch. 414, sec. 1. See Richardson v. Bd. of Educ. of Kansas City, 72 Kan. 629 (1906). There was at least one unsuccessful attempt to extend high school segregation to other cities. In 1911, a bill was introduced to amend the 1905 law to allow segregated high schools in all cities of the first class. The bill was reported favorably out of the House Committee on Cities of the First Class, but ultimately failed to become law. Kan. House Bill No. 264 (1911).

Legislation to expand the scope of permissible segregation to include cities of the second class was introduced in 1919. Kan. House Bill No. 9 (1919); Kan. Senate Bill No. 567 (1919). The bills engendered strong public reaction in favor of and against expanded segregation. See Kan. State Historical Society, Archives Dept., Governor Allen's Papers, Box 26, file no. 22, 'School Segregation', (1919). The legislation failed in both houses.

Although segregation in second- and third-class cities was never authorized by the Kansas State Legislature, it was practiced in many such cities through most of Kansas history. See Bd. of Educ. of the City of Ottawa v. Tinnon, 26 Kan. 1 (1881); Cartwright v. Bd. of Educ. of the City of Coffeyville, 73 Kan. 32 (1906); Woolridge v. Bd. of Educ. of the City of Galena, 98 Kan. 397 (1916); Webb v. School Dist. No. 90 in Johnson County, 167 Kan. 395 (1949) (cases involving segregation in cities of the second class).

43. The most important application of Kansas segregation law through the courts came with the introduction of junior high schools, as they were not mentioned in the Kansas school laws. Thurman-Watts v. Bd. of Educ. of the City of Coffeyville, 115 Kan. 328 (1924), held that ninth grade was part of high school under Kansas law, and therefore junior high school students could not be segregated in the ninth grade.

To comply with *Thurman-Watts*, the Topeka school board sent white students to

clearly settled by 1903. Smaller cities continued to segregate their elementary schools until ordered by the courts to comply with the law.[44] And black students and their parents in larger cities continued to seek access to the white schools from which they were legally excluded.[45]

Although Kansas statutes on segregation would be consistent over time, their very consistency would lead to a change in the permissible scope of segregation. The needs of school districts changed with population growth, yet Kansas maintained its increasingly anachronistic distinction between first- and second-class cities as those above and below 15,000.[46] Because the definition of first- and second-class cities remained the same, as Kansas communities grew in population, an increasing number would gain the authority to segregate.[47] By 1954, ninety percent of black Kansans would live in cities of the first class, so that the state's seemingly ambiguous policy would mean widespread permissible segregation in practice.[48]

Segregation and Black Education in Topeka

For the first superintendent of schools of Topeka, Kansas, black education was an important priority. In 1867, one hundred blacks were enrolled in an

---

junior high schools for grades seven, eight and nine, but sent black students to black elementary schools through the eighth grade, then to integrated junior high school for ninth grade only. This pattern of school attendance was challenged in 1941 as violating the requirement that separate schools must be equal. Graham v. Bd. of Educ. of the City of Topeka, 153 Kan. 840 (1941). The Kansas Supreme Court found that, due to the great differences in educational programs and facilities between grades seven and eight in the black elementary schools and the white junior high school, Topeka was not providing black students with an equal education. However, because grades seven and eight were considered elementary grades, the court did not require junior high school integration. It only held that if Topeka was to provide junior high schools for white children, it must do the same for blacks. 153 Kan. at 844–48. Topeka complied with the court order by integrating black seventh and eighth graders into the junior high schools. Kluger, supra note 19 at 379.

44. See cases cited in supra note 42.

45. Williams v. Bd. of Educ. of the City of Parsons [I], 79 Kan. 202 (1908); Williams v. Bd. of Educ. of the City of Parsons [II], 81 Kan. 593 (1910); Wright v. Bd. of Educ. of the City of Topeka, 153 Kan. 840 (1941) (school integration sought due to unequal conditions in cities of the first class).

46. When the legislature wished to distinguish between cities of different sizes for the purpose of education-related regulation, it simply created population groupings within the category of cities of the first class. E.g. Kan. Gen. Stat. sec. 72–1725, 72–1725a, 72–1726, 72–1737 (1949).

47. Compare Cartwright v. Bd. of Educ. of the City of Coffeyville, 73 Kan. 32 (1906) (Coffeyville as a city of the second class) with Thurman-Watts v. Bd. of Educ. of the City of Coffeyville, 115 Kan. 328 (1924) (Coffeyville as a city of the first class).

48. Joint Comm. of the National Educ. Assn. and the American Teachers Assn., *Legal Status of Segregated Schools* (Montgomery, Alabama, 1954) 14.

overcrowded one-room elementary school in which one teacher would teach all subjects to the fifty or so who attended each day. In addition, working people crowded into the segregated evening school which was maintained for several weeks during the winter. As Topeka expanded and improved its educational facilities and programs for the increasing population of white students, Superintendent L. C. Wilmarth urged the Board of Education to 'fully recognize the claims that the colored race have upon us for educational privileges', and to act promptly to provide additional facilities for black schools. As he wrote in his first report to the Board,

> It is plainly to be seen, that but a short time will elapse, ere the colored race by the general law of progress will be placed, side by side with us, equal participants in all rights, franchises and privileges of our government, qualified candidates for Legislative, Executive, and Judicial honors. Therefore it behooves us to be preparing not only for him, but ourselves, for the coming of changes by freely furnishing them with the best of educational advantages.[49]

Whether or not Wilmarth's successors provided black Topekans with an equal education, by the 1880s the city did provide four black schools.[50]

In one part of Topeka, there was partial elementary school integration as late as 1900. When the Lowman Hill area was annexed to the City of Topeka in 1890, only one school house existed in that new part of the city. It was attended by all children in the district regardless of race.[51] After the school burned down in 1900, the Topeka school board purchased a new site upon which to rebuild, claiming that the old site was unsanitary and inconvenient. It built a modern, two-story brick school building on the new site, and equipped it with new furniture and modern plumbing. The board then moved an old one-story structure to the original school site, equipping that two-room building with second-hand furniture. As the water mains for the city water supply stopped two blocks short of the old site, well water remained its sole water supply.[52] Once school was re-opened in the Lowman

49. Topeka Bd. of Educ., *History of the Topeka Schools* (1954) 110–11.

50. Ibid. at 113.
    The teaching staffs of the black schools were initially white. As Superintendent D.C. Tillotson noted in his report for the year 1886–87, '[s]ix years ago, with two exceptions, all the teachers in our colored schools were white', however white teachers were transferred once black teachers could be found. Quoted in ibid. at 115–16. After the first black students graduated from integrated Topeka High School in 1882, that school began to provide 'a small consistent flow of colored teachers to the community'. Ibid. at 116. Through hiring local and outside black teachers, Topeka eventually achieved completely segregated teaching staffs. Kluger, supra note 19 at 379.

51. Defendant's Return to Alternative Writ of Mandamus at 2–3 (May 1902), Reynolds v. Bd. of Educ. of the City of Topeka, 66 Kan. 672 (1903). There may have been occasional instances of school integration in other parts of the city as well. For example, after his mother petitioned the school board, Langston Hughes, the black writer, attended first grade in 1908 at Harrison School, which was considered a white school. Faith Berry, *Langston Hughes: Before and Beyond Harlem* (Westpoint, CT, 1983).

52. Plaintiff's Affidavit for Alternative Writ of Mandamus at 1–4, *Reynolds;* Defendant's

Hill District in early 1902, only white children were admitted to the new school building. Although the one-hundred and thirty whites occupied only four of the eight school rooms, black students were directed to the two room building on the old site.[53]

Black parents in the Lowman Hill District were outraged by the school board's action, and many responded by keeping their children out of school. According to the Women's League, an organization of black women in the Lowman Hill area, black parents would boycott the schools 'until the trouble is adjusted in some satisfactory way'. As they wrote to the Topeka Plaindealer, a local black community newspaper,

> if the board had given us equal school facilities for our children we would have had no grounds for complaint, though we were not in favor of separate schools, because we have not had one heretofore and it is not pleasant to have even the school house doors closed in one's face.[54]

The group did not want 'to appear stubborn or unreasonable, but simply ask for equal school facilities'.[55]

According to the Plaindealer, the black community was willing 'to agree to almost any sort of a compromise if the board had shown any spirit of conciliation, and would have let the matter drop if the colored children had been admitted to the sixth grade at the Lowman Hill School'.[56] However, when it met to consider the segregated schools controversy, the Topeka Board of Education was not in a compromising mood. The Board's 'attitude' foreclosed 'all possibility of compromise or setting the matter on any basis which has hitherto been proposed'.[57] Instead, Topeka blacks took the school controversy to the courts, as the Board's hard line position on segregation polarized the community. G. C. Clement, the attorney representing the black parents vowed to 'see these people through to the Supreme court of the United States, if need be, and spare my state this disgrace, if it takes the remainder of my life. I shall fight this miserable spirit of caste, and fight it to the last ditch.'[58]

Return to Alternative Writ of Mandamus at 4–5, *Reynolds;* 'Lowman Hill School', *The Topeka Plaindealer,* Feb. 1902.

53. There are conflicting accounts as to the number of black children involved. The plaintiff claimed there were fifty in the district. Plaintiff's Affidavit for Alternative Writ of Mandamus at 2, *Reynolds.* According to the defendants, there were about thirty-four black children enrolled in the two-room school, a larger number of black children than had ever been enrolled in the Lowman Hill district. Defendants' Return to Alternative Writ of Mandamus at 5, *Reynolds.* The difference may be due to a boycott of the segregated school by black parents. 'That School Question', *The Topeka Plaindealer,* Feb., 1902.

54. Ibid., quoting a letter to the Topeka Daily Capital.

55. Ibid.

56. 'The Lowman Hill School', *Topeka Plaindealer,* Feb. 1902.

57. Ibid.

58. Ibid.

Two months later, Clement filed a Writ of Mandamus in the Kansas Supreme Court on behalf of William Reynolds, a black parent whose son was excluded from the Lowman Hill School. Clement's most important legal argument was that racial segregation violated the state and federal constitutions. With the constitutional standard set by *Plessy v. Ferguson*,[59] he would not get far. The Kansas Supreme Court upheld the constitutionality of the Kansas school segregation statute, paving the way for an increasingly rigid and pervasive system of segregation in Topeka.[60]

Although *Reynolds* established the constitutionality of segregation in the Topeka schools, it was not the last time the city would be called upon to defend its practices in the Kansas courts.[61] For example, black education in Topeka was challenged as unequal in 1941. When the city established junior high schools,[62] it continued to segregate students through eighth grade, but not ninth grade, as Kansas law permitted.[63] White school children attended elementary school through sixth grade, junior high school for grades seven to nine and high school for grades ten to twelve. Black children, on the other hand, attended black elementary schools through the eighth grade, attended junior high for ninth grade only, and then attended the integrated high school. In *Graham v. Board of Education of the City of Topeka*,[64] blacks successfully challenged this pattern of schooling as providing unequal

---

59. 163 U.S. 537 (1896).

60. Reynolds v. Bd. of Educ. of the City of Topeka, 66 Kan. 672 (1903). See discussion supra at 359–61.

61. As the city's school system expanded in the early decades of the twentieth century, it maintained a limited number of black schools, so that many black children had to travel some distance to attend school. In 1930, Wilhelmina Wright sued the Topeka school board, claiming that the distance she had to travel to get to school constituted unequal treatment in violation of the *Plessy* standard. Wright lived a few blocks from Randolph School for whites, but was assigned to Buchanan School twenty blocks away. She claimed that her assignment to Buchanan was unreasonable due to the distance and the number of busy intersections she would have to cross. Wright did not argue that the facilities at the schools were unequal. Wright v. Bd. of Educ. of the City of Topeka, 129 Kan. 852 (1930). In a brief opinion, the court noted that, as a city of the first class, Topeka had maintained segregated schools for many years in accordance with state law. The city provided the plaintiff with bus transportation to and from Buchanan School, and the plaintiff did not allege that the transportation was inadequate. Consequently, the court held that Wright's assignment to Buchanan was not unreasonable. 129 Kan. at 853. Here and in other unequal treatment cases the Kansas Court did not compare the school board's treatment of whites with their treatment of blacks to determine whether the treatment of blacks was unequal. The sole question was whether the board's action regarding blacks, in isolation, was unreasonable. See Williams v. Bd. of Educ. of the City of Parsons [I], 79 Kan. 202 (1908); Williams v. Bd. of Educ. of the City of Parsons [II], 81 Kan. 593 (1910).

62. Topeka's first junior high school was established in 1914 or 1915. Plaintiff's Brief at 6 Graham v. Bd. of Educ., 153 Kan. 840 (1941).

63. See discussion at note 43, supra.

64. 153 Kan. 840 (1941). See note 42 supra, for a discussion of the ruling.

education for blacks in the seventh and eighth grades. Amid dissention in the black community stemming from the effect integration might have on the jobs of black teachers, the school board complied with the Kansas Supreme Court ruling by integrating black seventh and eighth graders into the junior high schools. Six black teachers lost their jobs, and two more were reduced to half-time.[65]

One year after the *Graham* ruling, Topeka hired a new school superintendent. Kenneth McFarland, a young, ambitious Kansan, was a gifted speaker who would provide forceful, perhaps overbearing, leadership in the Topeka school system during his tenure. Considered prejudiced and arrogant by many Topeka blacks, he held a hard line on segregation. In his racial ideology, McFarland invoked Booker T. Washington, suggesting that the only way to gain equality was to get a job and earn it. While he believed in segregation, he also believed in keeping separate schools equal, and tried to ensure that black students in Topeka were provided with equal opportunities.[66]

To enforce his policies on race, McFarland hired a black assistant, Harrison Caldwell, to supervise black education in Topeka. Caldwell used strong tactics to enforce a segregationist philosophy on black teachers, capitalizing on the insecurity created when blacks were fired as a result of *Graham*. Caldwell suggested that elementary school integration would lead to the elimination of black teachers from the Topeka schools. Shortly after he arrived, black teachers, responding to his pressure, increased segregation within their profession by forming a separate black teachers association.[67]

A focus of Caldwell's attention was Topeka High School. Topeka's only high school was considered 'a segregated school within an integrated school'.[68] Through 1949, classes were integrated but activities were not. Caldwell was ever vigilant to keep black and white students apart outside the classroom. He held separate 'good-nigger assemblies' for black high school students while whites attended chapel.[69] As one student later recalled,

Caldwell would tell us not to rock the boat and how to be as little offensive to whites as possible—to be clean and study hard and accept the status quo—and things were

65. Christopher A. McElgunn, 'Graham v. Board of Education of Topeka: A Hobson's Choice (1984) (unpublished paper, Washburn Univ. Law School) 20–21. Three of the teachers whose jobs were affected had some connection to the *Graham* litigation.

66. Kluger, supra note 19 at 379–83.

67. Ibid at 381.

68. Isabell Masters, *The Life and Legacy of Oliver Brown* (Ph.D. diss., U. of Okla., 1981) 31. Masters's dissertation overstates the importance of Oliver Brown's role in *Brown*. She presents some interesting information, however, including her own recollections from her experience as a black student at Topeka High and as a resident of Topeka during the 1930s and 40s.

69. Kluger, supra note 19 at 382.

getting better. Those who went along got the good after-school and summer jobs, the scholarships, and the choice spots on the athletic teams.[70]

Blacks were segregated from music groups, sports and student government. There was a separate black student council which sent the only black representative to the student government body composed of representatives from all student groups. Blacks had their own school 'kings and queens'.[71] One sport open to blacks was basketball through a separate black league. The black team, the 'Ramblers,' could not use the Topeka High team name or colors. They played home games at East Topeka Junior High.[72] Separate black teams were abolished when, with little fanfare, the school board rescinded its formal policy of internal segregation at the high school in 1949.[73]

By mid-century, Topeka was a city of over 100,000, and approximately 7.5 per cent of its residents were black.[74] Segregation in the city was not limited to its schools. Most of its public accommodations were segregated, even though Kansas law formally prohibited it.[75] Only one Topeka hotel, the Dunbar, would serve blacks, and most restaurants would not seat them. Of the seven movie theaters in town, five served only whites, one provided balcony seating only for blacks, and one theater was for blacks only. The municipal swimming pool at Gage Park was for whites only, with the exception of one day a year when it was open to the black community. Not everything in Topeka was segregated, however. There was no racial segregation in bus or train transportation.[76] And while many blacks lived in eastern Topeka, residential segregation was not absolute.

70. Samuel C. Jackson, quoted in Kluger, ibid.

71. Ibid. at 382; Topeka High School, *The 1947 Sunflower* (1947) 54, 56, 69 (school yearbook); Masters, supra note 67 at 31.

72. Julia Etta Parks, *The Development of All-Black Basketball Teams in Topeka High School, 1929–1949* (1982); Kluger, supra note 19 at 382.

73. Topeka Bd. of Educ. Minutes, Sept. 26, 1949.

74. Kluger, supra note 19 at 372.

75. 1935 Kan. Gen. Stat. 21–2424. Kansas law provided civil and criminal penalties against any person making 'any distinction on account of race, color, or previous condition of servitude' in the operation of a public accommodation licensed by a municipality. 1935 Kan. Gen. Stat. 21–2424.

   To circumvent the law, Topeka repealed its city ordinance which required the licensing of theaters and opera houses in the fall of 1947. Shortly thereafter, two black Topekans were refused admission to a Topeka theater. As they could not sue the theater owners for discrimination in what was now an unlicensed private business, they brought suit against the City of Topeka, challenging its authority to repeal its licensing requirement. Stovall v. City of Topeka, 166 Kan. 35 (1948). The Kansas Supreme found that the '[a]ppellants had no vested rights in the continued existence of the licensing ordinance and the city was at liberty to repeal it whenever it so desired'. 166 Kan. at 36.

76. Kluger, supra note 19 at 374–75.

Blacks also lived in mixed-race neighborhoods scattered through the rest of Topeka.[77]

After repeatedly requesting that the Board of Education reconsider its elementary school segregation policy, the Topeka NAACP, in conjunction with the NAACP national office, brought suit against the Board in 1951.[78] The district court ruled in favor of the Board. Although it found that segregation was harmful to black children, the three judge panel believed that it remained constitutional under *Plessy* until the Supreme Court reconsidered the wisdom of that ruling.[79] As the NAACP appealed, and, in the fall of 1952, the *Brown* case was consolidated with cases from South Carolina, Virginia and the District of Columbia, the focus of the legal battle shifted to Washington.[80]

IV. The School Segregation Controversy

A. The Politics of Ambivalence

Back in Kansas, a different battle was being waged, as state and local government officials awoke to the political implications of defending segregation. Proud of the Kansas free state heritage, many citizens were displeased that their state was involved in legal action which they associated with Southern racism. As school superintendent H.H. Robinson of Augusta, Kansas wrote Governor Edward Arn,

> I am surprised and I must say chagrined to learn that Kansas now classifies itself as one of the White Supremacy states as indicated by the case now before the United States Supreme Court. I have just finished reading a new and fine history of Kansas and found much of it thrilling and glorious. As I review those historical events which caused us to be called 'bleeding Kansas', I wonder how we suddenly find ourselves represented

77. See ibid. at 377, 408; Transcript of Record at 81–109, Brown v. Bd. of Educ., 347 U.S. 483 (1954).

78. Brown v. Bd. of Educ., 98 F.Supp. 797 (D. Kan. 1951).
    In 1948, the Kansas State Conference of NAACP Branches, and the NAACP national office supported the proposed filing of a desegregation suit in Wichita, Kansas, rather than Topeka. Wichita teachers mobilized against such an effort, however, and in December of 1948 the Wichita branch of the NAACP elected a new board opposed to desegregation litigation. The focus of desegregation efforts in Kansas then shifted to Topeka. See Mark Tushnet, *The NAACP'S Legal Strategy Against Segregated Education, 1925–1950* (Chapel Hill, 1987) 139–40.
    Because the background to the *Brown* litigation up through the district court trial is a familiar story as told by Richard Kluger in *Simple Justice*, see Kluger, supra note 19, this article will concentrate on the point in time after Kluger's version of the story, when the Topeka school board began to consider the wisdom of its involvement in the case, and the propriety of its segregation policy.

79. Brown v. Bd of Educ., 98 F. Supp. 797, 800 (D. Kan. 1951); Transcript of Record at 245–46, Brown v. Bd of Educ. 347 U.S. 483 (1954).

80. See Brown v. Bd. of Educ., 347 U.S. 483, 486–88 n. 1 (1954). A fifth case, from the state of Delaware, would later be included. Ibid.

before the Supreme Court opposed to those human rights for which our early settlers bled.[81]

Robinson was concerned that, through defending *Brown*, 'we are throwing the influence of our state against those principles for which we have always stood'.[82]

Many shared Robinson's view that participation in the *Brown* case involved the city of Topeka and the state of Kansas in matters that really concerned the South. It was in the South, after all, that 'real' segregation occurred, as far as many Topekans were concerned. While the white community[83] in Topeka paid little attention to black criticism of their own schools, they were outraged at Southern racial practices. For example, in June of 1950, the Topeka Daily Capital ran an editorial criticizing Georgia Governor Herman Talmadge for his vow to defy Supreme Court decisions finding certain forms of segregation in higher education to be unconstitutional.[84] According to the paper, '[a]s was to be expected, certain southernors are perturbed' about the decisions.[85] 'Southern states have

---

81. H. H. Robinson, Superintendent, Augusta Public Schools, letter to Kan. Governor Edward Arn, Dec. 10, 1953, Kan. State Historical Society, Archives Dept., Governor Arn's Papers, Box 62.

82. Ibid.

83. I recognize that the use of a term like 'the white community' reifies a group of individual human beings who, in fact, held a variety of views, some of which might conflict with my characterization of dominant white ideology in Topeka during this period. I do not intend to infer that all of white Topeka shared an identical consciousness. Similarly, in referring to 'the black community', I do not intend to downplay the variety of perspectives Topeka blacks held. Rather, I use such terms as shorthand to refer to those who have made their voices heard in the sources I have used. Given my sources, primarily school board minutes, newspaper accounts and court records, those whose ideas are represented are largely elites who were active in the city's political life.

84. Anti-Segregation Decision, Topeka Daily Capital, June 8, 1950. The cases that Talmadge was concerned with were Sweatt v. Painter, 339 U.S. 629 (1950), and McLaurin v. Oklahoma, 339 U.S. 637 (1950). *Sweatt* held that a separate black law school set up by the State of Texas could not provide an equal legal education in part due to differences in faculty and resources, and because black law students would not have access to the interaction with other students which was an important part of the educational environment at the state's law school for whites. 339 U.S. at 633–34. *McLaurin* held that an equal education was not provided to a black student admitted to an Oklahoma graduate school of education, but set off from other students through segregated seating in the classroom, the library and the school cafeteria. 339 U.S. at 641–42.

    On the day that the decisions were announced, Talmadge vowed that 'as long as I am Governor, Negroes will not be admitted to white schools'. He continued, '[t]he line has been drawn. The threats that have been held over the head of the South for four years are now now pointed like a dagger ready to be plunged into the very heart of Southern tradition.' 'Talmadge Defiant; Others Hail Court', New York Times, June 6, 1950, at 19, col. 2.

85. 'Anti-Segregation Decision', Topeka Daily Capital, June 8, 1950.

ignored the 14th Amendment almost since it was adopted in 1868. Educational facilities available to white students have been denied colored boys and girls.' Further, blacks were 'shamefully segregated' on trains. Following the Supreme Court rulings affecting their states, Texas and Oklahoma would now 'be obliged to admit colored students to classrooms on equality with whites. They have no other alternative.'[86] Notwithstanding historic racially discriminatory practices in Topeka and Kansas laws permitting segregation, the editorial characterized segregation as a peculiarly Southern phenomenon. 'Northern states have never practiced discrimination to the extent it has been prevalent in the South . . . . Only in the die-hard South have Negroes been segregated and thus denied their constitutional rights.' The recent Supreme Court decisions 'open [ ] the way for a square deal for a race that has been woefully mistreated in the southern states'.[87]

As a general rule, the local press simply ignored the black schools when reporting on educational matters in Topeka.[88] Black education was acknowledged only when something significant occurred that specifically concerned segregated education.[89] For example, one of the only news stories in the Topeka Daily Capital in 1950 that considered black education was a front page article announcing a 'new step to end school segregation'.[90] The article reported that the school board had voted to abolish the Office of Director of Colored Schools. This step would mean that black schools would not have their own administrator, but would be governed by the same administrative structure as the white schools.[91] Coming only a week after the editorial that had identified segregation as something practiced '[o]nly in the die-hard South',[92] the article would seem to contradict the paper's characterization of the peculiarly Southern nature of segregation. However, according to the

---

86. Ibid.

87. Ibid.

88. See, e.g., 'School Executives Into Second Day of Conference', *Topeka Daily Capital*, Feb. 3, 1950, at 6; 'Aim at Flag Hanging in Every School', *Topeka Daily Capital*, March 7, 1950, at 1; 'Teachers Face Tougher Tests', *Topeka Daily Capital*, April 13, 1950, at 1. The black newspaper, *The Plaindealer*, had moved from Topeka to Kansas City, Kansas by this time. It would occasionally report on matters concerning the Topeka schools when something particularly significant happened. See *The Plaindealer*, April 1953.

89. See 'Colored P.-T.A. Board to Meet', *Topeka Daily Capital*, Nov. 3, 1950, at 21; 'Honors Today From Colored P.-T.A.'s', *Topeka Daily Capital*, May 7, 1950, at 6C. When Oliver Brown attempted to enroll his daughter Linda in a white school, the incident was mentioned briefly in a routine story on the opening of the 1950–51 school year. The article appeared on page twelve next to the movie advertisements. 'Schools Get Down to Work Today', *Topeka Daily Capital*, Sept. 12, 1950, at 12.

90. 'New Step to End School Segregation', *Topeka Daily Capital*, June 15, 1950.

91. Ibid.

92. *Topeka Daily Capital*, supra note 85.

paper, while school segregation in Topeka was permitted under state law, ' "arbitrary segregation", as interpreted by the board, is not'. Abolishing the separate administrative office was the 'final policy step in the board's program to stop arbitrary segregation', which had also included an end to segregation at high school dances and in athletic competition.[93] Taken together, the article and editorial suggest that, for this newspaper, the form of segregation practiced in Topeka was somehow not of the Southern variety that so clearly violated the constitutional rights of Southern blacks.

Given the ambivalence of many toward school segregation in general, and the *Brown* case in particular, it is not surprising that neither the Topeka Board of Education nor the State Attorney General wished to be associated with the controversy. In a split vote, the school board decided not to defend itself on appeal. Board members justified their decision by the fact that the court had ruled in their favor on the question of the equality of educational opportunities. As purely local matters were no longer at issue, they felt that the Attorney General should be responsible for defending the constitutionality of the Kansas law.[94] Attorney General Harold Fatzer waffled in his response. During the summer of 1952, he told the Topeka school board that he intended to argue the case. He later changed his mind, insisting that the school board was responsible for defending its own practices.[95] With the Kansas case and three other school cases set for argument in the Supreme Court that December,[96] attorneys for the other states were concerned that the Topeka case would be decided by default.[97]

As state and local officials refused to budge, the Supreme Court forced the issue. On November 24, 1952, the Court issued an extraordinary per curiam order. The Court noted that no appearance had been entered by any of the Kansas defendants, and that counsel for the Topeka Board of Education had informed the court that the board did not intend to appear in oral argument or present a brief. The order continued,

Because of the national importance of the issue presented and because of its importance to the State of Kansas, we request that the State present its views at oral argument. If the State does not desire to appear, we request the Attorney General to advise whether the State's default shall be construed as a concession of invalidity.[98]

Harold Fatzer was not happy with the Supreme Court's order. The day after it was issued he rushed to Washington to confer with the Clerk of the Supreme Court. As he later reported to the Topeka Daily Capital, Fatzer told

93. *Topeka Daily Capital*, supra note 90.

94. 'Segregation Suit To Make History', *Topeka Daily Capital*, November 30, 1952. The vote was apparently taken during the summer of 1951.

95. Ibid.

96. Brown v. Bd. of Educ., 344 U.S. 1 (1952).

97. Paul Wilson, 'Speech on *Brown v. Board of Education*, May 1, 1981', 30 *Kansas Law Review* 15, 21 (1981).

98. Brown v. Board of Education, 344 U.S. 141, 142 (1952).

the Clerk that the Court's order was 'not a fair request. It is not the prerogative of the state executive department to concede the invalidity of any legislative act. That is for the courts to decide.'[99] Backed into a corner, Fatzer was forced to abandon his neutral stance. He first agreed to file a brief and later decided that the state would also participate in oral argument.[100] Yet Fatzer couched his capitulation in terms of his duty as Attorney General. In a lengthy public statement explaining his action, Fatzer noted that ' [a]s the chief law officer of the state, it is the duty of the attorney general to sustain any state statute which is attacked, as being unconstitutional. No official in the executive branch of the state government can concede the invalidity of any act of the legislative department . . . .'[101] Yet Fatzer felt that primary responsibility rested on the local level. 'I have always felt that the board of education had a plain duty to present oral argument to the court . . . It was they who, under the permissive Kansas statute, set up the particular system being attacked in this case.'[102]

Fatzer wished to make it clear that his decision to defend the suit did not mean that he, personally, or the State of Kansas favored a policy of racial segregation. 'Segregation, in the first place, is a local matter in Kansas', he insisted. Further, the state statute 'is permissive and it is not of major importance as it appears to be in the Southern States'. Fatzer believed that 'segregation in Kansas is rapidly being ended where practiced. Kansas has been making strides to abolish the injustice of segregation in the public school system and elsewhere.'[103] Perhaps in an effort to protect his political reputation from tarnish, Fatzer announced that 'I have never advocated or championed segregation and will not do so before the Supreme Court'. The state would restrict its arguments to the constitutional question of whether segregation was within the power of the state legislature in regulating education. Kansas would leave emotional appeals about the goodness or badness of racial segregation to other participants in the case.[104]

To further distance himself from the controversy, Fatzer would send Assistant Attorney General Paul Wilson to argue the case for Kansas. Wilson

---

99. 'Segregation Suit to Make History', *Topeka Daily Capital*, Nov. 30, 1952.

100. 'State to Defend School Statute on Segregation', *Topeka Daily Capital*, Dec. 5, 1952.

101. Ibid.

102. Ibid.

103. At that point Wichita and Pittsburg, Kansas, had already 'desegregated' their schools. Pittsburg closed its black school for financial reasons in 1950, firing its three black teachers and integrating black students into its white schools. Wichita went from a race-based to a residence-based attendance system. However, the school board drew attendance boundaries in such a way that the black schools remained all black and the white schools remained predominately or exclusively white. Because it retained substantial school segregation, Wichita did not fire any of its twenty-six black teachers. 'Future of State's Negro Teachers Found Uncertain', *Topeka Journal*, Jan. 14, 1954; 'Calm At School Ruling', *Kansas City Times*, May 18, 1954.

104. 'State to Defend School Statute on Segregation', *Topeka Daily Capital*, Nov. 30 1952.

was new to the Attorney General's Office. After some eight years of legal practice, he had come to work for Fatzer in part to gain appellate experience. He would present the first oral argument of his career before the U.S. Supreme Court.[105]

Not everyone on the Topeka school board agreed with the board's hands-off posture toward the case. At the October 6, 1952 school board meeting, board member Marlin Casey read a prepared statement criticizing his colleagues for their inaction. Casey felt that, as defendants in the *Brown* litigation, the board had a duty to defend its policies. He felt that the board's failure to take action reflected a desire to take an easy way out of a sticky political controversy. He suggested that

> [i]f the majority of the board is against segregation, as I assume they are by not defending this suit, then action should be taken to abolish it as the board can do under the present statute, and not take the weak position of letting the Supreme Court do it. Apparently the board would like to be in a position of saying to the colored people, if the Supreme Court holds the statute unconstitutional, 'We have helped abolish segregation by not defending this suit.' While on the other hand, they could say to the white people, 'We are sorry, there is nothing we could do, the Supreme Court has held the statute unconstitutional and therefore segregation must be abolished.'[106]

The Board of Education was not willing to follow Casey's suggestion, preferring a low profile on the substantive issue of segregation. However, the board did begin to prepare for the possibility that the Court might strike down segregation. The school board would not act on its own, but if the Supreme Court should abolish segregation, the board would be ready.

B. The Teacher Problem

In the spring of 1953, the Topeka papers reported that a 'purge' of black teachers had begun. Throughout the state 'a mass unannounced weeding-out of Negro teachers' was taking place in anticipation of a possible desegregation decision that might affect the upcoming school year.[107] In Topeka, the six newest black teachers were notified that their contracts would not be renewed. Wendell Godwin, the new Superintendent of the Topeka Schools, wrote the teachers that

> [d]ue to the present uncertainty about enrollment next year in schools for Negro children, it is not possible at this time to offer you employment for next year. If the Supreme Court should rule that segregation in the elementary grades is unconstitutional, our Board will proceed on the assumption that the majority of people in Topeka will not want to employ Negro teachers next year for white children . . . . If it turns out that

---

105. Wilson, supra note 97 at 20, 22–23.

106. Marlin Casey, Statement Presented to the Board of Education, Topeka Bd. of Educ. Minutes, Oct. 6, 1952.

107. 'Negro Teacher Purge Begins in Kansas', *Topeka Daily Capital*, April 6, 1953.

segregation is not terminated, there will be nothing to prevent us from negotiating a contract with you a[t] some later date this spring.[108]

The board only terminated the black teachers hired within the past year or two, as '[i]t is presumed that, even though segregation should be declared unconstitutional, we would have need for some schools for Negro children and we would retain our Negro teachers to teach them'.[109]

In response to pressure from the community and from one of its own members, the Board of Education reconsidered the firing of black teachers shortly after the initial decision hit the press. Nine Topeka NAACP members made an 'impassioned plea' that the teachers be reinstated.[110] Marlin Casey, the board's most outspoken advocate of segregation, moved that they be rehired.[111] Jacob Dickenson, Casey's 'arch antagonist',[112] tried unsuccessfully to table the motion regarding the teachers while the board reconsidered its segregation policy. When that move failed, he voted against the rehiring on the grounds that the board was not entitled to rehire teachers unless it had a place for them, and in order to have a place for them the board had to establish a policy on segregation and the employment of black teachers. Other board members refused to reconsider the Topeka policy until after the Supreme Court ruling came down. With a vote of three to three, the motion to rehire the teachers did not pass. Later during the same meeting the board hired seven new white teachers.[113]

The six black Topeka teachers would at least temporarily retain their jobs. In June of 1953, the Supreme Court called for reargument in the school segregation cases to be held the following October.[114] Under the assumption that a subsequent desegregation decree would not affect the 1953–54 school year, on June 15 the board rehired the teachers.[115]

C. Desegregation Kansas Style

When the Topeka Board of Education decided to postpone a reconsideration of its school segregation policy until after the Supreme Court ruling, the board had anticipated a resolution to the problem by the end of the

108. Wendell Gordon, letter to unidentified black teacher, reprinted in *The Plaindealer*, Apr. 1953.

109. Ibid.

110. 'Board Rejects Bid to Rehire Negroes Here', *Topeka Daily Capital*, April 21, 1953.

111. Topeka Bd. of Educ. Minutes, Apr. 20, 1953.

112. 'Firing Negro Teachers To Be Contested', *Topeka Daily Capital*, April 7, 1953.

113. 'Board Rejects Bid to Rehire Negroes Here', *Topeka Daily Capital*, April 21, 1953.

114. Brown v. Bd. of Educ., 345 U.S. 972 (1953). Reargument was scheduled following the death of Supreme Court Chief Justice Fred Vinson. Kluger, supra note 19 at 656.

115. 'Segregation Decision Reaction Is Mixed', *Topeka Daily Capital*, June 9, 1953; 'School Board Rehires Negro Teachers', *Topeka Daily Capital*, June 16, 1953; Topeka Bd. of Educ. Minutes, June 15, 1953.

1952–53 school year. The Court's postponement of the case and request for reargument caught the board by surprise. Its posture of neutrality would be difficult to maintain through another year. According to Superintendent Godwin, 'the board has sort of an agreement to take up the matter of segregation policy after the Supreme Court's decision was known, but I think the members may want to discuss whether the Supreme Court's failure to give a decision soon may change the board's course of action'.[116]

A newly constituted school board would meet to consider these questions in the fall of 1953. Marlin Casey, the board's most vocal supporter of segregation, Charles Bennett, Casey's closest ally, and Mrs. David Neiswanger[117] were replaced by three new members as a result of elections during the spring of 1953. The outgoing board members were the remaining three of the original six from the days of the McFarland administration.[118]

Very late one evening near the end of an unusually lengthy board meeting, the Topeka Board of Education considered the question of whether to continue segregation in the schools. It was 12:30 A.M. on September 4 when the bussing contract was about to be considered to continue transporting black children to segregated schools.[119] Jacob Dickenson, the new board president, offered a motion not on the agenda: 'Be it resolved that it is the policy of the Topeka Board of Education to terminate the maintenance of segregation in the elementary grades as rapidly as practicable.'[120] The motion was seconded, and Dr. Harold Conrad offered an amendment that no action to end segregation be taken until the fall of 1954. The amendment was defeated, which the Topeka Daily Capital took as 'indicating the board may not see fit even at that time to completely abolish the system of separate classes'.[121] Dickenson's motion passed with a vote of five to one. Former board president M. C. Oberhelman cast the only negative vote. He felt that the decision was 'ill timed'. Oberhelman was careful to note that he was 'not opposed to integration', however he thought 'we should have an orderly program in mind and a much more definite goal before we pass the

---

116. 'Segregation Decision Reaction Is Mixed', *Topeka Daily Capital*, June 9, 1953.

117. Unfortunately neither the newspapers nor the school board minutes disclose Neiswanger's first name.

118. The school board election in the spring of 1953 was very quiet on the segregation issue, at least according to the coverage provided in the *Topeka Daily Capital*. The newspaper's stories portrayed a bland campaign focusing on the candidates' records of community service, and ignoring the problems that the *Brown* case might create for the new board. See, e.g., 'Mrs. Shiner in School Board Race', *Topeka Daily Capital*, Feb. 1, 1953, at 1; 'Sheetz Enters School Race', *Topeka Daily Capital*, Feb. 12, 1953.

119. The only school bus transportation provided in Topeka was for the purpose of bussing black students to segregated schools.

120. Topeka Bd. of Educ. Minutes, Sept. 3, 1953.

121. 'School Board Votes End To Topeka Segregation', *Topeka Daily Capital*, Sept. 4, 1953.

resolution'.[122] Before adjourning, the board approved the bus contract for the 1953–54 school year, ensuring that, for the coming year at least, black children would still be bussed to achieve racial segregation.[123]

Just what the Topeka Board of Education intended to do to desegregate its schools was clarified somewhat at a board meeting the following week. Superintendent Godwin presented a report to the board, recommending a first step in the desegregation process. First, he emphasized four general points governing his recommendation:

1) That the termination of segregation should be done in a gradual and orderly manner.
2) That in his judgment it is a social impossibility to terminate segregation suddenly.
3) That speed with which segregation is terminated depends largely on the forebearance [sic] and self-discipline of both white and colored people.
4) That it is not possible to set an accurate time in which segregation is terminated completely.[124]

As a first step, Godwin recommended that black children residing in the Southwest and Randolph districts be allowed to attend those schools. However, any black student who wished to continue to attend black Buchanan School could do so, although bus transportation would not be provided. This move would affect approximately fifteen black students, and would take effect immediately. The board unanimously approved the Superintendent's recommendation.[125]

At the September 8 meeting, the board was called on to defend its decision to desegregate the schools. Edward Goss of the Topeka Civic Club asked the board how they could end segregation before the Supreme Court decided the issue. Board member Conrad explained that '[w]e feel that segregation is not an American practice'.[126] As the Topeka Journal reported, Conrad noted that

the subject had been under discussion for two years and there had been an informal agreement that segregation could not be continued because of the general trends in social and human development and that some time in the future, whether or not the Supreme court decided to end segregation, the board would do so in the best interests of the public schools and Topeka.[127]

The Topeka school board took further action to end segregation in its schools on January 20, 1954. Superintendent Godwin proposed that segregation be terminated at an additional ten elementary schools and partially terminated at another two. Under this second step, all black

122. Ibid.

123. Ibid.

124. Topeka Bd. of Educ. Minutes, Sept. 8, 1953. See also, 'Segregation Is Terminated at Randolph and Southwest', *Topeka Journal*, Sept. 9, 1953.

125. Topeka Bd. of Educ. Minutes, Sept. 8, 1953.

126. 'Segregation is Terminated at Randolph and Southwest', *Topeka Journal*, Sept. 9, 1953.

127. Ibid.

children residing in the ten districts could attend the white schools near their home, although they would 'be given the privilege of attending the nearest Negro school' if their parents desired. No transportation would be provided these students. The districts partially desegregated each had three black children geographically isolated from other blacks in the district. These children would be allowed to attend the white schools; the others would not. The justification given for this distinction was that the white schools had space limitations, so more integration was not possible.[128]

Step two of the Topeka program would affect up to 123 of the city's 824 black school children. It would leave nine of Topeka's twenty-two elementary schools completely segregated, four black and five white. The school board unanimously approved the plan, which would go into effect at the beginning of the 1954–55 school year. The primary problem with integrating the remaining white schools was reported to be the overcrowded conditions at the white schools, indicating that desegregation in Topeka was clearly contemplated as a one-way proposition.[129] In a matter-of-fact news story, the Topeka Journal reported the plan under the headline 'Segregation Ended in Twelve More Elementary Schools Here'. If there was any pronounced public reaction to the plan, the local papers did not choose to report it.[130]

D. The Brown Decision

When the *Brown* case was reargued before the Supreme Court in December of 1953, the Topeka school board filed a brief. This time they wished to have their say.

The board's brief dealt only with the remedial questions before the Court. They recommended that the Court not end segregation immediately, arguing that completely ending segregation would require 'difficult and far-reaching administrative decisions' which would affect nearly all school children, teachers, buildings and attendance boundaries, making 'a hurried and summary' change 'both impossible and impractical'. The board believed that under immediate desegregation, 'the attendant confusion and interruption of the regular school program would be against the public interest and would be damaging to the children, both Negro and white alike'.[131] Since the board had voted to desegregate, they felt they no longer had an active interest in the constitutional questions before the Court.[132]

The Supreme Court finally decided *Brown v. Board of Education* on May

---

128. Topeka Bd. of Educ. Minutes, Jan. 20, 1954.

129. Ibid.

130. 'Segregation Ended in Twelve More Elementary Schools Here', *Topeka Journal*, Jan. 21, 1954.

131. '"Gradual" Segregation End Sought', *Topeka Daily Capital*, Nov. 19, 1953.

132. 'In Court Paradox', *Kansas City Star*, Nov. 29, 1953.

17, 1954.[133] The Court found that the *Brown* cases squarely presented the question of whether school segregation, by itself, deprived non-white students of their constitutional rights, for in *Brown* the separate schools were equal or were being equalized.[134] In considering the constitutional question, the Court looked broadly at the effect of segregation on public education and the role education played in contemporary society. The Court found that '[t]oday, education is perhaps the most important function of state and local governments'. Education is 'required in the performance of our most basic public responsibilities', and is 'the very foundation of good citizenship'. Consequently, '[i]n these days, it is doubtful that any child may reasonably be expected to succeed in life if he is denied the opportunity of an education. Such an opportunity, where the state has undertaken to provide it, is a right which must be made available to all on equal terms.'[135] The court found that the intangible factors that had produced educational inequality in previous cases 'apply with added force to children in grade school and high school'. Relying on social science evidence that segregation harms children, the Court found that '[t]o separate [non-white] children from others of similar age and qualifications solely because of their race generates a feeling of inferiority as to their status in the community that may affect their hearts and minds in a way unlikely ever to be undone'. Therefore, 'in the field of public education the doctrine of "separate but equal" has no place. Separate educational facilities are inherently unequal.'[136] The Court reserved the question briefed by the Topeka Board of Education. More time, more briefs and more argument were needed before the Court would decide on an appropriate remedy.[137]

In Topeka, school officials hailed the ruling. School board president Jacob Dickenson felt it was 'in the finest spirit of the law and true democracy'. Superintendent Godwin said that the decision would have 'no effect upon Topeka schools because segregation already is being terminated in an orderly manner'. He thought that segregation would be terminated in Topeka 'before the Supreme court decides when and how it should be done'.[138] Attorney General Fatzer believed the ruling would present few problems for the state. 'Every city now under a segregation program should be able to make the change-over in two years.'[139]

---

133. 347 U.S. 483 (1954).

134. Ibid. at 492. The Kansas case was the only case where the lower court had found 'substantial equality'. Ibid. at 492 n. 9.

135. Ibid. at 493.

136. Ibid. at 494–95.

137. Ibid. at 495–96.

138. 'Segregation Already Ending Here, Say School Officials', *Topeka Journal*, May 17, 1954.

139. 'State Officials See No Trouble Adjusting to New Rule', *Topeka Journal*, May 17, 1954.

The Topeka NAACP was overjoyed with the *Brown* decision. Chapter President Burnett was 'completely overwhelmed'. '[T]hank God for the Supreme court. Their decision will enable me to pay my taxes with a little more grace . . . . We will celebrate and leave the rest to the court', he added. 'We believe we can depend on them.' According to Lucinda Todd, 'We may have a long time to go before segregation is actually abolished, but we are just thankful we have come this far.' Oliver Brown felt that the decision would 'bring about a better understanding of our racial situation', however he cautioned that 'this case has a deep bearing upon the hearts of our teachers. Certainly we must make an effort for them, also, for there are many I know are capable of teaching anywhere.'[140]

It would be one full year before the Supreme Court would rule on the implementation of *Brown*. By that time the Topeka school board would adopt one more step in their desegregation plan, a step which they would initially believe fully terminated school segregation in Topeka.

E. Topeka Takes Another Step

In February of 1955, the Topeka Board of Education considered Step Three of the Topeka desegregation plan. The proposal, which would go into effect in the fall of 1955, was designed to end segregation in all remaining schools. Black students within the remaining white districts would be able to attend the white school near them. Three black schools, Buchanan, Monroe and Washington, would be assigned attendance boundaries, and all children within a school's boundaries could attend that school. McKinley Elementary School, the fourth black school, was to be closed and placed 'on a stand-by basis'. No bus transportation would be provided for any children.[141]

Step three would change Topeka to a school system governed by neighborhood attendance boundaries, with two important exceptions. The plan allowed that 'any child who is affected by the changes in district lines herein recommended, be given the option of finishing elementary grades in the school which he attended in 1954–55, McKinley excepted'. Further, it provided '[t]hat entering kindergarten children in 1955–56, who are affected by the change in school boundaries as herein recommended, be given the option of attending the same school in 1955–56 that they would have attended in 1954–55 if they had been old enough to enter'.[142] The plan would get the Topeka school board out of the business of making attendance decisions based overtly on race alone. However, it would leave room for

---

140. 'Negroes Mark Court Victory Tuesday Night', *Topeka Journal*, May 17, 1954.

141. Topeka Bd. of Educ. Minutes, Feb. 7, 1955. In 1987, the district court found that '[t]he boundaries set around the former *de jure* black elementary schools after this case was remanded by the Supreme Court appear to have perpetuated the racial identity of those schools'. Brown v. Bd. of Educ., No. T-316, slip op. at 23 (D. Kan. April 8, 1987). See supra note 16.

142. Ibid.

individuals to avoid racial integration by exercising an attendance option. The board estimated that one third of the black students and all of the whites affected would opt to attend their old schools. The plan would increase the strain on already crowded previously white schools, while reducing enrollment at the black schools which, prior to desegregation, had more than enough space.[143]

Given the progress in Topeka toward desegregation, when argument was held for the third time in *Brown v. Board of Education*, Harold Fatzer was proud to go. The Attorney General told the Court in April of 1955 that no order would be required to end segregation in Kansas, as the state was complying with the previous year's ruling 'in good faith and with dispatch'. In Topeka, school segregation would be fully terminated by the fall of 1955.[144] However, the 'end of segregation' did not mean that some semblance of racial balance might be achieved in the Topeka schools. In a follow-up letter to the Supreme Court, Fatzer explained that the estimated school population in the formerly black schools was one hundred per cent black. According to Fatzer, this phenomenon was the result of several factors, including:

1. The schools were origionally built in predominantly colored neighborhoods because they were originally for segregated Negro children.
2. After the schools were built the Negro people who could do so, tended to move nearer to the Negro schools where their children were required to attend.[145]

Further, the options provided by the school board would enable any whites living in black areas to attend their old white school. In addition, 'persons who are dissatisfied with the schools their children will be required to attend during the school year of 1955–56, may have at least a year to move to a district of their choice'.[146]

As the Attorney General unabashedly told the Court, the former black schools in Topeka would remain black schools because previous school board policies had fostered residential segregation, and because the board now provided white people with a way out. Yet in spite of the fact that many of Topeka's black school children continued to attend all-black schools, Attorney General Fatzer and the Topeka Board of Education believed that segregation had ended. Clearly, racial isolation, by itself, did not constitute segregation in their eyes. However, it remains to be considered what the 'segregation' was that they had eliminated from the Topeka schools.

143. 'Board Takes Third Step in Integration', *Topeka Daily Capital*, Feb. 8, 1955; Casey, supra note 106.

144. 'High Court Told State Complying', *Topeka Daily Capital*, April 12, 1955.

145. Harold Fatzer, et al., letter to Harold B. Willey, Clerk of the U.S. Supreme Court, May 10, 1955, Kan. State Historical Society, Records of the Attorney General, File 851, 'Brown—Segregation'.

146. Ibid.

F. The Question of Good Faith

On May 31, 1955, the U.S. Supreme Court announced the remedial order in *Brown v. Board of Education*.[147] Because it believed that the implementation of *Brown* I would require attention to local conditions, the Court remanded the cases to the lower courts. In fashioning specific decrees, the lower courts would be guided by equitable principles, balancing the 'personal interest' of the plaintiffs in admission to non-segregated schools against the 'public interest' in eliminating a variety of administrative obstacles in an orderly manner. The Court noted that school authorities had the primary responsibility for solving local school problems, and consequently 'courts will have to consider whether the action of school authorities constitutes good faith implementation of the governing constitutional principles'. Once defendants had made a 'prompt and reasonable start toward full compliance', the Court felt that additional time might be required to handle administrative problems. However, '[t]he burden rests upon the defendants to establish that such time is necessary in the public interest and is consistent with good faith compliance at the earliest practical date'. And the lower courts were to ensure that the parties to the cases were admitted to non-segregated schools 'with all deliberate speed'.[148]

Brown II would be a license for delay and evasion in some Southern states, as the South prepared for a long period of resistance.[149] For Kansas, the Court had offered a welcome pat on the back, finding that 'substantial progress' had been made toward the elimination of segregation.[150] As the Topeka case was remanded to the district court, the defendants set out to show that they had acted in good faith to dismantle segregation. Judge Huxman and his colleagues in the district court set the terms of the discussion for argument on remand when they informed the parties that the only question at issue was whether the school board had acted in good faith to desegregate the schools. In a hearing on September 15, 1955, the court expressed reservations about the attendance options provided by the board, and requested both parties to submit briefs on the question of whether the board's plan was a good faith effort towards compliance.[151]

The board argued, first, that 'at the present time no child who resides within the Topeka public school system or district is denied admission to any school on the basis of race'. Therefore, 'the Board of Education has fully complied . . . in that race is no longer a determinative factor as to the right to attend any school in the Topeka public school system'.[152] However, they

---

147. Brown v. Bd. of Educ. [II], 349 U.S. 294 (1955).

148. Ibid. at 299–301.

149. See Wilhoit, supra note 17.

150. 349 U.S. at 299.

151. 'Segregation Brief Filed', *Topeka Daily Capital*, Oct. 21, 1955.

152. Defendant's Memorandum Brief on Plaintiff's Motion for Formulation of a Decree and

recognized that desegregation might not be fully achieved under their plan, and that the effects of the implementation of Step Three warranted study. Nevertheless, the board strongly defended its plan, particularly the questionable options.

The board noted that 'the options do not require compulsory segregation', and they 'apply to any child regardless of race'. The intent of the options was to permit 'any child affected by the boundary changes to finish the school which he previously attended'. Such a provision was important in part out of a concern that '[a] compulsory change of school affecting children of immature, elementary school age disrupts associations and conditions which may, in some cases, cause undesirable and unsettling psychological effects'.[153] In addition, however, the board had concerns which related to the phenomenon of racial integration itself.

> It must be granted that the transition from a segregated to an integrated school system is a radical one in the minds of some people. Some parents, regardless of race, may desire to make adjustments in their place of residence to conform with their personal feelings and those of their children to the change. While it is not the province of the Board or the Courts to determine such personal adjustments, it is proper for the Board and the Court to recognize that such adjustments may be made and to afford time therefor.[154]

This, the board added, was the primary motivation behind providing attendance options to entering kindergarten students. It gave parents at least a year to move to another attendance area. Not allowing for such private choice to avoid integration would involve the school board and the court in '*suddenly forcing* the change upon possibly unwilling persons, which is not what was intended by the decisions of the Supreme Court'.[155] Instead, the board argued, the Court acknowledged that '"private needs" and "private considerations"' should be taken into account when it allowed for 'a period of transition and adjustment'.[156]

The Topeka school board's plan left five schools all-white and three schools all-black as of September, 1955.[157] Even without the attendance options, much of this racial isolation would continue. The board maintained that it was not responsible for the racial composition of the schools when it resulted from the fact that blacks 'have chosen to reside and remain in' certain districts.[158]

In essence, the board understood its responsibilities under *Brown* II as

---

Judgment at 3, Brown v. Bd. of Educ., 139 F. Supp. 468 (D. Kan. 1955) [hereinafter cited as Defendant's Memorandum].

153. Ibid. at 5.

154. Ibid. at 6.

155. Ibid. (emphasis in original).

156. Ibid.

157. 'Segregation Brief Filed', *Topeka Daily Capital*, Oct. 21, 1955.

158. Defendant's Memorandum, supra note 152 at 6–7.

ending overtly compulsory race-conscious pupil assignment. Once it got out of the business of enforcing a formal color line, it was no longer engaged in 'segregation'. For the school board, the remaining racial isolation in the school system was the result of voluntary, private choice. Even when motivated by a desire to avoid integration, the board believed that such choice should be facilitated. To impede private, racially-motivated choice would again engage the school board in compulsion. Forcing integration on parents of school children became, for the board, an evil of the degree that forced segregation had so recently achieved.

As far as the plaintiffs were concerned, the 'crucial problem' to be considered by the court was 'whether there are any valid reasons of school administration which would warrant a delay in fully putting into effect a policy of nonsegregation in the public schools in Topeka'. The NAACP criticized the attendance options as facilitating white student transfers out of the remaining black districts. The effect of the options was that Buchanan, Monroe and Washington remained 100% black. They were simply no longer called black schools. Because the racial composition of these schools remained the same, '[s]egregation has not been terminated in the public schools in Topeka'. The plaintiffs felt that

> the problem that the defendants do not want to face up to is that of really integrating these former Negro schools into the total school system. Until they face that problem and make these schools a part of the total school system, in our opinion, they have not met their obligation under the Supreme Court decision.[159]

In evaluating the sufficiency of the school board's compliance, the plaintiffs urged that '[i]t must be remembered that this is Topeka, Kansas, and not Sumner, Mississippi. Good faith implementation in the two areas are certainly not identical.'[160] Because they felt the defendants had made no showing that delay was necessary, they asked the Court to find that the school board plan was inadequate, and to order full desegregation at once.[161]

In a brief per curiam opinion issued on October 28, 1955, the district court upheld the school board's actions. The panel felt that, in a number of respects, 'the plan does not constitute full compliance with the mandate of the Supreme Court, but that mandate implies that some time will be required to bring that about'. The elements of the plan which were problematic were 'mostly of a minor nature', and the court believed that 'no useful purpose would be served' by going into any of the details of the plan. However, the court did discuss one specific provision: the attendance option for kindergartners. The court did not 'look with favor' upon that rule, but because the school board had claimed it was a temporary measure, the court did 'not feel

---

159. Memorandum in Support of Plaintiffs' Claim that Defendants Have Failed to Meet Their Obligations Under the Supreme Court's Ruling at 5, *Brown v. Bd of Educ.*, 139 F. Supp. 468 (D. Kan. 1955).

160. Ibid. at 2.

161. Ibid. at 6.

that it requires a present condemnation of an overall plan which shows a good faith effort to bring about full desegregation . . . '.[162]

The court did not consider the existence of all-black and all-white schools as evidence of continuing segregation.

> Desegregation does not mean that there must be intermingling of the races in all school districts. It means only that they may not be prevented from intermingling or going to school together because of race or color.
>
> If it is a fact, as we understand it is, with respect to Buchanan School that the district is inhabited entirely by colored students, no violation of any constitutional right results because they are compelled to attend the school in the district in which they live.[163]

The court approved the board's plan as a 'good faith beginning to bring about complete desegregation', and retained jurisdiction for the purpose of entering a final decree.[164]

G. A Fourth and Final Step

The district court's ruling surely came as a relief to Topeka school officials. The court approved their handiwork and protected their autonomy regarding future school policy. The court also refrained from invalidating their efforts to facilitate parental avoidance of desegregation, although it was clear that the board would be required to take some further action to limit the frustration of desegregation resulting from private preferences.

Although the superintendent and the school board had, at one point, argued that segregation was completely terminated with Step Three, they now recognized that, at least in the court's eyes, something further was needed. Within two months, Superintendent Godwin came up with a plan to satisfy the district court's reservations. On December 21, 1955, he presented a proposed Step Four to the Board of Education. Godwin suggested, first, that the kindergarten option be eliminated for the 1956–57 school year, so that entering school children would be assigned to the school in the district in which they lived, regardless of preference to attend another school. Further, the nine black and eleven white children who exercised the option during the 1955–56 school year would not be entitled to continue in the schools they attended unless they moved into the proper district.

Secondly, all children moving into an elementary school district would be required to attend the school in the district in which they lived. This requirement was subject to two provisos: 1) Topeka would maintain, as it had for many years, optional attendance areas for neighborhoods between

---

162. Brown v. Bd. of Educ., 139 F.Supp. 468, 469–70 (D. Kan. 1955).

163. Ibid. at 470.

164. Ibid. On April 8, 1987, the district court found that the case had finally 'reached an appropriate denouement', and held that the school district was not responsible for the continuing racial imbalance in the schools, Brown v. Bd. of Educ., No. T-316, slip op. at 50 (D. Kan. April 8, 1987). See supra note 16.

two schools, and 2) 'traditional exceptions' to school attendance rules would be retained.[165]

For students in grades one through six, the options previously granted would remain unchanged. Sixty-two black and seventy-five white children had opted to attend schools outside of their attendance area. Those children would be permitted to continue in the schools they attended, however no future students would be entitled to exercise such an option. Superintendent Godwin recommended that no action be taken on Step Four until the January 18 board meeting so that the board could solicit views from the community.[166]

Representatives from the Topeka NAACP were not pleased with Step Four. They felt the options it retained would perpetuate racial segregation. Such delay in implementing full desegregation was harmful to the students segregated, and was 'creating a feeling of insecurity' among the black teachers at Buchanan, Monroe and Washington Schools.[167] At the January 18 board meeting, Mr. Burnett, President of the local chapter, appealed to the Board of Education to end segregation immediately by eliminating the options in Step Four. He claimed that, under the proposed plan, 'it would take seven long years to terminate racial segregation'. Burnett also commented that while the board spoke of the need to hire one hundred new teachers, 'nothing has been said about the integration of negro teachers'. These teachers 'had been completely left out of desegregation'.[168]

No discussion followed Burnett's remarks. Instead, school board member Nelda Shiner 'moved that Step IV in the gradual and systematic termination of racial segregation, as recommended by the Superintendent, and in compliance with the mandate of the U.S. Supreme Court and the U.S.

165. The 'traditional exceptions' were as follows:

> 1. A kindergarten or first grade child whose parents reside in Topeka and are both employed, may be granted permission to attend the kindergarten or first grade located in the district in which the adult who cares for the child during the day resides.
> 2. A child whose parents move into a different elementary school attendance district during the school year, may finish the year in the school he has been attending.
> 3. A child who has finished the fifth grade in an elementary school, and whose parents move into a different Topeka school attendance district, may attend the sixth grade of the school he attended in the fifth grade.
> 4. A crippled child may be given permission to attend an elementary school which is suitable in view of the nature of his handicap.
> 5. Pupils who are eligible for any phase of our special educational program which is not housed in the school district in which they reside may be asked to attend the school which does house that particular part of our program which meets the needs of those particular individuals.

Topeka Bd. of Educ. Minutes, Dec. 21, 1955.

166. Ibid.

167. Ibid.

168. Topeka Bd. of Educ. Minutes, Jan. 18, 1956.

District Court, be adopted'. The board unanimously approved its final step to desegregate the Topeka schools.[169]

Topeka's desegregation plan would, even in the eyes of the school board, retain some vestiges of racial segregation for several years.[170] However, Topeka school officials stood behind their remaining attendance options. They considered their policy as well within their rights under *Brown* II, for it protected the private interests of students who did not 'want the sudden disruption of their elementary school pattern'. As Superintendent Godwin noted, by proposing to remove these options '[w]hat you are talking about is compelling people to go to a school where they do not want to go'.[171]

The Topeka Board of Education had been compelling black children to attend certain schools against their will for many years. Successive school boards had based their decision to segregate on what they felt was best for white and black children alike.[172] Now that the board was getting out of the business of segregation, it wished to get out of the business of compulsion as well. When it meant controlling the choices that whites might make, compulsion became a dirty word.

V. Conclusion: The Limits of Good Faith

It would be quite a while before the Topeka school board found itself before the district court on the question of school segregation again. In the interim, Step Four would quietly progress. Judge Huxman and his district court panel had had their last word on the adequacy of the Topeka plan. They had entrusted desegregation to the school board's good faith efforts, and it was in the school board's hands that the authority and autonomy to enforce desegregation would remain.[173] Twenty years later, when the

---

169. Ibid.

170. The school board claimed segregation would be fully terminated in five years, while the NAACP claimed it would take seven years. Compare 'City School Segregation Nears End', *Topeka Daily Capital*, Dec. 22, 1955 (school board view), with Topeka Bd. of Educ. Minutes, Jan. 18, 1956 (NAACP view). It would actually take five and one-half years for those first graders exercising an attendance option in the 1955–56 school year to matriculate out of the elementary schools and into junior high schools.

171. 'City School Segregation Nears End', *Topeka Daily Capital*, Dec. 22, 1955.

172. See, e.g., Bd. of Educ. Minutes, Dec. 12, 1944; Return to Alternative Writ of Mandamus at 2, Reynolds v. Bd. of Education of the City of Topeka, 66 Kan. 672 (1903).

173. In granting nearly absolute autonomy to the Topeka school board in desegregating its schools, the district court was necessarily leaving room for majority interests to frustrate the enforcement of recognized minority rights. See generally Hochschild, *supra* note 5. Hochschild argues that data on school desegregation since *Brown* indicates that 'normal democratic politics' do not produce effective desegregation plans because desegregation strategies based upon popular control of the desegregation process tend to favor the white middle-class who, within the constraints of local

question of continuing segregation was raised by Topeka blacks and federal authorities, the board would claim that the court's acquiescence to their plan was evidence that they had fully complied with the law.[174]

In finding that the school board had acted in good faith, the district court was right in recognizing that the board's actions were motivated by a desire to rid the city of what they came to believe was wrong. *Brown v. Board of Education* had thrust the Topeka school board and its policy of school segregation before national attention, associating Kansas with the 'American dilemma' of the times.[175] As Kansans asserted the idealized heritage of their state, the free state, they wondered how and why Kansas was embroiled in a problem that really concerned the South. In response the Topeka Board of Education moved to distance itself from the conflict, and to distinguish itself from the South. In contrast to Southern resistance, the board voted to desegregate before the Supreme Court would require it to. There were limits to what the school board was willing to do, however.

The school board members could handle one-way integration. They had few problems with sending some of Topeka's black children to several predominately white schools. However, sending white children to the black schools would have forced the board members to face two questions they preferred to avoid. The first was the 'teacher problem'. If the school board retained three segregated schools, it could continue to employ black teachers in the schools, and gradually retire them, without being forced to choose between firing the teachers and having them teach in integrated schools.[176] The maintenance of segregated black schools also enabled the board to avoid either greatly increasing the proportion of blacks integrated into the formerly white schools or sending white children to black schools. By maintaining separate black schools, the board could keep the number of blacks at other schools artificially low. The board achieved its level of continuing racial segregation by straining the overcrowded white schools while the black schools continued to have plenty of room.

Even in implementing this limited, one-way integration plan, the Topeka Board of Education adopted a gradualist strategy, arguing that gradualism was the most sensible, rational means to achieve integration in Topeka. And while the board made passing reference to administrative difficulties that would require delay, the primary purpose behind the options in the plan was to facilitate parental avoidance of desegregation.

---

political processes, tend to be the participants who are more likely to gain power and whose voices are more likely to be heard.

174. See supra note 16.

175. See Myrdal, supra note 5.

176. As Linda Brown Smith remembers it, black teachers were gradually phased out of the schools as they retired. Interview by Richard Kluger, Kluger Papers, Manuscripts and Archives Dept., Yale Univ. Library. In 1987, the district court found that 'in the years immediately following the Supreme Court decisions, the district discriminated in the hiring and placement of minority staff'. Brown v. Bd. of Educ., No. T-316, slip op. at 32 (D. Kan. April 8, 1987). See supra note 16.

In this sense, the focus of the school board's efforts was not to alter the racial composition of the schools, but to privatize discrimination. While they acted to limit school board involvement in segregation, they also took affirmative steps to give parents the ability to continue segregation. Their explicit purpose here was to facilitate private racially-motivated attendance decisions.

In some ways the options in the Topeka plan are reminiscent of the so-called 'freedom of choice' plans adopted by many school districts to circumvent school desegregation after *Brown*. When we think of 'freedom of choice' plans in the early days of desegregation, it is usually with cases like *Green v. New Kent County*[177] in mind. In that case, previously segregated students were assigned to schools on the basis of their own preferences. The plan resulted in some blacks attending the white school, and no whites attending the black school. The Supreme Court found that the plan was an effort to circumvent *Brown* and avoid actual school desegregation.[178] Other communities also adopted plans which built in delay and escape clauses with the overt or covert purpose of frustrating the enforcement of *Brown*.[179]

The Topeka school officials approached desegregation from an entirely different perspective, however. They sought to distance themselves from the recalcitrant South and to be the first to actually comply with *Brown*. They embraced the *Brown* decision as an important and progressive step in U.S. race relations, and they claimed it was in keeping with the policies already adopted in Topeka. It is in the context of their desire to be the good guys and their desire to comply with *Brown* that the Topeka school board's adoption of its desegregation plan must be understood.

Having identified racial segregation as morally wrong, the board might have felt compelled to carry their new moral principle to its logical conclusion, even if it meant taking steps some of their constituents would be displeased with. Alternatively, the board might retreat from its moral principle. The board saved itself from such choices through an important rhetorical move. Once faced with the practical consequences of its decision to desegregate, the board's perception of the rights at stake suddenly broadened. Not only did blacks have a right to not be segregated, whites had a corollary right to not be integrated against their will. By casting white interests in terms of a right to be free from compulsory integration—essentially an associational right[180]—the school board could view the competing interests of whites and blacks in terms of competing values or rights on the same moral plane. In framing the issue as a liberty interest, rather than a right to actually

---

177. 391 U.S. 430 (1968).

178. Ibid. at 441–42.

179. See generally Jack Peltason, *Fifty-eight Lonely Men* (New York, 1961).

180. The school board articulated the rights at stake in terms of freedom of association which extended to both blacks and whites. In 1959, Herbert Weschler would argue that *Brown* should have been decided on such a 'neutral principle'. Herbert Weschler, 'Toward Neutral Principles of Constitutional Law', 73 *Harvard Law Review* 1 (1959).

integrated schools, the board could embrace the 'right' of whites not to be compelled to attend integrated schools with the same enthusiasm with which they had so recently embraced the right of blacks to not be segregated. By considering white interests in avoiding segregation as a right, and thereby framing the discussion of desegregation in terms of competing values, the board could limit the scope of what it believed it was required to do to desegregate, without seeming to descend from the moral high road the board believed itself to have taken. And because they viewed a balance of such competing values to be within the remedial framework contemplated by *Brown* II, they could justify the limits to their desegregation plan as in keeping with their efforts to comply with *Brown*. In this sense, the idea of competing values provided a way of talking about interests in avoiding integration in language other than the language of racism and recalcitrance. The board's interpretation of *Brown* II enabled it to use the case to legitimate continuing discrimination.[181] The focus on liberty also enabled board members to restrict their field of vision on the question of segregation to the actions they engaged in, and not to the results those actions achieved. Once they had essentially laundered the process by which they engaged in student assignment, segregation no longer existed, in their minds, regardless of whether actual school attendance patterns changed.[182]

In an effort to distance themselves from the racial practices they identified with the 'die-hard South',[183] the Topeka school board embraced an approach to race and school assignment which essentially assumed that the ideal society in which racism was not a factor in human motivation had already arrived in Kansas. From this perspective, any continuing racial isolation in the public schools could be seen as benign. Because racism had presumptively been eliminated from school policies, the board considered blacks to have no special claim to the school board's attention. As blacks and whites were now on equal footing, the desires of each group were entitled to equal weight. Color-blindness had become the order of the day. In the future society that had arrived in Kansas, whites and blacks had associational rights of an equivalent moral character. They could not be compelled to attend segregated schools or to attend integrated schools. In order to avoid such compulsion in violation of associational rights, the board constructed its policies to accommodate private prejudices.

In light of the limited nature of desegregation in Topeka, the question arises as to just what the board was up to in defining the problem and its solution in the way it did. A key to answering that question lies, I believe,

---

181. Similarly, as Alan Freeman has demonstrated, the Supreme Court would later find continued school segregation to be in keeping with the principles of anti-discrimination law. Freeman, *supra* note 20 at 1107–114 (1978).

182. In Freeman's terms, the board operated within the 'perpetrator perspective', viewing segregation in terms of their own acts, not the actual conditions of the schools. See ibid. at 1052–1057.

183. See *supra* at 370.

in the school board's efforts to distance itself from practices it identified as quintessentially 'Southern'. Topeka school officials had long practiced racial segregation and discrimination. However, to the extent the community was able to consider practices of others to be 'real' segregation and discrimination, and to the extent that they could distinguish their conduct from that of the other, they could think of themselves as doing something different from 'real' segregation and discrimination.

The phenomenon of defining oneself in reference to an 'other' manifests itself in group behavior in the way a group identifies who does and doesn't belong. As Kai Erikson has noted, communities identify their boundaries and thereby articulate their common character and values by defining and sanctioning deviance.[184] Public rituals of punishment or damnation serve to reinforce collectively held norms by illustrating what it is that violates the community's sense of its nature and identity. The identification of an 'other' as the damned, as engaging in behavior that violates community morality, can be one way a community articulates its cultural boundaries.

As racial segregation came to be identified as an American dilemma in the post-war period,[185] much of the country pointed a finger at the South which was seen as the source of the problem of racial injustice. Many Topekans viewed Southern racial practices critically, and saw Southern-style segregation as violating the constitutional rights of blacks. The paradox for the Topekans, however, was that, in blaming the South for segregation, they defined behavior *they themselves* participated in as deviant. Accordingly, if they wished to avoid the stigma they believed was attached to such behavior, they either had to stop doing it, or they had to come up with a way of understanding their behavior to be something different. The board took a middle course, altering their practices to a certain degree, and then interpreting continuing racial isolation in the schools as resulting from private, not public, choices.

Viewing the school board's desegregation decision as an effort to distance itself from villified behavior associated with the South, as an attempt to demonstrate that Southern forms of racism were beyond the bounds of what this Kansas community perceived of as moral, we can understand their decision to desegregate as an act of self-definition. The board hoped to distinguish itself from the deviant South and thereby place its actions firmly within what it considered to be proper American values. The scope of the school board's desegregation efforts was then bounded by the nature of their interest in the subject. They ultimately were not as concerned with affecting the character of the educational experience of black students, as with affecting the character of their own acts as school board members. Once they abandoned segregation as an express goal and cast continuing segregation as a purely private matter, they considered themselves to have acted

184. See generally Kai Erikson, *The Wayward Puritans* (New York, 1966) 5–29.

185. See generally, Myrdal, supra note 5; Warren, supra note 7. See also Kellogg, supra note 6.

to eradicate injustice, to have abolished segregation, even in the face of continuing racial isolation in the schools.

Although the school experience of many blacks and whites would remain the same, the reform-minded board members felt pride in the significant change they had brought to their community. And the change in Topeka was significant, albeit on the level of ideology. Through its efforts, the Topeka school board dramatically altered its perceptions of its own actions. The label of desegregation had replaced the old, evil label of segregation on Topeka's school policies. Hence, while 'desegregation' in Topeka did not end segregation in the schools, it was powerfully effective in enabling the school board members to feel good about themselves.

Ohio's Legislative Attack upon Abolition Schools

By Clayton S. Ellsworth

The efforts of the Ohio legislature to stamp out the teaching of abolitionism and the education of negroes in certain Ohio schools, especially in Oberlin College, offers a more comprehensive example of northern anti-abolition sentiment than the much better known Prudence Crandall affair in New England.[1] Although most of the other western states were linked to the South by the same ties as Ohio, and also possessed such colleges, partly sympathetic to the abolition movement, as Iowa, Illinois, Wabash, Beloit, and Albion, yet none of their legislatures took the propaganda of the schools as seriously as did the Ohio legislature.[2] The most apparent reason for its unique persecution of Oberlin College was Oberlin's prominence. By the winter of 1836-37, when the legislators first whetted their knives, Oberlin had opened her doors to negroes; her teachers and students had harbored fugitive slaves, and had become peripatetic lecturers for the American Anti-Slavery Society, a combination of activities which no other western college had made.

Before the legislators concentrated their attack upon Oberlin by attempting to repeal the charter of the college, they found time to express several annoying censures. Four sessions of the legislature balked at granting charters to student literary societies.[3] Furthermore, the trustees of the college were not per-

[1] The other schools involved were the Red Oak Seminary, and the Sheffield Manual Labor Institute which is mentioned in the body of the paper. By refusing to give the Red Oak Seminary a charter, the legislature killed that school before it started. Ohio *House Journal*, 38 General Assembly, 487; 39 Gen. Assembly, 191. Ohio *Senate Journal*, 39 Gen. Assembly, 493.

[2] The states included are those of the Old Northwest, and Iowa. Mary M. Rosemond, librarian of the Economics and Sociology Department of the Iowa State Library, Des Moines, Iowa, very kindly checked the legislative journals of that state.

[3] Ohio *House Journal*, 38 Gen. Assembly, 96, 182; 39 Gen. Assembly, 123. Ohio *Senate Journal*, 38 Gen. Assembly, 191, 192, 728; 39 Gen. Assembly, 131; 40 Gen. Assembly, 534, 535; 41 Gen. Assembly, 76, 670. *Ohio State Journal*, January 6, December 31, 1840; *Ohio Statesman*, December 31, 1840; Cincinnati *Philanthropist*, December 31, 1839, January 21, 1840; Cleveland *Daily Herald*, January 7, 1840.

mitted to enlarge their numbers from twelve to eighteen; and a bill incorporating the village of Oberlin was defeated by a one-sided vote.[4] The assemblymen also vented their hatred of Oberlin by refusing to give a charter to the Sheffield Manual Labor Institute, located near Oberlin and connected for a time with the college.[5] Although petty bills like these usually passed as a matter of routine, prolonged debates were focused upon the anti-slavery character of the college and the town.[6]

Many legislators yearned to take more stringent action by taking away the charter granted to the college in 1834, in the days of its innocency. Threats of repealing the charter were first heard during the turbulent session of 1836-37, when the legislators made three hostile sallies.[7] The first serious attempt to carry out these threats came three years later, when Senator Mathews introduced a repeal bill and an indignant petition from citizens of Lorain County, in which Oberlin is situated, praying

[4] Ohio *House Journal*, 35 Gen. Assembly, 338; Ohio *Senate Journal*, 35 Gen. Assembly, 206, *Ohio State Journal and Columbus Gazette*, January 20, 1837.

[5] Ohio *Senate Journal*, 35 Gen. Assembly, 444-45. *Ohio State Journal and Columbus Gazette*, February 28, 1837. Eventually after an amendment had been passed barring colored students from the school, the Senate agreed to the incorporation bill.

[6] It is probable that if the literary societies had been located elsewhere, their fate would have been different. During one of the hostile sessions similar societies at Marietta College and Miami University were granted charters. The objection of one legislator, who voted against one of the Oberlin societies, and who "did not want the statute books disgraced with the name of Oberlin. . . . It sent out scholars, who as school teachers, instill their abolition doctrines in the minds of our children," was typical. Cincinnati *Philanthropist*, January 21, 1840.

Opposition to the proposal to enlarge the number of trustees was led by two influential Democrats, Samuel Medary and John Patterson, who complained that Oberlin was "a hot bed of abolitionism," and that "the blacks and whites were placed on the same level there." *Ohio State Journal and Columbus Gazette*, January 20, 1837.

The sponsor of the bill to incorporate the village wrote that the objection to the bill "was because the name was Oberlin, and that you are considered especially friendly to the blacks." John W. Allen to Levi Burnell, Secretary of the Oberlin Collegiate Institute, March 27, 1837. John W. Allen MSS. (in the office of the treasurer of Oberlin College).

The school at Sheffield was refused a charter on the grounds that it was "too near akin to the Oberlin College," and consequently "it was to become the school of abolitionism." *Ohio State Journal and Columbus Gazette*, February 28, 1837.

[7] This was the session of the legislature that refused to incorporate the town, and the Sheffield Manual Labor Institute without an important amendment to its charter, and refused to permit the trustees of the college to enlarge their number.

for repeal.[8] He, also, published the results of an unofficial probe that he had made into the conduct of the school which showed: "From the president down to the tutor, they preach it [abolitionism] in the desk, inculcate it in common confab, and attend public deliberations for its promulgation."[9] More incriminating was the revelation that President Asa Mahan, himself, assisted by armed students, was guilty of helping fugitive slaves to escape detection.[10] The few friends of the college in the legislature insisted upon the corporate innocence of the school. Not entirely convinced by Mathews' report, the opponents of the college suggested that an official investigation be made by a joint committee of the House and Senate — a proposal that was defeated by a close vote. With this fortunate set-back, no more was heard of repeal that session.

By the time the legislature met again, Oberlin was a more dangerous enemy of the established order than ever before. Two agents of the college had returned from England, where they had obtained about $30,000 from British abolitionists. Enemies of John Bull (and who was not an enemy in the early forties?) accused Oberlin, among other things, of treason, the subjugation of American liberty, and the theft of negroes to be sold into the English army.[11] Oberlin's chances of retaining her charter were further weakened by the "Oberlin Negro Riot," which was serious enough, the *Ohio Statesman* said, "to throw gloom over the mind of every patriot and lover of his country."[12] While the legislature was in session a number of students and townspeople forcibly prevented the illegal return of two fugitives from Kentucky. The negroes after being lodged in the county jail, sawed their way to freedom. Although no legal proof was offered "a gang of Oberlin fanatical abolition anarchists . . . with saws, axes, etc.," was believed guilty of liberating the fugitives.[13]

8 James Mathews. Ohio *Senate Journal*, 38 Gen. Assembly, 197, 233, 370, 376. Cincinnati *Philanthropist*, February 25, 1840; *Ohio State Journal*, February 15, 1840. Herman Birch to Levi Burnell, January 30, 1840. Herman Birch MSS. (in the office of the treasurer of Oberlin College).

9 Ohio *Senate Journal*, 38 Gen. Assembly, 569 ff.

10 *Ibid*. Beyond a doubt Mahan had aided fugitives.

11 *Ohio Statesman*, December 25, 1840; Norwalk *Experiment*, May 6, 1840.

12 *Ohio Statesman*, March 13, 1841.

13 *Ibid.*; Norwalk *Experiment*, March 24, 1841.

As soon as news of the "riot" reached Columbus, a bill to repeal the college's charter was introduced. At this juncture the question of repeal became a lively factor in the fight between the two major parties. Hitherto, opposition to Oberlin had come from the Democrats, and such support as the Whigs had given was half-hearted and perfunctory. But the entrance of the Liberty party into Ohio politics the previous year, had forced the Whigs to make some concessions to their anti-slavery men, concessions which were gleefully labelled as abolitionism by the Democrats. At the risk of being partly identified with the anti-slavery movement, the Whigs, who had a majority, aggressively repelled the second annual onset upon the charter.[14]

Despite the numerical equality of the two parties in the next session of the legislature, the Democrats continued their attack upon the charter, and made the whole question, as one Whig complained, "a sort of tinder box — whenever touched it produces a flame." The Democrats ignited the flame by presenting two petitions with more than four hundred signers, who wished very much to see Oberlin "that great maelstrom of seditious faction . . . exerting a more potent influence in exciting sectional animosities and exasperated feelings . . . than all other malcontent institutions in the U. S.," abolished.[15] One petitioner, who did not doubt that a majority of the Oberlin people "are at heart Traitors to the nation," urged the repeal of the charter before war broke out with England.[16] In response to these petitions a repeal bill was reported with unusual quickness from the Judiciary committee of the Senate.[17] The hostile senators described Oberlin "as dangerous to liberty, law and morality, an excrescence upon the body politic," and "a subject of much odium with the people of the state."[18] When one lone Whig senator, who came from Oberlin's home county, asked the Democrats to state their charges more definitely, they pleaded that the matter was too unpleasant to discuss in detail. Finally the Democratic

---

[14] Ohio *House Journal*, 39 Gen. Assembly, 667, 694; *Ohio Statesman*, March 23, 1841; *Ohio State Journal*, March 24, 1841.

[15] *Ohio Statesman*, February 22, 1842. Ohio *Senate Journal*, 40 Gen. Assembly, 359, 424.

[16] *Ohio Statesman*, February 22, 1842.

[17] Ohio *Senate Journal*, 40 Gen. Assembly, 460, 505, 565.

[18] *Weekly Ohio State Journal*, February 23, 1842.

leaders begrudgingly accused Oberlin of encouraging mobs and aiding fugitive slaves.[19] Possessing a majority of only one in the Senate, the Democrats were ultimately forced to postpone the repeal bill until the next session, and to admit defeat in their third annual attempt to end Oberlin.

The following session, the one of 1842-43, opened more auspiciously for the Democrats than any session had before. With a sizable majority in the Senate, and a slight one in the House, they made a final bombastic attempt which almost annihilated the legal existence of the school. To increase the convictions of the legislators of the odiousness of Oberlin, a book, *Oberlin Unmasked*, was circulated among them. This lurid work written by an expelled student, depicted the Oberlin people as fanatical abolitionists, and amalgamists without benefit of clergy.[20] Some of the legislators must have found the book convincing, for in the long debate that followed the introduction of a repeal bill in the House the second day of the session, the old charges against Oberlin were repeated with added animosity. One of the leaders of the opposition who had been exposed to the "baleful influence" of Oberlin for eight years, and who "was familiar with its venomous and incendiary character, poisoning the minds of youth, and distracting the peace, dignity and morals of the State, under a plea of humanity and sanctity, but in defiance of every obligation of both," felt that the school had inflicted more evil upon the country than any other institution west of the mountains. "It was," he said, "a banditti of law breakers and negro stealers supported by enemies of this country abroad and emissaries at home." [21] Another said, "the institution was commonly

---

[19] James S. Carpenter, Whig from Medina and Lorain counties was the most important opponent of the bill. George W. Holmes from Hamilton County, and B. B. Taylor from Licking County were its principal advocates.

[20] Delazon Smith, *Oberlin Unmasked* (Cleveland, 1837). The senator from Lorain County wrote to his wife early in the session: ''I must say to you that you can have no conception of the opposition and prejudice existing against Oberlin College in the Legislature. This year it arises principally from numerous petitions presented last year . . . and from a book, 'Oberlin Unmasked,' passing round in the House, and a thousand unfavorable rumors, relative to amalgamation, fanaticism, harboring fugitive slaves, etc.'' Josiah Harris to his wife, Thanksgiving 1842, quoted in the appendix of James H. Fairchild, *Oberlin: The Colony and the College, 1833-1883* (Oberlin, 1883), 368-70.

[21] L. Byington from Hocking and Ross counties. *Ohio Statesman*, December 13, 1842; *Weekly Ohio State Journal*, December 14, 1842.

regarded by the citizens of Ohio as a nuisance and a disgrace to the State — a foul stench in their nostrils." [22] And a third, Caleb McNulty, author of the bill, added, "His county [Knox] was in the direct line taken by absconding niggers from the South to that institution, and his constituents complained of it as a very great nuisance. . . . It had been guilty of enormous outrages." [23] These diatribes forced the Whigs to take a new position of defense. Instead of stressing the corporate innocence of the college, they emphasized the corporate privileges of Oberlin by denying the legal right of the legislature to repeal the charter, thereby cutting the college loose from a large amount of property, without judicial proceedings. [24] The Democratic leaders, in turn, justified their action by reminding the Whigs of the repealing clause in the charter, although McNulty proudly announced, "the presence of the clause was a matter of the smallest conceivable consequence to him." To turn the legislature into a court was absurd. "Such is the course," argued one of the leaders, "some gentlemen advocate, and in a case as the one before the House, where the charges are not denied, and while a thousand emissaries are abroad, proclaiming their guilt, and scattering the seeds of iniquity on every hand." The bill was laid on the table by a vote of 36-35. [25]

The closeness of the vote greatly alarmed the college officials, who consulted Edward Wade, a lawyer and member of the well-known Wade family. Wade confessed that he was not certain of the best way for the college to defend itself, but finally advised the trustees and faculty to send statements to the legislature denying any violations of the charter, and to meet any investigating committee appointed by the legislature. This advice was followed. Wade, also, shrewdly comforted the Oberlin officials by assuring them that the legislature would not dare to repeal the charter, and if it did, no great harm would follow for "another Legislature would restore it without doubt and it would be such an ebullition of petty spite and venom as would operate to advantage decidedly." [26]

[22] James P. Henderson, Richland County. *Ohio Statesman*, December 13, 1842.
[23] *Weekly Ohio State Journal*, December 14, 1842.
[24] *Ohio Statesman*, December 13, 1842.
[25] Ohio *House Journal*, 41 Gen. Assembly, 7, 35.
[26] Edward Wade to Henry Cowles, December 16, 1842. Henry Cowles MSS. (in

The imminent possibility of repeal drew from the regular press the first sympathy, such as it was, that Oberlin had received. The *Ohio State Journal* wrote: "We have no particular sympathies with Oberlin; if guilty of any 'outrage' it is that of having contributed to the overthrow of the Whig party in the State; a party whose sense of natural justice and regard for public right, revolts from the turpitude of the measures now contemplated by those who owe their ascendancy to the untoward influences that radiate from Oberlin." [27] Other Whig papers copying the *Ohio State Journal* took much the same position by affirming that although Oberlin was getting its just dues for its support of the Liberty party, repeal without a fair trial was too drastic. Of greater significance was the almost unanimous silence of the Democratic papers. The *Lorain Republican*, the only Democratic paper to voice an outspoken opinion, wrote:

> If the proposed repeal would destroy the fanatical concern, the case would be different. But the only effect would be [to] irritate the motley stipendiaries, without producing any decided effect; and therefore, we must express our decided disapprobation of the measure.[28]

These comments did not deter the Democrats. Fortified by the fresh approval of the repeal bill by the judiciary committee, and by a paper signed by ten citizens, who testified to the integrity of the author of *Oberlin Unmasked*, they soon presented the bill again. Once more the measure was defeated by a close vote.[29] Thus ended the persistent attempts made in six sessions of the Ohio Assembly to suppress Oberlin and her ideals.

Why the Democrats abruptly ceased their struggle when they were so near to victory is something of a mystery. The sanctity of corporate privileges may have awed some. Perhaps friends of the college convinced them that Oberlin at its worst was not as offensive as they had imagined. Or the Democrats may have

the treasurer's office, Oberlin College). One representative, who had never met President Mahan, took the trouble to warn him: "The indications of the present would seem to be that it [repeal bill] would pass the house- [*sic*]. The charges brought are vague and indefinite — but violent vindicative in their character — introduced and sustained by the leaders of the Loco foco [*sic*] party in the house." Thomas Earl to Asa Mahan, December 9, 1842. Thomas Earl MSS. (in the treasurer's office, Oberlin College).

[27] *Weekly Ohio State Journal*, December 14, 1842.
[28] Elyria *Lorain Republican*, December 14, 1842.
[29] Ohio *House Journal*, 41 Gen. Assembly, 227.

realized that to repeal the charter would not necessarily have harmed the institution, and might even have helped Oberlin by forcing it into the limelight as a martyr.

If any of the Democratic leaders could have foreseen that Oberlin's fortunes would reverse so soon and so dramatically, their labors would have been still more determined. Within fifteen years, a gifted young professor, James Monroe, was elected to the Ohio House of Representatives where he became a leader of the radical wing of the rising Republican party. In this capacity he secured the passage of a personal liberty law, the main object of which was to nullify the Fugitive Slave Act of 1850, and introduced an amendment to the Ohio constitution authorizing negro suffrage. Furthermore, the community, by flagrantly violating the Fugitive Slave Act in the Oberlin-Wellington Rescue, unwittingly strengthened the Republican party by giving it a live issue with which to defeat the Democrats in the elections of 1860.

JIM CROW GOES TO SCHOOL: THE GENESIS OF LEGAL SEGREGATION IN SOUTHERN SCHOOLS

John Hope Franklin

A SURVEY of the history of the United States in the nineteenth century gives one the distinct impression that Jim Crow is the creature of a so-called free society. In the North, where freedom came relatively early, Jim Crow had an early birth and was nurtured, oddly enough, even by those who were committed to a loosely defined principle of universal freedom. The separation or exclusion of Negroes from the militia of several Northern states, their segregation in the schools of such states as Massachusetts and Ohio, and the clear-cut policy of excluding them altogether from certain other free states are cases in point. Such practices reflect at times a view, widely held even among those who were opposed to slavery, that Negroes were inferior and deserved special, separate treatment. At other times these practices betrayed an uneasiness among the white population that could be dispelled only by setting up adequate means of control that invariably involved separate arrangements of one sort or another. It is not an accident, therefore, that Jim Crow was practiced first in the very sections of the country that had eliminated slavery.

At the same time, the Southern slave states gave little thought to the problem of keeping the races separate. The entire situation was in the hands of white slaveholders who could relax or apply the controls as they pleased, without endangering or permanently altering the fundamental relationships in the social system. Thus slave children and white children could be cared for in the same nur-

MR. FRANKLIN is professor of history and chairman of the department at Brooklyn College. His books include *From Slavery to Freedom, A History of American Negroes* (1947, 1956), and *The Militant South* (1956).

sery and taught their first lessons together either by a white mistress or by a Negro nurse, who frequently had a major responsibility in transmitting the rudiments of the culture to the young of both races.

There was, under such circumstances, no thought or concern over Jim Crow; for this could not be a problem in a social order where the role of each member was rather carefully defined. Thus, too, Negroes and whites could consort together with impunity and produce a mulatto progeny that ran into the hundreds of thousands by 1860 without risking infracting the laws or even the customs of Jim Crow. They simply did not exist; and with the machinery for achieving and holding respectability securely in the hands of the whites, the ground rules, such as existed, were in their hands to manipulate according to their own whims or satisfaction.

At the end of the Civil War it was inevitable that Jim Crow would ultimately be embraced by those who sought ways to perpetuate in the new era the kinds of controls they had maintained during slavery. Its feasibility as a means of social, political, and economic control in a multiracial society had already been demonstrated. It mattered not that the North had begun to abandon *some* of its Jim Crow practices. There was still wide acceptance of them, even in the old abolitionist strongholds. And it was these *old* northern practices rather than new equalitarian ones that the South preferred to emulate. If the South was to remain a white man's country, as most Southern whites hoped and believed, then strict control of the Negro was desirable, nay, imperative. This was particularly true in the field of education.

In the ante-bellum South widespread illiteracy and the neglect of education were outstanding characteristics of the culture of the region. The aristocratic attitude that it was not necessary to educate the masses, the reluctance of the people to tax themselves for educational purposes, and the marked individualism of the people, born of isolation and the imperfect state of their social and political institutions, were among the factors responsible for this condition. Southerners saw little relation between education and life. Consequently, the view prevailed that those who could afford education could indulge themselves in securing it; and those who could not afford it lost little, if anything. This attitude was aptly summed up fifteen years after the close of the war by Virginia's Governor F. W. M.

Holliday who said that public schools were a "luxury . . . to be paid for like any other luxury, by the people who wish their benefits."

When the economic and social structure of the old South toppled at the end of the Civil War, the ex-Confederates immediately began to erect a new structure based on the old philosophy. Perhaps the war had smashed the Southern world, but it had left the Southern mind and will entirely unshaken. During the war, white Southerners had become more self-conscious than they had been before, more convinced that their way of life had superior validity, and more determined to hold fast to their own, to maintain their divergencies, and to remain what they had been and were. The smoke of battle had hardly cleared when the vanquished leaders, enjoying the autonomy inherent in presidential reconstruction, began to fashion their new world upon the model of the old, which they constantly held before them.

In considering an educational policy for the freedmen in the new order the ex-Confederates faced a real dilemma. Many were alarmed over the prospect of living among a huge mass of free, irresponsible, and ignorant Negroes. Perhaps Negroes should, therefore, be instructed in reading, writing, arithmetic, and the ways of Christian living. But many others were convinced that any intellectual elevation of the Negroes would merely make them difficult to control. Taking their cue from the views and policies of the ante-bellum period, they expressed vigorous opposition to "spoiling" Negroes by educating them. There were those, too, who strenuously objected to taxing themselves for the education of anyone, and certainly not Negroes! Finally, some remained under the influence of those Southern "scientists" and men of letters who had been insisting for a generation that Negroes were simply not capable of being educated.

While these and other considerations were present, it appears that the South was "in general, opposed to the education of the Negro." On Independence Day, 1865, the editor of the Charleston *Daily Courier* put it bluntly when he said, "The sole aim should be to educate every white child in the Commonwealth." A member of the Louisiana legislature said he was "not in favor of positively imposing upon any legislature the unqualified and imperative duty of educating any but the superior race of man—the White race." When he appeared before the Joint Committee on Reconstructon, James B. D. DeBow said that Southerners "generally laugh at the idea of the Negro learning. They have become accustomed to the idea that the Negroes are pretty stupid."

Opposition to the education of the Negro was widespread. In 1866 the Florida Superintendent of Education said that the white people of that state cherished a "deadly hatred to the education and elevation of the freedmen. . . ." In many places teachers in Negro schools were ostracized, and schools could operate only under the protection of federal bayonets. Within a year after the close of the war a reign of terror broke out in Georgia directed against Negro schools. In La Grange a mob burned a building where Negroes were taught, and in Columbus "some of the ladies of the town, 'of the highest standing in society,' were reported to have seriously planned to hang the Yankee teacher."

The dire poverty of the former Confederate states prevented the launching of elaborate programs of public education even where there was a desire to do so. In few instances did the whites regard it necessary to include Negroes in their modest plans. Even if they were of the opinion that Negroes should be educated, they could leave the task to the Freedmen's Bureau and other charitable and religious groups. Thus some states either ignored the question of Negro education or specifically excluded Negroes from public education. In 1866 the Georgia legislature enacted laws providing for a "thoroughgoing" system of free public education for any free white inhabitant between the ages of six and twenty-one. Texas wrote a similar provision into its fundamental law; the constitution of 1866 declared that the public school fund would be "exclusively for the education of all the white scholastics" of the state. It did provide, however, that when the legislature levied taxes for educational purposes the taxes collected from Negroes would be used for the maintenance of a system of public schools for "Africans and their children." Early in the following year Arkansas established a system of free public education limited to whites.

Some towns with control over their own schools seriously affected the education of Negroes by their policies. At the end of the war the city of Mobile, Alabama, merely assumed that its free schools were for whites and, consequently excluded Negroes. Then, in 1867, the Board of School Commissioners appointed a committee "to inquire whether our system of public instruction can be extended to the colored children of Mobile." In the following year the board extended its facilities and resources to Negro children in the primary grades. In Virginia, the city of Norfolk had a flourishing system of public education for whites for several years before it got around to setting up schools for Negroes in 1870.

In 1862 the Congress of the United States provided for the education of Negroes in the District of Columbia by segregating Negro taxes for the support of Negro public schools. It thus set a precedent that at least one Southern state followed rather closely: Florida in 1866 established a system of separate Negro schools to be financed by a tax of one dollar on all male persons of color between the ages of twenty-one and forty-five and fifty cents per month for each pupil. There is no indication that Negroes were relieved from the responsibility of paying taxes to support white schools.

A more vigorous prosecution of the idea of universal education was one of the results of the inauguration of radical reconstruction in the ex-Confederate states in 1867. Negro spokesmen called for free public education for the newly enfranchised freedmen. Leaders from the north, the so-called carpetbaggers, believed that an expanded educational program in the South would do much to improve the cultural and political life of the region. Augmenting this group were those white Southerners who had become committed before the war to the idea of universal education.

Universal education, even among carpetbaggers and Negroes, did not necessarily mean racially integrated schools. Most Freedmen's Bureau schools were segregated, in the sense that they were Negro schools. And the existent public schools were segregated, in the sense that most of them were white schools, with a gesture here and there toward Negroes in the form of separate schools with money raised among Negroes. But there was some reluctance to be explicit about segregated schools in the face of the equal protection provisions of the Fourteenth Amendment.

Alabama is an example of this cognizance of the possible implications of the Fourteenth Amendment for Southern school systems. The legislators had no taste for mixed schools, but they seemed to realize that it would be indiscreet to forbid them. Consequently in August, 1868, the Alabama Board of Education enacted a law that provided that "in no case shall it be lawful to unite in one school both colored and white children, unless it be by the unanimous consent of the parents and guardians of such children." It seems needless to add that this act established no integrated schools. Rather, it paved the way for a Jim Crow policy in public education in Alabama.

More typical on the question of mixed schools during the radical period was Mississippi's law, which was extremely vague on the subject. In the constitutional convention of 1868 there was some advocacy of racially integrated schools. No positive action was taken, however; and in the constitution that was ratified the following year there is no reference to segregation in the article on education. Nor was any color distinction made in the Georgia, North Carolina, and Texas constitutions of 1868, or in the Virginia constitution of 1870.

In Arkansas there never seemed to be any doubt about the wisdom or validity of separate schools, even during the halcyon days of the Radicals. The constitution of 1868 was silent on the racial question in public schools, but later in the same year the assembly took a position that ruled out any possibility of integrated schools. It instructed the state board of education to "make the necessary provisions for establishing separate schools for white and colored children. . . ." Tennessee had likewise segregated its schools from the beginning of Reconstruction.

Only two states were unequivocal in their legal provisions for integrated schools. In its constitution of 1868 Louisiana declared, "There shall be no separate schools or institutions of learning established exclusively for any race in the State. . . ." In 1871 the state forbade any racial discrimination in admission to schools for the blind, and in 1875 a law provided that there should be no discrimination in admission, management, or discipline of the new agricultural and mechanical college. Meanwhile, South Carolina had gone almost as far in its constitution of 1868, which declared that all public schools, colleges or universities supported in whole or in part by the public school fund "shall be free and open to all without regard to race or color."

It would not be too much to say that attempts to integrate schools were generally unsuccessful either in the states where the provisions were sufficiently vague to countenance them or where they they were expressedly authorized by law. The initial hostility of white Southerners to schools of any kind had been the most effective weapon against mixed schools. If Negro schools were burned, if white teachers of Negroes were ostracized, threatened, whipped, and chased from the community, any kind of schools for Negroes had little chance of succeeding. Mixed schools had no chance whatever. Even the friends of Negro education and many of those who frowned on separation were forced to the unpleasant but inescapable conclusion that the only real chance for success in the education of Negroes lay in the establishment and maintenance of separate schools.

For one reason or another many of the responsible leaders during the radical regime called for separate schools. Among these was Governor W. W. Holden of North Carolina, who hoped that the separate school would "equally enjoy the fostering care of the state." Another was Governor Robert K. Scott of South Carolina, who declared that while "God hath made of one blood all nations of men, yet the statesmen in legislating for a political society that embraces two distinct . . . races. . . must . . . take cognizance of existing prejudices among both." Such views contributed substantially to the establishment and perpetuation of separate schools.

While some Negroes resigned themselves to segregated schools as the only practicable solution to the problem, others were not so conciliatory. Most of the Negroes in the Mississippi constitutional convention of 1868 were in favor of mixed schools, which they viewed as the only means of securing equal advantages with the whites. On the other hand, meeting in convention in Nashville in 1879, a group of Negroes declared that "separate schools are highly detrimental to the interests of both races, and that such schools foster race prejudice. . . ." Negro members of Congress fought vigorously, if unsuccessfully, to keep the integrated schools provision in the civil rights bill of 1875 because they were convinced that there could be no equality in education in segregated schools.

Meanwhile, white Southerners who were opposed to mixed schools or to the education of Negroes altogether never relented in their fight. When equal educational opportunities were merely implied in legislation, its supporters were attacked as "imported amalgamationists." In Louisiana, where an attempt was made to establish mixed schools, the editor of the New Orleans *Times* predicted that such effort to annihilate "those great laws of distinction in race implanted by the Creator" would, perhaps, serve to destroy the school system. In South Carolina, at the state university, many white students and professors withdrew when Negroes were admitted, and the agitation against its integration all but wrecked the institution.

Here and there a few publicly supported mixed schools existed, and in one quarter there was even enthusiastic support on the part of some white Southerners. As late as 1875 ex-Confederate General P.G.T. Beauregard came out for mixed schools in Louisana on the ground that Southerners could win over Negroes by giving them the political and civil equality guaranteed them by the national and state constitutions. In 1874, supporting a national civil rights bill that included a provision for integrated schools, Representative C. B. Darroll of the same state praised its mixed schools. He declared that not only did white and Negro Republicans support it, "but many of the oldest and best of white citizens . . . have publicly in mass meetings and addresses heartily approved of all the features of the civil rights bill, including free schools to all."

Most of the mixed schools in the South, however, were the colleges, academies, and tributary grammar schools established and maintained largely by Northern philanthropic and religious societies. But mixed schools, public and private, were doomed from the outset. Their precarious position was constantly assailed by the majority of white Southerners who, by 1874, were powerful enough to have a good deal to do with preventing the inclusion of a provision for integrated schools in the proposed federal civil rights bill.

The advocates of Jim Crow in education found vigorous and enthusiastic support in the Peabody Fund. From its establishment in 1867, this Northern philanthropic agency founded by a Southern-born business man had opposed mixed schools in the South. In 1869-70 it had refused to contribute to the public schools of Louisiana because they were not segregated. The director of the fund, Barnas Sears, told the Louisiana Superintendent of Education that as long as the schools were so organized as to cause the greater part of the white population to be unwilling to send their children to them, the Fund could not contribute to them; and he diverted the Fund's resources to the support of white private schools. In 1874 Sears went to Washington to fight the "mixed schools" provision of the civil rights bill. When the provision was dropped from the bill late in the year, the fund and its officials took their share of the credit for the victory.

The involvement of Jim Crow in public education in the South steadily increased from the time the guns were silenced at Appomattox. At times it was fostered by the ex-Confederates during their period of home rule. At other times it was pushed by one group or another during the radical period: the Southern white irreconcilables, the Negroes who wanted an education more than they wanted integration, those radicals who saw in southern Jim Crow schools an extension of the practices in many Northern communities, and such foundations as the Peabody Fund which disposed of its funds in a manner designed to control policy.

When redemption came, the white Southerner, returning to the control of his government after an absence ranging from a few months to eight or nine years, began in earnest to put Jim Crow permanently into the public schools. This usually merely involved confirming in law a practice that had already become accepted. As the years passed, the ex-Confederate states became bolder in their insistence upon establishing Jim Crow schools in law. More and more, the early examples of Florida, Tennessee, and Arkansas in segregating became the accepted pattern. Georgia had made no color distinction in her formal legislation during the brief period of radical reconstruction; but when home rule was reestablished in 1870 one of the first steps the legislature took was the enactment of a law requiring school officials to provide for the "instruction of the white and colored youth . . . in separate schools." The law stated that the trustees of the school districts were to provide the same facilities for each race. This requirement was modified in 1872 when equal facilities were required "as far as practicable."

North Carolina was "redeemed" in 1870, but as early as November, 1868, the legislature had regularized and legalized the practice of Jim Crow in the schools. In 1876 Jim Crow education was written into the state constitution. In 1876 Alabama, now redeemed, deserted her equivocation of 1868 and wrote into her constitution that "separate schools shall be provided for the children of citizens of African descent." Since 1866 the constitutions and laws of Texas had been silent on the question of segregation: in 1873 the legislature took the first step toward legalizing Jim Crow by requiring the trustees of school districts to provide school houses "separating the children and so arranging the schools . . . that good order, peace, and harmony may be maintained in the schools." Three years later the state more unequivocally provided that "the two races shall always be taught in separate public free schools."

South Carolina and Louisiana, where the battle for integrated schools was most vigorously fought, surrendered to Jim Crow legislation in 1877. Since South Carolina did not repeal its constitutional ban on segregated schools until 1895, the state's dual system of public schools actually operated illegally between 1877 and 1895. Louisiana violated its own constitution for even longer, since it did not expunge its constitutional requirement for integrated schools until 1898. Jim Crow had become so powerful and the possibility of federal intervention had become so slight that the leadership in these two states thought nothing of violating the state constitutions.

In 1878 Mississippi required separate schools by law, and Jim Crow education was written into the constitution in 1890. Although Virginia did not enact its separate school law until 1882, its public schools had always been separate. A decade earlier, when W. H. Ruffner, the state superintendent, made his first annual report, he had proudly reported that there were 706 Negro schools among the 2,900 schools in the state.

Thus did Jim Crow become a part of the public school systems of all the ex-Confederate states. It was seized upon as an important instrument of control as the whites sought an acceptable subordinate relationship with their former slaves. By the end of Reconstruction Jim Crow in the schools had become an important means of social control and a device for perpetuating the ignorance of a great mass of blacks. Ignorance would, of course, make them unworthy to participate in the political life of the country. This view of the redeemers was supported by their calling attention to the corruption, waste, and inefficiency during the "years of darkness." They would overcome these deficiencies by retrenchment and improvement; and they would make permanent the time-honored relationship of the races by keeping them segregated. Somehow, retrenchment seemed to go well with segregation, particularly among a people to whom taxation for the support of education was repugnant.

Once the schools were clearly separated on the basis of race it became much easier for the redeemers to retrench without seriously affecting the schools for their own children. In some states expenditures for public education fell off as much as 20 per cent in the years following the overthrow of Reconstruction. While many white Southerners were not averse to slashing educational expenditures across the board, they went as far as possible in cutting expenditures for Negro schools *before* touching the white schools. To be sure, white schools were crippled all over the South, but it was the Negro schools that were all but destroyed at the hands of the enemies of education and of the Negro.

The way in which inequity in the treatment of Negro schools was not only perpetuated but magnified can be seen in what happened to the per capita expenditure for teachers' salaries in some Southern states. In 1871, the year after redemption in North Carolina, it was $.41 for whites and $.26 for Negroes. By 1910 it was $3.26 for whites and $1.38 for Negroes. In Alabama in 1875, the year after redemption it was $1.30 for whites and $1.46 for Negroes. By 1910 it was $6.19 for whites and $1.01 for Negroes. The material effects of Jim Crow could nowhere be more dramatically illustrated.

Once Jim Crow was firmly established in the public schools of the South, the inequities persisted and increased; and the conditions most destructive to the educative process in a democracy were created. White children were taught, if not directly then indirectly by their superior advantages, they they belonged to some kind of a master race. Even the rather dull minded among them, moreover, could see that they lived lives that contradicted the basic democratic tenets of equality and justice. For the Negro children the task was an almost impossible one: to endure the badge of inferiority imposed on them by segregation, to learn enough in inferior Jim Crow schools to survive in a highly complex and hostile world, and, at the same time, keep faith in democracy. For both Negro and white children, one of the most effective lessons taught in Jim Crow schools was that even in institutions dedicated to training the mind a greater premium was placed on color than on brains. True education in the South was languishing. Only Jim Crow was flourishing and making steady gains in the generation after the Civil War.

THE PERSISTENCE OF SCHOOL SEGREGATION IN THE URBAN NORTH: AN HISTORICAL PERSPECTIVE

by Vincent P. Franklin*

In 1967 the report of the United States Commission on Civil Rights entitled Racial Isolation in the Public Schools concluded that "seventy-five percent of the Negro elementary students in the Nation's cities are in schools with enrollments that are nearly all-Negro (90 percent or more Negro), while 83 percent of the White students are in nearly all-White schools. Nearly nine out of every 10 Negro elementary students in the cities attend majority-Negro schools."[1] The report stated that the "high level of racial separation in city schools exists whether the city is large or small, whether the proportion of Negro enrollment is large or small and whether the city is located North or South."[2]

These facts surprised many educators and social scientists since the major thrust of educational policy in the period after the Brown decision (1954) was integration and desegregation of White and Black in public schools. Another startling conclusion for many was the report that "racial isolation in the public schools is increasing. Over recent years Negro elementary school enrollment in northern city school systems has increased, as have the number and proportion of Negro elementary students in majority-Negro and nearly all-Negro schools. Most of this increase has been absorbed in schools which are now more than 90 percent Negro, and almost the entire increase in schools which are now majority-Negro." The Commission goes on to discuss the causes of increased segregation in the public schools. The fact that entire metropolitan areas are increasingly separated socially and economically is being reflected in the public schools. Housing policies and practices of both industry and government help to promote residential segregation by building homes at prices which only the wealthy can generally afford. Additional housing factors such as restrictive zoning ordinances, racially restrictive covenants which can be judicially enforced, and administrative determinations of building permits also help to increase the residential segregation.[3]

The report thoroughly documents the degree of racial segregation in the Nation's public schools and its possible effects on the educational outcomes of Black students. The Commission believes there is "a relationship between the racial composition of schools and the achievement and attitudes of most Negro students," that is, the fact that a student is in an all-Black school which is "generally regarded by the community as an inferior institution" places a stigma on the Black child that affects his achievement and attitudes as well as the attitudes of the teachers and administrators in the predominantly Black school.[4]

However, if one considers the total report, there is little attempt to present the problem of school segregation historically other than to demonstrate statistically that racial segregation in the public schools has increased since 1950. No attempt is made to discover whether the various problems stemming

---

*Vincent P. Franklin is in the Department of Education at The University of Chicago.

51

from racial segregation which affect the attitudes and achievement of Black students in 1965, were in existence in 1920, 1930, or 1940. Does the presence of school segregation in urban areas over long periods of time affect the possibility of desegregating the urban public school at present? In suggesting ways of dealing with problems of school segregation is it necessary to take into account past situations in the public schools in order to test the feasibility of implementing these recommendations? The historical analysis of segregation in the Philadelphia public schools and an analysis of the more important historical and sociological reasons for the persistence of school segregation in the urban North in general may shed light on the degree of pervasiveness of school segregation in the North and may also provide some historical insights into the situation of the Blacks in urban America.

Philadelphia was one of the first cities to establish separate schools for Blacks financed entirely by the public. Under the Acts of 1802, 1804, and 1809, the State of Pennsylvania made provision for the gratuitous education of the poor. In 1818 the first School District of Pennsylvania was laid out by the General Assembly to include the city and county of Philadelphia, and as a result five schools were established for poor White children in the city.[5] Although there was a large and growing Black population in Philadelphia at the time, "it is not probable that the white people of the state had for a moment contemplated the admission of negro [sic.] children into schools for their own children; hence only by granting separate buildings could negroes benefit by the law."[6] Therefore, the Pennsylvania Abolition Society which had been sponsoring private schools for Blacks in Philadelphia since the 1790's, but having problems maintaining them in later years, decided to donate one of its buildings (on Mary Street) to the School District in order to allow the Black population access to free public education. The remainder of the needed funds coming from the city, the Mary Street School for Colored Youth was opened in 1822.[7]

By 1850 there were eight "colored public schools" in Philadelphia with a total enrollment of 531. The quality of instruction in the public schools was reported as being "not as good as that in the charity (private) schools"; however, after the Civil War it was said that there was "noticeable improvement" in these schools.[8] In 1854, under the Common School Laws of Pennsylvania, there was a provision that "directors or controllers of the several districts of the State are hereby authorized and required to establish within their respective districts, separate schools for the tuition of negro and mulatto children whenever such schools can be so located as to accommodate twenty or more pupils; and whenver such separate schools shall be established, and kept open four months in any year, the directors or controllers shall not be compelled to admit such pupils into other schools in the district."[9] As a result of this statute all of the previously established separate public schools for Blacks in Philadelphia and throughout the State were sanctioned, and the door was opened for the establishment of others in the future.[10]

The Republican inspired activities on behalf of the civil rights of the Blackman on the national scene during the 1870's were matched by the activities of Republicans in Pennsylvania. The movement for the incorporation of a

52

414

section requiring desegregation of public schools into the Civil Rights Act pending in the national Senate, was followed by a movement in the General Assembly of Pennsylvania for the repeal of the separate school legislation of 1854. Passed by the State Senate on May 5, 1874, it failed to come to a vote in the lower house and was dropped.[11] The Civil Rights Act was passed by the U.S. Congress in 1875, but without the section calling for the desegregation of public education.[12]

The issue of separate schools was still not settled in Pennsylvania and again came to a head in 1881. In that year a Black parent, Elias H. Allen, appealed for a writ of mandamus to have his children admitted to the local White public school in Meadville, Pa. The county court decided that the Pennsylvania segregation law violated the equal protection clause of the Fourteenth Amendment to the Constitution and that the Black children should be admitted to the school closest to their home.[13] Meanwhile, a bill was introduced into the State Senate on April 1, 1881 for the repeal of the separate school provision of the School Laws, supported by petitions from the Pennsylvania State Equal Rights League, a Black civil rights group, and several other citizens of the State. The measure was quickly pushed through both houses and was passed with bipartisan support and signed by the governor on June 8, 1881.[14] The law was challenged in 1882 but was upheld by the State Supreme Court.[15]

The law of 1881 notwithstanding, the public schools in Philadelphia remained to a very great degree segregated. Writing in 1898, W. E. B. Dubois, in his famous sociological study of The Philadelphia Negro, reported that "this enactment was for some time evaded, and even now some discrimination is practiced quietly in the matter of admission and transfers. There are also schools still attended by Negro pupils and taught by Negro teachers, although, of course, the children are at liberty to go elsewhere if they choose. They are kept mainly through a loyalty to Negro teachers."[16] Although Blacks constituted only about four percent of the population of the city, and four percent of the school population, twenty-five percent of the Black students attended all-Black or nearly all-Black schools in 1895.[17] Therefore, one may conclude that the law of 1881 did not abolish the separate schools but merely gave the Black child the right to attend any public school to which he was eligible without regard to color.

From 1900, Pennsylvania statistics reveal that an increasing percentage of Black children of school age were attending school; however, it was significantly lower than for Whites. "In 1900, 54.1 percent of the native White and 44.3 percent of the Negro children between the ages of five and twenty were attending school. In 1910, the percentage for native Whites was 61.1 and 55.1 for Negroes; in 1920, the percentages were 65.4 and 59.4 respectively for native Whites and Negroes..."[18] As to why in 1912 Blacks in Philadelphia, and Pennsylvania were not attending school, Richard R. Wright, Jr. offers two important reasons: the first was "working parents"; the low economic status of the Negro required "that both of them be absent from their homes during the day," thus leaving the children to their own devices. The second was the inadequate training offered by the schools.

53

The Negro boy or girl who goes through the eighth grade,
can do nothing well. Very few of them go to the High
School because by that time they find that they are circumscribed by race prejudice which keeps them from open
competition, and they do not see that the four year course
in the High School would be of any special economic benefit
to them. It is a well known fact that a Negro girl finishing
eighth grade at present, has about as much chance economically, as her sister from the High School.... With Negro
young men who finish High School courses, there is often a
larger amount of discouragement. The reason is, that a
Negro boy is not permitted to enter competition for clerical
or other positions with his white classmates, though they be
no better intellectually or economically than he is. He is
not even half prepared for any other work and he must turn
to domestic service, where he is often held up by the
Negroes as sufficient proof for other boys and their parents,
that a High School course is useless for Negroes. [19]

The period from 1910 to 1920 saw the beginning of the great migration of
southern Blacks to the northern urban areas. The Black population of Philadelphia, for example, increased by 58 percent during that decade. [20] The over-
riding reason for this movement was economic. "Among the immediate economic causes of the migration was the labor depression in the South in 1914
and 1915 and the large decrease in foreign immigration resulting from the
World War." The boll weevil damaging large amounts of cotton crops in 1915
and 1916, the drop in the price of cotton, floods in the summer of 1915,
generally low wages and the increasing cost of living: all had the effect of
driving Blacks from the Southland. [21] There was also an increase in the number of jobs available to Negroes in the North. In Philadelphia the need for
workers for the Pennsylvania and Erie Railroads as well as "the industrial
plants situated in and adjacent to Philadelphia were... influencial in attracting
Negroes to the city." [22]

Although researchers agree that economics was the major cause, there
were other reasons for the movement of Blacks from the South. Ill treatment
received at the hands of the courts and the guardians of the peace constituted
one cause of the migration. [23] Another cause was the inadequacy of school
facilities. [24]

The inadequacy of the elementary school system for colored
children is indicated both by the comparisons of the public
appropriations already given and by the fact that attendance
in both public and private schools is only 58.1 per cent of
the children six to fourteen years of age. The average
length of the public school term is less than five months in
practically all the southern States. Most of the school

54

416

buildings, especially those in rural districts, are in
wretched condition. There is little supervision and
little effort to improve the schools or adapt their efforts to the needs of the community. [25]

Blacks left the South seeking better educational opportunities for their
children, and this large movement had significant effects on the northern public
school systems. In Philadelphia, throughout this century, the percentage of
Blacks in the public school population increased. In 1920, Blacks constituted
7.7 percent of the elementary school population and 3.2 percent of the secondary
school population. By 1925, Blacks made up 11.6 percent of the elementary and
3.9 percent of the secondary school population; in 1930, they accounted for 15.4
and 6.4 percent respectively of the elementary and secondary school population. [26] The percentage of Black children in the public school increased at a
much faster rate than did the percentage of Blacks in the population of the city
of Philadelphia. In 1920, Blacks constituted 7.7 percent of the elementary
school population and 7.4 percent of the city population. In 1940, Blacks made
up 13 percent of the city population and 20.5 percent of the school population. [27]

The results of this increase in the public school's Black population over
these years are several and germane to the discussion of school segregation.
A survey of the Philadelphia Public Schools conducted by W. A. Daniels in
1925 concluded that there were eight schools in the system with Negro principals, teachers and students. However, according to Daniels, segregation in
the Philadelphia public schools decreased from 1923 to 1925. "The number of
colored pupils in the separate schools in 1923 was 8718; in 1924, 8400; and in
1925, 7755....Six of the eight separate colored schools showed a smaller enrollment each year from 1923 to 1925."[28] Daniels states that although the
Black school population increased in those years, it did not lead directly to increased segregation; "the number of colored pupils in each mixed school is
small, (however) more than two-thirds of the colored elementary pupils, 68.2
percent, are in mixed schools."

At the same time, Daniels enumerated several of the difficulties faced
by Black students who attended the mixed schools. He reports that "it is not at
all uncommon for a Negro pupil 'belonging' to a mixed school by residence to be
asked by a White teacher or pupil 'Why don't you go to the ---- school WHERE
YOU BELONG?' The ---- school is invariably a school attended wholly or almost wholly by Negro pupils, and may be in another part of the city."[29] If the
principal of the school holds the same opinion as the White teacher or pupil,
"colored pupils are disposed of in summary fashion."

The degree of fairness accorded Black students in the mixed school was
also open to question. "Objection is raised to the fact that some principals
suspend colored pupils for certain offenses, but do not suspend White pupils
for the same offenses." The seating arrangement in many mixed classrooms
reflects "the attitude of the teachers, some of whom feel that Negro children
are mentally inferior to White children and, for this reason or for other reasons, should not be allowed to associate with White pupils...."[30] This points

55

up some of the reasons why many Black parents may have preferred to have their children attend all-Black (segregated) public schools. In any case, the report on the Negro in Pennsylvania by the Department of Welfare in 1927 reported that "In Philadelphia there are 12 schools which have 100 per cent Negro attendance. All the teachers are Negroes, including the principal. Negro children living in school districts bordering on the districts of these 12 schools are sent out of their district to the school having all Negro pupils and teachers, and White children living in the district of the schools having all Negro pupils and teachers are sent out of their district to schools which have 100 per cent White attendance."[31] This represents an increase of four schools in the two or three years of time between the two reports.

In 1940, it was reported that there were still only twelve schools that had "Negro principals, teachers and students." However, whereas in 1925, there were only twenty-two schools that had 40 percent or more Black students; in 1940, this number had increased to forty-five.[32] At the same time, it should be noted that all of the Negro teachers in the Philadelphia public schools taught only Negro pupils until 1934.[33] A group known as the Educational Equality League in that year petitioned the School Board of Philadelphia to halt the practice of assigning Negro teachers only to all-Negro schools, and allow Negroes to teach on the junior and senior high levels. By 1941, there was one Negro teaching on the junior high level, and eight Negro teachers who taught White pupils out of a total of 307 Negro teachers in the system. No Negro teacher taught on the senior high level in 1941.[34]

The report on Racial Isolation in the Public Schools found that in 1950, 63.2 percent of all Black elementary students in Philadelphia were attending 90-100 percent Black schools; and 84.8 percent were attending majority Black schools. In 1965, 72.0 percent of all Black elementary school pupils were attending 90-100 percent Black schools; and 90.2 percent were attending majority Black schools.[35] In trying to account for this great increase in school segregation in the various urban areas reported on, the Commission on Civil Rights discusses several important factors. School segregation "is perpetuated by the effects of past segregation and racial isolation. It is reinforced by demographic, fiscal and educational changes taking place in the Nation's metropolitan areas. And it has been compounded by the policies and practices of urban school systems."[36] The report goes on to discuss school district organization, population and economic trends (Whites moving out of the central city to the suburbs), as well as housing and fiscal policies. However, there was little or no attempt made to discuss exactly what or how "past segregation" caused racial isolation in the schools. Therefore, using data on Philadelphia, as well as several other northern cities, the author will attempt to delineate several of the historical reasons for the persistence of school segregation in the urban North.

Many social scientists have tended to view school segregation in the North as a recent occurrence. Their accounts would have Blacks encroaching on larger and larger areas of the cities, with Whites fleeing to the suburbs. This is the general impression one receives in reading the government report

56

418

on Racial Isolation in the Public Schools. Although this may account for the increase in segregation over the last fifteen or twenty years, it does not adequately explain the "historical" persistence of segregation in northern public schools.
As we have seen in Philadelphia, the primary reason for the persistence of
school segregation remains the attitude of the White population. The refusal
of the Whites to allow Blacks to attend the same schools became an accepted
tradition, later codified in School laws. The School Law of Pennsylvania in
1854 mandating the establishment of separate schools, was merely sanctioning
a situation that already existed. However, as long as the law was on the books
and enforced by school officials, segregation would continue in the public
schools of the state.

Laws sanctioning the existence of separate schools for Blacks were found
throughout the North in the nineteenth and twentieth centuries. In Ohio, the so-
called "Black laws" of 1802, 1804 and 1807 set the tone for legislation promulgated to "regulate" the Black population. State laws of 1848 and 1849 mandated
townships to provide separate educational facilities "under the general school
management, not under separate colored school directors." These statutes
were further bolstered by legislation for separate schools in 1853 and 1878.
These laws were finally repealed in 1886 "after a prolonged battle by the
A.M.E. Church and the National Colored Convention and numerous other
agencies and important individuals."[37] Delaware had provisions in the State
laws sanctioning separate schools throughout the twentieth century, as did the
State of Missouri. Legal school segregation ended in those states at the same
time that it ended in the South (1954).[58]

In some northern states no state law mandated the provision of separate
schools for Blacks, but the local communities passed such statutes, and their
legality was settled by the state Supreme courts. In New York, each of the
cases brought to contest local statutes requiring separate schools was decided
in favor of maintaining the separate schools. It was not until 1900 that a State
law was passed prohibiting the exclusion of a child from a public school on the
basis of color.[39] In New Jersey, local statutes existed in various communities
throughout the State sanctioning separate public schools for Blacks. In 1881,
the New Jersey legislature passed a law prohibiting the exclusion of children
from their local public school on the basis of color.[40] The Illinois Constitution
was silent on the question of separate schools, and the State court cases that
arose as a result of local laws were decided in favor of the statutes requiring
separation until 1908 when the Courts finally ruled that Black children cannot
be forced to attend separate Black schools.[41]

The most famous northern decision in favor of separate schools for
Blacks came from Massachusetts in 1849, in the case of Roberts v. the City of
Boston. This decision served as one of the precedents in the Supreme Court
case of Plessy v. Fergurson (1896) in which the doctrine of "separate but equal"
was sanctioned. Legal segregation in Massachusetts, however, ended in 1857.[42]

Although one finds that legal segregation ended in several northern states
as of a certain date, segregated schools persisted in those states because of the
patterns of residential segregation already established. In Philadelphia,

57

although there was no legal segregation after 1881, 100 percent Black schools persisted not only because "prejudice... works to compel colored children to attend certain schools where most Negro children go..." but also because the schools in the predominantly Black neighborhoods remained or became predominantly Black. [43] Residential segregation, therefore, can also be used to explain why school segregation persisted in the North.

R. R. Wright, Jr. comments that "in Philadelphia, the largest groups of Negroes are in the 7th and 30th wards, which contained in 1900, 10,462 and 5,242 Negroes respectively. The segregated communities were formed naturally; the first Negroes who settled for themselves settled in the places which they could secure employment. Others moved near them and so on, until there was a so-called settlement of Negroes. Race feeling, common interests, common bearing of racial prejudice, were among the things which tended to keep Negroes together." [44] The public schools in the areas of "Negro settlement" became predominantly Black, thus we have de facto segregation remaining after de jure segregation had ended.

In a study of Negro migration conducted in 1930, Louise Kennedy found that the reports on the effects of the migration on the northern cities were unanimous in "contending that there is residential segregation in the North and that migration has tended to increase the concentration of Negroes in certain districts." In specific reference to Philadelphia, it was pointed out that the migrants were practically forced to seek homes in the customary "colored sections." [45] "The housing problem was itself a result of the determination on the part of the white people that the migrant should live only in the part of the city in which Negroes had previously lived." [46] The report on the Negro in Pennsylvania of 1927 states that as a result of this situation there was great overcrowding in these Negro districts, and rents were very high. "The unskilled workingman who constitutes the mass Negro pays more for his housing in Philadelphia and Pittsburgh than does the white man. This is due, of course, to the fact that landlords take advantage of the great pressure on Negro housing resulting from the large number of Negroes in the two cities.... The Negro who pays the same rent as the white man, or even the Negro who pays more rent than the white, gets much inferior housing for his money." [47]

The concentration of Blacks into "ghettos" led to an increase in the amount of segregation in the public schools that served these communities. However, this "natural" segregation of schools does not account for the total amount of segregation in northern cities in 1930. "It is not unusual for colored children to be transferred or enrolled at the beginning, in a school which is predominantly Negro, even though another school may be nearer their homes. Likewise white children living in or near a neighborhood largely colored are sometimes sent to more distant schools in order to avoid mingling the races. [48] The increase in the Black population of the northern cities in the twentieth century accounts to a very great degree for the increase in the percentage of Blacks in these urban public school systems. However, the exit of the Whites from certain neighborhoods, the public schools, and eventually the cities themselves, also aided in the increase in segregation in the public schools.

58

The over-all effect of the great migration of southern Blacks to the urban North, therefore, was to assist in the persistence of school segregation.

At the same time, many educational problems were created for these northern school systems as a result of the migration of southern Blacks. As was noted above, the extreme inadequacy of the education provided for Blacks in the South meant that many children entered the northern schools with severe educational handicaps. However, there is little or no evidence that the public schools tried to solve or even deal with these problems or change their educational practices to conform to the needs of their new student body. Horace Mann Bond commenting on this situation in 1940 states that the "large, inflexible Northern school systems have as yet found no adequate adaptation to facilitate the acculturation of the undigested, and perhaps indigestible, Negro masses. The only solution so far attempted has been racial segregation."[49]

However, the fact that the education available to Blacks in the North was far superior to that found in the South, was used to excuse the failure to reform the educational practices in the North. It was argued that no matter how bad the education for Blacks was in these northern urban school systems, it was much better than the "completely inadequate" systems of the South.[50]

The educational problems of some Black students which were acute during the first half of this century became chronic after 1950, especially in those cities with a substantial percentage of Blacks in the school population. Educational research tended to emphasize integration or desegregation as means of improving the academic achievement of Black students. However, the implementation of these recommendations was slowed not only by the refusal of the federal government to enforce the Brown decision (1954) in the North against de facto segregation, but also because of the resistance of northern Whites to many desegregation plans. Meanwhile, the percentage of Blacks in the large urban school systems continued to increase until the 1970's when desegregation of many school systems would be virtually impossible because of a paucity of White students in the system. The only possible way of achieving the desegregation advocated by several educational researchers would be through plans for "metropolitan desegregation" in which a predominantly Black school system would merge (in one way or another) with a predominantly White school system. However, in districts where such a merger has been proposed or mandated by the courts, resistance by White parents has been great, and the matter may eventually have to be ruled on by the U.S. Supreme Court.[51]

In attempting to chronicle the reasons for the persistence of school segregation in the urban North, there are several more subtle factors that become apparent only after the more obvious ones have been dealt with. In reviewing the situation in Philadelphia, it becomes clear that there were some elements of the Black community which benefited from the persistence of segregated schools, especially in the early years. Dubois commented in 1898 that one of the reasons for the maintenance of all-Black schools after 1881 was "out of a feeling of loyalty to Negro teachers."[52] R. R. Wright, Jr. in 1912 found that the number of Negro teachers had increased over the previous ten years in Philadelphia. "This is largely due to the immigration of Negroes from the

59

421

South. Though Negro schools have no legal existence, Negro teachers, as a rule, teach only Negro children. There are more than sixty Negro public school teachers in Phila."[53] As long as these segregated public schools existed, Black teachers would have jobs. Teaching was one of the most prestigious and lucrative professions in the Black community. In the period from 1890 to 1940, the only jobs that were proscribed for Blacks were primarily in domestic services and the lowest levels of industry. The Negro professional class was made up of those persons who provided professional services for the Black community. Negro doctors, lawyers, teachers, etc., catered to other Negroes primarily and were usually prohibited from providing these services to Whites. However, the converse was not true, and therefore, it was believed that if mixed schools were advocated and brought about, Negro teachers would lose their positions and young Black college graduates would not be hired as teachers as quickly as Whites.

There is a good deal of substance to this belief. In New Jersey, in 1881, the effect of law which allowed Blacks to attend the local public school rather than separate schools, was weakened "by the ... acceptance of separate schools by Negroes of Fair Haven, for whose benefit the law was originally passed." The Negroes of Long Beach, New Jersey also requested separate schools the same year. "The attitude of the Whites against the admission of colored children into the schools, plus THE OPPORTUNITIES FOR TEACHING JOBS FOR MEMBERS OF THEIR OWN RACE, together with the influence of General Clinton Fiske, a man of high prestige among them, undoubtedly contributed to this decision on the part of the Negroes. The lack of unanimity among Negroes themselves has served to confuse the issue and to prevent the adoption of consistent policies governing the education of Negroes in New Jersey." (italics not in original).[54]

In Columbus, Ohio, the separate school for Negroes was demolished in 1882 and for thirty years thereafter Blacks "were admitted to the school nearest their homes. The colored teachers for the most part found other employment although a few were transferred to the other Columbus schools." In the 1920's, after a large influx of Blacks from the South, we find the restoration of separate schools.

> The reestablishment of schools for colored pupils after a 30 year experience of complete integration is noteworthy because of the controversy it generated. For over twenty years the question of integration versus segregation in the public school system divided the Negro group into two embattled camps. The controversy sent deep roots into the life of the Negro community which have not yet lost their virulence. However, it must be remembered in considering the schooling of Negro children in Columbus that the controversy which raged for so many years is no more peculiar to Columbus than is the racial pattern which provoked it.

60

422

WHATEVER POSITION ONE MAY TAKE ON THIS CON-
TROVERSY, IT IS NEVERTHELESS TRUE THAT THE
PUBLIC SCHOOLS PROVIDE AN IMPORTANT PART
OF THE GROUP'S PROFESSIONAL CLASS. THERE ARE
FOUR NEGRO PRINCIPALS AND SOME 80 TEACHERS,
THE LARGEST SINGLE PROFESSIONAL GROUP IN THE
CITY.[55] (italics not in original)

In Philadelphia, between 1930 and 1940 there was a decline in the White
public school population, but an increase in the Black school population. However, during those same years, the relative number of Black teachers in the
system declined, and there was an increase in the number of White teachers
with Black pupils.[56]

While some members of the Black community may have had a vested interest in the maintenance of segregated schools, there really was no consistent
opinion among Blacks or Whites as to the advantages or disadvantages of the
separate school before 1945. The report on the urban Black population in
Pennsylvania in 1941 discusses this dilemma. "In the matter of the establishment of separate schools, a board of education or a superintendent has many
complex problems with which to deal.... The Negro leadership is divided on
some main questions. This division both perplexes official White opinion and
affords it an opportunity to find a certain type of Negro leadership to support
its own attitudes, determinations, and actions.... No Negro leaders believe
that separate schools are ideal but some of them prefer to have separate
school(s) if Negro teachers, supervisors, and principals are otherwise excluded from the system. On the contrary, there are some Negro leaders who
believe it is better not to have these separate schools and who believe in using
all of the forces of democracy in having Negro teachers and pupils integrated
into the public school system as are citizens of other races."[57] Before 1947,
there was very little data which suggested that segregation had any damaging
effects on the Black child. In reference to school performance, there were
studies which reported that Blacks performed better in the segregated schools.[58]

Negro leaders throughout the country during the first forty years of this
century were divided on the issue of separate schools, and this division aided
in allowing segregation to persist in northern public schools. Kelley Miller, a
dean at Howard University, pointed out in 1921 that the question of whether
or not Blacks should have separate schools "is already a mooted question in
such cities as Philadelphia, Pittsburgh, Cincinnati, and Chicago. In Washington, Baltimore, St. Louis, and Kansas City, where separate colored schools
are maintained, there is a much larger enrollment of colored pupils in the
higher levels of instruction than in Philadelphia, New York, and Boston, where
the schools are mixed. The separate systems seem to invoke a keener incen-
tive and zest."[59]

W. E. B. Dubois and Horace Mann Bond also expressed positive opinions
about separate Black schools. They, and many other Blacks, pointed out "(1)
that mixed schools attend only to the needs of the white groups; (2) that social

61

423

discrimination practiced against Negro children in mixed schools is warping to their personalities; (3) that there are gains from segregated schools in increased administrative and teaching positions for Negroes; (4) that it is better to have segregated schools, fully controlled by Negroes, than mixed schools in which Negroes have no voice or administrative offices."

Charles Johnson, E. Franklin Frazier and many other Blacks, however, opposed separate schools, arguing "(1) that separate schools mean inferior schools for Negroes and (2) that Negroes can never participate fully and equitably in the life of the nation as long as they are forced to live a life apart, as a subject race."[60] In reference to higher education for Blacks, Carter G. Woodson, an outspoken critic of the education being received by Blacks in 1932 in both Black and White colleges, pointed out that "it may be of no importance to the race to be able to boast today of many times as many 'educated' members as it had in 1865. If they are of the wrong kind the increase in numbers will be a disadvantage rather than an advantage. The only question which concerns us here is whether these 'educated' persons are actually equipped to face the ordeal before them or unconsciously contribute to their own undoing by perpetuating the regime of the oppressor."[61]

This division of opinion among educators and leaders of the Negro continued throughout the first half of this century and had the consequence of not providing a solitary Black thrust for or against the increasing segregation in northern schools. Social science research however, starting around 1937, began to provide scientific data to support theories advocating integration in various aspects of American society. This research had the effect of shifting the opinion of many Americans, both Black and White, in a direction against racial segregation. The theories and findings of Robert Park, John Dollard, Samuel Stouffer, Morton Deutsch, Kenneth and Mamie Clark, Gordon Allport, and others, demonstrated either the positive effects of integration in various instances, or the negative effects of segregation in American society.[62] Much of this research was cited in support of the Supreme Court's decision in 1954 outlawing legal segregation in the public schools. However, although the climate of opinion in America shifted somewhat against segregation, there has been little change in the actual public school situation in the urban North, except that school segregation has greatly increased over the last twenty years.

The persistence of school segregation in the urban North has been one of the concomitant results of the interaction of historical and sociological phenomena surrounding Blacks in American cities. The federal government's report on Racial Isolation in the Public Schools describes in detail many of the demographic factors which tended to increase the degree of school segregation over the last fifteen or twenty years. Population movements, economic and social trends in northern metropolitan areas, fiscal policies, and housing patterns have had significant effects on school segregation, and there have been several historical factors that have accounted for the persistence of school segregation in the North. The existence of laws mandating the establishment of separate schools for Blacks in the northern states, residential segregation, the migration of southern Blacks to the northern cities were situations that tended to

62

424

perpetuate the existing system of school segregation. At the same time, Black vested interests in maintaining segregated schools, as well as the divided opinion among Blacks and Whites as to the advantages and disadvantages of separate schools, had the effect of allowing segregated schools to persist where they already existed. Only when the belief became general among Blacks that separate schools were detrimental to the self-esteem and school performance of Black children; and only after social science research provided scientific data supporting this belief, was there a strong thrust toward desegregation of the public schools.

The public school situation in Philadelphia over the last 140 years is a focal point from which to view the various causes of the persistence of segregation. But the situation in Philadelphia is illustrative of other northern cities. For example, in New York and Chicago, although Black teachers taught White students beginning very early in this century, this in itself does not discount the possibility of a Black vested interest in maintaining segregated schools. The racial attitudes and beliefs of White northerners made it necessary not only that separate schools exist, but also that Black teachers teach in them. The refusal of White teachers to work in Black schools in predominantly Black areas of the cities necessitated an increase in the number of Black teachers in the public schools. [63] Once these Black teachers had secured their positions, it is not very likely that they would support a change in the school situation, especially one that could possibly lead to their replacement by a White teacher.

A discussion of White racial attitudes should be endemic to any research on the segregation of Blacks in American society. However, it is often difficult to demonstrate when a "racial attitude" is operating as opposed to a perceived economic, social, or political necessity. There could be much debate over what a researcher may consider "racist" and how the individual (or group) perceives his behavior. Although "racist attitudes" were not dealt with specifically in this paper, one might infer that White racism was active in many of the situations presented and did have some effect on the persistence of school segregation.

Several other important conclusions can be drawn from the data presented, especially in reference to the current debate over school desegregation. In terms of historical development, we have seen that segregation in the North has a very long tradition, and that the issue of mixed, integrated, or desegregated education has been a subject of concern for a number of years. However, as an ultimate goal, desegregation has not been pursued for very long. And as to its success in urban areas--North and South--one must admit that it has been quite limited. [64] Segregation in the Philadelphia public schools and most northern urban systems is increasing and the possibility of desegregation is decreasing because of the large percentages of Blacks in city school systems. If desegregation on a large scale is to be attained, it would have to encompass entire metropolitan areas, rather than the area within the city school districts. At the same time, opposition has arisen to the various proposals for metropolitan desegregation, and it is possible that the forces which prevented the desegregation in northern cities for the last fifteen years

63

will come to play in preventing the implementation of metropolitan desegregation at the present. If one is concerned about ending segregation, or changing its patterns or degrees, it would appear helpful to have a clear understanding of those factors that allowed it to persist.[65]

Within the context of Blacks in urban America, one can conclude that the situation of Blacks in urban public schools has a distinct continuity. There is very little quantitative difference in the degree of segregation in the Philadelphia public schools between the 1870's and the 1970's. The vast majority of Blacks in the public schools attended all-Black or nearly all-Black schools in the 1870's, and the vast majority of Blacks in the public schools attend those same types of schools in the 1970's. The reasons for this situation are basically the same and were operating during both periods, though perhaps through different mechanisms.[66]

The idea of continuity in the situation of Blacks in the urban North is not new. Gilbert Osofsky in an article entitled, "The Enduring Ghetto," reviews the conditions of Blacks living in New York City in the nineteenth and twentieth centuries and concludes that "despite continuing efforts to effect racial reform, little has been accomplished that permanently improved the fundamental conditions of life of most Negroes in New York, nor any ideology nor program radically bettered the tone of race relations in the North, if the largest city is a suitable model."[67] The situation for Blacks in northern public schools also reveals a kind of continuity, and calls for desegregation or integration have contributed little toward changing overall patterns. To claim, as does Nathan Glazer, that Blacks are merely the "latest in a long stream of migrants" to the urban North and that their patterns of acculturation should resemble those of the "white ethnic groups" is to deny the continuity in the situation of Blacks in the North from the mid-nineteenth century to the present.[68] The persistence of school segregation, as well as other forms of segregation, requires a more viable interpretation of Black urban history than one that emphasizes the similarities in the conditions of the Blacks and the other "ethnic groups." The continuities of Black urban life over the past one hundred years demand an interpretation that not only explains the past situation, but also provides a foundation for future orientations.

NOTES

[1]U.S. Commission on Civil Rights, Racial Isolation in the Public Schools (Washington, D.C.: 1967), p. 199.

[2]Ibid.

[3]Ibid., pp. 20-25.

[4]Ibid., pp. 202-204.

[5]James Wickersham, A History of Education in Pennsylvania (Lancaster: Inquirer Publishing, 1886) pp. 263-268.

64

426

[6]Edward R. Turner, The Negro in Pennsylvania: Slavery - Servitude - Freedom, 1639-1861 (Washington, D. C.: American Historical Association, 1911), p. 130.

[7]Ibid., p. 131. See also Richard R. Wright, Jr. The Negro in Pennsylvania: A Study in Economic History (Philadelphia, 1912; reprint New York: Arno Press, 1969), pp. 124-125.

[8]Benjamin C. Bacon, Statistics of the Colored People of Philadelphia, (Philadelphia: Board of Education, 1856), pp. 4-6; Pennsylvania State Temporary Commission on the Conditions of the Urban Colored Population, Final Report to the General Assembly of Pennsylvania (Harrisburg, 1943) hereafter referred to as the Final Report on the Urban Colored Pop., pp. 382-383.

[9]The Common School Laws of Pennsylvania and Decisions of the Superintendent with Explanatory Instructions and Forms, prepared by Henry C. Hickock (Harrisburg: State of Pennsylvania, 1857), p. 15.

[10]A court case arose in 1873 over the implementation of the School Law mandating separate schools for Blacks. The School directors of Wilkes Barre, Pa. would not allow a Black parent to send his children to the local school, even though there was no separate school in the district (there were not twenty Black children in the district). The directors on their own sent the Black children to the separate school in another school district. The courts ruled that the directors could not refuse the admission of the Black children to the local White school according to the School Laws unless there is a separate school in the district. See Commonwealth ex. rel. Brown v. Williamson (Leg. Int., Vol. 30, p. 406) Common Pleas, Luzerne County, Penna., 1873.

[11]Ira V. Brown, The Negro in Pennsylvania History (Univ. Park, Pa.: Pennsylvania Historical Society, 1970), p. 52.

[12]John Hope Franklin, From Slavery to Freedom: A History of Negro Americans, 3rd ed. (New York: Knopf Press, 1967), p. 342.

[13]I. V. Brown, pp. 53-54.

[14]Journal of the Senate of the Commonwealth of Pennsylvania for the Session at Harrisburg on the 4th day of January 1881 (Harrisburg: State of Pennsylvania, 1881), pp. 696, 927, 969, 1091, 1335, and 1382.

[15]Kaine et al., School Directors, v. The Commonwealth ex rel. Manaway, (101 Pa. 490), 1881.

[16]W. E. B. Dubois, The Philadelphia Negro: A Social Study (Phila., 1899, reprinted New York: Schocken Books, 1967), p. 89.

[17]Ibid., pp. 90-96.

[18]Final Report on the Urban Colored Pop., pp. 383-384.

[19]R. R. Wright, Jr., pp. 189-190.

65

[20]Robert C. Weaver, The Negro Ghetto (New York: Harcourt, Brace Jovanovich, 1948), pp. 11-14.

[21]Emmett J. Scott, Negro Migration During the War (New York: Oxford University Press, 1920), pp. 14-17.

[22]Sadie T. Mossell, "The Standard of Living Among 100 Negro Migrant Families in Philadelphia," Annals of the American Academy of Political and Social Science, vol. 98 (Nov. 1921), 174.

[23]E. J. Scott, p. 19.

[24]Ibid., p. 18.

[25]Thomas J. Jones, Negro Education, vol. II, pp. 14-15, Bulletin, 1916, No. 30 of the U.S. Bureau of Education, quoted in Scott, supra, p. 19.

[26]Final Report on the Urban Colored Pop., p. 412.

[27]Ibid., p. 413.

[28]W. A. Daniels, "Schools," Negro Problems in the City, ed. Thomas Woofter (New York: Doubleday, 1928), p. 179.

[29]Ibid., p. 182.

[30]Ibid., pp. 182-183.

[31]Commonwealth of Pennsylvania, Department of Welfare, Negro Survey of Pennsylvania (Harrisburg: State of Pennsylvania, 1928), p. 58.

[32]W. A. Daniels, reports that there were twenty schools in this category in 1925; and Final Report on the Urban Colored Pop., p. 414, reports forty-five in 1940. See Daniels, p. 178.

[33]Albert P. Blaustein, "Report on Philadelphia, Pa.," U.S. Commission on Civil Rights, Civil Rights, U.S.A.--Public Schools Cities North and West (Washington, D. C.: U. S. Government Printing Office, 1962), 155.

[34]Final Report on the Colored Pop., pp. 418-419.

[35]U. S. Commission on Civil Rights, Racial Isolation in the Public Schools, p. 9.

[36]Ibid., p. 17.

[37]Fred A. McGinnis, The Education of Negroes in Ohio (Wilberforce, 1962), pp. 30-34, 57-63.

[38]Harry S. Ashmore, The Negro and the Schools (Chapel Hill: University of North Carolina Press, 1954), pp. 2, 101.

[39]Horace Mann Bond, The Education of the Negro in the American Social Order (New York, 1934; reprint New York: Octagon Books, 1966), p. 377. Bond provides an excellent summary of Negro education in the North, see pp. 367-379.

66

[40]Marion M. Wright, The Education of the Negro in New Jersey (New York: Columbia University Press, 1941), p. 200.

[41]Chicago Commission on Race Relations, The Negro in Chicago: A Study of Race Relations and a Riot (Chicago: University of Chicago Press, 1921), pp. 234-238.

[42]Leon Litwack, North of Slavery: The Negro in the Free States 1790-1860 (Chicago: University of Chicago Press, 1961), pp. 147-152; and Arthur O. White, "Integrated Schools in Antebellum Boston--The Implications of the Black Victory," in Urban Education, vol. VI (1971), 131-145.

[43]W. E. B. Dubois, pp. 349-355.

[44]R. R. Wright, pp. 64-65.

[45]Louise V. Kennedy, The Negro Peasant Turns Cityward (New York: AMS Press, 1930, reprint 1968), pp. 44-45.

[46]S. T. Mossell, p. 177.

[47]Commonwealth of Penna., Negro Survey of Penna., pp. 36-37.

[48]L. V. Kennedy, p. 193.

[49]Horace Mann Bond, "Negro Education" in the Encyclopedia of Educational Research, ed. Walter S. Moore (New York: 1941), p. 750.

[50]This point is made by many persons who studied the migration of southern Blacks to the North. See L. V. Kennedy, p. 200; and E. Franklin Frazier, The Negro in the United States (New York: Macmillan Co., 1949), pp. 444-446.

[51]Norman J. Chachkin, "Metropolitan School Desegregation: Evolving Laws," Integrated Education, vol. X, No. 2 (Mar-Apr., 1972), 13-26. This entire issue deals with the question of metropolitan desegregation. See also Paul R. Dimond, "Segregation, Northern Style," Inequality of Education, No. 9 (Aug. 1971), 17-23.

[52]W. E. B. Dubois, p. 89.

[53]R. R. Wright, pp. 80-81.

[54]M. M. Wright, p. 200.

[55]J. S. Himes, Jr., "Forty Years of Negro Life in Columbus, Ohio," Journal of Negro History, vol. 27 (1942), 136-140, 146.

[56]Final Report on Urban Colored Pop., p. 424.

[57]Ibid., pp. 424-425.

[58]L. A. Pechstein, "The Problem of Negro Education in the Northern and Border States," in Elementary School Journal, vol. 30 (Nov. 1929) 192-193.

67

For a discussion of the experiments which tried to demonstrate that Blacks learned better in separate schools, see, Howard H. Long, "Some Psychogenic Hazards of Segregated Education of Negroes," Journal of Negro Education, vol. 4 (July 1935), 337-340.

[59]Kelley Miller, "Education of the Negro in the North," Educational Review, vol. 62, No. 3, 136.

[60]Charles Johnson, Patterns of Negro Segregation (New York: Harper, 1943), pp. 23-24. The debate over the suitability of separate schools for Blacks was the subject of two important Yearbooks of the Journal of Negro Education, in 1935 and 1947. A perusal of these issues will show the shift in the opinion of Black leaders from 1935 to 1947 on the issue of separate schools. In 1935, there is a vigorous debate over the advantages and disadvantages of separate schools. In 1947, most of the writers condemn segregated schools and call for the end of de jure segregation in America. See the Journal of Negro Education, vol. IV (1935), and vol. XVI (1947).

[61]Carter G. Woodson, The Mis-education of the Negro (Washington, D.C., 1933, reprinted New York: Associated Publishers, 1972), p. XI.

[62]H. S. Ashmore, op. cit., p. 236; see also, David J. Armour, "The Evidence on Busing" in The Public Interest, No. 28 (Summer 1972), 92-93.

[63]U. S. Commission on Civil Rights, Civil Rights U.S.A., pp. 154-170.

[64]U. S. Commission on Civil Rights, Racial Isolation in the Public Schools, pp. 199-204.

[65]One example from the past may be used to demonstrate the point. The increase in the percentage of Blacks in the public schools led to an increase in the enrollment in the city Catholic school systems. It is very possible that metropolitan desegregation will lead to an increase in suburban Catholic school enrollment.

[66]In 1870 in Pennsylvania, Blacks attended segregated schools as a result of de jure segregation. In 1970 Blacks attended segregated schools because of de facto segregation. The effect is the same although the means was different.

[67]Gilbert Osofsky, "The Enduring Ghetto," The Journal of American History, 55 (1968), 255.

[68]Nathan Glazer discusses the eventual "acculturation" of Blacks in the urban North (as has already occurred for the other ethnic groups) in his article, "Blacks and Ethnic Groups: The Difference, and the Political Difference It Makes," Key Issues in Afro-American History, eds. Nathan Huggins, Martin Kilson, Daniel Cox (New York: Harcourt Brace Jovanovich, 1971), pp. 193-211. For another comment on the Glazer thesis, see William J. Wilson, "Race Relations Models and Ghetto Experience," Nation of Nations: The Ethnic Experience and the Racial Crisis, ed. Peter I. Rose (New York: Random House, 1972), pp. 259-275.

68

EDUCATION, EXPEDIENCY, AND IDEOLOGY: RACE AND POLITICS IN THE DESEGREGATION OF OHIO PUBLIC SCHOOLS IN THE LATE 19TH CENTURY

by David A. Gerber *

During the last century and a half, both Black and White parents have increasingly looked to education to provide the skills by which their children could attain security, self-determination, and status greater than, or at least equal to, their own. This striving to secure their children's future had immediacy for Blacks in the atmosphere of racial optimism and relative racial tolerance following the Civil War. Negroes took seriously their newly obtained promises of equal rights and full citizenship. Concerned with individual social mobility, they desired open access to the schools and universities, to political office, and to the professions. Group-minded Blacks, interested in framing strategies for the advancement of the entire race, stressed the need for articulate, educated leaders who would serve the race in two ways: creating programs for mobilizing Black resources for uplift and advancement, and communicating to Whites the desire of Blacks for equal opportunity and rights.

Although all would have agreed on the vital role of education--whether elementary, industrial, or collegiate--in racial and individual advancement, many Blacks in the years after emancipation would have disagreed on whether separate or integrated schools provided the best setting for the education of Black children. The question, of course, lost relevance as one moved south of the Mason-Dixon line, for with few exceptions the dual school system there was the relatively unquestioned product of the decade after emancipation. In the North, however, the possibility of integrated education continued to exist. Here the relative openness of race relations during the late 19th century and the impracticality of providing a separate school system for a small, scattered minority of the total school population combined to produce public debate and legislative action on school integration. The New England states either had not ever maintained dual school systems or had abolished them by 1870. In the Middle Atlantic and Middle Western states, however, dual school systems had been widespread during the ante-bellum period. In the four decades after emancipation, Iowa, Michigan, Illinois, Indiana, Ohio, New Jersey, New York, and Pennsylvania all dealt with the problem of integrated schools, resolving in favor of desegregation or local option. [1]

Northern Blacks were not united on the necessity of integration, however, and as the example of Ohio shows, their disagreements led them to ask larger questions about the role of education in the framing of strategies for racial advancement and, more generally, about the utility of separate racial institutions for an oppressed minority. Yet the tendency of debates among Black leaders to take on an ideological cast obscures the fact that many Blacks stood at a pragmatic midpoint on the question of school integration. Though concern for

---

*David A. Gerber is in the Department of History, State University of New York at Buffalo.

1

the larger problems of racial strategy was never completely absent, many seem to have wavered between support for separate or mixed schools in response to the practical problems of educating their children and maintaining racial peace in White-dominated communities.

In Ohio, where the state's separate school law was repealed in 1887 after almost a decade of debate in the legislature and within the Black community, the road to an integrationist stance was often paved with the frustration of years of unsuccessful effort to attain equal, though separate, facilities. The unwillingness or inability of school boards to provide quality education for Black children within the context of the dual school system tended to create among Ohio Blacks during the 1870s and 1880s the feeling that only identical facilities could be truly equal ones. Yet many Blacks also desired to have their children taught by Black teachers, for whom there was very little likelihood of employment in integrated schools in 19th century Ohio. Others, in an era of considerable economic deprivation and discrimination in employment, desired the income and socio-economic opportunity which separate schools provided the Black community.

The ideological debate over the utility of separation and the purposes of education in strategies for racial advancement was not resolved in late 19th century Ohio. Nor, in some local communities, did integration provide a resolution of the practical problem of finding the best setting for Black education. Indeed, when school integration did come to Ohio, it came in large part as the result of political forces outside the school debate. The failure of a number of Ohio school districts to desegregate after 1887, often with the tacit consent of Blacks to preserve the dual school system, revealed the extent to which the uncertainty of Black opinion lingered in spite of new educational opportunities made available by the larger society.

I

Ohio's dual school system was rooted in the oppressive racial conditions of the ante-bellum North, where law and custom combined to block entrance to the Southern Blacks and to proscribe the participation of Blacks in all areas of social and political activity. Ohio was no exception to the almost universal denial of public education to Blacks during the early 19th century, but as Black population grew in spite of repressive legislation, a reluctant state legislature was forced to confront the problem of Black education. Though the first Ohio school law was passed in 1828 and Blacks were taxed to support public schools, they were excluded from the school system created under the act, and no provision was made for their education until 1829. A general failure of local officials to comply with the 1829 law, however, caused its repeal two years later. Though Blacks continued to be taxed for support of the public schools, it was only through private academies, maintained by Black and White contributions, and through private tutors, that Black children obtained schooling. Finally, in 1848 and 1849, the legislature took definite steps to provide for Black public education with legislation obliging township trustees to use a pro-rated share of

2

the common school fund for the support of Negro education. [2]

The 1849 legislation was supplemented in 1853, 1864, and 1878 with laws seeking to define the number of Black children of school age necessary to create a Negro school district. The attempt posed serious problems for the legislature. The Black population of Ohio was comparatively small. Blacks remained largely rural until the 1880s and were scattered throughout the southern and central counties in small numbers in crossroads settlements, isolated farm districts, and villages. Given these conditions, it was impossible to provide schools convenient to all. But the problem was no doubt exacerbated by White school administrators who refused to consider the educational needs of Blacks. The net result was dramatically documented by the 1865 Annual Report of the Ohio Commissioner of Education, which disclosed that of the state's 626 school districts enumerating school-age Blacks, only 121 contained separate schools. Many of these·were so poorly located and widely scattered that a large number of Black children were actually denied schooling altogether. Thus, each successive piece of state legislation sought to lessen the number of Black children necessary to create a Negro school, until in 1878 no number at all was specified. In addition, township trustees were given the right to combine two or more regular school districts to create a larger district encompassing as many Black families as possible in order to draw more into the public schools. But the problem of providing adequate numbers of conveniently located schools for Blacks in the rural areas remained throughout the period prior to desegregation. [3]

In the 1850s, many of the larger cities and towns in the state and to a much lesser degree the rural areas, began to establish Black public schools, occasionally utilizing the buildings of the already existing Black academies. [4] At the same time, however, there were areas of Ohio where Black children were increasingly admitted to the regular public schools in the two decades before the Civil War, so that in 1865 almost a quarter of Ohio's school districts were integrated. These were generally districts where Blacks lived in small numbers--too small, in the minds of local officials, to justify the creation of a Black school. There were districts, however, where integration was genuinely esteemed for its own sake. In the Western Reserve of northeastern Ohio, a nine county area settled by New Englanders known for their partiality to the abolitionist and anti-slavery causes, Blacks were welcomed into the public schools. In Cleveland, for example, a staunchly integrationist Board of Education began to admit Blacks to the schools in the 1840s, and within the next two decades had begun the practice, rare for that time, of hiring Black teachers for the city's integrated classrooms. In nearby Oberlin, Blacks attended both the public schools and Oberlin College, where they made up from 5% to 8% of the graduates during the mid and late 19th century. [5]

As one moved south toward the Ohio River through areas of southern and central Ohio where the majority of Blacks in the state lived until well into the 20th century, the incidence of separation increased. In these areas Blacks often lived in an uneasy peace with Whites of southern nativity or ancestry who subscribed to southern racial mores. Here the color line was generally much

3

more rigid than in northern Ohio, and the resistance to integrated education was much stronger. In the majority of counties along and near the Ohio, the Little Miami, the Great Miami, and the Scioto Rivers, separate schools remained longer than in any other area in the state. They were present for at least two-thirds of the years between 1853, when the state began to gather statistics on the Black public schools, and the repeal of the separate school law in 1887.[6]

Because of Cincinnati's large and growing Black population during the ante-bellum years, and the early sense of community and development of group institutions among the city's Blacks, Cincinnati Negro education posed unique problems. Prior to the passage of the 1849 school law, after unsuccessful attempts to gain public funding, Cincinnati Blacks with the aid of White allies established several private Black academies, including a high school. These became public after 1850 and were supplemented by other Black schools in the city, catering to the needs of well over a thousand students and staffed by thirty Black teachers hired by Black administrators. Nowhere else in the state did a Black school system of this size develop.[7]

It was not unexpected that Cincinnati Blacks would be especially adamant in desiring control over a school system into which so much individual and community effort had gone prior to joining the public school system. After several years of indifference in response to Negro requests, the state legislature in 1856 established a Black Board of Directors, composed of three men to be elected by the adult males of the Black community, to superintend the administration of the Black schools. This Board of Directors was charged with submitting yearly financial reports and budgets to the Board of Education and the City Council, which controlled the allocation of school funds. Before this arrangement ended in 1875, when special school laws governing schools in individual large cities were repealed in favor of uniform statutes, and control of the Black schools reverted to the Board of Education and neighborhood school trustees, Black Cincinnatians had an unusual (for Ohio Blacks) opportunity to control their own educational affairs and to make their schools an object of community pride. Under the control of Black directors and school administrators such as Peter Clark, the principal of the Negro high school, these schools were run efficiently and professionally, and serious efforts were made to provide conveniently located schools and a curriculum similar to that available to White students.[8]

Yet, in spite of the good working relationship between Negro school administrators and the Cincinnati Board of Education both before and after 1875, and the excellent grasp of public school finances shown by Clark and others, the physical plants and pedagogical equipment of the Black schools were often antiquated and inadequate, and a shortage of teachers hindered the work of the high school.[9] Such a situation was by no means unique to Cincinnati, and indeed grew worse where Black populations were smaller and White officials less cooperative. Given the meager, albeit pro-rated, share of the school fund made available to Black schools, their physical plants were almost everywhere below the standard maintained for White schools. Before the Civil War,

4

it was not uncommon for Negro schools to be conducted in one room shacks or in the back rooms of Negro churches. After 1865, regular school buildings became increasingly common, depending on the wealth of the community and the willingness of White administrators. In some districts, however, older Negro schools or their substitutes were discarded only to be replaced by abandoned White school buildings, inadequate for Whites because of size and age. While no doubt better than the older Black schools, the abandoned White ones were themselves in poor condition. To Blacks surveying the failures of the dual school system to provide adequately for their children, no more obvious badge of inferiority could have been worn by Negro education than its inheriting of discarded White schools and equipment. [10]

In some districts, inadequacy of physical plant was supplemented throughout the period before 1887 by the weakness of curriculum, the lack of attention given the educational needs of various age-groups, and a shortage of faculty. Except in the larger cities, the Black schools were generally ungraded facilities in which a small number of teachers taught a relatively large number of pupils of all ages and all degrees of academic progress. In addition, high school instruction was almost nowhere present prior to 1865, and only provided occasionally thereafter through the creation of separate facilities or admission of small numbers of Blacks to the White high school. Blacks given neither opportunity were forced to seek private tutors for advanced instruction. In the eyes of many thrifty White school administrators, uninstructed by law and no doubt sharing to some extent contemporary notions of Black ability and the place of Blacks within the social order, there were not enough Black students to justify the hiring of more teachers, the creation of precisely graded schools, or the establishment of high schools. [11]

The most widespread problem posed by the dual school system, however, was the relatively greater distances which Black children had to walk in order to reach their inconveniently located schools. In the rural districts, under circumstances created by the joining together of several districts to create one outsized Negro school district, it was not uncommon for children to walk a total of ten miles a day to and from school. In the large cities (Cincinnati, Columbus, Springfield, Toledo, and Dayton) the situation was not much better, though distances were shorter. In the days before high density residential segregation, urban Blacks were often scattered throughout many of the wards of a city. In fact, during the years before World War I, only in a few of the larger towns (with populations in the 3,000 to 10,000 range) in central and southern Ohio did Blacks live in any individual ward in percentages greater than 50% of the total local Black population. Under such conditions, centrally located urban schools were usually difficult to establish, and even where school officials sought to provide them, the cost of accommodating everyone could be prohibitive. This difficulty, inherent in almost any attempt to create dual school systems in the North prior to the massive influx of southern Negroes during World War I, and the unwillingness or inability of school administrators to resolve it in the context of the dual school system, provided one of the most important cutting edges for Black protest against the dual school system. [12]

5

II

Both the qualitative and quantitative inadequacies of the separate schools were placed in sharp relief by the immense social and political changes in the race's civil status during the 1860s and 1870s. The sacrifices of Black troops during the Civil War, the emancipation of the slaves, and the egalitarian legislation of Congressional Reconstruction created a foundation for the maintenance and protection of Negro citizenship and increased the acceptance of racial equality. The decades after emancipation were ones in which a new pattern for race relations was sought in both North and South.

A pariah group in ante-bellum Ohio, Blacks now used their vote and the racial idealism of Reconstruction (and what remained of it after the 1870s) to secure a gradual widening of the scope of their rights. They and their White allies fought successfully in the state legislature for the repeal of the remaining ante-bellum Black Laws, the passage of civil rights legislation, and eventually the desegregation of the public schools. Blacks now sat in the legislature and on juries and rode free of harrassment on the streetcars of the large cities. This is not to say that there was no racial discrimination in Ohio, for prejudice manifested itself daily in vicious racial stereotypes, lack of employment opportunity, and, to different degrees in the various regions of the state, in discrimination in public accommodations. Doubtless the masses of Blacks remained entrapped in a debilitating cycle of poverty and lack of opportunity, scorned by the White majority and White institutions. But discrimination was informal and unfixed, and many Whites continued to be disturbed by its presence, especially when its objects were higher status Blacks with whom they shared a common life style and cultural values. During the late nineteenth century, the direction of race relations in Ohio was in favor of a legislative enlargement of Black rights and a growth of the opportunities to enjoy them. In the context of the new mood of race relations, the inadequacy of the dual school system, both as a means of educating Blacks and as a concession to the spirit of caste, was evident to many Blacks and Whites. [13]

Important too for the development of the Black community in Ohio were changes in the demography of the Black population after the Civil War. As the result of migrations from the South during and immediately after the war, the Black population increased from 36,673 to 63,213 between 1860 and 1870, a rise of over 72%. The in-migrants were spread equally over rural and urban areas, both of which experienced increases of nearly 13,500 each between 1860 and 1870. Urban areas, however, were coming to have a larger share of the total Black population. While except for Cincinnati there was little urban growth between 1810 and 1860, from 1860 to 1870 the state's Black urban population increased from 29.2% of the total Ohio Negro population to 38.4%. During the next two decades, as the result of migration from Ohio's rural areas and small towns to the cities, the percentage of Ohio Blacks in urban areas grew to 48.1% in 1880 and 58.7% in 1890. [14]

It is not surprising that the major confrontations on the school issue during the 1870s and 1880s took place in the cities and the larger towns, where

6

increasing school populations placed continuing pressure on antiquated, under-
staffed public schools to accommodate yet greater numbers of students. In
addition, urbanization accelerated the pace of socio-economic stratification
among Blacks and reinforced the assimilation of White middle class norms by
an aspiring Black bourgeoisie. In the context of urban culture and the urban
job market, the relationship between education and individual and group mobility was more obvious than in the rural setting. In an era of racial optimism,
the urban school became an important focus for Black aspirations and strategies
for racial advancement.

Symptomatic of the mobility conscious mood of many urban Blacks during
the 1870s were the frequent protests by Black parents for the initiation of high
school training for their children. Blacks agitated for high school instruction
(whether separate or integrated seemed unimportant) at Columbus, Xenia, and
Zanesville in 1873, and in the late 1870s and early 1880s, at Springfield,
Marietta, Lancaster, Urbana, Bellefontaine, Gallipolis, Circleville, and Portsmouth. In some cases, boards of education were willing to pay the expense of
maintaining separate high school instruction, though this was never costly.
The usual arrangement, made at Xenia, Gallipolis, and Zanesville, where
Black populations were relatively large and an especially vigorous White opposition to integration existed, was to have the principal of the local Negro
schools give advanced instruction to the few Black scholars seeking it. In addition, a small high school room was added to the Negro school. But Black
students were usually deprived of scientific, athletic, and other special equipment used by the White high schools. Where they were not, they often faced
the humiliating situation of having to use these at the White high schools at
special times and in isolation. At other locations, however, thrifty boards of
education, aware of the relatively few Black students seeking advanced instruction, opened the doors of the regular high schools. This, however, did not
jeopardize the local commitment to separate schools, for at Columbus, Springfield, and elsewhere elementary schools remained as separate following high
school desegregation as they had been before.[15]

The problem was not so easily resolved in the case of elementary schools,
where many more children of both races were involved. Prior to 1887, almost
everywhere that the elementary schools became the focus of serious community
racial conflict the pattern of developments was similar to that set at Toledo in
1869-1871. Dismissing integration as chimerical or not desiring it, Blacks
with the help of White allies petitioned for improvement of existing separate
schools, or for the creation of additional Black schools in more convenient locations, only to be frustrated by the indifference of local school officials of
their inability to ameliorate conditions. Faced with mounting protests from
Blacks to improve the separate schools, including the threat of law suits, and
confronted with the likelihood of increased expenditures if the dual school system was to be kept both separate and equal, school officials in Toledo opted for
integration. In that city, this was accomplished relatively easily, quickly, and
with little White resistance; but at other places (Columbus, for example),
school boards were more reluctant and the process took longer. Even in the

7

latter cases, a sustained White backlash was rare.

The outstanding exceptions to this pattern occurred at Steubenville, Marietta, Troy, and Piqua where in the early 1880s school officials decided independently of Negro demands to integrate the relatively small number of Black children into the schools. The expense of maintaining separate schools seems to have been crucial here. At Steubenville, for example, integration followed an attempt to create more precisely graded rooms for Black students, which left as few as six students per teacher; the impracticality of this arrangement led to integration. [16]

The experience of Columbus and Springfield illustrate these developments and are particularly important. After years of unsuccessful struggle for equal facilities, Blacks in both cities were to become the leaders in the struggle for repeal of the Ohio separate school law and in the articulation of a strategy for racial advancement based on mixing the children of both races in the public schools.

Negro public education at Columbus began in 1853 with the building of a small school southeast of downtown Columbus. But in the next several years, as the city's Black population began to congregate increasingly just northeast of the center of the downtown, another Black school was opened in the East Long Street area which was to become the heart of Negro Columbus in the next few decades. Here the Board of Education purchased a small old house at the junction of two alleys, which was converted into a three classroom school building, known locally as the "Alley School. "[17]

Black protests during the late 1860s focused on the failure of the Columbus Board of Education to distribute school funds equitably and demanded the creation of a Black Board of Directors, similar to Cincinnati's, to oversee the Negro schools. Failure to secure the necessary legislation from the General Assembly in 1869, and enfranchisement in 1870, led to a partial change in tactics. Though they continued to hope for some independent body to monitor the school board, Blacks now threatened to use their vote and to initiate a law suit to compel a fair apportionment of the school fund. [18] In 1871 the board acted. Blacks were given an antiquated, discarded White school building near the Alley School. The new school was named the Loving School, after their most articulate White ally on the school board, Dr. Sterling Loving. [19]

Population change quickly made this settlement obsolete. Between 1870 and 1880, Columbus' Negro population rose by 1,100 with concurrent increases in the number of Black students. The effect upon the Loving School was a tripling of its attendance between 1872 and 1879, straining both the physical plant and the small teaching staff. More importantly, the growing Black population did not settle only in the East Long Street area. Though the largest concentration of Blacks was in that area, smaller concentrations of from 6% to 10% per ward of the total Black population settled in north, south, and east Columbus wards. Complaints about the distance children had to walk from these wards to the Loving School, which led some parents not to send their children to school at all, now combined with criticisms of the inadequacies of the decaying school. In addition, the school board had to contend with a 56% rise in the

8

White population between 1870 and 1880 and subsequent overcrowding at many
of the already deteriorating White schools. Clearly, new schools were needed
for Whites, and if the dual school system was to be preserved, they were also
needed for the scattered, growing Black enclaves throughout the city and the
nearly 50% of the Black population living in the East Long Street area. Yet,
money was lacking. [20]

Integration seemed inescapable and the board eased gradually, though
haltingly, into this course. In September, 1881, faced with overcrowding,
Negro demands for new schools, and serious decay of the Loving School, it
voted to close the latter at the end of the school year and build another Black
school. The two actions were in a sense contradictory, for it was doubtful that
any adequate school building could be built before the Loving School was closed.
Then in June, 1882, when Blacks in southeastern Columbus demanded a separate school to relieve their children of the burden of long walks to school, the
board refused and invited them to send their children to the neighborhood
schools for Whites. Black parents throughout the city took up the invitation
when school opened in the fall, sending their children to the most convenient
schools. Integration brought little conflict; with almost half of the Blacks scattered throughout the city and the entire Black population constituting only 6% of
the total population, few Whites probably felt threatened enough to stage major
demonstrations against integration. [21]

Location and overcrowding also posed problems at Springfield, though
Black school conditions there were exacerbated by the hostility of the Board of
Education. A jump in Black population from 276 to 2360 between 1860 and 1880
had strained the Black Pleasant Street School to its limits. In addition, the
scattering of this growing population also made it inconvenient for most Black
children. In 1870 only 35% of the city's Blacks lived in the Third Ward where
the school was located; the remaining 65% lived in almost equal percentages in
Springfield's other four wards. [22] For years the Board of Education offered
little relief; indeed, when Blacks petitioned for more conveniently located
schools in 1872, they were treated, they said "with disrespect and effrontery."[23]

In 1881 local Blacks pressed for a final confrontation with the school
board. They were not united, however, and two factions arose with differing
interests. One group called for improvements in the existing system and desired a larger, more conveniently located Black school. Allied with them were
Blacks living in the northwestern part of the city whose children walked six
miles a day to and from the Pleasant Street School. Another group, composed
of parents living near the Pleasant Street School, though complaining that their
children had to walk past more convenient White schools to get to school, were
ready to argue against the principle of separation itself. While the board was
willing to cooperate with the former, it was adamantly against allowing Blacks
to attend White schools, and had the backing of an overwhelming majority of
Springfield Whites who voted against integration at referenda in the spring and
the fall of 1882. [24] Doubtless the rapid rise in Black population which resulted
in Blacks constituting 9.6% in 1870 and 11.3% in 1880 of the city's population,
a percentage equalled in few northern cities of comparable size in the 19th

9

century, helped to increase White hostility to integration.

Black integrationists and White allies, among whom was the editor of the influential Springfield Republic, pressed for a legal confrontation with the board, which agreed to participate in a test case in the federal courts contesting the principle of school segregation as a violation of the Fourteenth Amendment. Eva Gazaway, the daughter of a Springfield clergyman and one of the children refused admission at the White schools, was chosen as the plaintiff, and money was raised to finance the case. The suit was a tactical blunder by the Blacks, for by basing their case not on the essential inequality of their school system, inconvenient and overcrowded, but rather on abstract principle, they allowed the court to stay within the confines of an accepted judicial canon: that separation per se was not evidence of inequality. The case did not get beyond the federal District Court at Cincinnati where it was lost in November, 1882. [25]

The failure of the case left Springfield Blacks more vulnerable than ever to the vagaries of the school board. Though a teacher was hired for the Blacks in the northwestern part of the city, no school was built for them. In addition, in April, 1884, the board announced plans to build another White school without any mention of Black needs. In August funds earmarked for the Black school for 1884-1885 were cut. Finally, in 1884 the board used the expansion of the city limits to extend school segregation to Blacks in outlying areas who had been attending mixed schools but who were now forced into inconvenient separate facilities in the city or in areas just beyond the annexed territories. [26]

III

The emergence of militant integrationism at Springfield was part of a more general trend among vital segments of Ohio Negro opinion toward integrationism on the school question and the belief that school integration was absolutely necessary for securing racial equality. At the same time, the appearance of the integrationists and the threat of school integration mobilized Blacks who favored separate schools. The occasion for the first public confrontation between these two forces was the appearance in the Ohio House of Representatives in 1878 of a Republican-sponsored bill to repeal the state separate school law. The bill had no chance of passing in a legislature controlled by Democrats, but neither were Democrats prepared to be embarrassed in their quest for Negro votes as Republicans had hoped when they introduced the bill. The result was the school law of 1878 which made easier the creation of Black schools by ending the requirement that a certain number of school-age Blacks were necessary to establish a separate school district. [27]

The debate between the Blacks in 1878 was held in the pages of the Columbus press and prompted by the news that several Black teachers were lobbying for the defeat of the desegregation bill and were attempting to impress the legislators with the claim that Blacks desired a continuation of the dual school system. The teachers' efforts were revealed in a public letter written by Solomon Day, a Dayton teacher, who explained that while in abstract principle he was

10

not against mixed schools, "regarding the immediate and future interests of the colored race," integration would be a disaster. In the context of contemporary race relations, said Day, Whites would surely oppose Blacks teaching their children, and the Black teachers would lose their positions immediately. If the schools were integrated without assurances for the future employment of the teachers, they would have to search for work, they feared, in the South where separate schools were legion. Of integration, Solomon Day concluded:

> I know of no better scheme to reduce the most intelligent
> classes of colored people to penury and want, or to drive
> them from the state to become the victims of southern
> cruelty and barbarism....Where else is the colored
> teacher to go but the South?.... For the colored teacher
> to go South and carry his opinions with him is to die. [28]

Though Day and other teachers were not motivated solely by a desire to keep their positions, this was an important consideration, and some openly stated that they were not opposed to integration as long as it applied to faculties as well as student bodies. The teachers did indeed have a great deal to lose if integration was accomplished. The creation of Ohio's separate school system, with its 7,000 to 10,000 pupils during 1865-1887, had in turn created a self-conscious corps of Black educators, composed of teachers and school administrators, numbering between 144 and 262, and after 1878 consistently over 225. The great demand for Black teachers in Ohio and throughout the nation created high salaries, making teaching at once one of the best paying, most prestigious, and most readily available positions obtainable by educated Blacks in an era of employment proscription. In Ohio, in fact, Black teachers and principals of both sexes made as much before 1865, if not occasionally more in the case of women, as their White counterparts. [29] That salaries earned by Black teachers, representing the largest sustained income bloc taken by Blacks at the public till, were necessary for the support of Black families, enterprises, and institutions, and that there was little prospect they could be replaced were in themselves powerful arguments in favor of separate schools for some outside the ranks of the teachers. [30]

It was unfortunate that the exchange between the teachers and the integrationists began on this footing, for it tended to obscure larger issues and made it too easy for their opponents to identify every teacher who defended separate schools with a selfish and unprogressive espousal of inferior facilities. Actually many of the teachers and their Black allies had more in mind in opposing integration than Day's letter suggested and believed deeply in the benefits of separate schools, of Black teachers for Black students, and of separate racial institutions. They did not usually seek to argue that the dual school system, as it existed in Ohio, provided an educational setting equal in quality and convenience to that available to Whites, but maintained that, given the special needs of both the Black community and its children, separate schools brought benefits outweighing their inadequacies.

11

Throughout the continuing public interracial debate between 1878 and 1887 on the merits of school integration, the Black teachers' defense of separate schools on the basis of racial needs invariably had as its focus the corrective influence of the separate school and the sympathetic Black teacher upon the loss of ambition and damaged self-esteem of a Black child growing up in a racist society. Integrated schools, they in fact argued, would not only <u>not</u> serve the special emotional and educational needs of the Black children, but would daily exacerbate their difficulties by placing them in a demanding and hostile environment from which inevitably, predicted Ira Collins, the teacher-principal of the Hamilton Black school, "Many will absent themselves completely." John Q. Price, the teacher-principal of the Hillsboro school, pointed out that the Black students' poverty would affect the possibility of their regularly attending and succeeding in integrated schools. "Their parents are too poor to buy them the proper kind of clothes to wear," said Price, "And they will not stand being the objects of ridicule, preferring to live in ignorance." In addition, Price stated that many of his students had to work and could only attend school part-time, coming when they could for brief periods of instruction. "Some only stay an hour," he said, "But I let them, spending as much time as I can with them while they are in school, letting them leave when they have to." Indeed over 90 of Price's pupils were attending his school on this basis. Some of them were between the ages of 16 and 20 and still in the primary grades due to their inability to attend regularly. "Their pride will not allow them to be in class with the young[er] White children," he stated, and concluded that they would not receive such sympathetic understanding or attention from White teachers. [31]

If the Black teachers were seen to have a greater empathy with their Black students they were also considered important models for the intellectual and career aspirations of Black children whose social and cultural opportunities were cruelly limited by poverty, social isolation, and discrimination. Ira Collins warned that with labor unions drawing the color line, with prejudice keeping Blacks from clerkships in retail stores, and now with the teachers in jeopardy, "What has the average colored child to inspire him to educate himself?" W. O. Bowles, the teacher-principal of the Dayton Black school, cautioned against the taking away of this "opportunity for the development and employment of race talent," and pointed out the irony and ultimate destructiveness for the ambitions of Black youth of doing away with the almost unequalled opportunity which teaching represented in the name of racial advancement. [32]

For some, the defense of separate schools became quite naturally an integral part of a more general defense of separate institutions. "We have our own associations, churches, lodges, societies," Ira Collins said, "and it is but natural that we desire our own schools." For W. O. Bowles, the schools and other racial institutions became an important part of a comprehensive strategy for group development and the advancement of the race into the mainstream of American life. Though he considered such institutions the result of "a Chinese wall of prejudice and exclusiveness [which has] barricaded the way against the ambition and aspirations of the Negro," he felt that they nonetheless must

12

442

remain "until the causes which produced them shall cease to exist and to operate to our detriment." For the present, Bowles argued, moral and social uplift through self-help and greater racial pride, "will do more toward destroying
existing racial antipathy and securing us just recognition than any act of legislation compelling [inter] race associations." We need, said Bowles of the race,
"a manly independence to be secured by the accumulation of wealth, the improvement of morals, the development of intellect and the courageous support and
exaltation of our race institutions."[33]

Agreeing with Bowles, J. S. Waring, the principal of the Columbus Black
schools, compared the general position of American Blacks with other racial
and ethnic groups in examining the efficacy of separate development. The
United States is a pluralistic society, he stated, "homogeneous in neither language nor color." Yet the ethnic groups and racial groups within it were expected to conform to the social standards of the dominant culture if they wished
to attain full citizenship and acceptance. Until they assimilated these standards,
they suffered disabilities which added to the difficulties of acculturation. Waring sought the best setting in which a group might achieve devotion to new
standards while at the same time checking the debilitating effects of prejudice.
In integrated settings, he said, one has only the benefit of contact and that on
another's terms; thus, such settings were not necessarily "conducive to the
greatest growth and the highest culture of the individual or the masses of a
proscribed class" during its transitional period. What was needed instead
were institutions tailored to the psychological and social needs of the group.
Summarizing his views on group development, Waring said:

> All growth is from within outward, and is the result of
> exercise, and not merely of contact. Hence organizations,
> schools, and churches based on language and color may,
> during the period of transition of any class [i.e. group]...
> produce grander results than mixed organizations.[34]

While as desirous of eventual entry into the mainstream of American
society, school integrationists were less patient than Waring. "Ours is a work
of assimilation," said J. S. Tyler of Columbus in 1878 during a heated exchange
with Solomon Day," and the more vigorous and earnest the efforts the more
speedy the results." Tyler and others were concerned that inequality in the
present would postpone indefinitely full citizenship, social acceptance, and individual social mobility. While Waring and other teachers were prone to stress
the debilitating effects upon Black children of interracial contact in a White-
dominated setting, integrationists like Tyler stressed the dangers inherent in
the inequity of the separate school system. Led by Columbus and Springfield
Blacks prominent in the frustrating struggle for equal facilities in those cities,
the integrationists argued from bitter experience that separate schools could
never be equal in the context of American race relations, stressing the bias in
financial support, the inconvenient location of the Black schools, and the lack,
they spoke of occasionally, of adequately trained, pedagogically effective Black

13

teachers--a point dwelled on with greater candor than tact. Inferior schools, Tyler warned after systematically outlining the failings of the dual school system, would create adults inadequate in those qualities, "a well balanced brain and proper culture," which would speed social acceptance. As a parent, he said in defense of integrated schools: "I want my children to be brought up in immediate contact with everything that conduces to the development of these qualities among the Whites."[35]

Not only did the separate schools provide inadequate education, integrationists argued, but also they provided the key to the process by which the children of both races learned their place in the social order. The dual school system impressed upon them that the Black children, forcibly set apart in unmistakably inferior schools, were not the equal of their White peers. The lasting effects of such childhood experiences upon both races were vividly described by integrationists. The Reverend James Poindexter, a leading Columbus clergyman and school integrationist, stated that in separate schools:

> The White child imbibes the false idea that the color of his
> skin makes him the colored child's superior, while the
> colored child grows sour under the weight of invidious dis-
> tinctions made between him and the White child, and in many
> cases in the very beginning... loses that ambition which
> would be the greatest spur to his success in life.[36]

The only way, they reasoned, to break this cycle of White racial prejudice and Black degradation and to eliminate the images which sustained racial discrimination was to initiate among the children of both races contacts in the neutralized setting of the schools, before the children had been stamped with the hatreds and suspicions of their elders. The school integrationists were usually also concerned with more generalized efforts to end discrimination and change White attitudes, so that upon leaving school daily or upon graduating, the children would step into a more tolerant world. Yet they, much more than those who favored separate schools, tended to place a primary emphasis upon the schools in their general considerations of strategy for racial advancement. While the teachers who favored separate schools saw the school as but one link in a chain of racial activities and institutions working for group development and the eradication of prejudice, those who favored mixed schools tended to see the integrated school as the most important key to Black advancement. Impressed more than were the teachers with the new possibilities for race relations offered by the post-emancipation, post-Reconstruction North, and less sensitive to the need for the development of group pride and identity, they tended to believe that there was a single, integrated path to equality and social acceptance, and that it was shorter and less dangerous than the teachers argued.

Illustrative of the school integrationist's view of race relations was the ease with which they became allied on the school issue with Blacks from the Western Reserve of northeastern Ohio and in particular with Harry C. Smith, young editor of the Cleveland Gazette, which appeared in August, 1883. The

14

perspective of Smith, who was an outspoken fighter against the color line until his death in 1941, and other Clevelanders on both the school question and the problem of finding a racial strategy suited to the North was biased by the more tolerant racial atmosphere and the equalitarian traditions of the Western Reserve. In Cleveland mixed schools had been the rule for almost 40 years, Black teachers taught White students, and interracial contacts were generally freer and more frequent than in southern and central Ohio. Though showing concern for the future of the Black teachers, Smith tended generally, under the influence of his Cleveland experience, to believe that conditions to the south were as malleable as those around him. If Blacks simply exerted enough pressure, he thought, the teachers might be retained in integrated schools.[37]

For their sincere concern with equality and with the future of their children, the school integrationists never seem to have faced the inconsistent and cursory nature of their argument for school desegregation as it was presented by the teachers and their allies. Was not their often stated willingness, in the words of Tyler, "in good faith... to lay upon the altar every colored teacher, as an initiatory step to stamping out the infernal spirit of casts...,"[38] a concession to inequality and irrational prejudice? Was the school truly a neutralized setting if qualified Blacks could not find employment within it? What would be the effect upon the Black child of entering a White-dominated integrated school? Would White teachers prove effective, empathic instructors of Black children? Could the larger society be stripped of its racial prejudices enough to make the gains derived from school integration meaningful once the children left school?

The unknowns in the integrationist equation, the leap of faith which its espousal required, were probably not lost upon many Blacks. While some in southern and central Ohio communities were increasingly won over to integration through continual failure to achieve equality within the dual school system, and while others were seizing upon the changes in the race's civil status after the 1860s to believe equality was close at hand if pursued diligently, some were probably less optimistic and more circumspect. Perhaps as one moved downward past the upper reaches of the Black social scale, support for integration waned. More distrustful of Whites and White institutions, the masses may well have questioned school integration as a racial panacea and an aid for the individual child. Then, too, many Blacks, regardless of class, might have stood at some pragmatic midpoint. For the latter, support for the racial status quo in the schools might have been contingent on the belief that it could not be changed in their particular communities without drastically upsetting the delicate balance of local racial comity. Or they may have believed, regardless of larger consequences, that the dual school system was working effectively for their own children and that the Black community could not afford to sacrifice the economic opportunity which it created.

While it is difficult to weigh the strengths of both positions among the masses in central and southern Ohio Black communities, the lack of protest against school segregation is at least as impressive as the existence of support for integration. Given the inequities of the dual school system, protest and

15

support for integration such as were present in a number of communities might well be expected, especially among higher status Blacks, in the relatively open and promising racial environment of the post-emancipation North. Yet in other communities sustained protests either against inequality or for integration failed to materialize, and if separate schools were not always positively favored, neither were they despised; these communities were content to make the most of the separate opportunities they enjoyed. In Cincinnati, for example, where the separate schools were acknowledged by Peter Clark himself to be inferior in equipment and physical plant, [39] there is little evidence of continual protests against inequality and, until the appearance of the school desegregation issue in the legislature in the 1880s, no evidence of a widespread desire for integration. No doubt there the racial prejudice of an almost southern community combined with pride in the long established local Black schools, confidence in Black teachers (many of whom had been trained locally under the direction of Peter Clark), and relatively open channels of communication between Blacks and White school officials to stem discontent with inequality and the belief in the desirability and practicality of integration. In Dayton, however, Blacks more actively and directly expressed their belief that the dual school system served the interests of their children and the racial community-at-large. In 1884 and 1885, when the Dayton Board of Education threatened to integrate the public schools because of the expense entailed in creating conveiently located facilities for Blacks, many of them joined with W. O. Bowles in a vigorous and successful fight to retain the separate schools. [40]

Circumspection on the subject of the utility of integration also appears to have influenced the behavior in the state legislature of the race's first two elected members of the House of Representatives. Neither George Washington Williams of Cincinnati nor John P. Green of Cleveland who served in 1880-1881 and 1882-1883 respectively formally broached the subject, in spite of the concurrent struggles at Springfield and Columbus. Explaining his inaction, Green claimed that he and a White ally in the Senate were willing to open the question for debate, but that southern Ohio Republicans were adamantly against repeal of the separate school law and refused to allow it to become a part of the party's legislative program. They stated that Blacks neither desired nor asked for desegregation. Green, therefore, chose to call for petitions from Blacks and White allies requesting repeal. None was forthcoming during his term in office, however, lending support to the claims of Republican segregationists. [41]

IV

Yet in spite of the divisions and uncertainties of Black opinion, forces inside and outside of the school question were at work on the attitudes of both races between 1878 and 1884, when the next bill to repeal the separate school law was introduced by Representative John Littler of Springfield. These forces determined that the school question would become a major issue in the Ohio legislature during the 1880s. As we have seen, in the face of Black protests against unequal facilities in southern and central Ohio towns, school

16

boards were integrating both high school and primary grades rather than continue to pay the costs of maintaining dual school systems. Where boards were intransigent when confronted with Black appeals for equality, Blacks were becoming more prone to seek integration as a panacea for their complaints. Where school integration did occur, its failure generally to evoke sustained White resistance must have been encouraging to Black and White integrationists and White school officials. Finally, the conflict at Springfield smoldered on, and the conditions of Black education no doubt grew worse as Black population increased. While we have no direct evidence on Littler's motive in bringing the school issue back into the legislature nor on his ties, if any, with Black integrationists in Springfield, it certainly seems possible that Blacks and sympathetic Whites in that city could easily have come to the conclusion that the community's school crisis could only be resolved in the legislature.

Then too, the unstable political situation in the state, easily apparent in the 1883 state elections, if not a factor in the reopening of the school issue in 1884, was most certainly a factor in the eventual passage of the repeal of the separate school law three years later. The instability of Ohio politics was not new. Between 1873 and 1883, the Ohio Democrats posed a serious threat to the hegemony which Republicans had enjoyed in state politics during the crises of the late 1850s and the 1860s. Fluctuating control of both the governorship and the state legislature by the two major parties and relatively narrow margins of victory characterized the politics of the 1873-1883 decade. [42] Furthermore, third and fourth party movements, led by Greenbackers and temperance enthusiasts and reflecting the socio-economic and cultural conflicts of the emerging post-Reconstruction era, threatened to cut into the electoral support of both parties. In 1883, in an electorate of 718,000, Democrats gained 36,000 over their 1881 total to win the governorship by a mere 12,529 votes and took control of the state legislature, doubling their support in the Senate and nearly doing so in the House. [43]

Political instability and narrow margins of victory highlighted the importance of the Negro vote, which, estimated at 22,000 after the 1880 census, roughly approximated the margin of victory of Republican gubernatorial candidates in elections during 1873-1883. [44] Then too, Negro votes were obviously of importance in legislative contests in counties where the two major parties were almost evenly balanced, such as Clark County where Negroes were said to hold the balance of power between the Democratic city of Springfield and the Republican county. [45]

While Negroes were probably consistently Republican, and state elections doubtless decided by the votes of White independents, contemporary White politicians felt the need to court the Negro vote, which was often spoken of as a balance of power, to pad uncertain electoral tallies. [46] Normally, Democrats dismissed the Blacks, given their traditional loyalty to the party of Lincoln and the identification of the Ohio Democrats with the Democratic South. Yet the 1883 contest had been different, and Democrats claimed that 7,000 Blacks had voted for the newly elected governor, George B. Hoadley, a Cincinnati Democrat. [47]

17

The origins of the claim were several. Hoadley's Republican opponent, Joseph B. Foraker of Cincinnati, was by no means a popular candidate among Ohio Blacks in 1883. Rumors during the campaign accused Foraker of racial prejudice. It was well known that he had defended the Springfield Superintendent of Schools in the Gazaway case. Though Eva Gazaway's father had issued a public statement during the 1883 campaign declaring that Foraker had acted out of a sense of professional and personal responsibility (the Springfield school official was an old college friend) and had shown no racial prejudice in his dealings with the Black attorneys for the plaintiff, Black leaders such as John Green remained openly enthusiastic over the Foraker candidacy. [48]

On the other hand, Hoadley was a compelling candidate. An articulate foe of slavery and constant defender of Negro rights, Hoadley had been a Free Soiler and then a Republican until 1872 when he broke with the party over the Tariff issue. [49] He had thus secured during the 1883 campaign the articulate and unusually enthusiastic support of the small but influential group of Ohio Negro Democrats and Independents who had banded together in the last ten years in response to the Republicans' failure to secure justice for the southern freedmen and patronage for northern Black politicians. Most prominent among Hoadley's Black supporters was Peter Clark, the venerable principal of Cincinnati's Black high school. Clark, who urged upon Blacks a politics based on racial needs rather than gratitude for past favors, joined the Democrats in 1882 after almost a decade of flirting with political independence. While evidence indicates that most Blacks remained loyal to the Republicans in 1883, the articulate and vocal Black Democrats, whose party-financed newspapers (such as Clark's Cincinnati Afro-American) claimed a large Black defection to the Democrats, appeared to control many more votes than they actually did. [50]

In reward for Negro support or in hopes that such support would be increasingly obtainable, Democrats lost no time staking their claim to Negro gratitude. In his inaugural address, Hoadley called for the repeal of all racially discriminatory laws. Doubtless out of a mixture of conviction and (taking his cue from the growing integrationist sentiment among Blacks) political astuteness, he singled out the separate school law for its role in perpetuating caste relations in the state. In addition, once the legislature convened, Hoadley--in consultation with Peter Clark--immediately and with much fanfare guided through the legislature a state civil rights law to protect the rights of Blacks in public accommodations. Finally, as if these gestures of friendship were not enough from the race's historic enemy, the Democrats under Hoadley's direction gave Clark and a relatively large number of other Blacks re-spectable patronage positions. [51]

Hoadley, however, was considerably in advance of his party on the school issue, and it was perhaps as much to show the hollowness of Democratic promises on school integration as out of genuine commitment that Republicans like John Littler produced their own bill to repeal the separate school law. Introduced in January 9, just shortly after the start of the new session, the Littler bill got to the floor of the House before any Democratic school legislation which might have been intended.

18

Though Black integrationists made no sustained efforts during the session in behalf of the Littler bill, by February Negro teachers and school officials were well organized to protect their interests. Arguing that he was against integration unless it included the retention of Black teachers and claiming to speak for the majority of Ohio Blacks, Clark used his influence with the Democrats to secure an amendment to the Littler bill which allowed, upon petition of a majority of Blacks in any school district, the retention of separate schools. Clark and the Cincinnati teachers, with the unofficial support of the Cincinnati Board of Education, served as the chief lobbyists against wholesale integration during 1884 and 1885.[52]

The amended Littler bill reached a vote in the House on April 9. Democrats showed no sign of desiring to court the Negro vote on the school issue as they had done on the civil rights bill earlier in the session. Some Republicans, however, were not any more eager in behalf of integration. Though the bill received the vote of 40 Republicans and 10 Democrats to the 31 Democrats voting against it, it failed by only a few votes for want of a constitutional majority. Hurting the cause of repeal was the absence from the chamber of almost a quarter of the representatives, including 11 Democrats and Republicans from northern Ohio districts which had long ago done away with separate schools.[53] From Springfield and Cleveland came bitter criticisms of the teachers' lobby, which had unexpectedly come out against even the amended Littler bill just before the vote in the House and was credited by the Cleveland Gazette with changing the votes of at least 12 members of both parties who had been ready to vote for repeal.[54]

The school question was again debated during the 1885 legislative session. Hoadley once more recommended the repeal of all laws making distinctions on the basis of color and denounced separate schools. While Littler reintroduced his bill to repeal the separate school law--with a proviso for local option by Blacks--Republican Senator George Ely of Cleveland, who had a reputation among Cleveland Blacks as a crusader for Negro rights, introduced legislation in the Senate embodying Hoadley's more universal proposal. The Ely bill would repeal not only the school law but also the state's 1861 anti-intermarriage law, thus removing all of the remaining ante-bellum Black laws.[55]

The 1885 session witnessed important changes in tactics by both integrationists and separatists and by the Democratic majority. The integrationists had learned from their failure to organize in 1884 and took their cause to the halls of the legislature for the first time. Leading them and constituting the largest part of the Black pro-repeal lobby were Springfield Blacks who spent several months at the capital.[56]

The Cincinnati teachers also changed their tactics; desiring perhaps to lessen the impact of the bitter criticism of Peter Clark in the integrationist press and to have less attention called to their efforts, they hired a lobbyist.[57] Yet, there was serious trouble within their ranks, and they were for the first time encountering open, organized opposition in Cincinnati, their stronghold of support. During the 1884 session, grumbling among some Cincinnati Blacks about the teachers' lobby grew out of complaints about the inadequacy of

19

Cincinnati's own Negro schools and individual animosities against Peter Clark, but what discontent there was remained unorganized.[58] Now for the first time Blacks had begun to hold mass meetings to discuss the issue and to circulate pro-repeal petitions.

The growing reaction against the teachers among Cincinnatians was as much the result of conflicts in local politics as it was of a disgust with unequal school facilities. Many Blacks disliked the methods of the teachers' lobby; increasingly distasteful was its close relationship with the Ohio Democrats. Most Cincinnati Blacks were of course Republicans, and as such had occasionally met attempts by local Democrats to suppress their important vote in local elections. Prior to the 1884 fall campaign, these attempts were not serious, but on election eve in October of that year all previous efforts were eclipsed by unprovoked mass arrests of Black voters by Democratic police. The incident, more to be expected in the South than a northern city, left Cincinnati Blacks distrustful of their erstwhile Democratic allies and angry at the Blacks who supported and dealt with them.[59] In this climate of acrimony, Cincinnati Blacks began to step up their criticism of the teachers and particularly of Peter Clark, who as a Democrat was especially vulnerable. At a mass meeting early in February, 1885, a significant breach occurred when Charles Bell, the well-respected handwriting instructor of the Black schools, addressed the meeting by personal request to pledge that he would no longer support the teachers' lobby. The meeting then passed resolutions calling for repeal of the separate school law but agreeing to work for both the Ely and Littler bills, thus obscuring whether its true preference was the passage of local option or wholesale integration.[60]

The change in Democratic tactics was revealed when the Littler bill reached a vote in the House of Representatives on March 13. Democrats had been holding closed caucuses for weeks in order to calculate the political risks of opposing or backing repeal. The opportunistic decision of many of them to vote for repeal became clear in debates over the bill. Doubtless attuned to the opinions of the Cincinnati mass meeting a month before, and impressed by the activities of the Springfield lobbyists, Thompson of Cincinnati outlined the components of the situation for fellow Democrats. Proceeding from the premise that Blacks wanted repeal and would hold the Democrats responsible if it were not forthcoming, he warned that close contests in the coming fall elections might hinge on Black votes. Furthermore, he stated, if repeal were not achieved in 1885 and the Republicans won the fall elections, a Republican legislature would certainly accomplish it in 1886 and have the undying loyalty of the now-wavering Black vote.[61]

Thompson then introduced an amendment to the Littler bill nullifying the local option clause. Though there were bitter speeches against repeal by several southern and central Ohio county Democrats prior to the Thompson speech, the 59 to 13 vote in favor of the amended bill suggested that many Democrats respected his compelling political logic. All of the votes against the bill were Democratic, largely from southern and central county legislators, but 26 Democrats from northern and central Ohio and from Cincinnati--16 more than

20

450

had voted in the last session for the Littler bill with the local option clause--combined with 33 Republicans to vote for passage. The bill went then to the Senate where the school question had created intense political contention during the session. Senate Democrats, themselves divided on the question of repeal, had been loathe to take up both the school and the intermarriage issues at the same time, as the Ely bill required. Republicans, however, continued to press both issues at once in the hope of embarrassing them. When a Democratic bill dealing only with school desegregation finally reached a vote, it was defeated. Though five Democrats joined with eight Republicans to vote for repeal, ten Democrats voted against it, and many other members--mostly Democrats--absented themselves. The bill failed for want of a constitutional majority of 17. When the House bill finally reached the Senate, it fared little better. Action on the school question would thus have to await the state elections in the fall and the seating of a new General Assembly in January. [62]

While Foraker easily won election to the governorship in a return contest with the incumbent Hoadley (with the enthusiastic support of Black leaders whom he diligently courted), control over the new legislature was in doubt. Republicans had gained control of the House, whose membership included three Blacks, but the situation in the Senate was unclear. When the legislature convened, there were 17 Republican Senators and 20 Democrats, with four of the Democratic seats contested--ultimately successfully--by Republicans. [63] Though a bill sponsored by Rev. Benjamin Arnett, one of the new Black legislators, to repeal both the separate school and anti-intermarriage laws was passed by the House during the 1886 session, none was introduced in the Senate, because of its disorganization, until the final weeks of the session. [64]

But of great importance was a petition presented to the Senate signed by 3,000 Cincinnati Blacks, calling for repeal of the Black laws and finally placing them firmly behind desegregation. The petition signaled the collapse of the Cincinnati teachers' lobby; indeed from Cincinnati that spring came a report that Black teachers were already seeking positions outside Ohio. Though teachers from Xenia and Zanesville appeared before the Senate Committee on Schools to testify against integration, there never was any doubt that the vote in the Senate would be in favor of repeal if the four Republicans were seated. [65] It was no surprise then when the Arnett bill finally reached a vote in the upper chamber on February 16, 1887 and was approved, to the enthusiasm of several hundred Black spectators in the galleries, by a vote of 24 to 7. [66]

V

It was fitting that the largest celebration of the repeal of the Black laws took place at Springfield. There in March, at a rally attended by 2,000 Whites and Blacks from throughout the state, both Harry C. Smith and Rev. James Poindexter urged Blacks to take advantage of their new opportunity for quality, integrated education when the next school year began in the fall and pledged that the race was solidly behind the efforts of Black teachers to retain their positions. [67]

21

In most of the school districts still segregated at the time of repeal, Blacks did take advantage of their new educational opportunity. Whatever had been their feelings about the efficacy of separate schools, they seemed to arrive at the position that integrated education meant better opportunity for their children and a truer equality and fuller citizenship within the larger society. Some whose doubts lingered were perhaps helped to make up their minds by school boards which seized upon repeal as a means for closing the expensive separate schools which drained local resources.

But, as most probably were aware at the time and as future actions would prove, Black teachers and integrated schools were considered to be mutually exclusive. Whether school desegregation was accomplished without incident as at Springfield, Dayton, and the majority of desegregated school districts, or required the filing of law suits as at College Hill and Yellow Springs, or was accompanied by violence and intimidation of Blacks as it was in a few southern Ohio towns with relatively large Black populations, Black teachers were always the early victims of integration--fired as soon as it became apparent that local Blacks and school boards intended to abandon the dual school system. School board officials were often quite frank in asserting that the only way to retain the services of Black teachers was through the preservation of separate schools or the initiation of separate classrooms for Blacks within integrated schools.[68] While at Dayton the latter arrangement was eventually agreed to after almost a decade of unsuccessful attempts to secure the hiring of Black teachers, most no doubt felt that the price was too high.[69] Thus, between 1887 and the first World War years, only three of the state's integrated school systems (Cleveland, Youngstown, and Columbus) are known to have employed, as a regular practice, Black teachers (usually in very small numbers and often to the dismay of White parents) for integrated classrooms.[70]

Cincinnatians faced the dilemma of those who wanted Black teachers and integration in the years after 1887. Anxious to avoid a sudden influx of the city's more than a thousand Black pupils into the regular public schools, the Board of Education adopted a policy of gradual desegregation. It left the six Black elementary schools open, renaming them "Branch schools," staffing them with rehired Black teachers and opening them to students of both races who found them convenient (though fully expecting the only Blacks would attend). The plan worked well in the beginning because Cincinnati Blacks were content to send their children to the old schools. Indeed a month after the start of the 1887-1888 school year, the Cincinnati Superintendent of Schools reported that only 120 Black children had enrolled in schools other than the branches. Explanation by local Blacks of their seemingly contradictory desire for repeal and refusal to integrate focused on a wish to support the Black teachers who had faithfully served their children for many years.[71]

The Black community's willingness to forgive the teachers the methods they had used in fighting for their jobs, perhaps springing from the common understanding of the tragic ironies of racial advancement on terms dictated from outside the race, was touching. But after this initial show of support for the teachers, most Black parents began to remove their children from the branches.

22

By 1890 some 80% of the Black children were in integrated schools. As the branch schools disappeared, the teachers lost their positions. Finally in 1896, with some 13 Negro teachers still employed, the Board of Education announced it would no longer hire Black teachers and would allow the present number to diminish as the need for them declined. In spite of Black opposition, this remained the board's policy as long as integration was its goal, and the only Blacks employed as teachers at the end of a decade were those in the one remaining branch school which was located in a Negro residential area. [72]

Black teachers did remain securely in their positions, however, in the minority of school districts throughout southern Ohio which retained the dual school system. [73] In these districts the first day of school in the fall of 1887 brought few surprises, for usually there was little expectation on the part of either Blacks or Whites that desegregation would occur. It is, of course, difficult to judge whether separate schools were retained in these communities with the open consent of Blacks or because Blacks were coerced into accepting them. At Xenia, where many Blacks desired integration at first, local residential patterns easily established the basis for de facto school segregation which the school board then helped along through gerrymandering of school districts. But Xenia Blacks quickly accepted the will of the White majority, and the town's schools were segregated as late as the 1940s. [74] At Chillicothe, however, where residential patterns also established de facto segregation, Blacks did not seek integration until the 1890s when overcrowding at their schools forced them to stage unsuccessful protests against segregation. [75] In any case, the line between coercion and choice was no doubt thin in most places. If Blacks desired integration, they probably knew that pressing the issue might upset the delicate balance of local race relations, perhaps threatening their jobs, their peace of mind, and even their lives. [76]

Yet while coercion was a factor, there were also elements of choice. Separate schools were not everywhere scorned by Blacks. While in some districts law suits were being filed to force integration of children sent to formerly all-White schools in the face of White resistance, in other districts there was little sign of a desire for integration. In these districts, it was the tacit consent of Black parents which allowed segregated schools to remain even though they were illegal and were being replaced in other school districts in the state. Often, as at Gallipolis and eventually at Xenia, this consent was partly founded upon promises by local school boards of excellent facilities, highly qualified Black teachers, and a continuing commitment to equality with the White schools. At Xenia, the Board of Education answered post-1887 complaints against the inadequacy of the Negro schools with an expensive new building, an expansion of the Black high school to five rooms, and the employment of more teachers. Some might have seen this as a form of bribery, but their schools were a source of great pride for local Blacks and, in addition to furnishing jobs for 11 teachers and two janitors, served as one of the centers of local cultural and social life. [77] At other towns, however, such as Hillsboro where John Q. Price opened his school house in the fall of 1887 to all but one of his former pupils, the promise of equality was not necessary for the large

23

majority of Black parents as long as Black teachers were retained in Black schools.[78]

Thus, the uncertainties among Ohio Blacks on the school question continued into the post-1887 period. For the time being, the question had been resolved for all practical purposes in favor of the school integrationists. Yet after 1900, there was an increasing reaction in Ohio against integrated education, led by an informal alliance of prejudiced Whites and separatist-minded Blacks. In an era of deteriorating race relations, the quest for a quasi-autonomous, protective Black community on the one hand, and on the other the growing racial intolerance of the White majority, led to a resurgence of interest in separate schools. As Black populations grew in Cincinnati and Columbus as the result of pre-1916 Black migrations from the South, a separate school, staffed and administered by Blacks, was established in increasingly Black neighborhoods in both cities.[79] Moreover, a climate had been created in which de facto school segregation based on residential patterns would be relatively easily established to meet the educational needs of the massive Black migration from the South to the cities during the First World War years. The terms of the post-1900 debate over school integration within the Black community were the same as those of the 1870s and 1880s and are indeed similar to those present in the Black community today--a continuity that is sad testimony to how little the basic problems of being Black in American society have changed in the last century.

NOTES

[1]August Meier and Elliot Rudwick, From Plantation to Ghetto (New York: Hall and Wang, 1970), p. 161; Gilbert Stephenson, Race Distinctions in American Law (New York and London: D. Appleton and Co., 1910), pp. 177-189.

[2]Leonard Erikson, "The Color Line in Ohio Public Schools, 1829-1890," Diss., Ohio State 1959, pp. 54-71, 120-140, 174-177; Ohio, Laws, 1829, p. 72; Ohio, Laws, 1848-1849, p. 17.

[3]Ohio Laws, 1852-1853, pp. 429-453; Ohio, Laws, 1864, pp. 32-33; Ohio Laws, 1878, p. 513; Ohio Commissioner of Schools quoted in Charles T. Hickok, The Negro in Ohio, 1802-1870 (Cleveland: Western Reserve University Press, 1896), pp. 103-105; Erikson, pp. 228-230. Between 1853 and 1887, only once, in 1862, did the percentage of Negro children attending separate schools rise above 50%, for the most part during 1860-1887 remaining between 30% and 45% of the total Negro school-age population. But, while fluctuations in the number of children in separate schools was to some extent dependent on integration through local initiative, however, it is more than likely that many of those children not in separate schools were, because of poverty, the inconvenient location of nonexistence of schools, and other factors, not in school at all.

[4]Erikson, pp. 210-222; Frederick A. McGinnis, The Education of Negroes in Ohio, (Blanchester, Ohio: Curless Printing Co., 1962), pp. 45-49.

24

[5]Erikson, pp. 225-227; Cleveland Leader, March 21, 1860, March 27, 1863, August 9, 1876; W. E. Bigglestone, "Oberlin College and The Negro Student, 1865-1940," Journal of Negro History, LVI (July, 1971), 198; Hickok, pp. 103-105.

[6]Erikson, pp. 210-222. While only 32 of Ohio's 88 counties had dual school systems for 2/3 of 1853-1887, a total of 80 counties, including several in the Western Reserve, had separate schools for at least a year during this 34 year period.

[7]Erikson, pp. 92-94, 115, 209; Cleveland Gazette, September 6, 1886.

[8]Cincinnati Board of Education, Minutes, v. 1870-1873, p. 596 (June 16, 1873); v. 1873-1876, p. 203 (May 4, 1874), p. 413 (May 4, 1875), p. 475 (August 23, 1875), p. 519 (October 18, 1875), pp. 539-540 (November 29, 1875); Carter Woodson, "Negroes in Cincinnati Prior to the Civil War," Journal of Negro History, I (January, 1916), 17; Erikson, p. 208; John P. Foote, The Schools of Cincinnati and Its Vicinity (Cincinnati: C. F. Bradley and Co., 1855), pp. 92-93; Cincinnati Colored Citizen, May 19, 1866; Cincinnati Commercial, September 30, 1873.

[9]Columbus Ohio State Journal, February 11, 1878; Cleveland Gazette, March 29, 1884.

[10]Erikson, pp. 237-239.

[11]Ibid., pp. 246-247.

[12]Ibid., pp. 239-240. According to aggregate decennial census data for 1860-1910, in no individual ward in Cleveland, Columbus, Cincinnati, Dayton, Springfield, Toledo, and Youngstown, the largest Ohio cities, did over 50% of the Black population live during 1860-1910. Percentages of from 35% to 45%, present in the early decades, become rare after 1870. In the towns, however, percentages of between 50% and 80% were present, and though ward data for the towns are not available after the 1870 census, such concentration appears to have remained relatively constant through the years prior to World War I.

The following table suggests the patterns of concentration in Ohio cities and towns, in which separate schools existed.

I. Concentration of Black Population*

	1870		1890	
	total Black pop.	% of local Black population in largest Black ward	total Black pop.	% of local Black population in largest Black ward
Large Cities				
Cincinnati	5896	18.5%	11,655	13.6%
Columbus	1847	35.2%	5,525	22.6%
Springfield	1227	35.0%	3,549	27.6%
Dayton	548	31.9%	2,158	33.9%

25

Towns				
Chillicothe	774	73.4%	941	**
Gallipolis	740	87.1%	939	**
Portsmouth	870	60.9%	949	**
Xenia	1690	56.9%	1868	**

* No ward data available for 1880 for either cities or towns.
** No ward data available.

Source   U. S. Bureau of the Census, Ninth Census of the United States, 1870, I (Washington, D. C.: G. P.O., 1872), pp. 228-241, and Eleventh Census of the United States, 1890, I (Washington, D. C.: G. P.O., 1892), pp. 473-475.

[13]David A. Gerber, "Ohio and The Color Line: Racial Discrimination and Negro Responses in a Northern State, 1860-1915," Diss. Princeton 1971, passim.

[14]Ibid., pp. 10-35.

[15]Xenia Gazette, September 16, 1873; Zanesville Courier, September 2, 9, 10, 14, 1873; Columbus Board of Education, Annual Report...1882 (Columbus: n.p., 1882), p. 95; Erikson, pp. 25-253.

[16]Erikson, pp. 251-253; Leonard Erikson, "Toledo Desegregates," Northwest Ohio Quarterly, XXXXI (Winter, 1968-1969), 5-12; Joseph B. Doyle, Twentieth Century History of Steubenville and Jefferson County, Ohio...(Chicago: Richmond-Arnold Co., 1910). p. 395.

[17]Richard Clyde Minor, "Negroes in Columbus," Diss. Ohio State 1936, pp. 145-146.

[18]Columbus Journal, June 25, 29, 1867; Ohio, Senate Journal, 1869, pp. 94, 107, 183, 207, 254; Columbus Ohio State Journal, April 8, 14, September 27, 30, 1870. Columbus Blacks did eventually work out an arrangement with the Board of Education whereby an independent Board of Visitors periodically checked on conditions at the Negro schools.

[19]Minor, pp. 147-149. For complaints about the condition of the Loving School, Columbus Board of Education, Annual Report...1872-1873 (Columbus: n.p., 1873), p. 71; Annual Report...1876-1877 (Columbus: n.p., 1877), p. 166, Annual Report...1881-1882 (Columbus: n.p., 1882), p. 193.

[20]U. S. Bureau of the Census, Ninth Census of the United States, 1870, I p. 230, Eleventh Census of the United States, 1890, I, p. 474; Columbus Board of Education, Annual Report....1882-1883, p. 95; Erikson, "The Color Line in Ohio Public Schools, 1829-1890," pp. 272-284; Columbus Dispatch, September 22, 1880, February 9, May 4, June 1, 1881; Columbus Ohio State Journal, February 9, 1878.

26

[21]Columbus Dispatch, August 24, September 7, 28, 1881, September 5, 6, 20, 1882. One of the most significant benefits of integration was a rise in Negro enrollment because of the opening of the more convenient neighborhood schools to Blacks.

[22]U.S. Bureau of the Census, Ninth Census of the United States, 1870, I (Washington, D.C.: G.P.O., 1872), p. 228, and Eleventh Census of the United States, 1890, I (Washington, D.C.: G.P.O., 1892), p. 569; The History of Clark County, Ohio.... (Chicago: W.H. Beers and Co., 1881), pp. 526, 529; Springfield Republic, October 27, 1862; Cleveland Gazette, January 17, 1885.

[23]Xenia Torchlight, March 20, 1872.

[24]Springfield Republic, September 5, 13, 17, 1881; Cincinnati Enquirer, November 3, 1882.

[25]Springfield Republic, September 15, 27, 29, October 3, November 17, December 20, 1881, January 26, February 2, 1882; Cincinnati Enquirer, November 3, 1882. School integrationists throughout the state hoped for an appeal of the case, but Gazaway did not have the time nor money to press the matter; Springfield Republic, November 4, 9, 1882; Cleveland Gazette, January 5, 1884, January 17, 1885.

[26]Cleveland Gazette, January 12, April 12, August 30, 1884. Relief appeared possible in 1885 when a Republican school board decided to allow Black children to attend the schools nearest them, but leaving open the Negro school for those who wished to attend and rehiring its teachers. The decision left segregationists bitter, and they seized upon the deterioration of race relations occasioned by the use of Black strikebreakers in the city's farm machinery factories in the spring of 1886 to campaign for an overthrow of integration. Democrats promising to resegregate were elected to the board, and at the end of the 1885-1886 school year passed a resolution ordering Blacks back to the Pleasant St. School; Cleveland Gazette, July 24, 31, 1886.

[27]Ohio, House Journal, 1878, pp. 48, 647, 669-670; Ohio, Senate Journal, 1878, p. 801; Ohio, Laws, 1878, p. 513.

[28]Columbus Ohio State Journal, February 9, 1878. For the other letters in this exchange; ibid. February 7, 11, 14, 20, 21, 1878.

[29]Erikson, "The Color Line in Ohio Public Schools, 1829-1890," pp. 210, 216-219, 236. Unfortunately, no data on teachers' salaries were collected after 1865. We are probably safe in assuming, however, given the increase in Black population and the growing numbers of Blacks seeking education after emancipation, that the demand for Black teachers remained high as did the salaries paid them. Regional and sectional factors no doubt created differences around the country and within Ohio itself. The professional self-consciousness of the Ohio Black teachers was reflected in the organization in 1861 of an "Ohio Colored Teachers' Association"; Ohio Educational Monthly, v. 4 (1863), p. 159 (editorial).

27

[30] At a Columbus Black mass meeting held during the 1878 legislative session to discuss school integration, several speakers rose to warn of the economic consequences of school integration; Columbus Ohio State Journal, February 12, 1878. Thereafter, until repeal in 1887, the theme was introduced at least once at most major meetings held to debate the school issue.

[31] Cleveland Gazette, February 6, 1885; Hillsboro Gazette, March 5, 1887.

[32] Cleveland Gazette, February 6, 1885; Dayton Daily Journal, February 20, 1885.

[33] Cleveland Gazette, February 6, 1885; Dayton Daily Journal, February 18, 1885.

[34] Columbus Ohio State Journal, February 18, 1878.

[35] For Tyler's statement, ibid., February 11, 1878. A commonly held view among integrationists in regard to the qualifications of Black teachers seems to have been that of one Columbus integrationist who stated that the Black teachers, though admittedly working under poor conditions, were not "the equal in every regard of the best White teachers of the same grade."; ibid., February 11, 1878.

[36] Ibid., February 7, 1878.

[37] Cleveland Gazette, September 22, 1883, March 29, April 12, 1884, February 21, 1885, March 17, 1886.

[38] Columbus Ohio State Journal, February 11, 1878.

[39] Loc. cit.; Cleveland Gazette, March 29, 1884.

[40] Cleveland Gazette, August 9, 16, 1884, August 29, 1885; Dayton Daily Journal, February 14, 16, 18, 20, 1885. Both economic arguments for separate schools and fears for the fate of Black children in White schools were present among Dayton Blacks. When a local literary society held a debate on the question of school integration, the judges ruled that the integrationists had failed to refute the opposition's contention that mixing the schools would take thousands of dollars a year from the Black community and respectable employment from a number of Black women teachers; ibid., May 15, 1885. But another Black stressed that the issue was larger than employment: "It is our battle for the education, health and happiness of our little colored children, more than half of whom cannot afford to dress in the White folks' fashions or be prompt and regular in attendance at the White folks' schools."; ibid., July 25, 1885.

[41] John P. Green, Truth Stranger Than Fiction, 75 Years of a Busy Life ...(Cleveland: Riehl Printing Co., 1920), pp. 178-180; Cleveland Gazette, March 13, 1886.

[42] Taking the governorship, for example, between 1856 and 1873 no Democrat had been elected in eight gubernatorial campaigns, though Republican

28

458

margins of victory were often not very large. Profiting from the economic crises of the 1870s, however, Democrats began to make effective inroads into the Republican majority. They won the governorship in 1873, 1877, and 1883. Between 1873 and 1883, the margins of victory in gubernatorial elections were: 817; 5544; 22,250; 17,100; 26,662; and 12,529 in an electorate of between 449,000 in 1873 and 718,000 in 1883; see, Ohio Statistics, 1883, pp. 254-256.

[43] Thomas E. Powell, ed., The Democratic Party of Ohio...., I, (n.p.: Ohio Publishing Co., 1913), 288.

[44] For the claim that Blacks held the balance of power in Ohio politics, see, for example, Cleveland Gazette, September 1, 1883; Irvine Garland Penn, The Afro-American Press and Its Editors (Springfield, Mass.: Willey Co., 1891), pp. 193-194. Joseph Benson Foraker, the Republican nominee for governor in 1883, 1885, 1887, and 1889 remembered of those years, "The Negro vote was so large that it was not only important but an essential factor in our considerations. It would not be possible for the Republican party to carry the state if that vote should be arrayed against us."; Joseph Benson Foraker, Note from a Busy Life, I (Cincinnati: Johnson and Hardin, 1916), 177.

[45] In 1881, for example, 67 out of 105 seats in the legislature were won by less than 1,000 votes, and in 1883, 75 out of 105; see, Ohio, Statistics, 1881, pp. 352-355, and Statistics, 1883, pp. 312-315; and E. S. Todd, A Sociological Study of Clark County, Ohio (Springfield: Springfield Pub. Co., 1904), p. 91.

[46] See, n. 41, supra.

[47] Cleveland Plain Dealer, October 18, 1883; Cleveland Gazette, June 28, 1884.

[48] Foraker, 175-188; Springfield Republic, October 11, 1883. Ironically Foraker would one day become a champion of Black Americans. While serving in the United States Senate during 1906-1909, he emerged as the leading spokesman for 167 Black soldiers who were dishonorably discharged from the Army by President Theodore Roosevelt for refusing to testify about their alleged, but to this day unproven, participation in a shootout with Whites at Brownsville, Texas.

[49] Powell, 288-299; Wendell Phillips Dabney, Cincinnati's Colored Citizens... (Cincinnati: Dabney Co., 1926), pp. 87-88.

[50] New York Freeman, January 3, 1885; Celveland Gazette, March 8, 1886.

[51] New York Globe, February 2, 1884; Cleveland Gazette, January 12, 19, February 9, 1884; Cleveland Herald, September 16, 1884.

[52] Cleveland Gazette, February 16, April 19, 26, 1884.

[53] Cleveland Herald, April 8, 1884; Ohio House Journal, 1884, pp. 770-771.

29

[54] Cleveland Gazette, April 12, 1884.

[55] Columbus Ohio State Journal, January 7, 1885. A bill similar to Ely's had been introduced in 1884, but was quickly buried in committee; Cleveland Gazette, March 29, 1884.

[56] Columbus Ohio State Journal, January 1, 1885; Cleveland Gazette, February 28, 1885.

[57] Cincinnati Commercial Gazette, February 5, 6, 1885; Cincinnati Enquirer, February 11, 1885.

[58] Cleveland Gazette, March 29, April 12, May 3, 17, 1884.

[59] Cincinnati Commercial Gazette, October 15, 16, 18, 1884.

[60] Ibid., February 11, 1885.

[61] Ibid., March 14, 1885; Cleveland Gazette, March 14, 1885.

[62] Columbus Times, April 24, 30, 1885; Ohio House Journal, 1885, pp. 453-454; Ohio Senate Journal, 1885, pp. 735-736.

[63] Cleveland Gazette, June 13, 20, August 8, September 19, November 7, 14, 21, 1885, July 24, 31, September 25, 1886; Cincinnati Commercial Gazette, August 19, 29, 1885; Foraker, 175-200.

[64] Cleveland Gazette, January 9, 23, 30, February 6, 13, 28, March 6, 13, 1886; Columbus Ohio State Journal, January 13, March 11, April 2, 30, 1886; Ohio House Journal, 1886, pp. 95, 342; Ohio Senate Journal, 1886, pp. 44, 52, 592.

[65] Cleveland Gazette, March 27, June 19, 24, 1886. Peter Clark's effectiveness as a spokesman for the teachers was lost after he was charged with the attempt to bribe a witness in a case growing out of the 1884 mass arrests of Black voters in Cincinnati and, six months later, after nearly 30 years of service, fired by a newly-elected Republican school board; Cincinnati Commercial Gazette, November 29, December 1, 6, 19, 1885; New York Freeman, June 19, 26, July 3, August 7, 1886.

[66] Cleveland Gazette, January 15, 22, February 19, 1887; Columbus Ohio State Journal, February 17, 1887; Ohio Senate Journal, 1887, pp. 255-256.

[67] Cleveland Gazette, March 5, 12, 1887.

[68] Ibid., June 4, 1887; Zanesville Signal, September 12, 1887; Cleveland Plain Dealer, September 14, 1887; Jackson Herald, September 8, 15, 22, 1887.

[69] Richmond Planet, March 7, 1896.

[70] Cleveland Gazette, August 10, 1889, October 12, 1895, October 8, 22, 1898; Carrie Clifford, "Cleveland and Its Colored People," Colored American Magazine, IX (July, 1905), 372-373.

30

[71] Cincinnati Board of Education, Minutes, v. 19, "Special Report" (May 30, 1887), pp. 410-411 (June 20, 1887), pp. 494-495 (August 29, 1887). Cincinnati Enquirer, September 13, 1887; Cincinnati Commercial Gazette, September 16, October 18, 1887; Cleveland Gazette, June 25, September 17, 1887.

[72] Cleveland Gazette, June 15, 1889, September 13, 1890, April 25, May 16, 1896; Cincinnati Board of Education, Minutes, v. 23, p. 60 (August 30, 1897), pp. 347-348 (June 19, 1899), pp. 392-393 (August 28, 1899), p. 482 (May 7, 1900). The one remaining branch school, known after 1904 as the Frederick Douglass School, remained in existence during the 20th century.

[73] Columbus Ohio State Journal, September 12, 1887; Gallipolis Journal, September 7, 1887; Portsmouth Times, September 7, 1887; Cleveland Gazette, October 8, 29, 1887, September 29, October 25, 1888, July 27, 1895.

[74] Xenia Torchlight, September 14, 21, November 23, December 10, 14, 1887; Cleveland Gazette, September 18, 1888.

[75] Portsmouth Tribune, August 24, 1887; Jackson Herald, October 27, 1887; Cleveland Gazette, January 20, September 15, 22, 1894; Chillicothe Advertiser, November 1893, January, February, April, August, September, October, November 1894, passim.

[76] For several Ohio towns continuity between the separate schools of the pre-1887 era and those after is verified up to 1917 and 1947 in, Mame Charlotte Mason, "The Policy of the Segregation of the Negro in the Public Schools of Ohio, Indiana, and Illinois" (unpublished Master's thesis, University of Chicago, 1917); and G. Gwendolyn Brown, "The Influences Surrounding the Establishment of the Present Segregated Schools in Selected Cities of Ohio (unpublished Master's thesis, Howard University, 1947).

[77] R. R. Wright, Jr., "The Negroes of Xenia, Ohio: A Social Study," U.S. Department of Labor, Bulletin, N. 48 (September, 1903), 1020-1023, 1041-1042; Xenia Torchlight, November 12, December 17, 1887; "What Has Education Done for the Colored Woman," Voice of The Negro, I (July 1904), 296-197.

[78] Hillsboro Gazette, September 10, November 5, 1887.

[79] In neither neighborhood were Blacks in the majority. In Columbus, the result of this, as well as of the school board's prediction of some Black opposition and its desire for racial exclusiveness in the new Black school, was the gerrymandering of neighborhood school districts to conform to residential patterns. In Cincinnati, however, widespread Black support and a lack of desire on the part of the school board to have all neighborhood Black children in the new separate school made a gerrymander unnecessary. Dabney, pp. 235-236; Cincinnati Board of Education, Minutes, v. 29, pp. 563-564 (September 14, 1914), p. 593 (October 26, 1914); Mason, pp. 49-52; Minor, pp. 154-155; Columbus Board of Education, Minutes, May 11, 1908, August 3, 1908, August 31, 1908.

31

Desegregation in Nashville:
The Dynamics of Compliance[*]

By Hugh Davis Graham

By September of 1955, young Bobby Kelley was beginning to feel that keen sense of frustration with which older Negro students in Nashville, Tennessee, had long been familiar. Bobby would turn fifteen the following November. At the conclusion of that school year he would be graduated from his all-Negro junior high school and would be expected to enter Pearl, then Nashville's only Negro high school, the following September. For Negro high school students living in Bobby's neighborhood in East Nashville, this involved a daily round trip across the Cumberland River and through the downtown area to North Nashville, for Pearl is located there near the cluster of Negro colleges that includes Fisk University, Tennessee Agricultural and Industrial University, and Meharry Medical School. For Bobby, this daily trek would be particularly galling because he lived only a few blocks from Nashville's all-white East High School.

The previous year, Tennessee's archaic constitution had been revised for the first time in the twentieth century. That had been 1954, and an ironical year for the Constitutional Convention to reaffirm the traditional proviso that "No school . . . shall allow white and negro children to be received as scholars together in the same schools."[1] Shortly thereafter, as is well known, the United States Supreme Court held unanimously that "Separate educational facilities are inherently unequal" and as such violated the equal protection clause of the Fourteenth Amendment.[2]

In the light of the precedent-shattering Brown decision, and the court's somewhat cryptic order, delivered in May of 1955, that school desegregation proceed "with all deliberate speed," the Nashville School Board assigned its four-man instruction committee to study the problems posed by the task of desegregation, while the full nine-man board continued to abide by its traditional policy

---

[*] This paper was delivered before the Southern Historical Association, November, 1965.

[1] *Tennessee Blue Book 1957-58*, p. 282.

[2] *Brown v. Board of Education of Topeka, Kansas*, 347 U.S. 483, 74 Sup. Ct. 686, 98 L. Ed. (1954).

135

of maintaining a biracial school system.[3] As a consequence of the board's rather dilatory response, Bobby Kelly's father, proprietor of A. Z. Kelley's Barber Shop, filed an action against the school board in federal district court that September. *Robert W. Kelley v. Board of Education of Nashville* was a class action, seeking an injunction to require admission of children to Nashville's public schools without regard to race or color.[4] The time had arrived for Nashville to decide whether she was to comply.

Nashville in the mid-fifties was in many ways a typical southern city. Although its metropolitan area encompassed more than 350,000 citizens of Davidson County, the city's anachronistic municipal boundaries enclosed only half that number. Its unimpressive sky-line and the measured pace of its economic pulse contributed to the impression that Nashville's modest growth had not appreciably altered its gentle but pervasive southern tone since the ex-Confederate city had so grudgingly succumbed to Union armies almost a century earlier. Nor had the city's formal and informal biracial system been appreciably altered, or even substantially challenged, since the threat of Populism drove Tennessee's Bourbons to embrace the Jim Crow system late in the nineteenth century. But by the mid-fifties, an astute observer could perceive that an interesting variety of agents of change were combining to erode the once-firm basis of the old biracial order—agents whose potentially corrosive qualities were dramatically revealed by the catalytic Brown decision, but which were by no means created by it.

Foremost among these agents was a relatively large Negro community wherein growing dissatisfaction with the status quo combined with disproportionate political muscle to constitute a powerful and constantly escalating threat to the old biracial order. The Negroes' burgeoning postwar dissatisfaction with their ancient economic and social debilities was in large part a function of their exposure to the intellectual currents emanating from Fisk, Meharry, and A & I. Their political muscle was disproportionate to their numbers because restrictive city boundaries circumscribed most of the county's Negroes with proportionately fewer of its

[3] *Race Relations Law Reporter*, I (1956), pp. 1120-22.
[4] *Robert W. Kelley, et. al. v. Board of Education of Nashville*, 139 F. Supp. 578. Attorneys representing Kelley were Z. Alexander Looby, dean of Nashville's Negro elite, and Avon Williams, his aggressive junior law partner. Kelley was joined as plaintiff by twenty other Negro children and by two white children whose parents were teachers at Fisk.

whites—those whites of the lower economic echelons, for the most part, who could not afford to flee to the surrounding incorporated suburbs. As a direct result of this inadvertent gerrymandering, roughly one-third of Nashville's electorate was Negro, although less than one-quarter of Davidson County's population was Negro. And, unlike most southern Negroes, Nashville's were not largely disfranchised. They had infiltrated the franchise gradually over the years and had, until the postwar era, proven sufficiently docile and even malleable that Nashville's aspiring politicians had found that their modest demands and growing numbers made them profitable to court. Mayor Ben West had long and successfully courted their favor with his espousal of southern moderation. Two Negro politicians sat with nineteen whites on his city council. Finally, one of the nine members of the mayor's appointed school board was a Negro politician, Coyness Ennix.

No informed observer can seriously doubt that the majority of Nashville's whites clearly preferred the biracial system with which they had so long been familiar.[5] As a consequence, they were unhappy with the Brown decision and they anxiously wished that some way could be found whereby they might avoid its implications. Yet Nashville failed to respond in its racial crisis with the monolithic defiance of a Birmingham, and this was so primarily because several deeply rooted and institutionally encouraged counter-tendencies toward pluralism continually frustrated that powerful southern tendency toward defiance—or at least toward the rhetoric of defiance—that seemed to characterize so much of the southern white response during the late fifties.

The most visible institutions helping to produce the intellectual conditions for a questioning of the wisdom and efficacy of bald defiance were, in the Negro community, Fisk, Meharry, and A & I. They found their white counterparts in the triumvirate of Vander-

---

[5] In a poll conducted in 1958 in Knoxville, where the percentage Negro was less than half that of Nashville, not one of the 167 Knoxvillians who were polled would approve of enrolling one or two white children in a previously all-Negro school, and 71.8 per cent objected to enrolling one or two Negroes in a previously all-white school. All preferred that parents be able to transfer their children regardless of residential requirements. Ninety-four per cent opposed any racial integration that included sexually mixed classes also. Eighty-five per cent disputed that the Brown decision was legally the law of the land, and 70 per cent said they would support a legal battle against desegregation. See Douglas R. Jones, An Abstract of an Opinion Poll on Attitudes of White Adults About Desegregation in the Public Schools of Knoxville, Tennessee (Ph.D. dissertation, George Peabody College for Teachers, 1958).

bilt University, George Peabody College for Teachers, and Scarritt College. The presence of these six, plus an abundance of Protestant denominational colleges, had prompted chauvinistic Nashvillians long ago to style their city the "Athens of the South," and to erect, to the eternal astonishment of visitors, an exact and anomalous replica of the Parthenon.

That free institutions of higher learning tend to militate against monolithic tendencies, and, more particularly, should have the effect of encouraging moderation, is surely indisputable. But the importance of these colleges may be overly stressed. Nashville's basic social flavor partook far more of Protestant orthodoxy than of academe. An extraordinary sixty-seven religious periodicals were published in the city in 1957,[6] and 557 churches dotted its landscape—thereby providing one church for every 322 Nashvillians.[7] Historically, fundamentalistic Protesetant sects have, according to their inherent centrifugal tendency, and encouraged by the fervor native to the region, abundantly waxed and multiplied in Nashville. We know from experience that southern Protestantism has not only *not* been moderate on the racial question, but has seemed at times—and this is especially true of the evangelicals in which Nashville has been especially well endowed—to have been a center of energy and ideas for the defiant white. Nevertheless, a significant part of the Protestantism of the area worked in the other direction. This is not because Nashville's clergy and laity came earlier to the more moderate position on the question of racial integration now slowly emerging in southern Protestant churches. Rather, it was because so much of the city's religious establishment was, in financial resources and in personnel, gathered in the church-related colleges, denominational headquarters, boards of missions, religious publishing houses, and Vanderbilt's highly regarded Divinity School, thus providing Nashville with a large number of clergymen and laymen who, as Benjamin Muse has observed, did not have to answer directly to more conservative local congregations for their more liberal views concerning racial relations.[8] Their

---

[6] N. W. Ayer & Sons, *Directory of Newspapers and Periodicals* (Philadelphia, 1957), 927-30.

[7] Information obtained from the Nashville Chamber of Commerce through the courtesy of James Leeson, information director for the Southern Education Reporting Service, Nashville, Tennessee. SERS published, from September of 1954 through May of 1965, *Southern School News*, a monthly report highly regarded for its objectivity.

[8] Benjamin Muse, *Ten Years of Prelude* (New York, 1964), 115-21.

impact upon the Nashville Ministers Association and the Association of Churches, in conjunction with moderating efforts by relatively small Catholic and Jewish communities, provided a continued impetus toward a pluralistic climate of opinion.

Important as these various sources of moderate opinion were, however, their impact was discontinuous, spotty, and not likely of their own accord to be widely disseminated. The one institution uniquely capable of giving effective public voice to this body of opinion, of reflecting and magnifying its views, was the local press. Had that press been largely monolithic—as was that, for instance, of Birmingham or Dallas or perhaps New Orleans—the voices favoring compliance in Nashville would have been greatly muted—and who can guess the consequences? But the facts are that few cities in the nation possessed more vigorously competing and philosophically disparate newspapers than did Nashville.

My purpose in focusing on Nashville's press is not to suggest that journalistic pluralism is the *sine qua non* of moderation and the keystone of compliance. Obviously, the vigorously competitive press of Little Rock could not overcome Faubus' bold démarche. But contemporary students of social psychology have come increasingly to the view that a monolithic environment severely enforces a frightening degree of social conformity on the part of even the most sturdy of individualists.[9] A corollary of this is that pluralistic media tend to encourage the individual to respond more readily to the dictates of conscience. Thus, in the homely metaphor of Harvard social psychologist Thomas Pettigrew, pluralistic media would tend to bolster the independence of that kindly disposed southern white who would smile at a Negro if he were convinced that no one was looking.[10]

The journalistic spokesman for the forces urging compliance in Nashville was the morning *Tennessean*. Although the daily circula-

[9] For a brief review of the relevant literature and a description of experimental psychologist S. E. Asch's research, *see* Thomas F. Pettigrew, "Social Psychology and Desegregation Research," in *The American Psychologist*, XVI (1961), 105-112. Briefly, Asch's method was to put to an experimental panel of volunteers a series of questions that suggested their own rather obviously correct answers. In reality, only one panel member was a genuinely unknowing volunteer; all the rest were previously briefed confidants of Asch. The latter would all confidently describe a four-inch-long line as being five inches, for instance, and the pressure on the genuine volunteer to conform to the erroneous perception was found to be enormous—indeed, it was found to be alarmingly effective. When only one other member of the panel preceded the genuine volunteer in responding correctly, however, the degree of erroneous social conformity was drastically reduced.

[10] *Ibid.*, 109.

tion of the *Tennessean* was slightly less than that of either of the two Memphis dailies, its central location enabled it safely to boast of the largest circulation in the state. Because of this, and because Nashville was the capital, the *Tennessean* was probably the most influential newspaper in Tennessee.[11]

During the depression, the *Tennessean* had fallen into receivership.[12] In 1937, it was bought by an aggressive New Dealer, Silliman Evans. A native of Texas, Evans had been nurtured in the newspaper business there under the tutelage of Amon Carter, celebrated publisher of the Fort Worth *Star Telegram*. First a political reporter in Austin and later in Washington, Evans developed a taste for politics and an affinity for the populistic variety practiced by John Nance Garner, Jesse Jones, and Tom Connally. Prior to his purchase of the *Tennessean*, Evans had been a successful claimant of business acumen and political patronage in Washington. But he wanted to return to the newspaper business, and, more specifically, he wanted to create a southern voice in support of the policies of the Democracy of Franklin D. Roosevelt. The *Tennessean* was, after 1937, the only major daily in Tennessee that listed its political affiliation simply and faithfully as Democratic,[13] and it was in 1940 the only one of the state's eight major dailies to support the third term candidacy of Roosevelt.

Although the *Tennessean* always after 1954 avoided an outright endorsement of the Brown decision, it did state unequivocally the morning after the Brown case was decided that desegregation of public schools was now "the law of the land" and that the South could and should learn to live with it.[14] The court had "with sympathetic wisdom" allowed for a gradual adjustment, the editorial had observed, and the South would surely muster its better elements to solve this problem as it "had met and overcome other problems rooted in a departed past." "And in so doing," the *Tennessean* candidly concluded, Southerners will "be paying new honor to the principle of democracy they so readily profess but, on occasion, so reluctantly practice."

[11] The writer hopes that a brief stint in 1960 as a reporter for the *Tennessean* served to increase his knowledge without unduly interfering with his objectivity.

[12] For an engaging history of the *Tennessean* from an admittedly partisan source, see Jennings Perry, *Democracy Begins at Home* (Philadelphia, 1944). The following brief description of the early history of the *Tennessean* is based on Perry's volume.

[13] According to their political affiliations as listed in the Ayer directories. Most appended the suffix "Independent" to their Democratic affiliation.

[14] The Nashville *Tennessean*, May 18, 1954.

The editors of the *Tennessean* were justly proud of their largely successful role in combating the crushing embrace of the Memphis-based machine of Boss Crump during the forties, and of forging the alliance that was to destroy Tennessee's poll tax.[15] The powerful daily took its progressive politics seriously, but not quixotically. It could, to be sure, occasionally manifest a doctrinaire truculence, as in its perennial and sometimes purblind opposition to Governor Frank Clement. But on the whole, it seemed able to keep the distinction between its principles and its betes noires clearly in mind, and to retain its sense of humor.

The senior daily in Nashville was the *Banner*, established in 1876 and published by the prominent Stahlman family. The Stahlmans emigrated from Prussia in the 19th century, and through shrewdness, frugality, and hard work they had prospered well in Nashville. The editorial voice of the *Banner* had long been popularly equated with the voice of Nashville's business community, and while James G. Stahlman accurately and honestly reflected the views of Nashville's businessmen, he stubbornly and successfully refused over the years to be owned by them.

In 1954, Stahlman's *Banner* reached upwards of 90,000 mid-Southerners a day,[16] and few could have long remained unaware of his firm political convictions. Stahlman's profound conservatism reflected an intellectual affinity for the pessimistic anthropology of columnist David Lawrence and his confreres on the political right. The *Banner* not infrequently ran front-page editorials denouncing unequivocally and in somewhat baroque prose some encroachment on the sacred corpus of states' rights. A former liberal editor of the rival *Tennessean* referred to the *Banner* contemptuously as "spiritually the Southern edition of the Chicago *Tribune*."[17] The *Banner's* talented editorial cartoonist, James Knox, pilloried Stahlman's antagonists with an acid pen that was quick to link the NAACP-ADA-Leftist syndrome with the carpetbag, traditional symbol of Yankee exploitation, and with crass unconstitutional opportunism in general. Probably no editorial cartoonist enjoyed having his cartoons reprinted in so many southern newspapers as did Knox.

Like most newspapers in Tennessee, the *Banner* had greeted the

[15] See Perry, *Democracy*.
[16] Ayer, *Directory* (1954).
[17] Jennings Perry, Nashville, letter, January 30, 1964, to the writer.
[18] The Nashville *Banner*, May 17, 1954.

Brown decision with a responsible call for "calm appraisal" and a denunciation of "demagogic appeals."[18] But in simultaneously insisting that any solution to the problem of desegregation must "reconcile both the national interest and states rights on the Constitution," the *Banner* had hinted at the strict constructionist qualification that was to drive it into ever more intransigent opposition to desegregation as federal policy and states' rights seemed to grow increasingly irreconcilable.

The *Banner* couched its stout editorial defense of states' rights appropriately in the rhetoric of Calhoun, and, selectively, of Jefferson, always insisting that its construction of the federal system was logically simple, historically correct, and legally valid. Its editors were fond of metaphorically equating sociological jurisprudence with Pandora's Box, and contemporary liberal doctrine with the camel's nose—in the classical fashion of the *argumentum ad horrendum*.

Its efforts in this endeavor were bolstered in June of 1955—the month following the Supreme Court's order to implement the Brown decision with "deliberate speed"—by the formation of the Tennessee Federation of Constitutional Government.[19] The Federation was unapologetically a states' rights lobby directed, for the most part by respectable Nashvillians, toward the *Banner's* same high-minded goal of defending the Republic as the Founders had envisioned it. President of the Federation was Donald Davidson, highly regarded Professor of English at Vanderbilt and one of the twelve agrarians who had so dramatically taken their stand in 1930 against the encroaching industrial order. Directing its legal counterattack against the forays of sociological jurisprudence were Nashville attorney Sims Crownover, a Vanderbilt Phi Beta Kappa, and the erratic Jack Kershaw—sometimes realtor, attorney, and artist—who did not hesitate bluntly to suggest that Nashville close its public parks and that Tennessee abandon its public schools rather than desegregate them at federal behest.

Welcomed publicly to the lists the summer of 1955 by the *Banner*, the Federation warmed to the fight against federally coerced desegregation by denouncing the invasion of states' rights attendant unto the forced admission of Miss Autherine Lucy to the University of Alabama early in 1956, by praising the wisdom embodied in the so-called Southern Manifesto that was circulated

---

[19] *Southern School News*, August 1955, pp. 1, 16-17.

through Congress that spring, and by sponsoring speeches by Senators Strom Thurmond and James Eastland that summer.[20] But it was not until the following September that the Federation received its baptism of fire. That occurred in the crucible that developed rather surprisingly at Clinton—located near Oak Ridge, in East Tennessee's Anderson County. There, it will be recalled, the talented agitator and ardent segregationist from New Jersey, John Kasper, so fanned the flames of resistance that Governor Clement sent columns of National Guard troops and tanks rolling into the astonished little town.[21] The Federation had quickly appealed, first to the Anderson County Chancery Court and then to the State Supreme Court, to enjoin fifteen Negroes from entering Clinton's high school. When these appeals failed in the courts (thereby ironically hastening the day when Tennessee's Supreme Court would be the first among the ex-Confederate tribunals to declare that state constitutional requirements for school segregation must yield to the new federal interpretation), and when school desegregation became a *fait accompli* in Clinton, the Federation retreated to defend the threatened schools of the state capital. For in Nashville, Bobby Kelley's suit was docketed to be heard by Federal District Judge William E. Miller in October of 1956.

On October 15, Federation attorney Sims Crownover boldly petitioned Judge Miller for permission to intervene in the Kelley case on the grounds that the 14th Amendment was invalid.[22] The Federation's legal ploy pleased the *Banner* but struck the editors of the *Tennessean* as ludicrous and conducive not to constitutional government but to anarchy.[23] Despite whatever historical merit the Federation's case against the 14th Amendment might have possessed, however, Judge Miller denied the Federation's petition to intervene. Miller defended his denial by observing that Chief Justice Hughes had ruled twenty years previously that the question was a political one and as such was not justiciable.[24] Miller then ordered the Nashville School Board to provide the court, by

---

[20] *Ibid.*, March 1956, pp. 6-7.

[21] Useful accounts of the Clinton episode are the October, November, and December numbers of *Southern School News*, 1956; Wilma Dykeman and James Stokeley, *Neither Black Nor White* (New York, 1957), 350-56; and Muse, *Prelude*, 92-105.

[22] *Race Relations Law Reporter*, I (1956), pp. 1042-45.

[23] *Banner*, October 16, 1956; *Tennessean*, October 17, 1956.

[24] *Race Relations Law Reporter*, I (1956), pp. 1042-45. Hughes' precedent, as cited by Judge Miller, was *Coleman v. Miller*, in 307 U.S. (1936), p. 433.

no later than January 21 of the following year, 1957, with a plan for desegregating the city's public schools.

Two weeks later, the school board formally adopted, by a vote of eight-to-one (with Coyness Ennix dissenting), a plan calling for desegregation of only the first grade in September of 1957[25] On November 13, the board submitted the plan for Judge Miller's consideration. Testimony in the case revealed that the board had decided to begin with the first grade on an experimental basis because Nashville's principals and teachers, as educational experts, had recommended the plan with the observation that such young children were without racial prejudice and, of course, lacked potentially explosive sexual attractions.[26] The real key to the workability of the plan, however, lay in its liberal and rather ingenious provisions for transfer.

In pondering how best to modify its segregated school system, the school board faced a dilemma not unfamiliar to other American communities, whether their mode of segregation had been *de jure* or *de facto*. A generally conservative body of community leaders, the board members were interested in minimizing the degree of dislocation that could flow from such a fundamental social change, while not inviting the different but equally severe dislocations that would flow from leading the community in bald defiance. The best way to do this, they were convinced, would be to minimize the degree of desegregation while still appearing to comply with the law. It was in pursuit of some formula whereby, even while complying, such potentially explosive mixing might be minimized that Superintendent of Schools W. A. Bass and Assistant Superintendent William H. Oliver, in lengthy consultations with prestigious Nashville attorneys Edwin Hunt and Reber Boult, devised, in the finest tradition of conservative southern ingenuity, the following three provisions for transfer: children would be granted a transfer upon receipt of a written application by their parents or guardians (a) when a white student would otherwise be required to attend a school previously serving colored students only; (b) when a colored student would otherwise be requested to attend a school previously serving white students only; and (c) when a student would otherwise be required to attend a school where

[25] *Southern School News,* November 1956.
[26] *Race Relations Law Reporter,* IV (1959), pp. 590-94.

the majority of students in that school or in his or her grade were of a different race.[27]

The effect of such a racially triggered provision for transfer, if accepted by the courts, would be clear. No white parent could be compelled to send his child to a school or class where a majority was Negro. Thus, in effect, whatever degree of desegregation that was to occur would take place only in formerly all-white schools. In order further to minimize potential racial mixing, the board extended equal rights for transfer to Negro parents on the shrewd assumption that relatively few Negro parents in 1957 would want to send their first grade children to a predominantly white school that previously had been segregated. Finally, the board so effectively rezoned twenty-three of the city's thirty-six elementary school districts that potential racial mixing was even further reduced.[28] In accomplishing this rezoning, the board expressly denied that it was using race at a criterion. But Negroes with some justice claimed that the board could and did racially segregate the school districts by employing as zoning criteria certain specific qualities, such as low scores on reading and aptitude tests, which were in effect correlates of race. This strategem for discrimination was not new, of course; Southern states had historically disfranchised mostly Negroes by excluding from the franchise all illegitimate children, marriage partners in common law, convicted felons, and other categories that tended to include heavily Negro populations.

On January 21, 1957, Judge Miller accepted, over the objection of both the Negro plaintiffs *and* the Federation, the board's plan to desegregate the first grade only the following September as a prompt and reasonable start.[29] He added, however, that it was only a start, and he further ordered the board to submit, by no later than December 31 of that same year, a plan for desegregating all of the remaining eleven grades in the city's public school system.[30]

The board had planned well. Not only had Judge Miller accepted its timid first step toward desegregation, but the rezoning and the liberal provisions for transfer had so combined to reduce racial mixing that the degree of genuine integration was to be relatively miniscule. Of Nashville's approximately 37,000 public school stu-

[27] *Race Relations Law Reporter*, II (1957), p. 22.
[28] *Southern School News*, October 1957, p. 6.
[29] *Race Relations Law Reporter*, II (1957), pp. 21-25.
[30] *Ibid.*

dents, roughly 10,000 were Negro.[31] But only 3,400 students would enter the first grade in September of 1957—1,400 of them Negro. After rezoning, only 115 Negro children were eligible to attend desegregated first grade in eight of the city's 36 elementary schools. Of these 115 Negro children, parents of 96 immediately requested and promptly received transfers to all-Negro schools—a fact that proved to be particularly galling to the local chapter of the NAACP which had financed the Kelley litigation.[32] Predictably, parents of all 55 of the white children required by the new zones to attend previously all-Negro schools requested and were promptly granted transfers.[33] Thus Nashville's desegregation, scheduled for September of 1957, was to involve only nineteen six-year-old Negro first graders scattered throughout six elementary schools.

The board had planned well in a dual sense. Not only did its form of compliance avoid extensive desegregation, but the nature of the actual integration was such as to discourage white resistance. The nine Little Rock Negroes, scheduled simultaneously for desegregation in Arkansas, were teenagers whose attendance at one centrally located high school would provide a single dramatic focal point for initiating social change.

In addition to the tactical differentials involved in the desegregation of Nashville and Little Rock, other important dissimilarities obtained between the two ostensibly similar situations which worked toward moderation or grudging compliance in Nashville. The most important of these, in the long run, proved to be the marked difference in the quality of leadership exerted from the statehouse. Governors Frank Clement of Tennessee and Orville Faubus of Arkansas had both been popularly regarded as southern moderates, and by some even as liberals. But both governors were politicians of considerable skill; neither could be expected to ignore the rising cacophony of segregationist dissent that the Brown decision had sparked. Clement, reelected under the new constitution to a four-year term in 1954, was constitutionally barred from succeeding himself. But he well knew that the national Democratic party had historically placed a high premium on moderate southern Democratic politicians who could woo the southern vote from the

---

[31] Statistics concerning Nashville's school system are derived from a detailed review of the Kelley case before the Sixth Circuit Court of Appeals, June 17, 1959, Nos. 13,748; 13,749. *Race Relations Law Reporter,* IV (1959), pp. 584-603.

[32] *Southern School News,* October 1957, p. 6.

[33] *Ibid.*

number two spot on the national ticket while not alienating northern Democrats. When Clement's biennial legislature met in 1955, a few unhappy legislators from heavily Negro and Dixiecratic West Tennessee had attempted to ram nullificationist laws through the General Assembly.[34] But Clement, who dreaded the political embarrassment that such brazen defiance would cause him, had forthrightly vetoed the bills as attempts "to circumvent the efficacy of the recent opinion handed down by the Supreme Court of the United States banning segregation in public schools."[35]

In the two years that intervened before the legislature reconvened in January of 1957, however, several events had occurred which tended to dilute the governor's progressivism. He had keynoted the Democratic National Convention in the summer of 1956 and had openly courted the Truman wing of the party in his quest for the vice-presidential nomination. But the prize went instead to his fellow Tennessean, Senator Estes Kefauver. Further, the turmoil at Clinton and elsewhere throughout the South had heightened racial tensions and narrowed Clement's room to maneuver. Many of the newly elected legislators had promised the disturbed voters back home that they would defend the southern way of life in the General Assembly. The *Banner* and other segregationist newspapers in Tennessee—especially the Chattanooga *News-Free Press* and the Memphis *Commercial Appeal*—had openly backed the demands of the Federation and other ad hoc segregationist lobbies that Tennessee adopt a defense patterned after Virginia's attempt at "massive resistance."[36]

Rather than allow himself to be boxed in by this swelling segregationist drumfire, Clement responded with a bold stroke that further revealed his political acumen. In an extraordinary move, he appeared on January 9 before a joint session of the 80th General Assembly.[37] The two galleries in the house chamber were early filled on a non-segregated basis, and the corridors were jammed with milling people and watchful policemen. The governor began by observing that "no law, no traditional decree, can erase

[34] For a review of the history of the Stainback bill, *see Southern School News,* January 6, 1955, p. 14; February 3, 1955, p. 16; March 3, 1955, p. 15; and April 7, 1955, p. 16. Generally, for a review of Tennessee's response to desegregation, *see* my doctoral dissertation, Tennessee Editorial Response to Changes in the Bi-Racial System, 1954-60, to be published in 1967 by Vanderbilt University Press.

[35] Frank G. Clement, as quoted in *Southern School News,* April 7, 1955, p. 16.

[36] *Banner,* December 4, 1956.

[37] *Southern School News,* February 1957, p. 10.

three hundred years of history." But, "in our recognition of the existence of different backgrounds," he added, "we must not overlook the fact that the Negro is equal to the white in the eyes of the law, and in the sight of God."[38] The young and somewhat evangelistic governor proceeded to recognize that the Negro rightfully refuses to accept a place in society "if that place is set in shame and degradation. When the Negro reads the Declaration of Independence, when he hears our leaders speak of the rights of man, he knows that he is a man, he knows that he is an American, and he will never be content to be treated as anything less."[39] If the governor's remarks were less than a clarion call for civil rights, they were at least on a par with anything that the President of the United States had said concerning the Negroes' rightful place in American life.

Having reasserted his moderation on the racial issue, Clement then outlined his program. It included recommendations for five acts.[40] The first, the so-called school preference act, would authorize local school boards to maintain racially separate schools for children whose parents "voluntarily elect" that their children attend school only with members of their own race. Specific procedures for such voluntary parental election, however, were conspicuously absent from the bill. The second, the pupil placement act, would authorize school boards to assign pupils on the basis of varied standards, ranging from location of residence to "the possibility or threat of friction or disorder among pupils or others." The remaining three bills were relatively minor measures designed to assist in the implementation of the first two.

With masterful ambiguity, Clement's package hinted at a formula for maintaining segregated schools while falling short of a specific blueprint. On January 10, Clement had his lieutenants introduce into both houses his five bills; the legislature responded to the governor's prods by quickly approving them.[41] Clement's strategy of preempting the field of segregationist legislation with relatively mild and ambiguous laws had worked admirably. He had dished the defiant segregationists as Disraeli had dished the Whigs. He let it be known that any stronger proposal, such as abolishing public schools or abandoning laws compelling attendance, would be

[38] Frank G. Clement, quoted in *ibid.*
[39] *Ibid.*
[40] *Race Relations Law Reporter*, II (1957), pp. 215-22.
[41] *Southern School News*, February 1957, p. 10.

vetoed. When the legislature subsequently passed a bill modifying compulsory attendance laws, the governor promptly vetoed it and the veto stood.[42] Out-maneuvered, the defiant segregationist legislators responded by introducing a lengthy resolution, grandiosely entitled the Tennessee Manifesto, in vitriolic denunciation of the Supreme Court. The resolution, which of course only expressed the sense of the 80th General Assembly and required neither the Governor's signature nor any specific action, was passed by the legislature with a whoop. The General Assembly then adjourned, on March 22, sine die.

At the conclusion of the legislative session, the *Tennessean* complimented Clement with a rare show of commendation.[43] In an editorial that covered one-third of a page, the *Tennessean* complimented the governor more for what he did *not* do than for what he did. He wisely did not contemplate abolishing the system of public schools or repealing the law compelling attendance. He did not propose to transfer to the state powers that traditionally had belonged to local school officials. Nor did he attempt to force the diverse schools of Tennessee into one procrustean mold. Finally, he did not make his provisions mandatory for local officials. The *Tennessean* was especially pleased that the governor had echoed its theme that only *compulsory* segregation was unlawful. But it was quick to deflate the chimerical notion—soon to be trumpted by the *Banner*—that the first of the five bills—the school preference law—embodied a way somehow to avoid any desegregation at all. That act, declared the *Tennessean,* was "either unconstitutional or meaningless." Such voluntary segregation would indeed in all probability be a general phenomenon, but "school boards need no special powers to permit it, and they can be cloaked with none."

When Judge Miller accepted, on January 21, the school board's decision to desegregate the first grade in the following September, the *Banner* had editorially called the ruling "considerate," observing that it was the most gradualistic option realistically available to the court.[44] But as spring faded into summer and desegregation became more imminent, and as the battle over the civil rights bill in the Congress further heated the air in Tennessee, the *Banner* began to hedge on its earlier approval of the school board's fall commitment.

[42] *Ibid.,* April 1957, p. 12.
[43] *Tennessean,* January 10, 1957.
[44] *Banner,* January 22, 1957.

The *Banner* here reflected as well as encouraged a segment of local opinion, hardening into a defiant mood as the deadline approached. Early that summer, an ad hoc segregationist group organized in Nashville as the Parents' School Preference Committee.[45] Child of the Federation and prompted by its advice and encouragement, the Parents' Preference Committee began to press the school board to abandon its plan to desegregate in September. On June 24, the *Banner* editorially endorsed the new group's aims.[46] Three weeks later, the *Banner* argued editorially that the board should reconsider its plan because the new state law providing for preferential assignment of pupils had been signed forty-four days *after* Judge Miller's ruling of January 21 that the board should proceed.[47] Thus, the *Banner* concluded, the board should provide, in accordance with the new law, "separate schools for white and Negro children whose parents, legal custodians or guardians voluntarily elect that such children attend school with members of their own race."

Concurrently, the Parents' School Preference Committee circulated a petition designed to enable parents to "voluntarily elect" to send their children to schools attended exclusively by members of their own race. The *Banner* editorially insisted that the 6,000 signatures ultimately claimed by the Parents' School Preference Committee were a reasonable request to postpone all desegregation and give Tennessee's new laws a chance to work.[48] Sufficient pressure was brought to bear on the school board to prompt it to instruct its attorneys, Hunt and Boult, to argue before Judge Miller that the previously accepted plan to desegregate the first grade should be abandoned and that the voluntary three-school system should be given a chance to work.

Pressure exerted on the school board by local segregationist whites that summer had surely been severe. But it is arguable that the school board was prompted to strike this new defensive posture in part out of a strategic need to counterbalance the Negro plaintiffs' complaints that the court-approved desegregation was too token and too slow. Thus the court was left in effect to defend the original plan as a moderate middle way between extremes.

---

[44] *Southern School News*, August 1957, p. 6.
[44] *Banner*, June 24, 1957.
[47] *Ibid.*, July 13, 1957.
[48] *Ibid.*, August 23, 1957.

Whatever the complex motivation behind the board's new retreat might have been, however, the more sanguine hopes of the
Banner and the segregationist groups to stem the tide that summer were short lived. On Saturday, September 7, just two days
before the Negro children were scheduled to enter Nashville's
previously white schools, Judge Miller abruptly declared Tennessee's new school preference law to be "patently and manifestly
unconstitutional on its face."[49] The *Tennessean* welcomed the decision with an I-told-you-so, and the *Banner* demanded immediate
appeal—in apparent unawareness that Judge Miller's retention of
jurisdiction made immediate appeal a legal impossibility.

The next day, Sunday, September 8, Nashville Police Chief
Douglas E. Hosse issued a public statement declaring that he
would arrest anyone who attempted to intimidate children or
parents at the desegregated schools.[50] On Monday, September 9,
115 policemen were on guard as nineteen Negro first graders
entered six previously all-white schools. During the day, the ubiqui-
tous John Kasper, recently convicted of contempt of court in Knoxville and out on bond pending appeal, appeared with protesting
segregationists at several of the schools. There were minor scuffles
and the beginnings of a boycott at the desegregated schools, but
police sternly maintained order. Late that evening, unknown dyna-
miters blasted into the midnight sky one wing of the Hattie Cotton
School, where one six-year-old Negro girl had attended school during the day. Having lost their appeal to avoid any desegregation,
determined municipal officials and school board members stayed
up most of Monday night in Hunt and Boult's law office gathering
evidence to support pleas to Judge Miller for injunctions against
die-hard segregationists who were prone to violence. Sensing the
mixed emotions of Nashville's white police officers, Boult felt constrained to remind them that they must enforce the law impartially.

As all schools but Hattie Cotton opened Tuesday morning, Nashville's police cracked down firmly on the protesting segregationists.
Barricades were thrown up, demonstrating groups were dispersed
and nineteen arrested for violating Judge Miller's injunctions. Within a week, Hattie Cotton School was back in operation and the

---

[49] *Race Relations Law Reporter*, II (1957), p. 975.
[50] The details concerning Nashville's response to the racial violence prompted by
desegregation are derived from *Southern School News*, October 1957, p. 6. Muse's
brief account in *Prelude*, 115-21, is also useful.

boycott was beginning to crumble. By the end of the month, attendance was reported back to normal throughout the school system, and eleven Negro children were still attending previously all-white schools. With difficulty not unmixed with pride, Nashville had honored at least the procedural dictates of an unpopular law.

With the crisis successfully passed, Nashville's troubled compliance—reluctant and token as it was—was, like Clinton's of the year previous, a *fait accompli* not to be reversed. Having failed to convince Judge Miller that Tennessee's new school preference law was constitutional, Hunt and Boult retreated to the pupil assignment law—the second of Clement's laws—urging that the suit be dismissed because the plaintiffs had not exhausted their new administrative remedy by appealing not to the courts but to a school board newly armed with powers to reassign pupils.[51] In response to this plea, Judge Miller wryly observed that "To require the plaintiffs to go before a board committed in advance to a continuance of compulsory segregation would be to require them to perform a futile act. . . . "[52] With recourse to both laws thus exhausted, the school board proposed that the remaining eleven segregated grades be desegregated on a grade-a-year basis. According to this plan, Nashville's public schools would be completely desegregated by 1968, when the recently integrated first graders would graduate from high school. This accorded well with Judge Miller's notion of deliberate speed, and he consequently approved of the board's grade-a-year or stairstep plan, thereby relinquishing jurisdiction and permitting appeal.[53]

The Negro plaintiffs, unsatisfied with the grade-a-year plan's token and exceedingly gradualistic character, appealed Judge Miller's ruling to the Sixth Circuit Court of Appeals in Cincinnati. Attorneys Hunt and Boult promptly cross-appealed, thereby once again sandwiching Nashville's modest plan, with its controversial transfer provisions based upon racial criteria, between two apparent extremes. On June 17, 1959, the court of appeals affirmed Miller's

[51] Generally, sources describing the legal history of the Kelley case were the appropriate volumes of *Race Relations Law Reporter* and numbers of *Southern School News*. These, however, were supplemented by personal interviews with Edwin Hunt, Reber Boult, Avon Williams, and William Oliver—all during the second week of August, 1965.

[52] *Race Relations Law Reporter*, III (1958), p. 183.

[53] Memorandum Opinion, District Judge William E. Miller, June 19, 1958, in the case of *Kelley v. Board of Education*, Civ. No. 2094, *Race Relations Law Reporter*, III (1958), pp. 651-55.

judgment.[54] Plaintiffs immediately appealed to the Supreme Court for a writ of certiorari. In response to this plea, three of the high court's liberals—Justices Douglas, Brennan, and Chief Justice Warren—voted to review the Kelley case on the grounds that the provisions for transfer "explicitly recognize race as an absolute ground for the transfer of students between schools, thereby perpetuating rather than eliminating discrimination."[55] But conspicuously and critically absent from the court's liberal ranks was Mr. Justice Hugo Black of Alabama, who, by voting with the majority not to grant certiorari, thereby insured that Nashville's stairstep plan would afford that city, and the numerous southern communities that subsequently adopted the Nashville plan, security in their grandualism during what Muse has called those critical *Ten Years of Prelude* in which the pattern of the South's response to school desegregation emerged.

In 1959, then, the Supreme Court granted implicit approval to a process of school desegregation that was designed to bridge a dozen years before all twelve grades in the city's public schools were desegregated. Four years later, however, in 1963, the same court unanimously held, in the case of *Henry C. Maxwell v. County Board of Education of Davidson County, Tennessee,* that the same racially triggered transfer system of which it had earlier approved in the Kelley case "lends itself to the perpetuation of segregation." "Indeed," held Justice Clark, "the provisions can work only toward that end."[56] Perhaps it is more attributable to the wisdom than to the inconsistency of the court that what was approved as a prompt and reasonable start in 1959 was regarded as all *too* deliberate speed in 1963.

By 1963, 773 Negroes were attending school with 16,177 white children in Nashville's public schools, and 244 Negro children were

---

[54] *Race Relations Law Reporter,* IV (1959), pp. 584-602. Thurgood Marshall, respected attorney for the NAACP, was scheduled to represent the plaintiffs before the Sixth Circuit Court of Appeals in Cincinnati, but Marshall's airplane was grounded on the east coast by inclement weather. Thus, Marshall was unable to argue the appeal and the burden was carried by Looby and Williams. Attorneys Hunt and Boult privately expressed their delight at this development.

[55] *United States Reports,* December 14, 1959, 361 U.S. (U.S. Government Printing Office, 1960). Appealing unsuccessfully for certiorari on behalf of the plaintiffs were Z. Alexander Looby, Thurgood Marshall, Jack Greenberg, Constance Baker Motley, and James N. Nabrit III.

[56] *Maxwell v. County Board of Education, Davidson County, Tennessee,* United States Supreme Court, June 3, 1963, 83 S. Ct. 1405. *Race Relations Law Reporter,* VIII (1963), pp. 377-79.

attending Davidson County's public schools with 51,744 whites.[37] It was still tokenism, to be sure, and the all-Negro schools of 1953 were still the all-Negro schools of 1963. But the percentage of Negroes attending public school with whites in Nashville was constantly, if slowly, escalating, the trend seemed—at least in the short run—to be irreversible, and the public peace was being maintained with decreasing difficulty. Nashville, in other words, was making a successful if gradual transition toward approximating that familiar pattern of *de facto* school segregation that obtained in most northern cities.[58]

But none of this slow progress toward integration ever directly benefited Bobby Kelley. Bobby was never permitted to attend a desegregated public school in Nashville—although, significantly, one of his little brothers was subsequently permitted to do so. After graduating from all-Negro Pearl High School, Bobby earned his bachelor's degree from all-Negro Tennessee Agricultural and Industrial University. The final irony, however, in a story that is replete with irony, is that Bobby Kelley, after failing to obtain federal court orders to desegregate his own environment in Nashville, finally achieved desegregation through another federal agency— a fledgling agency, which flew him to Africa in the process of accomplishing it. For Bobby Kelley, at this writing, is teaching as a Peace Corps Volunteer in Malawi.[59]

---

[37] *Statistical Summary 1962-63* (Nashville, 1963).

[58] *See* Jerrold L. Footlick, "Schools and Race in the South: The Human Problem," in *The National Observer*, November 15, 1965, p. 1.

[59] Personal interview with Michael McCone, former Peace Corps Representative in Malawi.

Acknowledgements

Graham, Howard Jay. "The Fourteenth Amendment and School Segregation."
Buffalo Law Review 3 (1953–1954) 1–24. Reprinted with the permission
of the University at Buffalo, State University of New York. Courtesy of
Yale University Sterling Law Library.

Bickel, Alexander M. "The Original Understanding and the Segregation
Decision." *Harvard Law Review*, 69:1 (November, 1955) 1–65. Reprinted
with the permission of the Harvard University. Copyright 1955. Courtesy
of Yale University Sterling Law Library.

Wechsler, Herbert. "Toward Neutral Principles of Constitutional Law." *Harvard
Law Review* 73:1 (November, 1959) 1–35. Reprinted with the permission
of the Harvard University. Copyright 1959. Courtesy of Yale University
Sterling Law Library.

Pollak, Louis H. "Racial Discrimination and Judicial Integrity: A Reply to
Professor Wechsler." *University of Pennsylvania Law Review* 108:1
(November, 1959) 1–34. Reprinted with the permission of the *University
of Pennsylvania Law Review*. Copyright 1959.

Black, Charles L., Jr. "The Lawfulness of the Segregation Decisions." *Yale Law
Journal* 69:3 (January, 1960) 421–30. Reprinted by permission of The
Yale Law Journal Company and Fred B. Rothman & Company. Courtesy
of Yale University Sterling Law Library.

Bell, Derrick A., Jr. "*Brown* v. *Board of Education* and the Interest-Convergence
Dilemma." *Harvard Law Review* 93:3 (January, 1980) 518–533. Reprinted
with the permission of the Harvard University. Copyright 1980. Courtesy
of Yale University Sterling Law Library.

Avins, Alfred. "De Facto and De Jure School Segregation: Some Reflected
Light on the Fourteenth Amendment from the Civil Rights Act of 1875."
Walter E. Dellinger, III. "School Segregation and Professor Avins' History:
A Defense of *Brown* v. *Board of Education*." *Mississippi Law Journal* 38:2
(March, 1967) 179–247; 248–253. Reprinted with the permission of The
University of Mississippi. Courtesy of Yale University Sterling Law Library.

Beezer, Bruce. "Black Teachers' Salaries and the Federal Courts Before *Brown
v. Board of Education:* One Beginning for Equity." *Journal of Negro
Education* 55:2 (Spring, 1986) 200–213. Reprinted with the permission of
Howard University. Courtesy of Yale University Seeley G. Mudd Library.

Cohen, Ronald D. "The Dilemma of School Integration in the North: Gary,
Indiana, 1945–1960." *Indiana Magazine of History* 82:2 (June, 1986) 161–
84. Reprinted with the permission of Indiana University. Courtesy of the
Indiana Magazine of History.

Diamond, Raymond T. "Confrontation as Rejoinder to Compromise: Reflections on the Little Rock Desegregation Crisis." *National Black Law Journal* 11:2 (Summer, 1989) 151–176. Reprinted with the permission of the University of California, Los Angeles, School of Law. Courtesy of Yale University Sterling Law Library.

Dickens, Milton and Ruth E. Schwartz. "Oral Argument Before the Supreme Court: *Marshall* v. *Davis* in the School Segregation Cases." *Quarterly Journal of Speech* 57:1 (1971) 32–42. Reprinted with the permission of SCA Publications. Courtesy of the *Quarterly Journal of Speech*.

Du Bois, W. E. Burghardt. "Does the Negro Need Separate Schools?" *Journal of Negro Education* 4:3 (July, 1935) 328–335. Courtesy of Yale University Seeley G. Mudd Library.

Dudziak, Mary L. "The Limits of Good Faith: Desegregation in Topeka, Kansas, 1950–1956." *Law and History Review* 5 (Fall, 1987) 351–391. Reprinted with the permission of the Cornell University Law School. Courtesy of the *Law and History Review*.

Ellsworth, Clayton S. "Ohio's Legislative Attack upon Abolition Schools." *Mississippi Valley Historical Review* 21:3 (December, 1934) 379–86. Courtesy of Yale University Sterling Memorial Library.

Franklin, John Hope. "Jim Crow Goes to School: The Genesis of Legal Segregation in Southern Schools." *South Atlantic Quarterly* 58:2 (Spring, 1959) 225–35. Reprinted with the permission of the Duke University Press. Courtesy of Yale University Sterling Memorial Library.

Franklin, Vincent P. "The Persistence of School Segregation in the Urban North: An Historical Perspective." *Journal of Ethnic Studies* 1:4 (Winter, 1974) 51–68. Reprinted with the permission of Western Washington University. Courtesy of Yale University Sterling Memorial Library.

Gerber, David A. "Education, Expediency, and Ideology: Race and Politics in the Desegregation of Ohio Public Schools in the Late 19th Century." *Journal of Ethnic Studies* 1:3 (Fall, 1973) 1–31. Reprinted with the permission of Western Washington University. Courtesy of Yale University Sterling Memorial Library.

Graham, Hugh Davis. "Desegregation in Nashville: The Dynamics of Compliance." *Tennessee Historical Quarterly* 25:2 (Summer, 1966) 135–54. Reprinted with the permission of the Tennessee Historical Society. Courtesy of Yale University Sterling Memorial Library.